Governing the Global Clinic

The Chicago Series in Law and Society

Edited by John M. Conley, Charles Epp, and Lynn Mather

ALSO IN THE SERIES:

Sunbelt Capitalism and the Making of the Carceral State
by Kirstine Taylor

Speaking of Crime: The Language of Criminal Justice (Second Edition)
by Lawrence M. Solan, Peter M. Tiersma, and Tammy Gales

Dual Justice: America's Divergent Approaches to Street and Corporate Crime
by Anthony Grasso

Big Money Unleashed: The Campaign to Deregulate Election Spending
by Ann Southworth

The Making of Lawyers' Careers: Inequality and
Opportunity in the American Legal Profession
by Robert L. Nelson, Ronit Dinovitzer, Bryant G. Garth,
Joyce S. Sterling, David B. Wilkins, Meghan Dawe, and Ethan Michelson

The Crucible of Desegregation: The Uncertain Search for Educational Equality
by R. Shep Melnick

Cooperation without Submission: Indigenous
Jurisdictions in Native Nation-US Engagements
by Justin B. Richland

BigLaw: Money and Meaning in the Modern Law Firm
by Mitt Regan and Lisa H. Rohrer

∴

Governing the Global Clinic

∵

HIV AND THE
LEGAL TRANSFORMATION
OF MEDICINE

Carol A. Heimer

THE UNIVERSITY OF CHICAGO PRESS
CHICAGO AND LONDON

The University of Chicago Press, Chicago 60637
The University of Chicago Press, Ltd., London
© 2025 by The University of Chicago
All rights reserved. No part of this book may be used or reproduced in any
manner whatsoever without written permission, except in the case of brief
quotations in critical articles and reviews. For more information, contact the
University of Chicago Press, 1427 E. 60th St., Chicago, IL 60637.
Published 2025
Printed in the United States of America

34 33 32 31 30 29 28 27 26 25   1 2 3 4 5

ISBN-13: 978-0-226-83862-5 (cloth)
ISBN-13: 978-0-226-83864-9 (paper)
ISBN-13: 978-0-226-83863-2 (e-book)
DOI: https://doi.org/10.7208/chicago/9780226838632.001.0001

Library of Congress Cataloging-in-Publication Data

Names: Heimer, Carol Anne, 1951– author.
Title: Governing the global clinic : HIV and the legal transformation of medicine /
    Carol A. Heimer.
Other titles: Chicago series in law and society.
Description: Chicago : The University of Chicago Press, 2025. | Series: Chicago
    series in law and society | Includes bibliographical references and index.
Identifiers: LCCN 2024035546 | ISBN 9780226838625 (cloth) | ISBN 9780226838649
    (paperback) | ISBN 9780226838632 (ebook)
Subjects: LCSH: HIV-positive persons—Legal status, laws, etc. | HIV infections—
    Prevention—Law and legislation. | AIDS (Disease)—Patients—Legal status,
    laws, etc. | AIDS (Disease)—Law and legislation. | Law and globalization.
Classification: LCC K3575.A43 H45 2025 | DDC 344.04/369792—dc23/eng/20240805
LC record available at https://lccn.loc.gov/2024035546

♾ This paper meets the requirements of ANSI/NISO Z39.48-1992
(Permanence of Paper).

In memory of Art

Contents

List of Abbreviations ix

CHAPTER ONE
Deep Law: Governing the Global Clinic · 1

CHAPTER TWO
Where the Action Is: Taking Standardized
Rules to Unstandard Clinics · 34

CHAPTER THREE
The Mushroom Cloud of Rules · 75

CHAPTER FOUR
The Variability of Universals: What HIV
Clinics Do with Clinical Guidelines · 123

CHAPTER FIVE
Rules, Credibility Struggles, and Institutionalized Skepticism
in Clinical Research: Constructing Trustworthy Data · 164

CHAPTER SIX
Disciplining Medicine: What Happens When
Guidelines Are Hardened by Law · 205

CHAPTER SEVEN
Strategic Uses of Ignorance in HIV Clinics · 236

CHAPTER EIGHT
"Wicked" Ethics: Compliance Work and the
Practice of Ethics in HIV Clinics · 262

CHAPTER NINE
Moral Worth and the Legal Turn in Medicine:
From Scientific Claims to Moral Obligations · 287

Acknowledgments 317
Appendixes 323
Notes 325
References 347
Index 379

Abbreviations

ABC	Abstinence, Be faithful, use Condoms
ACTG	previously AIDS Clinical Trials Group, now Advancing Clinical Therapeutics Globally for HIV/AIDS and Other Infections; an HIV/AIDS research network funded by the US NIH
ACT UP	AIDS Coalition to Unleash Power (US)
ADAP	AIDS drugs assistance program
AE	adverse event
AETC	AIDS Education and Training Centers (US)
AIDS	acquired immune deficiency syndrome; the late stage of infection with HIV
ALP	AIDS Law Project (South Africa)
AMA	American Medical Association
ART	anti-retroviral therapy
ARV	anti-retroviral drugs
CD4	cluster of differentiation 4, a type of white blood cell that helps the body fight infection
CDC	Centers for Disease Control and Prevention (US)
CMS	Centers for Medicare and Medicaid Services (US)
CPG	Clinical Practice Guidelines
CRC	contract research center
CRF	case report form
CTU	clinical trials unit
DAIDS	Division of AIDS, subpart of the National Institute of Allergy and Infectious Diseases (NIAID), within the National Institutes of Health (NIH), within the US Department of Health and Human Services
DHHS	Department of Health and Human Services (US)
EBM	evidence-based medicine
EGPAF	Elizabeth Glaser Pediatric AIDS Foundation
FDA	Food and Drug Administration (US)

FDC	fixed-dose combination
FWA	Federalwide Assurance (US)
GCP	Good Clinical Practice, guidelines and training regimens under the aegis of the International Council for Harmonization of Technical Requirements for Pharmaceuticals for Human Use (ICH)
GFATM	Global Fund to Fight AIDS, Tuberculosis and Malaria, also known as Global Fund
GMHC	Gay Men's Health Crisis (US)
GPO	Government Pharmaceutical Organization (Thailand)
GPO-VIR	an inexpensive, generic fixed-dose combination anti-retroviral (Thailand)
HAART	highly active anti-retroviral therapy, now simply called ART
HIPAA	Health Insurance Portability and Accountability Act (US)
HIV	human immunodeficiency virus, the virus that causes AIDS
HPTN	HIV Prevention Trials Network (US NIH)
HVTN	HIV Vaccine Trials Network (US NIH)
IAC	International AIDS Conference
IAS	International AIDS Society
IAS-USA	International Antiviral Society–USA
ICH	International Council for Harmonisation of Technical Requirements for Pharmaceuticals for Human Use
IHR	International Health Regulations
IMPAACT	International Maternal Pediatric Adolescent AIDS Clinical Trials (US NIH)
IRB	institutional review board
JCAHO	Joint Commission on Accreditation of Healthcare Organizations, now simply Joint Commission
KS	Kaposi sarcoma
MCC	Medicines Control Council (South Africa)
MOPH	Ministry of Public Health (Thailand)
MSF	Médecins Sans Frontières (Doctors Without Borders)
MTN	Microbicides Trials Network (US NIH, terminated in 2021)
NGC	National Guidelines Clearinghouse (US)
NIAID	National Institute of Allergies and Infectious Diseases (US)
NIH	National Institutes of Health (US)
OHRP	Office of Human Research Protections (US)
OI	opportunistic infection
PCP	pneumocystis carinii pneumonia, now called pneumocystis jiroveci pneumonia
PEPFAR	President's Emergency Plan for AIDS Relief (US)
PI	principal investigator

PICT	provider-initiated counseling and testing
PMTCT	preventing mother-to-child transmission
QA/QC	quality assurance/quality control
RCT	randomized controlled trial
RCT	routine counseling and testing
SAE	serious adverse event
SOP	standard operating procedure
TAC	Treatment Action Campaign (South Africa)
TASO	The AIDS Support Organization (Uganda)
TRIPS	World Trade Organization Agreement on Trade Related Aspects of Intellectual Property Rights
UNAIDS	Joint United Nations Programme on HIV/AIDS
VA	Department of Veterans Affairs (US)
VCT	voluntary counseling and testing
WHO	World Health Organization
WMA	World Medical Association
WTO	World Trade Organization

[CHAPTER ONE]

Deep Law

Governing the Global Clinic

Pestilence and disease are generally believed to lie in the domain of the biological sciences and medicine. But social arrangements—and in particular law—also have crucial roles to play. *Governing the Global Clinic* asks how the introduction of more legally inflected ways of doing things has altered the work of healthcare and how the effects of legalization vary across sites. But it also challenges readers to reconsider the impulse to use law— broadly conceived to include both "hard," binding forms such as statutes, and "softer," nonbinding forms like guidelines—as a way of organizing and governing social life.

To this end, the book braids investigations of three transformative events—the "legalization" and globalization of medicine and the advent of HIV/AIDS—in a study of how laws, regulations, and other rules have actually been used in research and treatment in HIV clinics. It investigates what happened when laws, regulations, and guidelines, generally created for use in the clinics of rich countries, were transported to new sites where they confronted the realities of medical care, clinical research, and healthcare administration in poorer countries. I ask whether the rules were used differently in countries such as Uganda and South Africa, where AIDS reached truly epidemic proportions, than in the US, where infection rates remained comparatively low. The book also considers how the character of the medical-legal regime varied with the identities of people initially understood to be at risk for HIV/AIDS—homosexuals or IV drug users (in the US), sex workers (in Thailand), or heterosexuals (in Uganda and South Africa).

The project thus combines an examination of what has happened at the level of national and international policymaking with a close look at how the plethora of laws, regulations, rules, guidelines, codes, protocols, frameworks, and standard operating procedures (SOPs) actually affected how healthcare workers went about the daily work of conducting research on HIV and caring for people living with HIV/AIDS. The bulk of the research was conducted in HIV clinics in the US, Thailand, South Africa, and Uganda, and focused on how clinic workers worked with the rules, including how they learned about the intricacies of the rules, how they determined which rules were binding and which merely guidance, what they did when rules did not fit the situation, and how they balanced conflicting rules. Interviews with government official responsible for HIV policy, key researchers and activists, and writers and disseminators of guidelines and regulations supplemented clinic fieldwork and filled in details about the global, national, and local contexts.

In the book I transform these individual encounters with laws and rules into general knowledge. The book aims for a rich account of how the "legal turn" in medicine affected treatment and research, facilitating the rapid creation and diffusion of knowledge about HIV and shaping patterns of access to drugs. But it also asks whether some ways of formulating, adapting, and using law, guidelines, and other prescriptive statements are especially likely to support rather than undermine the agency and sense of responsibility of clinic workers.

In effect, then, the book makes the case for studying the legal turn in healthcare, and in social life more generally, by studying a specific, but highly consequential, global case that coincides with the growth of legalism and so allows us to see clearly what a lushly developed, highly pluralistic system of rules looks like. But we cannot understand how such a complex system of rules actually works without studying it on the ground—in this instance, as clinic-level law. In highlighting the part played by rules in the unfolding of the HIV/AIDS epidemic, I demonstrate the extent to which contemporary life is ordered by rules rather than other mechanisms that might instead be called on to do this work. Although rules are represented as universal, neutral mechanisms for creating order and getting things done, such deep law[1] is not nearly so innocuous as claimed, and many of its effects are invisible to participants. As they create order, rules both open up new possibilities and delegitimate and foreclose alternative, less legalized ways of engaging with others and creating order. They reshape our thinking about moral worth, creating advantages (what we might call legal endowments) for some while disadvantaging others. Rules and laws also focus attention and channel resources, sometimes resulting in positive effects but sometimes creating blind spots, tunnel vision, and ethical lapses. HIV counseling and testing regimes illustrate the role that legal supports play and show what is at stake with increased reliance on law and legalistic modes of governance in healthcare.

The Stakes of Legalism: Legal Supports and Barriers in HIV Testing

In early 1985, the US Food and Drug Administration (FDA) granted a license to Abbott Laboratories for an HIV antibody test. Until that point—four years into the epidemic—there had been no way to verify that a person was infected with the virus. Because clinicians were often unsure that the illness they were observing was HIV, they could not be confident that they were using their limited medical tools appropriately. Gay men worried about protecting themselves and exposing others, but often did not know whether they were infected. In addition, there was no way to determine whether blood and blood products were tainted with HIV. Initially deployed to protect the US blood supply, the first test kits went to Irwin Memorial Blood Bank, which, Randy Shilts observed, "had the dubious distinction of dispensing more AIDS-tainted blood than any other blood bank in the country" (Shilts 1987, 539). "From now on," Shilts continued, "the chances of contracting AIDS through a blood transfusion were effectively eliminated. . . . That much was simple, but it was probably the only simple aspect of the enormous implications that the beige plastic kits held for the future of the AIDS epidemic" (1987, 539).

At first glance, the HIV antibody test and the procedures for using it might seem to be largely technical matters, yet these technical matters were deeply intertwined with law and carried a great deal of weighty social baggage. The test was ultimately used to diagnose and treat individuals—just as other diagnostic tests are—as well as continuing to be used to protect public resources such as the blood supply. But the licensing and diffusion of the antibody test were highly contested and occurred in tandem with the adoption of a host of rules, regulations, and statutes (Shilts 1987, 539–43). Worried that the test would become a tool for discrimination against people infected with HIV and against gays generally, gay rights groups filed a petition in US federal court to block the licensing of the test. With additional labeling and guarantees that the test would be used only in blood banks and laboratories, gay rights groups ultimately withdrew their suit.

Such solutions were only stopgap measures, though, and approaches to testing were anything but uniform at the beginning. California and New York, the main sites for AIDS activism in the early 1980s, took quite different paths. California set aside funds for testing sites and passed laws to protect people who decided to be tested. These legal protections included mandates for pre- and post-test counseling and provisions for anonymity and confidentiality, elements that became standard practice in HIV testing. During the period before the testing sites opened, though, the director of the California Department of Public Health invoked emergency powers to prevent blood banks from revealing the results of antibody tests to anyone—employers, insurers, but also the people whose blood was being tested. The interests of blood banks, worried about being inundated with gay men hoping to learn whether they were infected, took precedence over the interests of individual patients. Worried about possible civil rights violations and the questionable clinical value of the test, New York's gay leaders, in contrast, opposed HIV antibody testing and demonstrated with the slogan "no test is best" (Johns, Bayer, and Fairchild 2016, 134). Given the strength of these sentiments, the New York Health Commissioner issued a public order that laboratories could conduct antibody tests only for scientific research. The net effect in these early days was that the blood supply was protected but individual testing was prohibited.

From the outset, then, HIV testing protocols differed greatly from the public health testing strategies used to prevent the spread of other infectious diseases. This human rights approach to HIV testing, often referred to as voluntary counseling and testing (VCT) or client-initiated testing, was crafted and institutionalized in Western democracies, especially in the US where HIV/AIDS disproportionately affected stigmatized groups such as gay men and injection drug users. These groups had good reason to worry about stigma and discrimination as well as the legacy of mandated testing, public health registries, and even quarantines associated with public health laws (Bayer 1991; Johns, Bayer, and Fairchild 2016). Promoted by international HIV/AIDS, healthcare, and human rights organizations, these counseling and testing protocols were adopted by many national governments, written into policy, and often backed up by statute. Over time, legal protections of the confidentiality of HIV test results and legal requirements for lengthy pre- and post-test counseling became the standard, diffusing around the world along with the test kits themselves. This cascade of legal and quasi-legal moves ended up "hardening" the counseling and testing protocols, reducing the room for adjustment as the world of HIV testing and treatment evolved.

In the ensuing decades, policymakers, activists, people living with HIV, and health workers remained concerned about the appropriate role of counseling, confidentiality, consent—the 3 Cs—in HIV testing. In fact, different groups' positions on the meaning, advisability, and importance of the 3 Cs were neither identical nor entirely stable, varying over time as well as with social and geographical location.

Generally speaking, the protocols were more warmly received in the global North than in the global South, both because of the nature of the epidemic and prevailing norms. The low-prevalence, concentrated AIDS epidemic of the richer countries of the global North, disproportionately transmitted through stigmatized gay sex or IV drug use, differed from the higher-prevalence, generalized AIDS epidemic in many countries of the global South, where HIV, though still a stigmatized disease, was more often transmitted through heterosexual sex, which is not itself seen as disreputable. Moreover, the rights discourse championed by human rights groups did not always align with the more communal norms of people living with HIV in the global South (Englund 2006; Angotti 2012; Vernooij and Hardon 2013).

Yet the safeguards of VCT were sometimes quite important in the global South, particularly in societies where the legacies of colonialism permitted routine disregard for the rights of people from lower social strata. In post-apartheid South Africa, for instance, the military, mine owners, and many employers of domestic workers initially tried to make preemployment HIV screening mandatory (Heywood and Cornell 1998). But implementation of testing protocols remained uneven. Stakeholders were not equally invested in the VCT testing protocol. In Malawi, for instance, although the "proponents," employed as bureaucrats by the government or NGOs, formally defended the 3 Cs, they did not always prioritize them in practice (Angotti 2012). Because the ethics of VCT protocols often conflicted with moral concern for the people and communities they were tasked with helping, the HIV counselors—"implementers"—often felt morally compelled to make adjustments to mandated practices, including violating confidentiality to protect families and sexual partners (Angotti 2010, 2012).

Resource constraints and local working conditions often exacerbated these conflicts and enlarged the gap between what was legally required and what caregivers actually did. The problem was not generally the law, which was "very clear," I was told by a South African worker who trained HIV counselors and testers. But it was not always obvious how the rules mapped onto local situations, and even when they agreed with its objectives, healthcare workers confided that they were often frustrated in their attempts to implement the VCT protocol. Staff shortages presented a major problem in resource-constrained societies. Recognizing that testing and treatment generally could not be put on hold until all of the legal niceties were worked out and resource shortages resolved, clinic staff developed accommodations. Some of these became sufficiently established to have such well-understood labels as "silent testing," "consent by proxy," and "passive approval."

Implementation of VCT seems to have been uneven in richer countries as well, though. Although US agencies such as the Centers for Disease Control and Prevention (CDC) and the governments of individual states invested in building, fine-tuning, and institutionalizing counseling and testing infrastructure and the supporting legal architecture, assessments by reviewers and scholars alike found that the counseling and testing routines were not being implemented as designed (Sheon 1999; Fincher-Mergi et al. 2002; Johns, Bayer, and Fairchild 2016). According to one director of an HIV testing, prevention, and treatment facility, "No one followed the [counseling] guidelines—ever—and the quality was poor" (Johns, Bayer, and Fairchild 2016, 140).

Even though VCT protocols were difficult to implement initially, one might have expected levels of compliance to improve over time as protocols were adjusted and clarified and as the people tasked with counseling and testing received further training and gained experience. But that is not what happened. Instead, VCT simply outlived its utility. The increasing prevalence of anti-discrimination law and legally backed formal codes of ethics for medical workers made some of the robust protections of the VCT protocols less important.[2] Primarily, though, advances in HIV treatment and increasing availability of effective therapy boosted the payoff for knowing one's HIV status and correspondingly diminished reluctance to test. In the long run, client-initiated testing, including the VCT protocol, was largely supplanted by provider-initiated counseling and testing protocols (PICT), also referred to as routine counseling and testing (RCT). But the "long run" was perhaps longer than it needed to be.

In the meantime, the discussion about modifying testing protocols and associated legal frameworks was tense. Many health workers cut corners, while others spoke their minds in the face of colleagues' allegations that any modification was a step away from honoring patients' rights. As the options for diagnosing and managing HIV changed, elaborate counseling and testing protocols began to discourage testing and siphoned off resources that could be better used for treatment. In the view of Edwin Cameron, Justice of the Supreme Court of Appeal of South Africa, who was himself HIV positive, counseling and testing protocols became "a barrier to diagnosis and treatment" and "a source of risk and harm" (Cameron 2007, 106).

Reversing course on VCT was neither quick nor easy, though, given the commitment of key organizations such as the CDC, WHO, and UNAIDS (Joint United Nations Programme on HIV/AIDS) to VCT and the thorough institutionalization of the VCT regime. Over the years since testing began, the human rights approach of VCT had been codified in statutes, guidelines, and protocols, and built into training programs and organizational routines.

Although the first endorsements of routine testing occurred in 1987 (before the VCT regime was fully codified), transitioning from VCT to RCT took decades. Moreover, because implementing the VCT regime at scale had required new funding streams to enlarge and support cadres of counselors, these funding streams created constituents who became invested in the VCT regime. This was particularly true in resource-constrained societies where livelihoods often depended on funds from abroad, a point brought home by Swidler and Watkins's (2017) astute analysis of AIDS altruism.

The switch to RCT unfolded on somewhat different timetables at the CDC than at the two UN bodies, WHO and UNAIDS. When testing first became possible in 1985, no treatment was available and experts disagreed about what a positive test meant for transmission of the virus through sexual contact or during pregnancy. That uncertainty, coupled with concerns about privacy and discrimination, spoke to the importance of investing in pre- and post-test counseling. Only a couple of years later, though, the implications of a positive test were clearer, and the CDC gradually began to endorse routine testing. When effective treatment became available (starting in 1996), pressure to "normalize" HIV testing increased (Institute of Medicine 1999; Johns, Bayer, and Fairchild 2016). But only in 2006 did the CDC guideline writers "advocate routine voluntary HIV screening as a normal part of medical practice, similar to screening for other treatable conditions" (CDC 2006, 5).

WHO began recommending a transition to more routine testing and cautiously encouraging scaled-back counseling procedures as early as 2002, when one publication noted that "the demanding procedures inherent in the VCT approach may now inadvertently draw a high level of attention to HIV in a way that impedes the 'normality' of seeking and accepting HIV testing" (WHO 2002). By 2004, a joint policy statement from UNAIDS and WHO acknowledged that "the current reach of testing services remains poor," with only 10% of people who needed testing because of possible HIV exposure actually having access to testing (UNAIDS and WHO 2004). Noting that approximately 80% of people living with HIV in low- and middle-income countries did not know that they were infected and citing the evidence that testing rates improved with PICT, in 2007 WHO and UNAIDS finally came around to strongly urging provider-initiated testing (WHO and UNAIDS 2007a; see also WHO and UNAIDS 2007b, the testing guideline).

These new policies did not receive unqualified support at UNAIDS. In particular, members of the UNAIDS Reference Group continued to champion a human rights policy (Bayer and Edington 2009). Although WHO HIV/AIDS Director Kevin De Cock, who had previously worked at the

CDC, was mindful of these disagreements and the "sensitivity about un-due American influence" (Bayer and Edington 2009, 316), he emphasized the urgency of the change in testing procedures: "Without a major increase in HIV testing and counselling in health facilities, universal access to HIV prevention, treatment and care will remain just a noble goal" (WHO and UNAIDS 2007a).

Nevertheless, making the switch was not simply a matter of declaring a new policy. In the rush to protect the rights of people with HIV, activists and healthcare workers had welcomed legal actors' help in creating appropriate rules and the infrastructure to ensure that they were followed. Both national and international bodies supported the involvement of legal actors. WHO, for instance, saw international legal instruments such as UNGASS, UNAIDS, and OCHR guidelines and declarations[3] as "vital components of the rights-based approach to HIV testing and counselling services" and noted that signatory countries were "required to adhere to the principles laid down in the instruments" (WHO and UNAIDS 2005, 13–14). But as the tide turned and the public (Kaiser Family Foundation 2006; Baggaley et al. 2012) and entities such as the CDC and WHO began to support RCT, existing legal mandates undoubtedly slowed and complicated the transition from VCT to RCT. The legal supports, previously seen as essential to the HIV counseling and testing regime, now had become substantial impediments to change.

The WHO and UNAIDS guidance continued to stress that rights were not being abandoned with the move to RCT, reiterating that commitment in both 2005 and 2007: "the '3 Cs' [consent, confidentiality, and counselling], advocated since the HIV test became available in 1985, continue to be underpinning principles for the conduct of HIV testing of individuals" (WHO and UNAIDS 2005), and "in all cases of HIV testing and counselling, the 3 Cs . . . must be respected" (WHO and UNAIDS 2007a).[4] Importantly, though, the list of rights expanded rather than contracted, and the first right now listed was people's "right to know their HIV status" (WHO and UNAIDS 2005).

Yet it is hard to see how the changes in procedures could have been experienced by healthcare workers as anything other than a speed-up. Workers already felt that they were being asked to do more work than they could manage and to take on tasks they were not legally permitted to perform. How could they increase the number of HIV tests they performed simply because HIV testing was now supposed to be part of their routine or had been added to the list of patient rights? In a legal and cultural context that had put so much emphasis on consent, confidentiality, and counseling, the repeated assertions that the 3 Cs remained in place put healthcare workers in an awkward spot. Simpler rules had become more complicated: counseling was mandated, but counseling had been scaled back; consent was mandated, but it was now opt-out rather than opt-in; confidentiality was required, but with some exceptions. The message about the fundamental importance of increased testing seemed likely to get lost in a legalistic tangle. And indeed, by 2017 the 3 Cs had morphed into the 5 Cs, now including "correct results" (a set of requirements about quality assurance systems and standards) and "connections" (requirements for links to prevention, treatment, care, and support services) (WHO and UNAIDS 2017).

The dilemmas faced by guideline writers in the US were somewhat different. As the Institute of Medicine and the CDC began to recommend RCT in many situations, the CDC also acknowledged that this recommendation was at odds with the law of many states, urging that "jurisdictions should consider strategies to best implement these recommendations within current parameters and consider steps to resolve conflicts with these recommendations" (CDC 2006). That mildly stated acknowledgment of a need for adjustment and harmonization rather understated the problem, though, according to commentators. Gostin (2006), for instance, remarked that state laws "could stand as a barrier to implementation of CDC guidelines." But these barriers seemed not to have been factored into the modified guidelines: "The CDC and commentators have acknowledged that states' laws might limit implementation of routine testing; however, none of the discussions have seriously addressed the extent of these potential legal barriers" (Wolf, Donoghoe, and Lane 2007). Agreeing about the mismatch between the CDC's new guidelines and existing federal and state legal provisions, some commentators were less concerned about these misalignments because they believed states (and professional associations) were moving to close gaps (Bartlett et al. 2008). Yet others observed that some recently amended state-level statutes had not moved in a direction that facilitated routine testing (Wolf, Donoghoe, and Lane 2007). Even at the federal level, some policies could be read as inconsistent with the CDC's attempt to routinize HIV testing. Medicare, for instance, did not at that time cover HIV screening (Bartlett et al. 2008), and Medicaid, partly controlled at the state level, does not always cover routine HIV testing (Kay, Batey, and Mugavero 2016).

To summarize, then, as rapid testing and effective treatments were developed, a fragile consensus in support of routine testing was reached—but only after a long period of arcane discussion and disagreement about how to balance human rights and public health approaches to HIV counseling and testing. By this time, "only lawyers and sophisticated advocates [could] understand these arguments" Corrine Carrie of the New York Civil Liberties Union admitted (Bayer, Philbin, and Remien 2017, 1263). As is common with policy changes, implementation of RCT took some time, not least because of the difficulty of harmonizing policies, laws, regulations, and guidance at the international, national, and subnational levels with the new WHO and CDC guidelines. To be fair, though, this was not just a matter of implementation but de-implementation,[5] as legal frameworks that had supported VCT were dismantled to make possible a new RCT regime. Although the legalization of the counseling and testing regime may have been important at the outset, the elaborate legal edifice did complicate the switch to RCT.

Getting testing policies and procedures right is essential to ending the HIV epidemic, a point increasingly recognized in discussions of HIV policy. Getting tested is the first step in the "treatment cascade" of testing, treatment, and viral suppression. Only after people have tested positive can they be brought into healthcare systems for management of opportunistic infections (OIs) and the anti-retroviral therapy (ART) that will suppress the virus. Over the years, UNAIDS has articulated a series of goals intended to quell and then end the HIV/AIDS epidemic: "3 by 5," "90-90-90," and now "95-95-95."[6] Notably, achievement of the goals has depended on the success of the first step, a point increasingly made both by policymakers and scholars. Speaking at the International AIDS Conference in Bangkok in July 2004, for instance, Jim Yong Kim, director of the WHO AIDS program, explicitly noted the link between testing and WHO's and UNAIDS's commitment to treatment: "With the possibility of treatment, we feel it is critical to routinely offer testing and counseling in all health care settings" (Kim 2004). Over time, indicators of adequacy of testing programs began to appear in the annual reports put out by UNAIDS and WHO alongside other statistics. Eventually the favored indicator came to be percent of people living with HIV who knew their HIV status.

This attention to testing emphasized the importance and distinctiveness of this first step. Testing is crucial because it is the point where people first come into contact with healthcare workers who might diagnose and treat their HIV infection. Any hope of interrupting the chain of HIV infection thus depends, even more than one might expect, on testing. The self-evident part of this story is that people who are being treated and have achieved viral suppression are quite unlikely to transmit the infection. But painstaking research using 2009 data showed that the likelihood of transmission declines at each step in the HIV treatment cascade (Hall et al. 2015; Skarbinski et al. 2015). In the US, for instance, nearly a third (30.2%) of the new HIV infections were attributable to the 18.1% of the people living with HIV who had not yet been diagnosed. The transmission rate dropped modestly simply with testing and then much more substantially as people moved into treatment, received ART, and achieved viral suppression.[7] What proportion of the new infections are attributable to undiagnosed people living with HIV obviously depends not just on the transmission rate but on the percentage of the HIV-infected population that has not been tested.

The successes in managing the HIV epidemic are real, and they include successes in biomedical products and processes as well as innovations in social programs and global cooperation. But the failures are real as well (Darrow 2021). Although death rates have dropped and lifespans and quality of life have improved for people living with HIV, the epidemic has not been brought to an end. And, crucially, for far too long many people living with HIV were not being tested. At the time the CDC revised its testing recommendations in 2006—more than two decades after the first tests became available—about a quarter of the people living with HIV/AIDS in the US did not know their status (Branson 2007). In 2014, when UNAIDS announced its 90-90-90 target, only 45% of people in sub-Saharan Africa living with HIV knew their status (UNAIDS 2014, 18).

The language of cascades helps when thinking about the balance of successes and failures because it highlights the interdependence of the steps in HIV testing and treatment. To take the 90-90-90 goal as an example, not reaching the first target—90% of people living with HIV knowing their status—almost inevitably dooms the program. Some effects of low testing rates cannot be overcome by higher rates of treatment and viral suppression of those who did test. In particular, lower rates of testing mean more transmission of HIV, as noted above, as well as higher mortality rates because people who test late begin treatment later in the course of their infection when their health often is already quite compromised (Bartlett et al. 2008; Bendavid et al. 2010). In one systematic analysis of the HIV treatment cascade, Levi et al. (2016) showed that globally the largest failures ("breakpoints") to meet the 90-90-90 targets occurred at diagnosis. Rather than 90-90-90, Levi et al. (2016, 3) estimated that what had been achieved was 54-76-78. The ultimate result was that only an estimated 32% achieved viral suppression, rather than the 73% that would have been virally suppressed if all targets had been met. Much of this gap of 41 percentage points was attributable to the failure to achieve a high level of testing, the first target in the treatment cascade.

Given the historical context in which HIV emerged, it had been hard to get consensus, at the CDC but especially at WHO and UNAIDS, that testing guidelines should recommend routine, provider-initiated testing (RCT or PICT) rather than insisting on client-initiated VCT. And given the legacy of legal protections put in place early in the HIV epidemic, preparing new guidelines was necessary but hardly sufficient. With the deeply persuasive talk about protecting the rights of people living with HIV, VCT norms and policies had been thoroughly institutionalized through reference to global human rights declarations, endorsement by professional societies, and national and subnational laws. Changing guidelines was thus only the first step, albeit an essential one.

The cascade metaphor used to discuss treatment is therefore also useful in thinking about the de-implementation of the legal edifice surrounding HIV testing. The three steps in UNAIDS's goals—diagnosis, treatment, and viral suppression—are all medical matters. That said, testing, treatment, and viral suppression do not occur in a social vacuum but unfold in professional, social, and legal contexts. Because the gay men who were the main people confronting the uncertainties of the new disease also experienced considerable stigma and discrimination, an especially robust legal edifice grew up around HIV testing. That edifice now had to be de-implemented in a long series of steps spread over many years. In the US, although the CDC issued its revised testing guidelines recommending routine testing in 2006, the legal edifice supporting VCT was not fully dismantled until 2018, when Nebraska, the last holdout, finally ceased requiring written consent for HIV testing. Given the early opposition of New Yorkers to testing even with legal protections, it is perhaps not surprising that New York was the other laggard, only completing the legal de-implementation process in 2014. Summary statements about timelines do not convey just how protracted, complicated, and contentious the de-implementation process can be. Here some numbers help convey the challenge of de-implementation. Between 2006, when the new CDC guideline were issued, and 2010, the New York state legislature introduced 169 HIV-related bills (Bayer, Philbin, and Remien 2017, 1261). But did New York's restrictive laws really make it difficult for physicians to do HIV testing? On that point, the New York Medical Society had complained bitterly that "for over 20 years, physicians and other health care personnel have not been allowed to offer HIV testing as part of the standard tests that are offered patients" (Bayer, Philbin, and Remien 2017, 1261; see also *New York Times* 2006).

Between the start of the HIV pandemic and the end of 2023, an estimated 88.4 million people had become infected with HIV, 43.3 million people had died from AIDS-related illnesses (630,000 of those in 2023) (UNAIDS 2024). Although diagnostic tests were first developed in 1985 and effective treatment that dramatically reduced transmission rates became available in 1996, there were still 1.3 million new infections in 2023 and 5.4 million of the 39.3 million people living with HIV did not know they were infected (UNAIDS 2024). It is hard to know for sure, of course, what difference a speedier transition to RCT might have made, but existing statistical work on the high HIV transmission rates of people who are infected but not yet diagnosed coupled with the shockingly low level of testing suggest the devastating costs of the protracted de-implementation process necessitated by the earlier rush to law as a way of firming up protections for people living with HIV. It is far from clear that the rigidity that came with the use of legal tools was worth the price in new infections and abbreviated lifespans.

To add a bit more perspective, consider the excess deaths from the AIDS denialism of the South African government during the Mbeki regime (discussed more later in the book). Those denialist policies are estimated to have resulted in 330,000 excess deaths and 35,500 excess infant infections (Chigwedere et al. 2008). The excess deaths from a cumbersome HIV testing guideline that had outlived its original purpose were surely far more numerous than those attributed to Mbeki's unscientific policies. That suggests that it is worthwhile to think carefully about the negative as well as the positive effects of adding legal supports to healthcare guidelines. Introducing excessive rigidity into rapidly changing arenas like medicine, which may be better served by flexibility, potentially can cause considerable harm. Perhaps doctors do not need to become more like lawyers. These questions about what happens when we turn to law to help manage the work of medical staff and to aid in the governance of healthcare organizations are the core subject of this book.

The History of HIV as a History of Rules

The history of HIV, often written optimistically as a history of scientific progress, political activism, and increasing tolerance, is also a history of rules: laws, regulations, guidelines, and SOPs. The preceding account of HIV testing shows in concrete terms how true this is. In the early 1980s, when caregivers began to think they were seeing something new without yet knowing what it was, no one really knew what to do about HIV. Caregivers treated OIs but were unsure why previously rare infections were occurring more frequently and why these infections coincided with worsening health and eventual death. During this period of overwhelming uncertainty about what was causing illness and equally high uncertainty about how to prevent, mitigate, or cure the illness, the absence of systematized knowledge was felt acutely. People wanted guidelines so they could more confidently diagnose and treat the new disease.

Gradually the uncertainty receded. The causal agent was identified—people now knew what caused the previously unexplained illnesses. Diagnostic tests were developed—people could now find out whether they were infected. Eventually, scientists and pharmaceutical companies succeeded in developing anti-retroviral drugs (ARVs) that combatted HIV rather than just treating OIs. Soon after that, HIV researchers learned that a cocktail of three or more ARVs, working to control the virus in different ways, was far more effective in controlling HIV than mono- or dual-therapy. As these discoveries were made, the new knowledge was translated into clinical guidelines—rules about how to test people for HIV and how to read the tests, when to start therapy, what prophylaxis should be given before patients were ready for anti-retrovirals, what drugs should be included in a multidrug regimen, how to monitor progress and how often to check CD4[8] levels and viral loads, when to modify a regimen, what therapies should be used to prevent transmission of the infection from a mother to the unborn child, or what kind of prophylaxis to give to prevent infection after a needle-stick injury. Rules are a key part of the decrease of disorder and of medical workers' mastery over new diseases.

But rules do more than just organize and transmit medical knowledge. The guidelines for HIV testing, for instance, are as much about social matters as biological ones. To be sure, these guidelines specify how to collect and process biological samples. But in mandating pre- and post-test counseling and rigorous protection of confidentiality, the guidelines also govern the relationships among the people brought together by the disease and their attempts to cope with it. In addition, they arrange and legitimize the work of clinic staff, for instance, specifying who can counsel patients or prescribe drugs. And, when coupled with constitutional guarantees of healthcare, health insurance contracts, and the rules of philanthropic programs, these guidelines undergird claims on resources to support prevention, testing, and treatment. When embedded in research protocols, they form part of the edifice for the creation of new medical knowledge. But to accomplish all this, HIV-specific rules and guidelines must be used in tandem with other rules, thus necessitating the creation of vast networks of interconnected clinical guidelines, regulations, accounting rules, SOPs, formal laws, and even international treaties.

The most visible of these HIV-related rules have been noisily and publicly contested. Could the bathhouses of San Francisco legally be shut down? Could the patent rights protected by TRIPS (the Agreement on Trade-Related Aspects of Intellectual Property Rights)[9] be waived on the grounds of national emergency so that poorer countries such as Thailand, South Africa, or Uganda could produce or procure drugs to treat their HIV-infected citizens? Could courts require the South African government to offer treatment to HIV-infected pregnant women to reduce the odds that their infants would be born infected? How should the collection of information about the disease (through mandated reporting and contact tracing) be balanced against the civil rights of those being tested? When should it be permissible to violate the usual rules about confidentiality to protect others who might have been exposed to HIV?

Many other rules, especially those not tethered to formal law, are less visible to the public. Struggles over adoption and implementation of these rules have often occurred outside of public view. Clinical guidelines are especially important in marking progress in the battle against HIV. In the very early days, clinical guidelines were largely absent because there was little or no knowledge to systematize. "You might as well drink your shampoo," one doctor remarked about one "cure of the day" (Monette 1988, 109). No one knew how the disease would unfold, how much time a person would have between one OI and the next, or how often a person could bounce back from PCP.[10] Patients, their lovers, friends, and families spent their time "trying to figure out patterns that hadn't been reported yet" (Monette 1998, 123). Only very gradually did the chaos of this early period give way to more orderly methods of managing the disease. Along the way were many false starts, and provisional rules and guidelines had to be dismantled and practices and programs de-implemented. Some drugs proved ineffective or too toxic. Others had intolerable side effects. Clinical guidelines also had to be modified to take account of situations different than those for which they were originally crafted: new drugs were created and regimens formulated; regimens were modified for women, including pregnant women, and children; procedures were created for treating people coinfected with TB, malaria, or hepatitis; "salvage" regimens were developed for those who were "failing" treatment. And because the conditions of poor countries differed vastly from those of rich ones, guidelines about the "staging" of the disease and initiation of treatment had to be modified for use in places where laboratory tests were unavailable and people might not know whether their weight had decreased by 10%.[11] Adjustments also had to be made for changes in the virus as resistant strains became increasingly common.

Typically, rules come in complex combinations of technical and legal, shaped by solid knowledge and substantial uncertainty, and fought over by people with deep moral convictions, professional commitments, economic interests, and personal stakes. Looking at the role played by these rules, I show how deeply contemporary life has been reordered by the choice to use rules to organize the work of governance. What happens to these rules is by no means obvious, and I therefore trace the life course of rules (like the VCT rules) as they are created, transported to new settings, and implemented, invoked, ignored, violated, rejected, or reworked. But we should also acknowledge that rules are not neutral. Rather than simply creating order, they reshape the social order, conferring legitimacy on some actors and taking it away from others. They bolster claims on resources for some claimants but not for others; they increase the legitimacy of some professions but decrease the standing of others. And the process of creating, disseminating, modifying, and working with rules consumes vast resources, whether or not there are any spare resources to devote to rulemaking or adjudication.

This increased tendency to organize the medical work of HIV/AIDS around rules did not occur in a vacuum, though. Before examining the ubiquity and use of rules in HIV/AIDS more deeply, I offer some background on the legalization and globalization of healthcare since the last decades of the twentieth century. I also explain the choice of HIV/AIDS as a lens for looking at these recent changes.

Legalized Medicine in a Globalized World

The number of bodies issuing rules about healthcare, the number of rules issued, and the number of activities governed by rules all have increased (Heimer, Petty, and Culyba 2005; see also Timmermans and Berg 2003). This pattern of growth occurs partly because new forms of governance join old ones rather than replacing them. Policymakers often layer new rules on top of old ones rather than doing the extra work of de-implementing and stripping away irrelevant or counterproductive elements that are deeply embedded in organizational and professional practices. Thus, in US healthcare, professional, public, managerial, and market governance mechanisms are bewilderingly layered and interwoven (Scott et al. 2000, 348–49), yielding both a larger number of rules and a different mix of rules than in the past. Professional self-regulation has now been joined by mandates emanating from state bodies and third-party payers. The resulting formal laws, official regulations, clinical guidelines, research protocols, rules of quasi-official regulatory bodies such as the Joint Commission (and its international counterparts), policies of insurers and other third-party payers, and organizational policies and SOPs are all authoritative statements intended to shape the activity of participants in healthcare settings. Moreover, with ramped up pressures for accountability (Power 1997; Strathern 2000; Espeland and Vannebo 2007) in healthcare as in other fields of endeavor, new occupations and professional associations have arisen to write, revise, and track rules; monitor work and ensure adherence to rules; examine the credentials of staff members; assess the appropriateness of billing; and settle disputes.

In effect, the increasingly legalistic approach to healthcare imports law, legal actors, and legalistic, rule-driven ways of doing things into healthcare work, professions, and organizations. With some exceptions, though, the law transported across the boundary into healthcare is soft rather than hard, gray-letter rather than black-letter law. The legalization that has occurred in the world of medicine thus can fruitfully be compared with soft legalization chronicled by scholars studying international relations and international organizations. The more "legalized" arrangements—"hard law"—are those in which parties are clearly and unconditionally obligated to follow the rules, the rules clearly define the conduct that is required, permitted, or prohibited, and authority has been delegated to third parties to interpret and implement rules, to resolve disputes, sometimes even to make additional rules (Abbott et al. 2000; Abbott and Snidal 2000). Less legalized arrangements can be "softer" on any or all of these three dimensions, and obligation, precision, and delegation need not move in tandem.

In the world of healthcare, legalization arises both from the efforts of governments and formal legal systems and from the legislative, interpretive, and oversight activities of other entities that govern subparts of healthcare, often with some degree of government involvement. The dimensions of legalization remain the same, but the mechanisms are somewhat modified when governance is carried out by nonstate actors. Almost inevitably, "law" in the realm of healthcare is somewhat softer because its rules may not be fully articulated with the laws and regulations of the formal legal system. Because the boundary between state and nonstate regulatory bodies is porous, though, states sometimes economize on start-up costs and evade political controversy by drawing on nonstate bodies to perform regulatory activities on their behalf. Even though it is generally less hard, nonstate regulation often comes with well-developed mechanisms for monitoring and enforcement, a good deal of precision in the rules and routines themselves, and bodies charged with settling disputes.

Some of the complexity of the system of governance in the world of healthcare arises because of its decentered, multicephalic character.[12] Healthcare has many fiefdoms, each governed semiautonomously by its own "legislators," "executives," and "courts." What is being governed is sometimes a geographical area (think of the national and subnational ministries of health). But often entities being governed are analytically distinct but empirically overlapping functions such as research, treatment, drug distribution, training of healthcare personnel, and payment for goods and services. Moreover, although they may seem to be distinct and may be pursuing somewhat inconsistent objectives, these fiefdoms often overlap in space and time, sometimes creating chaos and confusion even as they aim for order. Too many regulators seem just as able as too many cooks to spoil the soup. Further complicating matters, some of these rules span national borders because in contemporary medicine, research, training, and even some treatment draw funding and personnel from distant places.

To be clear, though, this legal turn in healthcare is not simply a US phenomenon, though it has certainly been pushed forwarded by the US. Rather, it is intertwined with the globalization both of healthcare and law. Because disease is no respecter of borders, medicine and healthcare have almost necessarily been global as well. Since antiquity, people and their governments have been attempting to reduce the spread of infectious diseases (McNeill 1976), creating rules about quarantine, gathering officials to discuss how to align commercial interests and public health, and eventually creating international treaties (such as the International Health Regulations), global networks of laboratories and surveillance systems, and compacts for sharing information and biological samples.

The unfolding of the HIV/AIDS epidemic has both driven and been shaped by the new globalism and legalism of medicine and healthcare. Initially reacting defensively to health threats from abroad, people and governments put in place rules that reinforced boundaries. Later, these same actors were somewhat more likely to reach across borders to offer help, although often that help continued to advance national interests. As they both shored up boundaries and reached across them, actors often employed legal and quasi-legal tools.

To date, much of the research on the globalization of law has looked at the processes through which transnational laws, regulations, standards, and norms emerge, diffuse across national borders, and are adopted as national policy. It has focused on state change (Shaffer 2012, 242–43) through national statutes, cases, and regulations (Halliday and Osinsky 2006) across a variety of legal domains. Further, as Munger (2012) notes, much of this scholarship has examined formal institutions of law and the elite lawyers— and elites more generally—who create, resist, or facilitate adoption of new national laws, regulations, or governance structures (see Dezalay and Garth 1996, 2002, 2010; Halliday and Carruthers 2007). In contrast, scholarship on domestic and transnational social movements in processes of democratic transitions and rights-claiming highlights the role of non-elites and activists (see Klug 2000; Merry 2006b; Munger 2008–09; Kay 2011). These non-elites and activists—who may act in concert with elites or who may themselves be elites in their local settings—prompt adoption of new laws, legal reforms, and legal frameworks.

These processes of transnational diffusion, adoption, and adaptation occur within fundamentally unequal governance systems in which norms, rules, and resources often move from the global North to the global South (Silbey 1997). To be sure, normative frameworks and model laws also move on South-South and South-to-North routes. Yet in the midst of these transfers, all too often rules, priorities, and policies crafted in the places marked as "global" (e.g., Geneva, where WHO sits) come to be interpreted by those powerholders as "universal" ideals that should govern globally. However, these new laws and norms reflect what Santos (1995) calls "a globalized localism"—something (an object, a law, a language) that is the product of a very specific place and time that serves the interests of particular powerholders but that is described as global or universal once it has spread transnationally. As the book will demonstrate, many of the new laws and norms developed in the global North and introduced under the banner of universal best practices are revealed to be quite specific and laden with moral and cultural assumptions that may not resonate with or complement preexisting norms and routines in other parts of the world.

Yet, as Klug demonstrates, both elite and non-elite actors may strategically use, adapt, and deploy norms and laws originating in distant locales for their own purposes, a process that results in hybrid rules that in turn influence global discourse and practice. Klug argues for "a dialectical understanding of the relationship between the global and local in which local agency deploys global forms and is both reshaped in the process and contributes to the continuing reformulation of global alternatives" (2002, 277). Klug's hybrid rules recall the mutually constitutive processes of transfer, uptake, and iterative modification that Halliday and Carruthers (2007) refer to as the "recursivity" of law.

Governing the Global Clinic extends this scholarship on the global reach of law to a new setting—medicine—with a focus on meso- and microlevels of analysis that operate below the level of the nation-state. I ask how law operates in healthcare, a domain outside of the formal institutions of law and, to date, largely neglected by the scholarship on the globalization of law. In this new domain, mechanisms of transfer, sources of authority, and enforcement often do not require formal national policy adoption and may bypass the nation-state altogether, particularly when both creators and enforcers of new rules and norms (such as the FDA) lie outside the national jurisdiction of countries where these rules are being used.

Moreover, the invocation of law in the domain of medicine often involves a transformation of law and a rethinking of the meaning and relevance of traditional categories of hard and soft law. The rules governing the practice of medicine involve both hard law and soft law, and sometimes also a de facto conversion of hard law into soft law in the absence of enforcement mechanisms within this new domain. Formal law may involve the police and surveillance powers associated with the public health functions of the state, such as mandatory reporting of new infections or forcible quarantine of individuals exposed to highly infectious, untreatable, and/or fatal viruses. But formal law may also involve threats of medical malpractice lawsuits or legal determinations of who may consent to medical procedures on behalf of dependents or those with cognitive impairments.

However, more influential in many ways in the routine practice of medicine are the pressures to recognize, attend to, and comply with the soft law associated with the rules, reporting requirements, and anticipated sanctions of entities that govern subparts of medicine through government-like legislative, interpretive, and oversight activities. By training attention on meso- and microlevels of analysis, I highlight processes of adoption, adaptation, resistance, and sometimes mutual adjustment at the "messy leading edge of institutionalization" (Heimer 2013, 142) in the HIV clinics where I conducted my research. Despite the absence of strong enforcement mechanisms, such soft law can transform the daily routines and practice of medicine and directly impact clinical research and patient care.

This simultaneous globalization and legalization of medicine has created an unsettled and often incoherent structure of governance that requires continual tinkering, as clinic workers weigh priorities and adjust to local circumstances. This unsettled, incoherent governance structure nevertheless has powerful effects.

HIV/AIDS as a Strategic Case for Studying the Legalization of Medicine

So far I have described a general tendency toward increasing legalism and an accompanying increase in globalism in healthcare. I have stressed that by legalization I mean the propensity to turn to rules (including, but not limited to, formal laws) as a way to solve problems. These new rules have not always been easy for medical actors to work with, and, as I will show, the repeated use of legal solutions has created a host of unintended effects. HIV/AIDS provides an especially good lens for examining the legal turn in healthcare and the effects of deep law on clinic life.

The first mysterious cases of HIV appeared in 1979, concentrated among gay men in New York and San Francisco. Initially trivialized, the HIV pandemic has strained the capacities of healthcare systems around the world and wreaked havoc in poor countries. As of 2023, 43.3 million people had died of AIDS since the beginning of the pandemic. Annual global deaths peaked in 2004, when an estimated 2.0 million people died from HIV; by

2023, that number had dropped to 630,000. New infections peaked at an estimated 3.2 million in 1996, but had dropped to 1.3 million new infections in 2023. By 2023, 86% of people living with HIV knew their status, and 77% of people living with HIV were accessing treatment. In part because treatment allows people who are infected to live much longer, the number of people who are living with HIV has continued to rise, reaching an estimated 39.9 million in 2023.[13] Usually studied as a medical and public health problem, the epidemic clearly has economic, political, and social causes as well as biomedical ones. In particular, the legal turn in healthcare has been critical in shaping responses to HIV/AIDS.

HIV, often tagged as a global disease, originated in central Africa but did indeed move from country to country. But it did not simply move by itself. Instead, it moved through the unwitting actions of people. Moreover, insofar as people's patterns of behavior changed in ways that facilitated the spread of the virus, the changes were much more complex than the increased travel to which the spread of infectious diseases is often attributed. Instead, the virus's movement was facilitated by a much more multidimensional globalism.

HIV is a bloodborne disease most often transmitted through sexual activity. But as Pepin (2011) and many others point out, sex is generally a rather inefficient transmitter of the virus. Blood transmission is more efficient than sexual transmission. Ironically, colonial disease eradication campaigns, in which unsterilized needles were used for vaccinations and shots, were an important early amplifier of the disease. But sex also became a more efficient transmitter when economies collapsed and the exclusion of women from the cities of colonial Belgian Congo led struggling "femmes libres" to take on many clients rather than continuing the customary practice of serving a stable group of three or four men. In this instance, the economic collapses can be traced to the joint effects of rapid urbanization (particularly in Brazzaville and Léopoldville, now Kinshasa), as Africans were enlisted to supply raw materials for the Allied effort in World War II, and then subsequent economic decline of urban areas as Whites fled during independence movements.

It was also during the post-independence period that HIV likely moved from Congo to Haiti. Why Haiti? Belgian colonial education policies meant that there were few educated Congolese citizens to fill administrative and teaching positions when independence came to Congo. Well-educated, French-speaking, Black Haitians, able to earn more than they could at home, migrated to post-independence Congo to staff government bureaucracies and schools. Some of these workers acquired HIV during this sojourn, carried the virus back to Haiti, and transmitted it to others. Haiti then contributed its own HIV amplification program in an unhygienic, poorly regulated Port-au-Prince plasma center that exported blood products to the US, infecting both Haitian plasma donors and American recipients of these blood products, and adding to the effects of gay tourism.

So, although HIV/AIDS is a profoundly global disease, the spread of the disease is not just a matter of the economics and geography of tourism, and especially sex tourism, but instead includes colonial labor and health policies and investments in education, the spread of guns, world wars, trade in raw materials, independence movements and UN interventions, and the harvesting of blood and other biological products in poor countries and their subsequent sale to rich countries—all legally mediated phenomena.

Once the virus was identified, both the legalism and the globalism of HIV continued to affect how things unfolded. Because they were often in a quandary about how to respond to the AIDS epidemic, medical caregivers and researchers' responses have been strongly shaped by the new laws, rules, and protocols of the medical world. Rules for testing and diagnosis, as well as for classifying cases, have continued to evolve as researchers make new discoveries about symptom patterns, develop laboratory tests for verification, and adjust protocols for use in countries with inadequate laboratory facilities. These definitions and rules are important in the collection of statistical information about disease prevalence, but also create legal entitlements to treatment, social services, and insurance for patients and entitlements to payment for physicians and clinics. Access to pharmaceuticals has been shaped internationally by TRIPS and by the subsequent loosening of that agreement's rules in the Doha Declaration. But drug access has also been shaped by the FDA's drug approvals process and judicial decisions ordering governments to supply drugs.

But if the legalization of medicine has affected how care is delivered and research conducted in HIV, HIV has also contributed to the legalization of healthcare in what is clearly a recursive system. This pressure for increased legalism occurs at all levels: in the research rules of AIDS research networks, intensive research monitoring programs, insistence that testing follow the rigorous VCT protocols, attention to guidelines (and perhaps even increased adherence to guidelines) in treatment programs, and legal contestation over rights to treatment. As one example, although healthcare organizations have long had guidelines about infection control, anxiety about the spread of infection through contact with bodily fluids increased markedly with HIV. First created in 1983 for preventing the spread of HIV and other bloodborne pathogens, the CDC's recommendations on Universal Precautions have become standard of practice in many healthcare settings around the world (CDC 1988). Likewise, although many of the rules of the research world existed long before HIV, AIDS heightened consciousness about these rules, partly because activist patients pressed to be included in decision making about research and agitated for speedier access to new drugs (Epstein 1996). In the long run, stakeholder participation in policymaking matured and became institutionalized, for instance, in National Institutes of Health (NIH) requirements for community advisory boards.

As a lens for studying the legalization of healthcare, then, HIV/AIDS provides a felicitous case, in part because of the historical timing of the epidemic. Enterprises bear the imprint of the era in which they were born (Stinchcombe 1965). Because the research, treatment, and governance cultures of HIV medicine were being formed at the time when medicine (and especially US medicine) was becoming more legalistic, the organizational and institutional cultures surrounding HIV bear an especially clear imprint of the new legal regime. It should therefore be easier to study the legalization of medicine here than in most other medical fields.

Clinics as Strategic Sites for Studying the Legalization of Medicine

If the history of HIV is in part the story of the legalization of healthcare, with a host of rules on a stunning array of topics being created, disseminated, and adopted, it doesn't end there. Creation of rules is one thing; use of rules is quite another.

Some rules that guide HIV treatment and research are made in the clinics where research and treatment occur, but most are made elsewhere (though they may be adjusted somewhat at the clinic level). Governments and government agencies make many of the rules about the conduct of clinical research, the approval of pharmaceuticals and medical devices, as well as creating core regulations governing healthcare and health professionals. Professional societies develop clinical practice guidelines. University (or research center) ethics review committees (in the US, institutional review boards) are responsible for implementing national laws and international codes. But we can only know how these rules are used by looking at what happens when the rules arrive in the clinics—the primary worksites of the legal system of HIV medicine. There the story is likely to be much more complicated than the rulemakers might have imagined. Practice rarely conforms exactly to rules, for the good reason that rules cannot anticipate the astonishing variability of the real world. But knowing what use people make of rules—as guidelines that will need modification, as starting points that allow workers to coordinate their activities, as ways of establishing who is in charge—should show us why some rules "work" and others do not.

In many organizational settings (e.g., hospitals, factories, universities), those who devise rules believe they have developed superior methods for performing key tasks, whether those tasks are treating patients, assembling cars, or compiling grades. Rules are intended to ensure that tasks are carried out "correctly." If several equally good methods are available, choosing one will make coordination easier, whether the activity occurs in a laboratory, pharmacy, or operating room. Written in the days before clinical practice guidelines and governance protocols were ubiquitous, Bosk's (1979) classic book on the training of surgeons shows how seriously physicians have taken rules, including the largely arbitrary local rules of procedure that make teamwork possible in high-pressure settings such as the operating theaters Bosk studied or the HIV research projects examined in this book.

Even though "everyone knows" that people do not religiously adhere to rules, rules and guidelines remain important. Studying the use of an oncology research protocol and the cardio pulmonary resuscitation (CPR) protocol, Timmermans and Berg (1997) found that participants often did not follow the script. Protocols were not "prescriptions" imposed on docile participants, they argue, but instead tools by which participants remind each other what they are supposed to do. This reminding takes into account both participants' objectives and the features of the materials with which they are working. Rather than dictating exactly what should happen, then, a CPR protocol is one tool among many that medical workers use to decide how to treat a drowning victim versus someone being resuscitated after a hanging. Because of the inherent impossibility of writing standards that take sufficient account of the variation that workers encounter, then, protocols are only modestly authoritative: "Medicine doesn't fail to meet the standards: the standards fail to meet reality" (Mol and Berg 1998, 10).

These questions about *how* rules matter and for what and what happens when people have different expectations about how rules are to be used can be answered only with detailed ethnographic observation. Because many rules recede into the background as they come to seem "natural" to workers, it is not easy for workers to report on rules. *Observing* must therefore supplement *asking*, and in the case of the rules about HIV/AIDS, that observing needs to occur in clinic settings.

In effect, then, I make a case here for studying the legalization of medicine by studying a specific case that coincides in time with the growth of legalism and whose international character allows us to see the lushly developed, highly pluralistic system of rules. I also argue that we cannot understand how such a complex system of rules actually works without studying it on the ground—in this case, as clinic-level law.

Clinic-Level Law and the Legalization of Medicine: Gaps and More Gaps

This book poses a series of questions about the governance of healthcare and the clinics where so much medical work occurs. More specifically, it asks about legal solutions to problems of regulation and governance, with both "legal" and "regulation" defined broadly. Within "legal solutions," I include a stance to problem solving that takes the formulation, dissemination, and application of rules as a core part of regulation and governance. And I include in regulation not only the regulatory activities of state agencies but also similar activities by a wide variety of other entities.

The central questions that animate the research are by no means mine alone. In essence, they are all about one or another sort of gap: about interpreting the regulatory landscape as filled with gaps, about filling these alleged gaps with rules, and about creating new gaps between rules on the books and rules in action. Although stating it this way suggests a sequence (see gap, fill gap, create different kind of gap), in fact these processes go on simultaneously. For instance, the impulse to create rules is not simply a response to a (previous) interpretive act. Rather, the assessment of the regulatory landscape can just as well occur as rules are being created or even after they have been inserted into the situation.

Above I note medicine's turn to rule-based governance—what I call legalization—in the waning decades of the twentieth century. Medical practitioners have long argued about the extent to which medicine is an art or a science. At stake here is what role clinical guidelines and other rules should play in the practice of medicine. Although it is rare to insist that medicine is and should be only art or only science, caregivers and policymakers often disagree about how closely physicians and other healthcare workers should adhere to clinical guidelines and who should be empowered to decide whether deviation is appropriate. Advocates for the legalization of medicine argue that rules and guidelines bring several advantages. On average, they reason, patients are better served when doctors and other caregivers follow rules because carefully written guidelines assess and summarize the latest research and show how it bears on particular medical problems, a complex cognitive task that is difficult to perform adequately and consistently. Guidelines also can help with the efficient allocation of resources by suggesting which tests are unnecessary and which expensive medications and therapies offer no advantages over cheaper alternatives. And by reducing practice variations, guidelines may make healthcare fairer, decreasing discrepancies between treatments received by rich and poor. More rules, in this way of thinking, mean better medical outcomes.

This vision of rules is hardly unique to the medical world. Similar arguments appear, for instance, in the sociolegal discussions of "access to justice" and "rule of law." There, as in the literature on clinical guidelines and evidence-based medicine (EBM), rules are seen as solutions—ways to introduce and mandate effective and efficient practices, increase predictability, level the playing field, and control (inappropriate) discretion. Despite the similarities, important differences exist between attempting to standardize medical practice and attempting to increase civil justice or encourage judicial independence.

Legal tools do not always match the problems people are trying to solve, as research on access to justice demonstrates. When ordinary citizens encounter problems with landlords, neighbors, spouses, or governmental bodies, they may not turn to the law for help (Merry 1990; Sandefur 2008, 2009). Some problems clearly are addressed by law, others clearly are not, and many require reformulation before they fit into legal categories. In addition, legal solutions can be expensive and time consuming. They may require an initial investment in learning what the law is and finding legal assistance. They may be inflexible. And not everyone believes that the law is available to them or likely to be on their side (Ewick and Silbey 1998). Often people seem to conclude that nonlegal solutions are as good or better that what law offers (Sandefur 2009). Despite this, those concerned with increasing access to justice continue to look primarily at access to *legal* solutions, apparently believing that increases in access to justice depend on increased access to lawyers, paralegals, and others who can work with and through the law.

Rule of law research takes a similar stance on the desirability of introducing more law. Rather than addressing the problems of individuals and families, though, recent rule of law literature focuses on economic and political development, often using the concept of rule of law to "champion our way of doing something over someone else's" (Ohnesorge 2007, 102). Without much thought about whether alternative principles are ordering activity, other states' political and economic failings are attributed to the absence of the rule of law. Rule of law modifications in one arena (such as the economy) are expected to spill over into other arenas (such as human rights). In addition, the rule of law agenda has broadened to include "just about everything one might associate with fair and just governance" (Ohnesorge 2007, 106). In short, in the name of protecting loans, international financial institutions such as the World Bank have legitimated micromanagement by insisting that other countries run their affairs (and not just their economic affairs) legalistically.

But have access to justice and rule of law advocates either imagined or misunderstood the gaps they are attempting to fill? Sociologists, sociolegal researchers, and regulation scholars have noted that new rules and regulations often are layered on top of preexisting norms, customs, and commitments, with outcomes then shaped jointly by the old and the new (Silbey 1997; Klug 2002; Merry 2006a; Bartley 2011; Swidler and Watkins 2017). Development scholars have similarly noted the disadvantages of "institutional monocropping" as a development strategy (Evans 2004) and the advantages of drawing on local expertise and local preferences in crafting rules and institutions (Ostrum 1990; Sen 1999). An older literature on legal pluralism acknowledges the existence of multiple systems of rules—rules of First Nations or ethnic groups exist alongside state law; rules of religious bodies and states govern overlapping terrains.

Finally, as law on the books becomes law in action, street-level bureaucrats (Lipsky 2010) and other workers must craft translations and make rules fit the circumstances in which rules are being implemented. In this process, the old truisms of sociology make their appearance. Those who are rich, well educated, well connected, White, male, and so forth frequently draw on rules that were crafted with their situations in mind (see especially Lempert and Sanders 1986, 430–38; Minow 1990), have those rules interpreted by people who are similar to them and sympathetic to their circumstances, and encounter rules in action that work to their advantage. When rules pit the interests of individuals against those of organizations, the latter generally are repeat players with deep pockets of expertise and funding (Galanter 1974; Edelman and Suchman 1999). Whatever their intended purpose, because rules are written, interpreted, and applied by people with power, the introduction of "more law" into new settings often reinscribes and recreates old inequalities (Black 1976).

The impulse to legalize is often partly an attempt to decrease (bad) discretion. But discretion is required to make regulations work as intended, and some designs or ad hoc adjustments do protect people's capacity to make the system work better (Silbey 2011), a point that has been illustrated in such diverse arenas as the regulation of science labs in the US (Huising and Silbey 2011), the securing and monitoring of microloans by Mexican bank officers (Canales 2011), and the social problem solving of a subset of Brazilian prosecutors (Coslovsky 2011). "Relational regulation" or "sociological citizenship" often can correct the official system, stretching and reshaping formal rules so they are responsive to empirical realities (Silbey 2011).

My argument, then, is that the legalization of medicine is very much in the spirit of other moves to solve problems by introducing more law and in particular the kinds of rules that emanate from rich countries such as the US. But this study is distinctive in several ways. First, this book is about medicine rather than civil justice, the economy, nation building, or any of the other realms where sociolegal scholars have either studied or advocated legalization—in effect, the introduction of more law. By posing these questions about medicine and by investigating a field of medicine that has a global character, we are able to think about how legalization works across both professional and national boundaries. In this case, rules are exported from richer countries (especially the US) to poorer ones, often as part of the infrastructure that comes with access to research and treatment funds. This movement of rules across national borders is almost inevitably accompanied by difficulties adapting rules to new settings and skepticism about compliance. At the same time that rules are being carried across national borders, this legalistic way of working is also spreading to new professions. The work of medical caregivers has not always been so closely governed by rules, and indeed rules have been used differently—with more autonomy and discretion—than in law.

Questions about preexisting rules also have a different character in medical arenas. The dispute about whether medicine is an art or a science is, in part, a fight about how much the rules of thumb of particular practitioners or clinics should be respected. By now, ample evidence demonstrates that benchmark medical conditions are not managed uniformly even within countries. Unsurprisingly, those "practice variations" are magnified in cross-national comparisons, particularly if those comparisons include indigenous practitioners, whose practices have usually been viewed skeptically by Western medicine.[14] But the discomfort of Western-trained caregivers with indigenous medicine tells us much about what happens when dominant rule systems fail to acknowledge preexisting systems of governance. Some Western-trained caregivers acknowledge the de facto layering of medical regimes and try to incorporate traditional caregivers; many others do not. Western-trained caregivers also often fail to acknowledge the limits, biases, and cultural foundations of Western medicine, for instance, by incorporating their own religious beliefs into their practice while decrying the "superstition" of traditional caregivers. Medicine's rules and practices are also always layered on a relatively ungovernable stratum of patients' own practices, a rough edge in rich countries and perhaps an even rougher one in countries where community elders may oppose treatment in "Western" clinics.

Moreover, in this situation, the rules themselves are highly variable. Some are about medicine, others about research, ethics, training and certification of workers, or financial accounting. And the rules whose meaning is being negotiated have a variety of often ambiguous statuses. Some are formal law, others are regulations, and still others are much softer kinds of rules. This book thus allows us to think about what happens when negotiations over the meaning of rules occur a bit further beyond the range of formal law, where the shadow of law is (perhaps) less dense and where other professions support competing systems of rules and norms (Heimer 1999). Yet the influence of law remains surprisingly strong. When people are unsure whether rules have the backing of law, they nevertheless worry a great deal about whether what they are doing is legal. To some degree, this seems to be because the organizations they work for are deeply worried about organizational consequences of legal infractions.

This study also acknowledges the complexity of the social worlds in which rules are being implemented. HIV clinics function as intermediaries between patients and other organizations, often translating patients and their actions into more bureaucratically acceptable categories. Clinic staff members are sometimes simultaneously part of the "developed" world—working in the realm of biomedicine, training in a "Western" medical tradition, prescribing drugs and therapies created in the global North, and often accountable to donors from the global North—and part of the "emerging economies" in which they reside and from which their patients are drawn. More than most people, then, these clinic workers are equipped to help their patients understand what the clinic and its external supporters require and to make the lives and experiences of these patients legible to external bodies.

Although this is a book about clinical guidelines, rules for the conduct of research, and regulations governing the work of clinics, it does not aim simply to say whether the rules work. Rather, its objective is to look at what happens when the impulse to govern through rules leads to the dissemination of rules to places quite different from those where they were originally formulated. Just as the rules of the global North do not work quite the same way when transported to the global South, so the tools of law have some surprising effects when imported to the realm of medicine. At their worst, they create confusion about what the rules are and who has the authority to make decisions. At their best, they open opportunities to talk about what we owe one another and to ratchet up our sense of obligation to our fellows.

Overview

Clinic staff members work with three main types of rules: clinical guidelines and other rules about how to do medical work, protocols and associated rules about how to conduct research, and administrative rules that shape clinic governance and accounting. Although the main objective varies from one type of rule to another, these rules share common patterns that are analyzed here. To understand the effect of the legal turn in medicine and healthcare, I focus particularly on the rules governing treatment and research, core matters for medical workers; I weave in comments on administrative matters as appropriate.

HIV is often described as the first truly global disease. Yet, as this introduction suggests, HIV is likely also the first truly "legalized" disease in the sense that legal forms have shaped HIV treatment and research from the outset, a point illustrated by the legal infrastructure surrounding HIV counseling and testing. Deep law has penetrated more deeply into the world of HIV than into many other areas of healthcare, and we cannot understand what happened in HIV without seeing the complexly global and legal nature of the disease.

The laws, guidelines, and other rules intended to shape the work of HIV clinics are part of the legal turn in healthcare and of the ongoing globalization of healthcare. Both legalization and globalization introduce standardized practices—those laws and guidelines—into healthcare organizations dispersed around the world. In a recursive process, they both assume and create uniformity. And yet, these standardized forms encounter a world—the clinics, their workers, and their patients—that is not nearly as uniform as anticipated. Although the objective is to provide relatively uniform care guided by clinical and research rules, the variability among clinics and research facilities makes this challenging. Chapter 2 begins with an abbreviated history of the globalization of healthcare, focusing on the parts that most affect HIV treatment and research. After briefly explaining important national differences in the experience of the HIV epidemic, the chapter provides detailed portraits of five clinics—two in the US, and one each in Thailand, South Africa, and Uganda—where I gathered the ethnographic material and interviews used in this book. These introductions to the clinics lay a foundation for the closer analysis of the work of treatment and research and how clinic staff engage with the rules that are intended to shape their activities.

The complex legal environment in which HIV clinics are embedded originated in inchoate initiatives that gradually coalesced into mutually reinforcing strands beginning in the middle of the twentieth century. After cataloging key changes in the legal environment of medicine (especially US medicine) and placing those changes in a broader historical context, chapter 3 examines the subjective experience of those working with the rules. The chapter asks how the proliferation of rules came to feel like a "mushroom cloud" of rules, in the words of one administrator I talked with. Within the clinics, as the book explains, global rules have not simply been adopted and followed. Instead, they have been deciphered, tinkered with, and harmonized with local rules. They also have been avoided, contested, gamed, and sometimes outright violated.

Clinical guidelines are intended to increase the likelihood that physicians in different locations and kinds of healthcare organizations will draw on the scientific consensus and provide their patients with essentially the same treatment. And yet, as chapter 4 shows, purportedly universal clinical guidelines look considerably more variable as they enter actual clinics and are put to use. Clinical guidelines have implicitly imagined a world that is biologically variable but socially uniform, but the world beyond the clinic doors is not uniform, and some of that social variability impinges on the clinics. This chapter explains how clinicians, pressured to adhere to clinical guidelines, carefully signaled their support for guidelines at the same time that they judiciously tinkered with rules to take account of local contexts, including variations in clinic resources and staffing, the availability of medications and laboratory tests, and local customs and patient needs and resources. All five of the clinics used clinical guidelines, but they worked with them in somewhat different ways. Despite these differences, guidelines did establish standards for treatment and shape understandings about what kind of care patients were entitled to receive. When clinics were not able to live up to those expectations, guidelines made it harder to ignore the gap and increased clinicians' (and activists') resolve to do better.

Both clinical guidelines and the rules governing clinical research aim to increase uniformity and raise standards, but with somewhat different purposes. For clinical guidelines the goal is improved care. The objective of research rules is to ensure the trustworthiness of research findings so that data may be aggregated across sites and used both in drug approval processes and in the preparation of clinical guidelines. In analyzing how clinics work with research rules, chapter 5 argues that a multilayered system of "institutionalized skepticism"—consisting of carefully vetted routines, training programs, records, and staff—has been used to make clinic-level scientific data credible in the global world of HIV clinical research. Yet, once again, uniform rules confront locally variable work settings, creating significant challenges especially for researchers in poor countries. Not only do these researchers need to use a disproportionate share of their resources to meet global standards, but they also must produce extra evidence to convince distrusting research monitors that they are adhering to the rules.

Chapters 4 and 5 discuss what clinic staff actually do when they work with the guidelines, protocols, SOPs, and other rules that are intended to shape and govern clinic life. The next three chapters consider some unexpected effects of these systems of rules. Moving beyond national and clinic-level variations in the use of treatment rules, chapter 6 explores how the experience of the legalization of medicine varied from one healthcare occupation to another, depending on the nature of staff members' work, their position in the clinic hierarchy, and the training they receive on legal and quasi-legal matters. The legalization of HIV care has introduced rules that have felt doubly unfamiliar because they entailed imports both across national borders—as rules move from the global North to the global South— and across professional boundaries—as lawyerly ways of interacting with and using rules were imported into healthcare professions. But because clarity about what was scientifically or medically appropriate did not always lead to clarity about what was legally required or socially acceptable, the new rules often created confusion about what course to follow.

Chapters 7 and 8 consider some of the blind spots created when healthcare organizations face unrealistic mandates. In many organizations, workers find that they must develop work-arounds to complete required tasks. Particularly in politically fraught arenas with publicly announced goals organized around careful compromises, workers know they must toe the line or at least appear to do so. HIV treatment and research have been contentious because of both the stigma of HIV infection and the precariousness of rich countries' support for programs located beyond their borders. Aware that continued support depends on delicate compromises, clinics do their best to conceal their failures to follow the rules exactly. For that reason, clinics not only produce knowledge—scientific advances from clinical research and practical knowledge about how to provide treatment in resource-constrained clinics—but also produce ignorance as they conceal information about compromises that funders and regulators might view skeptically. Social scientists often investigate how organizations and individuals use information and knowledge, but they have been slower to recognize that ignorance is an important resource that also gets deployed strategically. Chapter 7 asks what it is strategic for clinics to conceal and what methods they use to keep discrediting information hidden.

Ethics regulations also produce blind spots, as chapter 8 shows. Clinics conducting research are required to follow carefully crafted and thoroughly institutionalized ethics rules, including rules about initial and ongoing review of projects, recruitment and retention of research subjects, informed consent, and the treatment of research subjects. But these rules of "official ethics" say little about many other ethical issues that arise in the work of HIV clinics engaged in research and treatment. Yet the silence of official ethics is not exactly neutral, both because it implicitly suggests that other moral and ethical issues are less important and because clinics often have little time and few resources to devote to "ethics on the ground." Chapter 8 discusses how official ethics developed, systematically compares official ethics and ethics on the ground, describes the compliance work associated with official ethics, and elucidates the link between official ethics and organizational interests.

Although the aspirations of law may be noble, the legalization of healthcare has not always brought the anticipated results. In particular, although increased legalism has brought some of the expected benefits of higher, more scientifically defensible treatment standards, it has also created confusion about the status of rules. And although legalization may have increased the trustworthiness of research results, it has also introduced rigid compliance bureaucracies that sometimes conflict with and undermine indigenous systems of professional and lay morality and may encourage dissembling because of extreme pressures to follow impossible rules. Drawing on observations in both the five clinics and the larger world of HIV treatment and research, the concluding chapter asks about the very special conditions under which increased legalism enlarged clinic workers' understanding of what they owed their patients and research subjects. These felicitous conditions have been somewhat more common in HIV than in other fields of medicine, in part because early HIV activism brought together medical caregivers, scientists, patients, research subjects, regulatory personnel, government officials, and even an occasional pharmaceutical company staff member. Such encounters created a culture more fully attuned to moral worth and more deeply informed by and respectful of the experiences of diverse groups of stakeholders. That in turn encouraged deeper deliberation about how to temper the excesses of legalism and harness rules to keep the focus squarely on improving the welfare of desperate patients and research subjects.

[CHAPTER TWO]

Where the Action Is

Taking Standardized Rules to Unstandard Clinics

For most people, healthcare settings remain a world apart from everyday life. In these places of intense fear, sorrow, hope, and joy, people confront their own and others' mortality but also experience the miracle of healing and the magic of birth. Clinics are fateful places, sites of problematic, consequential action for both patients and caregivers; they are also places where people spend long, dull, uncomfortable hours just waiting.[1]

Although the experience of hospitals and clinics as alien spaces may be universal, people's experiences in clinics are not in other respects uniform. Patients and families who come to HIV clinics in the US, Thailand, South Africa, and Uganda—the countries where the research for this book was conducted—come to rather different places, arrive there in quite different ways, and are treated in somewhat different manners. The objective of the rules that govern the clinics is to introduce a modicum of uniformity, at least in medically crucial parts, into otherwise variable circumstances. Yet that attempt is only partially successful, in part because the boundaries between human bodies and the social contexts in which they exist are highly permeable, altering the character of apparently uniform diseases and modifying the effects of allegedly standardized interventions.

In line with this expectation of uniformity, HIV is often said to be the first truly global disease. Although this claim seems overstated, HIV has surely combined local and global elements in different proportions than previous pandemics. HIV/AIDS has clearly accelerated globalism in healthcare as people worked across borders to conduct research, develop treatments, and prevent the development and diffusion of drug-resistant strains of the virus. Yet in other respects, HIV is not the same disease in the many countries to which the virus has spread. Deep inequalities have persisted in access to prevention, testing, and treatment, as well as in attention to creating relevant knowledge and useful remedies.

Seeing HIV as an international, universal disease is both an illusion and an aspiration. It is self-evident that neither HIV nor the world in which it exists can be described as homogeneous. That does not mean it is futile to create standards for this unstandard world, though it suggests we should anticipate variability in outcomes when we attempt to standardize engagements with a world or a disease that is in fact not uniform. Like all models and simplifications, standards come with scope conditions; they fit some situations better than others. Attempts to treat HIV with standardized clinical guidelines, to conduct clinical studies with research protocols, and to orchestrate the work of clinics with government regulations, clinic policies, and standard operating procedures (SOPs) therefore offer countless examples of what happens when the world of standards encounters a world that is not itself standardized (Timmermans and Epstein 2010). By looking closely at how clinic workers and patients in five very different HIV clinics grapple with the frequent mismatches between what standards are intended to do and what they accomplish, even after considerable tinkering and adjustment, we are able to appreciate the full range of responses to the introduction of standardized ways of working.

This chapter lays the foundation for the book's investigation of how global treatment and research regimes work on the ground by first considering the increases in the globalization of healthcare that might create some uniformity in how clinics and other healthcare organizations manage illness and disability. Despite the globalization of some aspects of healthcare, important differences remain and the chapter then goes on to illustrate just how much "the ground" itself actually varies. In the five clinics where I interviewed staff members and watched them work, the virus may be essentially the same— although some variations do exist in the virus itself—but much else is different. In some clinics, most patients are gay men; in others, heterosexual women and men dominate the clinic population, with children also arriving for treatment. In all of the clinics, staff worry about whether patients will show up for appointments and adhere to treatment regimens, but those concerns are intensified where many patients are too poor to travel to the clinic or to secure the food needed to accompany medications. Some clinics have ample resources; others lack HIV medicines and the basic supplies and instruments that richer clinics take for granted. Doctors, nurses, and administrators are overworked in all of the clinics, but in some sites staff members work truly grueling hours because their patients will otherwise receive no care at all. In all of the clinics, medical challenges are commonplace, but care is far more routinized (or routinizable) in some clinics than others.

The portraits of the five clinics will start to show why, despite their appeal, universal rules, guidelines, and protocols often fail to live up to their promise. Standards and rules may appear to be simple solutions to problems—ways of organizing activity, ensuring consistency, and perhaps even increasing fairness or at least predictability. Yet much sociolegal and science studies scholarship suggests that this depiction misleads as much as it clarifies. Among the questions this book attempts to answer, then, are when, how, and with what effect globalized clinics can be governed with universal rules and whether it is possible to secure some of those anticipated benefits of universalism with less fully universal rules.

Globalism in Healthcare

HIV convinced many people that their own health and that of their compatriots cannot be secured without attending to the health of their neighbors. At least some of the move to global governance in healthcare arises, then, from the desire of rich countries to protect their citizens.

Although HIV was identified by researchers in France and the US, the virus originated in central Africa. Press coverage of Avian flu, the Ebola and Marburg viruses, TB, West Nile virus, Zika, and other infectious diseases suggests that Americans, and surely people in other countries as well, now rightly fear global health crises and understand how easily diseases are transported across national borders by human and nonhuman carriers. The COVID-19 pandemic reinforced concerns that global and domestic public health systems are ill prepared to deal with such devastating diseases.[2] Some part of the legalization of medicine therefore concerns improving global public health governance to secure the health of domestic populations, particularly in rich countries. The guidelines, protocols, and regulations used in HIV clinics are ground-level elements of this global regulatory system.

At its core, globalization is about a change in how much people and organizations engage with, take their cues from, and coordinate with extra-local entities (Keohane and Nye 2000; Cockerham and Cockerham 2010). It is therefore about changes in networks, practices, and cultural understandings. To say that healthcare has become more globalized, then, means that how people think about health, medicine, and healthcare now depends on how both locals and people at some distance think about these matters; that those engaged in the work of healthcare are more likely than in the past to be embedded in networks that span national boundaries (Chorev and Schrank 2017); and that the work of healthcare now relies on technologies, material objects, and practices, including regulatory practices, that closely resemble those used by organizations and people elsewhere. Some of these new, globalized ways of thinking and working are freely adopted; others may be imposed.

The drivers and effects of globalization are quite diverse. Countries may be globalizers without being globalized when practices and products mostly flow one direction. It would be incorrect, then, to suggest that globalization is everywhere and in all details the same. Rich, middle-income, and poor countries relate differently to the globalization of healthcare, with some countries more fully incorporated into global networks and others more detached. Such differences are consequential for where rules and practices originate; how rules, regulatory systems, knowledge, and materials diffuse; and what happens when global health regimes attempt to govern differently situated facilities—like the five clinics discussed here—with similar if not identical rules.

Although the worlds of medicine and healthcare may now be more thoroughly globalized than in the past, some elements of globalization, including measures to track and prevent the spread of infectious diseases, have been in place since the sanitary conventions and quarantine programs of the mid-nineteenth century (Carvalho and Zacher 2001; Fidler 2001, 2004; Packard 2016). With these global pacts and the development of vaccines and antibiotics, infectious diseases were thought to be on the verge of eradication. Rich countries refocused on treating chronic diseases and the bodily deterioration of old age. Health campaigns stressed lifestyle issues, suggesting that people should take responsibility for their own health by improving their diets, increasing exercise, and giving up or moderating the use of tobacco, alcohol, and recreational drugs (Petersen and Lupton 1996). Decreased concern about contagious diseases also meant less pressure for cross-national coordination of health campaigns. And, indeed, until the 2005 revision, the International Health Regulations (IHR) required reporting on only three diseases.

The prediction that infectious diseases would soon be vanquished proved premature, however (Barrett et al. 1998). Not only have many infectious diseases not been conquered, but treatment and eradication have become more difficult with the development of drug-resistant strains of diseases such as TB and malaria and with reinvigorated resistance to childhood vaccination programs and treatment protocols. In addition, completely novel infectious agents—notably SARS (severe acute respiratory syndrome), MERS (Middle Eastern respiratory syndrome), Candida auris, COVID-19—have continued to emerge. The 2005 revision of the IHR focuses on mode of transmission, infectiousness, and virulence, providing tools to guide decisions about which infectious diseases and other threats to health warrant coordinated global action (Gostin and Sridhar 2014; Gostin and Katz 2016).

At the same time that the perception of threat has gone global, the perception of rights has also gone global. This perspective was articulated in the 1948 UN Universal Declaration of Human Rights, which included a right to health, and later spelled out in a series of covenants and declarations.[3] Subsequent expansion of rights to health and healthcare, often more theoretical than real, has come when countries have adopted new constitutions that include health and healthcare in the package of constitutionally protected rights, changing understandings of what the right to health means.

Moreover, rich countries are increasingly expected to shoulder some responsibility for the health of citizens of poorer countries, for instance, by providing technical, logistical, and financial assistance in creating and maintaining public health capacities (Katz et al. 2012).

Global health programs have grown dramatically since the advent of HIV (Gostin and Sridhar 2014), with the efforts of HIV activists leading to larger pots of funds being available not just for HIV but for other diseases and health conditions as well. These funds have supported the development of global tracking systems, including ProMED-mail, the Global Public Health Intelligence Network (GPHIN, the "rumor list"), the Global Outbreak Alert and Response Network (GOARN), and medical whistleblowers.[4] This system for reporting on and tracking disease, including both seasonal influenza and new infectious diseases, is well developed and linked to production of vaccines. Yet we know that availability of vaccine is hardly uniform and that richer countries receive more than their share of prophylaxis and treatment. Nevertheless the simple existence of such statistics demonstrates the increasing integration of countries into a global health reporting system.

Globalization has altered patterns of movement of patients, with patients traveling to hospitals and clinics known to offer better care, shorter queues, or lower prices. In the early days of HIV, patients sometimes crossed borders to obtain treatments not offered in their home country. Once effective treatments were developed and knowledge was disseminated in clinical guidelines, differences among countries in treatment regimens decreased. What remained, though, were differences in people's and countries' access to skilled caregivers and appropriate pharmaceuticals (especially beyond the first-line regimens) and capacity to pay for treatment.

The era of HIV has brought substantial changes in who gives care and in arrangements for training. Generally, in the US and other rich countries, the balance among subvarieties of medical workers has shifted over time. More doctors are specialists; fewer are general practitioners. At the same time, physicians' assistants and advance practice nurses have stepped in to provide the primary care previously supplied by general practitioners. Moreover, in these same countries, more medical care is now delivered by workers who have migrated from or been trained in other countries. The persistent drain of skilled medical workers from countries with the most pressing needs has led to complaints about the ethics of richer countries' recruitment practices and attempts to limit recruitment from poorer countries (e.g., the Kampala Declaration of 2008, issued by WHO, acting as the host organization for and secretariat of the Global Health Workforce Alliance). Interestingly, though, the globalization of healthcare has created conflicting pressures. Rich countries use attractive employment opportunities to entice medical workers away from poor countries while the flow of funds to poor countries for treatment and research programs creates both increased employment opportunities in poor countries and some pressure for rich countries to curb their voracious appetite for the skilled workers of other nations. And although the workers may migrate to rich countries seeking employment, medical workers flow in both directions for training, research, and short-term placements.

Complicating this already complex picture is the incommensurability of healthcare worker training in different countries. Because the credentials of rich countries are highly respected, rich-country doctors, nurses, and even medical students can easily work abroad, but foreign medical workers must go through elaborate credential checks to work in the US and other rich countries. This allows richer countries to staff philanthropic programs and to offer a hand during crises, but it also may allow unlicensed caregivers to practice above their competence in poorer countries (Sullivan 2016). HIV clinics are popular sites for "clinical tourism" (Wendland 2012) and for what we might call "research tourism" as well.

The production and dissemination of scientific knowledge also has become increasingly global. Clinical research is now routinely conducted multinationally,[5] with both benefits and costs. On the positive side, it brings the researchers and clinicians of poorer countries into contact with the researchers of richer countries, providing access to the research funds of richer countries and opportunities to build skills, networks, and careers. In the US, patients are particularly eager to participate in clinical trials during the period when therapies are being developed for new diseases or when other therapies have failed (Shilts 1987; Epstein 1996). In poorer countries, clinical trials are often the only route to treatment rather than an option to pursue after other treatments have failed.

Although they gain much from clinical research, the medical organizations, researchers, and patients or research subjects of poorer countries often participate as unequal partners in research enterprises. Research activities are strongly shaped by research protocols and by general rules about how research is to be conducted. For the most part, these rules have been developed in the global North and diffused along with research funds to other countries. Organizations outside the US have smaller research budgets, have less infrastructural support already in place, and often receive more scrutiny by research monitors (Heimer and Gazley 2012). Treated as "hands" rather than "heads," researchers in other countries often are incorporated initially to help gather data rather than to write scientific papers or generate research topics (Gazley 2011). Partnerships with poor countries are valuable especially because they offer lower research costs and large pools of potential research subjects (Petryna 2009). Moreover, these patients are more likely to be "treatment naïve" and so especially valuable as research subjects. In addition to meeting simple numerical targets, the research subjects of poor countries may also help projects meet mandated targets for diversity in research subjects because African non-Whites are treated as interchangeable with African Americans (Epstein 2007). Despite what the clinics of poorer countries bring to the table, research rules, along with journal publication agendas and publication standards, all help perpetuate the disadvantages experienced by researchers from poorer countries.

The process of distributing the materials of healthcare, such as pharmaceuticals and medical devices, has also become more global (King 2002). Pharmaceuticals are big business, reaching across national borders. Although some pharmaceutical companies are strictly local, many are multinational organizations, producing drugs or pharmaceutical components in one country for final assembly and distribution in other countries. Pharmaceutical companies are therefore subject to regulation in multiple countries (Braithwaite and Drahos 2000) and seek markets and consumers in multiple countries. Trade negotiations, trade treaties, and domestic and international law (especially having to do with intellectual property) all are consequential for the distribution of drugs and medical devices. Because the US market is so large, multinational manufacturers of drugs and medical devices want to be able to sell their goods in this lucrative market and therefore seek Food and Drug Administration (FDA) approval, giving the US an especially important role as a regulator of medical products.[6] This means that patterns of production and distribution end up influencing research, with the result that all of them are more global than in the past, but with the US being a globalizer (a shaper of the process) and many other countries being more globalized (more influenced by the process).

The poorest countries often do not have much capacity to produce drugs and medical devices and therefore are net importers of both. But as long as incomes remain depressed, imports will also remain limited. Imports may be somewhat higher than one might imagine, though, largely because of international support for healthcare. Yet when such aid is provided, it often comes with strings attached. Donors sometimes specify that funds may be used to purchase only brand-name drugs produced by the pharmaceutical companies of their nations, although such requirements tend to be couched in more neutral terms having to do with drug quality (Klug 2008). Upper-tier resource-constrained countries such as South Africa, with sizeable upper classes with purchasing power on par with the citizens of rich countries, may have some capacity to produce drugs domestically, especially when they partner with richer countries and secure licenses from them (as the generics manufacturer Aspen did in South Africa) (Klug 2012).

Middle-income countries often have the capacity to produce at least some pharmaceuticals and medical devices. Before TRIPS (the Agreement on Trade-Related Aspects of Intellectual Property Rights), middle-income countries often produced drugs for both domestic use and export, undercutting the expensive products of richer-country pharmaceutical companies. As TRIPS provisions gradually came into force, these countries were prohibited from producing cheap drugs for sale beyond their borders, even with the adjustments offered by the Doha Declaration (Klug 2008, 2012; 't Hoen 2009). Countries vary, though, in how much they focus on domestic needs. As Eimer and Lütz (2010) document for HIV/AIDS drugs, at roughly the same level of economic development, India produced pharmaceuticals for export but Brazil produced drugs for domestic use, with the result that a much higher proportion of HIV-infected people in Brazil received anti-retroviral therapy (ART) than in India (see also Biehl 2009).

This more globalized world, in which both people and microbes move more easily between countries than in the past, is also a world shaped by large institutional actors. Yet the institutional environment of global public health is not a unified environment. Instead it is composed of overlapping networks of public health organizations; sponsors of research (including HIV/AIDS research); organizations concerned with pharmaceutical production, regulation, and trade; professional associations of physicians, nurses, pharmacists, and other healthcare workers; certification and standard-setting bodies; and even activist groups. In this complex field, key institutional actors sometimes work in concert and sometimes oppose one another, promulgating rules that are unlikely to be fully consistent and helping to produce the erratic globalization described above.

As they reacted to threats to global public health, governments, intergovernmental actors, and NGOs often employed legal and quasi-legal tools. The unfolding HIV/AIDS epidemic has both driven and been shaped by the globalism and legalism of healthcare. This book helps us see just how deeply global governance has penetrated the daily activity of HIV clinics around the world.

Localizing Global Phenomena: Site Selection

To suggest that the legalization of healthcare must be understood as a global phenomenon but studied very locally in the clinics (or other healthcare organizations) where rules are used offers only modest guidance about where to conduct research. Although many factors shape how rules are received and used in clinics, several stand out as particularly important: engagement in global rulemaking, national wealth and level of development, features of the HIV epidemic, and government stance on the epidemic. With these four criteria in mind, I delved into the literature on the HIV epidemic in various regions and countries, ultimately deciding to conduct my study in the US, Thailand, South Africa, and Uganda. As table 2.1 shows, these four countries offer ample comparisons on key dimensions.

Although laws, rules, guidelines, regulations, and norms often claim to be neutral and universal, in fact they are strongly shaped by temporal and geographic origins (Lempert and Sanders 1986; Minow 1990). As in many other spheres, the US and a handful of other rich countries play an outsized role in shaping the global governance of healthcare, whether they work bilaterally or through multilateral organizations. The US presence is simultaneously welcomed and resented because the US often governs with a heavy hand. Many of the rules and regulations used in HIV treatment and research originate in the US and are sent abroad along with the funding. As table 2.1 suggests, the US is a rulemaker in global public health; Thailand, South Africa, and Uganda are more often rule receivers.

In healthcare, as in many other arenas, a country's wealth shapes possibilities. Richer countries are generally able to offer a wider variety of health services and are particularly advantaged in being able to provide services that depend on new technologies. Wealthier countries are also more likely to have well-developed pharmaceutical industries, more healthcare workers per capita and better-trained workers, more hospital beds and other facilities per capita, and fewer shortages of medicines and supplies. The US is much richer than Thailand, South Africa, and Uganda, as shown by the table's income figures (from the period during which my field research was conducted). In addition, South Africa has an exceptional level of inequality, with a Gini coefficient of 64.8. Although both are much poorer than the US, Thailand and, to a lesser degree, South Africa have the capacity to produce at least some of the drugs used to treat HIV patients.

Because this is a study about HIV/AIDS, two other considerations shape the suitability of particular countries as research sites. First, the HIV epidemic varies a good bit from one country to another. In some countries (typically richer countries of the global North and West), the epidemic is a concentrated epidemic that began among gay men and diffused slowly to other groups, such as intravenous drug users and people with hemophilia. Although the epidemic has spread into the heterosexual population (in the US, spreading especially rapidly among African Americans and some other minority groups), it generally has spread slowly and thus has not become a generalized epidemic. In some other countries, the epidemic began as a generalized epidemic, affecting heterosexuals. Where the epidemic has been a generalized epidemic, the rates of infection have also been higher.

TABLE 2.1. Country Variations on Key Dimensions for Site Selection

	US	THAILAND	SOUTH AFRICA	UGANDA
Role in global governance	Global rule maker	Rule receiver; resists some rules; adapts rules for local use and for particular population groups	Rule receiver; adapts rules for local use and for particular population groups	Rule receiver; adapts rules for local use and for particular population groups
Level of wealth and development	Rich	Intermediate in wealth	Intermediate in wealth but exceptional inequality, with wealthy White minority and much poorer Black majority	Very poor
	2007 GDP per capita: $48,050 2007 Gini: 40.8	2007 GDP per capita: $3,935 2007 Gini: 39.8	2007 GDP per capita: $6,662 2005 Gini: 64.8	2007 GDP per capita: $402 2005 Gini: 42.9
	Strong pharmaceutical industry	Moderately developed pharmaceutical industry capable of producing HIV drugs	Pharmaceutical industry not fully capable of producing HIV drugs	Essentially no domestic pharmaceutical production
Nature of HIV/AIDS epidemic	Concentrated (initially mainly gay men, then IV drug users and people with hemophilia)	Generalized heterosexual (but initially thought to be concentrated in sex workers)	Generalized heterosexual (although began as concentrated epidemic of gay men)	Generalized heterosexual
Government stance on HIV/AIDS	Open	Open	Denial (especially 1999–2007)	Very open

As summarized in table 2.1, the US has a concentrated epidemic, while the other three countries have generalized epidemics.

Finally, as table 2.1 shows, the national governments of these four countries have had varying reactions to the epidemic, an important point given their role as promulgators of rules and regulations and sponsors of guideline-writing projects and research, treatment, and training programs. In the earliest days of the epidemic, people with HIV, their families and friends, and AIDS activists despaired over US government apathy. President Ronald Reagan made no major policy statement about AIDS until May 31, 1987, by which time more than 20,000 Americans had died of the disease.[7] But although some US government programs have included questionable policies (including the anti-prostitution pledge and the requirement that substantial proportions of prevention budgets be reserved for abstinence-only programs), the US government has been a key sponsor of HIV research, a generous donor to AIDS treatment programs, an important participant in multilateral anti-HIV efforts, and an underwriter for the infrastructure and institutions that have created and disseminated treatment guidelines. The government is not a unitary actor, and, contrary to the standard historical narrative, conservatives were not united on AIDS policy (Brier 2009). Surgeon General C. Everett Koop, the President's Commission on HIV/AIDS, the State Department, the US Agency for International Development, and even the CIA all advocated policies that diverged from the recommendations of Reagan and Gary Bauer, who spearheaded Reagan's HIV/AIDS effort. To be sure, the record is mixed, but overall the US has not hidden its head in the sand.

In contrast, some other national governments have been reluctant to acknowledge their countries' HIV/AIDS epidemics. Such denialism has taken many forms. Perhaps the most devastating was the AIDS denialism propagated by Thabo Mbeki, president of South Africa from 1999 to 2008. Mbeki cast doubt on scientific research, discredited medical treatment programs, and spent very sparingly on all things HIV-related (Fassin 2007; Nattrass 2007; Decoteau 2013). His wrongheaded policies led to countless deaths, unnecessary suffering, and preventable spread of the virus. Although Mbeki's stance was surely the most extreme, many African countries were reluctant to publicize their epidemics. When the Corporation for Public Broadcasting sought to create a documentary about the HIV/AIDS epidemic in Africa, only Uganda agreed to allow researchers to film. Uganda's stance on the documentary was quite consistent with its openness to discussing HIV and President Yoweri Museveni's early support for HIV/AIDS programs. HIV/AIDS programs in Uganda and other resource-constrained countries have drawn heavily on the resources of foreign governments and

NGOs. In Uganda, the first country to receive funds from the US President's Emergency Fund for AIDS Relief (PEPFAR), the government's welcome has been crucial to the success of these programs. Many countries, including Thailand, have been somewhere in the middle, more open to HIV/AIDS programs than South Africa but not as proactive as Uganda. Although in the long run Thailand developed a vigorous HIV/AIDS program that included free anti-retrovirals and a locally produced generic combination drug, its earliest responses left much to be desired. Officials demonized sex workers and drug users, suggested that these groups were the source of the problem, and refused to acknowledge an unfolding general epidemic.

These four countries have played important but quite different roles in the HIV epidemic and therefore make for especially illuminating comparisons. Given its leadership role in HIV/AIDS research and treatment, it was imperative to include the US. Given the importance of Africa in the HIV/AIDS epidemic, it would have been folly not to include African countries in the study, and Uganda and South Africa provide useful contrasts because of their governments' opposing stances. Selecting a country at an intermediate level of development was more difficult given the many options. In HIV/AIDS, an important threshold is crossed when a country has a domestic pharmaceutical industry capable of producing anti-retroviral drugs (ARVs). Thailand is among the countries that produce generic anti-retrovirals and was an attractive option also because of its initial focus on curtailing the spread of HIV by regulating sex work. Over time, Thailand became an increasingly useful case when it moved onto the international stage as host of the biannual conference of the International AIDS Society and later engaged in legal battles with major pharmaceutical companies over compulsory licenses for HIV medications.

I did my research in HIV clinics that were involved in both treatment and research—one each in Thailand, South Africa, and Uganda and two in the US (appendix A, which can be accessed online at this book's page at the University of Chicago Press website, provides additional detail about my research process). With the help of research assistants, I observed the full round of activities in all five clinics, with some variations in what we observed because clinic activities and physical layouts differed. Many of the topics I was interested in were somewhat sensitive. In our first days in each clinic, staff members nervously joked about whether my team and I were actually there to see whether they were doing things properly. As our research unfolded, though, we gained access to the formal meetings and informal discussions that surround research and caregiving. We shadowed staff members as they treated HIV patients (in Uganda we did not accompany physicians into examining rooms), gathered data from their research subjects, worked with the data they had collected, and discussed ongoing projects. We attended staff meetings and training sessions. And we often sat in as research monitors and site visitors did their work and as staff members discussed monitors' reports. We also talked with the full range of staff members, both informally as they worked and in more formal interviews, including physicians, nurses, lab workers, administrators, social workers, students, and volunteers. Although we inevitably encountered patients and research subjects, they were not the focus of our study. We asked their permission to observe as physicians and nurses worked with them. We stepped out of the room when our presence would have been awkward or embarrassing, exchanged a few pleasantries, and thanked them for so graciously allowing us to sit in. Many of them were amused to find that their caregivers taking their turn as research subjects in our study. We also interviewed people who did HIV work in a variety of other settings, including government bureaucracies, ministries of health, NGOs, and other clinics, using those interviews mainly to fill in gaps in what we learned in the target clinics.

In keeping with widely shared norms on confidentiality, I pledged to conceal the identities of the clinics and individuals (both clinic staff members and unaffiliated experts) who participated in my research. I assigned pseudonyms to the clinics (as well as some individuals) to help readers distinguish among them. I named the clinics for deceased AIDS activists from the countries in which the clinics were located. Although these pseudonyms retain some national flavor, the names are primarily an opportunity to remind readers of the urgency, uncertainty, and fear of the early days of the epidemic and the audaciousness, bravery, and selflessness of many of the people living with the disease.

The sketches of the clinics, to which I now turn, provide essential background for the rest of the book by showing just how challenging it is to attempt to offer universal, more or less standardized, care for HIV patients in circumstances that are anything but uniform.

Robert Rafsky Clinic, USA

Robert Rafsky[8] Clinic is located in a major metropolitan area in the Midwest. In the US, the HIV prevalence rate is generally higher in major urban areas than in other locales, and this metropolitan area is no exception. During the period of our field research, roughly 2003–7, the metropolitan area's rate of new AIDS diagnoses hovered around 17 cases per 100,000 annually.[9] By the end of 2007, this geographical area had about 180 AIDS cases per 100,000 population (and therefore, obviously, a larger number living with HIV infection, with or without an AIDS diagnosis). In the US, although the HIV epidemic began among gay men, it gradually expanded to include an increasing number of heterosexual men and women, particularly African Americans and Latinos. Although these changes were reflected in the clinic's patient population, the clinic requirement that patients be insured meant that minorities remained underrepresented during my study period. According to the 2010 Census, the city was about a third African American and about 30% Latino. African Americans were (and continue to be) overrepresented among the city's HIV-infected population, which was about 55% African American and around 20% Latino, but underrepresented in the clinic's patient population, which was about 25% African American and a bit over 5% Latino. At that time, women were 20% of the city's HIV-infected population but more than 25% of the clinic's patient population. The clinic's strong gynecological and obstetric program likely elevated the female population above what it might otherwise have been.

Housed on an upper floor of a major medical center, Robert Rafsky Clinic carefully conceals its mission. No signage identifies it as an HIV clinic. The receptionist answers the phone with a bland building name and floor, never mentioning the clinic's mission. During my time there, some family members accompanied patients to the clinic without ever knowing that their relative was being tested or treated for HIV. The medical center is located in a congested downtown area, flanked by tall buildings. Street parking is scarce and parking garages are costly, but the medical center is only a short walk from bus and rail lines, making it possible for patients to reach the clinic by public transport.

Robert Rafsky Clinic, founded in 1988, engages in both treatment and research. It offers a wide range of services for people with HIV, including initiation on ART, adjustment of treatment regimens, treatment for AIDS-related infections and medication side effects, consultation with patients' primary care physicians, instruction about HIV medications, nutritional counseling, obstetric and gynecological care, home care coordination, social work services, and referrals for dental, psychiatric, and legal services. In addition, patients receive opportunities to participate in clinical trials, some industry-sponsored, others funded by the US government through the National Institutes of Health (NIH) Division of AIDS.[10]

As will become apparent, clinics adopt different stances on how treatment and research should be related.[11] Some clinics intermingle the two; others insist on rigidly separating research from treatment to avoid conflicts of interest. At Robert Rafsky, it can be difficult to say definitively which spaces, activities, people, and funding streams are being used for treatment, research, and training. This intertwining also can create ambiguity about which rules apply. Although people loosely speak of the clinic as housing both research and treatment, when they make more careful distinctions, they say that the clinic provides treatment. Thus there is a director of the clinic, who oversees caregiving; a head of research, who directs the clinical research program; and a head of infectious diseases, who runs the training program for the affiliated medical school. In fact, all of these actors engage to greater and lesser degrees in all three activities—caring for patients, conducting research, and teaching and training students. Lower-level staff are more often specialized, though. Thus the nurse manager of the clinic is not much involved in research, and some nurses do no research work. Other nurses spend the bulk of their time on research. But at Robert Rafsky, all research nurses work some "clinic hours" each week because the head of research believes that caring for ordinary patients gives research nurses a perspective on the evolution of the disease not available from working only with the more select population of research subjects.

The allocation of duties affects what people do, who they work with, and where they do their work. If we grossly oversimplify and envision the clinic space as a Venn diagram, the treatment part of the clinic's work extends toward the hospital and the research part of its work extends toward the medical school and university. In fact, the clinic's tentacles reach even farther. Fellowships bring young doctors from around the country and abroad to work at Robert Rafsky. And the research group has close ties to several other clinics that belong to the "clinical trials unit" led by its research director. Finally, Robert Rafsky staff are deeply involved in international work, especially in training HIV practitioners and researchers in sub-Saharan Africa.

It is the work with patients and research subjects themselves that is especially likely to be confined to the clinic proper. Patients coming for treatment meet their caregivers in the clinic. There they see nurses and doctors to start ART, to assess the continuing efficacy of the regimen and renew prescriptions, and to manage side effects and opportunistic infections (OIs). They also see lab workers who collect specimens, social workers who help with financial and other nonmedical matters, pharmacists who advise on their drug regimens, and receptionists who schedule subsequent appointments. Patients are sometimes sent to other areas of the medical facility for tests not routinely done in the clinic, and, of course, they are sometimes hospitalized due to complications, serious illness as their regimens fail, or completely unrelated conditions.

Likewise, when research subjects come for "study visits," research staff meet them in the clinic. Research subjects interact with general clinic staff who draw blood and sign patients in. However, the bulk of research subjects' time in the clinic is spent with research staff—nurses and doctors—whose interactions with them are guided by research protocols that specify what medications to administer and what specimens and data to gather at each visit. After research visits, research nurses log data into case report forms. Data are then entered into the computer, with multiple quality control checks by local staff and visiting research monitors.

The financial aspects of clinic life are just as convoluted as the research protocols. Funds for HIV-related work come primarily from three sources: support for treatment, support for research, and support for faculty members. The bills for treatment are mainly paid by private health insurers, although some patients are covered by Medicare or Medicaid. Robert Rafsky makes insurance coverage a precondition of treatment, referring patients without insurance to a nearby public clinic. Research funds come primarily from the NIH, although some research funds also come from pharmaceutical companies or from the university. Finally, some of the doctors are medical school faculty and receive part of their support from the university.

I observed the activities of staff members in many different positions, but I spent especially long hours with Richard, the lead researcher. I attended meetings with him, listened in on conference calls, observed him seeing patients and research subjects, talked with him informally, and interviewed him more formally in tape-recorded sessions. My time with Richard confirmed some of my preconceptions about the worklives of prominent AIDS researchers and disconfirmed others. He had an exceedingly full agenda, starting work early in the morning and continuing at least into the early evening. During that time, he moved among tasks, including core scientific activities, such as writing papers, drafting presentations, preparing grant proposals, conducting study visits, planning research, and discussing research anomalies and problems; oversight of scientific work, such as discussions with research coordinators about institutional review board (IRB) submissions and discussions with administrators about budgets; mentoring of younger colleagues; and a lot of hands-on doctoring.

Seeing him especially as a researcher, I sometimes had to be reminded that Richard was also a caregiver. When I once asked how he could track a change in the lung function of one patient, he gently chided me: "It's not as impersonal as you think, Carol." And clearly his patients didn't see him as impersonal, unapproachable, or uncaring. For example, one late-middle-aged White man with a rash got an immediate appointment, a careful examination, and a new prescription, accompanied by consideration about how the new medication—not a "study drug"—would be paid for and stern reminders that he could never again take the drug that had caused the rash. But at this same meeting, the patient raised concerns that his "buffalo hump" was returning and sought advice on hair loss. That same day, an

African American woman consulted Richard about switching drugs so she could have another child. Richard carefully walked her through the alternatives, discussing what was known about how alternative regimens would affect both her and the fetus. And again he verified insurance coverage for the drugs and then informed her that there would be no charge for this visit. He also promised that they would monitor her closely during pregnancy. She too consulted Richard about other concerns, including surgery to redistribute fat to compensate for facial wasting. As she prepared to leave, the patient thanked Richard and told him that he "had always done right" by her. Later he confided that this patient had come close to dying some years earlier when her HIV went untreated because she lacked health insurance. Richard's good rapport with patients sometimes annoyed nurses when appointments occasionally ran too long as conversations wandered into topics that served no obvious medical purpose. Those same nurses who were occasionally annoyed also cited Richard as an exemplar on matters of ethics—not because he adhered strictly to official rules of ethics but because he had a robust ethical compass. When I attended a dinner honoring Richard's work, I noted that a few long-standing patients had been invited to celebrate alongside his many colleagues. He was clearly a major player in HIV research and treatment, serving on advisory panels for both the NIH and PEPFAR.

With more resources at their disposal, the staff members of Robert Rafsky Clinic should have had little difficulty complying with the rules and regulations of HIV treatment and research. Even at Robert Rafsky, though, the rules chafed enough that staff members groused about the rules on a daily basis. Confident about the quality of their work, they nevertheless complained about nitpicky research monitors. Annoyed about endless IRB requirements, they grumbled when the IRB panel asked a key researcher to answer additional questions about a multisite research project, an intrusion that seemed unwarranted and even illegitimate to research staff.

Billing issues came up frequently, but they got sustained airings at infectious diseases faculty meetings. At one meeting, an administrator presented material about year-to-year changes in reimbursements, showing a recent drop in the proportion of patient visits categorized as highly complex and therefore warranting high billing rates. The discussion about the categorization of patient visits raised related questions about who could write notes, check recommendation boxes, and so forth. The doctors, who apparently had different practices, were confused about the rules on who was permitted to write notes in the file. They were concerned simultaneously about what was legal, what was pedagogically effective and appropriate, and what was useful. For instance, no one wanted to trivialize medical students' work by excluding their notes, but it was not legal for medical students to check the recommendation boxes or for their notes to be the only notes in a file. Yet too many notes made for confusing medical files. And, of course, the physicians also balked at redoing perfectly adequate work simply to comply with rules. As the billing discussion unfolded, it became clear that no one in the group was entirely sure how to use the new forms that had been imposed/inflicted on them. But their discussion did lead to some clarity about how "double billing" might occur when patients were seen at the clinic and then reassessed by different staff members during hospital admission. Both of these examinations were "high complexity" and billed as such. Some clinic workers said that when they admitted a clinic patient to the hospital, they simply wrote a follow-up note rather than a fresh assessment that would result in another large fee. But they all agreed that this sensible practice did not translate into any clear policy about how to deal with the ubiquitous forms.

Moving on, the administrator handed out packets that translated the clinic-level figures into individual-level figures so department members could see how they contributed to the drop in clinic reimbursements. As they looked through their respective packets, Richard became animated, laughed uproariously, and showed his sheet to his colleagues, who also chortled. "Does this mean I lost $27,000?" he asked. He was amused and incredulous, but not upset. The loss seemed large, but it was unclear how it had arisen or what it would mean for the institution. Richard himself was not affected by the "loss"—his salary was fully covered by grants. Although the loss figures were not "wrong," they seemed to be an artifact of administrative procedures that failed to capture the reality of clinic, hospital, and medical school work. Such glitches had consequences, but the status of the group and the individual participants did act as a buffer. Rather than feeling individually responsible, they assigned blame to the system and the rules. They rolled with the punches and got on with their work.

Although they uniformly endorsed the importance of rules, staff members were frustrated by rules that did not sufficiently respect their expertise, integrity, or demands on their time. Yet they also sometimes acknowledged that they were better situated than others—that complying with rules was almost certainly easier for them than for HIV researchers and caregivers in other countries or even at poorer institutions in the US. "Americans have a bad reputation as being piggy, always wanting things done our way," one physician confided. "So the folks in other countries are intimidated and hate us at the same time that they admire us. And, of course, all of this is complicated by the fact that a lot of the research money comes from the US."

Robert Rafsky was the clinic where my project team began data collection. We gathered data in this site off and on for two years. Although I have a great deal of fieldwork and interview data from this clinic, Robert Rafsky was the site about which there was the least publicly available material. Perhaps in keeping with its strong emphasis on privacy, it did not maintain much of an online profile; no articles touted the accomplishments of the clinic or introduced its satisfied or redeemed patients. In this, as in many other things, it presented a sharp contrast to the Bobbi Campbell Clinic.

Bobbi Campbell Clinic, USA

Bobbi Campbell[12] Clinic, a highly regarded facility affiliated with a large public hospital, cares for the poor patients of the southeastern metropolitan area in which it is located. For the US, this metropolitan area has a rather high HIV burden. Between 2003 and 2007, the metropolitan area's rate of new AIDS diagnoses hovered around 24 cases per 100,000 annually. By the end of 2007, this geographical area had about 250 AIDS cases per 100,000 population and therefore, obviously, a larger total number living with HIV infection. As was the case for Robert Rafsky Clinic, men were overrepresented in Bobbi Campbell's patient population during my study years. Roughly 78% of patients were male and 42% were men who had sex with men. Ten percent were IV drug users. At Bobbi Campbell, 72% of patients were African American, a figure only partly accounted for by the city's substantial minority population and the overrepresentation of minorities in the population of poor people that the clinic serves.

Serving a largely uninsured population of patients and research subjects, Bobbi Campbell Clinic provided a useful contrast to the Robert Rafsky Clinic and a salutary reminder that in the US, the availability of medical care has historically depended on whether a person (or their spouse or parent) had a job that provided health insurance.[13] In a clinic such as Bobbi Campbell, care is paid for largely through the federal Ryan White HIV/AIDS Program (which covers HIV/AIDS care for patients who cannot afford it), Medicaid, Medicare, and the state's AIDS drug assistance program. Generally speaking, clinics find it more difficult to abide by the rules of government funders than the rules of private insurers, although this may be partly because clinics that rely on government funding also have fewer staff members to sort out billing problems. None of these payers provides generous funding, and this state does not spend lavishly on healthcare for its poor citizens. A bit of additional help comes from pharmaceutical company philanthropic programs, but those slots are very limited.

Bobbi Campbell Clinic opened in 1986 and moved to its present site, a spacious but institutional facility, in 1993. Some of the treatment staff have HIV themselves and sometimes share this information with patients when doing so seems appropriate and helpful. Although the clinic has many selling points, easy access is not one them. Bobbi Campbell is hard to access without a car. For the clinic's mostly poor clientele, getting to the clinic can mean spending an hour or more on public transportation. Sensitive to these difficulties, clinic staff try to schedule patients' HIV-related appointments on days when other appointments are booked, for instance, with clinic dentists, nutritionists, mental health staff, or social workers.

Clinics differ in their philosophies on how to combine treatment and research. Although this clinic was deeply involved in both, the clinic's medical director felt strongly that research and treatment should be kept separate. To minimize potential conflicts of interest, he insisted that all research subjects have primary care physicians not connected to the research projects in which they were participating.

This clinic is involved in many of the same research areas as Robert Rafsky Clinic, but Bobbi Campbell is less involved in research and more engaged in treatment than Robert Rafsky. Although Bobbi Campbell Clinic is part of a clinical trials unit, it is not the primary site. That means it is less likely to take the lead in decisions about what research projects to participate in and shoulders a bit less of the administrative burden that comes with research. That said, the administrative work of keeping abreast of IRB submissions and renewals and tracking the research paperwork remains very substantial.

The paperwork burden associated with Bobbi Campbell's public funding is probably more intensive than that associated with the insurance-based funding that supports caregiving at Robert Rafsky. For instance, the Ryan White program requires that Bobbi Campbell Clinic have clinic guidelines (which Robert Rafsky Clinic does not have). Documentation requirements associated with funding are arcane and cumbersome. At Bobbi Campbell Clinic, problems arise from the extremely detailed specifications for billing records. For instance, to receive full reimbursement, special code numbers and explanatory notations must be added when a patient session covers more than a single medical problem. Staff are taken to task by hospital administrators over inadequate documentation and retrained to keep proper notes on patient visits. At both Robert Rafsky and Bobbi Campbell, complexity of visits is difficult to anticipate and difficult to capture efficiently in billing records. In both clinics, staff feel annoyed by the overlay of administrative requirements that, from their perspective, distract them from the important work of caring for patients. But the situations of the two clinics differed both in the specificity of requirements (more detailed in the public clinic) and in how far the requirements penetrated (only physicians were affected in the private clinic, both physicians and lower-level caregivers were affected in the public clinic). Moreover, the financial precariousness of the public clinic meant that threats to its income had to be taken very seriously.

A nurse auditor, meeting with staff members at Bobbi Campbell, informed the group that they were "on the list with the highest error rate for modifier 25," the code that signals more than one medical problem had been covered in a patient encounter. They had also been "double-billing" because they improperly coded patient visits. Incredulous laughter broke out when the auditor added that they had "a 100% error rate" in one part of their work. A long, confusing, and sometimes boisterous discussion ensued, with both the nurse auditor and the clinic staff growing increasingly frustrated. Under consideration were a series of worksheets that staff members were expected to use to document patient visits, but the worksheets were anything but straightforward. They attempted to capture information about skill level and time requirements for caregiving tasks, billing arrangements for different categories of health professionals, facility versus professional fees, and Medicare versus Medicaid rules. In addition, a recent rule change recategorized some "procedures," making them part of routine care and so no longer coded or charged separately. To make matters worse, the forms seemed to have envisioned a work environment with doctors and nurses, covered by professional fees and facility fees respectively, but made no provision for mid-level professionals such as physicians assistants and nurse practitioners. "My level doesn't count anymore," one nurse practitioner commented ruefully. "It never did!" another caregiver retorted.

As the back and forth continued, the tension became palpable. When one doctor suggested that "the policy needs to change," the nurse auditor said defensively that "all [she is] doing is complying with Medicare regulations." Pressing her on this point, the doctor said the auditor was "wrong about the regulation" and "need[ed] to re-read it." When the auditor demurred that she was there "to teach them why they are noncompliant," another staff member suggested that she was targeting the wrong group and should instead be talking to the people who actually do the billing because "this is a clerk and billing issue." In other clinics, a discharge nurse either filled out the forms or checked them, but Bobbi Campbell had no discharge nurse.

The financial stakes were high. "It sounds like we're doing a lot of work and not billing for it," the clinic director observed with chagrin after the auditor's departure. Worrying about the financial consequences, he suggested that "someone needs to educate the providers individually because a memo won't do it." Conceding that some providers' professional services weren't being billed and that it wasn't clear how to reassign this administrative work, he acknowledged the complexity of the problems: "That's step one!" The room burst into laughter. Attempting to stave off despair, he encouraged staff members not to turn on each other and to take a deep breath. "Can we bill for that [breathing]?" someone quipped. Although the financial nitty gritty threatened to interfere with providing care, it was clear where people's primary commitment lay: "Although I work for finance, my allegiance is to IDP [the infectious disease program]," one financial counselor declared.

To receive ART in this clinic, a patient had to have a previous AIDS diagnosis (meaning that the disease had progressed substantially) or a CD4 count of 200 or less. Several years later, the clinic was still using this cutoff even though the guidelines now recommended initiation of ART when a patient's CD4 count dropped to 500, a modification from the previous recommendation that therapy begin when the CD4 count dropped below 350. Other clinics adjusted their practice as the recommendations changed, but Bobby Campbell's funds were simply not adequate to start people on drugs at earlier stages in their illness.

Although Bobbi Campbell staff members were similarly exasperated by rules about clinical research, IRB reviews, and funds for treatment, differences in the balance between research and treatment, in funding sources, and in adequacy of resources altered the tone of their frustration. Bobbi Campbell staff members worried somewhat less about research-related rules both because they did less research and because they were not their clinical trials unit's lead clinic. Fiscal pressures were more intense at Bobbi Campbell than at Robert Rafsky, though. A much higher proportion of Bobbi Campbell's funds came from government payers, who tended to be less generous and more rigid than insurers. In addition, because they were unable to send their indigent patients to other clinics, Bobbi Campbell staff had little choice but to work through the intricate rules of the various programs that might pay for patients' medications. Fiscal pressures that might be irritating at a well-resourced clinic like Robert Rafsky were instead a crisis at Bobbi Campbell with its much tighter budget. For Bobbi Campbell staff members, then, the rules especially challenged their sense of themselves as responsible caregivers, able to provide the kind of care they thought their patients deserved.

Crossing national boundaries to the Thai, South African, and Uganda clinics brought a host of differences, some due to the nature of the epidemic, others to cultural differences, and still others to resource shortages.

Cha-on Suesum Clinic, Thailand

Thailand is not a rich country, but it is also not a poor one. Its citizens are well educated (93.5% are literate) and enjoy quite a high standard of living. Moreover, it has a relatively good healthcare system, and HIV is covered by the Universal Coverage Scheme (also known as the 30 Baht Scheme).[14] Perhaps especially important, Thailand has a sophisticated domestic pharmaceutical industry capable of producing ARVs and has for some time treated its citizens with GPO-VIR, a locally produced combination ARV.[15] The Thai government has taken advantage of provisions in the 2001 Doha Declaration on the TRIPS Agreement and Public Health that allow governments to issue compulsory licenses to circumvent burdensome patent agreements in the case of national emergencies. The pharmaceutical companies and the US government have disputed these compulsory licenses, creating considerable tension between Thailand and the US. Pharmaceutical companies once subsidized Thai researchers' travel to international conferences; after the issuing of compulsory licenses, they terminated support. In the US, such a dispute would be unlikely to reach the attention of ordinary citizens, but one informant told us that at the height of the dispute, Bangkok cab drivers sometimes refused to drop passengers at the US embassy.

Because HIV was seen initially as a disease of sex workers, the Thai government attempted to control the epidemic by regulating sex work.[16] The government also introduced harsh punishments for drug use in a vain attempt to control HIV by reducing the population of IV drug users. Over time the epidemic became a more general epidemic, though both homosexual men and IV drug users continued to be overrepresented. The prevalence rate remained relatively low.

Cha-on Suesum[17] Clinic is located on a busy Bangkok boulevard. With a skytrain stop nearby, it is easily accessible by public transportation. Because the clinic buildings are in a compound, sheltered from the street noise by a thick wall, the clinic itself feels calm. While we were engaged in fieldwork, a family of friendly puppies gamboled about the courtyard. One building is reserved for research offices. Visits with patients and research subjects occur in a second building, which also houses offices on an upper floor. Much treatment occurs in a nearby, loosely affiliated university hospital where some clinic staff members hold appointments.

Founded as an international research consortium in 1996, Cha-on Suesum Clinic was created to bring clinical research to resource-limited settings and to make HIV treatment affordable and available in the countries most affected by the epidemic. Although it began as a purely research enterprise, the clinic's work has always included a care component because researchers engaged in clinical trials necessarily provide care for their research subjects. More important, though, as the first research projects neared completion, the researchers realized that they needed to ensure continuing access to treatment for their research subjects and adjusted their program. They filled the gap with "observational studies" that tracked the medical course of the people who had been enrolled in the clinical trials, much as has been done since 1983 on a larger scale in the US by MACS (the Multicenter AIDS Cohort Study) (Evans 2009; Detels et al. 2012). By now, the reports of the clinic acknowledge dual goals: "setting up and participating in clinical trials" and providing "continuous care for our patients."[18]

Superficial similarities hid important differences among the clinics. As is common in all but the richest countries, all parts of the clinic's program were oversubscribed during the period of my observations. Cha-on Suesum's director pointed out that the "shaky financing" for ARVs and medical care in Thailand made clinical trials very attractive for patients. But, he added, the situation was unlike the US where the "attraction was to receive the newest treatment, rather than any treatment." Roughly 1,500 people were enrolled in Cha-on Suesum's clinical trials, with another 300 people waiting to be enrolled as study slots became available. Another 500 or so patients were enrolled in the continuing-care, post-treatment observational studies. Because the NIH, an important sponsor of Cha-on Suesum's research, did not pay for drugs, the clinic and its patients often scrambled to secure sometimes scarce and often very expensive drugs. Poor access to basic medical care also shaped the clinic's stance on the relationship between treatment and research. For Cha-on Suesum, the director informed me, the issue was "not so much about an ideological stance as about convenience." The group strongly believed that their research subjects should receive HIV care from some clinic and preferred that they receive it at Cha-on Suesum so that they didn't have to spend their time going from one place to the next to get treatment. Thai patients didn't have "the luxury of so much choice."

For the most part, staff members at Cha-on Suesum had the materials and professional qualifications needed to follow clinical guidelines, research protocols, and other kinds of rules. But for two key reasons, they remained at a disadvantage compared with staff at the US clinics. First, as careful and well trained as they were, Cha-on Suesum staff members had been trained initially on a different set of rules, with different conventions about privacy, error correction, and so forth. They were accustomed to working in a different language. Their research priorities, including which drugs to include in clinical trials, differed somewhat. Second, these staff members also felt under siege. They worried, with some reason, about being judged as inferior. Whether the topic was submitted samples, research records, or proposals for new research, they felt their work always had a strike against it because they were located "in the boonies."

In one telling example, a member of my team observed the work of an onsite monitor for a research project. Joel, one of the handful of foreigners working at the clinic, checked a box of blood samples that was being prepared for shipment from the Thai clinic to an affiliated US site. It was a long process: going to the lab, retrieving the samples from the $-80°C$ freezer, donning latex gloves (more complicated this time because of a defective glove), verifying that the box contained the right number of tubes per patient, and checking that samples were boxed in the same order as listed on the manifest. This sounds complicated and tedious, but fairly straightforward. But at room temperature, condensation forms around the tubes, so they freeze to the box; latex gloves slip on the tubes; tweezers have to be located to gently ease the tubes out of the box. And it was imperative that the samples remain frozen.

As the tubes were being extracted, a question arose about how many tubes there were supposed to be for each patient. It was three per patient for the last shipment, but no one knew for sure about this shipment, so the manual had to be located and the information retrieved. This took ten minutes. Together the lab manager and Joel leafed through the binder until they found the information: eight tubes per patient for this shipment. That question settled, they turned to comparing the rows of samples in the box with the labels on the manifest. And then more trouble. Joel called over the tech and the lab manager and showed them that the numbers in the box didn't match the order of the labels affixed to the manifest. The square box had ten rows of slots with ten slots per row. The first row contained eight vials from the patient in position 1 on the manifest, followed by two empty spaces; the second row contained eight vials from the patient in position 2, but right next to patient 2's eighth vial was a vial from the patient in position 11. Joel was quite upset, trying to figure out what was going on. The tech finally explained that he had put the first ten patients across, one per row. For the 11th and 12th patients, he had rotated the box and put them in vertically, leaving empty the last two spots in the first and tenth rows. "May di, may di!" (not good, not good), Joel exclaimed. He demonstrated proper procedures for the tech—all vials in order with no gaps—saying, "you have to do it this way or what's her name will throw them away." The tech argued that his way was okay, but Joel was emphatic—"it says in the book you cannot." The tech and lab manager spoke for a moment in Thai, then the tech opened another box and began to reorder the vials.

At the time, Joel explained to my ethnography team member that the "NIH just can't cope" with any variation in routine. In an aside, he added that the tech had "quite logically filled the boxes in a way that the sample sets would be kept together." But the tech was not given this modulated response; the tech heard only "not good, not good" and "the book says you must do it this way." As others continued checking numbers on vials and manifests, filling in forms, and adding signatures, my coworker took another look at the lab manual. Nowhere in the thirteen pages of shipping instructions and sample shipping forms could she find an instruction about row order; the instructions said only that all of the labels for a particular patient at a particular visit had to be "on the same shipping log and in the same row" pertaining to the manifest rather than the packing box. Would the NIH actually throw out the samples as Joel alleged? That may not have mattered. What did matter was that Cha-on Suesum staff members, including Joel, had become convinced that the NIH was unlikely to give them the benefit of the doubt. Cha-on Suesum workers had become so nervous about the rules, so concerned with complying exactly, that they routinely accepted the ratcheting up of demands, including Joel's insistence on repacking samples despite his own admission that the lab worker's solution was "quite logical."

This anxiety about outsiders' assessments of their work also fostered a careful defensiveness in how they presented policy decisions to outsiders. At one point Cha-on Suesum doctors began doing annual pap smears for all women patients. Cervical cancers count as an "end point" in HIV research, and they wondered whether an increased capacity to detect cervical cancers would introduce bias into research results of multisite studies if only one site in a multisite study was doing pap smears. But annual pap smears were "already standard of care in the West," one doctor pointed out, so they wouldn't be the only site doing them. "Why would we need permission [from the study sponsors]?" the clinic head pointedly asked, if cervical cancer is a valid endpoint and annual pap smears are already standard of care in the West. Thinking further, they wondered whether telling the sponsor they had begun doing annual pap smears would suggest that the Thai research team had been "behind" as compared to Western clinics. Another team member thought pap smears were not standard of care in Latin American sites. Ultimately they decided to simply tell the sponsor that they were now doing annual pap smears and to "suggest that other countries—like Latin American ones—might wish to follow Thailand's example."

Cha-on Suesum Clinic had an extremely ambitious research program, funded by Thai government sources, the NIH, and pharmaceutical companies. Because Cha-on Suesum researchers were eager to control their own research agenda, they kept salaries artificially low, diverting funds to a research kitty that would allow them to plan and initiate their own projects even when outside funding was unavailable. This was particularly important, they believed, because international funders were often reluctant to support projects designed to address issues of special concern to the Thai population. With their research kitty, they initiated studies of lower dosages, appropriate for smaller Thai people, and studies of renal problems, a special problem for Thai HIV/AIDS patients. When the Fifteenth International AIDS Conference was held in Bangkok in July 2004, Cha-on Suesum's researchers were given prominent roles, validating their investments in research.

In the long run, Cha-on Suesum Clinic also became an important regional player, developing research collaborations with Laotian, Vietnamese, and other Asian partners, and creating programs to train others to do clinical research and manage and treat HIV patients. Although staff members of the two African clinics we studied were similarly involved in international, regional, and national research, policy, and training programs, the heavier burden of HIV in South Africa and Uganda meant that staff members were more constrained by the truly crushing workloads within their clinics.

Gugu Dlamini Clinic, South Africa

South Africa straddles the divide between rich and poor countries. Some South Africans—mostly Whites and especially those residing in the cosmopolitan cities of the richer provinces—live much like people in Europe or North America. Others—especially those with dark skins residing in the rural areas of poorer provinces—live more like people in poorer African countries. Indeed, according to the usual indicators, such as the Gini coefficient, South Africa is one of the most unequal societies in the world.

South Africa reported its first case of HIV in 1982. Like many things in South Africa, HIV is unequally distributed. During my first visit to Durban, another (White) guest at the bed-and-breakfast where I was staying was surprised to hear that her country had an HIV problem. South Africa's history with HIV has been marked by the Mbeki government's policy of AIDS denialism.[19] The result has been an escalating epidemic in a country that arguably had the resources to do a much better job of managing HIV. Yet all of this occurred in a country being radically reconfigured with the transition from apartheid to majority rule in 1994, holding the first truly democratic elections in April 1994, and replacing its interim constitution with a permanent constitution in 1995. The political history of the country is crucial for understanding the HIV epidemic in South Africa because the epidemic is in fact two different epidemics (Abdool Karim and Abdool

Karim 2002). The first, resembling the HIV epidemics of richer countries, occurred among homosexuals, drug users, and people with hemophilia. The heterosexual epidemic followed somewhat later. The strains of HIV in the two groups are different. It is the heterosexual epidemic that has been particularly explosive.

It was because of the comparatively high rate of HIV infection, which then stood at 40% in KwaZulu-Natal (KZN), that I decided to do my research in Durban. The population of KZN, an eastern coastal province of South Africa, is predominantly Black African (86.0% in 2007), with a smattering of Indians and other Asians (8.1%), Whites (4.4%), and "Coloreds" (1.4%). Most of the Black Africans are Zulu speakers (80.0% of the total; 3.5% are Xhosa speakers) and most of the rest of the population are English speakers (13.4% of the total; 1.5% are Afrikaans speakers). In 2007, just over 10 million people lived in KZN, making it the second largest province in the country. About 3.5 million resided in Durban, the second largest city in South Africa.

Although Gugu Dlamini[20] Clinic does have university affiliations, they are somewhat looser than those in the other clinics I studied. During my first visit to South Africa, I conducted background interviews in both Durban and Cape Town, regularly asking respondents where I should site my ethnographic work. Because South Africa has had a policy of dispersing research rather than concentrating it in a few facilities, several promising clinics were ruled out because they were so small that my presence would disrupt clinic routines. The few large research clinics that existed often did only research, sending their research subjects elsewhere for treatment.[21] Several options remained. One I ruled out because it was so closely affiliated with US research that it was often seen as simply an outpost of the NIH. Several others were ruled out serendipitously by a university strike, which would have made it impossible to receive timely ethics clearance for my project.

Gugu Dlamini is part of a long-standing, highly regarded hospital. Entering the hospital grounds, one navigates a narrow lane, almost an alley, with buildings and parking lots on either side and "park homes" (trailers) packed into yards and plazas to accommodate the overflow. Pedestrians trudge up and down the hill on which the hospital compound is located, dodging vehicles whenever they need to cross the lane. Uniformed guards stand at the entrances to parking lots and buildings, helpfully opening gates and giving directions, but also casting a watchful eye on those entering and leaving. Rising several stories above the street, the main hospital building is the most prominent element of the landscape and is clearly labeled with the hospital's name and logo.

Noting the increasing prevalence of HIV among their patients, the hospital superintendent had decided to establish an HIV clinic at the hospital. The resulting HIV clinic—Gugu Dlamini—grew rapidly. The clinic proper is housed in its own walled compound with a parking lot, courtyard, and backyard, two large, sturdy buildings, and a few park homes. On most mornings, the main waiting area is crowded with patients and family members sitting in rows of stackable plastic chairs. At the front of the room, receptionists sit at desks behind a grille, busily registering patients, taking payment for monthly fees, scheduling appointments, and handing out stickers to indicate patients' places in several possible queues. At the start of the day, though, work is suspended for half an hour or so for the (Christian) prayer service.

By local standards, the clinic is spacious, with several reception and waiting areas, treatment rooms, a small lab, a clinic pharmacy, a few offices, collective work rooms, a staff tea room, and a large room for staff meetings, seminars and continuing education sessions, and batch training sessions for patients preparing to start ART. Importantly, this space also brings some modicum of privacy for patient examinations and counseling. And there are bathrooms—not something to forget, both because clean, working bathrooms with toilet paper, soap, and paper towels are a luxury in poor countries, but also because these bathrooms, open to staff and patients alike, also contain condom dispensers.

The clinic accepted local patients who could afford the modest monthly copay and who met criteria for starting ART. Gugu Dlamini's patient population was almost entirely Black, though it included a small number of Indians and Whites. Although the clinic is located in Durban, many of the patients come from poor Black "suburbs" such as Umlazi and KwaMashu (the township in which Gugu Dlamini had lived). Because of its excellent reputation, the list of people wishing to receive treatment at this clinic was always long, even after the government rollout of ARVs began, and the clinic adopted strict rules about its geographic catchment area to help control the queue. The justification for these rules was that people had to be able to come to the clinic on a regular basis for follow-up care and to get their next batch of pills. The staff feared, with some justification, that patients who lived too far away would default on their treatment.

The clinic had instituted user fees because of a strongly held belief that people would be more likely to value the care they received if they helped pay for it. The fee was relatively low, but some patients were nevertheless unable to afford the payment. The clinic had provisions for delaying payment and used donated funds to cover the fees of a few patients. The intention was that lack of a fee should not prevent any current patient from coming to the clinic. Yet there was some evidence that patients sometimes skipped appointments when they couldn't pay their fees.

Gugu Dlamini Clinic had both pediatric and adult HIV programs. It offered assessment, treatment for OIs and side effects, medication training (including nutritional counseling), psychosocial services, on-site access to pharmaceuticals, and ART. There was a play group for the youngest HIV patients and a support group for older children. The staff worked closely with parents and other caregivers—HIV-infected children were often orphans being cared for by relatives. Staff interfaced with schools and helped with disclosure as children became old enough to understand the nature of their illness. The excellent prenatal program was located in a separate space. According to more than one informant, this prenatal program was seen as a "jewel in the crown" or a "thorn in the side" of the provincial health department, depending on whether provincial authorities were bragging about successes or annoyed at the failures of other programs.

Gugu Dlamini Clinic had a well-developed system for bringing people into treatment. People who tested positive for HIV (at the hospital testing site) were referred to the clinic for "staging." They did not actually become clinic patients, though, until they needed ART. In the interim, the clinic referred them to local community health clinics for prescriptions for prophylactic antibiotics (Bactrim) to stave off OIs during the early stages of the disease.

In fact, there were always more people ready for treatment than could be accommodated. The testing program kept a queue for the pretreatment training program, but clinicians often felt compelled to make adjustments to the list. Too often, people did not get tested until they were so ill that treatment could not be delayed until the next time the class was offered. As I noted earlier, at the time of the research, guidelines recommended that treatment begin when the CD4 count dropped below 250[22] or when the patient had AIDS-defining illnesses. Assessing these components is the core task of staging the disease. Many South African patients were already clinically ready to begin treatment by the time they were tested. A few had CD4 counts in double or even occasionally single digits and were coinfected with TB.[23] These people and their "treatment buddies" were allowed to jump the queue and enroll in the next available training class. In some cases, this expedited start still did not save their lives.

The clinic's treatment program drew on other sources of funding beyond what user fees brought in. Receiving money from PEPFAR and from the South African government shaped Gugu Dlamini Clinic practices in distinct ways. To meet the considerable tracking and reporting requirements of funders, the clinic created a monitoring and evaluation program and regularly reported clinic program data (e.g., numbers receiving treatment;

numbers lost to follow-up or death; percentages of men, women, and children). The clinic was also required to participate in regional conferences to share best practices with other clinics receiving PEPFAR monies. The Durban clinic was well regarded in this user group and seen as a source of many good ideas.

South African government rules pushed the clinic to make other modifications. As the government began to make funds available for treatment, the Durban clinic thought carefully about whether to participate. Obviously Gugu Dlamini welcomed the opportunity to stabilize its funding stream—it was never clear how long PEPFAR funds would continue—and to expand its treatment program. But clinic staff worried about some of the strings attached to the government program, including the obligation to use the official first-line drug regimen, a drug combination they (correctly) believed posed life-threatening risks to some of their patients. As it became clear that the government rollout program was more flexible than staff originally expected, they decided to participate. These new monies allowed the clinic to initiate more patients onto ART, but created a fresh challenge because clinic staff could not shoulder the extra work of caring for the additional patients. To manage ongoing care for these patients, Gugu Dlamini formed ties with a group of community clinics, some of which were not full-fledged clinics but community organizations offering very basic medical services. Gugu Dlamini staff worked out a division of labor in which they initiated patients on therapy, cared for them until they were stable, and then passed them on to partner organizations for ongoing management, with detailed protocols for referrals back to Gugu Dlamini if problems arose.[24]

In comparison with the US, Thai, and Ugandan clinics, Gugu Dlamini Clinic did relatively little research, and none of that research involved clinical trials. In partnership with a US university, the clinic had recently begun research on drug resistance and adherence to drug regimens. Mindful of the good quality of its medical records, the Durban clinic also increasingly saw these records as a "goldmine" of data that its staff and others could use for research purposes. Like the other clinics, Gugu Dlamini aspired to combine research and treatment, believing that each enriched the other. But in contrast to the Ugandan and Thai clinics that began with research and moved toward treatment, Gugu Dlamini's trajectory was from treatment to research.

Staff members at Gugu Dlamini Clinic often remarked that they were building the ship as they were attempting to sail it. In both African clinics, staff members faced clinical challenges not fully anticipated by the guidelines and rules. Working with patient populations that included women, some of whom were pregnant, and children meant caring for people whose bodies worked quite differently from those of the men for whom clinical guidelines were initially written. Because Gugu Dlamini staff members had only recently started to do much clinical research, they were figuring things out in that realm as well. But in contrast to some of their Thai and Ugandan counterparts, Gugu Dlamini staff seemed to feel that their work as clinicians and researchers was respected. They tended to receive accolades as their work was held up as an example for other clinics in conferences and user groups. In part this was because of the funding sources that supported their work. In their research program, they partnered with a US university program that was helping them learn the ropes. More critical reviews likely lay in the future, but clinic workers hadn't yet experienced the rules as standards against which they were measured regularly and episodically found wanting. They were not naïve about possible effects of time-consuming and critical reviews, though, and that concern led them to delay a decision to participate in a government drug provision program until they were convinced that the rules were less draconian than they had feared. More than in other clinics, then, Gugu Dlamini staff members' experience of rules and regulations aligned with ideals about what such measures should accomplish. To be sure, staff members sometimes groused about rules, but they also felt that the rules were generally helpful in guiding their work and that they were empowered both to adjust rules and to create new ones as needed.

Philly Lutaaya Clinic, Uganda

Kampala, like Rome, is a city built on seven hills, and like Rome it now spreads up, around, and beyond the hills. In Kampala's early days, competing religious groups mostly claimed the hilltops. One hilltop, though, is crowned by Mulago Hospital, the national referral hospital, which shares a site with Makerere University Medical School. A host of clinics, research facilities, training centers, staff residences, and medical suppliers sprawl over the steep hillside. A few gardens and trash heaps flank the road; goats graze on the lawns and wander into the road; roadside vendors offer clothing and shoes, phone calls and phone cards, and food and drink, working either from crowded closet-sized stalls or simply spreading their goods out on the grass. Most goods are sold in small quantities—a quarter cup of roasted peanuts sealed into a tiny plastic bag; single cigarettes.[25] Young men line up on their boda-bodas (a term that includes motorbikes, bicycles, and even, jokingly, children's tricycles), chatting and soliciting customers from among those who look reluctant to trudge up the hill.

Philly Lutaaya[26] Clinic, located near the top of the hill, is initially a challenge to find. Many Kampala buildings and their adjacent parking areas are located inside walled compounds. Access usually requires passing through a gate, explaining one's business to a guard, and perhaps showing an identification card. As they leave, visitors might be asked to open purses, tote bags, or briefcases, allowing guards to verify that none of the enterprise's property is being carried out. My white skin and middle-class garb meant that I got a less thorough check than would be the case for arriving or departing Black Africans. In my daytime observations, I never noted anything of a threatening nature either from guards or those entering or exiting, hardly surprising given that this was a medical facility. I was a bit surprised, then, to learn from the clinic's site security SOP that the guards are armed. The clinic's daytime guards are in fact clinic employees armed with bows and arrows (which I never saw).[27] The night guards are employees of a security firm and armed with guns.

Over the years of my research, Philly Lutaaya's facility grew by leaps and bounds. Initially the clinic occupied a single two-story concrete building and a few "containers."[28] By the end of my project, the clinic was overflowing not just the original structure but also a new four-story concrete edifice and the smaller buildings that housed the food program and handicraft ("income generating") project. The facility was still crowded. For instance, four or five medical officers (doctors with an undergraduate medical degree) shared a single large office (so private interviews were still nearly impossible). But crowding was relative, and the clinic did have a storage room for clinic records (a huge step up from the open-air "cage" with floor to ceiling stacks of file folders that I had seen at the nearby hospital), an enclosed play area for the many small children who came for treatment or accompanied mothers to their appointments, a spacious dining and meeting area, and a large conference room, as well as the usual treatment rooms and offices. The furnishings were adequate, but not plush—no carpets on the concrete floors; glass windows to close against chilly evenings or rainy days, but no screens; electrical outlets and computers for key workers, but still shortages of even rudimentary medical equipment like otoscopes; clean bathrooms, but still large plastic garbage cans filled with water for flushing and handwashing when the piped water stops flowing. Although drug "stockouts" became less common over time, clinic staff had to make ad hoc adjustments because they could never count on having the supplies they needed. For example, the clinic did not stock bottles for dispensing drugs. To solve this problem, one enterprising clinic worker asked local restaurants to save empty half-liter water bottles for the clinic. One morning she arrived for work with a giant garbage bag full of empty bottles, which could now be sterilized and filled with ARV syrups for HIV-infected infants.

Except in the early morning or late afternoon, the wooden benches that lined the walls of the waiting room and hallways at Philly Lutaaya were crowded with patients. Women also sat on the waiting room floor on woven mats, nursing babies and watching over toddlers. Although many youngsters occupied themselves with the toys and "boda bodas" in the play area, where a play supervisor kept a watchful eye on them, some children chose to remain at their mothers' sides. The clinic offered a welcoming environment for children. They tagged along with staff (including me), grabbing a friendly hand and wandering down the hall or up the stairs for a while before becoming bored and returning to their mothers or playmates. Although some of the children were clearly ill, with the most visible problem being skin diseases, they came to the clinic carefully dressed, babies swathed in spotless blankets, little girls with hair braided and beaded, little boys wearing carefully matched outfits, and all of them wearing shoes.

In addition to waiting, eating was another key activity in the clinic. Although some clinic workers complained about the quality of the food, for many patients what mattered was that they received food at all. The clinic served a midmorning meal of porridge and tea and a more substantial early afternoon lunch. Staff members ordered their food, but patients and those accompanying them simply received bowls of whatever was on offer that day—typically several starches (such as matoke, the steamed green bananas that are the national staple, maize, white rice, sweet potatoes, or "Irish" potatoes) with some protein such as meat or fish or a groundnut sauce and greens or other vegetables. The food was a big draw for clinic patients, some of whom lived in quite precarious situations, and staff worried that they were encouraging patients to come early and stay late to receive the free meals. But as long as the patients were present, staff members also felt that they needed to eat something. Ugandan hospitals do not usually feed patients, making the clinic unusual in this respect.

The hardships faced by Philly Lutaaya patients shaped clinic programs in many other ways as well and generally meant a closer tie between the clinic and its "participants," as they are called, than was the case in the US. For instance, when a pregnant woman with HIV enrolled in the program to prevent transmission from mother to child, the clinic would gather location information (somewhat complicated in Uganda) for the woman, as well as for her mother in the rural home and another close friend or relative. "Health visitors" were part of every Philly Lutaaya team, and participation in study or treatment programs generally required consenting to be "visited." "They call us spies," Faith, the health visitors supervisor joked. "If the woman goes 100 miles away, we'll still go and pick her up to come to her appointment. She might be sick and weak. Her husband might have died, so she goes home to the rural area. Then she's far away and can't manage to get in. We trace her, give her money to pay for transportation to come in for her scheduled visits." For the most part, health visitors seemed to be a welcome presence. They received participant confidences (one woman in dire circumstances proposed to come live with her health visitor), frequently troubleshooted, and acted as liaisons between participants and other clinic workers. Their role required considerable social skill because their visits could signal that a woman had HIV and lead to shunning by neighbors or abandonment by a partner or his family. At the same time, the health visitors provided important protection for women being ferried to and from the clinic by the clinic's male driver. In Ugandan culture, it would be improper for a woman to be alone in a vehicle with a man who was not her husband. Faith illustrated this point: "One husband was told that his wife had been seen being dropped off episodically by another man and the person giving the information even gave the registration number of the vehicle. It was very fortunate that there were two of them in the car this time [the health visitor and not just the driver]. The husband was ready to shoot the driver when they arrived. The husband was a soldier. The health visitor was able to explain what it was about and everything turned out ok." In a second case, the mother had not disclosed to her husband and he concluded that the driver was the father of their baby. With the health visitor's help, the woman was able to disclose to her husband and assure him that her absences from home were clinic visits not assignations.

Originating as a research facility, Philly Lutaaya was formed in a partnership between faculty members at US and Ugandan medical schools. That it began as a research facility has deeply shaped the clinic's trajectory. As was the case with all of the clinics I studied, the focus was specifically on HIV, an important matter because it meant that all of the clinics were roughly the same age, having been created in the mid-1980s. This clinic's first study concerned the transmission of HIV from pregnant women to their babies, which has remained a core area of research at Philly Lutaaya, with studies of drug regimens, adherence, breastfeeding, and the like. At the time of my four-month research stint in early 2005, the clinic was engaged in a half dozen research projects funded through the NIH Division of AIDS (DAIDS) and the CDC (Centers for Disease Control and Prevention) and had plans for additional studies.

The clinic had also developed a pediatric program that combined research and treatment, and two treatment programs (a maternity program and a family-centered care program) running alongside its research projects. Often participants transitioned from research projects to treatment programs, and, in fact, the treatment programs were formed because staff needed some way to meet the continuing needs of research subjects. Patients sometimes participated in treatment and research simultaneously. Although the research tended to focus almost exclusively on mothers and infants, the treatment programs were broader, offering care to the whole family and defining "care" expansively to include psychosocial programs, food and nutrition programs, and an income-generation program, as well as the more usual tracking of disease progress, provision of treatment for OIs, and ultimately treatment with ARVs. Clinic staff also provided training in HIV medicine in programs that mainly drew practitioners from central Africa.

Not surprisingly, the staff grew as rapidly as the buildings, reaching just over 250 members (some working full time, others part time) by early 2005. Yet even with these numbers, staff members felt that they always had more work than they could manage. Not only had participant numbers grown, but it was hard to refuse care to participants' family members, explained Pamela, a physician who was also an eminent researcher. "You think of a mother bringing her child for research and then the little kid who is not in the research not being able to get care—it just doesn't make sense." Approximately 70% of their encounters with patients were sick visits, she clarified. "When we look at the diaries . . . the routine visits are really very few. They can be manageable. It's the sick visits that are so many." Describing her routine, Pamela told us that she typically arrived at 7 a.m. and stayed until 8 p.m., adding that only in the middle of the night did she have any time to write articles.

The boundaries between Philly Lutaaya and the other organizations with which it worked were necessarily porous. Patients or research subjects belonged simultaneously to the clinic and to the other organizations. For instance, a woman who took part in a clinical trial investigating mother-to-child transmission was also a patient in an antenatal clinic (as they are called in Uganda) and in the maternity ward. When patients needed to be hospitalized, clinic doctors arranged admission to a nearby hospital. During hospitalization, care of clinic patients was transferred to hospital doctors, with some continuing (and sometimes uncomfortable) consultation and oversight from clinic staff. Staff members also belonged to multiple organizations. Although the hospital and the clinic were separate entities, they had overlapping staffs. Some clinic nurses also were employed by the hospital, especially in the antenatal units, and some of the doctors served as medical school professors or had teaching roles in hospital-affiliated institutes. The tension between hospital and clinic-based staff seemed especially acute when clinic staff had to ensure that hospital staff followed research proto-cols exactly and adequately documented their work.[29] Some of the quality control and quality assurance work of the clinic focused on these interfaces.

As noted, staff members at Philly Lutaaya Clinic in Uganda shared their South African counterparts' sense that they were writing the rules as they went along. But the experience of Ugandan clinic workers was distinctive in several ways. First, the balance between research, with more stringent rules, and treatment, with somewhat laxer guidelines, differed. Ugandan staff members were much more deeply involved in research, with the result that Philly Lutaaya staff more often encountered strict, critical regulators rather than friendly site visitors eager to observe best practices to share with others. Moreover, Philly Lutaaya's own rule writing was often oriented to the NIH's requirements about SOPs rather than to local clinical chal-lenges. In addition, at the time of my main field observations, Philly Lutaaya had recently experienced a very public dressing down over issues about re-search records. Although they were completely vindicated in the long run, the experience made Philly Lutaaya staff extraordinarily sensitive both to the need to keep meticulous records and to the costs of outsiders draw-ing unfounded conclusions before bothering to ask questions. More than their counterparts at other sites, then, Philly Lutaaya workers felt that they needed to be sure to have in place the right rules, appropriately adjusted for the peculiarities of their setting, and that they needed to document that they had followed the rules or have written contemporaneous explanations for why they had deviated from guidelines. One could not miss the daily dis-cussions about rules and adherence to rules or the fact that staff members were so committed to transparency that they were willing to air this dirty laundry with a researcher studying them.

Finally, compliance with rules is immeasurably harder when the mun-dane materials for compliance are absent. Records are harder to keep without ample paper, file folders, locking file cabinets, measurement in-struments (such as blood pressure cuffs), stat labs to produce test results, computers, photocopy machines, reliable electricity, and so forth. Staff shortages obviously amplify other resource shortages, as do obligations to train people to do their work in conformity with "foreign" rules.

Comparing Countries, Comparing Clinics

All five HIV clinics included in this study engaged in both treatment and research, which might suggest that the work being done in them would be quite similar. And in some respects it was. But as the sketches of these clinics make clear, context matters, and the clinics differed both because of the countries in which they were located and because of local institutional environments. (For more details on the latter, see table A.1 in appendix A, available online at this book's page at the University of Chicago Press website.) Even when people follow the same protocols and guidelines to study and treat the same disease, many features of the local environment impinge on clinic work, in part because unexamined assumptions about patient populations and work practices underlie the protocols and guidelines. For instance, adhering to clinical guidelines is easier in well-resourced clinics and when working with well-nourished patients whose medical histories do not include bouts of TB or malaria. Likewise, training staff members to adhere to US research conventions, whether they are about accounting, recording data, or protecting confidentiality, is easier when they are not already accustomed to working with somewhat different local research rules.

Even though all of the clinics offered ART during the period of my research, treatment programs were more fully established and better funded in some clinics than others. By the time I began my research, ART and research programs were well established in both US clinics, although funding for treatment continued to be a challenge at Bobbi Campbell. The Ugandan and South African fieldwork was conducted as Philly Lutaaya and Gugu Dlamini were participating in the early stages of large rollout programs, funded by international donors and national governments, to provide antiretrovirals through HIV clinics. The Thai government's program, organized around GPO-VIR (the locally produced generic), had been in place for a little while at the time of our fieldwork.[30]

All five of the clinics engaged in research, although their programs differed. Robert Rafsky, Cha-on Suesum, and Philly Lutaaya all had vigorous research programs. Bobbi Campbell's program emphasized treatment more than research. Gugu Dlamini did less research than the other five clinics but had a strong affiliation with a US university and was expanding its research activities, focusing especially on the development of drug resistance. The scaling up of research at the South African clinic provided an opportunity for me to observe organizational learning. Conversely, Philly Lutaaya was in the process of adding more care independent of its research programs. Thus, the Ugandan clinic allowed me to observe a different kind of organizational learning—perhaps better described as "unlearning"—as staff members figured out how to scale back research-related services that required resources unavailable in a sustainable clinic treatment program in a poor country. Although the clinical and research programs in the US and Thai clinics were more settled, these clinics continued to initiate new studies. Preparing for new studies often required clinics to redeploy and retrain staff, procure equipment, and institute new recordkeeping routines, as well as make arrangements for new treatment interventions. The Thai researchers were eager to design research responsive to local issues and sensitive to Thai conditions as well as to participate in internationally funded multisite studies.

In the five clinics, I observed variation in the overlap between research and care ranging from nearly complete overlap to almost none. Because all of the clinics were outpatient facilities, care was shared with or taken over by others when patients required hospitalization. At Philly Lutaaya and Cha-on Suesum, essentially all outpatient care was initially provided through research. Therefore, clinical needs often had to be fit around research protocols. With the recent addition of grant-funded treatment programs at Philly Lutaaya Clinic, treatment no longer needed to fit the strictures of the research program, although treatment programs could also impose severe constraints. At Cha-on Suesum, care continued to be given under the umbrella of research, but that umbrella had been enlarged to accommodate research subjects who cycled off studies but had no other way to access HIV/AIDS treatment.[31] At Robert Rafsky Clinic, there was some overlap between research and care. Both took place within the same facility, with research nurses and physicians engaging in both clinical and research work. Most research subjects were also clinic patients. When study subjects required HIV treatment beyond what a study provided, they usually got that care in the clinic, with expenses covered by their own insurance. Whenever changes had to be made to their medications, the research staff consulted with research subjects' HIV care providers to encourage them to make changes that complied with the research protocol when possible. However, medical needs were supposed to come first, and the research staff did not discourage or prevent research subjects from receiving needed medical treatment even if that meant losing them from a study. At Bobbi Campbell Clinic, research and care were treated as discrete activities. The research and treatment units were housed in the same building but operated separately. In fact, to prevent research subjects from confusing research with treatment, the clinic's policy required that research subjects not be seen by their primary care physicians when they came for study visits. How the Gugu Dlamini Clinic in South Africa was going to manage the overlap between research and care was less clear, because the clinic had not yet fully developed its research program. These clinic-level policies about the proper relationship between treatment and research were, among other things, policies about how to work with two (or more) sets of sometimes aligned, sometimes conflicting rules and protocols—a daily challenge that was generally managed smoothly but occasionally created real headaches.

HIV may appear to be the same disease the world over and that may lead to expectations that clinical guidelines crafted in one place will work well in another. And multisited clinical research depends on uniformity in data collection procedures so that data may be aggregated across sites. Yet as these clinic sketches show, these universal rules are being inserted into clinics that are anything but uniform. The worlds of HIV treatment and research are not so easily standardized as factory assembly lines—or even as the world apparently envisioned by guideline writers and regulators. That does not mean that rules and guidelines are useless, but only that clinic workers cannot simply "apply" the rules but must instead either rework square-peg rules or modify round-hole clinics to enable a match that allows the rules to do at least some of the work they are intended to do.

Conclusion

In the struggle against HIV, the vision of the disease as a global health problem, the obvious connections among countries as the virus spread around the world, and the pledges of international bodies to press for equitable access to prevention and treatment have created a misleading illusion of uniformity. Among the forces that might contribute to genuine uniformity are the rules, regulations, and guidelines that govern clinic life. Because these rules ostensibly focus on viruses and pharmacological agents, they have tacitly assumed that uniform rules are appropriate tools to increase uniformity in treatment, thereby furthering such goals as reducing "practice variations" (different treatments for the same conditions) and decreasing "healthcare disparities" (inequalities in access and outcomes).

The chapter began the work of assessing the tools and, to some degree, the goal itself. This task is reminiscent of debates about equal opportunity versus equal outcomes. To be sure, viruses (and other infectious agents) and medicines are constant enough across time and space that we would not argue that medicines available to treat HIV in rich countries would not work in poor countries and therefore should not be provided. And we would not argue, as some have, that citizens of poor countries are "inferior" patients on whom expensive medications should not be wasted. Yet we need not go to these extremes when we acknowledge differences among clinics and the people they serve. The clinics and the countries in which they are located differ, and some of their differences are consequential.[32] But even in rich countries, clinics, medical workers, and patients do not fully conform to the expectations of those who make the rules. At the very least, rules designed to create uniformity nearly always create some discomfort. They may be "nitpicky" and annoying, and they may therefore be resisted. More serious problems arise, though, when rules fit so badly that they undermine research or treatment or siphon off resources desperately needed for core tasks.

As we have seen, the five clinics are rather different places. With so much variability in patients and research subjects, caregivers, researchers, and clinics, it behooves us to ask how clinic staff actually work with the purportedly uniform rules, regulations, and guidelines that are intended to shape their work and produce standardization in both treatment and research. Are the rules in fact uniform when they arrive? Do they remain uniform as staff begin to work with them? And what effects flow from these attempts to standardize? With a clearer picture of the clinics themselves, we are now ready to pose these questions.

[CHAPTER THREE]

The Mushroom Cloud of Rules

Early in my research, I interviewed an administrator associated with Robert Rafsky Clinic. He had been reluctant to talk with me, convinced that he had nothing useful to share. Jim, as I'll call him, had demurred that he was only familiar with rules about governance and knew nothing about other kinds of rules, seemingly unaware just how deeply entwined governance was with research, treatment, and training. In fact, he surprised us both. Jim had a great deal to share, so much that I mostly confined myself to taking notes (he preferred that to audiotaping), interrupting only occasionally to verify my understanding by restating key points. He talked steadily through our allotted time, continuing to offer explanations and further examples even as I stowed my pad and pen and rose to leave for my next interview.

I had begun my discussion with Jim, as I often did, with a brief recap of the topic of my research, which I had described more fully in the handout I included with the interview request. Employing a meaning so common that it can be found in most dictionaries, I used the word "mushrooming" to describe the rapid increase and spread of rules. Aiming for a neutral tone, I meant only to suggest that mushrooming had happened, not that it was either inherently good or bad. But although I had aimed for neutrality, I soon learned that my respondent's experience of rules was anything but neutral. Over the course of the interview, Jim offered detailed examples of the challenges of reconciling the conflicting rules that impinged on collaborating entities such as the hospital that housed the HIV clinic, the foundation ("faculty practice plan") that handled physician salaries, and the medical school that employed him and many clinic staff members. The problem was made worse, he suggested, both by the rapid increase in the number of rules—which he estimated to have doubled in just the previous three years—and by the "tunnel vision" exhibited by colleagues who did not consider how policies affected other entities in the network. But such complexities were inescapable, he believed, because "there's little any of us can do that impacts only one of these entities." Near the end of his impassioned account of this byzantine regulatory environment, Jim returned to my reference to mushrooming. But to my astonishment, my reference to the mushrooming of rules had now become in his narrative a much more sinister "mushroom cloud of rules."

This was not just an isolated assessment of an overwrought administrator. Expressions of impatience, bewilderment, frustration, and even outrage over laws, rules, guidelines, and policies were exceedingly common in all five fieldsites (and also came up in interviews with respondents unaffiliated with these clinics) and ranged across topics. In a comment that could have been made at any of the five clinics, one Robert Rafsky worker remarked that sometimes she and her colleagues "just look at each other and say, 'it's all rules; all we do is deal with rules.'"

This chapter considers how the "legal environment" of clinics has changed, cataloging key modifications and placing those changes in a broader context and then turning to the subjective experience of those working with the rules. In essence the chapter asks how the "mushrooming" of rules came to feel like a "mushroom cloud" of rules—or, according to O'Reilly and Berry (2011), a "tsunami." The last sections of the chapter offer an overview of clinical guidelines and rules about the conduct of research, the main rules that shape the clinical and research work of HIV clinics.

The chapter, admittedly, gives a US-centric account of how individual strands developed and became interwoven. This focus on the US is intentional, but comes with costs that should be acknowledged. Because the US plays an outsized role in the global governance of healthcare and especially HIV care, explicating the intertwined elements of American healthcare regulation provides an important foundation for understanding the US's dominating but not fully consistent interventions in other countries. This initial US focus risks suggesting by omission that there is little to know about domestic healthcare regulation in those other countries. As the book unfolds, I attempt to correct that impression by showing how the global regulation of HIV clinics often went astray by taking too little account of local regulatory systems and cultures. But this chapter's single-country focus does permit me to show in some detail how disparate elements came to be woven into a loose fabric and, especially important, to move more quickly to examining the work of research and treatment in the five HIV clinics I studied.

The Mushrooming of Rules and the "Legalization" of Healthcare: How It Happened

The mushrooming of rules that began to accelerate in the 1960s is the result of a confluence of factors, making a concise account difficult. What is clear is that, before the middle of the twentieth century, US healthcare operated with relatively little interference from outsiders. The deference accorded to US physicians, painstakingly described by Paul Starr (1982), together with the origins of hospitals as charitable institutions, often sponsored by religious bodies, meant that physicians and healthcare organizations were frequently exempted from regulation when other entities were not. To be sure, those working in healthcare had long welcomed government intervention on some points, for instance, seeking state governments' assistance with the licensing that enabled dominant groups of practitioners to exclude competitors. For a variety of reasons, though, starting in the mid-1960s and accelerating as time went on, courts and legislatures became more inclined to intervene, and physicians themselves more often urged clearer guidelines for medical work, sometimes even participating in enforcing those standards.

This new framework for the practice of medicine—though labeling it a framework may exaggerate its coherence—emerged from the actions of a wide variety of players. Acting independently at first, but more often with reference to one another as time passed, these actors still did not quite achieve "concerted action." Rather than coordinating, entities noted and sometimes made use of one another's work, attempting to discern order in the chaos of new regulatory efforts and, when possible, exploiting opportunities opened up by others' actions. We should be careful not to make these initiatives sound too entrepreneurial or visionary. Often these regulatory efforts were instead cautious, conservative moves intended to protect an advantageous position, avoid political controversy, make others do the heavy lifting, or bring legal rulings into alignment. And, of course, some interventions were intended simply as resource grabs, with stronger actors introducing rules that might legitimize their greed.

Here I briefly untangle some of the main threads of this increased legalism to show where these strands originated and how they have been woven together to form a strong and constraining, if rather inelegant, fabric. Although some of this new legalism was grounded in formal law, restricting our gaze to formal law would lead to a gross underestimate of the magnitude and effects of these changes. In the healthcare arena, the "hard law" created by legislatures and elaborated through court cases has been supplemented by considerable "soft law," quasi-legal instruments of governance that are less binding than hard law.[1]

Among the many threads out of which this fabric is woven, I here trace the contributions of six that seem particularly consequential. Especially important, first, are the rules, regulations, and policies created by physicians themselves to raise the standard of professional practice. Although physicians have long worked with some form of guidelines, recent initiatives have brought more systematic production and dissemination of guidelines and a stronger grounding of clinical guidelines in scientific evidence. These changes in the nature of clinical guidelines provide a foundation for other regulatory initiatives, many of which have come from outside the medical academy. In particular, those who pay for healthcare and for clinical research have insisted on their right to ensure that funds are spent well. Increases in public funding for healthcare thus also brought a second set of rules and regulations in the form of increased public (or semipublic) oversight of caregivers and healthcare organizations. A third set of rules was crafted especially by the private insurers, who orchestrate payment for healthcare, and the healthcare organizations, where care is actually provided. Like public payers, private insurers and healthcare organizations were concerned with the relationship between the adequacy of care and the funding streams that covered healthcare costs. But because insurers and healthcare organizations must keep their eyes on the bottom line, this third set of rules was focused on healthcare as a business enterprise and was as much about protecting profits and forestalling liability as about providing good care. Although at first glance the rules seem to be about appropriate, safe care, disputes between payers (insurers) and recipients (healthcare organizations) over what care will be covered and when reimbursement will be declined suggest that both parties are deeply invested in creating rules that work to their own advantage.[2] But rules were also crafted, fourthly, by regulatory bodies. Some of these regulatory bodies originated as government agencies; others came into existence at the behest of nongovernmental bodies such as professional associations, but in the long run have functioned as semiofficial regulators. During this time period, fifthly, public outcry over well-publicized abuses created pressure for more attention to patients' rights and to protections for human research subjects. The rights of patients and research subjects have then been institutionalized in both statutes and case law; in the routines of healthcare and research organizations; and in new professions such as bioethics and research administration. Sixth, and lastly, legal academics have helped introduce some order into thinking about the relation between law and medicine, offering courses on health law, putting together textbooks, and launching journals.

As will become clear, these six threads cannot be described as either empirically or analytically distinct. At most, they have discernibly distinct starting points and some distinctive features, but each of the threads quickly became entangled with one or more of the others. The discussion that follows therefore tacks back and forth between analytical distinctions and historical events, showing how the legalization of healthcare, originating in a series of rather independent actors and episodes, was gradually consolidated into a more coherent, consistent set of regulatory interventions pushing toward increased formality and increased external control. As a reference point for this unfolding discussion, table 3.1 lays out a rudimentary timeline that juxtaposes milestones for the six threads, giving some sense of when each strand emerged and how rapidly it developed. Table 3.2 focuses on the six strands individually, offering a compressed portrait of each. The remainder of the chapter fills in the details that show the dynamic process by which the fabric was woven—and indeed continues to be rewoven.

CLINICAL GUIDELINES AND EVIDENCE-BASED MEDICINE: LAYING THE FOUNDATION FOR EXTERNAL CONTROL

Clinical guidelines (sometimes called "clinical practice guidelines" or "clinical protocols")[3] are one of the most important forms of medical soft law. In essence, they are rules that translate the findings of medical science into "recipes" that tell medical caregivers how to respond to a patient's medical condition—for instance, what medications to give in what dosages or when to do surgery given a patient's symptoms, medical history, and personal characteristics. As part of this translation, clinical guidance is often embedded in technologies—algorithms and decision support tools—that come close to concealing any remaining clinical discretion.

Clinical guidelines have been around since at least the fourth century BC, when Plato commented (in *The Statesman*) on the creation of codified rules to govern clinicians' practice and even anticipated legal enforcement of compliance with such guidelines (Hurwitz 1999). Contemporary clinical guidelines differ from the clinical guidelines of the past, though. In the past, standards were likely to be based on physician experience, a practice sometimes characterized as "eminence-based medicine" (Millenson 1997). In contrast, today's guidelines are usually "evidence based," relying on the huge growth of medical research, particularly outcomes research, and on systematic assessment of both the quality of evidence and the efficacy of interventions. The use of systematic methods and statistical techniques, including meta-analyses, to assess the effectiveness of medical interventions (Rosoff 2001, 2012; Chalmers, Hedges, and Cooper 2002) is arguably one of the most consequential changes in this broad process of legalization.

The clinical guidelines of today depend on the technology of randomized clinical trials (RCTs) and the statistical techniques to assess and aggregate the results of such clinical trials. As in other endeavors, the early phases unfolded slowly with an accelerating pace as the elements that now

TABLE 3.1. Timeline of Major Milestones in Legalization of (US) Healthcare

DATE	CLINICAL GUIDELINES AND EBM	PUBLIC PAYMENT FOR HEALTHCARE AND RESEARCH	BUSINESS OF HEALTHCARE: PRIVATE INSURERS AND HEALTHCARE ORGANIZATIONS	REGULATORY AGENCIES	SOCIAL MOVEMENTS AND PUBLIC PRESSURE	HEALTH LAW
1900s				1906: FDA created (major increases in authority in 1938 and 1962)		
1910s						
1920s			1929: Blue Cross created			
1930s			1939: Blue Shield created	1938: increase in FDA authority with legislation requiring premarket review of new drugs and banning false information re: therapeutics on labels		
1940s	RCTs provide evidence about effectiveness but seen as "oddity"	1945: NIH (created in 1930) begins giving research grants	1945: McCarran-Ferguson Act provides for state rather than federal regulation of insurance and exempts health insurance from antitrust laws			
1950s				1951: Joint Commission created (with somewhat different name)		1953: first law-medicine program established at Case Western Reserve

1960s	1965: Medicare and Medicaid programs created		1962: increase in FDA authority leads to creation of drug approvals process requiring demonstration of substantial benefit of new drugs	1965: *Griswold* begins to establish right to privacy for reproductive care	1960: first health law textbook published
			1965: Joint Commission becomes semiofficial regulator, accrediting organizations and programs so they can receive Medicare and Medicaid monies		
1970s	1970s and thereafter: Wennberg and Dartmouth Atlas Project investigate practice variations		1972: Office for Protection from Research Risks created 1977: precursor of Centers for Medicare and Medicaid Services created	1972: *Canterbury* ruling establishes right to informed consent 1973: *Roe* consolidates right to privacy for reproductive care 1976: *Quinlan* begins to establish limited right to die	1975–76: several health law journals begin publication
1980s		Medical-industrial complex comes into existence with horizontal and vertical integration and industry concentration		1980s: AIDS activism adds pressure for legislation and modification of agency procedures	

(Continued)

TABLE 3.1. (*Continued*)

DATE	CLINICAL GUIDELINES AND EBM	PUBLIC PAYMENT FOR HEALTHCARE AND RESEARCH	BUSINESS OF HEALTHCARE: PRIVATE INSURERS AND HEALTHCARE ORGANIZATIONS	REGULATORY AGENCIES	SOCIAL MOVEMENTS AND PUBLIC PRESSURE	HEALTH LAW
1990s	1990: Institute of Medicine calls for clinical practice guidelines 1998: National Guidelines Clearinghouse created	1990: Ryan White Care Act provides funding for domestic AIDS care		1992: Office of Research Integrity created		
2000s		2003: PEPFAR provides funding for global HIV/AIDS care				
2010s	2018: ECRI Guidelines Trust takes over work of National Guidelines Clearinghouse	2010: Obamacare increases public funding for health insurance				
2020s		2023: Inflation Reduction Act allows negotiation of some drug prices				2023: 189 health law programs ranked by *US News and World Report*

TABLE 3.2. Key Strands in Legalization of (US) Healthcare

STRANDS	TIMELINE AND KEY ACTORS	FOCUS, RELATION TO HEALTHCARE, EFFECT ON LEGALIZATION OF HEALTHCARE
Clinical Guidelines and EBM	1940s, RCTs, providing evidence about effectiveness of interventions, begin but remain "oddity" into 1960s 1972, Cochrane, *Effectiveness and Efficiency* (evaluation of National Health Service in UK) 1970s and thereafter, clinical decision trees (Eddy) 1970s and thereafter, practice variations (Wennberg and colleagues involved in Dartmouth Atlas Project) Mid-1980s on, EBM textbooks begin to appear 1990, Institute of Medicine calls for clinical practice guidelines to standardize clinical work 1993, Cochrane Collaboration (UK) (later renamed Cochrane) creates 13-country network to encourage evidence-based healthcare grounded in systematic reviews and guidelines 1993, US Agency for Health Care Policy and Research (later renamed Agency for Healthcare Research and Quality) launches program to create evidence-based guidelines 1993–2000, McMaster University hosts Evidence-Based Medicine Working Group 1995, EBM journal, *Clinical Evidence*, begins publication 1998–2018, National Guidelines Clearinghouse managed database of clinical guidelines and related documents; many functions subsequently transferred to ECRI Guidelines Trust	<u>Focus</u>: Offering guidance to caregivers through clinical guidelines; producing reviews of RCTs of healthcare interventions, including treatments, diagnostic tests, screening procedures; training caregivers to use decision trees and practice EBM; reducing practice variations among caregivers, organizations, and locales. <u>Relation to healthcare</u>: Largely internal to medical world (in sense that rules are created by clinicians and medical researchers), though seen by some as threat to practitioner autonomy. <u>Effect on legalization</u>: Formal but flexible, though less flexible when adopted by other actors (e.g., governments, insurers). Basis for much of regulatory work of other strands/actors.

(Continued)

TABLE 3.2. (*Continued*)

STRANDS	TIMELINE AND KEY ACTORS	FOCUS, RELATION TO HEALTHCARE, EFFECT ON LEGALIZATION OF HEALTHCARE
Public Payment for Healthcare and Research	1930, Hygienic Laboratory (first created in 1901) becomes NIH 1945, after NIH received congressional authorization to fund extramural research in 1944, finally has sufficient funds to offer research grants by end of subsequent year; eventually becomes major funder for clinical research 1965, Medicare and Medicaid programs created 1990, Ryan White Care Act creates program to pay for domestic AIDS care 2003, PEPFAR created as response to global HIV/AIDS, continuously renewed 2010, Patient Protection and Affordable Care Act (ACA or Obamacare) signed into law, making health insurance more widely available in the US 2023, Inflation Reduction Act gives government the right to negotiate prices of some prescription drugs for Medicare beneficiaries	<u>Focus</u>: Accepting public responsibility to provide for health of citizens and advance of medical knowledge; setting agenda for public health, including adjusting for new threats to health; responding to public pressure; providing funds for healthcare and research. Accountability for efficiency and effectiveness. Fiscal concern about controlling cost of healthcare. <u>Relation to healthcare</u>: Largely external to medical world, but some positions occupied by medically trained personnel. <u>Effect on legalization</u>: Increase in formality and rigidity. Route to regulation of private healthcare organizations through power of purse. By acting through government-created regulatory bodies and privately created entities, creates pathway for legalization of healthcare.
Business of Healthcare: Private Insurers and Healthcare Organizations	1929, creation of program that eventually becomes Blue Cross health insurance plans, covering hospital services; marks the beginning of both nonprofit and for-profit insurance to cover medical expenses rather than just to replace workers' lost income 1939, formation of first Blue Shield insurance plan covering physician services 1945, McCarran Ferguson Act returns insurance regulation to the states, with result that insurance programs evade federal government oversight and are not covered by antitrust legislation; partial repeal in 2021	<u>Focus</u>: Ensuring profits of insurers and healthcare organizations. For insurers, refusing to pay for procedures and therapies not considered effective. For healthcare organizations, preventing lawsuits. Dominated by organizational/corporate interests, so pursuit of profitability plays big role. <u>Relation to healthcare</u>: External to medical professions but closely involved with medical care. Private payment for healthcare is simultaneously about payment (so aligns with public payment) and about the business of healthcare (so aligns with healthcare organizations). Hospital administration is about both provision (so aligns with interests of government and nonprofits, including religious bodies) and management and payment (so aligns with insurers). Both hospital administration and private health insurance combine nonmedically trained staff with medically trained or dual-degreed staff.

Business of Healthcare: Private Insurers and Healthcare Organizations	1980s and thereafter, large healthcare corporations ("medical-industrial complex") become important element of healthcare system, bringing shift from nonprofit and government to for-profit companies, horizontal integration with less local control, vertical integration with many phases of healthcare within single organization, and industry concentration 1982, merger creates Blue Cross Blue Shield Association 1994, some BSBC licensees become for-profit entities, greatly increasing their profits	<u>Effect on legalization</u>: Heavy involvement of both the American Hospital Association and AMA in determining form of health insurance programs (what would be covered, who would receive reimbursement). Although insurance increased likelihood that medical bills would be paid, it also reduced physician control of healthcare. Consolidation of hospitals likewise increased formality of rules governing activities of physicians and other healthcare workers. Two main effects, then: guidelines become more like "hard law" because both insurers and hospitals insist on adherence to guidelines and add enforcement; autonomy of healthcare workers further decreased by obligation to follow hospital rules, some created by medically trained workers, others not.
Regulatory Agencies	1906, Pure Food and Drug Act creates the FDA 1938, Federal Food, Drug and Cosmetic Act increases FDA authority by requiring premarket review of new drugs and banning false labeling re: therapeutic benefits 1951, Joint Commission on Accreditation of Hospitals created (changes in name and scope of activities over the years; now referred to simply as Joint Commission)	<u>Focus</u>: Responding to public demands for reform and regulation; fleshing out and implementing legislation. <u>Relation to healthcare</u>: Variable relation to healthcare. In some instances, originated within healthcare sector (e.g., Joint Commission), often initially as handmaid of professional associations. Now often independent quasi-legal bodies. Some regulatory agencies created at behest of government specifically for regulatory purposes. Others independent and function as business enterprises.

(Continued)

TABLE 3.2. (*Continued*)

STRANDS	TIMELINE AND KEY ACTORS	FOCUS, RELATION TO HEALTHCARE, EFFECT ON LEGALIZATION OF HEALTHCARE
	1962, Kefauver-Harris Amendment further increases FDA authority by requiring evidence of substantial benefit for new drugs and therefore ushering in the drug approvals process 1965, Joint Commission acquires semiofficial status when it becomes the organization that has "deeming authority" to accredit healthcare organizations and programs, making them eligible to receive funds from Medicare and Medicaid. Although Joint Commission's reach expands over the years, other organizations now also have "deeming authority." 1972, Office for Protection from Research Risks created; replaced in 2000 by Office for Human Research Protections (OHRP) 1977, Health Care Financing Administration formed to coordinate Medicare and Medicaid; renamed Center for Medicare and Medicaid Services (CMS) in 2001 1992, Office of Research Integrity created	Effect on legalization: Instrumental in enlarging volume of regulations and guidance, in some instances directly linked to statutes, in other instances less tethered to formal law. Regulatory agencies often given responsibilities as part of approval process for payment (e.g., by Medicare and Medicaid or by government bodies funding research).
Social Movements and Public Pressure	Patient rights, including: • 1972, *Canterbury v. Spence* requires informed consent for treatment • 1965 and 1973, *Griswold v. Connecticut* and *Roe v. Wade* recognize right to privacy in reproductive decisions • 1976, *In re Quinlan* establishes a limited right to die Disease-constituency activism (e.g., AIDS activism starting in 1980s) pressuring for particular pieces of legislation or for modification of agency procedures	Focus: Especially focused on rights: of patients (and their families) and research subjects. Pressure often arises as response to abuses. Relation to healthcare: External to healthcare, though some participants are medical professionals; usually formal and often entails pressure to create new rules or regulations, though can also be pressure to modify existing rules. Effect on legalization: Social movement activities somewhat independent of other strands. Effects especially through court cases and legislation, which then lead to procedures and practices for demonstrating and documenting compliance.

| *Health Law* | 1953, Law-Medicine Center, the first such program, established at Case Western Reserve University
1958, Law-Medicine Research Institute established at Boston University
1960, William Curran publishes first health law textbook, *Law and Medicine: Text and Source Materials on Medico-Legal Problems* (though preceded by Elmer Brothers' text on "forensic medicine" in 1914)
1960, *Medicine, Science and the Law* begins quarterly publication, with focus especially on forensics
1975–76, *American Journal of Law and Medicine*, the *Journal of Medical Ethics* and the *Journal of Health Politics, Policy and Law* all begin publication with other journals following in short order
2023, 189 health law programs are ranked by *US News and World Report* | <u>Focus</u>: Creating legal framework for emerging field of law. Training lawyers and others for law-related work in healthcare organizations and for health law teaching and research.
<u>Relation to healthcare</u>: External to healthcare, though some participants have medical training and some activities (courses in health law) occur in medical schools.
<u>Effect on legalization</u>: Responsive to health social movements—through analysis of legislation and judicial decisions. Also responsive to demand for training from key professions and organizations. |

seem crucial to clinical trials were added: systematic administration of the test (for instance a specified dose of a carefully prepared pharmaceutical compound), comparison of the test with an alternative (perhaps a placebo, perhaps an alternative treatment), appropriate composition of the groups receiving the experimental and control treatments, adequate numbers of research subjects in all arms of a study and sufficient duration of trials so that results were reliable, and so forth. RCTs were being done occasionally in the 1940s but remained relatively rare for quite some time. Writing in *JAMA* in 1992, the Evidence-Based Medicine Working Group asserted that "in 1960, the randomized clinical trial was an oddity. It is now accepted that virtually no drug can enter clinical practice without a demonstration of its efficacy in clinical trials" (1992, 2420). Only in the 1970s did researchers begin to collate RCTs into clinical guidelines.

The core insight that medical practice should be grounded in scientific evidence seems to have occurred to several people simultaneously, although they reached this conclusion via different routes and used somewhat different language to describe their emerging conviction. An early advocate was Archie Cochrane, a remarkable British epidemiologist who did pioneering experimental work. His pathbreaking *Effectiveness and Efficiency* (1972) reviewed the National Health Service and articulated the fundamental importance of using solid evidence, preferably from RCTs, to assess the effectiveness of medical interventions. Cochrane urged not only primary research but also the creation of a system of reviews of RCTs. The Cochrane Collaboration (now simply Cochrane), established by his colleagues in 1993 as a thirteen-country network, has specialized in producing high-quality reviews of clinical research in a wide array of fields (Chalmers, Dickersin, and Chalmers 1992).

Beginning in the 1970s and taking a somewhat different tack, John Wennberg and his Dartmouth Atlas Project[4] colleagues used Medicare data to document "practice variations" in the provision of medical care (Wennberg and Gittelsohn 1973; Relman 2010; Wennberg 2010, 2011). They categorized medical care as falling into three groups: effective, preference sensitive, and supply sensitive. In their view, variations in the first were unwarranted and indicated an undersupply of care, variations in the second were acceptable if patients were well informed, and variations in the third were physician driven and suggested inappropriate overuse of medical care, a problem likely more common in the US than elsewhere. Also worried about unwarranted variations in medical practice, the Institute of Medicine's 1990 report called for clinical practice guidelines to standardize medical work (Institute of Medicine 1990).

Even the term "evidence-based" seems to have been brought into the lexicon by several people. David Eddy, David Sackett, and Gordon Guyatt all began using variants of the phrase simultaneously. Attempting to create decision trees for clinical decision making, Eddy discovered just how little evidence supported many long-established treatments and began to urge that medicine should be evidence based (Eddy 1996, 2011). Sackett and Guyatt began teaching physicians to practice evidence-based medicine (EBM), writing textbooks and creating residency programs at McMasters University with that focus (Sackett et al. 1996; Evidence-Based Medicine Working Group 1992; Zimerman 2013; Djulbegovic and Guyatt 2017). The Evidence-Based Medicine Working Group at McMasters University (1993–2000) and the EBM journal *Clinical Evidence*, which began publication in 1995, were important steps in institutionalizing this approach to healthcare (Eddy 2005).

Soon, the idea that medical practice should be grounded in science and organized around systematic, evidence-based guidelines was being endorsed by such bodies as the Institute of Medicine (now the National Academy of Medicine) (1990, 2011). One result has been an "explosion" of clinical practice guidelines (O'Brien et al. 2000, 1078)—and more groups producing them. According to the AMA's 1996 *Directory of Practice Parameters*, 1700 clinical practice guidelines were created between 1970 and 1995, with almost half of them written between 1993 and 1995 (O'Brien et al. 2000, 1078). In 1990, 26 physician groups were involved in developing clinical practice guidelines; by 1994, more than 60 organizations were producing guidelines (Walker et al. 1994; Sheetz 1997, 1348, citing Ayres 1994). These guideline-writing groups include federal and state agencies, professional specialty groups and societies, and third-party payers (Merz 1993), but guidelines are also produced by some large research organizations and even malpractice insurers. From 1998 to 2018, the National Guidelines Clearinghouse (NGC) maintained a website index of guidelines.[5] The service provided by NGC was especially important because guidelines are updated frequently (1197 of the 1970 indexed guidelines had been updated since the website started). Although NGC closed in July 2018, this does not signal any decreased importance of guidelines. Many of NGC's functions have been taken over by the ECRI Guidelines Trust,[6] although the work of tracking and archiving guidelines also seems to be increasingly decentralized, with guidelines compiled for medical specialties by specialty professional associations.

Along with this numerical increase came a shift in how guidelines are used. Once merely informative, clinical guidelines are now behavior modification tools aimed at shaping and correcting the activities of medical workers and even patients. They often are adopted by healthcare organizations with a clear expectation that physicians and other employees will adhere to the guidelines. How authoritative the guidelines are meant to be varies from one guideline producer to the next. Mello, for instance, describes the guidelines of malpractice insurers as falling "somewhere between payer guidelines and professional societies' guidelines on the continuum of authoritativeness" (Mello 2001, 652).

By the time the HIV epidemic arrived in the early 1980s, guidelines had become an established part of healthcare, at least in the US. More than in long-standing fields, guideline culture was able to take hold in HIV medicine without competition from norms and practices that predated the advent of guidelines and EBM. In the culture and practices of HIV medicine both in the US and in other countries, then, guidelines have played an outsized role. Whether they are doctors and nurses, social workers, or administrative personnel, clinic staff generally express irritation about rules. But they complain less about clinical guidelines than other kinds of rules. This is not because clinical guidelines are easy to apply, though. In fact, guidelines can be quite difficult to use when they are written in rich countries and subsequently transported to poorer countries where conditions are very different or when guidelines written initially for adult men are redeployed without sufficient modification to guide care for women or children. Despite these caveats, guidelines more than other rules are experienced as useful rather than burdensome, perhaps because they are written largely by clinicians for clinicians. They are thus "internal" regulation and are "informal" in the sense they come with an assumption that some adjustment will be needed for the very particular circumstances of individual clinics and even individual patients.[7] Often, guidelines have been treated as flexible rules of thumb created by doctors for doctors—essentially, tools of the trade.

Nevertheless, a few key changes have made clinical guidelines feel a bit less like "indigenous rules." First, as guidelines have become more firmly tied to evidence, the likelihood of them changing from one year to the next has increased. And as the rules have become more complex, practitioners sometimes depend on cut-down versions, perhaps produced by their colleagues for their particular facility. Caregivers often make heavy use of the charts and tables that accompany the voluminous guidelines. In rich countries, practitioners increasingly rely on handheld electronic devices to quickly guide them through the welter of detail. In addition to being more detailed and more likely to change from one year to the next, guidelines are also more likely to be enforced, particularly by the government bodies or insurers who pay for care. Because of these changes, guidelines now are less "soft," even if they have usually not quite become "hard law." Caregivers are constrained or incentivized to follow the guidelines even when adherence is not fully mandatory.

In some places and for some caregivers, though, the hardening of guidelines, and their distortion as they are deployed for purposes other than simply guiding medical work, may "denaturalize" guidelines and move them into the same category as other externally imposed rules. We will return to this problem repeatedly in the chapters that follow as we examine the alienation and loss of agency that has accompanied these changes. It is this transformation of clinical guidelines as they are used by other actors and entangled with other kinds of rules to which we now turn.

PUBLIC PAYMENT FOR HEALTHCARE AND RESEARCH: DEMANDING FISCAL RESPONSIBILITY AND ACCOUNTABILITY

The signing of the Medicare and Medicaid legislation in 1965 brought a sea change in US healthcare, making healthcare more readily available to both elderly and poor patients. This legislation also dramatically changed the legal environment of healthcare, vastly increasing the volume of rules that caregivers and healthcare organizations had to attend to.

Although other industrialized countries had begun to think of healthcare as a government responsibility, the US has been and continues to be a laggard in this regard. Medicare is a large and by most accounts very successful federal program. But unlike many other countries' national healthcare programs, Medicare is restricted to the elderly (and a handful of other groups, such as people with end-stage renal disease). In keeping with Americans' valorization of choice, Medicare is a system of payment rather than a system of provision,[8] meaning that although the government pays for care, patients choose who will provide the care and where it will be provided, although some caregivers are unwilling to accept Medicare patients because its reimbursement rates are lower than those of private insurers. Each of these features—that it is a federal program, that it is paid for but not provided by the government, and that it covers only limited groups—has affected the kinds of rules that were created to regulate Medicare.

In contrast, Medicaid, which funds healthcare for people who are poor or disabled,[9] is a joint federal and state program. Like Medicare, though, Medicaid helps cover the costs of care but allows patients to choose their caregivers, again assuming that caregivers are willing to accept Medicaid patients. Medicaid programs are administered by the states, with the federal government paying a portion of each state's Medicaid costs.[10] The portion covered by the federal government varies from one state to another, with some states receiving 50% of the cost of their Medicaid programs from the federal government and a few receiving reimbursements in the range of 70–75%, depending on per capita income and other factors.[11] Because the exact arrangements for Medicaid vary from one state to another, the rules also vary from state to state.

Although the federal government did not create its own regulatory agency to govern Medicare and Medicaid, it did create the Centers for Medicare and Medicaid Services (CMS). This body set many of the basic rules for Medicare and Medicaid, including establishing the parameters for the accreditation process required for a facility or program to be deemed eligible to receive Medicare or Medicaid reimbursements. Until recently, the core requirement for reimbursement was that organizations and programs be accredited by the Joint Commission (discussed in more detail below). And because essentially all healthcare organizations receive funds from Medicare or Medicaid, this stipulation meant that, for all practical purposes, accreditation had become mandatory in US healthcare (Ruggie 1992). All this was accomplished with a fiscal tool and without creating an official regulator.

For HIV specifically, Medicaid has been an important source of funding, partly because many of the people infected with HIV are poor, but also because people often qualify for disability funds as the disease progresses. Three other sources of government funding also have profoundly shaped both the lives of people who have HIV/AIDS and those who work with them. Domestically, the Ryan White HIV/AIDS Program has paid for much of the care for HIV patients who lack other sources of funding. The Ryan White program covers the cost of drugs through its AIDS drug assistance program (ADAP). In addition, the US government has provided considerable support for treating people with HIV in other countries through the President's Emergency Plan for AIDS Relief (PEPFAR), created by George W. Bush. The funding for HIV flows from these key programs but is supplemented with funds from other government programs (e.g., Medicaid, Medicare, the CDC [Centers for Disease Control and Prevention], the VA [US Department of Veterans Affairs]).[12] Finally, both in the US and abroad, the public purse pays for a good deal of AIDS-related research and training and provides care for people participating in clinical trials. Research on HIV has been largely funded through the National Institutes of Health's Division of AIDS.[13]

The National Institutes of Health (NIH), the US government agency with primary responsibility for biomedical and public health research, grew very gradually from the Marine Hospital Service (created in 1798) and its Hygienic Laboratory (established in 1887). It was recognized by law in 1901 when the US Congress allocated funds to construct a building to house the lab's public health and infectious disease research. According to NIH historian Victoria Harden, this pattern of creating government services only through appropriations bills was quite common, in part because the government was not entirely convinced of the utility of these entities and so "chose to preserve the option of divesting the government of them simply by not renewing their funding" (Harden, n.d.). Over the years, the agency's portfolio expanded to include new responsibilities, such as the regulation of biologics such as antitoxins and vaccines[14] and research on the pollution of rivers and lakes. Nonmedical personnel (PhDs rather than just MDs) were incorporated into the agency's professional workforce. Extramural grant programs and intramural fellowship programs were added to the intramural research program following the passage of the Public Health Service Act of 1944 (Public Law 10).[15] New divisions and institutes were created in response both to scientific advances and to the advent of new health problems (such as HIV/AIDS). The agency's name was changed to the National Institute of Health in 1930 and then to the plural form (Institutes) in 1948 to acknowledge the additional topics and groups of researchers that had been brought under the NIH umbrella. And the budget expanded dramatically as scientists, legislators, and the public came to believe that the government should play a major role in health-related research.

From the outset, key functions of the NIH (and its predecessor organizations) were to provide rules (e.g., to regulate biologics) and to ground those rules in robust scientific research. But the rules were not just the result of the research; they also guided the research process. This was particularly apparent when the NIH began to conduct and sponsor clinical research. Histories of ethics regulation initiatives in human subjects research offer somewhat different accounts of how such regulation came about, some suggesting essentially that ethics regulation was "in the air" after WWII and the Nuremberg trials, others that the NIH was proactive in putting protections in place, and still others that the NIH put protections in place only after abuses came to light. For my purposes, the origin story matters less than the regulatory effect. Whether or not one believes that human subjects research now does a better job of attending to ethical questions (Heimer and Petty 2010), what is clear is that attention to ethics has introduced a host of rules that researchers are now obliged to attend to.

Although government funding for treatment and research has been a boon to patients, caregivers, and researchers alike, it has also brought a nearly endless stream of rules in its wake. And unlike the clinical guidelines discussed above, these are not rules generated by caregivers or researchers to govern their own activities. Rather, these rules have been crafted externally and are generally experienced as "foreign," particularly when transported for use in clinics outside the US. Moreover, the rules often feel like an unnecessary and distracting irritant because rather than directly improving patient care, they demand that the already scarce time of caregivers be diverted from patient care or research to administration. Unlike the rules about universal precautions, for instance, no one feels that their patients' health would be immediately jeopardized by ignoring these administrative rules. Nevertheless, because the flow of funds is contingent on following these rules, clinic staff generally feel compelled to abide by them, however arcane, cumbersome, and unnecessary they may seem.

The government payers were themselves the source of some rules, but the influence of government funding on the legalization of healthcare goes well beyond the rules emanating directly from government bodies. Government payers also altered how rules crafted elsewhere were used and experienced. For instance, because programs such as the Ryan White program required that recipient clinics specify which guidelines they were using, guidelines became "harder." And government requirements that healthcare organizations and programs be accredited before they could receive Medicare and Medicaid funds hardened the rules of accrediting organizations such as the Joint Commission. And even when governments created rules de novo, as occurred with the Common Rule on human subjects research (discussed more fully later in this chapter), the effects could be much more extensive than anticipated, for instance, because the legislation led to the creation of federal agencies such as the Office of Human Research Protections (OHRP), to innumerable regulations and guidance (see OHRP 2019), and to the creation of associated review and enforcement bureaucracies inside universities and other research organizations (Heimer and Petty 2010; Babb 2020).

THE BUSINESS OF HEALTHCARE: USING
FORMAL RULES TO INCREASE PROFITS

Despite the substantial role governments play in paying for and overseeing US healthcare, the role of private entities, such as insurers and healthcare organizations, remains substantial. Private enterprises both pay for healthcare and receive those payments. Private insurers, often working hand in hand with employers, pay for healthcare but also make hefty profits both from underwriting, when premiums exceed reimbursements, and from investing the premiums between the time when policyholders pay for insurance and get reimbursed for care. Hospitals and other healthcare organizations receive much of the money spent on healthcare by governments, private insurers, and individual patients. That many US healthcare organizations have historically been legally categorized as nonprofits does not substantially diminish their interest in keeping prices high, particularly when the most lucrative services and centers can be spun off into "profit centers," leaving behind the parts of the organization that lose money.

As they jockey over charges and payments, healthcare organizations and insurers are not simply governed by the rules generated by other parties such as governments. Instead, they actively shape the legal environment of healthcare, generating policies and rules that shape the activities of those they interact with. And because they are often larger, stronger, and more experienced than other parties, they, like other repeat players (Galanter 1974; Edelman 2016) generally shape the rules of the game to favor themselves. For the health insurance companies that began to appear in the 1930s, this has meant assiduously attempting to preserve their lucrative exemption (under the 1945 McCarran-Ferguson Act, partially repealed in 2021) from antitrust laws and other regulation (Jost 2009; Reich 2010; see also Starr 1982). It has also meant establishing rules about what the insurance policies will and will not cover (medications, procedures, caregivers, facilities) and creating systems for verifying that requested reimbursements fall within policy parameters. "Because insurers usually draft contracts, which the insured often never even sees until a claim is made" (Jost 2009, 7), policyholders and caregivers are often making healthcare decisions with precious little information about policies, exceptions, and caveats.

For healthcare organizations, which have rapidly grown and consolidated into a "medical-industrial complex" (Relman 1980), some of the most important procedures concern billing and price setting (Starr 1982). Insurers and government organizations do sometimes push back against the exorbitant prices set by US healthcare organizations and pharmaceutical companies, but equally often they simply pay what hospitals and drug suppliers ask. As Rosenthal (2017) notes, although patients and their families are urged to gather information and consider their options, this is often quite unrealistic because hospitals refuse to share information, information is presented in an uninterpretable form, or patients lack the leverage to configure healthcare teams or select therapies and medications. And, of course, patients often face significant constraints at the point when healthcare is needed. No one can do comparison shopping for emergency room services. Even for nonemergency care, comparison shopping is difficult because patients are systematically denied information about the cost of services provided through complex contractual arrangements between medical institutions, medical caregivers, and third-party payers.

In principle, insurers should be acting as their policyholders' agents, intervening to secure reduced prices from healthcare organizations. In fact, they often do not negotiate reduced prices because they expect the cost of negotiation to exceed its benefit (Rosenthal 2017). One might hope that large insurers, acting on behalf of substantial numbers of patients and the employers with whom insurance arrangements were negotiated, would use their leverage for the benefit of patients. Yet they apparently prefer to pass costs on to consumers. It is perhaps not surprising, then, that the portion of healthcare costs (including insurance premiums, deductibles, copays, and other out-of-pocket expenditures) paid by workers who have employer-sponsored health insurance has risen disproportionately (Kaiser Family Foundation 2012, fig. 15; Rae, Copeland, and Cox 2019). In some cases, negotiation over key elements is explicitly prohibited by law. For instance, until 2023, the government was forbidden to negotiate with pharmaceutical companies to secure lower prices for drugs in some of its programs, most notably on behalf of Medicare Part D beneficiaries (Cubanski et al. 2019). In other cases, such as Medicaid, the VA, and the ADAP that provides drugs for Ryan White program participants, negotiation over prices is allowed.

Viewed from the perspective of healthcare workers and the clinics where they work, this complexity (particularly in the hybrid US healthcare system) wastes precious time and money[16] and generally makes life much more difficult as insurers, healthcare organizations, and professional staff (often working through "faculty practice plans"[17]) all attempt to claim their portion of the healthcare dollars. Staff members must spend time determining what procedures and medications are covered by insurers and government programs, deciding what procedures and medications to recommend given existing funding constraints, allocating costs and reimbursements among various parties, and finding other ways to cover essential expenses when core payers decline reimbursements. They must also explain these administrative details to patients and research subjects. Meticulous records must be kept and filed to justify billing. And, as the administrative staff in all five clinics repeatedly reminded their colleagues, if they fail to keep abreast of changes in rules and policies, they will be required to undergo remedial trainings to ensure that the clinic does not lose money.

Because both physicians and insurers work with guidelines, their interactions around those guidelines makes the process of "hardening" especially visible. When physicians draw on guidelines in caregiving and consider how closely guidelines match particular patients' situations, they do retain some discretion. They lose some of that discretion, though, when insurers are the ones assessing the fit. Doctors are frustrated when insurers refuse to pay for the medications and therapies they prescribe and annoyed when they must spend time crafting justifications to convince reluctant insurers to grant exceptions (Wynia et al. 2000; Werner et al. 2002). Guidelines do not inherently offend healthcare workers, then; rather, what offends them is the assumption that guidelines are "right" and the displacement of discretion from frontline healthcare workers to outsiders. Caregivers would agree that healthcare organizations need rules and often find that rules and policies facilitate their work, yet they may also find that organizational rules conflict with their obligations as caring professionals (Chambliss 1996; see also Zussman 1992).

Whether or not the individual tasks of tracking and accountability have been put in place with the best of intentions, it is nevertheless clear that the whole is much more—and much worse—than the sum of the parts, exactly because these systems of rules intertwine. The result has been a shift in the balance of time and attention away from the direct patient care physicians were trained to provide to activities that they pejoratively categorize as "bureaucratic tasks." One observational study found that physicians spent nearly twice as much time doing administrative work as seeing patients (Sinsky et al. 2016). Those "bureaucratic tasks" regularly top US physicians' lists of dissatisfaction with their jobs (Peckham 2015; see also Brown and Bergman 2019, who also discuss nurses' dissatisfaction with paperwork). Attempts to ameliorate the problem (e.g., by introducing electronic medical records) seem only to have made things worse, in part because of the ease with which new reporting requirements can be folded into electronic systems (Ofri 2017). With the mushrooming of requirements for documentation, US physicians and nurses increasingly report burnout and consider leaving their professions or creating new institutional arrangements such as concierge practices that reduce the burden of administrative work, sever some ties with rule-bound payers like governments and insurers, and strengthen ties with patients (who may pay retainers). Rather clearly, care-givers feel differently about rules intended to protect patients than those intended to protect profits.

REGULATORY AGENCIES: CREATING
COMPLIANCE BUREAUCRACIES

Although rules come from many sources—and indeed this is part of the problem—a few rulemakers dominate the regulatory landscape for healthcare organizations receiving public funding. Unlike many other countries, the US has no centralized body responsible for health policy or for regulating healthcare, in part because under the US Constitution (Tenth Amendment) any power not specifically given to the federal gov-ernment belongs to the states (or the people). Regulation therefore occurs at the behest of both federal and state authorities, often working through a mix of private and public bodies. This mix of public and private regula-tion means that regulatory coverage is sometimes thin and at other times exceedingly dense.

Among the most important regulators of US healthcare are the Joint Commission and the Food and Drug Administration (FDA). Their regula-tory efforts are supplemented by many state-level bodies, such as those that regulate, license, and discipline healthcare practitioners (Horowitz 2013). And for the many healthcare organizations that also conduct research, reg-ulations emanating from the NIH, the OHRP,[18] and a host of subsidiary or-ganizations join the regulations of the FDA and the Joint Commission in shaping their work.

The Joint Commission[19] is not a government agency but a nonprofit, tax-exempt organization that has garnered a semiofficial status because of its role in accrediting healthcare organizations and programs so that they will be deemed[20] eligible to receive Medicare and Medicaid reimbursements. At present, although the Joint Commission accredits the vast majority of US healthcare organizations and programs, it does not have a monopoly[21] because its statutorily grounded accreditation authority, granted in 1965, was removed by 2008 legislation. Since that time, the CMS has overseen the conditions and terms of deeming authority, now granted to additional organizations.[22] In addition, some states have developed their own licens-ing procedures, use other accrediting bodies, or conduct joint surveys with the Joint Commission. Because Medicare and Medicaid funds are so important to their fiscal health, healthcare organizations and programs are careful to track the rules of the Joint Commission and the calendar of regularly scheduled accreditation reviews, while remaining mindful of the possibility of unscheduled, unannounced visits.

In contrast to the Joint Commission, the FDA[23] is a US government agency, created in 1906. Scholars concur that the FDA is an exceptionally strong agency whose policies have shaped drug innovation and development processes, vast parts of the world economy, and many details of daily life (Carpenter 2010). Indeed, by some assessments, the FDA "is arguably the pivotal regulatory body in the modern liberal state" (Ferejohn 2012, 797). The FDA would seem to belie my claim that the legalization of healthcare is a creation of the second half of the twentieth century. Yet a closer look shows that the FDA's regulatory teeth were cut relatively late as responsibilities were added and its budget increased. Particularly important were the 1938 Food, Drug, and Cosmetics Act, passed after the Elixir Sulfanilamide tragedy, and the post-thalidomide 1962 Kefauver-Harris Amendment. Only with the passage of the Kefauver-Harris Amendment did the US require that all new drug applications provide evidence from human clinical trials that a drug was both effective and safe (see also Djulbegovic and Guyatt 2017, 415). This new rule ushered in the modern drug approvals process and helped consolidate the legal turn in healthcare by interweaving two previously autonomous developments, namely the development of clinical guidelines and the growth of regulatory agencies, both driven by demands for a more solid evidentiary foundation. Yet it would be a mistake to conclude that the FDA's role has been shaped exclusively by statutory provisions. Instead, as Carpenter (2010) shows, accomplishing its regulatory objectives has regularly required that the FDA engage in action that went considerably beyond its legislative mandate, with statutes following rather than leading agency action in a process that Eskridge and Ferejohn (2010) label "administrative constitutionalism."

By now the rules of the FDA, which is funded both by budget appropriations and user fees,[24] shape the activities of both those marketing, prescribing, and dispensing drugs and those conducting research with an eye to selling those drugs in the US, a key market for pharmaceutical products, as well as in other countries. And, as with accreditation, a host of other organizations help researchers and drug developers conduct their work in an FDA-compliant fashion.

For those engaged in clinical research and other research with human subjects, the OHRP, under the auspices of the Department of Health and Human Services, is a crucial gatekeeper. Although OHRP issues rules and guidance, researchers orient especially to the local IRBs that review and authorize their research projects. Although essentially all researchers concur on what core ethical principles should guide human subjects research, these principles have been translated into a set of rather rigid rules, often embedded in technologies such as algorithms and decision support tools, enforced by an extensive bureaucracy that generally expands but is occasionally trimmed back. Although almost all of the work is delegated to local IRBs, which enjoy considerable autonomy, anxiety about possible penalties (which can extend well beyond an individual project to an entire university) has led IRBs to rather slavish rule following (Bledsoe et al. 2007; Heimer and Petty 2010; Stark 2012; Babb 2020). During some periods, local IRBs enforced rules so strictly that OHRP occasionally reminded them of existing wiggle room (Babb 2020).

Although US healthcare is often characterized as being a loosely regulated, market-driven system, it more correctly is described as inconsistently regulated. Several powerful bodies—some public, others private, many with monopolies or near monopolies—regulate some parts of the healthcare world while other portions receive considerably less regulatory attention. Pharmaceutical products, for instance, go through quite rigorous testing before being approved, while the pricing of such products and other healthcare goods and services receives little attention (Relman 2010; Rosenthal 2017, 2020). Healthcare organizations and programs go through thorough accreditation reviews, and physicians and other healthcare workers receive training, licensing, and continuing education. At the same time, it is well known that professional review boards are dominated by the regulated groups and are quite reluctant to punish their own (Horowitz 2013). Yet the same facts that make regulatory coverage uneven also make the rules quite onerous—they come from disparate sources, provenance and legal status is difficult to discern, and those subject to regulation may be quite uncertain what the rules are let alone what consequences follow from failure to abide by them. Healthcare workers might well prefer to trade the looser but rather unruly system of rules of the hybrid US system for closer government regulation if they got greater certainty as part of the bargain. Although large healthcare organizations may benefit from being able to game the loose, unruly system, for those lower in the hierarchy, the hybrid system mostly brings the obligation to sort through a welter of inconsistent rules. Insofar as externally imposed rules (linguistically marked at Robert Rafsky as "what they want") undermine well-established professional practices (linguistically marked at Robert Rafsky as "you always, you must"), the current hybrid system of regulation and accreditation likely "leaves too much room for focusing on things that aren't important, often leading to a lot of work but not better care" (Jha 2018).

PUBLIC PRESSURE: USING LAW TO RESHAPE THE AGENDA

Although the increased pressure for attention to patients' rights is often categorized as a movement, the pressure from the public has been neither sustained nor unidirectional. Social movement scholars have noted the paradox that American health-related activism seems both ubiquitous and largely absent (Levitsky and Banaszak-Holl 2010). On the one hand, healthcare has often been an important concern, for instance, of workers negotiating contracts, retirees worrying about covering rising medical bills, people with preexisting conditions concerned about losing insurance coverage, or HIV patients angry about the government's reluctance to adequately fund HIV research, testing, and treatment. On the other hand, no large-scale movement for access to healthcare has grown from such collective action in the US.

Three different kinds of effects of social movements seem particularly important to the legalization of healthcare. First, social movements and political pressure have often focused on inequalities in access (Brown et al. 2004). In some instances, this activism has been organized around the needs of particular vulnerable groups, such as children, or people with specific healthcare needs, including people with mental illness, addictions, or illnesses or health conditions that have not received adequate attention or funding (Brown and Fee 2014). Over time, disease-constituency activism has sometimes been transformed into broader mobilization (Epstein 2016; Best 2019). Often social pressure comes from patients and family members, but in some instances, healthcare professionals have been especially effective advocates for expanded access to care (Harris 2017a, 2017b). Second, social movements and activism also have been organized around protecting patients and expanding and institutionalizing patients' rights, including patients' right to be fully informed about treatment and research and the corresponding obligation of caregivers and researchers to seek consent after supplying information and answering questions. Often activism occurs in response to well-publicized abuses, such as the experimentation on children institutionalized at Willowbrook (Rothman and Rothman 1984), but the patients' rights movement also drew energy and inspiration from other rights movements of the 1960s and 1970s. And, like those other movements, the patients' rights movement has been strongly shaped by the involvement of lawyers, including in iconic cases establishing the right to informed consent (1972, *Canterbury v. Spence*), the right to reproductive privacy (1965 and 1973 rulings in *Griswold v. Connecticut* and *Roe v. Wade*, respectively), and the right of guardians to withdraw life support in some limited circumstances (1976, *In re Quinlan*) (Rothman 2001; Heimer 2010; Beauchamp 2011). Finally, beyond insisting on the right of patients to participate in decisions about their own care, some social movement actors have pushed for greater inclusion of affected laypeople (patients, family members) in crafting healthcare policy (see, e.g., Epstein 1996 on HIV). Each of these has added pressure for increased legalization in healthcare, in part as an unintended consequence of expansion of rights to particular kinds of care (Pryma 2020).

Although we often think of social movements as targeting the state, health-related collective action in the US has not been so singularly focused. In part this is because "the state" is amorphous and complex, with healthcare policymaking, funding, and regulation often controlled by subnational or local bodies. Equally important, because professional and industry associations, insurance companies, pharmaceutical companies, and healthcare organizations also play large roles in shaping healthcare, health-related activism has sometimes taken aim at these actors.

Moreover, the social movement literature mainly asks about major social change—how major policies have been altered (or not) as a result of health-related activism. This literature is less likely to ask about the more incremental change represented by modifications in the legal environment of healthcare. But asking about the legal environment of healthcare is important because modification of the rules is often a first step in the larger policy transformations that social movements seek. For instance, in the US, activism seeking subsidized care for HIV patients worked through the creation of a new program, the Ryan White Care Program, as well as through modification of Medicaid rules. In both cases, though, the new policies came with a host of rules. And whether the result is major social change or incremental change, lawyers are increasingly likely to be part of the group of professional and lay experts who work in the space between fields to co-produce solutions (Eyal 2013b; Pryma 2020).

THE BIRTH OF HEALTH LAW: ASSEMBLING THE LEGAL TOOLKIT

One might expect that the academic field of health law would shape the process of legalization in healthcare. In fact, the relationship between the two is more reciprocal. Rather than driving legalization, the academic discipline of health law developed in tandem with increased legalism.

Legal academics concur that health law began to take shape as an academic field in the US only in the 1950s and early 1960s when casebooks on health law began appearing and health law programs were created. To be sure, there had been scattered courses and publications before that time, but the field was less developed in the US than in Europe. In the early years, classes on health law were generally taught in schools of medicine or public health, where health law specialists held appointments, rather than in law schools. The first centers specializing in health law came into existence in 1953 (Case Western Reserve University) and 1958 (Boston University). By 2023, 189 such programs were listed in the *US News & World Report* rankings. Specialty journals began to appear in the 1970s.

The mission of early health law casebooks seems to have been to "convey to law students a sense of the field as it had been developed by physicians" (Hall 2006, 349, discussing the orientation of William Curran, author of the first casebook). Following a trajectory common in other "law and a banana" fields (Annas 1989, 553), the "octopus of health law" (Hall 2006, 356) developed more as legal commentary on a growing list of topics of concern to the healthcare industry and health professionals than as an intellectually coherent field. Rather than asking how law might best contribute to governance in this new field, legal scholars joined practitioners in a more reactive, accretive, essentially atheoretic enterprise of asking how existing law impinged on or should be adapted for use in the world of healthcare. Although this approach is sometimes productive, it also fosters convoluted legal reasoning and sometimes absurd comparisons (often referred to as "legal fictions") that may overlook crucial differences between life-and-death medical care and other kinds of services.

Emerging legal fields undoubtedly need some measure of each of these elements. In this instance, health law needs the perspectives of those working in healthcare as well as those more deeply grounded in law. And, of course, legal fields should adjust to changes in the world—it is deeply disconcerting, for instance, that the second edition of Curran's casebook (Curran and Shapiro 1970) completely ignored the 1965 introduction of Medicare and Medicaid (Hall 2006, 349). Nevertheless, one could argue that incorporation of new knowledge—and implicitly new policy—has been a particular strength of some parts of the legal infrastructure of healthcare, such as clinical guidelines (Heimer 2006).

Over time, core texts in health law have begun to tease out an underlying rationale for the field, suggesting principles that might foster more coherence in health law[25] and support interventions to shape that law moving forward. Among other things, that might mean showing how legal tools, sometimes understood as isolated instruments, can instead be seen and deployed as a toolkit with individual tools working on different elements of a common project. Although this introduction of organizing principles is significant, it matters that health law academics continue to track changes in the quasi-legal environment of health law and remain open to a broad definition of "law." For the administrators and medical professionals working in healthcare organizations, the distinctions between "hard" formal law and "softer" legal or quasi-legal forms such as regulations and clinical guidelines may be hard to discern. An expansive approach by legal academics could undoubtedly help people without legal training understand the implications of being at one or another point along the continuum between formal law and the less formal norms of medical practice. Understanding that continuum would equip practitioners to think more clearly about when "rules" might better be institutionalized as law and when less binding, more easily modified forms might serve healthcare better.

From Mushrooming to Mushroom Cloud: The Experience of Legalization

In all of these arenas—government funding of healthcare, regulatory oversight, insurer verification, the emerging field of health law, and so on—rules have mushroomed, with more rules on the books from one year to the next. Rulemaking endeavors that started as separate enterprises also bled into one another, as existing rules and routines were put to new uses. Although it may seem efficient to repurpose existing almost-adequate rules rather than creating new ones, making rules serve multiple purposes often transforms them so they perform their original functions less well.

Medical records are a good example of this. Originally created as doctors' private notes (Timmermans and Berg 2003), these records eventually moved from doctors' homes into the offices of healthcare organizations. Such records are now compiled by a host of actors and serve a variety of purposes, including communication among caregivers tracking a patient's care and providing data for research, evidence for legal cases, and support for billing. This "efficiency" does not make everyone happy. When records are used in billing, physicians are pressured to provide evidence to justify charges, but that may not be the evidence they need to communicate to other caregivers (Heimer 2008). Although physicians can be trained to write records that support billing, it is not clear that this is desirable. Spending time adding information for billing takes physicians' attention away from clinical tasks; scanning records that contain extraneous information may undermine medical work by making it harder for caregivers to focus on the most important clinical information.

Mushrooming rules like these may begin to feel like a mushroom cloud when individual rules, regulations, and routines are made to serve multiple, overlapping, but not fully consistent purposes. People asked to comply with rules may then find that complying in a way that serves one purpose can easily—and frustratingly—be read as noncompliance with another objective.

As rules become more numerous and complex, organizations and individuals seek ways to manage the associated workload. Often this means creating new administrative support positions, a practice especially common in research administration. In all five clinics, research coordinators (with titles varying from one site to another) tended the interface between clinic work and regulators. They ensured that paperwork was filed correctly and on time, that copies of key documents were readily available in electronic and paper form, that staff members were given timely reminders of upcoming regulatory tasks, and so forth. Although these "compliance workers" felt themselves to be full members of the clinics where they worked, they were also proud of their mastery of the rules, their superb organizational skills, and their good relations with regulators. Doing their jobs well depended on developing the forms, tracking sheets, and explanatory documents that made tasks easier for their clinic colleagues and, in turn, meant growing their own jobs. It was no longer sufficient to keep a file of a study's signed consent forms. As IRB-associated work became more rule bound, the research coordinators were obliged to track additional documents as well: the signed consent forms, of course, but also the various versions of consent forms and explanations for changes in those forms.

It would be alarmist in the extreme to claim that the growth of rules is as significant or explosive as an atom bomb. Nevertheless, a close look at some of the indicators of "mushrooming" shows that they cross into the territory that Jim, the administrator, described as a "mushroom cloud." When the rules have become so cumbersome and so arcane that additional specialists are required, we have evidence that speaks as much to the experience of the rules as their volume. Ironically the creation of positions for specialists who might help ameliorate these problems can backfire and make matters worse. Specialists tasked with "supporting" staff members as they navigate the changing regulatory landscape often end up with close affiliations with the more enduring repeat players whose rules they are interpreting, adopting their perspective rather than seeing things through the eyes of the oneshotters they are supposed to assist. Carl Elliott (2007) noted a similar shift in the perspectives of ethicists as they became more closely allied with the hospital organizations and medical staff they worked with regularly. Repeat players both provide the rationale for "compliance work" and help organize career opportunities for that kind of work (Elliott 2007; Babb 2020).

Thus far, this chapter has reviewed the key legal influences on the world of healthcare to assess whether there is some merit to the contention that healthcare is indeed more closely regulated (using that term loosely) than in the past. When we look at the causal side of this equation, we indeed see changes that suggest a broad-based cultural change in the direction of amplified legalism. Pressure for closer regulation of healthcare has come from multiple sources: courts and legislatures, regulatory agencies, professional societies and less formal groups of professionals, organizations where healthcare and health-related research are sited, public and private bodies that pay for healthcare, and patient movements. This does not mean, however, that they have always seen eye to eye on what the rules should be.

So, yes, the rules have mushroomed. But what about that mushroom cloud of rules that Jim complained about at Robert Rafsky? Why were caregivers, researchers, and administrators so often annoyed by the rules? The answer, I suspect, is that the more numerous, "harder" rules all too often constrained, overburdened, and sometimes even confused workers without actually improving the lot of patients or research subjects. A clearer picture of some of the core rules and regulations governing work in HIV clinics—some general, others specific to HIV/AIDS—will provide a firmer foundation for the analyses of chapters that follow.

Governing HIV: Clinical Guidelines and Research Administration

Healthcare organizations have long been constrained by rules. They are complex organizations, after all, accustomed to managing flows across organizational boundaries, whether those flows are of patients or other clients; medical and nursing students and other trainees; permanent and temporary workers; inspectors and regulators; medical records and other information collected and disseminated for many purposes; medical and other supplies; clinical samples; and, not least, simply money. These flows have long been shaped and governed by rules, with the intensity of regulation increasing over the years.

Yet in the US, at least, the tie between top healthcare workers and healthcare organizations healthcare has been unusual. Although many healthcare workers have been employees of the healthcare organizations, physicians often have not. Physicians' work has spanned organizational boundaries because they have cared for their patients both in the hospitals where they had admitting privileges and in their own offices. They have divided work between themselves and ancillary workers. They often have shared work with other physicians in group practices and through referrals to specialists. Despite being embedded in multiple organizations, all of which experienced the mushrooming of rules, physicians and physician-scientists nevertheless retained considerable autonomy. But has physicians' autonomy decreased as legalism gradually encroached on core clinical and research activities, the work of the most skilled medical professionals?

To study these changes, we need to look closely at the rules that govern the "guts" of caregivers' and researchers' work: clinical guidelines and other rules that shape clinicians' work as they treat patients, on the one hand, and research protocols, ethics regulations, and other rules that govern research activities, on the other. These kinds of rules intrude on the "technical core" (Thompson 1967) of medical caregiving and clinical research. Beyond a crude (illustrative more than exhaustive) listing of what rules now shape the work of HIV clinic staff members, we need some sense of where the rules come from, what their legal status is, and how much they actually constrain physicians' and clinical researchers' activities.

The daily work of clinic HIV specialists is guided by clinical guidelines for testing for HIV, staging the disease, managing opportunistic infections (OIs), resolving coinfections, initiating treatment, adjusting for and managing side effects, monitoring the progression of the disease and watching for indications that patients are not complying with the regimen or need to be switched to another regimen. These HIV/AIDS specific guidelines also build on the foundation of previous generations of scientists' and clinicians' thinking about how to translate medical science into medical practice. Because of the changes in the legal environment of medical work described earlier in this chapter, the five clinics I studied all used clinical guidelines. They did this both as a matter of convention—that is simply how medical staff were trained to do their work—and because governmental bodies or third-party payers required them to use guidelines. But for a variety of reasons that are explored later, the five clinics used guidelines in somewhat different ways.

Table 3.3 provides an overview of the most influential clinical guidelines for the treatment of HIV-infected adults and adolescents that shaped the HIV clinics' work at the end of my time in the field. Written for adults and adolescents, the guidelines also served as a starting point for creating additional guidelines for treatment of other groups, including pregnant women, children, or people with coinfections. Supplementary guidelines covered related activities such as counseling and testing or provided advice on the

TABLE 3.3. Clinical Guidelines (for Treatment of HIV-Infected Adults and Adolescents)*

ENTITY PRODUCING OR ADOPTING GUIDELINE	WHAT IS IT? HOW UNIVERSAL IN REACH?	HOW "HARD" OR "SOFT" IS IT? (HOW OBLIGATORY? HOW PRECISE ARE THE REQUIREMENTS? ARE THERE PROVISIONS FOR DELEGATION/ENFORCEMENT?)
	1. International Treatment Guidelines (Treated as international resource; widely used as reference; sometimes created at the behest or with the sponsorship of international body.)	
US DHHS/CDC (Jan. 2008 revision)	*Guidelines for the Use of Antiretroviral Agents in HIV-1 Infected Adults and Adolescents.* Produced and regularly updated by the DHHS Panel on Anti-retroviral Guidelines for Adults and Adolescents, a working group of the Office of AIDS Research Advisory Council. The first versions of these guidelines were aimed at the US population and therefore offered little guidance on how to apply the guidelines in resource-constrained settings. Subsequent versions more easily adapted to other settings. Available on website.	Generally, international treatment guidelines are not legally "obligatory" unless made so by other entities (e.g., government, clinic, third-party payer). In some places, caregivers might be held liable (e.g., malpractice suit for failure to give patients care that complied with guidelines). Guidelines are very precise. No provisions are made for delegation or enforcement.
WHO (2006 revision)	*Antiretroviral Therapy for HIV Infection in Adults and Adolescents: Recommendations for a Public Health Approach.* Available on website. 132 pp. Specifically written for resource-constrained settings.	Same as above.
IAS-USA (2006 revision)	*Treatment for Adult HIV Infection: 2006 Recommendations of the International AIDS Society–USA Panel.* Available on website and published in *JAMA*. 17 pp.	Same as above

MSF	*Clinical Guidelines: Diagnosis and Treatment Manual.* HIV guidelines are included in this general manual, which is "for curative programs in hospitals and dispensaries." Available on website. Section on HIV is 13 pp.	Available for use by others; not clear whether guidelines are binding on MSF clinics. Guidelines based on those issued by bodies such as WHO.

Examples: South Africa, Thailand, Uganda; not US	Available on websites. Typically modified from WHO guidelines to take account of local conditions. Apply universally within country.	Mandatory for health facilities participating in government treatment programs. Recommendations very precise. Some provisions for delegation (e.g., about mandatory reporting when switching regimens).
AETC (2006 ed., updated July 2007)	*Clinical Manual for Management of the HIV-Infected Adults.* Available on website. 400 pp.	Training arm of US Ryan White Program. Not legally obligatory beyond Ryan White recipients; very precise; no provision for delegation. Designed especially for training HIV care providers. Includes information from DHHS, CDC and WHO, so more "derivative." Ryan White Program grantees (such as Bobbi Campbell Clinic) required to specify which guidelines they will use.

(Continued)

TABLE 3.3. *(Continued)*

ENTITY PRODUCING OR ADOPTING GUIDELINE	WHAT IS IT? HOW UNIVERSAL IN REACH?	HOW "HARD" OR "SOFT" IS IT? (HOW OBLIGATORY? HOW PRECISE ARE THE REQUIREMENTS? ARE THERE PROVISIONS FOR DELEGATION/ENFORCEMENT?)
	4. Clinic Treatment Guidelines	
Bobbi Campbell Clinic (US), Cha-on Suesum Clinic (Thailand), Gugu Dlamini Clinic (South Africa), Philly Lutaaya Clinic (Uganda)	Available to clinic staff (e.g. in treatment rooms). Updated episodically, especially when new guidelines are released by WHO or DHHS, when national governments modify their guidelines, or when funding bodies change their rules.	Typically mandatory within clinic, though staff generally sensitive to need for flexibility. Very precise; more precision added through reference to other guidelines. Oversight sometimes mandated (e.g., by requiring formal discussion of regimen changes).

* There are many other guidelines, e.g., covering HIV in people within particular lifecycle stages (e.g., children), with particular conditions (e.g., pregnancy), or with coinfections (e.g., TB, hepatitis). There are also guidelines for sensitively addressing identity or lifestyle issues (e.g., in transgender patients), offering care in particular practice settings (e.g., dentistry), offering particular services (e.g., counseling, testing), managing special problems (e.g., occupational exposure), or carrying out particular tasks (e.g., developing treatment guidelines). The guidelines referenced here were in use during the time of my fieldwork and interviews (ca. 2003–8). More recent versions can be found on the websites of major guideline writing organizations.

management of HIV risks associated with particular situations, such as occupational exposure.

A small number of organizations produces these core guidelines. (See top panel, "International Treatment Guidelines.") As table 3.3 suggests, the treatment guidelines that are referenced most often are those issued by the Panel on Antiretroviral Guidelines for Adults and Adolescents of the Department of Health and Human Services (DHHS 2008), WHO, and the International AIDS Society–USA Panel.[26] These guidelines are widely disseminated and available to anyone with internet access. Guidelines are updated periodically as new drugs and new scientific results become available.[27] Releases of new guidelines are important events, with public announcements (often at major scientific meetings), press releases and embargo dates, news articles, and brief summaries of the main differences between the new guidelines and previous ones.

These core international guidelines are often adopted and modified by other bodies. International NGOs such as Médecins sans Frontières (Doctors Without Borders) draw on these international treatment guidelines to produce manuals for use in clinics, dispensaries, and hospitals, making adjustments for local conditions and the availability and cost of drugs. (See the second panel of table 3.3, "International NGO Treatment Guidelines.") NGO guidelines are used by the facilities and personnel of the NGOs that produce them (and therefore are more constrained by them) but also become a resource for HIV workers in other organizations, where the level of constraint may vary widely depending on whether these guidelines are simply seen as one source among many or as templates that might be adopted, with or without further adjustment.

The international treatment guidelines are also a resource for national level activities. (See the third panel of table 3.3, "National Treatment Guidelines.") At that level, they may be incorporated into training manuals (e.g., by the AIDS Education and Training Centers [AETC], a US organization), adopted as national guidelines (typically in somewhat modified form, e.g., with some drug combinations chosen as the national first- and second-line regimens). For example, Thailand, South Africa, and Uganda all had national guidelines and sometimes had provincial guidelines as well. Although US government bodies, namely the DHHS and CDC, write some of the highly influential HIV treatment guidelines, these guidelines are not adopted as official US guidelines, and US facilities are not required to adhere to them. The caveat here is that the Ryan White program, the largest US government program providing funding for domestic HIV care, mandates guideline use. Facilities receiving Ryan White funds are also required to specify which guidelines they are using and to undergo training provided by the AETC.

Finally, many clinics either adopt existing guidelines as official clinic guidelines (as Bobbi Campbell Clinic did) or customize guidelines for use in their facility. (See the fourth panel in table 3.3, "Clinic Treatment Guidelines.") Such customization may involve producing very compressed guidelines for quick reference in clinic treatment rooms, as was the case at Gugu Dlamini Clinic, with instructions about where to find fuller guidelines as needed. Clinic-specific guidelines may also take account of local health conditions and resource constraints, as occurred at Philly Lutaaya. Each update of the international treatment guidelines then leads to a cascade of updating by NGOs, national ministries of health, education and training centers, and local treatment facilities whose guidelines are based on these foundational guidelines.

These clinical guidelines tell several stories about the legalization of healthcare. First, they tell us that the translation of scientific knowledge into a form that can be used by healthcare workers is an enterprise that is now organized around specific rules and norms. That is, guideline writers not only instruct practitioners about what they should do but also assess the evidence supporting these recommendations using a rather rigid set of rules. The DHHS, for instance, uses a two-part rating scheme that specifies the strength of its recommendation (with ratings running from A to E)[28] and assesses the quality of the evidence supporting that recommendation (rated as I, II, or III).[29] The ideal would be to increase the certainty of recommendations (more rated A or E) and the quality of the evidence (more I or at least I and II). And indeed, that does seem to be the case. Petty (2008) finds that over time HIV guidelines have increasingly been based on evidence from clinical trials (I in the rating scheme) rather than expert opinion (III).[30]

The guidelines tell a second story about how legalization constrains the activities of caregivers. Guidelines issued by bodies such as WHO and DHHS are usually (but not always) considered "guidance," meaning that medical workers are expected to draw on their training and judgment as they use guidelines to help them decide how to proceed. That said, embedded in that guidance is a lot of professional soft law and some hard law. The soft law includes innumerable embedded assumptions about standard medical practices learned as part of professional training. Such soft law remains largely implicit, but may sometimes become more explicit if and when these tacit rules have not been followed. Somewhat "harder" are the sometimes explicitly articulated regulations specifying which professional workers can carry out particular tasks, regulations that are backed up by other rules about the training and certification of professional workers. An example of this would be rules about who can provide HIV counseling and testing, rules that troubled staff members both in South Africa and the US because their colleagues were sometimes being asked to do tasks they were neither legally empowered nor trained to perform.

Legalization enters by yet another route as guidelines or elements of guidelines are adopted by other bodies, such as insurers or other payers. In these instances, guidelines become a mechanism for holding clinics and their workers accountable for providing high-quality care (as indicated by adherence to guidelines) with the threat that payers will not cover the cost of care that fails to conform to guidelines. Although details varied, all five clinics encountered this kind of fiscal pressure to follow guidelines. For example, Gugu Dlamini could not receive funding from the South African government anti-retroviral rollout unless it prescribed the government-approved regimen and followed government rules about exceptions, and Bobbi Campbell had to say which guidelines it was following and undergo AETC training to be eligible for Ryan White funds.

Finally, clinics or other organizations (such as NGOs) may further the legalization associated with guideline use by adopting clinic-level guidelines and strongly encouraging or even mandating their use. As guideline use has become the accepted, institutionalized way of doing medical work, clinics face considerable pressure to formally state that their work is organized around clinical guidelines. By preparing clinic-level guidelines, clinics may improve the match between guidelines and local conditions, facilitate attention to guidelines, and increase local peer pressure for adherence. But this account perhaps understates the importance of changes in clinic culture that accompany the legalization of healthcare. Yes, the layered legalization spelled out in table 3.3 has increased pressure for adherence to the now-harder rules of HIV treatment. At the same time, though, standardized guidelines have helped foster a universalistic clinic culture that views healthcare as a fundamental human right. But we should not forget that the legal turn and its mushroom cloud of rules sometimes make staff members feel that minding the p's and q's of regulations can keep them from getting on with their work.

Turning to research governance, I use the example of ethics regulation to illustrate how these rules unfold and become more specific and constraining, ultimately leading to detailed directives about how to conduct research that will be deemed scientifically and (in this case) ethically acceptable. Some parts of the regulatory framework for clinical research focus on safeguarding the quality of the science; examples include the rules of Good Clinical Practice (GCP),[31] the regulations and standard operating procedures of labs and clinics, rules about the inclusion of diverse subject populations, and the research protocols for particular clinical trials. Other, overlapping rules focus on ensuring that research with human beings is conducted ethically.

Among the most important of the project-specific rules focused specifically on biomedical science are the research protocols themselves—the recipes about how particular research questions are to be explored. Because they aim to produce closely comparable data in dispersed sites, clinical research protocols are extremely detailed. They include very full instructions about what procedures are to be carried out, when, by whom, with what instruments; what drugs are to be given on what timetable to the various "arms" of the study; what information is to be collected (laboratory tests, physical observation) and how it should be recorded and stored; what kinds of research subjects are to be enrolled in the study and what categories of people should be excluded; what procedures should be used to elicit and verify participant consent; what to do if research subjects experience adverse events (AEs) (adverse events such as drug side effects or illnesses) or SAEs (serious adverse events)[32] and how they should be reported. Staff must be trained on each new research protocol. Because some protocol elements are common, though, experienced staff find that a new protocol means mastering details and variations rather than learning from scratch the language of SAEs, CRFs (case report forms), IRBs (institutional review boards), and so forth.

Rules about the ethical conduct of research, as table 3.4 shows, begin with the articulation of principles, often at a supra-national level. These principles are then made more concrete in statutes, regulations, and guidance, typically crafted at the national level but sometimes aiming for effects beyond national boundaries. And finally, the principles, statutes, and regulations shape research infrastructure and detailed instructions provided by research sponsors, networks, sites (including universities, clinics, and research institutes), and individual protocols. The declarations, reports, statutes, guidance, regulations, and associated research infrastructure outlined in table 3.4 tell a story of a rather uneven pushing of the envelope on universal rights of human research subjects and a companion story about enforcement mechanisms. But they also tell a story of decreasing discretion and displacement of attention from research and caregiving activities to nitpicky rules that seem likely to meet legalistic goals without always making human subjects research more ethical.

The articulations of principles (top panel of table 3.4) began as a largely hortatory exercise. Although the entirely admirable principles articulated in the Nuremberg Code, crafted as an antidote to Nazi doctors' medical experiments, were incorporated into the UN Declaration of Human Rights,

TABLE 3.4. Rules for the Conduct of Research

CORE ELEMENTS	WHAT IS IT? HOW UNIVERSAL IN REACH?	HOW "HARD" OR "SOFT" IS IT? (HOW OBLIGATORY? HOW PRECISE ARE THE REQUIREMENTS? ARE THERE PROVISIONS FOR DELEGATION/ENFORCEMENT?)
	1. Articulations of Ethical Principles (often international)	
Nuremberg Code (1947)	Hortatory articulation of principles; 10 conditions that must be met for research on human subjects to be acceptable; stated universalistically.	Few mechanisms for implementing provisions of Nuremberg Code, which has not been accepted as law by any country or as an official code of ethics by any professional association. Nevertheless considered to be key document because of its influence on subsequent legal documents on human rights generally and ethical treatment of human research subjects specifically. Subsequently reflected in UN Universal Declaration of Human Rights, so "accepted in principle" by each of the 193 UN members. Nuremberg Code influence also clear in reports, rules, codes and regulations discussed below.
Declaration of Helsinki— Ethical Principles for Research Involving Human Subjects (adopted in 1964, revised 9 times, most recently in 2013; under revision in 2023 and 2024)	Hortatory articulation of principles; stated universalistically.	Adopted by the WMA, an international organization to represent physicians and ensure their independence. (WMA has memorandum of understanding with WHO affirming cooperation between the two organizations.) Not legally binding but has had substantial effect because of its influence on national legislation and regulations. Seen as significant attempt by medical community to regulate itself. Morally binding for physicians, who are expected to adhere to its standards, which are often more stringent than national laws and regulations. Widely cited in ethical regulation of research on human subjects.
Belmont Report: Ethical Principles and Guidelines for the Protection of Human Subjects of Research (1979)	Hortatory articulation of principles by US national body; stated universalistically.	Issued by the National Commission for the Protection of Human Subjects of Biomedical and Behavioral Research (in existence 1974–78). Commission activities and Belmont Report led directly to US legislation on protection of human research subjects.

(Continued)

TABLE 3.4. (*Continued*)

CORE ELEMENTS	WHAT IS IT? HOW UNIVERSAL IN REACH?	HOW "HARD" OR "SOFT" IS IT? (HOW OBLIGATORY? HOW PRECISE ARE THE REQUIREMENTS? ARE THERE PROVISIONS FOR DELEGATION/ENFORCEMENT?)
Good Clinical Practice (GCP) (finalized in 1996, went into effect in 1997; under revision in 2023)	International quality standard that speaks to such matters as the rights of human subjects and volunteers in clinical trials, standards on how clinical trials should be conducted. It defines roles and responsibilities of IRBs, clinical research investigators, clinical trial sponsors and monitors.	GCP is under the aegis of the ICH. GCP was developed by the tripartite International Conference on Harmonisation, a steering committee that included the regulatory authorities of the EU, Japan and the US. Individual countries or groups of countries then craft statutes and regulations from the GCP standard. GCP was adopted by law in some Asian countries as early as 1998 and by Thailand in 2000. With the adoption of the UK Medicines for Human Use (Clinical Trials) Regulations in 2004 and the EU Directive on Good Clinical Practice, compliance with GCP is a legal obligation in the UK and much of Europe for all trials of investigational medicinal products. Since 2006, the US has cited GCP as its touchstone for how to conduct research rather than citing the Declaration of Helsinki. The NIH requires that investigators and staff working on NIH-funded projects be trained in GCP.
	2. Ethics Statutes, Regulations and Guidance (national in origin but having effects beyond national boundaries)	
45 C.F.R. 46, the Code of Federal Regulations Governing the Protection of Human Subjects in Research (Research Act of 1974)	Statute. Protection of human subjects in any research funded by DHHS. Subpart A, relabeled the Common Rule, was revised in 1991 to apply to any US government–funded research. Further revised in 2017 to reflect changes in research practices in intervening years.	Code itself is hard law and so obligatory. Guidance issued episodically by the OHRP is "softer" and therefore not always obligatory. Because staff members of the IRBs of many entities treat the Guidance as obligatory, it is in practice obligatory for many individual researchers. This statute was preceded by the Public Health Service Policy on the Protection of Human Subjects (1966).
Federal Wide Assurance (FWA) (part of 45 C.F.R. 46) (2005)	Statute. Clarifies that rules apply universally, including to international sites doing US government–funded research.	Hard law, reaching into other countries via funding mechanism (if funded by US government, adherence to these regulations is mandatory).

	3. Research Infrastructure, Research Practices (at varying levels)	
Research sponsor and research network conventions	Research sponsors and research networks have conventions that standardize some features of research—not the scientific core but lab procedures, reporting conventions, research and grants administration. Applies to entities receiving research monies or participating in research network activities; not confined by national borders.	Combined hard and soft law. Obligatory to comply with 45 C.F.R. 46 (hard law), but additional prescriptions associated with collection of data, monitoring of study, etc. not always obligatory. Examples: sample SOPs often adopted by all or most research entities receiving funding from a particular sponsor; use of mandated third-party monitor; use of particular laboratories or data analysts.
Clinic, university, or research institute practices	Universities and other entities conducting research have policies, conventions, and norms, which vary from one entity to another, about how to conduct ethics review, how to review grant proposals before submission (e.g., whose signatures must be affixed), etc. Also SOPs about laboratories, data processing, review of personnel qualifications, etc. Applies to all researchers affiliated with the clinic, university, or research institute that are conducting research under its auspices.	Soft law in sense that no legal consequences, but investigators can be prohibited from conducting research if do not meet requirements of entities like IRBs. IRB approval often required for submission of grants or for publication of research results.
Research protocols	Recipes for conducting research, including instructions for selecting and recruiting research subjects, instructions about randomizing subjects to various arms of study, what to do with or to subjects at various points in the study, what data to collect and how to record it, what to do when AEs and SAEs occur. Applies to anyone engaged in activities associated with the particular protocol.	Soft law in sense that no legal consequences, but nevertheless obligatory; extremely specific; delegated enforcement by research monitors, committees to review SAEs, etc.

this did little to make them enforceable. The advances offered by the Declaration of Helsinki[33] a decade and a half later were still at the level of principles, but went considerably further than the Nuremberg Code.

The Helsinki Rules have been revised repeatedly to close loopholes that had permitted the exploitation of research subjects in poorer countries and to resolve long-standing disagreements about ethical pluralism versus ethical universalism. Concerns about clinical trials on transmission of HIV from mother to child led to vigorous debates about research ethics.[34] The first clinical trial on mother-to-child transmission found that a six-month course of the anti-retroviral AZT (azidothymidine, also known as zidovudine or ZDV) coupled with a six-week course of AZT for the newborn dramatically reduced the odds of transmission of HIV to the baby. Following this first study, this long-course AZT regimen became the standard of care for pregnant women living with HIV in rich countries. But AZT was both expensive and quite toxic. In poorer countries, the cost of the drug and the necessity for extensive monitoring meant that the long-course AZT regimen did not become standard of care during pregnancy. These concerns about cost and toxicity stimulated subsequent maternal-infant transmission studies investigating the efficacy of a short course of AZT. To the consternation of many observers, in these clinical trials, US research subjects in the control group received the full course of AZT, while pregnant women in poorer countries received a placebo.

In the ensuing years, the Helsinki Rules have been revised to limit the conditions in which placebo trials are ethically permissible and to insist that the standard of care offered to control groups in clinical research projects cannot differ from one part of the world to another.[35] Although the NIH website comments that the Helsinki Rules are "currently in use throughout the world," it is far from clear what that means given that there is no mechanism for encouraging, let alone requiring, anyone to abide by the principles articulated in the Declaration of Helsinki. Many decisions about the ethical conduct of research are made locally and depend on how the Helsinki Rules have been incorporated into national law.

Resulting from the investigation of the abuses of the Tuskegee syphilis study and other research using vulnerable groups (prisoners, orphans), the Belmont Report mostly reiterates principles spelled out earlier in the Nuremberg Code and the Helsinki Rules. Yet its status as a set of US home-grown principles to correct home-grown abuses surely made its message more urgent. Because US and Japanese research abuses were largely swept under the rug when Nazi abuses were prosecuted in the Nuremberg trial, acknowledgment of at least some US research abuses was especially important.

GCP, an international quality standard intended to govern human subjects research, went into effect in 1997. It, too, articulates ethical principles without being legally binding. But GCP differs from the other statements of ethical principles in several important respects. First, GCP was developed by an international group that included regulatory authorities from the EU, Japan, and the US, but unlike other statements of ethical principles, it was crafted with pharmaceutical industry involvement. GCP is under the aegis of the International Council for Harmonisation of Technical Requirements for Pharmaceuticals for Human Use (ICH), a nonprofit legally registered in Switzerland that brings together regulatory authorities and representatives of the pharmaceutical industry to discuss and work out scientific and technical aspects of pharmaceutical development and registration.[36] Second, GCP addresses technical matters as well as the ethics of human subjects research. Although its regulations cover the rights, safety, and confidentiality of research subjects, GCP also lays out regulations intended to ensure that the data and reported results of clinical trials are credible and accurate and will be accepted by the regulatory authorities of the countries that have signed onto GCP. It bears mentioning that GCP has its critics, some of whom label it the "bronze standard," noting that there is no evidentiary support for its standard, that important constituencies were omitted during its development, and that it adds "expense without benefit" (Grimes et al. 2005, 172–73).

Individual countries or groups of countries then craft domestic statutes and regulations from the GCP standard. Some Asian countries adopted GCP as law as early as 1998; Thailand adopted it as law in 2000 (Vijayananthan and Nawawi 2008). Following the adoption of the UK Medicines for Human Use (Clinical Trials) Regulations in 2004 and the EU Directive on Good Clinical Practice, compliance with GCP is a legal obligation in the UK and much of Europe for all trials of investigational medicinal products.[37] The US government cites GCP as its touchstone for how to conduct research rather than citing the World Medical Association's (WMA) Declaration of Helsinki. It dropped references to the Declaration of Helsinki in 2006 over objections to revisions that limited the role of placebos and increased trial sponsors' responsibilities to research subjects (Wolinsky 2006).[38] Although compliance with GCP is not statutorily required, the FDA's website on regulations relating to GCP and clinical trials provides links to both the extensive regulations themselves and to the equally extensive preambles to these regulations, which offer information on why the regulations were proposed, how the FDA interprets the meaning and impact of the regulations, and the FDA's review and commentary on any public comments.[39] In addition, the NIH requires GCP training for investigators and staff conducting NIH-funded research.

As noted, both GCP and the Belmont Report have their effects by being endorsed and taken on board by regulatory authorities of nations involved in clinical research. This is a key part of the legalization of biomedical research. Beyond acknowledging ethical lapses, the investigation of US research abuses summarized in the Belmont Report also did lead to the creation of mechanisms to force researchers to attend to the rights of their human research subjects. With passage of 45 C.F.R. 46, the protection of human research subjects became "hard law." (See the second panel of table 3.4.) The enforcement mechanisms for the statute were radically decentralized. The law was to be implemented largely by the IRBs of universities and other research centers. IRBs have zealously created the administrative apparatus needed to enforce the law (Heimer and Petty 2010; Babb 2020), often so eager to comply that they have treated the "guidance" episodically issued by the OHRP as law.[40] Concerns with protecting funding streams have played a substantial role in this (Bledsoe et al. 2007).

Over the years, the reach of these rules has been extended. The rules first applied only to research funded by the DHHS; subsequently section A of the statute was amended and named the Common Rule, with coverage extended to all government-funded research involving human subjects. An especially important change occurred in 2005 when new legislation created the Federalwide Assurance (FWA) rules and extended coverage to US government-funded research being carried out in other countries. This latest change in some ways mirrored the Helsinki Rules since both sets of rules aimed to close loopholes that for a time allowed rich-country researchers to conduct research in foreign countries in ways that would not have been permitted on their own soil. Yet those changes, often lauded for increasing parity between rich- and poor-country research subjects, have created fresh difficulties by overlooking crucial differences (e.g., in culture and the availability of resources) among countries where research is being conducted.

Both the more scientifically oriented rules about research and the rules for the ethical conduct of research become more detailed as they reach the level of research networks that sponsor research; universities, research institutes, and clinics that carry out research; and the research protocols that guide individual projects. Although these rules often look like soft law, they have been hardened through ties to statutes. Moreover, although enforcement has been delegated, research organizations and researchers are mindful of the consequences of failing to abide by the rules. IRBs, particularly, have frequently enforced the rules with a rather heavy hand, often seeming to be more attentive to the interests of the research portfolios and research dollars flowing into universities than to the needs of the human research subjects the rules allegedly protect.

Conclusion: Why Legalization Matters

As is the case with any contemporary legal system, traces of rule origins are found in current codes and practices. This is easily seen for the legalization of healthcare where one can find clinic-level evidence of the effects of all six of the historic strands that coalesced to form the complex governance system for HIV treatment and research.

The evidence of legalistic impulses shows up in the guidelines and other attempts to systematize and justify the daily work of clinic staff members. To be sure, these intramedical impulses are reinforced by outside pressures, yet it would be a mistake to think there is no local interest in figuring out how to do things. At Gugu Dlamini Clinic, for instance, the pediatricians not only consulted frequently about their cases but also kept notes on their work and were translating these notes into proto-guidelines that could be used by their colleagues.

The influence of payers on rule development likewise could be seen in all of the clinics. As government anti-retroviral rollout programs were developed, clinic staff were acutely aware of the rules about which expenses were covered and which were not and what workers needed to do to get those reimbursements. At Bobbi Campbell, for instance, public payment covered only patients who resided in the geographic catchment area, necessitating routines for gathering information about residence and for referring ineligible people to other facilities.

Although none of the clinic workers thought of themselves primarily as being "in the business of" healthcare, they were nevertheless mindful of the effects of their work on the fiscal health of their clinics and the organizations with which the clinics were affiliated. Even at Robert Rafsky, easily the best resourced of these five clinics, caregivers were attentive to clinic rules about patients' capacity to pay for their care, either through insurance or through study participation. In all of the clinics, attention to these bread-and-butter constraints was built into intake procedures and the check-ins each time a patient returned for an appointment.

Also near the surface were concerns with the rules of regulatory bodies. A first glance might suggest that regulators were only episodically on workers' minds—just before an accreditation review for a program or a monitoring visit for a research project, for example. But clinic workers were continually preoccupied with rules and regulators, in part because it simply was not possible to put things in order for a regulatory visit if staff had been disregarding the rules between visits. At both Philly Lutaaya and Cha-on Suesum, clinic staff worked hard to craft and institutionalize practices that were more fully aligned with the official rules.

That social activism had influenced clinic routines would have been obvious to even casual observers. Perhaps it did not occur to previous generations of caregivers that they had to inform patients and seek their consent before embarking on treatment or enrolling them in clinical trials. Yet even the newest hires in the five HIV clinics were aware of the centrality of informed consent, though a couple of decades into the epidemic they may not have understood the role that activists had played in pressing for confidentiality in testing and treatment for the highly stigmatized disease. That the counsel-test-counsel routine had become part of clinic practice and culture was clear from the discomfort around proposed modifications as HIV testing was mainstreamed and began to be performed routinely alongside other medical tests.

Finally, although the influence of health law as an academic subspecialty was not as apparent, its existence surely shaped the substance and form of legal expertise in healthcare organizations. When caregivers were uncertain about legal constraints—for instance, wondering what they should do when a child's parents opposed treatment or what they were required to do when a caregiver sustained a needlestick injury—they were likely to be referred to the hospital legal department. Hospital lawyers were conversant with this body of law and could guide clinic staff in deploying the elements of a legal toolkit, up to and including working to revise statutes—like those on custody of orphaned children in Uganda—that did not serve patients well. Likewise, caregivers in contemporary clinics often received episodic training (continuing education sessions) that included some discussion of the law that impinged on their field of practice.

For the most part, clinic workers did not think about the threads from which this legal fabric was woven. But like Jim, the administrator who complained about the mushroom cloud of rules, they often seemed to feel they were spending too much time attempting to reconcile the requirements of the cloud of rules that seemed to be all around them.

[CHAPTER FOUR]

The Variability of Universals

What HIV Clinics Do with Clinical Guidelines

The arrival of HIV and the discovery of its cause created a critical juncture in the world of healthcare and medicine. Not only did HIV change how governments and healthcare organizations monitored human populations globally, it also ushered in laws and regulations that did not exist or were little used before the advent of the virus, changing how healthcare systems monitored themselves and how doctors did their work. Drawing on the ethnographic and interview material from the five clinics, this chapter uses the example of one kind of regulatory instrument—clinical guidelines—to think about variability in the diffusion and use of rules explicitly crafted as universals. It also points out that guidelines seem to imagine a world that is biologically variable but socially uniform. Adjusting to biological variability is part and parcel of the work of guideline writing. Yet how guidelines fare— what purposes they serve, how they are used, and what they can and cannot accomplish—depends at least as much on the social variability of the worlds into which they are introduced as the biological variability of a disease and the bodies of the people living with it.

Daniel, a Philly Lutaaya physician, was deeply involved in the regional infectious diseases training program. Sitting in on his training sessions with regional doctors showed me how sophisticated caregivers actually use treatment guidelines. A summary of one case discussed in these sessions gives a glimpse of how the doctors brought guidelines, local constraints, and the particularities of the case together to arrive at treatment recommendations. The distilled information in clinical guidelines helped physicians sort through case complexities just as they would in richer countries. But in Uganda, the cases were more complex because, on average, patients were sicker. And at every step, doctors also had to maneuver around severe resource constraints.

The training program doctors and I spent most of our time squeezed together on a hard wooden bench in Daniel's small office, some of us sitting forward, others sitting back, creating just enough space for us to scribble notes in the notebooks we all carried. The discussion unfolded with Daniel offering a few facts about a case, asking the students what they would do, and then gently and patiently pointing out other factors they should consider. After some discussion, he would reveal how he had treated the patients, how their illnesses unfolded—sometimes responding to treatment, sometimes not—and how he had adjusted treatments along the way.

At the start of the first session, Daniel invited us to accompany him as he examined a patient whom he described as "very ill." When we arrived, the woman was lying on the examining table fully clothed (no hospital gowns there), with her husband standing beside her. Explaining that we were part of a regional program to teach doctors to treat HIV, Daniel asked the woman's permission to discuss her case with us, assuring her that she could decline his request. Daniel expected the couple to be sympathetic to his request—she was a nurse, her husband a lawyer. In telling us their occupations before we left his office, Daniel had explained that the couple fully understood the gravity of her situation and could be relied on to follow his instructions.

After a brief physical examination and some discussion of symptoms, we returned to Daniel's office. The patient was very ill with HIV, but she also had TB. And she was three months pregnant. Her CD4 count was 8, a perilously low number. Even in very poor countries such as Uganda, doctors aimed to commence treatment when a person's CD4 count fell to 200. Daniel opened the discussion by asking the students how they thought the woman's TB should be treated given her pregnancy and extremely low CD4 count. It was clear that her TB had to be treated, he clarified, so the question was whether they should simultaneously start anti-retroviral therapy (ART) for the HIV or hold off on that. And here the pregnancy complicated matters. Nevirapine, one of the drugs in the first-line HIV regimen, interacts with TB drugs, but the drug one would ordinarily substitute for nevirapine had recently been reclassified as unsafe for pregnant women because of an association with neural tube defects in fetuses.

Several of the students asked Daniel whether it wouldn't be sensible to terminate the pregnancy. Given the value placed on children in central African cultures, this was a surprising question, suggesting mainly that the students understood the bleakness of the woman's situation. Daniel carefully answered that he would not urge termination if there were other options. The couple had experienced two previous pregnancy losses and very much wanted this baby. Discussing other details about her pregnancy and effects of HIV on women's reproductive systems, Daniel noted that the woman would have six months to regain her health before delivery. Inserting another brief lecture, this time on "vertical transmission" of HIV from mother to child, Daniel allayed some of the students' concerns about whether the woman's low CD4 count suggested a high viral load, making it likely that the infection would be transmitted to the fetus. Only 20% of HIV-infected newborns become infected in utero, he explained. Fully 60% are infected during delivery. If the woman started treatment immediately, her viral load should be undetectable by the time of delivery, reducing the risk of transmission from 23% to just 1%. Adding another mini-lecture about recent results on alternative regimens for expectant mothers, Daniel noted that the multidrug highly active anti-retroviral therapy (HAART) he was proposing works considerably better than the national PMTCT (preventing mother-to-child transmission) program, which relies on a very affordable single-dose nevirapine regimen (one dose for the laboring mother, one for the newborn) but only reduces transmission to 12%.

Daniel then returned to his question about how to sequence the TB and HIV treatments. TB is often masked by HIV, and the guidelines for treating people who are coinfected had not been fully worked out. The students observed—correctly—that one generally begins by treating TB. In this case, though, Daniel pointed out, HIV treatment couldn't be deferred. With her very low CD4 count, the woman would get one opportunistic infection (OI) after another; if ART was delayed by two months, she might well die from one of those infections.

A lengthy discussion of possible anti-retroviral drug (ARV) regimens ensued. Some drugs are known to endanger fetuses; others have not been studied in pregnant women. The effectiveness of drugs varies with what else is in the regimen. Some drugs that might be good choices for pregnant women were too expensive or unavailable in Uganda. With two of the options, patients had to be monitored especially carefully for life-threatening side effects, some of which were more common during pregnancy. Moreover when liver problems develop, guidelines specify earlier discontinuation of drugs in pregnant women than in other patients.

And should they do something to stave off OIs during the period before the woman has benefited from the TB and HIV treatments? The usual recommendation would be to give prophylactic Bactrim. But Bactrim may cause fetal abnormalities in both the first and third trimesters of pregnancy. The odds were small, though, Daniel added, and doctors do have to weigh the costs and benefits. His main concern was that the patient might develop either PCP (a form of pneumonia), toxoplasmosis, or some other dangerous OI. And then Daniel added what seemed like a very ordinary recommendation for pregnancy—the woman should have a multivitamin—except that he explained that some research suggested the vitamins might have the added benefit of slowing HIV disease progression.

After this preliminary discussion of options, Daniel revealed the course of treatment he had followed and the ups and downs the woman had experienced. In particular, she had developed cryptococcal meningitis, which he had diagnosed with a serum crag test (the low-cost test used in resource-constrained countries) and treated. But now her headache had returned, suggesting a recurrence of meningitis, and the group concluded that he should treat her with fluconazole for about eight weeks and then continue with a lower maintenance dose. And again, her very low CD4 count came into play because the maintenance dose of fluconazole would have to be continued until multiple CD4 counts of 200 indicated that her depleted immune system had recovered. The discussion continued, touching on the cost of drugs, what the government treatment recommendation would be, whether his recommendations would differ for a patient in a private clinic, concerns about sequencing ARVs to reduce the risk of "running out of options" when patients develop drug resistance or sensitivities, and whether the woman's confusion was encephalopathy or just transient delirium. Daniel also noted that he always gives patients a card with phone numbers for a physician, pediatrician, health visitor, and counselor. "And this one rings often," he said, an observation that seemed to give him some comfort.

Although we discussed other cases, this one illustrates how clinicians commonly use guidelines while remaining attentive to the complexity of illness in poor countries and the challenges of making adjustments at every step. The complexities and complications are staggering and multiplicative. For instance, in poor countries with limited options for anti-retroviral treatment, the expense of resistance testing means that when a patient is experiencing treatment failure, rather than just switching out the one drug to which the virus has developed resistance, clinicians have to switch out the whole regimen because they cannot determine which drug is the culprit. And so in the catch-22 pattern so common in resource-constrained countries, the screws are tightened and an already difficult situation becomes even more challenging.

With the example of Daniel's training session to illustrate the stakes, the remainder of the chapter reviews the role clinical guidelines are expected to play in universalizing treatment and then looks at what clinics actually do with guidelines, showing the lack of standardization at the core of this standardization project and raising questions about the utility of clinical guidelines as a tool for decreasing practice variations and achieving the goal of treatment equity.

Treatment Equity and the Politics of Guidelines

Almost from the start of the epidemic, those working in HIV stressed universal access to treatment and the imperative to break down social barriers to care. Over the past several decades, scientists, caregivers, policymakers, and activists alike vociferously proclaimed their commitment to treatment equity at major HIV/AIDS conferences. At the International AIDS Conference (IAC), an event where major scientific breakthroughs are announced and agendas set, universal access became a mantra quite early. The first conference gathered 2,000 scientists and public health officials in Atlanta in 1985.[1] Dr. Bila Kapita, a Congolese physician, drew attention to the global reach of the epidemic when he spoke about HIV/AIDS in Africa at the 1986 Paris conference.[2] For this groundbreaking speech, he received a prison sentence (subsequently suspended).[3] Over time, the IAC has come to be a more or less amicable HIV-focused melding of science, public health, politics, and practical concerns. In recent years, scientific forums, user roundtables, and social science panels have run alongside demonstrations both inside the conference and on the streets of host cities.[4] The more rough and tumble activities of the Global Village (introduced at the 2004 Bangkok conference) joust for space and time with slick pharmaceutical company displays.[5] Especially well attended are the featured panels announcing major scientific breakthroughs, the speeches of activists and political leaders, and the moving memorials for lost comrades, as I observed when I attended the 2004 and 2006 conferences.

The 1996 Vancouver and 2000 Durban IACs were particularly important in advancing the goal of universalism.[6] At the Vancouver conference, scientists announced recent studies demonstrating that HIV/AIDS could be treated effectively with a cocktail of drugs, carefully selected so that their varying mechanisms for combatting the virus made viral replication essentially impossible.[7] As the 1996 conference theme of "One World, One Hope" emphasized, triple-therapy (as it was often called) and the Lazarus syndrome (in which desperately ill patients regained their health) meant there were now meaningful interventions to universalize. Yet, in a world marked by gross inequalities in wealth, equalizing access to treatment would prove remarkably difficult. At the 2000 Durban conference, where the location put social factors high on the agenda, momentum began to build for making universal access something other than a slogan.

This chapter follows the struggle for treatment equity—for universal access—into the clinics, where that treatment actually occurs. Clinical guidelines, and in particular HIV treatment and testing guidelines, are a core element of the global universal HIV/AIDS treatment regime. Indeed,

HIV/AIDS could almost be described as a poster child for guidelines. If ever there was a disease whose management might be deeply influenced—perhaps even governed—by guidelines, it would surely be HIV/AIDS. And yet, as Daniel's training sessions and this chapter show, once they enter actual clinics, purportedly universal clinical guidelines begin to look considerably less universal and have not yet led to universal access to treatment.

HIV/AIDS arrived on the medical landscape at a propitious moment in the history of clinical guideline writing and use. Clinical guidelines "attempt to bridge the gap between producers and consumers of health care research . . . [they] seek and synthesize sound evidence, assign values to outcomes, generate recommendations and try to influence what clinicians do in the hope that reduced practice variation, lower costs and improved health outcomes will result" (Hayward 1997, 1725). By the time the first HIV/AIDS ARVs had been developed in 1987,[8] clinical guidelines had been in use for sufficiently long to have evolved from an ideological program into a set of practices. Medical practitioners had learned how to incorporate the newest and most scientifically sound medical knowledge and how to translate that knowledge into prescriptions for action whose strength varied with the magnitude of the expected effect and the quality of the evidence.[9] Moreover, practitioners were starting to understand some of the barriers to adoption and use of guidelines.[10] Practitioners thus had the capacity to create guidelines, and the pressure to use them was unusually strong.

In addition, from the mid-1980s onward, HIV was understood to be a global disease calling for global solutions, including global guidelines. This commitment to a global fight against the disease was manifested in the creation of a host of global institutions and included a resolve to offer treatment to rich and poor alike. Clearly no one was naïve enough to imagine that all of the privileges of wealth and position would be eliminated, yet in the world of HIV medicine, the intent seemed to be to reduce substantially the effect of entrenched inequalities. In particular, as effective treatments became available to the citizens of rich countries, caregivers, scientists, activists, and those personally affected by the disease seemed to believe that the citizens of poor countries should also be assured access to these new treatments. Indeed, as noted above, pledges to that effect were made in public forums such as the international conferences[11] and institutionalized in the 3 by 5 Initiative and its successors.[12] Guidelines were a key part of the technology deployed to achieve universal treatment. The dream of treatment equity is still a dream, to be sure, but the vigorous pursuit of that dream has brought treatment, albeit unevenly, to many who otherwise would have received nothing (Heimer 2018; Nolen 2023).

Indeed, over the past several decades, HIV clinical guidelines have been deeply consequential in both symbolic and practical terms, despite the evidence that practitioners often do not follow them (see, e.g., Cabana et al. 1999). Symbolically, the guidelines have suggested that in the realm of HIV/AIDS, there are not rich and poor or deserving and undeserving patients, just sick people who need care. Practically, guidelines have turned attention away from questions of whether to provide treatment to questions of how to provide treatment. As it became politically unacceptable to suggest that poor-country patients could not manage complex regimens and therefore should not receive the expensive medications, scientists and caregivers worked to adapt guidelines, routines, and even the drugs themselves to make treatment more accessible. Treatment guidelines emphasized that treatment for some particular medical condition should vary only modestly from one place to another, and then primarily in response to the patient's condition. In attempting to reduce practice variations, then, clinical guidelines become tools for treatment equity.

Therefore, although treatment guidelines are represented primarily as translations of scientific findings into useable action guides, they are not politically neutral. Politics are not simply left at the clinic threshold. Guidelines themselves, the aspirations they embody, and how they represent those aspirations are political matters. In some cases, de facto rights to treatment begin to blossom even where formal legal rights to care do not exist (Heimer and Tolman 2021). But additional politics, sometimes uncomfortably at odds with the universalizing thrust of the guidelines, gets smuggled in along with the rules, hidden in the intricacies and obscure clauses of guidelines, standard operating procedures (SOPs), and protocols. But as clinics begin to implement guidelines, the focus shifts to practical constraints and a fresh set of challenges, which also are not politically neutral. As the examples in this chapter show, it would be foolish to overestimate the role of guidelines in raising the floor of clinical practice. Guidelines are not a panacea and cannot accomplish much without appropriate infrastructure and adequate resources.

Clinical guidelines are called on to do multiple tasks in both instrumental and symbolic registers. Guidelines have proliferated, Weisz et al. (2007) argue, because they offer an additional tool for regulating the quality of medical practice, supplementing the credentials granted by medical schools and state bodies. Such supplementary tools are particularly important in HIV care because of the variability in HIV caregivers' qualifications; desirability of transferring caregiving to less expensive, more readily available medical staff who often have lesser qualifications ("task shifting"); concerns about accountability to government bodies, private payers, and international donors; and worries about the competence of patients.

As treatments for HIV became available, they were typically administered by doctors with assistance from nurses. But the qualifications of a "doctor" vary from country to country. For instance, the main medical degree (MD) is a four-year postgraduate degree in the US, but an undergraduate degree in many other countries, including both South Africa and Uganda, where a five-year (or sometimes six-year) program leads to a Bachelor of Medicine and Bachelor of Surgery degree (MBChB). In Thailand, a medical degree (MD) is awarded after a six-year program that admits students after high school graduation; students with bachelors' degrees can enroll in a five-year program (Yamwong 2006; Mei et al. 2022). Similar variations occur in training programs for nurses, pharmacists, phlebotomists, and other medical workers. Beyond the basic training programs, systems of testing and credentialing also vary from one country to another.[13] Such cross-national variability in training and credentialing inevitably raises questions about the staffing of HIV treatment programs. If clear clinical guidelines for testing and treatment specify in detail what is to be done at each stage in the disease, though, the training and qualifications of those who provide the care may matter somewhat less. That is, standardization in procedures can substitute to some degree for standardization in training and credentialing.

Many countries are unable to staff HIV treatment programs adequately because they have too few physicians and nurses, another barrier to universal treatment. Clinical guidelines offer some help here. In addition to providing detailed guidance on treatment, they can help with allocation of tasks. Because they specify which kinds of care can be provided by staff with different types and levels of expertise and tell caregivers when to consult more expert clinicians, guidelines can be used to organize task shifting. To compensate for staff shortages, many HIV clinics shift responsibility for stable patients from the most skilled practitioners to other caregivers. Such task shifting might occur within the facility in which patient begin treatment, or patients might be "down-referred" to an affiliated satellite clinic, perhaps closer to their residences,[14] as occurred in South Africa (Heimer 2013). Generally, supplementary local guidelines are written for caregivers taking on work previously allocated to more highly trained workers. Such guidelines specify which tasks less credentialed staff can perform and when they must refer patients to better-trained specialists. Finally, treatment protocols can be used to tell caregivers how to prepare patients to adhere to complex medical regimens and how to discern when patients are not adhering. Abbreviated versions of those same protocols can also tell patients what they are supposed to do—when and how to take their medications, what side effects might occur, and when those side effects merit medical attention.

Initially a strictly medical project, the introduction of clinical guidelines has been overlaid with other projects, perhaps especially an accountability project. With this layering, the legalization of medicine began to shape and sometimes interfere with the practice of medicine as traditionally understood and experienced by physicians and other key medical workers. The original thrust of evidence-based medicine (EBM) was to offer physicians the tools to practice better medicine and to lower healthcare costs (Timmermans and Kolker 2004, 182; Weisz et al. 2007, 691–92). Over time, though, scholars, hospital administrators, third-party payers, and policymakers noted that simply offering tools had not led to widespread use of those tools (Cabana et al. 1999, 1458; Timmermans and Kolker 2004, 186–87).[15] Insurers and government agencies began to employ fiscal pressure to modify medical practice, for instance, shortening hospital stays in the US and denying payment for tests and procedures that fell outside payer guidelines (Ruggie 1992; Scott et al. 2000). Moreover, given the high anxiety about malpractice suits in the US, it was not lost on either clinicians or administrators that guidelines might provide a defense if and when patients sued (Mello 2001). Guidelines have thus also played a part in accountability, where they have often served as comparison points in assessing compliance and making decisions about reimbursement.

Although increases in attention to accountability are ubiquitous in healthcare (Emanuel and Emanuel 1996; Timmermans 2005), accountability pressures have been especially acute in HIV. Governmental and private funders of healthcare had to be convinced to pay for care for "undeserving" patients suffering from a stigmatized, "preventable" disease. As funders were persuaded to pay for treatment, they continued to insist on high standards of accountability (Collins, Coates, and Szekeres 2008), undoubtedly in part because of lingering suspicions about the worthiness of care recipients. When US dollars were sent abroad to support treatment, program managers needed to demonstrate that the funds were being used "appropriately" and efficiently, including offering evidence that patients were using the scarce and expensive drugs as prescribed—in the right combinations and on the correct tight schedule.

Guidelines thus appear to be a flexible, efficient way to bridge gaps, increase reliability, and ensure accountability. But "appear" is an important word here. Guidelines do not always fit the situation as well as guidelines writers have hoped. Tinkering with a guideline to make it fit may consume vast resources. Following a guideline may require more skill than anticipated. Necessary supplies may not be available. Guidelines may conflict with well-established ways of doing things. Making resource flows contingent on following guidelines may encourage some dissembling about how closely staff members adhere to guidelines. Paradoxically, then, evidence suggests that guidelines cannot produce the uniformity that is their primary objective, and, insofar as they do produce some modicum of uniformity, they arrive at it by different paths.

Puzzling Variations in How Clinics Work with Guidelines

Guidelines were used in all five clinics where my team and I observed the work of clinic staff members, but how they were used varied from one clinic to the next. This section reviews what we learned about how practitioners actually worked with guidelines. Insofar as guidelines were used to "guide practice," what that phrase meant seemed to vary among sites, with looser interpretations in some places and stricter interpretations in others. For instance, clinics that were deeply involved in research were likely to incorporate new research findings into their practice rather than simply following preexisting guidelines. And when funders required clinics to adhere to guidelines, clinics used guidelines somewhat differently than when clinics were less constrained.

ROBERT RAFSKY CLINIC

"Is the clinic officially governed by a set of guidelines for anti-retroviral therapy, or is this just something all the physicians independently keep up with?" we asked one Robert Rafsky physician. "I would say independently keep up with," she responded without hesitation. Although there were no official clinic HIV/AIDS treatment guidelines at Robert Rafsky, the private HIV clinic in the US, guidelines did shape clinic activity. Robert Rafsky clinicians evinced a strong belief in EBM, stating that they "generally follow what would be national guidelines" and that they used guidelines to train students, residents, and fellows. As they were issued, new guidelines were discussed in journal club (Petty 2008). In one journal club meeting, for instance, physicians discussed new guidelines from the Centers for Medicare and Medicaid Services' National Pneumonia Project, which recommended the timely administration of ARVs to reduce mortality rates. As research protocols were crafted by Robert Rafsky's researchers, clinical guidelines were included in the background sections or appendices. When research protocols were prepared for foreign sites, Robert Rafsky researchers made sure the information packets included international clinical guidelines as well as the domestic guidelines of the country where the training was to be conducted. And although the HIV clinic had no clinic guidelines, guidelines for specific purposes and subgroups of staff members were crafted and regularly updated. For instance, guidelines for everything from handling abnormal lab results to arranging home healthcare had been created to guide nurses' work. And the hospital with which Robert Rafsky was affiliated had guidelines, for instance, for the use of anti-microbials.

At times, staff members adopted an almost jocular attitude toward guidelines, noting that medication lists had not been updated to make them consistent with the guidelines. But generally their comments suggested that guidelines were taken very seriously. Although no one told infectious-disease fellows which guidelines to follow (several were mentioned approvingly), the fellows were expected to refer to guidelines as they worked and to master the logic and evidence behind the guidelines. As one leading physician explained: "The key is that you sort of get behind the guidelines, understand the rationale for them . . . because even the fellows in clinic, we're training them to be experts too. It's not enough that they can read the guidelines and spit it back. They have to know what's going on behind the guidelines and understand the rationale and if the guidelines really fit for this individual patient because the guidelines don't always fit, and so they have to know that." Clarifying this point, he added that it would not be sufficient to consult the tables (such as the charts laying out alternative regimens) or even to consult the accompanying text; rather, staff at this clinic were expected to "go to the original source." Completing his train of thought, the physician emphasized that this was the special obligation of an elite training institution such as Robert Rafsky: "We try to train people to not just accept the guidelines, for example, but to question the guidelines and to look behind them and look at the numbers and look at the actual studies and look at the methods of the studies and look at how they did things and see if it really makes sense."

BOBBI CAMPBELL CLINIC

Following guidelines was seen as a quality of care issue at Bobbi Campbell Clinic, the US public HIV/AIDS clinic. Bobbi Campbell received much of its funding through the Ryan White HIV/AIDS Program, which required the clinic to affirm that it was following guidelines. In theory, the clinic head noted, this could create problems, for instance, if staff members used a recently introduced, improved anti-retroviral regimen that had not yet been incorporated into the guidelines. Although this issue about discrepancies among guidelines was seen as a mostly theoretical problem, Bobbi Campbell's clinic director noted that a recent letter in *JAMA* commented on a discrepancy between a state standard of care and the national guidelines. A suit had been brought against a physician for not meeting the state standard of care when he was instead following the national guideline (Merenstein 2004). As Bobbi Campbell's director suggested, physicians may sometimes feel pressure not to adjust their practice to take account of the latest scientific information.[16] The clinic director also seemed to see guidelines as a "shield" for practitioners. But rather than the usual claim that adherence to guidelines might protect practitioners in legal proceedings (Mello 2001, 648; Rosoff 2001, 328), he instead saw guidelines as stiffening the spines of clinicians and helping them justify their decisions when patients pressed for faddish or inappropriate treatments—for instance, when patients come in wanting the exact drugs that were prescribed for their friends.

Although Bobbi Campbell staff members were more likely than their counterparts at Robert Rafsky to talk of "following guidelines" and "conforming to guidelines," they too noted that they had some flexibility. Such flexibility was less apparent in the early stages of treatment than in later stages, when more adjustments were required. The clinic had created its own provider manual that included treatment guidelines, making them easily available for the staff to refer to. Commenting on the complexity of guidelines and the importance of keeping up to date in this rapidly changing field, the clinic coordinator also remarked that keeping abreast of the changes only seemed possible in a clinic context blessed with a large group of providers and support staff. Although there appeared to be less emphasis on evaluating the quality of evidence behind the guidelines, the staff at Bobbi Campbell nevertheless actively engaged with guidelines, and guidelines seemed to play a particularly important role in new staff training. Believing that they should "follow" guidelines, staff members also acknowledged that guidelines could not cover all contingencies. As the clinic director put it, "DHHS guidelines are standard, but best judgment is still practiced. If [a] patient won't take optimum therapy because of side effect[s], for example." When gaps were encountered, the clinical coordinator stressed, the more experienced staff were important resources, helping junior colleagues to interpret and assess when the guidelines "cannot give you what you need" in the way of definitive answers. Such situations appeared to be rather common in this particular clinic because many of the patients had multiple health problems that were not fully addressed in the guidelines.

CHA-ON SUESUM CLINIC

At the Cha-on Suesum Clinic in Thailand, special emphasis was placed on adapting guidelines (e.g., the WHO guidelines) for local use. Although staff in the US clinics noted that guidelines did not cover all of the circumstances they encountered, Thai staff were particularly frustrated by the large number and great variety of gaps. In their experience, international guidelines did not adequately deal with more than a few situations they commonly encountered. Under the testing guidelines then in place, for instance, clinic staff were not catching cases of women infected during pregnancy, a particularly important failure because the high viral load of the early infection period increases the likelihood of transmission to the baby. The guidelines also were insensitive to variations among populations, specifying doses that were inappropriately high for Thais, who are smaller on average than people from Western countries. Such overmedication wastes precious drugs and results in higher rates of side effects. Moreover, the guidelines tended not to incorporate generics into the regimens[17] and largely ignored cost. One clinic staff member complained that the guidelines did not give advice about what to buy when a clinic cannot afford to stock all of the options. A local NGO staff member echoed this concern: "They issue guidelines, but then they don't think about how people are going to source these drugs." In adjusting for these lacunae, the staff of Cha-on Suesum also were troubled by the paucity of evidence to guide their modifications.

Kowit, the scientific director, saw the clinic's special niche as creating evidence-based guidelines to support clinical decision making based on resources available in resource-limited settings. Concerned about cost, the clinic used a first-line regime based on GPO-VIR, the very modestly priced Thai generic combination anti-retroviral. When their search for evidence yielded only limited useful data, the Thai Government Pharmaceutical Organization (GPO) commissioned a small study to address key remaining questions. With this additional evidence, the Thai guidelines recommended GPO-VIR as the first-line regimen, although Kowit noted that doctors needed to step up doses gradually and be alert for the toxicities associated with nevirapine, one element of this combination.[18]

Cha-on Suesum staff members were deeply involved in guideline writing both domestically (serving on committees at the Ministry of Public Health [MoPH]) and internationally (serving on a WHO committee to write guidelines for resource-limited situations). But, as Kowit observed, implementation was a major challenge: "No matter how good" guidelines are, if they do not reach the people who need them, they remain useless. The staff of Cha-on Suesum Clinic not only disseminated guidelines in Thailand but also offered training for medical workers from Vietnam, Cambodia, and other Southeast Asian countries. Carefully walking trainees through the international guidelines, Thai staff explained how to adapt guidelines to local circumstances. For instance, when one member of a visiting Vietnamese delegation asked whether they shouldn't get a resistance profile before starting treatment, their Cha-on Suesum host acknowledged that such testing would be optimal and was recommended by the guidelines, but went on to explain that in resource-constrained countries, very expensive resistance testing had to be reserved for later when the patient's drug regimen needed to be adjusted. (In fact, as Daniel, the Philly Lutaaya doctor, told his students, in poor countries resistance testing is prohibitively expensive and can't be done even when regimens need to be modified.) Care providers in resource-limited countries instead needed to focus on CD4 counts. During a subsequent presentation to this same delegation, a second Cha-on Suesum doctor pointed out that many of the drugs suggested as substitutes for first-line regimens were very expensive and rarely available in resource-limited countries. In essence, she explained, there was no second-line regimen, making strict adherence to the first-line regimen all the more important. One high-level Cha-on Suesum staff member, originally trained as a nurse, spent much of her time visiting Cambodian and Vietnamese clinics to help them get up to speed on guideline use and such research-related procedures as adjusting dosages for pediatric studies. Like other clinics, then, Cha-on Suesum linked guidelines to training. But their work as guideline writers and trainers regularly extended far beyond the clinic threshold.

GUGU DLAMINI CLINIC

"We need guidelines, but we also need flexibility and nuance," the director of Gugu Dlamini Clinic noted. "It's like we're sailing a ship and building the ship at the same time," another staff member memorably observed. Although guidelines were crucial to their work, South African clinic staff also sometimes felt that they were "ahead of the guidelines." By this, they meant that they were capable of noting where the guidelines did not fit and modification might be needed to prevent harm. But, the clinic director added, "you feel guilty, sheepish, that you are not following the guideline" because "you don't want therapeutic anarchy." Staff members talked of "maturing" as a province and country, not only learning how to use ARVs but also how to use guidelines.[19] As in Thailand, the South African clinic staff worried about adjusting guidelines to take account of resource constraints.[20] But in addition to worrying about which drugs and laboratory tests were possible given the realities of the clinic budget, they were aware that failure to follow guidelines could jeopardize the entire government HIV/AIDS treatment program (e.g., by facilitating the development of drug resistance and necessitating the use of expensive second-line and salvage treatments), creating a countrywide disaster.

Although the staff of Gugu Dlamini were not much involved in crafting national or provincial guidelines, several staff members had invested heavily in preparing streamlined clinic guidelines. These simultaneously offered guidance on the most common clinical problems (and referred clinicians to the full guidelines for other matters) and made adjustments for what was available in the clinic and hospital.[21] These clinic guidelines were readily available in folders in treatment rooms. In some subfields, such as pediatric AIDS, where national guidelines were less adequate, clinic staff had developed a strong oral tradition through close consultation as they "popped into each other's room regularly" to discuss cases and treatment plans. With both of the pediatric AIDS specialists about to go on maternity leave, they were quickly codifying their practices to ensure that their expertise was available to others in their absence.

Of course, not everyone was equally involved in crafting guidelines. To ensure that others were nevertheless tracking guidelines and modifications of guidelines, Gugu Dlamini Clinic staff regularly included formal discussions of guidelines in their continuing education seminars; their multisited, multinational discussions of cases; and meetings for subgroups of clinic staff. In these discussions, they reiterated the importance of guidelines as a teaching tool, a foundation for the practice of less experienced clinicians, a mechanism for ensuring continuity of care as patients moved from one facility to another, and a tool for husbanding healthcare resources. Although guidelines were part of assessment processes, clinic staff, confident in their practice, expressed relatively little concern about compliance with guidelines and appraisals of their performance. Yet, in their quest for discipline and uniformity, Gugu Dlamini staff sought balance, reminding each other that guidelines were "not hard and fast rules" and that they had to be "prepared at every turn to do things differently if [they] felt it was in the individual's interest."

PHILLY LUTAAYA CLINIC

Working with extremely constrained resources, the staff of Philly Lutaaya Clinic in Uganda were acutely aware that their practice often failed to conform to international standards. Because of time and resource constraints, for example, the clinic often initiated ART before viral loads and CD4 counts could be checked, in contravention of the international WHO guidelines. This worried staff members because their clinic had received such intense scrutiny.

Generally speaking, research programs are monitored more closely and held to more exacting standards than treatment programs. The Thai and Ugandan clinics, both deeply involved in clinical research, had suffered under the gaze of research monitors. In both cases, their work was found wanting, and they had been required to do a good bit of explaining and documenting. In both cases, the clinics also redesigned clinic procedures and retrained staff, ultimately setting things right. Because variability is much more acceptable in treatment programs than in research (where aggregation of data depends on uniformity), program site visitors rule with a lighter hand than research monitors. But even light oversight is oversight, and the South African and Ugandan clinics were obliged to host site visitors and participate in user groups as a condition of receiving foreign (mostly US) support for their treatment programs. Philly Lutaaya thus received a double dose of oversight, since its activities were scrutinized by both research monitors and site visitors. With several treatment programs and five active research studies, the clinic "basically always [had] monitors" on site. Moreover, these regulatory workers were all foreign nationals and thus, to varying degrees, were unfamiliar with local conditions.[22]

Given this expectation of intense foreign oversight, guidelines took on special significance at Philly Lutaaya. More than in the other clinics, guidelines were understood as a dialogue with outsiders, a way to demonstrate competence and compliance. Although clinic guidelines had been written in the past, over the years they had ceased to be a touchstone for clinic practice. The problem was not that staff members were doing their work haphazardly. But their work might look haphazard to site visitors, research monitors, program officers, and other outsiders because their practices were not always codified and were different from US practices. Philly Lutaaya staff members therefore undertook an extensive guideline-writing project to formalize and document their practices. Without this documentation, they worried that monitors and site visitors "could read variability [from rich-country practices] in treatment decisions as people really not knowing what they're doing." Elaborating this point, they discussed how the guidelines should then inform the writing of medical records, specifying who was making the clinical assessments, how frequently the patient had been seen, and so forth, so that it was clear that a judgment was involved and that any deviations from guidelines were based on clinical assessments about what was appropriate rather than ignorance of the standards. A frequently referenced example here was lifesaving transfusions for anemic newborns. Guidelines typically specified that blood tests should precede such transfusions. But in Uganda, this sequencing of test and intervention was often impossible because laboratories did not operate around the clock or on weekends. Under these circumstances, staff members might draw the sample before transfusing but conclude that they could not safely wait for test results before giving the transfusion. With appropriate guidelines and inscriptions in the medical records, they hoped to forestall questions about such deviations from the standards of practice in richer countries.

In fairness, some staff members did believe there was too much "practice variation" within the clinic and that some of their colleagues needed to reeducate themselves about the guidelines. In one long discussion, as some staff members delicately talked "flexibility," others less delicately suggested that it would be more honest to talk about "variations in competence" and "lack of clinical skills." These physicians thus believed that the guideline-writing project was important both to improve the work of their clinical staff and to make their practices legible and legitimate to outsiders.

As in the other sites, guidelines were also a tool for training. Like the Thai clinic staff, the Ugandan physicians were deeply involved in domestic and regional training programs.[23] Inviting his students to think through treatment decisions in several complicated cases, Daniel, the Philly Lutaaya physician discussed earlier, led the group to think through the intricacies of the ARV treatment guidelines. As the cases made painfully clear, applying the guidelines was not a simple exercise. "So these are general guidelines that have to be used in the context of the overall situation of the patient— you have to look at the full clinical picture," Daniel concluded. And, of course, "looking at the full clinical picture" required different skills and tests in poorer countries than rich ones.

CLINIC COMPARISONS

Guidelines are clearly an important element of HIV clinic environments. But although the five clinics worked with guidelines in roughly the same way, some significant variations remained. Table 4.1 summarizes the five clinics' patterns of guideline use. Of the eight uses of guidelines observed in the clinics, three were universal. In all five clinics, guidelines were discussed in a variety of formal sessions, such as journal clubs, continuing education seminars, and clinicians' own meetings to keep abreast of changes in recommended practices, consider the evidentiary support for guidelines, and think about which guidelines would be helpful in their particular clinic. Beyond these formal collective discussions, in all five clinics, staff members referenced guidelines in their own daily work when they pondered courses of action and puzzled over unusual cases. They also used the guidelines to legitimate their clinical decisions, citing guidelines as they wrote medical records. In all five clinics, guidelines were also used for local training

TABLE 4.1. How Five HIV Clinics Work with Clinical Guidelines

	ROBERT RAFSKY (US PRIVATE)	BOBBI CAMPBELL (US PUBLIC)	CHA-ON SUESUM (THAILAND)	GUGU DLAMINI (SOUTH AFRICA)	PHILLY LUTAAYA (UGANDA)	TOTAL (# CLINICS USING GUIDELINE/TOTAL # CLINICS)
Universal Uses of Guidelines						
Clinic staff discuss guidelines in formal meetings.	yes	yes	yes	yes	yes	5/5
Clinic staff reference guidelines to guide or legitimate individual practice.	yes	yes	yes	yes	yes	5/5
Clinic staff use guidelines for local training.	yes	yes	yes	yes	yes	5/5
International Guidelines May Require Adjustment Because of Resource Constraints or Patient Demographics						
Clinic staff write or modify guidelines for clinic use.	no	no	yes	yes	yes	3/5
Guidelines Necessary or Helpful for Funding and Legitimacy						
Clinic adopts guidelines as clinic standard.	no	yes	no	yes	yes	3/5
Clinic staff reference guidelines to guide or legitimate clinic practice.	no	yes	no	yes	yes	3/5
Participation in Guideline Writing Indicates Global or Regional Status						
Clinic staff disseminate guidelines, use guidelines for external training activities.	yes	no	yes	yes, but modest	yes	4/5
Clinic staff serve on external guideline-writing committees.	yes	no	yes	no	yes	3/5
Guideline Use Inversely Correlated with Resources and Global Position						
Total (# uses of guidelines/clinic)	5/8	5/8	6/8	7/8	8/8	

purposes. As junior colleagues were taught the intricacies of HIV treatment (e.g., in residency and fellowship programs or the Ugandan sessions run by Daniel), more senior staff members repeatedly sent them off to read the guidelines.

In some clinics, though, guidelines had to be adapted before they were much use either in guiding and legitimating clinical work or in training students. At Robert Rafsky and Bobbi Campbell, staff members did not write guidelines specifically for clinic use because existing guidelines worked well in these sites. In contrast, staff members at Cha-on Suesum, Gugu Dlamini, and Philly Lutaaya often found that existing guidelines did not work well for their patient populations, either because guidelines were written for a different demographic group (adults rather than children, men rather than women) or a different social context (where caregivers would be able to order laboratory tests to assess disease progress or where patients could afford food and drugs).

Guidelines also served clinic interests as well as being useful to individual staff members. In three clinics (Bobbi Campbell in the US, Gugu Dlamini in South Africa, and Philly Lutaaya in Uganda), specific guidelines had been adopted as the clinic standard. In these three clinics, guidelines were explicitly used to guide and justify the work of the clinic as a whole. In the other two clinics (Robert Rafsky in the US and Cha-on Suesum in Thailand), staff members were less constrained; physicians were free to consider the recommendations of the existing guidelines (e.g., those disseminated by WHO, DHHS/CDC, IAS-USA, AETC) and make decisions for themselves. Although guidelines lent legitimacy to clinical decisions in all five clinics, the legitimacy of the clinic was clearly more precarious in some sites than others.

In some cases, interactions around guidelines connected clinic workers to peers beyond their own institution. For instance, guidelines were referenced in training programs that extended beyond the clinic, though such training sessions did not take the same form in all five clinics. At Robert Rafsky, researchers included HIV treatment guidelines in the packets of materials they used to train partners in other countries. Daniel and other staff members from Philly Lutaaya participated in a regional training program on HIV medicine, emphasizing the importance of HIV treatment guidelines in the sessions I observed. In the training sessions that Cha-on Suesum ran for HIV workers from other Southeast Asian countries, clinic staff walked trainees through explanations of EBM and then carefully reviewed the HIV treatment guidelines for resource-limited countries. Neither Bobbi Campbell nor Gugu Dlamini held formal training programs that extended beyond the clinic. As I was leaving the field, though, Gugu Dlamini was creating a down-referral program to transfer patients to lower-level partner clinics once they had been stabilized on ART. The training of staff members at the partner organizations would include discussion of HIV treatment guidelines, although partner clinic staff would not be practicing independently.

In some instances, guideline writing connected clinic staff members to the wider world of HIV treatment. In three clinics (Robert Rafsky, Cha-on Suesum, and Philly Lutaaya), eminent staff members participated in prestigious guideline-writing bodies that assessed evidence and wrote guidelines designed for general use. This activity was sponsored either by government bodies (such as the country's ministry of public health or the US DHHS/ CDC), by intergovernmental organizations (such as WHO and UNAIDS), or by professional associations (such as IAS-USA).

Explaining Clinic Differences in Guideline Use

Guidelines are intended to reduce practice variation and to introduce uniformity in its place. Yet researchers have generally found that the effect of clinical guidelines is more modest than proponents hoped (Hayward 1997; Cabana et al. 1999; Timmermans and Kolker 2004; Weisz et al. 2007).[24] Although there seems to be considerable variability in how deeply guidelines penetrate into the work of caregiving and how thoroughly the activities of medical caregivers are organized by clinical guidelines, researchers have not asked about systematic variations in guideline use among fields of medicine or across healthcare organizations. Below, I suggest that clinical guidelines might be expected to figure more prominently in HIV medicine than in other fields and explain the historical, institutional, and task-related reasons why that might be the case. I then use these general arguments to revisit and elucidate the clinic-level differences in guideline use discussed above.

WHAT FACTORS MIGHT EXPLAIN WHY CLINICS DIFFER IN GUIDELINE USE?

Although HIV crossed the species barrier some time ago, medical workers became aware of HIV only in 1981. The date when medical professionals and scientists first began to track HIV as a coherent and recognizable set of symptoms matters because many of the conventions and practices for managing a disease depend on what organizational forms and routines are available at the time people start to believe they are seeing a new disease. The organizations in a field bear the imprint of the industry's founding era,

Arthur Stinchcombe (1965) points out, with considerable stability in the practices and forms after that point. The same is clearly true for healthcare as an industry (think of the organization of core medical professions and the division of labor among them), and we might expect it also to be true for the various fields of medical practice. Therefore, it is deeply consequential for HIV that it was "born" in the EBM era. These founding-period or *institutionalization effects*—the first of the six causal factors introduced here—thus suggest that HIV medicine and the HIV clinics in which care is delivered are likely to have been strongly imprinted with the conventions and practices associated with guidelines and EBM.

Although guidelines and descriptions of best practices are the accepted, even mandated, modes for coordinating work, disseminating accumulating knowledge, and standardizing practices, these founding-period effects might be exaggerated or muted depending on other aspects of the institutional environment of a particular clinic.[25] How a particular clinic codified emerging treatment practices might thus depend both on the codification methods of the field (HIV/AIDS) and the codification methods circulating in the local environment, with some differences between stand-alone clinics and hospital-based clinics. We might also expect variations in pressure to make a show of adopting and using guidelines (Meyer and Rowan 1977; Powell and DiMaggio 1991), depending on how thoroughly particular clinics were embedded in a "guideline regime."

Whatever the period in which a field of medicine is born, we might also expect to find differences in guideline use related to the age of the field. New diseases or medical conditions pose a different set of challenges than older, better-understood ones. These *disease-novelty effects*, the second causal factor, occur when people are working with a new disease and subsequently diminish with the maturing of a field as people learn to manage that disease.[26] Disease-novelty effects might predict greater attention to guideline writing in the early periods as practitioners attempt to sift, record, and disseminate their rapidly evolving ideas about how to do things and their accumulating evidence about the efficacy and efficiency of their practices. Although we would expect heighted activity in the first years, we would also expect bursts of vigorous writing and revision of guidelines with new discoveries and inventions. Because HIV medicine is a young field, we might expect to see more interest in guideline production and dissemination than in fields where new knowledge is not being produced so rapidly. We would expect disease-novelty effects to be stronger in some of the clinics, more muted in others, because of their varying relations to knowledge production (e.g., clinical trials) but also because of variability in knowledge translation. In some clinics, new research results were easily incorporated.

In others, because of resource constraints and mismatches between study and treatment populations (e.g., research on men might not be immediately applicable to pregnant women), considerable work was required to translate research results into practice.

A third causal factor, *coordination effects*, suggests that guidelines and other rules may be especially likely to be used in subfields, locations, or periods of time where the work of practitioners must be tightly coordinated, as occurs in surgery (Bosk 1979) or trauma medicine. For the most part, HIV medicine does not require close coordination. However, more coordination is required in situations like childbirth and medical emergencies where HIV infection is especially likely to be passed from one person to another. In those situations, people may be more inclined to adhere to universal precautions, the guidelines designed to manage the dangers of contact with the blood of people infected with HIV.[27] In addition, extra coordination—albeit not the tight coordination of trauma medicine—is required for the task shifting that accompanies attempts to introduce economies of scale into HIV treatment programs. As work is passed from the most expert practitioners to less expert workers and as resources are dispersed across a larger landscape, guidelines have been used for coordination. For this reason, national rollouts are likely to sharply increase pressure for adherence to guidelines.

From the outset, HIV/AIDS clinics had to look for ways to accomplish more with less and to justify their use of resources. In both comprehensive national rollouts, often funded by international donors, and smaller-scale programs, the adoption, creation, or citation of guidelines is often taken as evidence that resources will be used efficiently, effectively, and safely, moves that would be familiar to neo-institutionalists (Meyer and Rowan 1977; Powell and DiMaggio 1991; Edelman 2016). Such evidence may be particularly important when the clinics of poorer countries receive monies from richer countries and donors. These *accountability effects*, a fourth causal factor, may also help explain variability in guideline use. Although the push for EBM has not been primarily motivated by demands for more accountability, it has surely been magnified and accelerated by such pressures, which are ubiquitous in modern life (Power 1997; Espeland and Vannebo 2007). Infusions of funds, whether for treatment or research, typically are accompanied by an obligation to report on how funds have been used. Reimbursements and continued funding often depend on claims that treatments and other interventions are medically and scientifically appropriate, claims that are supported by referencing a field's clinical guidelines. Regulators or funders may therefore monitor clinics' use of guidelines and introduce incentives to increase conformity to guidelines. In addition, caregiving organizations may also police themselves by requiring subunits to monitor and report on their conformity to guidelines.

Although guidelines are collective products, relationships with those collective products vary, and we might expect that people who participated in writing guidelines (local, national, or international) would have a deeper knowledge of those guidelines and a stake in their use. This *ownership effect*, the fifth causal factor, might mean that guideline writers would be more disposed than other clinicians to use guidelines in training or to reference guidelines in discussions with colleagues. Because guidelines are especially likely to be written in the early phases of field development, we might expect that ownership effects would be concentrated especially in the group of scientists, caregivers, and policymakers who participated in crafting a field's first guidelines. When guideline writing is an ongoing activity, though, because a field continues to experience rapid change or because clinics must produce clinic-level guidelines, we might expect a more enduring ownership effect, still concentrated in the individuals who specialized in guideline writing.

Finally, guidelines may help resolve disputes among specialists or legitimate the actions of low status or previously disempowered people. Because of these *legitimacy effects*, a sixth factor influencing guideline use, we might expect explicit reference to guidelines to come from those who are worried that others may doubt their competence or challenge their decisions. Note that legitimacy effects and ownership effects lead to different predictions about who would be especially enthusiastic about guidelines. Legitimacy effects predict that more precariously positioned people would be especially likely to draw on guidelines, while ownership effects predict that guideline writers, who are often higher-status people, would be especially likely to champion guidelines. But both are predictions about how healthcare workers will behave as they work with others who have a different relation to guidelines. That is, they are predictions about how guidelines work in social interactions.

Some of these six causal factors are about nature of the work, others about the relationship between worksites and the environments in which they are embedded; some work at the level of a field of medicine (here HIV/AIDS), others at the level of the clinic or program; still others affect individual clinicians as they interact with others. Yet all six suggest that guidelines would be especially important in HIV as compared with other fields of medicine.

PRESSURES FOR GUIDELINE USE IN THE FIVE
CLINICS: SIMILARITIES AND DIFFERENCES

The five HIV clinics studied here differ somewhat in how they work with clinical guidelines, as the material presented above and summarized in table 4.1 show. Now I ask whether and how pressures for guideline use vary from one clinic to the next. Specifically, I look at whether institutionalization effects (#1), disease-novelty effects (#2), coordination effects (#3), accountability effects (#4), ownership effects (#5), and legitimacy effects (#6)—the six factors discussed above—impinge on some clinics more than others. I also consider whether the presence or absence of these factors helps to account for variations in how intensively clinics use guidelines and what they do with them. Table 4.2 summarizes the findings about how the clinics vary on these predictors of guideline use.

All of the clinics work in a guideline environment. In that sense, the founding-period institutionalization effects should affect all five clinics in similar ways. Yet guideline-based practice is demonstrably less fully institutionalized in some settings than in others (table 4.2, row 1). And that means guideline use is more visible in some clinics than in others, fading into the background in practice settings where EBM was well established and had become naturalized (Douglas 1986) by the time of HIV's arrival and remaining in the foreground where EBM was just gaining a toehold.

At both Robert Rafsky and Bobbi Campbell, staff members were accustomed to organizing their work around guidelines, protocols, and SOPs. They considered guideline use a normal part of the practice of medicine. They regularly used guidelines in training, consulted guidelines when carrying out activities that were a bit out of the ordinary, and noted the differences among guidelines in the strength of the recommendation and the quality of the evidence. In the other three clinics, guideline use was less fully institutionalized. At Cha-on Suesum Clinic, for instance, although the most senior staff members were well versed in guideline use, lower-level staff, particularly at the satellite clinics, needed instruction in how to work with guidelines and protocols. That guideline use was not fully institutionalized became painfully apparent when the clinic hired internal monitors to instruct on documentation standards and encourage adherence to guidelines and protocols. (This was especially true in research, but spilled over into treatment.)

At Gugu Dlamini in South Africa, clinic staff also were attempting to reorganize their work around guidelines and SOPs. This was truly a work in progress. The pressures of high staff turnover, coupled with staff absences for maternity leave or training programs and the arrival and departure of medical interns every few months, made written clinical guidelines a necessity. Standards simply could not be carried in the informal culture and conveyed through day-to-day interactions. Abbreviated versions of core HIV/AIDS guidelines were available in examining rooms, but other guidelines (e.g., on managing HIV/TB coinfection) were still being distilled from larger compendiums. Pediatric guidelines were not yet completely codified. The pediatric source material was less adequate, and the clinic staff were aware that they were working things out as they went along. Guidelines and procedures for social service work were crucial to successful HIV/AIDS treatment, but staff were still sorting out issues about financial arrangements, disclosure, and legal custody of children while I was in the field. Although staff members clearly believed they should organize their work around codified routines and procedures, their work was fraught with ambiguity. Where should they look for guidance when there was little scientific authority? Clearly they had to comply with the law, but sometimes they were uncertain what the relevant law was or what it implied for their work.

Staff members at Philly Lutaaya in Uganda were also deeply involved in guideline writing. Although clinical guidelines for the clinic had been written at some point in the past, over time the connection between the guidelines and caregiving had become looser. To some degree this seemed to have been because practices changed as new drugs became available and as information accumulated about what did and did not work. And, of course, updating guidelines required more time and attention than was available in an overburdened clinic. According to some staff members, work continued to be guided by norms despite the shift in the balance between the oral and written cultures. Other staff members were more critical, suggesting that preparing new guidelines, more closely tied to international guidelines and more strongly grounded in the research literature, would definitely standardize and improve the clinic's work.

From the outset, HIV research and treatment have been strongly shaped by the guideline regime that had recently come to dominate the most sophisticated medical settings. Yet the extent to which each of the five HIV/AIDS clinics had embraced guidelines depended both on the codification methods of HIV/AIDS as a field and the challenges to codification in the local environment. Even though guidelines and best practices had become the accepted way to organize work and incorporate scientific advances, the magnitude of these institutionalization (founding-period) effects varied across the clinics. Moreover, guideline use tended to be less fully institutionalized in the global South because clinic staff were less fluent in guideline use at the beginning of the period, because they operated with

TABLE 4.2. Pressures for Guideline Use: Variations among Five HIV Clinics

	ROBERT RAFSKY CLINIC (US PRIVATE)	BOBBI CAMPBELL CLINIC (US PUBLIC)	CHA-ON SUESUM CLINIC (THAILAND)	GUGU DLAMINI CLINIC (SOUTH AFRICA)	PHILLY LUTAAYA CLINIC (UGANDA)
			Effects at Clinic Level		
(1) Institutionalization (founding-period) effects	Staff accustomed to working with guidelines and documentation. Embedding in existing hospital may mute HIV institutionalization effect.	Staff accustomed to working with guidelines and documentation. Affiliation with large hospital may mute HIV institutionalization effect. Exaggerated HIV institutionalization effect because of reliance on Ryan White funds earmarked for HIV treatment. Guideline use mandated by Ryan White.	Some staff less accustomed to working with guidelines and documentation. Challenges in early period and in coordinating work of core clinic with subsites for research or with outside caregivers for treatment. Institutionalization process very visible (with internal monitors).	Staff less accustomed to working with guidelines and documentation. Institutionalization process very visible (with form creation, guideline writing, and creation of monitoring and evaluation program).	Staff less accustomed to working with guidelines and documentation. Challenges in early period and in coordinating with outside caregivers for treatment. Institutionalization process very visible (with guideline writing and creation of QA/QC program).
(2) Disease-novelty (age) effects	Shows up especially in use of guidelines for training, in participation on guideline teams, and in preparation of materials for non-US partners.	Shows up especially in use of guidelines for training and in selection of (updated) official clinic guidelines.	Shows up especially in use of guidelines for training, in modification of guidelines for local patient populations, in creation of materials for training external groups, and in participation in external guideline-writing groups.	Shows up especially in use of guidelines for training and in creating, modifying, and compressing guidelines for clinic use.	Shows up especially in use of guidelines in training, in creating guidelines for clinic use, and in participation in external guideline-writing groups.
(3) Coordination effects	Coordination between caregivers and researchers may encourage guideline use.	Coordination between caregivers and researchers may encourage guideline use.	Coordination between caregivers and researchers may encourage guideline use. Guidelines may help coordinate with outside caregivers.	Coordination between researchers and caregivers is relatively new. Coordination important in down-referral program associated with treatment rollout.	Coordination between caregivers and researchers may encourage guideline use. Guidelines may help coordinate with hospital.

(4) Account-ability effects	Accountability to research funders and insurers. Disputes over billing.	Accountability to research funders and government. Explicit government requirement to have clinic guidelines.	Accountability to funders, esp. Thai government (though not as intense as some of other government requirements).	Accountability to US donors and South African government with rollout (though accountability less intense than anticipated).	Accountability to funders, esp. US donors.
			Effects at Individual Level and Clinic Level		
(5) Ownership effects	Active involvement in national and international guideline production.	Active involvement in crafting/selecting local guidelines.	Active involvement in national and international guideline production.	Active involvement in crafting clinic-level guidelines. Active involvement in formulating episodic challenges to elements of national/provincial guidelines.	Active involvement in crafting local guidelines. Active involvement in writing international pediatric guidelines (esp. for resource-constrained settings).
(6) Legitimacy effects	Not much of a consideration because of high status of clinic doctors and researchers.	Not much of a consideration; few challenges to legitimacy.	Important consideration in relations with external bodies and foreign colleagues. Threats real, have been experienced in research program (requirement for extra monitoring).	Important consideration in interactions with donors and (to a lesser degree) with government. No real threats.	Important consideration in interactions between clinic and hospital and with foreign donors. Threats real, have been experienced in research program (major investigation).
			Conclusions		
	Guideline use muted. Rules often become background. Wide discretion in how guidelines used.	Guideline use explicit, in part because required by Ryan White Care Program.	Guideline use explicit. Clinic staff aware of poor match between international guidelines and Thai context.	Guideline use explicit. Clinic staff aware of poor match between international guidelines and South African context. Clinic staff especially mindful of challenges of resource constraints and cultural differences.	Guideline use explicit. Clinic staff intensely aware of poor match between international guidelines and Ugandan context. Clinic staff especially mindful of challenges of resource constraints, cultural differences and intensity of prevailing health needs.

severe resource shortages, and because extra work was required to adapt guidelines to local conditions.

I suggest above that a disease-novelty effect might increase guideline use. But because HIV/AIDS had been a recognized disease for a quarter century by the time of my research, the pressure to use guidelines to create some semblance of order was slowly diminishing. But, as the tumultuous history of the first decades suggests, this was still relatively early days for HIV/AIDS treatment. That the first important steps of identifying the disease, creating diagnostic tools, learning how to prevent transmission, and developing effective treatments had been completed did not mean that management of HIV/AIDS had become entirely routine. Many promising treatments had to be discarded when longer time periods and more evidence showed that they were ineffective or even dangerous (Epstein 1996; Engel 2006, esp. 127–45). Over the years, innovation has continued at a rapid pace as new populations gained the attention of medical caregivers, new side effects were discovered, and combination therapies (including drug cocktails and "boosting") were found to be more effective than single drugs. In addition, pharmacological preventives were added to behavioral ones, treatments were adjusted for old age (a challenge not anticipated in the early days), and discoveries were made about the benefits of starting treatment earlier in the course of the disease.

All in all, disease-novelty effects have persisted, and guidelines have remained important as a means of systematizing and disseminating new knowledge, although admittedly this new information is now added to a substantial substrate of established scientific and practical knowledge. The importance of new knowledge did vary from one clinic to the next (table 4.2, row 2), though. "It's the responsibility of the head of department to ensure that our standards are equivalent to the best standards," said the superintendent of the hospital with which Gugu Dlamini was affiliated. "So, yeah, guidelines will have to be revised. If your management of diabetics changes, your management of infections changes, depending on what the current resistant strains are. Your management of HIV is probably the most rapidly changing field right now, so every six months, there's something new coming out." The director of Gugu Dlamini similarly remarked that the "unknowness" of HIV made it different from either surgery or diabetes, where adequate handbooks were readily available for use in training. Acknowledging the burden of preparing plans and reports for funders and the accountability pressures from the government, she nevertheless suggested that it was primarily the newness of HIV that made the HIV clinic staff feel such pressure to record and systematize what they were learning. Their new knowledge needed to be accessible to others.

Although the five clinics all treated HIV/AIDS patients and conducted research, the degree to which they were working at the forefront of medical knowledge varied. Established guidelines tended to work relatively well at Robert Rafsky and Bobbi Campbell Clinics. Their patient populations and clinical contexts were the ones for which the guidelines had been written. Of course, they faced challenges with complicated cases. And, of course, there were some constraints on resources, particularly at Bobbi Campbell.[28] Nevertheless, by the end of my research period, neither US clinic felt a need to substantially rewrite guidelines to do its work. The match between the clinical challenges and the guidelines was sufficiently close that existing guidelines generally served their purpose.

In contrast, the other three clinics remained in a period of rapid learning. At Cha-on Suesum in Thailand, clinic staff felt strongly that clinical guidelines needed to be recrafted to offer lower-dose options for smaller people. This, they hoped, would reduce the side effects their patients were experiencing, although they believed some of these side effects were attributable to genetic variations between Thais and Western populations and meant that first-line regimens should be tweaked accordingly. Their guidelines also needed to incorporate recommendations for regimens built around GPO-VIR, the locally produced fixed-dose combination (FDC).[29]

In addition, Cha-on Suesum, Gugu Dlamini, and Philly Lutaaya Clinics all worked with substantial numbers of pediatric patients. Because the epidemic in richer countries was initially concentrated among gay men, IV drug users, and people with hemophilia, information on the treatment of children had accumulated slowly.[30] Pediatric formulations of some key drugs were unavailable. For infants, syrups were preferable to pills, but when syrups were unavailable, pills had to be split, crushed, and mixed with liquids or foods. Because infants often spit out the foul-tasting medicines, staff then had to give parents guidance on whether to readminister the medications. Core measures of the progress of disease, such as CD4 counts, also had to be adjusted for children. Medication schedules and procedures had to be synchronized with school schedules and the schedules of parents or other caregivers.[31] Eventually, staff had to decide how to manage HIV/AIDS in adolescents and when to transfer patients from pediatricians to staff members who treated adults. Beyond these basic questions about medical care, staff members also worked with social services staff members to figure out when and how to inform children about their illness, how to protect confidentiality (of mothers as well as children) while sharing information with the full range of people who cared for the children, and what to do when parents and children disagreed about treatment.

In these three clinics, preparation of guidelines for treating pregnant women and HIV-infected children became a special focus. Both the paucity of information and the challenges of local resource constraints made adjustments necessary. In richer countries, the babies of HIV-infected women had long been delivered by caesarian section (see ACOG 2001). Reviewing an article on the management of pregnancy and childbirth in HIV-infected women, Philly Lutaaya physicians noted that no babies were delivered by prescheduled C-sections in the affiliated hospital's maternity ward. Any planned caesarian was inevitably displaced in the queue by emergency deliveries until it became an emergency itself. In these circumstances, the task of the healthcare workers was to develop the safest alternative method that was realistic given their clinic's resources. In Uganda, as Daniel explained to the doctors he was training, that meant offering a single-dose nevirapine regimen that would reduce transmission to 12% even though it was theoretically possible to reduce mother-to-child transmission to just 1% with an ARV cocktail. But following that guideline was nevertheless crucial because reducing transmission from 23% to 12% would still save a lot of babies. Thus, clinical guidelines ended up being quite important for Thai, South African, and Ugandan clinics as they struggled to treat populations of patients initially largely overlooked in the US and international guidelines: smaller adult patients, children, and expectant mothers. Although they were not themselves "novel," these patient populations posed novel management problems necessitating substantial adjustment of generic international guidelines. And these three clinics worked creatively and industriously to codify their local knowledge into new clinical treatment guidelines.

Guidelines are also especially helpful when work requires unusually careful coordination. Although the work of treating HIV/AIDS patients generally does not require the minute-to-minute coordination and careful sequencing of surgery, coordination effects do play some role in HIV/AIDS (table 4.2, row 3). For example, the infectiousness of the disease has encouraged close adherence to universal precautions. Moreover, although HIV/AIDS care is very often provided in specialty clinics (like the five discussed here), caregiving responsibilities were divided among clinic staff members and spanned the boundaries between the clinics and other healthcare organizations. Inside the clinics, caregiving was often shared by research and treatment staff, with work coordinated by clinical guidelines and research protocols. When patients had to be hospitalized, treatment was provided jointly by hospital staff and clinic staff, again with coordination organized around guidelines.

Coordination was not always smooth, though, especially in locations where guideline use was not as fully institutionalized. That sometimes led

Gugu Dlamini doctors to provide the TB treatment (as well as the HIV treatment) of TB/HIV coinfected patients so they could make sure it was done properly. The complicated treatment history of one young Zulu woman, coinfected with HIV and TB, illustrated why and how this would happen. Language barriers complicated the appointment from the outset. Christiaan, the doctor, seemed to understand Zulu although he did not to speak it; the patient used some English but mostly spoke to him in Zulu. (Christiaan did bring in a Zulu nurse as the appointment ended to verify that he and the patient had correctly understood each other.) Christiaan had the woman's medical record to refer to and that helped him fill in gaps. He proceeded slowly, repeating a lot, and apologizing when he needed to take time to write things down. After being treated for TB meningitis—"TB in [her] head," was how she described it—for nine months, the woman was diagnosed with abdominal TB and had been receiving treatment for that for six months. From his physical exam and her recent X-ray, Christiaan concluded that she still had TB in both her lungs and abdomen. Her belly was soft and swollen as if she had never been treated for abdominal TB, he explained to me later, adding that he was worried that she had MDR (multidrug resistant) TB. In addition to TB and HIV, she also had a variety of other ailments, most crucially PCP (pneumonia), one of the common OIs that occurs with HIV. Christiaan gave the woman her prescriptions and sent her off to the hospital pharmacy to get them filled with instructions to return immediately to him so he could explain to her how she was to take the various tablets. He also informed her that she must come back the next week for him to check on her PCP. And, apparently worried about the lack of continuity in the care she had received, he told her that when she be-gan ART—which would happen as she began to recover from the TB—she should return to him in particular at least for the initial visits.

Inserted into this long conversation was some crucial information. The woman asked Christiaan why one clinic had prescribed two tablets per day when the previous clinic had given her three tablets per day. Christiaan pa-tiently questioned her about where she had been getting treatment and why she had switched clinics. Her care had been transferred to a clinic closer to her home, she explained, and without spelling this out fully she told Christiaan that she had been given the two-dose regimen when her mother had gone to fetch the medicines because she herself had been too weak to go to the clinic. It was just after she recounted this part of the saga that he suggested that she get her TB treatment at Gugu Dlamini. She would like that, she affirmed. Christiaan did not go so far as to blame the TB clinics for the deterioration in the woman's condition, but he clearly felt she needed to be tracked more closely, with attention to both her TB and her HIV. Staff members worked valiantly to coordinate care with other institutions—when patients were not yet sick enough to come to Gugu Dlamini for HIV treatment, when patients were transferred to other institutions because they could not afford the modest copays, or when patients moved out of the clinic's catchment area—but they were not always convinced that their colleagues in other institutions knew how to treat complex cases or understood the importance of follow-up.

Philly Lutaaya staff similarly were often quite unhappy with the treatment their patients received in the local hospital and tried to get nonclinic caregivers to organize their work around clinical guidelines. They often reported disagreements with other physicians about how to sequence the early stages of treatment for people coinfected with TB or malaria and HIV, as Daniel noted. They were also distressed when very young infants were sent home rather than being kept in the hospital when they were ill. Some of these babies died because they could not be returned to the hospital quickly enough to get lifesaving care. In both situations, Philly Lutaaya staff felt that some of the difficulties in coordinating care arose because hospital staff were not on the same page as them about guideline use. Thai clinic staff likewise complained about difficulties coordinating care with primary care physicians or pharmacists who were not orienting to the same set of rules and guidelines.

Guidelines also were crucial in coordinating care as HIV/AIDS treatment programs expanded beyond core clinics. When South Africa's national treatment program began, Gugu Dlamini began recruiting partner clinics to take over the care of patients who had already begun ART and were now stable. This division of labor would allow Gugu Dlamini to scale up the number of patients receiving therapy. But safe down-referral of such patients required scrupulous coordination around common guidelines so that patients could be passed smoothly back and forth between the more skilled caregivers of the core clinic and the less fully trained staff of satellite clinics (Heimer 2013). According to one local consultant I interviewed, potential down-referral sites were not always receptive to being handed a set of guidelines that would dictate the terms of interaction between the core clinic and its partner. Some of these partners—municipal clinics, for example—were accustomed to working with SOPs and guidelines. Because they were already part of the medical world, they were comfortable with outsiders "coming in uniform" and giving structured presentations about medical procedures. Other down-referral sites, some of which had been only marginally involved in medical work, would not take kindly to being handed a set of already prepared guidelines. In the consultant's view, coordinating work with this second group of sites required that Gugu Dlamini staff "sing and dance together" with them before jointly working out ground rules for their relationship. Ultimately, coordination would be around the guidelines, but the sites first had to be introduced to the culture of SOPs, guidelines, and EBM. In summary, coordination effects made guidelines especially important in poorer countries where more task shifting was required and clinic staff were under pressure to transfer care of stable patients to less specialized neighborhood or community clinics. But these were also places where guideline use was less fully institutionalized.

The ubiquity of accountability in contemporary societies added another pressure for guideline use, yet accountability demands varied from one clinic to another (table 4.2, row 4). All of the clinics faced pressures to account for themselves, spending countless hours documenting compliance. Still, some clinics were more insulated from these pressures than others, and that meant guidelines played a somewhat different role in accountability. At Robert Rafsky, clinic staff were accountable to insurers, funders, and research oversight bodies, as well as to the hospital and university in which they were embedded. Yet the pressures they experienced differed somewhat from those experienced in other clinics, as two incidents illustrate. First, the clinic experienced a precipitous decline in revenues when insurers concluded that the evidence in their medical records did not support their billing. In essence, insurers believed the clinic was overcharging by claiming to have offered more complex services than it had actually provided. This problem, which would have been a real disaster in most clinics, led to a long, not very successful, series of attempts to improve the production of records and the process of distilling billing information from those records (see also Heimer 2008, 39–40). Second, on the research side, clinic staff worried that inadequate enrollments in studies might lead to a decrease in funding. Although both of these were questions about performance and accountability, neither led to deep reflection on guidelines or altered how staff members used guidelines. Insurers were not doubting the appropriateness of the medical care given by Robert Rafsky physicians, and research funders were not questioning whether Robert Rafsky researchers were adhering to research protocols.

Bobbi Campbell staff faced no special accountability pressures on the research side. As a subsite of another clinical trials unit, they were somewhat insulated from accountability pressures. In contrast, the accountability pressures on Bobbi Campbell's treatment program were quite intense. The clinic received much of its treatment funding from the Ryan White program, a federal program that required participating clinics to specify what guidelines they were following. But although the clinic had to justify its reimbursement claims, with special pressures to follow routines for documenting instances when multiple services were provided in a single visit (the "modifier 25" issue), and although the clinic was required to specify which guidelines governed its practice, outsiders were not casting doubt on the quality of the clinic's work and its adherence to those guidelines—they were just (mostly inadvertently) making life miserable for Bobbi Campbell staffers. Experiencing this as a "clerk and billing issue," clinic staff did not feel that their medical work was being indicted.

At all of the other clinics, though, accountability pressures did lead to heightened scrutiny and raised questions—justified or not—about clinic competence and adherence to guidelines and protocols. The staff at Cha-on Suesum Clinic were accountable to both foreign funders and to the Thai government. In that clinic, accountability pressures originated in the research program when research monitors raised concerns about deviations from standard research practices. Working with the embedded monitor supplied by one of their research sponsors, clinic staff developed an internal monitoring program to avoid further violations of standard research practices. In the long run, this internal monitoring program grew into a universal program to ensure the quality of all the clinic's work. Heightened sensitivity to guidelines, in this case, did originate in external accountability but was magnified by the clinic's proactive response to the possibility of further scrutiny.

A similar response occurred at Philly Lutaaya, where intense research-related scrutiny raised questions about the adequacy of recordkeeping and the quality of care provided to research subjects and other patients. Although the clinic was entirely vindicated in the long run, the experience of such scrutiny prodded staff to create a top-to-bottom, multistage quality assurance/quality control (QA/QC) program. At the same time, though, clinical staff embarked on the guideline-writing program (discussed earlier in this chapter) intended to update existing guidelines, codify current practices, and create new guidelines that were consistent with the latest research but useable in the Ugandan context. As they drafted and reviewed guidelines, they also reminded each other of the importance of consulting guidelines in their daily work, writing detailed medical records, and explaining any deviations from guidelines. Although Philly Lutaaya had a good reputation both locally and internationally, staff felt they needed to prove themselves and address any lingering doubts after the recent harsh reviews. Accountability pressures were especially intense at this clinic both because of this review and because of the clinic's deep dependence on external funding (primarily from the US) for both research and treatment.

Staff members at Gugu Dlamini Clinic were also very sensitive to accountability pressures, but had not in fact received much critical scrutiny. Their research program, as noted before, was less developed than the research programs of the other clinics. As they moved into conducting more research, Gugu Dlamini's staff members were being mentored by partners at an eminent US university. As the senior partner in the research, the US university took most of the responsibility for ensuring compliance with standard research practices. Given how the funds were routed, Gugu Dlamini was insulated from oversight by entities other than its research partners. Because they understood that accountability pressure would increase in the future, Gugu Dlamini staff were eager to develop appropriate routines and infrastructure. As noted earlier, the site visits of treatment programs are often more collaborative than the monitoring visits of research programs, and this had certainly been the experience of Gugu Dlamini staff. Nevertheless staff members prepared carefully for site visits. Their preparation was rewarded with considerable praise both during the visits and during subsequent "user meetings" where clinics receiving funding from the President's Emergency Plan for AIDS Relief (PEPFAR) shared best practices.

In addition to the (muted) accountability from research funders and foreign supporters of its treatment program, Gugu Dlamini also faced accountability pressures from the South African government. These pressures increased as more funding became available for treatment. Perhaps because the Mbeki government's previous HIV/AIDS policies had been so wrongheaded, clinic staff had little confidence that the rollout policies and implementation would be sensible. Foremost in their minds were concerns about the first-line regimen, which included d4T, a drug whose side effects included life-threatening lactic acidosis.[32] The clinic had purchased special equipment to test for lactic acidosis, which was especially common among people with a high body mass index. What worried clinic staff was the requirement to get permission before switching patients off the first-line regimen. If getting permission took any time at all, patients could die. Gugu Dlamini staff pessimism seemed justified given that they had failed to convince government guideline writers to take account of the lactic acidosis problem as they prepared their recommendations. Given their concerns, clinic staff considered not participating in the rollout even though that would mean forgoing the much-needed government funding that participation would bring.

As it turned out, program officials were considerably more flexible than clinic staff had feared. At least for Gugu Dlamini Clinic, "get permission" seemed not to mean "get permission in advance." Program officials were satisfied if clinic staff informed them after switching a patient off the first-line regimen. Neil, a doctor who was deeply involved in preparing compressed forms of guidelines for clinic use, remained unhappy about the need to comply with government guidelines, which he regarded as a "political game." As he explained, "The problem with our Department of Health

HIV guidelines is that we are starting at the same place America started when they first had this problem with HIV. We're not learning from that experience. So we are using a lot of the old drugs that most of the first-world countries are not using anymore, [with all] the toxicities and side effects and problems that they bring to the patients." The Department of Health guideline seemed to him a move backward from Gugu Dlamini's previous practice, which was grounded in the clinic's own painstaking study. Neil expected that the government would eventually change its policy given the strength of the evidence, but in the meantime, Gugu Dlamini had little choice but to comply. Its compliance was coupled with close monitoring of patients, though, and a group pledge to immediately change the regimen of any patient showing signs of illness and then "deal with the legalities of it later on." Given its prominence, health officials would have had egg on their faces had Gugu Dlamini Clinic declined to participate in the government rollout. But then again, the South African government had not seemed to mind the egg in the past.

These tensions between Gugu Dlamini and the South African government were especially important because they simultaneously illustrate the use of guidelines as shields (Mello 2001; Rosoff 2001) and show that the effectiveness of defensive weapons depends on what armaments the other side is deploying. Accountability pressures spurred Gugu Dlamini's leaders to use science-based guidelines as shields. Although they were inclined to respect the government's guidelines, their willingness to adhere to its rules came with limits grounded in EBM. But such defensive moves may prove ineffective if the other party is less fully embedded in an EBM and guideline culture. In such instances, those with power can decide that accountability is simply about following the rules whether or not those rules take account of the latest scientific findings.

Not all of the observed effects were at the clinic level. Both ownership and legitimacy effects had individual-level as well as clinic-level effects. In particular, some staff members enthusiastically embraced guidelines, participating in writing and adjusting guidelines for the larger HIV/AIDS community or for their own clinic, while others were more reluctant users of guidelines. I had expected the "ownership effects" that arose from participation in guideline writing to vary across time and place, with stronger experiences of ownership in the first cohorts of HIV caregivers and researchers and in places where crafting guidelines for local use continued to be necessary.

In all five clinics, but for somewhat varying reasons, ownership effects increased the prominence of guidelines in clinic work (table 4.2, row 5). When clinic staff participated in drafting national and international guidelines, this honor might be expected to shape clinic attitudes toward guidelines. In the three clinics most deeply involved in research—Robert Rafsky, Cha-on Suesum, and Philly Lutaaya—clinic staff had participated in guideline writing. The effect of such participation seemed more muted at Robert Rafsky than at Cha-on Suesum or Philly Lutaaya, perhaps because the status and self-assurance of Robert Rafsky's researchers buffered them from many pressures at the same time that inclusion of personnel from a prominent US clinic seemed less remarkable than inclusion of Thai or Ugandan researchers. At Bobbi Campbell and Gugu Dlamini, guideline writing was focused especially on selecting, producing, or adapting clinic-level guidelines. But at both Gugu Dlamini and Philly Lutaaya, guideline writing combined local and extra-local orientations. As mentioned above, although Gugu Dlamini staff were not yet deeply involved in research and so not fully integrated into research and guideline-writing circles, their successes had been noted and lauded in regional gatherings for recipients of PEPFAR funding. And Gugu Dlamini had not been shy about disagreeing with government bodies about the first-line regimen or about policies to prevent mother-to-child transmission. Nevertheless, their guideline writing was primarily focused on the clinic itself. Guideline writing seemed to be a collective activity for the pediatric team, perhaps because staffing issues arising from the pediatricians' own pregnancies increased the pressure to codify practices. In the rest of the clinic, guideline writing was a more individual endeavor, taken on especially by Neil, the physician who enjoyed the intellectual challenge of distilling information from the voluminous international and national guidelines. At Philly Lutaaya, as observed earlier, the crafting of local guidelines was a collective activity, with tasks parceled out and resulting guidelines discussed in staff meetings.

Finally, guidelines can be useful tools when disagreements arise about what should be done (table 4.2, row 6). Challenges to legitimacy can be either individual-level or clinic-level phenomena. Others might question the decisions of a particular practitioner or they might question the practices of the clinic as a whole. Note, though, that when legitimacy challenges occur at the individual level, more precariously positioned staff members and higher-ranked staff members might employ guidelines somewhat differently, with the former citing guidelines in support of chosen but disputed courses of action and the latter championing guideline writing as a method for moving forward.

With the exception of disputes over funding, reimbursement, and routine regulatory reviews, the appropriateness of clinic activities had not been challenged at either Robert Rafsky or Bobbi Campbell. Reference to guidelines was thus a routine part of maintaining legitimacy. Legitimacy was more precarious at the other three clinics, where clinic or staff practices had been questioned. At Cha-on Suesum, although questions were raised by outside research monitors, concerns about legitimacy were widely diffused among clinic staff. Senior physician researchers felt that they had to justify and defend their practices in ways that would not have been necessary for their Western peers. Lower-level staff members complied, indeed overcomplied, with regulations so they would never "look stupid" to outsiders (Heimer and Gazley 2012).

As its director and other informants liked to point out, Gugu Dlamini Clinic was sometimes seen as the "jewel in the crown" of the provincial health ministry, suggesting it had high legitimacy, and at other times described as a "thorn in the side" of that same ministry, suggesting that the appropriateness of clinic practices was sometimes challenged. One of the points of contention, the clinic's practice of switching patients off d4T, is worth revisiting. The disagreement about the presence of d4T in the government's first-line regimen showed how guideline use was influenced by the need to coordinate work, by concerns about accountability, and now, finally, by the need to establish the legitimacy of clinic practices. In discussions with government health officials, Gugu Dlamini staff consistently drew on their meticulous treatment records and the guidelines they had developed for switching to alternative regimens. Guidelines were thus crucial in establishing the legitimacy of clinic practice and simultaneously providing an acceptable language for questioning government policies.

In contrast to Gugu Dlamini's experience, at Philly Lutaaya challenges to legitimacy came from outside the country. Philly Lutaaya staff members felt they needed both to be consistent in their practice and to base their practice on written guidelines so that others—including monitors—could not misunderstand variance from standard (international) practices as them "not knowing what they were doing." In their view, they had important local knowledge, unavailable to outsiders. But this knowledge had to be translated into accepted formats—guidelines—before it could be understood by outsiders and used to legitimate the (unconventional) local practices. Both the local guideline-writing project and staff contributions to the new pediatric HIV/AIDS handbook displayed this nuanced understanding of their situation. Their legitimacy was precarious, at least in some circles, and could be shored up by the use of guidelines, but only if those guidelines simultaneously drew on local knowledge, conceded the limitations of that knowledge, and took the form outsiders preferred. The usual story of the neo-institutionalists in sociology (Meyer and Rowan 1977; Powell and DiMaggio 1991) is that form and substance may become decoupled when actors seek legitimacy by adopting the trappings of change without actually modifying entrenched practices. In an interesting twist on the neo-institutionalist story, although Philly Lutaaya's legitimacy concerns did dictate the packaging, that packaging was adopted precisely to make substantive change acceptable to outsiders. Adopting the form made it possible to smuggle in the substance. Substantively important local knowledge was legitimated by being packaged in internationally accepted institutional forms.

Overall, these six factors—institutionalization, disease-novelty, coordination, accountability, ownership, and legitimacy effects—help us understand the variation in guideline use across the five clinics. I examined how the clinics responded to the newness of HIV/AIDS and the challenges of treating their particular patients, the demands for close coordination given their specific mix of activities, the institutionalization of guideline use in their environment, the accountability pressures they faced, the sense of ownership that came with guideline writing, and the questions they encountered as individual practitioners and as a clinic about the legitimacy of their work. These factors, I suggest, help explain why guidelines were more likely to fade into the background at Robert Rafsky and were more explicitly referenced in the other clinics. At Cha-on Suesum, Gugu Dlamini, and Philly Lutaaya, clinic staff were intensely involved in modifying global guidelines, which, for a variety of reasons, fit poorly in their clinics. Guidelines were also very much on the minds of practitioners in these three clinics because of thinly veiled or explicitly articulated doubts about the quality of their work. Guidelines are, then, a key element not just in guiding clinical work and research but also in justifying and explaining local practices to outsiders.

Conclusion

Clinical guidelines have implicitly imagined a world that is biologically variable but socially uniform. Thus the original guidelines did a better job of helping practitioners cope with variability in OIs, side effects, and disease progression than in helping them adjust for variations more deeply grounded in the social than the biological world. In fact, the first guidelines considered only a limited range of biologically based differences because they incorporated the usual blinders of medical science: they assumed an adult male body. Adjustments thus had to be made for the bodies of women, children, and people who were smaller or larger than the average person from the global North. But such adjustments for biologically based variability are relatively easily incorporated into guidelines, guideline writing, and guideline use. They are part and parcel of what clinical guidelines are about.

More important challenges to guidelines come from variations in the social circumstances of patients and variability in how healthcare is delivered. For one thing, the social situations of patients are quite variable. Some only come to medical facilities when they are already very ill, others come much earlier. Some face dire consequences if others learn that they have HIV; others can disclose without fear. Local customs on marriage, sexuality, and infant feeding magnify the consequences of HIV infection in some societies more than others. But caregivers also vary, and guideline adoption and use is affected by the adequacy of their knowledge base and the pressures they face, both positive and negative, to use guidelines. The material worlds in which guidelines are used also matter. Guidelines are much harder to follow when basic equipment is scarce and sophisticated lab tests cannot be performed. And, of course, it matters that guideline use is embedded in organizational environments that vary in whether guideline use is mandated, regularly available continuing education helps caregivers keep abreast of guideline changes, and healthcare professionals are obliged to draw on guidelines as they report regularly and systematically on their work.

For these reasons, the fate of clinical guidelines depends as much on the social world in which guidelines are written, disseminated, and used as on the accuracy and comprehensiveness of their match to biological phenomena. As Timmermans and Epstein remind us, "Tinkering, repairing, subverting, or circumventing prescriptions of the standard are necessary to make standards work." Even when clinical guidelines must be remade to fit local circumstances, then, "it would be wrong to consider these standards as failures because a standard's flexibility is often key to its success" (Timmermans and Epstein 2010, 81). Guidelines are often written in the centers of power, as we know, and therefore reflect the knowledge and interests of those locations. Rather than furthering a goal of uniformity, then, they support a particular uniformity, empowering the groups that developed the standard in the first place and delegitimating and disadvantaging groups that must tinker with the standard and translate their data and experience into institutionalized formats. Often those translations can be made, but only with substantial expenditures of resources by already disadvantaged groups. If indeed flexibility is generally the key to a standard's success, that flexibility is often bought with the resources of those who have the least to spare.

Equally important, it is not clear that the dissemination of clinical guidelines will contribute much to the goal of ending practice variations. Even if guidelines were entirely successful in inducing uniformity in what physicians and other caregivers do, other important factors that shape access to treatment are not in the hands of healthcare workers. To be sure, it has been important to demonstrate the feasibility of treating HIV with ARVs in poor countries. This has meant rewriting clinical guidelines, training caregivers, and instructing patients. But access to treatment also requires, at the very least, that drugs be priced at levels that make them affordable in poor countries, whether that comes about through purchasing consortiums, bilateral and multilateral aid programs, private philanthropy, government provision, or more sane and humane pharmaceutical pricing. And beyond that, any hope of bringing the AIDS epidemic to an end almost certainly depends, among other things, on reductions in the many gross inequalities that permitted the disease to take root and spread in the first place.

Clinical guidelines, like many other universalistic rules, surely introduce a modicum of fairness, but it is often a narrow, restricted fairness confined to the topics covered by the guideline. In a sense, the guidelines produce an essentially parochial fairness that is a counterpart to their local universality. In later chapters I consider both the positive and negative effects of the legal turn in healthcare, including the increased emphasis on clinical guidelines. In some instances, more rules simply turn caregivers into rule followers, but sometimes rules instead lead caregivers to more deeply consider what they owe their patients.

[CHAPTER FIVE]

Rules, Credibility Struggles, and Institutionalized Skepticism in Clinical Research

Constructing Trustworthy Data

> It [the quest for the cause of AIDS] is a story of commitment and dedication to mankind and of tireless, often brilliant detective work within the magic and marvelous world of modern medical technology. But it is also a story of cut-throat competition and bare-knuckled politics, of individual ego and national pride, and of the kind of intense pressure on human beings that often brings out the worst in even the best, and can result in lying, cheating and outright fraud.
>
> James D. Squires (1989, 1)

In the drama of emerging infectious diseases, science often has a starring role. It is scientists who determine whether an outbreak is a new disease or simply a recurrence of an already known illness. Scientists also develop the diagnostic tests that allow doctors to determine which patients have the new disease. And, perhaps most important, scientists develop, assess, and refine treatments. But although scientists' contributions to identifying and combatting emerging infectious diseases are vital, their work can be deeply controversial, particularly during the confusing early period when false moves are nearly inevitable. People confronting the terrifying uncertainties of new diseases may find it hard to put their faith in painstaking but maddeningly slow scientific research. They may wonder whether parts of the cumbersome review and testing protocols of risk-averse agencies like the Food and Drug Administration (FDA) could be reworked or temporarily suspended to save lives and prevent the spread of the new disease. They may worry that the alliance between scientists, doctors, and pharmaceutical companies may have distorted research and drug development agendas to the detriment of patients.[1] During these early days, desperately ill people may also consider alternative therapies that seem to promise so much more than Western medicine can offer.

Although public skepticism about HIV science has largely subsided, in the early days of the epidemic, scientists had every reason to feel that they were under siege with attacks coming from many sides. Some disputes took the form of measured disagreements in professional journals; others spread into popular discourse and even onto the streets in noisy, theatrical demonstrations; still others led to lengthy, full-scale investigations and even to negotiations among heads of state. Because patients and family members, funding bodies, and other stakeholders repeatedly raised questions about the qualifications and intentions of researchers and the integrity of the research process, shoring up the trustworthiness of science has been a central aspect of the global regulation of clinical trials.

Moreover, the work of ensuring the trustworthiness of scientific data is a fundamental part of the research process—omnipresent, even when public controversies subside. Organized skepticism, Robert Merton claimed, was one of the central norms of science, "both a methodological and an institutional mandate" (1949/1968, 614). By this he meant not only that scientists believe in bold questioning of received wisdom but also organize their work to encourage and support a skeptical approach to knowledge, including systematic testing of facts and a willingness to revisit and revise conclusions in the light of new evidence (Merton 1973; Hallonsten 2022).

The claim of this chapter is that the credibility of contemporary clinical research—and science more broadly—depends not just on organized skepticism of the sort that Merton described but on a more thoroughly institutionalized skepticism equipped with a painstakingly fleshed out and even fetishized set of rules (the "mushroom cloud"). These rules allow scientists to rebuff the charges of outsiders and to claim, with the endorsement of "disinterested" others, that they have done science properly, that their representations of their work and their findings are honest and accurate, and that their data are trustworthy. Here I explore what science workers have done at the core of their own enterprise to stave off challenges and to protect their borders. In the era of accountability, that means not just following a set of rather rigid rules but also providing evidence that the rules have been followed. Both instrumental and symbolic effects matter here. Science thus depends on a "contract" between funders and scientists, as well as between researchers and research subjects, and the scientists must demonstrate that they have adhered to their side of the contract.

Early Controversies in HIV Laboratory Research: Scientific Reputations and Downstream Effects

Two of the most public of the early controversies in HIV science spilled across continents, showing that HIV scientific controversies are as global as the disease itself. These two disputes, over precedence and the factual correctness of key findings, strongly resemble the scientific credibility contests analyzed by Gieryn (1999), while bearing the imprint of the increasingly legalistic environment in which biomedical scientists work. The fight over precedence came first.[2] No sooner had the virus been identified in 1983 (by Luc Montagnier, Simone Barré-Sinoussi, and their colleagues at the Pasteur Institute in France) and definitively linked to AIDS in 1984 (by Robert Gallo and his colleagues at the US National Institutes of Health) than the disputes began. Should Gallo receive credit for the first pathbreaking discoveries in HIV/AIDS science, or did that honor belong to Montagnier and Barré-Sinoussi? As is common in such disputes, the stakes went beyond the reputations of individual scientists to include the prestige of host countries and claims on patents and the resulting income streams. Thus the dispute over precedence erupted in 1985 as patents were being issued for the first HIV blood test. Although US President Reagan and French Prime Minister Chirac worked out an agreement to split patent royalties evenly, this did not resolve key questions about the relationship between French and US strains of virus and the allocation of credit in papers authored by Gallo and his associates.

The *Chicago Tribune*, Congressman John Dingell, the Office of Scientific Integrity (OSI), the Office of Research Integrity (ORI),[3] and an appeals board in the Department of Health and Human Services (DHHS) all were involved in the case against Gallo and his associate Mikulas Popovic. Eventually, Gallo was able to convince investigators that contamination rather than theft explained the similarity of the French and US viral strains. And in the view of the DHHS appeals board, ORI investigators who had worried about discrepancies between lab records and published papers had placed too much weight on a few words and notations written by Popovic, who had "limited English skills" (*New York Times* 1993). Gallo and his associates had surely given too little credit to other researchers, but perhaps investigators were overreacting to essentially normal scientific practices. In some senses, a final verdict was rendered by the Nobel committee, which awarded the 2008 Nobel Prize to Montagnier and Barré-Sinoussi while passing over Gallo (Cohen and Enserink 2008).

Although the controversy eventually lost steam, the long-running investigation of Gallo and his team signaled significant changes in the relationships among scientists, regulatory bodies, journalists, and the public, changes that together suggested an increase in skepticism about biomedical science.[4] No longer would it be acceptable for intellectual stars to hoard resources and credit, actions now seen as damaging to the scientific community. No longer could the raw intellectual talent of team leaders compensate for lax oversight of the daily work of science. No longer could scientists expect journalists to write admiringly about their discoveries while ignoring the underbelly of science (Cohen 1991). No longer would scientists be trusted to carry out their work without formal regulatory oversight in the form of rules, guidelines, and regular monitoring. These new norms are embodied in practices designed to create trust in clinical trials, practices that are the subject of the remainder of this chapter.

Questions about credibility and trustworthiness figure in the second controversy as well, albeit this time with a shift in focus from key personnel to the plausibility of central findings in HIV/AIDS science. Despite Gallo's claims, neither his contributions and nor those of other HIV scientists were undisputed. In particular, Peter Duesberg and other AIDS denialists cast doubt on the claim that HIV (the virus) caused AIDS (the disease), as Gallo, Montagnier, Barré-Sinoussi, and the HIV/AIDS establishment claimed. Scientific reputations were at stake in this second controversy as well, but so too were claims on state purses to support treatment programs. If AIDS was not actually caused by HIV, then treatment was at the very least inappropriate and perhaps extremely dangerous.

Duesberg and other denialists argued that the correlation between HIV and AIDS was spurious, and that HIV was a benign virus, essentially a "harmless passenger" (Duesberg 1989, 1998; Cohen 1994, 1643; Specter 2007). Duesberg, a molecular biologist who did some of the earliest work on retroviruses, had not himself carried out any AIDS research.[5] Yet Duesberg's views were influential, perhaps partly because of his stature as a member of the National Academy of Sciences and recipient of prestigious scientific awards and grants. Duesberg offered alternative hypotheses, including that AIDS was caused by recreational drug use, by poverty and deprivation, or even by the anti-retroviral drug AZT. In the early days of the controversy, HIV scientists engaged with Duesberg, but as it became clear that he could not be persuaded by point-by-point refutations of his arguments or by the accumulating evidence, Duesberg's reputation as a contrarian hardened.

Although Duesberg mis-aimed his attack, elements of his conspiratorial perspective resonated in some circles. Whether or not AZT caused AIDS, drug companies had an indisputable stake in selling pharmaceuticals, and ties between scientists and pharmaceutical companies had both upstream effects on research agendas and downstream effects on drug production and provision (Angell 2005). Claims about the absolute or comparative efficacy of drugs, particularly when based on industry-sponsored studies, merited a closer look. Moreover, although Duesberg was not an ideal figurehead for those espousing anti-establishment or anti-Western approaches to science, such subaltern perspectives might have hoped to get a fuller hearing with him as an ally. Yet healthy debate can easily turn into a deeper and less responsible rejection of scientific practices and standards. In the US, frustration with the pace of AIDS research and rejection of scientific authority on the grounds that the "real experts" experiencing the disease were often not at the table (Monette 1988; Callan and Turner 1997) may have made some clinical research less efficient, for instance, when research subjects shared pills, smudging the bright line between experimental and control groups.

But that frustration also infused fresh ideas from lay participants, drew large numbers of eager research subjects into clinical trials, and intensified pressure to consult affected communities and improve FDA review procedures (Epstein 1996).[6] As the epidemic unfolded, many in the AIDS community experienced disappointments when promising drugs proved ineffective or had unacceptable side effects. Over time, AIDS activists, and particularly those who had participated in HIV science policymaking, became more supportive of science—more convinced of the utility of adhering to research protocols and waiting for the results of clinical trials. Among those activists was Robert Rafsky, whose name serves as a pseudonym for one of this book's research sites.

In other locales, though, AIDS denialism, sometimes with Duesberg's participation, led to stubborn rejection of scientific work and "Western" approaches to prevention, testing, and treatment, and an embrace of "traditional" medicines for which there was no supporting evidence (Specter 2007).[7] Many laypeople (perhaps including Thabo Mbeki, then president of South Africa) found it difficult to decide who was right. Moreover, the legacy of colonial health programs and medical experimentation on vulnerable or disadvantaged populations made many of those affected by HIV deeply suspicious of mainstream science (Crane 2013). Unethical experimentation was not simply a distant memory. New evidence about historical episodes continues to be uncovered, with just enough instances in the present to make people reluctant to participate in clinical trials or treatment programs.[8] The results, particularly in South Africa, were a stalled rollout of treatment programs, a rapid and preventable spread of the virus, and hundreds of thousands of "excess" AIDS deaths (Mbali 2004; Nattrass 2007; Chigwedere et al. 2008; Decoteau 2013; Harris 2017a).

Admittedly the patients who turned up in the HIV clinics I studied were probably predisposed to accept the legitimacy of Western medicine. Yet, even in this group, doubts surfaced episodically and reactions were sometimes tinged with skepticism about Western science and medicine. In South Africa, particularly, the clinic staff worried that patients were either substituting traditional medicines for their anti-retrovirals or mixing the two. In a particularly troubling case, a mother who had initially sought treatment for her adolescent daughter apparently changed her mind after being pressured by traditional healers. The girl's health had been improving, and she herself wanted to receive treatment. When her mother stopped picking up her drugs, asserting that the girl still had plenty, the girl's condition deteriorated quickly. Worried that the girl's "therapeutic options [were] being destroyed," the medical staff felt they had to discontinue treatment. When social workers visited the home, the mother taunted them for their acceptance of White people's medicine, adding that traditional medicines were "what's good for a Black person." As the head of the Gugu Dlamini social work team observed, "When the Minister of Health says that it's ok to use traditional medicines as well, that makes it hard for us."

Besides the troubling therapeutic disagreements between traditional healers and Western practitioners in places like South Africa, some of the "noncompliance" that so frustrated caregivers may also have resulted from an unvoiced skepticism about the efficacy of Western medicine. That skepticism may have been harder to quell when the cultural and religious commitments of Western practitioners remained uninterrogated even as traditional practices were prohibited or treated with suspicion. The presence of clergy was especially common in clinics and hospitals that received substantial support from religious organizations. Gugu Dlamini's workday began with prayer, and references to Christianity were woven into clinic activities. Although some traditional African religious practices were tolerated in the clinic and hospital, others were excluded on the grounds that they were either disruptive or harmful.

One conversation with a doctor, who seemed to be a careful and kind practitioner, led me to wonder whether some Christian religious practices might contribute to skepticism about Western science and medicine. I spent several hours with him as he saw patients. Between patients he spoke about how he understood the relationship between medicine and spirituality. Commenting that "some problems were spiritual rather than strictly medical," he explained that in some cases the blackened flesh that would usually suggest gangrene might instead be caused by witchcraft. In those cases, the appropriate course was to cast out the spirit after which the blackened flesh would clear up. He also discussed instances where people's breathing difficulties might seem to be caused by asthma or other medical ailments but were actually caused by spirits (he mentioned Kali, the Indian deity) lodged in the lungs. Once the spirits had been exorcized, the patient's respiration would improve. As his patients prepared to leave the examining room, he often suggested that they should come visit the religious organization with which he was affiliated, the site where these exorcisms occurred.

Despite the nearly universal rejection of Duesberg's views in HIV science circles, the critique of AIDS denialists could not be summarily dismissed because of the questions it raised about what makes someone an expert and what makes experts trustworthy. Where the Gallo/Montagnier controversy raised questions about what goes on in the inner sanctum of science, the denialists raised questions about how the inner sanctum is constituted. In essence, these are questions about what makes science credible. What is it about the way they do their work that gives us confidence in the findings of some scientists and efficacy of some medical practices, while doubting others? And what is it about scientific credentials and training that makes us trust the claims of some scientists and physicians, while doubting the claims of others? Both controversies had important and far-reaching implications for the trustworthiness and credibility of scientific work and medical practice, particularly in the HIV/AIDS context, and for the continuing elaboration of a regulatory system to govern clinical research, including in the five clinics.

From the Bench to the Clinic: Scientific Credibility in Clinical Trials

Concerns about personnel and procedures are especially visible elements of disputes about the credibility and trustworthiness of scientific work. Both popular and social science discussions focus on challenges to the credibility of individuals at the top of the hierarchy of scientific workers—essentially a "great man" analysis of scientific credibility. Thus we read about Charles Darwin versus Alfred Russel Wallace or, in HIV science, Robert Gallo versus Luc Montagnier. To be sure, there is some acknowledgment that science is not done solely by individuals—we may read about Luc Montagnier's collaborator Françoise Barré-Sinoussi or Robert Gallo's colleague Mikulas Popovic. But we hear remarkably little about other research team members.

For social scientists, the exclusive focus on project leaders seems surprising. A major accomplishment of science studies has been to demonstrate the overwhelmingly social character of scientific activity. As science studies scholars note, the work of science is not so much discovery as co-construction or coproduction. Scientific facts are not simply biding their time, waiting to be discovered. Without (usually) denying the objective existence of some scientific truths, science studies scholars have shown that people do not simply read facts off the world or use instruments to see what is waiting to be seen. Rather scientists have to be taught to use the instruments, to identify and name what they are seeing, to make distinctions that are anything but obvious, and to see and interpret the world in ways that speak legibly to an emerging consensus or paradigm. And that constructionist project is inevitably collaborative. "Great men" are joined by scientific peers with whom they cooperate and compete, but also by a host of usually unnamed people who collect and prepare specimens, carry out experiments, record and analyze data, file reports, manage documents, and track correspondence. The famous laboratory studies of Bruno Latour (1987), Steve Woolgar (Latour and Woolgar 1979), Karin Knorr Cetina (1981, 1999), Michael Lynch (1985), and others have thus alerted us both to the true nature of scientific work and to the complex staffing required to do science.

That science is a deeply collaborative project has implications for the credibility of science. The trustworthiness of scientific findings depends not only on the talent, integrity, and meticulousness of a project leader but on the quality and dedication of the rest of the staff. Moreover, collaborative coproduction is particularly complex in clinical trials because they often are dispersed over many sites and depend on sophisticated contributions from a host of ancillary personnel—primary care physicians, laboratory technicians, statisticians, IT staff—as well as dedicated clinical trials team members, including principal investigators (PIs), research coordinators, research nurses, regulatory affairs specialists, and quality control workers. In addition, clinical trials depend on collaboration with lay research subjects, whose participation can make or break a research project. We therefore need to ask how the process of creating trust is different for this kind of deeply collaborative work than for work that involves (or is perceived to involve) great scientists working alone.

Although scientific controversies are surely about the quality of the science and the integrity of scientists, the credibility of science also depends on how scientific work is presented to and received by audiences, as cultural sociologists would lead us to expect (Griswold 1987). In medical science, public trust is especially important, not just because costly research depends on large contributions from the public purse[9] but also because scientists need willing subjects to participate in clinical trials and confident patients to take the resulting drugs once the scientific work is complete. Yet while science and technology studies scholars have examined what people actually do when they are doing science—how they make facts and convince other scientists that they are onto something—Gieryn (1999) argues that they have not dug as deeply into the equally social process of producing "science." These phases in which scientific work is presented as science and consumed and used by nonscientists also need to be unpacked. Just as "nature outdoors underdetermines its inscriptions [by scientists]," so "upstream science substantially underdetermines the epistemic authority that marks its consumption downstream," Gieryn observes (1999, viii and ix–x).

Importantly, epistemic authority is historically contingent. How epistemic authority is constructed varies from one time and place to another, as Gieryn's case studies demonstrate. It is also more precarious in some periods and locations than others. In the world of HIV clinical research, as in many contemporary scientific fields, epistemic authority is constructed largely through a process of crafting rules for how scientific work is to be done and then assessing whether science workers have adhered to those rules. Some of the rules address questions about personnel—who is authorized to carry out particular tasks and how workers should be trained and certified. Other rules and guidelines are more procedural, specifying at a granular level exactly how scientific work is to be conducted: for example, the rules of Good Clinical Practice (GCP), rules for the ethical conduct of research (which overlap with GCP), the protocols for individual research projects, rules of major funding sources (e.g., NIH), rules for review and approval of drugs and devices (e.g., those promulgated by the FDA), and research sites' SOPs.

Formal rules can shore up credibility in multiple ways. On the one hand, formal rules may be settled summary statements about what has worked in the past, with their credibility depending on a form of replication at the level of procedures rather than full-scale studies (Freese and Peterson 2017). Such replication does not lead to publications but instead results in "craft knowledge" (Collins 1974, 2001; Mulkay 1984) passed on in rules, conventions, and standards. These kinds of rules figure prominently in clinical research protocols, with their lengthy specifications of when and how procedures should be carried out, which data should be collected and on what timetable, and which symptoms should be tracked and how their severity should be "graded." Such formalization allows people to take some things for granted and to build on others' work rather than starting from scratch (Stinchcombe 2001). On the other hand, rules may be needed to standardize work and coordinate activities, even when no strong reason supports preferring one procedure to another. Many clinic SOPs are examples of this second kind of rule. In practice, the analytic distinction between evidence-based, replicated rules and coordinating rules gets blurred in the fashionable rhetoric of "best practices," which implies that clinic rules have a strong evidentiary base that may not actually exist.[10]

These rules look universal and seem to address important concerns about patient safety, data quality, and comparability of data from multiple sites. Yet, as sociolegal scholars often point out, legal systems (including both "hard" and "soft" law) tend to favor already advantaged groups (Galanter 1974; Lempert and Sanders 1986; Edelman and Suchman 1999). Moreover, biases in written rules often are magnified as law on the books becomes law in action (Lempert and Sanders 1986; Edelman 2016). Whatever the credentials of HIV researchers and ancillary staff members and however carefully they do their work, the rules that guide their work are biased in favor of rich-country research facilities whose research practices served as the template as rules were being constructed. Rather than being fully universal, then, rules and regulations crafted in rich countries such as the US can feel like awkward transplants when deployed in the resource-constrained clinics of poorer countries. Only with additional expense and effort can these rules be adjusted to local circumstances (Klug 2002; Merry 2006a, 2006b; Bartley 2011; Petty and Heimer 2011; Heimer and Gazley 2012; Heimer and Morse 2016). But because the rules help establish epistemic authority, the poor fit and the continuing need for tinkering mean that the credibility of poorer clinics and those who work in them is automatically questioned. Seen in this light, the exaggerated, ultra-careful rule following of clinics "in the boonies" (as one Cha-on Suesum worker put it) looks like a sensible risk-reduction strategy.

Accountability in Clinical Research: Monitoring Regimes and the Reshaping of Clinic Work

Depending on whom one asks, clinical research is either a key contributor to improvements in health and welfare, an engine for producing vast wealth for pharmaceutical companies, or an unethical system in which disadvantaged people are induced to participate in research that ultimately benefits other social groups. How one assesses the benefits of clinical research surely also affects one's perspective on where to focus regulatory attention. Regulations and incentive systems might be designed, for instance, to increase the speed and efficiency of research, reduce the self-interested behavior of pharmaceutical companies and researchers, decrease the exploitation of research subjects, or require that research be relevant to the needs of those who serve as research subjects.[11] Given the diversity of these regulatory objectives, a sprawling regulatory apparatus has grown up to govern clinical research and hold research organizations and researchers accountable.

In contemporary US medical research and healthcare, professional accountability, economic accountability, and political accountability all play a role (Emanuel and Emanuel 1996).[12] In principle, we might want medical scientists and caregivers to be held to standards developed and enforced by professional peers (professional accountability); to be held accountable in a market, with investors, payers, and patients deciding which services to buy, from whom, and at what price (economic accountability); and to be required to answer to a larger community, in which caregivers, researchers, patients, research subjects, and other interested parties interact as "citizens" for decisions about the package of services to be offered or the priority of research questions (political accountability).

Contemporary accountability regimes often use rankings to create competitions among organizations (or subunits or individuals) and to induce improvements in performance. But as Espeland and Sauder (2016) note in their research on law school rankings, leaders throw themselves into the competition, attempting to rise or at least not to fall in the rankings. However sympathetic one might be to improving performance, using resources wisely, and being responsive to key constituencies, it is hard to ignore the negative effects of ranking systems: distortion of production systems as organizations devote disproportionate resources to producing anything that improves ranking, increased anxiety and decreased morale among organizational participants, and a flocking of clients to highly ranked organizations or individuals even when differences in rankings are small. Although many accountability regimes work through rankings and competition, others, like the institutional review board (IRB) regimes governing human subjects research (Bledsoe et al. 2007; Heimer and Petty 2010; Babb 2020), work by tracking compliance with rules, imposing punishments for infractions, or requiring remediation when rules are violated. As one might expect, both kinds of accountability regimes foster reactivity, although the distortions produced by the two systems are somewhat different.

Accountability in HIV clinical research includes both ranking regimes—focused especially on success in enrolling research subjects—and regimes organized around adherence to rules. Both forms of accountability are at least partly responses to external pressures, namely the concerns about the legitimacy of science discussed above. They are institutionalized means of solidifying credibility in the face of multifaceted skepticism—skepticism that spilled over into research funding, research administration, and research activities. In effect, the skepticism of outsiders was answered with accountability regimes that brought skepticism inside. Outsiders might think that some clinics were likely doing a better job than others, but the research networks could demonstrate that they had already taken account of that, not only tracking performance but requiring clinical trials units (CTUs), which might be which might be a single clinic or a lead clinic along with its subsites, to explain their failures and provide plans for improvement. And if outsiders might have doubts about whether research clinics had collected and reported their data properly, the research networks had thought about that as well and scrutinized clinic work. Moreover, responding to the scrutiny of external monitors, many clinics created internal quality assurance and quality control (QA/QC) systems that brought skepticism into the clinic itself.

But these two forms of accountability do not impinge equally on all clinical research facilities. Although all five clinics were engaged in research, they had varying relations to the world of clinical research (some clinics simply did more research than others) and to research funders (some clinics' ties to funders were mediated by research collaborators). In the clinics I studied, accountability was largely focused on producing data that met the requirements of the research project and was therefore primarily organized around complying with rules. The competitions of ranking regimes, focused especially on recruiting and retaining research subjects, directly affected only a few of the clinics but had indirect effects on others.

Researchers at Robert Rafsky closely tracked how they compared with other research clinics, and their discussions about indicators and rankings tell us much about how accountability processes work when they are not quite so narrowly focused on a single number such as a rank. At Robert Rafsky, successes and failures in enrolling research subjects were discussed at every weekly research meeting. Enrollment figures were aggregated by the research network to produce rankings of CTUs.[13] As new figures became available, staff discussed where they stood in relation to other prominent research clinics, strategizing about how participation in particular studies might affect their place in these rankings. Rankings mattered both because of the prestige associated with being a highly ranked CTU and because rankings had some effect on clinic resources.

Although a clinic or CTU's rank depended on enrollments, the relationship between the two was not straightforward because enrollments were weighted by the difficulty of locating, screening, enrolling, and retaining patients for specific studies. But the funds allocated to clinics did not correlate in any exact way with their rank. Some funds were associated with studies, with part of the monies allocated simply for a site's participation in a study and the rest varying with the number of research subjects the site enrolled for that study. But other funds were allocated simply by virtue of a clinic's status as a CTU in a particular research network.[14] The networks episodically ran recompetitions to determine which clinics and CTUs would be allowed to participate in research organized by the network. Research clinics thought carefully about whether to participate in particular studies, considering how much each enrollment counted (generally, one point per recruit, but in one tempting study, five points per recruit), whether the clinic had any comparative advantage in recruiting research subjects, and the balance between the costs of gearing up for a study and the income and other benefits from participation. Study size also mattered—no one wanted to retool for a study that would enroll only one or two subjects per site, unless the study was unusually prestigious, lushly funded, helped key patient groups (e.g., with access to promising experimental treatments), or asked particularly important scientific questions.

That CTUs were evaluated on multiple criteria was clear from the thick sheaf of papers included in the annual site performance evaluation for Robert Rafsky's CTU. The AIDS Clinical Trials Group (ACTG) Site Evaluation Subcommittee conducted the evaluation, in which accrual played a significant role, though it was by no means the only indicator considered. Of the twenty-six indicators, only twelve were related to accrual (including cost per accrual and accrual of subjects from minority groups).[15] In addition to commenting on the site's performance on the twenty-six indicators, the document included graphs showing the performance of all thirty-four CTUs on each of these indicators. After all this comparison, though, the final result was not a single number but a list of indicators on which the unit met the standard, performed especially well, or failed to meet the standard. Units that failed to meet a standard were required to respond in writing with explanations and plans for remedial action, transforming the rankings competition into a hybrid rankings-and-rule-following accountability regime.

In the other four clinics, accountability pressures were even less tethered to rankings. Although Cha-on Suesum Clinic also was deeply concerned with its standing in the research world and was intensely aware of the disadvantages it and other non-American clinics faced in US-based competitions, its staff members had little to say about rankings. Instead they worried about what kinds of studies they could participate in and what tasks they were assigned in the collective work of research—whether their collaborators were interested only in their "hands" or also valued their "heads" (see Gazley 2011, 48–49). Philly Lutaaya staff were less overtly engaged in the competition, perhaps because they competed as the junior partner of a prominent US research university. Bobbi Campbell staff did track enrollment figures, but because they were a subsite rather than a CTU, the main responsibility for tracking their standing lay with the lead clinic. Gugu Dlamini was less involved in research but was affiliated with staff at a very prominent US institution, and its standing in the world of research depended much more on this affiliation than on its own capacity to attract research funding or research enrollments. But clinic staff nevertheless were careful to comply with research rules because they believed their data would be a "gold mine" and they wanted to be able to vouch for their quality.

The evidence from this group of research clinics may tell us less about the anxieties associated with rising, staying in place, or falling in the rankings and more about pressure to keep on top of compliance work. Perhaps because clinic evaluation and ranking were focused on regulation and governance more than on marketing, anxiety was less about falling in the rankings than about explaining failures, undergoing thorough examinations of records and procedures, and producing plans for improvement. To be sure, there is some competition over which clinics will be invited to participate in clinical trials and how much funding they will receive. But more important is the scrutiny of a clinic's products. Are their data clean and reliable? If not, scientific findings might be challenged, patients harmed, FDA approvals delayed or derailed, or drugs recalled. Client choice plays only a minor role and is not affected by clinic rankings in any direct way. Admittedly, patients do sometimes decide where to enroll as research subjects and may seek care in clinics with especially strong, well-funded research programs, but such competition among clinics is rare and is essentially limited to US clinics. As a general matter, clinics enroll research subjects in a geographical catchment area and do not attempt to entice research subjects to choose their clinic over a competitor's.

The work of Theodore Porter and of Michael Power helps us think about what these accountability regimes are trying to accomplish. Porter (1986, 1995) focuses particularly on the production of uniformity, Power (1997, 2003) on pressures for accountability. Porter argues that pressures for standardization, quantification, and curbs on discretion are likely to be especially intense in places where elites and experts have been distrusted (as has occurred in the US). Pressures for rules and protocols also increase when experts arrive at embarrassingly different answers or when external bodies can take advantage of dissensus. All of these pressures exist in clinical trials. In the wake of the research scandals and the patients' rights movements, demands for transparency, uniformity, and accountability have increased. One result has been an increase in the extent to which medicine is governed by formal rules.

In clinical trials, pressures for uniformity are especially intense because of the dispersion of research over a large number of sites. Despite repeated attempts to produce uniformity, uniformity remains elusive. When patients are given a fixed dosage of an experimental drug, the hope is that their bodies will react in similar (if not identical) ways. Yet how bodies respond to medication depends on a host of things, including, most fundamentally, body weight. Doses are generally adjusted for children but are less likely to take account of the very substantial weight differences among adults. Uniformity in dose, then, occurs at the expense of uniformity in ratios of drugs to body weight. This can be quite consequential with relatively new drugs. Thai researchers, for instance, hypothesized that differences in body mass might explain why Thai patients experienced more side effects than Western patients receiving anti-retroviral drugs (Gazley 2011).

But it is not just research subjects' bodies that differ. Other features of the scientific situation are likely to differ as well, making adherence to rules difficult. In accountability regimes, though, following rules exactly is what is required, and monitors visit frequently to check on adherence. This situation puts staff in a bind. On the one hand, their job is to follow rules. On the other, as highly trained professionals, their charge is to know when the rules are inappropriate and modifications of procedures are therefore warranted even if not explicitly permitted.[16]

Monitoring regimes have disproportionately focused on one side of that equation, creating elaborate auditing systems. In effect, these monitoring regimes have institutionalized skepticism. Subjected to intense scrutiny, clinic staff struggle to convince monitors that they are trustworthy, attempting to demonstrate that they follow the rules as closely as possible, deviate only in very minor ways, understand the purpose of the rules, and believe in the scientific objectives. Moreover, as will become clear below, staff take pains to demonstrate that their deviations are rule- or norm-governed rather than haphazard—that any flexibility is orderly flexibility.

Just as ranking systems end up reshaping the behavior of those being ranked, so monitoring regimes reshape the activity of monitored clinics and the daily work of people subjected to the skeptical gaze of auditors (Power 1997, 2003; Espeland and Vannebo 2007; Espeland and Sauder 2009, 2016; Heimer and Espeland, n.d.). We know that people are now spending considerable time doing compliance work—demonstrating that they have met requirements and complied with regulations. But because the fundamental issue here is whether anyone can trust their performances and representations of themselves, much of that effort is devoted to demonstrating trustworthiness.

The remainder of the chapter examines accountability regimes operating in clinical research settings as regimes of institutionalized skepticism. It asks what specifically organizations, groups, and individuals do to establish trust in regimes of institutionalized skepticism. My contention is that the establishment of trust—and it does occur—requires work on several fronts simultaneously. In effect, clinics create elaborate systems designed to reassure skeptics at each point where questions might arise. And although critics can be reassured, their confidence in a clinic and its workers (and, thus, in the clinic's data) must be continually refreshed. Trust has a limited lifespan because institutionalized skepticism introduces fresh skeptics into the system episodically as personnel are added or rotated between sites. And just as organizational life can be distorted by too much attention to ranking systems, so aberrations also arise when people believe that others distrust them unfairly.

Institutionalized Skepticism, Evidentiary Packages, and the Construction of Trustworthy Data

Institutionalized skepticism is grounded in an assumption that a carefully constructed and rigorously enacted system of mandated reports and audits will yield trustworthy assessments of the quality of the data and of those producing the data, ultimately increasing the trustworthiness of the science itself. Yet there are limits to what can be accomplished through rules, reports, and audits, not least because of the practical constraint that auditors cannot distrust everything and everyone. For this reason, auditors need to figure out what and whom they can trust and therefore how they should structure their work, allocate their time, and focus their attention. For clinic staff members facing an audit, the corresponding challenge is to figure out how to convince research monitors or other auditors of their data's trustworthiness.

The research programs of these five clinics are highly structured variants of treatment programs. Much of the day-to-day work is done by specially trained research nurses, also called study nurses. Patients are enrolled in trials as subjects, assigned randomly to experimental or control arms, and scheduled for a series of study visits over the duration of the research project (several months to several years). For each study visit, the protocol specifies physical exams to be conducted, blood samples to be drawn, questionnaires to be administered, and medications to be dispensed and adjusted. After visits, study nurses complete the case report forms (CRFs) and other documentation. Often, data are collected in many clinics simultaneously and pooled for statistical testing to establish safety and efficacy. In clinical trials of new drugs, study records may be submitted as part of an application to the FDA, the key gatekeeper for both US and international pharmaceutical markets. Both government and industry sponsors place a premium on flawless documentation and periodically send research monitors, whose work is described more fully below, to examine clinic records for accuracy and compliance with protocols and the rules of GCP.[17]

Commenting on the ubiquity of regulatory oversight, one research physician at Philly Lutaaya observed that "with quarterly monitor visits and five studies, we basically always have monitors here." But there are several distinct types of oversight. Besides the "monitoring" of research projects by external regulators and the "site visits" to clinic treatment programs, healthcare organizations also episodically underwent "accreditation reviews." The work of these external evaluators was supplemented by clinics themselves. Responding to the pressure to pass muster, they created or shored up internal QA/QC programs and hired data managers and, particularly in Uganda and Thailand, internal study monitors.

Research monitors conduct inspections to assure the integrity of clinical trial data. Monitors spend most of their time going through CRFs and "source documents" such as medical records[18] to check whether nurses gathered mandated data and dispensed the right medications. They also verify that symptoms are graded, recorded correctly, and properly followed up. They check dates and signatures on forms, including records of when and by whom errors were corrected. And they carefully inspect regulatory documents such as informed consent forms.

Monitors are typically US or European nationals employed by international contract research organizations, objective third parties hired by research sponsors such as the NIH or pharmaceutical companies to ensure that study data will pass muster with entities like the FDA. Arriving at the clinic with rolling suitcases, monitors looked like they might be preparing for a lengthy trip. The suitcases are loaded with books of general rules, miniaturized research protocols, forms to use in their work, and lists of files to review and items to check—not exactly light reading. At each monitoring visit (typically one to three days), monitors review a portion of the records, conduct a formal debriefing, and eventually produce a written report (submitted to the clinic and the study sponsor).

Were it possible to have entirely trustworthy and competent people carrying out research, the entire edifice would, in theory, be unnecessary. Such a possibility seems remote in a world with incentives for dishonesty and researchers who may not know each other personally even when they work on the same study. Researchers may face conflicts of interest because they earn fees as speakers or consultants or have financial stakes in companies and products related to their research. They may also be concerned about their reputations, vying for the right to claim precedence on important discoveries. More mundanely, PIs are likely to worry about research funding, which may support the whole complement of affiliates, including core researchers, administrators, nurses, social workers, and postdoctoral fellows that a research program employs. Moreover, the overhead from a research project helps support university research infrastructure. That means there is considerable incentive both to do things correctly—because that ensures the continuity of the enterprise—and to cut corners (or worse) when the funding program is threatened and a few "minor" misrepresentations might patch things up. Everyone is aware of these temptations and can tell a story or two about someone who behaved dishonestly (see, e.g., Heimer and Gazley 2012, 853–54).

In clinical research, trustworthiness is constructed as a layered system with the layers necessitated by the institutionalized obligation and thoroughly inculcated inclination to be (or appear to be) suspicious of each presentation of evidence, whether that evidence is the data, the source material from which data are extracted, accompanying notes and explanations, or even oral discussions and justifications. In essence, the assumption is that the trustworthiness of an enterprise is increased with each additional layer of evidence and with the cost and difficulty entailed in manufacturing false evidence that remains consistent with previous elements of the evidentiary package.[19] Each layer of evidence brings an additional opportunity for inspectors to interrogate the evidence and those presenting it.[20] Just as Latour and Woolgar (1979) argued that facticity in science is established by surviving repeated challenges, so here the trustworthiness of a clinic's data is similarly established by surviving repeated grilling as one layer after another is subjected to skeptical review.

The interlocking parts of this layered system, as summarized in table 5.1, include trustworthy rules and routines, and even subroutines for deciding when modifications were acceptable; trustworthy training, certification, and accreditation programs; and procedures for creating trustworthy records. These layers and the people responsible for them address different components of trustworthiness—different ways that a research program might prove deficient, each of which also represents a distinct avenue to dishonesty and a distinct site for verification. In each of these layers, however, it is neither possible nor advisable to create systems of rigid adherence. Thus, as discussed below, the layered system included a fourth element: the clinics either drew on or developed systems of orderly flexibility to maintain trust even when small deviations were needed, either because of ill-fitting rules or because things had gone awry. Moreover, additional elements were added serially to these three core layers as accountability pressures escalated, for instance, when clinics had difficulty convincing outsiders that their work had been carried out competently and with integrity. The complexity of this interlocking system helps explain why it was hard for anyone to think about what all these rules added up to and why even the monitors, specialists in rule enforcement, had trouble tracking the details and felt they needed to come prepared with rolling suitcases stuffed with miniaturized rule books.

TABLE 5.1. Constructing Trustworthy Data: Elements of Layered Systems

	WHAT LAYER ACCOMPLISHES	EXAMPLES
Rules, Routines and Schemas	Creates plans to standardize clinic work	Clinical guidelines Research project protocols GCP SOPs Charts for grading symptoms for reporting AEs and SAEs
Trustworthy Training	Builds on normal professional training to produce workers who can be expected to understand assigned tasks and have skills to perform them	IRB training Special training for specific clinical trials Continuing education sessions on selected topics Remedial training sessions as needed
Trustworthy Records	Accurate, complete, verifiable data Data adequate for submission to FDA as element of drug approval process	Checking CRFs against original sources Error corrections with complete and legible trail of corrections Design and use of appropriate forms and cheat sheets Removal of "distracting" information from core records during inspections
Orderly Flexibility and Respect for Norms	Acknowledges that even with excellent planning, unforeseen circumstances will arise Portrays gap-filling solutions as thoughtful, methodical	Two methods: (1) Consultation with colleagues or with "authority" (e.g., protocol team) to get consensus on how to deal with gap (2) Demonstrations of respect for norms to signal intention to follow rules whenever possible and as closely as possible and to return to strict rule following after resolving gap

TRUSTWORTHY RULES, ROUTINES, SCHEMAS: PRODUCING UNIFORM WORK PLANS

It is the trustworthiness of routines that makes it possible for workers to say for sure what they did as they produced, gathered, and manipulated data, and to provide convincing evidence to others, including distant colleagues, skeptical monitors, dubious regulators, and critical reviewers of journal submissions. And because rules are seen as essential to producing trustworthy performances, the production of rules becomes an important focus of organizations conducting clinical research.

The trustworthiness of rules and routines depends on strategic combinations of standardization and variation. The scientifically significant part of the package of clinical research "legal system" is spelled out in a research protocol carefully prepared by the protocol team to test key hypotheses about new medications or therapies while holding everything else constant. Clinical research protocols necessarily vary from one study to another because they are testing potential advances at the leading edge of medical science. At the same time, though, this variation among protocols is combined with standardization across the research sites conducting a study so data from multiple sites can be pooled. Each research protocol is intended to govern only the activities associated with a particular research project and therefore to apply only to those involved in that study and only for the duration of that project. But during the period and for the people it is intended to govern, the protocol is applied very strictly. Adherence to protocols is absolutely fundamental to modern clinical research, especially when studies must recruit research subjects with unusual combinations of traits to demonstrate the efficacy of experimental drugs or other therapies. Clinic staff may find it challenging to adhere to protocols if those protocols make too many assumptions about clinic routines or clinic resources. For this reason, protocols specify only core procedures and make sure to provision research clinics so that they all have the materials and equipment needed for a particular study (Petty and Heimer 2011).

The objective of uniformity is different for protocols than for other kinds of rules such as SOPs. Protocols are intended to produce uniformity across sites; other rules more often aim to produce uniformity within a site. These more mundane and less scientifically significant parts of research work are often encapsulated in SOPs. SOPs are often standardized across studies, but can be allowed to vary somewhat from one site to the next. SOPs can be adopted for a clinic as a whole or for a particular study. Often both kinds of SOPs are in place.

Like much of the machinery of accountability regimes, SOPs are a peculiarly Western phenomenon. Because the US plays such a dominant role in global medical research, its research practices are adopted by or imposed on researchers in many other countries. This export of US conventions is not always smooth, though (Heimer and Morse 2016). In other countries where written SOPs may not be the customary way of standardizing work practices, imported off-the-shelf SOPs may fit poorly. Thus, although US researchers may be able to insert off-the-shelf SOPs into their proposals and work routines, research organizations in other parts of the world may need to begin by reshaping SOPs to make them serviceable. Without such adjustments, researchers may be unable to follow SOPs, and the resulting deviations may bring flurries of questions from research monitors or expand the final error lists in monitoring reports. Monitors might wonder whether researchers' practices were shaped by some alternative standard or simply varied in an unregulated and unpredictable fashion. Especially suspicious monitors might even wonder whether researchers were attempting to conceal something. Did staff members simply need additional training, or were infractions so serious that staff members should be replaced and data discarded? In the extreme, should the site be banned from participation in future research projects?

The existence of SOPs is thus taken as a first piece of evidence that staff members are doing their work in an orderly fashion. But although research places a premium on uniformity, the policy on SOPs reveals a more flexible stance than might be expected. A clinic often can get by with a variant of the prescribed practice as long as that variant is incorporated into its local SOPs. Of course, this tolerance of codified variations does not extend to the key manipulations being investigated in the research, where much less variability is acceptable.

In essence, much as Thompson (1967) argued that organizations protect their technical cores, the closer clinic work is to the core scientific question, the stronger the insistence on uniformity. How much and what kind of variation can be tolerated depends on how those variations in procedure might affect essential measurements. Research nurses and other staff members carefully study the research protocols of the studies they work on and often receive formal training on the protocol. Protocols provide details about schedules and procedures for core manipulations of the study and exhaustive instructions for making biometric measurements and collecting and processing specimens, sometimes even insisting that specimens be sent to research laboratories rather than being processed in hospital labs. But for less scientifically significant matters—measurements that are not the focus of the research but are instead checks on the overall health of the research subject—what matters is that the clinic does its work in a consistent way rather than that all clinics use identical procedures. That consistency will allow a clinic to detect changes over time, for instance, in a patient's weight or the results of tuning fork tests for peripheral neuropathy. Because some comparisons require consistency across clinics while others require only consistency within a clinic, codified variations are acceptable for some routines even though rigid standardization is required in others.

An example from Robert Rafsky illustrates this point about when variability can be tolerated. One research monitor uncovered a number of relatively small errors. Most were trivial mistakes that occurred only once. But the monitor did note a pattern of "systematic errors" associated with how patients were weighed. Were Robert Rafsky research nurses weighing patients without their shoes, as the research protocol specified, the monitor wondered. The records were not clear, so the monitor asked for more documentation on this point. "It's enough to drive you crazy," the monitor remarked to one research nurse, acknowledging the nitpickiness of the research protocol and her monitoring. Near the end of their conversation, the monitor returned to the question about how research subjects were being weighed. If the clinic were to revise its SOP to specify how clinic patients were to be weighed, she observed, this SOP could be used to fill the documentation gap without creating additional work for the nurses. Without such an SOP, research nurses would need to note each time whether patients had removed their shoes before being weighed. Because monitors accept an SOP as evidence that staff members are following a routine—though why they expect better adherence to an SOP than to the research protocol is not entirely clear—a clinic often can get by with a variant of the prescribed practice as long as that variant is incorporated into its local SOPs. Because the objective here was to track whether patients had lost or gained weight, consistency in weighing procedure mattered more than which procedure was used.

The premium placed on having established procedures was no secret. As a condition of funding, the NIH requires that sites have SOPs. For US clinics, this requirement is unproblematic. The SOP requirement does add a layer of constraint, but because clinics already have SOPs in place, little additional work is required. Although several staff members at Robert Rafsky did complain about needing to produce additional SOPs because of the requirements of ACTG, this seemed to be more a matter of compiling existing SOPs than starting from scratch.

In contrast, clinics in poorer countries may not have SOPs in place. The Ugandan clinic was a case in point. Although Philly Lutaaya researchers had been collaborating with US researchers for more than a decade and a half by the time I arrived, they had continued to operate less formally than many US institutions. When an NIH grant mandated that Philly Lutaaya have a full suite of SOPs, clinic staff discovered that they had some room for maneuver because NIH rules allowed them to tailor SOPs to their site. This discovery allayed concerns about the poor fit between the model SOPs and Ugandan working conditions. Ugandan clinic staff needed to be consistent in how they did their work, of course, but except for those scientifically sensitive procedures laid out in the study protocol, they did not need to do the work exactly as it would be done in a richer country. In fact, insisting that staff use off-the-shelf SOPs would have undermined Philly Lutaaya staff members' capacity to work consistently.

Still, when Philly Lutaaya staff embarked on their SOP writing project, no one imagined just how much time and effort would be required. But the resulting rules fit the clinic well because they were responsive to the local context and allowed staff to adjust for worrisome deficiencies. For example, until they revised their SOP, Philly Lutaaya staff had found it difficult to comply with rules about serious adverse event (SAE) reporting, a grave matter given the emphasis placed on timely reporting of SAEs in clinical research. SAEs were being identified by staff but were not being reported because the existing SOP was unclear about who held that responsibility. After the new SOP assigned that responsibility to an SAE coordinator, the problem was solved.

Although I had expected Ugandan staff to chafe against ill-fitting rules, in the long run Philly Lutaaya staff were more satisfied with their clinic's rules than were their counterparts in other clinics. Summarizing the local attitude, one staff member approvingly commented that "the SOPs ensure that we're doing things in a planned way." When SOPs were adjusted to local conditions, staff members could work in the prescribed orderly way. Before these adjustments, clinic staff either worked haphazardly as they vainly attempted to follow ill-fitting rules or they appeared to be practicing haphazardly when they were in fact adhering to an alternative routine that had not been fully documented. For Philly Lutaaya staff, then, the time spent crafting bespoke SOPs was time well spent.

Clinic staff are, of course, accustomed to working with rules. Indeed, as medical professionals, they assume their work should follow the norms of their disciplines. What is uncomfortable for them, though, is the extensiveness of the rules, the assumption that everything has to be governed by a rule, and the continual introduction of new rules or variants of rules. As one employee of an affiliated clinical research center explained, "You look at any of these regulations at times and you go, 'Were they really thinking?' . . . Because what you get is . . . what I call a second-grade syndrome where you get a second grader or a third grader and there was somebody in the back of the classroom who was bad and the teacher said, 'If so and so doesn't sit down, we're all going to lose recess.' And so the rule for the class, the really rigid, kind of overkill, rule was instituted for that one bad person. And that seems to be what often happens. It's that we've had somebody be bad and . . . the response to that is to make a rule that is just kind of crazy-making for everybody."

This proliferation of rules means that staff members do not experience rules as being all the same. One Robert Rafsky nurse alerted us to this variability as she described a typical study visit. Referring to research practices as "what they want" nurses to do, she said that nurses frequently needed to check study documentation to figure out what was required. Nurses checked study protocols to determine what forms to complete at particular visits, how to instruct patients to prepare for upcoming study visits (was this a "fasting visit"?), or how to adjust a medication dose (a task assigned to physicians in normal medical care) according to a study's dosing schedule. In contrast, discussing practices associated with ordinary nursing work, such as collecting blood, the nurse said "you have to," "you always," or "you must." The nurse's shift in language signaled that although the rules of nursing had become naturalized (Douglas 1986), many rules of the research world were still part of the foreground—unnatural, convoluted ways "they" want things done rather than the normal way members of a practice community do things as a matter of course.

In their speech and patterns of work, clinic staff thus distinguish the internalized norms of medical practice, on the one hand, from the externally imposed and somewhat artificial rules of research protocols and SOPs, on the other. Although people follow the internalized norms of practice simply by virtue of having been trained as a nurse, doctor, or phlebotomist, they do not automatically and without thought adhere to many of the rules of research. Increases in the number of externally imposed (not yet naturalized) rules therefore necessarily create more work because of the need to doublecheck the rules. Over time, some of the rules of research do come to seem more natural, and indeed, one objective of Philly Lutaaya's extensive QA/QC program seemed to have been to make research practices feel more like "we always" rather than "what they want."

It was because the rules of research had not been fully internalized, though, that research required the frequent and extensive training to which I now turn.

TRUSTWORTHY TRAINING: PRODUCING UNIFORM WORKERS

It is an inescapable fact that research protocols and SOPs have to be implemented by people and that the people introduce a sometimes helpful, sometimes destructive variability even when the rules themselves are invariant. The variability people bring can be helpful because intelligent adaptation—orderly flexibility—can save the day when the unexpected occurs or when local circumstances fail to meet assumptions embedded in protocols. But variability can harm when workers have not understood the protocol or mastered essential techniques. Mandated training is intended to address both mastery and variability, ensuring the first and curbing the second. With trained workers, drawing on their general knowledge and following the protocol and the SOPs, clinical research can be trusted, or at least that is the hope.

Clinical research necessarily requires people to do novel things. But only if these novel tasks are performed—or appear to be performed—in an orderly, replicable way will any new knowledge be accepted as legitimate scientific advance. To be sure, the work of clinical research builds on existing foundations of standard professional training.[21] But even experienced researchers find that the work is just different enough and the need for precision so urgent that some additional training is needed to ensure that they understand the rules and have requisite skills for each new research protocol. Unlike clinical practice, research work requires elaborate screening of potential participants, informed consent procedures during enrollment, and meticulous recordkeeping, all tasks that staff members get trained to perform correctly. In addition to these elements, more arcane protocol-specific training may be required for skin-pull measures, neuro reflex testing, and so forth.

In all five clinics, my team and I witnessed nonstop training, including continuing education sessions, GCP training for new staff members, training on new research protocols, training on new equipment and new software, training on new forms, conflict of interest training, training for IRB certification or recertification, AE training, and training on new QA/QC programs. And that list is by no means exhaustive. We observed clinic staff members training each other. We also observed clinic staff members preparing training materials and conducting training sessions for outside groups. At Cha-on Suesum, for instance, staff members conducted regional training programs for staff members from Cambodian and Vietnamese institutions aspiring to partner with international clinical research teams. Likewise, Robert Rafsky staffers put together packets of training materials for affiliated African sites and traveled to those sites to conduct in-person training sessions on clinical research practices. As they prepared to train people in other countries, staff members at both Cha-on Suesum and Robert Rafsky were mindful of the need to adjust SOPs and training materials for the local context of their trainees. They wanted to avoid asking people to do things that were actually impossible given local resource constraints, professional training, and previous work experience. Training was so integral to clinic life that clinics in poorer countries, already struggling to keep positions filled, carefully staggered absences for training to avoid disrupting clinic work.[22]

Staff reactions to the frequent training ranged from appreciative to annoyed. Although they often resented the time required for training, as long as new protocols and equipment required new procedures, clinic staff preferred to undergo training rather than find themselves penalized for making mistakes. And for workers in poorer countries, the per diems that came with offsite training were valuable supplements to meager household budgets (Smith 2003; Swidler and Watkins 2008; Watkins and Swidler 2013) Beyond a certain point, though, training could seem redundant and silly, perhaps more designed to protect the institution from liability than to teach new skills. Moreover, in some non-US sites, all this training and proceduralism was sometimes seen as a reflection of US preferences rather than what the clinics would choose for themselves. At Philly Lutaaya, for instance, staff members discussed how the rigid proceduralism of SOPs sometimes jeopardized good studies and good care. When there were few genuinely new skills to be learned, staff members sometimes became irritated or impatient, grousing that the seemingly endless attention to training and rules interfered with getting on with the work. Yet staff members generally expressed their dissatisfaction through humor and muted resistance rather than outright rebellion.

Even when training seemed largely irrelevant, staff members generally went along, if a bit grudgingly, as an episode at Robert Rafsky Clinic shows. Following an IRB proclamation that all researchers participating in federally funded studies had to be trained in research ethics, the medical school with which Robert Rafsky was affiliated was requiring all research staff to complete the University of Miami's online modules. Robert Rafsky staff members decided to prepare for these tests as a group. Introducing the upcoming training for IRB recertification as "a necessary evil," one staff member observed dryly that even though the doctors had already trained them on this material, "the IRB also feels the need to train you." Staff members snickered as he noted that the material was at an eighth-grade level. An administrator did much of the legwork for the review sessions, downloading the modules and assigning the research team's nurses, doctors, and support staff to walk the group through the material and the associated quizzes. Because the "biomedical course" included a module on social science research, even I was given an assignment. Most staff members expressed some cynicism about this extensive review and retesting process while signaling their support for ethical research. Staff members joked about selling the answers to the doctors who failed to show up for review sessions they were supposed to run, cleared their throats loudly to signal that the correct answer was being read, reminded colleagues that test-taking skills were as important as content, and grumbled about statute numbers and acronyms. Mixed in with the levity, though, were serious discussions—not about statute numbers, of course, but about the ethical dilemmas that actually seemed relevant to the clinic's research. Research staff reflected on which ways of recruiting were ethical. If study nurses did clinic duty and so were caregivers as well as researchers, could they legitimately approach patients about participating in studies? They talked through what "coercion" meant when patients could get the newest drugs only by participating in clinical trials and wondered how they should think about the incentive effects of providing free medications for people who lacked health insurance.

Redundant training was not the only problem, though. Mandatory training sometimes missed its mark and even misled because it corresponded so poorly with actual research tasks. As one Robert Rafsky research nurse explained, "lots of times it's not anything like what you're really going to be doing." This nurse was being trained on an electrocardiogram (EKG) machine supplied by the industry sponsor. Because it differed from the equipment used at Robert Rafsky, she had to adjust procedures so they fit the locally available EKG. And because the instructions assumed nurses would input data directly into the computer—which nurses rarely did—she had to go into the system to compose a list of the data she would need to gather before conducting the study visits.

Such adjustments were even more elaborate and time consuming in resource-constrained countries where studies routinely made inappropriate assumptions about what equipment would be available. At Philly Lutaaya, for instance, even blood pressure kits and otoscopes were in short supply. In one meeting about a newly developed QA/QC program, a staff member urged her QA/QC colleagues to remember that even when staff received good training, features of the work environment could make it hard to correctly implement the routines they were taught: "If people don't have any place to sit while they do their work, they are less likely to fill out forms correctly or to check them. If there is not a clock, they can't document the time if they don't themselves own watches. If there is not a locking cabinet, they can't store their work securely. You can't tell people not to leave forms in the pocket of the binder if you don't supply them with a hole punch so that they can prepare the forms to file in the right sections of the binder."[23]

In both research and treatment programs, staff members in poorer countries repeatedly found that they lacked the resources to implement the routines they had just learned. But the situation of research and treatment programs were somewhat different. First, because research protocols are about testing new drugs, therapies, and procedures, research programs necessarily required more frequent training and retraining than occurred in treatment programs. Despite that, the gap between needed and available resources was somewhat smaller in research programs because sponsors were careful to supply the tools and resources required to do the research (Petty and Heimer 2011). Because they drew up their plans with richer countries in mind, though, research sponsors might nevertheless not fill all the gaps.

In research clinics, then, training seemed to be a "go-to solution" whenever problems arose. Staff members were required to undergo training or retraining at Philly Lutaaya when there were widespread data problems, at Cha-on Suesum when the clinic received a devastatingly bad monitoring report,[24] and at Robert Rafsky when reimbursements dropped and administrators concluded that physicians did not know how to write medical records that were adequate for billing (Heimer 2008).

Training requirements were especially intense in poorer countries' clinics, and were generally intended to introduce research culture and skills to sites where research sponsors and heads of research teams either believed they were lacking or thought others would believe they were lacking. "We're research experienced, they're not," explained a US regulatory affairs specialist working at Philly Lutaaya. In some cases, though, apparent lapses seemed likely to have arisen not because local staff were poorly trained but because they had originally been taught different rules. A subsite of Cha-on Suesum, for instance, was cited for leaving patient names on files. Although this is a clear violation of US research rules, my team and I were repeatedly told that Thai rules permitted inclusion of names. Walking us through specimen labeling conventions, one doctor explained that such labels must have two unique identifiers. Noting the three identifiers on the label he had in hand—date of birth, patient identification number, and name—he added that using the name may seem unusual, but that in Thailand "no-one cares so they use it on everything." A subsequent encounter confirmed that inclusion of names was routine when a patient brought along specimen tubes all labeled with her hospital ID number, research clinic study number, and name. Pointing to the photocopy of a patient's hospital identification card, the physician again noted that inclusion of names and other identifying information is entirely routine in Thailand. Acknowledging the difference between US and Thai practices, he laughingly added that "this would be completely unacceptable in the US, but is ok in Thailand because the patients don't care."

When they were convinced it was necessary, though, staff members did manage to unlearn old practices. Another example from Cha-on Suesum illustrates the arduous process of retraining to eliminate old practices. Pointing to the many "strike-outs" in a file, one foreign staff member explained that these were actually an important achievement. Initially the Thai nurses had not understood the importance of being able to follow the logic of a change in the record—the corrected entry, but also what was recorded initially and who made the change. Wishing to produce neat records, the research nurses "went around with great pots of white-out, not understanding that this was wrong." He joined the project specifically to provide the repeated training necessary to change such practices and was therefore justifiably proud of the messier but more complete record of original notations and initialed, dated corrections. And Cha-on Suesum had also managed to eliminate patient names from study records at the main site, where Western research culture was stronger and trainings occurred more frequently, although lapses still occurred at their subsite.

Clearly, these training sessions had both symbolic and instrumental effects. Outsiders such as research monitors checked the files to verify that staff members had received the specific training required for particular studies, that certifications were kept current, and that staff had appropriate credentials. Training did not guarantee that a study would be conducted properly of course; if it did, all the monitoring and QA/QC checking would have been unnecessary. But appropriate training was expected to increase the likelihood that research would be done carefully and correctly. Staff members themselves apparently also endorsed this view as they requested additional training, attended trainings, prepared training materials, and trained others. But they also had a clear-eyed understanding that training was a mixed bag. Chiding each other over mistakes, they teasingly threatened to send colleagues for more training. Expressing mild irritation over minor disagreements with monitors, they ruefully joked that if they failed to write the records in the prescribed manner, "they could put us through training."[25] Even the most jaded participants in the clinical research community seemed to agree that training mattered even if some training sessions were unnecessary and others were not very good. With these minor quibbles and occasional bursts of irritation, training remained an article of faith. Endorsement of this highly ritualized practice signaled membership in the community of researchers as well as one's intention to abide by its rules.

TRUSTWORTHY RECORDS: THE RIGHT
INFORMATION RECORDED THE RIGHT WAY

Carefully spelled-out rules and thoughtful training were important, to be sure. But ultimately what mattered was the records—the data—that would allow conclusions to be drawn about the efficacy of novel therapies. No surprise, then, that research monitoring programs focused especially on verifying the trustworthiness of records. But even at this final stage, where one might expect an emphasis on outcomes rather than appearance, appearance remained important. The data needed to be complete and correct—good enough to be used in drug approval submissions to the FDA. But the records also needed to look the right way.

Staff members prepared carefully for regulatory encounters, hoping to create a first impression as a compliant clinic and creating props that would bolster that impression as the visit unfolded. The monitors expected staff to prepare, but what they had in mind was setting up a dedicated workspace, reminding people to be available to meet with the monitor, and gathering files and other requested materials. Monitors did not want a rehearsed performance—site visits are supposed to check on the normal round of activities.

In fact, staff preparations were usually extensive and tailored to very specific regulatory audiences. As a first step, staff brought the physical space into rigid compliance with the actual and implied regulations. They cleaned the space, tucked things away, closed doors, and threw out expired medicines. They prepared props, always mindful that props that will perform well for research monitors are not the same as those needed for an accreditation review. Medical records and CRFs received particular scrutiny during preparations for research monitor visits. Just before an ACTG monitoring visit, Robert Rafsky's weekly QA/QC meeting was devoted to previsit preparations. The clinic staff used special forms to preaudit the specific patient files they had been told would be inspected. They debated about which additional files monitors might request once they arrived, ultimately agreeing also to preaudit the files of the one study that had not been reviewed during recent monitoring visits. Likewise, at Cha-on Suesum Clinic, the team for one multisite project gathered patient files from their subsites. Although clinics did much eleventh-hour polishing, they understood that these final preparations should supplement rather than substitute for regular QA procedures. Because monitoring and other kinds of review happen so frequently, clinics are always preparing. Preparation for regulatory encounters penetrated deeply into clinics' day-to-day work.

This preparation served three purposes. First, orderliness signaled "regulatedness." Signs of minor noncompliance—open doors, stray coffee cups, medical supplies conveniently awaiting use on countertops—were carefully eliminated with the hope that the orderliness of the space would be taken as an indicator of the orderliness of the work. Second, by smoothing the background and eliminating "noise," the staff hoped to allay suspicion. Finally, the preparation of props ensured that any file picked up from a desk had already been checked and was therefore "clean," allowing the clinic staff to control the performance. Clinic staff aimed to be proactive, directing the monitoring visit, rather than reactive.

Monitoring programs verified the trustworthiness of data—the final layer of trustworthiness—by carefully checking data sources (e.g., medical records) against the CRFs where study data are recorded. Did the source data exactly match the extracted data? If not, could the discrepancy be explained? They also looked for any anomalies that might indicate modifications of the data, and for that reason insisted that changes be made in a manner that allowed the full story of original inscription and modification to be traced with full details about who gathered the data from the patient, who extracted the data (e.g., from a medical record) and prepared the initial research records, and who corrected those records. This was the sequence of record production that had tripped up the Thai research staff. Monitoring programs' focus on these very issues shows why mastering this sequence was consequential.

Although it may seem extreme, checking handwriting is common practice in research monitoring, and it does sometimes help uncover fraud. For instance, an investigation of the fraudulent practices of a Chicago-area HIV research coordinator began when a research monitor noted anomalies in signatures on consent forms and other documents (Callahan 2010; Heimer and Gazley 2012). The infractions, uncovered in 2008 and 2009, were serious: forged or missing signatures; falsified records of physical examinations, electrocardiograms, and laboratory results; enrolling of patients without adequate checks on their eligibility; and disappearance of more than 200 tablets of investigational drugs. The infractions were committed by a research coordinator who had also been embezzling the research subjects' stipends. The FDA charged that Daniel Berger, the lead researcher, had "failed to protect the rights, safety and welfare of subjects under [his] care, repeatedly or deliberately submitted false information to the sponsor and repeatedly or deliberately failed to comply with the cited [federal] regulations, which placed unnecessary risks to human subjects and jeopardized the integrity of data."[26] Berger was permitted to continue doing research but with an outside monitor regularly reviewing his work; these restrictions were removed in 2014.[27] Accounts like this vindicated monitors' inclination to check that all i's were dotted and t's crossed and were repeatedly referenced by monitors. Research staff listened to those accounts with interest and trepidation, knowing what such celebrations of meticulous monitoring presaged for them.

Aware that they were being scrutinized, staff members sought to produce records that were in fact trustworthy but also looked trustworthy. This meant being attentive both to the rules about how records should be produced (e.g., corrections by strike-out not white-out) and to matters that might raise the eyebrows of research monitors. At Robert Rafsky, Kay, one of the research nurses, was questioned about why some research records were written in a different hand. Her answer was innocent enough: when she went on vacation, a colleague had substituted for her. Under such circumstances, research nurses leave detailed instructions for their colleagues so that the collection and recording of data will go smoothly. But after eyebrows were raised over differences in handwriting, Kay added another step to her vacation routine. She instructed colleagues to record information on sticky notes, allowing her to complete the records in her own hand when she returned to work.[28]

My team and I observed similar attentiveness to the preferences of research monitors and the norms of oversight agencies in Thailand. An internal monitor at Cha-on Suesum Clinic generated forms to remind doctors what information to gather at each patient visit so study nurses would have the data needed to correctly fill out the CRFs. Even these cheat sheets came under scrutiny. Because the internal monitor believed that the NIH disliked "a whole lot of prompting and tick boxes," he revised his cheat sheets to conform to his understanding of these new auditing standards. Rather than tick boxes and blanks to be filled in, his forms now included lines for "MD Notes"—which he believed the NIH preferred. He still prompted the doctors for all the information, but his cheat sheet looked less rehearsed and more like forms used in "a normal doctor visit." Another Cha-on Suesum staff member, responsible for training people in other sites, seemed to agree that it was appropriate to scrutinize descriptions of procedures as well as a clinic's data and records. She told us, for instance, that she would be "very suspicious about [its] procedures" if a clinic planned for its consent process to take less than an hour. In her view, such a plan was clear evidence of taking inappropriate shortcuts in a crucial part of the research process.

In addition to noting what practices led monitors to raise their eyebrows, research staff in some clinics believed that it was better to provide no more than the requested information. Extra information might raise suspicions that the staff was "protesting too much" because they had something to hide or might simply provide additional points to be probed. In preparing for monitoring visits, staff members took great pains to convey an impression of orderliness and compliance, hoping thereby to allay any suspicions. "A 'good' site is one where there are more 'questions' than 'findings,'" a couple of monitors explained as they reviewed documents at Robert Rafsky. "You can spend four hours figuring something out and then ultimately decide it's okay. It's basically detective work, sort of like '20 questions.'" It was this "detective work" that staff members hoped to circumvent. Before one monitoring visit, Kay talked with the data manager about which files were being requested and which parts of the study would be reviewed. Kay thought out loud about whether to leave her personal notes in the file. These notes contained useful information—sometimes more than the protocol required. Because a skeptical monitor could always use them against the clinic, Kay decided to remove the notes. After several encounters in which monitors conveyed their inclination to trust her records, Kay changed her mind about leaving her notes in the file. Nevertheless, this incident shows just how carefully research nurses strategize about what information to share. In effect, the notes point out that the records might not have been constructed exactly as mandated by the rules—otherwise there would be nothing to explain. The notes might therefore reinforce trust or they might undermine it.

Although staff members in rich-country clinics thought it safer not to give extra information that might increase scrutiny, the staff of clinics in resource-constrained countries had a different view. Because experience had taught them to expect suspicious monitors and intensive reviews, they prepped extensively and supplied extra information at the outset, both to reassure monitors that their actions were carefully thought out and oriented to protocols, guidelines, and other rules, and to explain the many adjustments that were inevitable in their clinics. Although my team and I observed monitoring and other regulatory work by both insiders and outsiders in all five clinics, we noted that the Ugandan and Thai sites had especially extensive internal research monitoring. During the period of my fieldwork, Philly Lutaaya Clinic in Uganda developed a multilayered QA/QC program, in part as a response to previous experiences of intensive oversight that required much extra work from clinic staff to correct misunderstandings. At Cha-on Suesum, internal research monitoring initially focused on two studies that had run into difficulties with external monitors, but ultimately grew into a clinic-wide program.

Other scholars have argued that internal monitors can sometimes be more effective than external regulators (Rees 1988; Flood and Fennell 1995). In the clinics I studied, outsiders more often wrote formal reports with relatively little opportunity for correction of errors "off the book." However, astute clinic workers watched for cues about monitors' preferences (e.g., whether they disliked tick boxes) and made adjustments that they hoped would meet with monitor approval in the future. Internal monitors, in contrast, happily represented themselves as the local experts on the standards and practices of international clinical research, helping correct errors in preparation for visits by external monitors. With a foot in both worlds, internal monitors could help with judgment calls about how important it was to have English translations of records in Cha-on Suesum's subsite or what Philly Lutaaya should do when its slender resources made it impossible to photocopy hospital source documents to place in the clinic's files.

In years past, anxiety about monitors sometimes outstripped skill and led clinic staff astray. As mentioned earlier, Cha-on Suesum's research nurses, likely in an abundance of caution, had initially gone about their work with "great pots of white-out" to produce neat, clean, error-free CRFs. As clinic staff learned the rules—in part from the embedded monitors—they added new routines and adjusted their presentation of data so that it conformed in both substance and style and brought them ever closer to the allegedly universal standards.

Producing records that would be deemed trustworthy thus entailed attending both to content and form. Over time, clinic staff became adept at both parts of this work, though each new study brought new rules and fresh challenges that were almost inevitably more daunting in poorer clinics than in their richer counterparts.

ORDERLY FLEXIBILITY AND RESPECT
FOR THE NORMS

Because no system of rules can cover all contingencies, legal systems generally have some provision for filling gaps in an orderly way, whether by judicial decisions, mediation, agency rulemaking, or some other mechanism. As the five clinics conducted their research, they episodically encountered situations where rules simply did not offer adequate guidance and compliance was difficult if not impossible. In these anomalous situations, staff members bent over backward to provide evidence of their good-faith attempts to follow the rules, and their reactions provide further evidence of the importance of trustworthiness. They aspired to craft solutions that looked less like slapdash fixes and more like solid, masterful repairs that were deeply respectful of the rules. They hoped to look like skilled, careful, honest researchers capable of both planning ahead and flexibly adjusting when things went awry. Above all, no one wanted to look sloppy, careless, or unscrupulous.

Research teams repeatedly encountered gaps in all five clinics. If the rules fit well, a trained researcher generally could implement the rules without too much trouble. Even very experienced staff admitted to having trouble mastering the rules, though. One experienced researcher at Bobbi Campbell Clinic noted that after working on one study for two years, she still found new things when she went back to read the protocol book. But reasonably often the rules did not speak so clearly to the situation. When this happened, workers consulted colleagues, sometimes spending hours tacking between the rules and the case before ultimately deciding what to do.

This prolonged tacking between rules and case is well illustrated by one SAE report at Robert Rafsky. The case was discussed at the research meeting two weeks in a row, with an intensive work session after the second meeting. The pharmacist, a nurse practitioner, and the research coordinator did the bulk of the work, although two physicians also chimed in. In the early stages, they discussed what exactly the problem was and what label should be affixed. Were they seeing transient heart palpitations arising from the patient's distress over his father's death? That would not be an SAE. Or was this bradycardia that should be reported as an SAE? They looked over the patient's medication list, test results, and documentation from his recent hospitalization, concluding that the appropriate label was "cardiac arrhythmia." His symptom pattern would have been ranked as "grade 2," but the hospitalization automatically bumped it up to "grade 3." Together they crafted the prose, but only the nurse practitioner, who was a "clinical" member of the "responsible parties" list for the study, was eligible to sign the report. As they approached the end of their work, they kept returning to the question of whether the condition was study related. "Can we say it's 'not' or 'definitely not related' to the drug?" the pharmacist asked. They looked at the SAE instructions and discussed the options listed there. The category they were most comfortable with—"probably not related"— was not one of the options. They talked this through referencing what they knew about the study drug, the comments of one of the doctors, and the fact that reporting was mandated for any grade 3 symptom. But they also considered whether their impulse to report the problem meant that at a gut level they believed the arrhythmia might actually be study related. Circling around what exactly the "awareness date" was, they worried both about when they first received the news about the patient's medical condition and whether they were still in the mandated reporting window. And they discussed SAE rules, what documentation to include, where to file the report, and the grading of symptoms, among other topics. They reasoned that if they had been unsure how the rules applied, monitors might also have questions, and they wanted their solution to appear orderly and thoughtful. All this uncertainty and consultation about a relatively mundane research task—SAEs are rather common—occurred in the best resourced of the five clinics, where staff members were sophisticated, well trained, and very experienced in the intricacies of clinical research.

Rather than filling gaps as they arose, clinic staff also sometimes tried to anticipate where gaps would occur and created clinic-level guidelines to fill the holes. Here their work resembled that of government agencies writing regulations and guidance to spell out how statutes should be applied in particular circumstances. This kind of gap filling occurred especially in Uganda, where intense scrutiny from outsiders had motivated staff members to embark on the extensive clinical guideline-writing program discussed previously. Philly Lutaaya's staff hoped to forestall any suspicion that they were practicing haphazardly by providing explicit rules that did double duty, guiding their practice and explaining their practices to outsiders.

Philly Lutaaya staff were also concerned about SAE reporting. Seeing researchers struggle with SAE reporting in multiple sites, one might conclude that there were systemic problems with SAE reporting, and the commentary of Ugandan researchers seemed to support this. At one point, Philly Lutaaya staff—both Ugandans and ex-pats—worried about whether to lump symptoms together into a single SAE or report multiple SAEs (examples included dehydration, vomiting, diarrhea, and fever; malaria and anemia; and seizures in the context of other symptoms in infant patients). "We need guidelines on lumping together symptoms as a single AE or SAE," one staff member declared, adding that "you need to use your judgment, but we need to have a consistent thought process on this." The group discussion acknowledged both the utility and the limitations of guidelines. Additional guidelines might help but could not fully solve the problem. And for that reason, they needed to demonstrate that they had followed a "consistent thought process." Where other clinics might have been satisfied to troubleshoot as problems arose, Philly Lutaaya's history of outside scrutiny made them feel that once again they should go the extra mile to establish a general procedure rather than just making a one-time decision.

Finally, in a few cases, staff members consulted the protocol committee, either because they remained uncertain about the appropriate course of action or because the rules required that the protocol committee be consulted. If the protocol is the core of the "legal system"—the "statutes"—of a particular study, the protocol committee is then the body primarily responsible for creating the rules in the first place and filling in remaining interpretive gaps. The questions taken to the protocol committee often spanned the boundary between science and patient care. Protocols generally had quite strict rules about when patients had to be taken off a study regimen to protect their health. This might entail a brief hiatus with the patient being put back on the regimen once the symptoms abated or lab values improved. But detailed as they were, the protocols still did not cover all contingencies, and the site PI might need to refer the case to the study protocol committee for its verdict on such matters as whether a patient could rejoin the study.

As this analysis suggests, the orderliness of the system is produced jointly by the rules and by the tight control of the process of crafting acceptable exceptions. The orderly flexibility of clinical research is notably more collective than the individual discretion discussed in research on street-level bureaucrats (Lipsky 2010; Brodkin 2012; Hupe 2019). In effect, clinical researchers are often seeking an assessment of the alignment between proposed solution and the original rule before acting. Orderly flexibility thus yields both flexibility and a check on flexibility, preserving trustworthiness all the way through the process.

Even with these other safeguards in place, though, the system for producing trustworthy data ultimately rests on a bedrock of the trustworthiness of the people conducting the research. At some point, then, the monitors and other people assessing a project must decide whether they can trust a research team. Typically this is a global assessment of the staff and site—tentative and subject to reversal, to be sure, but nevertheless an assessment understood by staff members and monitors alike as signaling a change in the tenor of reviews. If reviewers do decide that a clinic's team is trustworthy, they will continue to be thorough in their work, with both announced and unannounced elements, but staff members will sometimes be given the benefit of the doubt when anomalies are uncovered; researchers' explanations will not immediately be greeted with suspicion.

During the period when monitors appear to be weighing their preliminary conclusions about the research staff's competence and trustworthiness, clinic workers sometimes offer up additional confirming evidence and supportive statements to nudge monitors in the direction of trust, a rather Goffmanesque approach (Goffman 1969). This might done by showing understanding of and respect for the deeper norms, perhaps during discussions of other teams' lapses. For example, monitors talked with Kay, the Robert Rafsky research nurse, about a physician who "need[ed] some lessons in error correction." On a previous occasion, the monitors had talked with Kay about the lapses of a former colleague and about a patient who failed to disclose a key symptom. When Kay jokingly asked whether she would get put in jail for her own errors, the monitor laughed, categorizing her errors as "just small stuff." Not missing a beat, Kay retorted that she "sweat[ed] the small stuff too!" "Good!" the monitor exclaimed. The monitor also praised the records as "vastly improved" after Kay took over one study from a recently departed colleague. Kay subsequently said that she was happy to "take *full responsibility*" for a study that had been hers from the outset.

One might think no one would be so foolish as to openly disrespect the norms. Yet reckless displays of disrespect do occur, sometimes with very serious consequences. One research monitor talked about a research coordinator (not affiliated with my fieldsites) who had filled in patients' temperature and blood pressure measurements weeks in advance of study visits. Some prefilling of forms is common, but it is limited to inserting patient identification numbers, the site number, and so forth. In this case, though, the research coordinator erroneously reasoned that more extensive prefilling was okay because some measurements are only tangentially related to study questions. In fact, changes in temperature and blood pressure may indicate that something is amiss and are therefore important elements of AE detection and reporting. The research coordinator's willingness to falsify data—and her apparent naïveté about the scientific importance of vital signs—indicated a profound mismatch between the norms of the clinic and the norms of science. That this was a systemic problem became clear when the PI seemed unconcerned about the breach. "So how did we do other than that?" he asked the monitor during the debriefing. Concluding her story, the monitor confided that the site was probably being closed over this infraction.

The other end of the continuum was staked out by such staff members as the regulatory affairs specialists (titles vary) at Bobbi Campbell and Philly Lutaaya Clinics. These two staff members were unnervingly conversant with the rules (in both cases, not so much the protocols as IRB and site compliance matters) and reliably on top of schedules and deadlines. Other staff members sometimes grumbled about being nagged by these fastidious colleagues, but their attention to detail and demonstrated willingness to toe the line usefully signaled a clinic stance of deep respect for the rules. The presence of such true believers did much to shore up trust in those clinics' work.

As the tidy legalism of clinical research administration and monitoring confronted the still unruly world in which that research is conducted, two core principles—orderly flexibility and respect for the norms—shaped staff members' responses. In aiming for orderly flexibility, staff members looked for adjustments that came as close as possible to abiding by the rule. This often meant consulting colleagues or asking someone "official," such as the protocol team, to offer an opinion or make a decision about whether a proposed adjustment was acceptable. Alternatively, when anomalies could be anticipated, clinic staff might prepare alternative versions of rules to cover those situations. In displaying respect for the norms, staff members intended to convince monitors that they were acting in good faith, doing their best to adhere to the norms of science endorsed by monitors and staff members alike, and taking responsibility for the quality of their work. They intended to convey that monitors could be confident that clinic staff were following both the letter and the spirit of the rules. Careful and thorough though monitors were, they could not check everything, and staff members aimed to suggest that the unexamined records were just as rule-conforming as the records that had been inspected. Better yet, they hoped to convince monitors that the high quality of the work they saw indicated that clinic staff members and monitors were really on the same side and that clinic researchers believed in the rules every bit as much as the monitors did.

Conclusion

To wrap up this analysis of the legalization of clinical research, I return to some of the core questions of the book. What happens when more legalistic forms of governance are introduced in not just medical caregiving but also the work that medical staff do as scientists and researchers? How comfortably does such legalism fit into the clinics of poorer countries where research and treatment are especially likely to be fused?

A central claim of this book is that different professions work with rules in different ways and that introducing more soft law into medical settings entails not just a tightening up of regulation but a shift in how regulation is done. For many years, the norms and rules of medicine have been understood as guidelines to be used with discretion and respect for the diversity of patient circumstances. As guidelines have been more fully codified, though, and as sanctions have been attached to "noncompliance," both expectations and practice have changed, although not always as quickly or fully as guideline writers might have hoped. Moreover, although medical practice has changed slowly, associated reviews of practice (e.g., by insurers and government payers) have changed more rapidly.

But these tentative conclusions speak differently to the infusion of legalistic ways of working and thinking in clinical research. Although clinical research is conducted in medical settings—in this case, the five HIV clinics featured in this book—and although many of the workers have been trained in core medical professions, they understand themselves to be doing something different when they engage in clinical research. Seeing themselves as scientists or as ancillary workers contributing to a scientific enterprise alters their perspective on their work and the patients/research subjects with whom they work. In short, it is not just the rules and norms of medicine that apply, but the rules and norms of science.

Even when they are pressured to follow guidelines and reduce practice variations, healthcare providers are also taught to adjust to the needs of their particular patients. In research, in contrast, pressures for uniformity are intensified, with the result that rules are firmer and less amenable to interpretation and adjustment. "Local universals" are thus less likely in research than in clinical work.

That said, the norms of science were probably never quite as Robert Merton described them. But if those exalted norms never quite matched what transpired in the past, the gap is almost certainly larger in the era of "big science." Today's biomedical science workers are not working in isolation, making judgment calls on their own, deciding alone how to balance risks and benefits. Instead, in ways large and small, they find themselves compelled to adhere to rigid rules even when following the rules may actually harm their research. For example, when her patient got stuck in traffic, a Robert Rafsky research pharmacist resigned herself to discarding (or not drawing) a valuable sample as the rules required even though she believed that being a minute or two late would make no difference whatever in her pharmacokinetic study. Even at the top of the hierarchy, individual scientists do not get to make their own decisions about changes in the direction of a research project. Instead, site PIs consult a protocol team about deviations from a collective plan. This is bureaucratized, organizationally based science, conducted in modern medical facilities and dispersed across multiple sites. Among other things, this way of doing science places a premium on the rules that ensure that data from those dispersed sites are sufficiently comparable that they can be aggregated to draw meaningful, robust conclusions. Of course, scientists have always worried about replicability, but this is replicability on steroids.

In addition, the embedding of science in organizations means that scientists face constraints and opportunities that have little to do with science and much to do with the organizations in which they make their careers. By now, the sub rosa focus is on protecting research dollars flowing into universities and other research establishments (Bledsoe et al. 2007), and that focus shapes many details of how rules and regulations are administered. Whether strict compliance is always necessary for the advance of science may be quite a different question than whether strict compliance keeps the research dollars flowing.

The formalization of the processes for creating and updating routines (such as the SOPs mandated by the NIH, including the SOP for revising SOPs) is mirrored at other levels. Just as SOPs are intended to ensure reliable performance in the workplaces of clinical research, so standards for SOP topics, SOP writing, and SOP revision are intended to ensure SOP coverage and quality. But how can we be confident that staff members know how to carry out the task specified by the SOPs? To ensure that, workers are required to undergo initial training and episodic retraining. And increasingly, special certifications are required for particular kinds of tasks—for lab workers and nurses, to be sure, but also for research administrators or IRB professionals (certified IRB professionals, or CIPs, and certified IRB managers, or CIMs). And the adequacy of training and testing, in turn, is ensured by professional societies and accreditation programs (such as those that review and accredit human subjects protection programs).

Finally and importantly, the work of accountability provides career opportunities for an increasing number of workers. Compliance work is work, after all. Each layer of nested verification systems creates work, and while from some perspectives this siphons off scarce resources from core scientific activities, from another perspective, it creates solid careers, particularly as these positions become institutionalized and organized into hierarchies backed up by recognized credentials.

The growth of nested verification systems to ensure trustworthiness surely in part responds to the vital importance of trust in research. Science is worth little if we cannot be confident that scientific findings have been honestly and competently produced and can be compared and added to results from other sites so that scientific knowledge is cumulative. But whatever the initial intention, verification systems now have lives of their own. Accountability has become a watchword of contemporary life (Espeland and Vannebo 2007), as thoroughly institutionalized in science as in other fields. And if institutionalization is largely driven, as Meyer and Rowan (1977) and others argue, by the need to convince interaction partners (suppliers, consumers, funders) of an enterprise's legitimacy, this is even more the case when what is being institutionalized is procedures for demonstrating legitimacy. In this case, then, process and substance lock hands, powerfully advancing accountability regimes.

When all is said and done, we still need to ask whether these attempts to make science more trustworthy actually make science better. If attending to the increasing number of rules deflects attention from thoughtful science, delays important scientific projects, focuses too much attention on the theatrical aspects of compliance, consumes resources sorely needed for other uses, and makes participation more difficult for researchers in resource-constrained countries, then perhaps these attempts to increase trustworthiness via increased legalism come at too high a cost.

[CHAPTER SIX]

Disciplining Medicine

What Happens When Guidelines Are Hardened by Law

In 2004, a Thai study (Lallemant et al. 2004) published in the *New England Journal of Medicine* established that "dual anti-retroviral prophylaxis" was much more effective than a single-drug regimen in preventing mother-to-child transmission (PMTCT) of HIV.[1] WHO quickly adopted this regimen as its standard. Despite WHO's endorsement, South Africa continued to offer a one-drug regimen for PMTCT until 2008.

HIV policy was a flash point in South Africa during Mbeki's presidency, with exceedingly slow adoption of key programs. Considerable political pressure and a 2002 court order were required to induce the South Africa government to implement any PMTCT program, making its lengthy delay in adopting the two-drug standard explicable though not excusable. The South African evidence on the efficacy of the two regimens was striking. In KwaZulu-Natal (KZN), where the national single-drug regimen was also endorsed by provincial authorities, the mother-to-child transmission rate was 23%. In contrast, the Western Cape's provincial health department broke with the national government and adopted the two-drug regimen and achieved a transmission rate of less than 5% (Dugger 2008b). Admittedly, the South Africa's single-drug regimen was cheaper but, because the price of AZT had dropped, the two-drug regimen was not exorbitantly expensive, and the returns from investing in PMTCT programs are substantial.[2]

Adopting a guideline as official government policy has important effects that go beyond what professional and scientific bodies achieve when they create guidelines. In South Africa, the national and provincial governments' adoption of the single-drug PMTCT regimen as official policy proved consequential. In May 2007, a group of KZN doctors pressed the provincial health department to allow them give the two-drug regimen. It was unethical, they argued, to use the single-drug regimen when they had the capacity to deliver better treatment. But Sandile Buthelezi, responding for the province, denied their request, saying that the budget did not provide for the added cost of the AZT. Referring to the Western Cape policy, he added

205

"I am wary of us undermining national just because of what other provinces are doing" (Dugger 2008a).[3]

Colin Pfaff, acting medical manager of Manguzi Hospital, where 36.3% of pregnant women were HIV positive (TAC 2008a), raised additional funds so he could give his patients the second drug. Although one might expect the province to applaud Pfaff's resourcefulness, the KZN Department of Health instead charged him with misconduct for "acting beyond his authority" and "without prior permission of his superiors" (TAC 2008a). Outraged medical groups insisted that Pfaff's action fell well within the bounds of professional discretion. When the charge was withdrawn, Francois Venter, president of the South African HIV Clinicians Society, credited the health worker campaign and the "spontaneous outpouring of anger at the news that Colin was being disciplined for doing his ethical duty" (TAC 2008b).

Extreme examples such as this can sometimes bring into sharp relief tendencies that have previously been obscured. This case helpfully shows what can happen when medical and legal components are interwoven in treatment guidelines and alerts us to healthcare providers' discomfort with the legalization of clinical guidelines. Only with the melding of legal and medical elements could Pfaff's normal use of medical discretion to provide superior treatment be judged an inappropriate exercise of legal discretion.

Medical practitioners, accustomed to working with guidelines, seem nervous about some guidelines, irritated by others, and welcoming of still others. This chapter compares two main types of guidelines used in HIV clinics, purely medical guidelines and medical guidelines that have an interface with the legal system. It argues that the discomfort clinic staff experience when they encounter guidelines with a legal interface arises from their lack of expertise in legal matters. Taught to be flexible users of guidelines, medical staff expect to use their judgment about whether and how guidelines apply to any particular situation. When they encounter "hardened" guidelines, expert clinic staff discover that they are not expert in all of the kinds of knowledge embedded in these new types of standards. Although the rules of medicine may remain flexible and relatively "soft," the rules of law can be rigid and "hard." We might, then, expect medical workers to be more resistant to forms of legalism that tether clinical rules to formal law and more willing to embrace rules that are more decoupled from formal law.

The chapter thus develops an argument about the relationship between standards, expertise, discretion, and flexibility and offers an explanation for why the law seems especially "foreign" to groups of people who are otherwise quite accustomed to working with law-like guidelines.[4] I focus especially on treatment guidelines and on variation in the importance of the legal interface. Although generally guidelines are supposed to reduce uncertainty, they have that effect only when there is a match between the knowledge base referenced in guidelines and the training of those who work with them. That condition is met with strictly medical guidelines that reference scientific studies, but is less likely to be met when the guidelines also draw heavily on law.

New Rules, New Anxiety

To be sure, this interweaving of medical and legal is not exactly new,[5] although my contention is that its scale and the imperiousness of some of the rules are unprecedented. In earlier research on infant intensive care units, I noticed that staff were continually referencing rules such as protocols, guidelines, and standard operating procedures (SOPs) (Heimer and Staffen 1998). Moreover, staff members often expressed concern about whether what they were doing was "legal." They might worry, for instance, about whether they were legally empowered to take custody of an infant whose parents opposed a medically necessary blood transfusion or whether they had the legal right to refuse to send a child home with parents who had not learned how to manage ongoing medical problems. Sometimes it seemed that their concern with legality had displaced a concern with what was ethical. Undoubtedly this new focus on legality was influenced by the patients' rights movement, worries about medical malpractice suits, and the intense scrutiny associated with the US Baby Doe regulations.[6] Staff members were encountering more rules—some of which they had themselves written— and were more worried about them.

As arrangements become more legalized, the parties to whom the rules apply are more clearly and unconditionally obligated to follow the rules; the rules are more precise, with little room for discretion or interpretation; and provisions may even have been put in place for third parties to resolve disputes and make additional rules (Abbott et al. 2000). In the world of healthcare, "legalization" may arise in a variety of ways, for instance, from formal legal systems and governments or from the legislative, interpretive, and oversight activities of other entities that govern subparts of medicine. The dimensions (degree of obligation, precision, and delegation of dispute resolution) may be similar, but inevitably the mechanisms are somewhat modified when the "government" is not a state but is a less fully institutionalized entity that has government-like functions. Almost inevitably, "law" in this realm is somewhat "softer" because its rules often are not fully articulated with the laws and regulations of the formal legal system.

Yet, in some instances, there are well-developed mechanisms for monitoring and enforcement, a good deal of precision in the rules and subrules, and instruction on how to figure out what to do when a situation is not covered by the rule.

Some of the complexity of the quasi-legal system of the medical world arises because of its multicephalic character. This system contains many fiefdoms, each with its own "legislators," "executives," and "courts." But because what is being governed may not always be a geographical area but might be semi-independent functions such as research and treatment, these fiefdoms overlap in space and time, sometimes creating chaos rather than order. Adding further complexity, these rules sometimes span national borders.

With all of this quasi-legal complexity, we must start by asking what clinic workers actually know about the provenance and legal status of the rules they encounter. Clinic workers may not know, for instance, which rules are mandated by national law and so are especially obligatory. Some rigidity is added to guidelines when they are reinforced through adoption by a national government, third-party payer, or clinic. But perhaps it doesn't matter that some rules come from a research bureaucracy, as opposed to originating in national law on human research subjects, or being put in place by quasi-public regulatory bodies like the Joint Commission. Does the different legal status of guidelines and regulations affect clinic work, and do clinic staff generally know which rules are intended only as guidance and which (like research protocols) are intended to be followed exactly?

Guidelines as Mechanisms for Managing Uncertainty

The core of medical work is diagnosing, offering prognoses, and treating patients. The practice of medicine is grounded in scientific knowledge that doctors, unlike the rest of us, are expected to have mastered. Yet medical professionals have not always had much expertise, as Starr (1982) reminds us in his history of American medicine. As the body of scientifically grounded medical knowledge has grown, though, mastery of that corpus has become a challenge (Becker et al. 1961), making decision supports such as clinical guidelines crucial to the practice of medicine.

Clinical guidelines attempt to summarize research in any given area and to formulate that summary as a recommendation about what to do, accompanied by assessments of the quality of the evidence, how strongly it supports the recommendation, and supporting references.[7] Guidelines can be either deterministic, branching, or some combination of the two (see generally UNAIDS 1999, 10). Deterministic guidelines are more restrictive and offer a fixed list of elements to be used as a recipe for action (e.g., how to deal with a life-threatening condition). Branching guidelines, in contrast, guide a clinician's actions in an unfolding situation, recommending one or more courses of action at each point in a decision tree. Most of the guidelines discussed in this chapter are branching guidelines. Branching guidelines often incorporate flow diagrams or algorithms and typically build on information gathered by the clinician as the situation unfolds. In effect, deterministic guidelines are "harder" than branching guidelines because they mandate a course of action rather than having practitioners choose among several possibilities.

Clinical guidelines are intended to reduce uncertainty about medical care, including caregivers' uncertainty about what to do and patients' uncertainty about whether their caregivers know what to do. For the most part, these uncertainties concern core medical matters. Yet there are many more uncertainties faced by clinic workers, clinics, and patients. For instance, practitioners and the clinics in which they work face uncertainties about whether they will be paid for the services they provide. If we think of clinical guidelines as a language that caregivers use to talk with each other about what care to give, they also become a way to conduct a dialogue with insurers, government agencies, and other third-party payers. When an insurer adopts a particular guideline, it agrees to pay for treatment that aligns with that guideline. Likewise, when governments adopt a specific guideline, they agree to a payment scheme whereby they cover services, supplies, and medications that are administered to a particular population by a specified category of practitioners working in a particular type of facility as long as that care complies with the guideline. Guidelines can thus be used to reduce uncertainties about not only medical care (by reducing practice variation) but also fiscal uncertainty. Finally, guidelines can reduce legal risks for practitioners and the medical facilities in which they work. If medical workers follow guidelines, this should reduce the likelihood of malpractice suits and perhaps give them a stronger defense in the event of a suit. A clinic's adoption of clinical guidelines signals to a variety of publics that it is a careful, law-abiding enterprise.[8]

Generally, clinical guidelines become "harder" and more mandatory as they are adopted as guidelines by successive layers of governments and medical organizations. The main bodies issuing HIV guidelines include the US Department of Health and Human Services (DHHS) working with the Centers for Disease Control and Prevention (CDC) and the National Institutes of Health (NIH), WHO, and the International Antiviral Society–USA (IAS-USA).[9] The HIV treatment guidelines issued by the DHHS and

CDC, WHO, or the IAS-USA do not really constrain anyone until they are adopted by some other entity. As they are adopted by governments, insurers, or clinics and modified to suit the circumstances and purposes of those entities, the guidelines become more constraining. In part this is because the rules are no longer just about what treatments work best but about how to allocate scarce resources among competing parties and how to manage some of the risks faced by clinics and governments. The same points could be made about guidelines for testing, PMTCT, changing regimens, and so forth.

Legal and Medical Content in Clinical Guidelines

Guidelines issued by the DHHS and CDC, WHO, or IAS-USA are complex medical documents without administrative or legal content. As guidelines are adopted by governments and clinics and adapted for specific populations and constraints, administrative and legal content gets added. Generally speaking, because the objective of clinical guidelines is to use carefully assessed scientific information to standardize medical work and reduce "practice variations," the core medical content of guidelines is essentially fixed from one location to another. But, as this chapter shows, there is more to these rules than the purely medical content, and the administrative and financial arrangements and legal content vary a good bit from one country to another and even from one clinic to another.

Although a complete discussion of the use of clinical guidelines would also include an analysis of administrative and financial elements to complement the discussion of legal elements of clinical guidelines provided here, a quick word about these administrative and financial matters will have to suffice. If anything, administrative and financial elements are even more variable than legal content. Clinics generally draw on a wide variety of resources, including payments from patients, reimbursements from insurers and governments, program grants from large donors, and monies from pharmaceutical company philanthropic funds. Each source of funds comes with its own strings—lists of items for which funds can and cannot be expended, mandated reporting schedules, and so forth. As the "strings" are transformed into routines and embedded in locally designed forms, people forget the origins of the obligations. If users are asked why they record a particular bit of information, many will not remember that the obligation to collect that information originated in a donor contract or government mandate. A similar kind of forgetting occurs when legal content is transformed into local routines.

Although all clinical guidelines have legal content, this legal content often is not made explicit, creating confusion about the legal status of the actions described in clinical guidelines. Table 6.1 summarizes the legal content of several clinical guidelines that are especially important in HIV medicine, including guidelines for testing to see whether people have been infected with HIV; guidelines for starting patients on ART; guidelines for switching patients from one treatment regimen to another, either because they cannot tolerate the regimen or because it no longer keeps the virus in check; guidelines for preventing transmission during pregnancy, childbirth, or breastfeeding; and guidelines for treating HIV-infected children. Clinical guidelines are meant to be used by particular professional groups. Which professional groups are empowered to carry out the actions spelled out in a particular guideline depends on the laws and regulations of the country, state, or province where the guideline is being used. In an appendix on guideline appraisal tools, the UN guideline for guideline development (a bit of bureaucratic excess reminiscent of the SOP on revising SOPs) urges that guideline writers be explicit on this point: "Is there a description of the professional groups to which the guideline is meant to apply?" (UNAIDS 1999, 27). To take one example, in a South African guideline on PMTCT (published just after our field observations had been completed), a diagram shows that it is a "registered health professional" who prescribes AZT and orders a CD4 count (Department of Health, South Africa 2008b, 18). The announcement of the new policy is even more explicit on this point: "The two drugs used in the programme—AZT and nevirapine—are schedule 04 medicines and therefore have to be prescribed by a medical officer after an appropriate assessment of the patient" (Department of Health, South Africa 2008a, 1).

Medical staff interact with medical elements of guidelines in a different way than they interact with the legal elements. Much of the training clinic staff receive is on the *medical* part; their expertise and previous professional training is as *medical* caregivers; their professional identity is as doctors, nurses, pharmacists, or laboratory workers. The complexity of medicine is part and parcel of the job in a way that the administrative and legal complexity is not. Medical or scientific complexity is expected, even interesting and challenging; legal complexity is unnerving, disconcerting, and anxiety-producing. Uncertainty about medicine or science stimulates problem solving; uncertainty about law, because law lies outside the core expertise of medical workers, tends to induce paralysis.

TABLE 6.1. Legal and Medical Elements of Clinical Guidelines

GUIDELINES*	MEDICAL ELEMENTS IN GUIDELINES	LEGAL ELEMENTS IN GUIDELINES
Testing Guideline	Medical elements present, relatively constant across settings, not complex. Testing staff typically a mix of specially trained counselors and nurses.	Legal elements often specifically addressed (e.g., in 2006 CDC revised recommendations for testing), but laws highly variable by locale and in flux. Legal issues: Is informed consent required? If so, must it be written consent? When is counseling required? (Pretest, post-test, or both?) Must exposed partners be notified? Must HIV infections be reported to the state? (Can reporting be anonymous?) At what age can children and adolescents consent to testing? Can patient blood be tested even without consent when health workers receive needlestick injuries?
PMTCT	Medical elements present, some variability across settings (because rich countries have option to start women on ARV and to deliver surgically), complexity depends on whether pregnant women receive full ARV or prophylactic regimen. Typically done by doctors.	Legal elements usually addressed only indirectly (e.g., in South African 2008 PMTCT guideline: women "should be given routine information about voluntary HIV testing and the PMTCT programme"). Legal issues: Will women be tested routinely as part of antenatal care? Are signed consent forms required? Will women be required to take prophylaxis to protect their babies?
Treating HIV-Infected Children	Medical elements present, some variability across settings because of drug availability, quite complex (partly because less is known about pediatric HIV). Always done by doctors.	Legal elements sometimes addressed directly (e.g., in South African pediatric guidelines). Legal issues: At what age can children consent to testing and treatment? Who can consent on behalf of a young child? What should medical practitioners do if parents oppose treatment?
Initiating ARV in Adults and Adolescents	Medical elements present, relatively constant across settings, but with some variability because of drug availability, complex. Typically done by doctors, though sometimes by specially trained HIV nurses; ARV training often done by specially trained counselors.	Legal elements usually addressed only indirectly. Legal issues: Are patient training programs mandated? Do doctors have discretion over which regimens to use or are limits placed by the ministry of health (or similar entity)?

TABLE 6.1. (*Continued*)

GUIDELINES*	MEDICAL ELEMENTS IN GUIDELINES	LEGAL ELEMENTS IN GUIDELINES
Switching Regimens	Medical elements present, somewhat more variable across settings because of variations in access to alternative regimens and adequacy of lab facilities, highly complex. Always done by doctors. When adjustment is because of side effects, switching may be less medically complicated than when switching is necessitated by drug resistance; when resistance is suspected, patient often referred to doctor specializing in this problem.	Legal elements usually addressed only indirectly. Legal issues: Does the government program provide for switching regimens? Must physicians request permission or notify a government body before switching patients to alternative regimens?

* These guidelines do not stand alone but typically appear alongside other guidelines in the HIV guidelines and recommendations issued by a guideline-writing panel, a ministry of health, or a clinic.

TESTING GUIDELINES (1): CHANGING NEEDS, LAGGING RULES

It is perhaps in HIV-testing guidelines that legal elements are most fully articulated. By the time I was completing my field observations, the strictly medical components of HIV testing had become uncomplicated, with multiple testing options (antibody tests using blood, urine, or mucosal swabs), some offering results in minutes. Arrangements for HIV testing were controversial from the outset, though, as I note in the book's opening pages. In the early days of the HIV epidemic, frightened people called for quarantines and for excluding HIV-infected children from schools, insurers canceled the health insurance policies of those who tested positive, legal protections for HIV-infected people had not yet been put in place, and medical caregivers could offer little more than treatment for opportunistic infections and palliative care at the end. It was in that social environment that HIV testing guidelines were first developed. Given the concerns about confidentiality and people' reactions to the news that they had a fatal disease, the routines mandated that testing be fully voluntary with counseling before and after the test itself.

Over the years, policymakers, caregivers, and activists became less supportive of voluntary counseling and testing (VCT) and began to favor routine counseling and testing (RCT), always with the possibility of "opting out" of the test. The idea was that caregivers should incorporate HIV testing into routine healthcare, screening for HIV just as they would screen for any other serious, treatable health disorder (see, e.g., CDC 2006, 2–7). Because caregivers now had something to offer their HIV-infected patients and because people do better if they are treated sooner rather than later, testing was no longer simply about protecting other people's health. Although the CDC has recommended changes in how HIV testing is done in the US, HIV testing has been governed by state laws and regulations, which have varied a good bit from one state to another.[10] The National HIV/AIDS Clinicians' Consultation Center (2011) provides a compendium of state laws on HIV, but its "Quick Reference Guide" often points to areas where the law is unclear. As the 2006 CDC testing guideline noted, "at least 28 states have laws or regulations that limit health-care providers' ability to order diagnostic testing for HIV infection if the patient is unable to give consent for HIV testing, even when the test results are likely to alter the patient's diagnostic or therapeutic management" (2006, 6). Only the District of Columbia, which at the time had the highest rate of new cases in the US, had adopted a vigorous program of routine testing (DeParle 2006).

At Philly Lutaaya Clinic in Uganda, one of the founders of the facility, a medical school professor and prominent HIV researcher, passionately advocated routine testing, emphasizing the impossibility of preventing the birth of HIV-infected babies if women were not tested in pregnancy. In his view, "with a deadly disease like AIDS it does not make any sense to leave counseling and testing voluntary while with a disease like syphilis all mothers have to undergo a test."[11] Other staff, including counselors, disagreed, arguing that women had many reasons not to be tested and that it was wrong to second-guess them.

The Ugandan testing guideline, issued in provisional form in February 2005, went further than the guidelines of other countries in distinguishing levels of consent required in different settings. Using "HIV Counselling and Testing (HCT)" as the umbrella term, the introduction commented that "testing may be voluntary but other times the testing is carried out under different circumstances where voluntarism does not apply" (Uganda 2005, 1). The chief innovation introduced in the 2005 guidelines was RCT for HIV in clinical settings, with some attendant modifications in the counseling process. For situations in which people "seek out service of their own will," VCT remained the model. The document also introduced ways of doing testing where the degree of voluntarism was diminished (some select employment situations or cases where people were "applying for a particular service or privilege") or entirely absent (in criminal situations, where consultation with the attorney general's office was required), or where people were unable to consent because they were legal minors or had disabilities that made full consent difficult (Uganda 2005, 3–4). Recognizing that parents and guardians might not always see eye to eye with children, the Ugandan testing guideline provided both for children to refuse HIV tests (even when parents were urging testing) and to test without the approval of their parents or guardians starting at age twelve (Uganda 2005, 22). The guideline also acknowledged that there would be some children who were emancipated at even younger ages because they were themselves parents, heads of households, or abandoned (Uganda 2005, 22). In practice, such children were not likely to make their way to an HIV clinic. But the Ugandan guidelines did at least reduce ambiguity about their legal status should they arrive at the clinic door. With legal impediments minimized, medical staff were more likely to be able to move on to testing and treatment.

In South Africa, sentiment seemed to be shifting toward routine testing. Among the most eloquent advocates for routine testing was Edwin Cameron, a judge on the Supreme Court of Appeal. In a lecture honoring deceased AIDS activist Ronald Louw, Cameron reviewed the history of HIV testing in South Africa before arguing that it was time to dispense with the "fuss and palaver and hullabaloo" that accompanied testing (2007, 105). At Gugu Dlamini Clinic, staff members were fully aware of these ongoing conversations and seemed uncomfortable about their testing routines. The clinic's director attended Cameron's lecture, questioning him about the legal and ethical implications of switching to routine testing.[12] But the clinic's counseling-testing-counseling routine was thoroughly institutionalized, so for the time being they continued to do their work just as before. They did worry, though, that in simply "inviting" people to be counseled and tested they were supporting laws and policies on confidentiality that assume HIV is stigmatizing.[13]

Particularly in PMTCT programs, staff expressed discomfort about moves toward routine testing, in part because they were uncertain about precisely where the law came down on provider versus client-initiated testing. Many practitioners were intensely concerned with preventing transmission to babies and found it nearly impossible to believe that prospective mothers would not share their sentiments. This tended to make them feel that if a woman was reluctant to have the test it must mean that she had not understood the grave risk to her baby or that the risk could be substantially reduced with prophylaxis. The "fall off" at every stage between presentation of information, individual counseling, testing, receiving prophylaxis for herself, and receiving prophylaxis for the baby was difficult to explain and tended to make staff favor routine testing.[14] Yet the law in South Africa had not moved very far in that direction. The January 2008 regulations said that women "should be given routine information about voluntary HIV testing and the PMTCT programme" (Department of Health, South Africa 2008b). With the inclusion of both "routine" and "voluntary" in the regulations, this was not quite the "opt out" arrangement that people like Cameron advocated. After all of the parsing of words in the discussion of testing, the guideline did not actually use language that gave a clear signal that it meant "opt out" rather than "opt in" (as in the past).

TESTING GUIDELINES (2): CONFIDENTIALITY, LOCAL PRESSURES, FOREIGN RULES

Confidentiality was another important element of testing, though questions about how to handle confidentiality also extended well beyond testing to treatment and research. In all five clinics, staff seemed uncertain about what protecting confidentiality actually meant. Although they were fairly confident that they understood the rules in the abstract, clinic workers often were less sure about how the rules applied to particular situations. All rules require pragmatic adjustments and tacit knowledge to work. But pragmatic adjustments and local tacit knowledge were often delegitimized in the highly legalized environment of HIV work, particularly in locales where foreign funding came with unfamiliar rules.

At Robert Rafsky, clinic workers were scrupulous about concealing even the identity of the facility as an HIV clinic. In answering the phone, they referenced the floor and the building, but did not say anything so obvious as "HIV clinic." Oddly, this meant that the clinic lost the opportunity to educate patients by stocking the waiting room with relevant literature. Other clinics did not feel that confidentiality necessitated such extreme measures. When friends or family members were unaware that the person they were accompanying was being tested or treated for HIV, the secret was easily kept by staff. Although Robert Rafsky staff members agreed that a patient's medical information was not to be shared with outsiders, they seemed uncertain about how the rules applied to discussions among themselves about the patients they shared. In staff meetings, one nurse tended to refer to patients by initials rather than names. Worried that she had modified her practice because she felt I should not be privy to confidential information, I checked with a leading researcher. No, he assured me, it was rather that the clinical staff had been thoroughly drilled on HIPAA (Health Insurance Portability and Accountability Act) regulations. In any case, he added, in his view we were all (me included) within the circle of confidentiality. But there lay the problem—although they felt they could not do their work unless their colleagues were within the sphere of confidentiality, no one seemed sure how and to whom the confidentiality requirements applied.

At Cha-on Suesum Clinic in Thailand, some parts of clinic work were supposed to be governed by *farang* (foreign, in fact predominantly US) rules about confidentiality. That meant, among other things, that names of research subjects were supposed to be excluded from some kinds of records and should not be easily visible on others. Thailand has a long history of concern with ethics in medicine and biomedical research, as the head of the local institutional review board (IRB) reminded me.[15] But Thai medical workers had not always adopted the same solutions as those promulgated by the US government in HIPAA, and some Thai staff members, including an in-house research monitor at Cha-on Suesum, believed that patient names could be retained on records to facilitate nurses' work. Only at the last stage, when information was moved to the research case report forms (CRFs), did names need to be expunged from records. Yet this account wasn't entirely consistent with their practice, the Thai interviewer working with my research group pointed out. Patient names continued to appear on CRFs in some subsites. In response, the monitor reiterated her previous explanation: "That was because the site [runs] their work by calling the name of the patient not the ID code. So, they need to put the name on the CRFs to make the work easily flow. They cannot remember the [identification] number of the patients. This can be acceptable during the [clinical] trial only, but not when the documents would be archived." The monitor then explained additional protections put in place to protect confidentiality, such as requirements for signatures of anyone accessing the records that had been placed in archive boxes in the last stages of a project. Apparently an extra step had been inserted: removing identifying information just before CRFs were archived.

When Thai researchers carried out clinical studies partly funded by the US government, though, they were obliged to adhere to a host of US rules. Despite considerable training on these rules and general agreement about the principles, people often discovered that they had overlooked instances where local practice and international rules had not been fully harmonized, a point raised in interviews with doctors and research administrators as well as in-house monitors. Discussing the overall level of compliance with the rules of good clinical practice (GCP), one in-house monitor explained that in the past they had used only local standards, but that now they followed GCP standards 50% to 60% of the time, which she thought was adequate for a post-marketing study like the one they had been discussing. The monitor estimated that in the next couple of years the subsites would be in compliance with GCP 70% to 80% of the time. Compliance was higher—80% to 90%—at Cha-on Suesum and at more centrally located subsites, she added. As this interview with the in-house research monitor suggests, it was not always entirely clear which Thai conventions had to be modified to fit US rules and which could be left undisturbed.

Confidentiality issues were not limited to preparation of records, though. Sometimes staff members were pressured to reveal information to other people, such as employers. Staff generally knew that this was prohibited; moreover these rules aligned closely with their own instincts. But occasionally they would be caught off guard, for example, by a patient requesting them to tell an employer that a test result was negative. In other cases, despite the best efforts of the clinic, husbands, mothers-in-law, or neighbors sometimes became suspicious, as happened when Philly Lutaaya "health visitors" dropped in to check on mothers who missed appointments or when mothers were ferried home by clinic drivers.

But there were also times when the rules seemed to require that information be revealed. In South Africa, for instance, when HIV-infected patients were not practicing safe sex and had not disclosed to their partners, Gugu Dlamini Clinic staff were permitted—indeed, obliged—to inform the partners so that they could protect themselves. Of course, there were legally mandated steps along that path to disclosure, including that clinic staff must first put patients on notice, allowing them time to make the revelation themselves. Equally troubling were instances where very ill adult patients had not informed their caregivers—generally, their mothers—that they had AIDS. Staff members found these situations agonizing. Torn between their obligation to protect the confidentiality of the patient and an equally strong obligation to protect the welfare of the patient's partner or caregiver, staff members often stalled because none of the options seemed acceptable.

That the rules were cumbersome and never quite fit the real-life circumstances became clear in the long training sessions I attended as well as in interviews and more casual conversations. Although it might be "obvious" to neighbors, family members could be quite blind: "It's different when this is the person you sleep next to every night," one counselor poignantly observed, adding her own family's experiences into the mix. Moreover, clinic staff believed that patients' extreme reluctance to disclose to caregivers was sometimes matched by mothers' equally deep resistance to putting any barrier between themselves and their children. "She would not want to be left with the memory of touching her child with gloves on the last day," one counselor noted sadly, recounting how a now-infected mother gently cleaned the bloody nose of her son with her bare hands the day before he died, unaware that he had AIDS.

Even more common, though, was the situation that arose in Uganda, where one of Philly Lutaaya's treatment programs required that people disclose to their intimate partners. This was a family-oriented program whose objective was to get the whole family treated. But all staff knew of instances where telling the partner had gone very badly. Husbands did occasionally beat their wives or throw them out of the house, leaving the woman and the couple's children homeless and without any financial support. Did it make sense to insist that an HIV positive woman run this risk? Staff members noted that the program aimed to improve the health of HIV-infected parents and their children and wondered how that could be accomplished if a woman lost her tie to the man who put food on the table for her and their children. At first blush it would appear that this program, partly supported by US funds, violated confidentiality rules. Strictly speaking, though, the program rules did not violate the letter of the law because staff were not themselves informing anyone of their partner's HIV infection. Yet these program policies did seem to staff to conflict with the spirit of the law. Aware that legal scrutiny was more intense than it had been in the past, staff members pondered how to balance medical goals and legal requirements.

PREVENTING MOTHER-TO-CHILD TRANSMISSION: MEDICAL CONSENSUS, INCONSISTENT LEGAL AND POLITICAL SUPPORT

As they worry about legal issues, staff members often reflect on how the law balances the interests of one party against those of another and how the law facilitates or undermines medical work. Such questions are especially prominent in PMTCT programs, where the rights of mothers—for example, not to be tested or to decline treatment—may conflict with the rights of their fetuses to be protected from infection. Although doctors, and especially pediatricians, feel strongly about protecting the health of unborn babies, the conflict between maternal and fetal rights is much more vigorously debated in the US than in Thailand, Uganda, or South Africa, perhaps because pregnancy is more medicalized in the US and the state has sufficient resources to follow through with a full program of prophylaxis during pregnancy. Although access to testing and treatment has improved over the years,[16] poorer countries often have not been able to offer anti-retroviral therapy (ART), provide caesarian deliveries when indicated (e.g., when the mother has not achieved viral suppression), or provide baby formula to prevent transmission via breastmilk. Because the state cannot make good on a threat to protect the child against the mother's wishes, doctors may be less eager to use the muscle of the state to induce unwilling mothers to accept treatment. Only in the US has there been much talk about protecting fetuses from "irresponsible" mothers.[17] Such talk may also be more common in the US because of the association of HIV with IV drug use. When HIV is a general heterosexual epidemic, as it is in Africa, women who are HIV positive are not automatically assumed to be inadequate mothers. Because of the ambiguities about how fully the law supports coerced testing or treatment of pregnant women, staff members in the five clinics often felt unsure of the legality of pressing women to be tested and treated during pregnancy.

The South African case usefully illustrates the conundrums medical workers encounter when medical consensus, here about PMTCT, embodied in international clinical guidelines is not supported by law but is instead undermined by legal and political authorities. The foot dragging of the South African Department of Health during the Mbeki era (1999–2008) is an important backdrop for any discussion of the South African PMTCT guideline during that period. There was ample information about the magnitude of the HIV epidemic in South Africa and the transmission rate from infected women to babies, and nevirapine prophylaxis had been used successfully in other developing countries. Yet the Department of Health did not offer prophylaxis for pregnant women until ordered to do so by the Constitutional Court (TAC 2001; Department of Health, South Africa 2002). Another court case was required in 2007 to force the government to offer dual anti-retroviral prophylaxis for pregnant women (TAC 2007). In the meantime, Manto Tshabalala-Msimang, the minister of health, so frequently expressed her opposition to ART that her resignation was publicly called for at the Toronto AIDS conference in 2006 and in a letter from sixty international AIDS experts, who reminded President Mbeki that "garlic, beetroot and lemons are not alternatives to efficacious medication" (Louw 2006; see also BBC 2006; Blandy 2006). Even when an official guideline was put in place, it was clear that the national government was not enthusiastic about treatment. Despite official policies supporting treatment, drugs were not supplied and protesters were arrested (Blandy 2006). The 2008 South African PMTCT guideline acknowledged some of the contention but omitted mention of pressure for the two-drug regimen, claiming that "the Department of Health implemented the court rulings to the letter and the PMTCT programme is now widely available" (Department of Health, South Africa 2008b, 24).

But where did provincial governments stand during the period when the national government refused to offer PMTCT prophylaxis? The provincial government of the Western Cape elected to use provincial funds for a dual anti-retroviral program when the national government was still not fully supporting even the nevirapine-only program. But the Western Cape was anomalous, both richer than other provincial governments and more willing to challenge the national government. In KZN, the provincial health department that sometimes described Gugu Dlamini's successful PMTCT program as "a thorn in [its] side" specifically mentioned its unwillingness to break with national policy as it brought charges against the acting medical manager of Manguzi Hospital for offering dual anti-retroviral prophylaxis to his patients.

The South African national PMTCT guideline was largely silent on any controversial matters. It alluded to staff qualifications ("professional nurses" were mentioned as those who should get training); distinguished between "health care providers" and "health care workers" with citations to statutes; and stated, in both the text and graphs, that it was a "registered health professional (in line with the relevant legislation and regulations)" who would prescribe drugs (Department of Health, South Africa 2008b, 34, 9–10, 17–19 and 29, respectively). It mentioned that professional nurses "should be trained in performing the rapid HIV tests and on the importance of confidentiality" (South Africa 2008b, 34). It discussed the role of provinces in implementation (South Africa 2008b, 70) and provided detailed discussion of reporting (South Africa 2008b, 62–68). In a section on "guiding principles," it summarized the "rights of women, pregnant women and mothers to information, treatment, management and care"; discussed what was entailed in "protecting and respecting children"; and laid out the "duty and responsibility of ALL health care personnel" (South Africa 2008b, 27). Given that this document was produced under pressure from activists and the courts, it may not be surprising that rights to testing and treatment received more attention than rights to refuse testing or treatment. On any conflict between maternal and child rights, the document was silent, stating only that "the child's best interest is of paramount importance" (South Africa 2008b, 27). Throughout, the language was either of "offering" women counseling, testing, and PMTCT interventions or of "informing" them about HIV and PMTCT (see, e.g., South Africa 2008b, 29, 30). When offered the test, a woman was "asked to provide verbal and written consent to the testing" (e.g., South Africa 2008b, 30), but the document acknowledged that she "may refuse an HIV test" (South Africa 2008b, 30). Women who refused testing were to be offered counseling and testing at each subsequent visit. Earlier portions of the document suggested that refusals of testing would be followed by "post-refusal counselling" (South Africa 2008b, 11).

As a guideline moves from being a treatment guideline offered as guidance for professionals to being a set of recommendations promulgated by a government to create rights (for patients) and obligations (for care providers), the balance between law and medicine changes. The South African PMTCT guideline differed strikingly from the DHHS guideline for PMTCT (DHHS 2007) in use at that time. In particular, the South African guideline had much more *law* in it: lists of statutes on professional jurisdictions, reporting obligations for clinics, lists of rights of women and children. It also had medicine and science in it, of course, but a lower proportion of the pages were devoted to these topics, with much less space allocated to review of the scientific evidence supporting recommendations. In part this is because guidelines adopted by governments and clinics for their specific jurisdictions are intended to be used in conjunction with the guidelines of bodies like WHO and the DHHS on which they are based. In addition, though, national guidelines are intended not just to instruct medical workers on issues of medical science but also to remind them of the legal constraints within which they must practice. Where the law is out of sync with the medical consensus on what is appropriate, rather than helpfully legitimizing medical practice, statutes and regulations may instead undermine medical authority and paralyze medical practitioners.

PEDIATRIC HIV: UNCHARTED MEDICAL TERRITORY, UNHELPFUL LAW

Only in resource-constrained countries are there many HIV-infected children. Although practitioners in poorer countries have often relied on the guidelines developed in richer countries as a starting point for treating adults, rich countries had less to offer for the treatment of children. In the South African and Ugandan clinics, treatment of children was a high priority. At Philly Lutaaya, most of the children being treated were quite young and therefore under the wing of parents or guardians. Because their patient population included the full range from infants to adolescents, Gugu Dlamini's staff often found themselves confronting legal and ethical questions for which no one had clear answers.

The pediatricians at Gugu Dlamini Clinic were enthusiastic about the "superb" South African pediatric AIDS guidelines (Department of Health, South Africa 2005). But unfortunately, there were problems with dissemination, and no one could get copies of the guidelines. "They're probably sitting in an unopened box in someone's office and that person hasn't a clue that they're there," one pediatrician joked as she listed the people she had telephoned in her attempt to get copies of the booklet. The pediatric guidelines were clear and comprehensive with a practical, humane tone. These guidelines provided a solid foundation that allowed Gugu Dlamini pediatricians to "reason together," as they put it, to figure out how best to meet the needs of individual patients. On nonmedical points, though, the guidelines seemed less confident.[18] For instance, the section on adherence confessed that it was "originally written with adult patients in mind"

(South Africa 2005, 96). How one would ensure that children or adolescents being initiated on ART truly understood that they had to adhere to these rigid drug regimens for the rest of their lives was far from clear. The section on legal issues opened with a carefully crafted statement that touched on intertwined obstacles to normal consent procedures but did not always offer clear solutions. Ordinarily only a parent or legal guardian could consent to testing and treatment for children under fourteen. But some flexibility was necessary, the document acknowledged, explaining options for legal appeals, expansion of the group of adults who could give consent, and lowering of the age of consent to twelve and even younger for exceptionally mature children (South Africa 2005, 108).[19] The document continued by observing that when many adults have died of AIDS, children end up living in "informal care situations without legal guardians to assist them" (South Africa 2005, 108), adding that "abandoned children have the same rights as other children" (South Africa 2005, 109). One social scientist involved in a project on AIDS orphans in Uganda noted that children had sometimes "been succeeded" (passed from one relative to another as family members died of AIDS) as many as three times in three years. Often, guardianship decisions were made only when children were orphaned, and they were rarely formalized.

In addition, the legalities of guardianship might simply be ignored in practice. Whoever repeatedly brought a child to the clinic was treated as the legal parent or guardian. Questions about familial ties were asked when forms had to completed, but the answers often had little bearing when it came time to get consent for treatment. The staff worried more about ensuring that a consistent, identified person—a parent, granny, aunt or uncle, or even an older sibling—was caring for the child and was committed to tracking a complicated treatment regimen and schedule of clinic visits. When an orphaned child lived in a large household, it was not always obvious which person was tracking the child's treatment.

Questions about family ties became more fraught as clinics considered who qualified for care as part of a clinic's "family package." Staff were inclined to be generous, both because they were deeply committed to getting people treated and because they understood that target children were more likely to remain healthy if their caregivers were healthy enough to earn a living and provide childcare. Although they were also inclined to be generous, administrators were under pressure to keep clinic commitments within manageable limits and to protect the clinic income stream by adhering to the rules of granting agencies.

Especially troubling, though, were the cases where parents or guardians seemed unable or unwilling to get treatment for children or where parents and adolescents disagreed about what to do. One adolescent girl, whose case was discussed repeatedly in Gugu Dlamini staff meetings, had been on and off treatment as her mother's willingness to let her receive antiretroviral drugs (ARVs) waxed and waned. Concerned that "her therapeutic options [were] being destroyed," the girl's pediatrician noted her rising viral load and worried that it would be "disastrous" if she became resistant to the first-line regimen while staff worked things out with her mother. Home visits by Gugu Dlamini delegations made little progress. Sometimes the mother was not home. When she was home, she accused them of "behaving like Whites" rather than considering "what's good for a Black person." Sometimes she threatened not to let her daughter participate in the adolescent support group, a program the child enjoyed. Over several months, the counseling staff and medical team discussed initiating legal action against the mother. Although a consultation with a local AIDS law group convinced staff that they were legally empowered to intervene on behalf of the child, it was never clear *how* to intervene. Rights not attached to clear mechanisms often mean little. Rights have to be claimed, and almost by definition vulnerable children cannot claim their rights, in part because they lack crucial resources such as transportation and legal advice. Moreover, it often is not clear that a child will be better off being removed from the home even if parents or other caregivers are not supporting treatment. By the end of my months in the field, the girl's situation remained unresolved.

In these pediatric cases, the law appeared to have something to say, yet its message was unclear. The laws seemed to offer tools, yet the tools were difficult to access and use and not always very helpful. Treating HIV-infected children was difficult under the best of circumstances. The purely medical problems were challenging; often doctors were working in new medical terrain as they adjusted dosages for infants and children or made adjustment for puberty. Yet doctors felt they had the tools to tackle the strictly medical problems. When families or guardians were unwilling to let children be treated or did not give medications properly, medical and counseling staff felt much more helpless. To solve those problems required a different set of tools—tools that clinic staff either lacked or did not know how to employ.

INITIATING THERAPY AND SWITCHING REGIMENS: MEDICAL TROUBLESHOOTING, OFFICIAL RIGIDITY

Compared to the intractable uncertainties that arise because of the different interests and needs of mothers and children and those that arise sequentially as children grow into more autonomous beings, the more mundane uncertainties of initiating ART and switching regimens seemed almost trivial. Staff members may wonder whether pretherapy training is legally mandated or merely advised. They may be uncertain about the legal acceptability of their ad hoc solutions when patients fail to complete training but desperately need to start therapy. Or, in a country offering a limited range of ARVs, they may be unclear about the rules for switching a patient from a first-line regimen to a more expensive second-line regimen. These are situations that require considerable medical troubleshooting, especially when a patient is "failing" treatment. Too-rigid laws may reduce room for maneuver.

In South Africa, as the government rollout finally began, Gugu Dlamini Clinic staff worried about decreased flexibility in dealing with these medically complex cases. In the past, because their funding did not come from the government, they had been able to make decisions about regimen changes without being constrained to consult anyone beyond their own staff. Now, as they understood it, they were obliged to submit requests to government officials before making regimen changes. As mentioned before, Gugu Dlamini's doctors were convinced that the official first-line regimen often led to lactic acidosis, a life-threatening side effect. When this side effect was detected, a regimen change needed to be made quickly, leaving little time for the back and forth the government seemed to be envisioning. The clinic had purchased a handheld blood lactate analyzer and developed its own routine for managing lactic acidosis. Staff were unwilling to return to their previous way of practicing, which they believed endangered a subgroup of patients. Although the clinic had collected evidence to support its internal guideline, the government had not even begun to track this side effect.

Gugu Dlamini staff identified three intertwined problems: the regimen itself, the inadequate mechanisms for reporting and tracking serious side effects, and a cumbersome process for switching patients to second-line regimens. In a system oriented to public health, as the South African system was, more attention was given to formulating a set of alternatives that would work for the infected population than for individual patients. In Thailand, Uganda, and South Africa, the interests of individual patients did not trump collective interests as they often would in the US. In these countries where policymakers struggled to find affordable treatments during a catastrophic epidemic and ministries of health worried that AIDS would swallow the whole health budget, it was imperative that patients adhere to their regimens so the less expensive first-line regimens could be preserved as a treatment option for as long as possible. Public health officials thus tried to ensure that doctors moved patients to second-line regimens infrequently and only for sound reasons.

In this climate, clinic doctors had good reason to expect that the government would devise a complicated routine and that the ominous language about "getting permission" truly meant that permission had to be received in advance of the switch. The South African government's previous HIV policy failures did nothing to allay their fears. But not following the rules might jeopardize Gugu Dlamini's status as a rollout site and its access to funds to cover the expenses of hundreds of patients. Their concerns proved to be unfounded, though, and, at least for the staff of this very reputable clinic, "ask permission" actually meant "inform us after the fact."

This example illustrates how the intertwining of legal and medical constraints can create complex dilemmas for healthcare workers. Gugu Dlamini Clinic doctors believed they had solved an important medical problem—deaths from a side effect associated with one of the drugs in a common first-line regimen—and done it better than most other sites. But as medical experts, they were ill equipped to take on the legal and regulatory questions that came with participation in the government rollout. For these clinicians, discretion to make *medical* decisions was central to their understanding of their ethical and legal obligations as physicians. A legally based limitation on that discretion was therefore hard to accept.

Guidelines and Skill: Expert Work and Task Shifting

Clinical guidelines are procedural standards, compressed summaries of voluminous scientific studies presented as suggested courses of action. One common misconception is that scripts and guidelines are only useful for coordinating and managing the work of unskilled workers. But guidelines, protocols, and scripts can also help organize the more complex activities of highly trained workers.[20] Whether the objective is schematic processing with simpler tasks or deliberative processing with more complex ones, guidelines and scripts help direct and control attention.[21] Training and practice turn both simple and complex activities into routines and establish habits. With repetition, people become competent users of complex scripts such as clinical guidelines and are then able to skillfully adapt to unforeseen circumstances (Dewey 1930), reducing error, saving time, and economizing on thought.

To enact guidelines, users generally need to draw on tacit knowledge transmitted in interactions between experienced and novice users. Even when people have acquired the basic skills and professional training necessary to use these guidelines, though, differences in skill and training remain. In the five clinics, all elite facilities, guidelines were widely used. The difference between skilled workers and others was not about whether they used recipes and routines but how they used them. For skilled workers, routines can be a foundation for flexible adaptation (Feldman and Pentland 2003). People use guidelines less flexibly when they are just learning, and indeed their teachers may require more rigid adherence to rules during apprenticeship. For instance, the heads of the surgical services Bosk (2003 [1979]) studied expected their residents to follow prescribed routines exactly. Admittedly, surgery is an especially hierarchical field because routines are needed to coordinate complex activities in the operating room. But those same routines also facilitated residents' learning and made their inputs more predictable. Although junior staff's limited skills meant they needed to follow rules exactly, senior surgeons used rules more flexibly, adjusting as circumstances required. Senior doctors' capacity to adjust and correct meant that subordinates' technical errors often were less worrisome than one might expect—as long as juniors did not compound the problem by failing to communicate quickly and thoroughly (a normative error, in Bosk's taxonomy) when they made mistakes.

Their discussions made clear that medical staff in my fieldsites believed guidelines helped them reliably achieve better results. They referred to guidelines in discussing the mistakes of other practitioners, for instance, commenting (at both Gugu Dlamini and Cha-on Suesum) on doctors who ignorantly started patients on mono- or dual-therapy instead of multidrug regimens or who didn't know that TB looks different in people who also have HIV and so failed to diagnose and resolve TB before starting their patients on ART (at Philly Lutaaya Clinic in Uganda). They also referred their students to guidelines and went over guidelines in teaching (most notably when a group of us squeezed together on a hard wooden bench to receive instruction in Daniel's office in Uganda). Aware that guidelines are "always in development," doctors also talked about which guidelines did not fit local conditions. For instance, doctors at Cha-on Suesum Clinic and other Thai clinics believed that in some crucial respects their Thai patients' bodies differed from those of "Western big guys" and that dosages and regimens needed to be modified accordingly (Gazley 2011, 96–132). Similarly, the doctors at Gugu Dlamini Clinic believed that recommendations about first-line regimens needed to be modified to include a warning about lactic acidosis in people with high body mass indexes.

In these examples, the conversation could move to a higher level, pose more complex questions, and fine-tune solutions because caregivers could start with the guideline as a base. Much of the literature discusses guidelines as a floor beneath the feet of practitioners, a minimum level of performance. As a floor, guidelines should help physicians reduce error, incorporate new scientific findings into their practice, and track side effects, complications, and drug interactions. Yet floors can also be foundations for even better performances. In several of the clinics, staff were actively involved in writing guidelines, sometimes working with international bodies (with clinic doctors' names appearing in the credits) but more commonly simply reworking guidelines for clinic use. At Philly Lutaaya, doctors were preparing clinic guidelines on a long list of topics and were meeting regularly to review the drafts. At Gugu Dlamini, Neil seemed to enjoy compressing voluminous guidelines for hospital use and other doctors regularly updated loose-leaf binders of key guidelines to keep handy in the clinic's examining rooms. Other staff used guidelines to craft forms that reminded their colleagues and patients of the schedules of visits, when visits required lab tests or fasting, or when annual pap smears were due. That there were guidelines available as references, as starting points for conversations, as documents from which schedules of lab tests could be extracted meant that conversations were more detailed and more sophisticated than they would be if everyone had to reinvent the wheel for each task.

But the good effects of standards come about only when people "actively submit" to standards (Timmermans and Berg 2003). Neither standards nor workers can produce the results alone. Results are instead produced by the interaction of workers and guidelines, the outcome of workers allowing their work and thought to be shaped by the guidelines. Put differently, the most positive results of these guidelines are achieved when workers use them as a basis for further deliberation, employing guidelines mindfully rather than robotically. Rather than providing a way to avoid thought (Heimer 2008), then, this use of guidelines *encourages* and *disciplines* thought. The examples discussed above illustrate this effect. The South African pediatricians began with national pediatric guidelines that they fine-tuned to meet the needs of individual patients. These same physicians made larger adjustments to guidelines when treating adolescents. Also at Gugu Dlamini, physicians very carefully worked out an alternative guideline on d4T and lactic acidosis. And at Philly Lutaaya, Daniel explained to his students how to manage TB/HIV coinfection coupled with a very low CD4 count and how to adjust the treatment plan further to protect a patient's pregnancy. In all of these cases, existing guidelines established a starting point, suggested a basic methodology, and provided a long list of things to keep in mind as physicians considered courses of treatment for individual patients and appropriate adjustments for their clinic's ongoing work.

Importantly, those guidelines that serve as the foundation for the work of the most skilled experts can also be used to reorganize work, shifting tasks from scarce, expensive workers to more plentiful, less expensive, and less skilled personnel. Scholars have debated about whether the use of scripts and guidelines deskills work, potentially threatening the jobs of skilled workers—as Braverman (1974) predicted. Yet the evidence on this too-simple hypothesis is quite mixed, both because employers not only deskill or dumb down some jobs but also reskill and upskill others and because workers find ways to protect their jobs and resist deskilling (Attewell 1987; Tilly and Tilly 1997; Iskander 2021). And sometimes workers welcome scripting because it guides them through difficult or awkward situations. Leidner (1993), for instance, found that workers trying to sell life insurance in the living rooms of strangers appreciated the help offered by scripts, though workers selling hamburgers in a fast-food franchise resented requirements to follow scripts that forced them to push customers to make additional purchases.

Medical staff, likewise, have mixed reactions to scripts, often taking notes on protocols to prepare them to interact smoothly with patients, but also frequently either deviating from informed consent scripts or making wry jokes to smooth over the awkwardness of scripted interactions. Within the medical world, one can easily find instances of both deskilling, as tasks once done by physicians are delegated to less skilled workers, and upskilling, as ever more complex tasks and new occupations are added to the mix in healthcare organizations.

At least since the Industrial Revolution, employers have understood that output can be increased by routinizing work and standardizing components. That in turn has fostered the hope that once routines have been established, the work can be done with less skilled employees, stretching the budget and expanding the workforce at the same time. And indeed that is what many public health programs and individual clinics (Heimer 2013) hope to accomplish in resource-constrained settings and what sponsors and global health organizations advise, though they also urge that task-shifting programs follow guidelines about how to reallocate work (WHO, PEPFAR, and UNAIDS 2008). If anti-retroviral rollout programs are to succeed, they will have to use less trained medical workers to do tasks initially assigned only to the most skilled physicians (Callaghan, Ford, and Schneider 2010), though some observers warn against adding extra tasks to the work packages of less qualified workers (Philips, Zachariah, and Venis 2008), the very problem experienced by lay HIV counselors in South Africa.

Often the objective in standardization is not to do the same thing with cheaper labor but to do something more or better with skilled labor, a point emphasized by the designers of checklist programs to reduce infection rates in US hospitals (Gawande 2009; Pronovost and Vohr 2011; but see Bosk 2023). Skilled workers may be able to move more quickly through their work and do it with fewer errors when the steps are spelled out in a guideline. When workers orient to the same guideline, they may be more successful in handing off work to a colleague midstream, an important point given increased regulatory attention to handoffs as a source of error (Cohen and Hilligoss 2010; Szymczak and Bosk 2012). They may spot anomalies more quickly and see how to manage them when guidelines point out the main variations that are likely to arise. The trick, then, is to use guidelines to increase the capacities of *all* workers—so both less and more skilled workers are doing better work than they would without the guidelines. The best guidelines do not shut off thought but instead guide people to think about particular topics. For the most skilled workers, guidelines may encourage deliberation on nonroutine questions because there is less need to expend time and energy thinking about the areas where medical science has reached consensus. Because doctors can consult the charts about recommended combinations of anti-retrovirals, they can focus on how to manage troubling cases of patients who are failing treatment or who seek care only when they are already desperately ill. For less skilled workers, attention may instead be focused on determining when patients need to be referred to more skilled caregivers, a particular concern in the task shifting that accompanies rollouts of anti-retroviral programs.

Healthcare Experts, Legal Novices: Legalization and Limits on Discretion

Guidelines give some workers the right to use their judgment while curtailing the discretion of other workers. Historically, the right to use discretion has depended on professional norms, professional hierarchies, and organizational rules. Chambliss (1996), for instance, notes that although nurses are trained to be caring professionals, their capacity to exercise professional judgment is severely curtailed. As hospital employees, they are expected to adhere to hospital policies; as subordinates in the medical hierarchy, they are required to follow doctors' orders.

Important as organizational rules and professional hierarchies are in the medical world, constraints on the exercise of professional judgment arise in other ways as well. Discretion may depend, for instance, on rules imposed by outside bodies such as governments, as Dr. Pfaff learned. The legalization of healthcare has reduced the discretion of many groups of health professionals, in some cases by restricting what they are legally permitted to do and in others by creating uncertainty about what is legally permissible. Worried about avoiding legal liability, healthcare organizations and many healthcare workers may overcomply, particularly in periods when the law is in flux.[22] Although discretion surely depends on status and professional qualifications, when guidelines are endorsed by government bodies and in one way or another buttressed by law, staff members who lack legal training lose some of their capacity to use discretion. Highly placed, skilled users of medical guidelines may nevertheless be untrained, unskilled users of the legal part of guidelines. As medical guidelines are legalized, then, even high-status medical staff lose some of their capacity to adapt.

As summarized in table 6.2, different categories of workers have different experiences with guidelines and are differently affected by the medical and legal elements in those guidelines. This is partly a matter of skill base—medical guidelines are, of course, about medicine, so workers at the top of the medical hierarchy are most likely to have the training that will make them facile users of the guidelines. But it is also a matter of status. Although neither doctors nor nurses are likely to have the legal training that would equip them to be facile users of the legal elements of medical guidelines, the legal system gives more rights to doctors and fewer to nurses. Doctors generally have more privileges and more capacity to exercise discretion, but nurses usually have more legal cover than doctors if following rules or orders results in bad outcomes. Counseling staff are more likely than most medical staff to work at the interface of law and medicine. They typically are not legally trained, though, which can make for considerable anxiety about what they can and cannot do. In the clinics and hospitals of rich countries, some ancillary staff are likely to have received a bit of training on legal matters—a few workshops perhaps, similar to the ones that occurred at Gugu Dlamini Clinic. Hospitals also may employ in-house legal counsel or hire legal consultants, especially in richer countries. Generally speaking, though, medical and legal expertise tend to be located in different people and perhaps even in different parts of the organization. All this makes for complex relationships to guidelines and other rules, particularly rules most firmly tethered to formal law. It is not simply that some people have the skills to use guidelines while others lack those skills. Instead it is that people

TABLE 6.2. Occupation and Expertise: Medical and Legal Competence

TYPES OF WORKERS	MEDICAL ELEMENTS	LEGAL ELEMENTS
Medical Doctors (Physicians, Medical Officers)	Fully competent to deal with medical elements. But multiple kinds of expertise are recognized: training in infectious diseases and HIV medicine; medical specialty (such as obstetrics or pediatrics); and special expertise in HIV-related issues such as opportunistic infections, or drug resistance.	Typically not legally trained. Often legally empowered to carry out particular actions. Because of lack of legal training, unlikely to know limits, exceptions, etc. Common reaction is caution.
Nurses (Professional Nurses, Licensed Practical Nurses, etc.)	Competent in many medical matters, but subordinate to doctors. Specialist nurses may practice with little supervision from doctors. In some locales, nurses can prescribe some categories of drugs.	Not legally trained. Legal empowerment narrower in scope than is the case for doctors. Typically practice under the supervision of doctors with some legal cover provided by doctors.
Other Medical Staff (Pharmacists, Phlebotomists, Lab Workers)	Competent in specialty, but perhaps not in the matters generally addressed in clinical guidelines.	Not legally trained. Empowered to carry out specific activities only.
Counseling Staff (Psychologists, Counselors, Peer Counselors)	Generally not competent on medical matters, though usually more knowledgeable than general population. May be trained to do HIV testing and counseling (also psychological counseling for psychologists). Often interact with patients.	Generally not legally trained. Many of their activities put them at boundaries jointly governed by law and medicine. Sometimes great uncertainty and anxiety about which actions are legally permissible and which are prohibited.
Ancillary Staff: Administrators, Financial Officers, Legal Counsel (Positions, Titles, Job Descriptions Vary by Locale)	Generally not competent in medical matters. May have little or no contact with patients.	Generally not legally trained (exception is legal counsel, but not all institutions have this position), though some knowledge of law. Many of their activities put them at boundaries of medical institutions, which are often jointly governed by law and medicine. Often consulted by others about which actions are legally permissible and which are prohibited.

are skilled users of different element of the guidelines, and often no one is expert in the full package.

The Locus of Discretion in Law and Medicine

The management of discretion varies by field. In medicine, discretion is local and is concentrated in doctors. In law, in contrast, discretion is concentrated at the appellate level rather than at the first encounter between case and law (Llewellyn 1960; Stinchcombe 2001).

In any given medical institution, the right to interpret and adjust is typically in the hands of the doctors first encountering a case; interpretation and adjustment generally do not have to wait for the judgment of higher-ranking, specialist doctors. One needs to be careful not to overstate this point, though. Within medical institutions, occupations are partially ranked, with doctors having authority over nurses and so having a larger sphere of discretion than nurses. Within this system of ranked occupations, though, nurses and other professionals (phlebotomists, physical therapists, various technicians) do retain some control over their separate jurisdictions and some discretion within that special sphere despite the overall dominance of doctors. And within the sphere of doctors, some medical problems require referral or consultation and some categories of doctors (interns, residents) have less autonomy.

In addition to tailoring their actions to fit the cases they encounter, in many places doctors also can modify the rules that they work with so that these rules have a better fit with the stream of cases they typically encounter. To put it differently, the medical "law" that doctors work with can be adjusted in the place where this "law" encounters the "cases." Clinical guidelines can be recrafted to be local, site-specific "law," and physicians also often make rules that apply to the group of subordinates they supervise and with whom they share cases (Bosk 2003 [1979]).

As medicine has become more legalized, though, this local flexibility has diminished. More of the work of doctors (and other medical workers) has come to be organized around clinical guidelines, a distinctive set of techniques for assessing, organizing, and transmitting medical knowledge. Guideline culture in turn has shaped, constrained, and disciplined the dialogue between new cases and the corpus of medical knowledge. That dialogue between cases and existing medical knowledge would look quite different if placed in the context of a less law-like way of summarizing knowledge—such as on-the-job learning, rules of thumb, or medicine as art rather than science. At the same time that the dialogue between medical knowledge and cases is organized around guidelines, guidelines have been adopted as standards of practice by governments, granting bodies, insurers, and clinics. As the soft law of medicine is hardened, doctors are more often required to justify their decisions to senior doctors or external review panels. Discretion is thus less local, more constrained by medical "law," and more subject to review.

Conclusion: Doctors within Borders

It would be a mistake to overstate the uniformity of arrangements for social control and governance in medical care. Although I argue that medicine has become more legalized in recent decades, with the regulation of medicine becoming more formal and more organized around explicit rules, it is nevertheless more legalized in some places and less legalized in others. Table 6.3 summarizes this variability by comparing systems of medical "law" along two dimensions: whether guidelines speak to medical matters and whether they speak to legal issues.

In some locations and time periods, guidelines play only a small role if they exist at all. In "preguideline" situations, guidelines do not speak clearly to either legal or medical issues. The practice of medicine is not strongly regulated either by a body of peers working with codified scientific knowledge distilled into guidelines or by state bodies attempting to regulate the work of professionals.

Under conditions of "professional dominance" (Light 1994), the medical profession works autonomously, and guidelines primarily address medical matters and are largely silent on legal questions. If states are involved in the regulation of medicine, it will often be because they are enlisted by one branch of medicine in a battle to delegitimate competitors (Starr 1982).

TABLE 6.3. Guidelines and Jurisdiction in Healthcare

	GUIDELINES SILENT ON MEDICAL ISSUES	GUIDELINES SPEAK TO MEDICAL ISSUES
Guidelines Speak to Legal Issues	State dominance: healthcare fully controlled by state and legal professionals	Shared jurisdiction: healthcare jointly regulated by professions and state
Guidelines Silent on Legal Issues	Pre-guidelines: no formal regulation	Professional dominance: healthcare fully in jurisdiction of health professionals

Medicine can also be the handmaiden of the state, though, and in such circumstances, the state decides how medicine will be practiced and with what purposes. In situations of "state dominance," guidelines will especially address the legality of procedures such as abortion or involuntary hospitalization of people judged to be mentally ill, rather than addressing strictly medical and scientific issues.

Increasingly, though, guidelines have both medical and legal content. With "shared jurisdiction," the coverage of guidelines is extended and questions are raised about the allocation of medical resources. But the increasing emphasis on rules often comes with an increased rigidity that undermines the local adjustment that is the hallmark of medicine. Doctoring within borders established by the state has its costs.

This chapter has looked at how the use of medical guidelines changes when those guidelines include a legal element. Because clinic staff lack expertise in legal matters, they are often uncomfortable with these legal interfaces. In long years of training, medical staff are taught to use guidelines flexibly. They are reminded that it is their responsibility to assess whether and how guidelines actually apply. Although clinical guidelines allow doctors to stand on the shoulders of generations of other doctors and scientists, they are instructed to remain mindful of the need for flexibility. Their medical training thus equips them intellectually and morally to make judgment calls about when and how guidelines should be put aside. But doctors may not know when to put the law aside or how that can be accomplished even when their medical training suggests that it is necessary.

[CHAPTER SEVEN]

Strategic Uses of Ignorance
in HIV Clinics

In Western culture it is assumed that sound decisions require good information. As the evidence about HIV clinics and the research and treatment
carried out in them suggests, this assumption is as common for healthcare
organizations and the medical and ancillary staff employed by them as for
other kinds of organizations and their staff members. Yet the link between
information and decision making often is weak. Organizations collect
much more information than they have any hope of using. In collecting
this apparently useless information, they signal that they are the kinds of
organizations that make decisions rationally and that they have collected
appropriate information to guide those decisions (Feldman and March
1981). Because the collection and use of information is generally mandated
by rules, regulations, and routines, organizations are also signaling that they
are law-abiding entities.

Given the symbolic importance accorded to information (at least in
Western societies), though, the absence of information is also significant.
To collect information on something signals one's attentiveness and the importance of the topic. What, then, does it mean *not* to collect information,
to be ignorant on some subject? Not collecting information implicitly signals that something is not worth attending to, yet explicitly announcing that
something is unimportant is a risky strategy because it draws attention. A
safer alternative, then, is to bury difficult or controversial facts by making
them inert, for instance, by creating piles of paper that give an illusion of
knowledge or by keeping facts separate from contextual information. In either case, awkward facts are furtively made unavailable for discussion and
decision making.

In this chapter, I examine strategic uses of ignorance to refine the perhaps overly rational portrait of HIV clinics created by the earlier discussions of treatment guidelines and clinical research. I show how the heavily
legalized and documented institutional landscape of HIV clinics produces
the conditions under which information is distributed, sequestered, or

strategically decompiled. This process of rendering facts inert serves to protect a variety of interests—public health initiatives, research projects, donor funding streams, and so forth—and deflects attention from certain truths about broader socioeconomic problems or the pragmatic nature of clinical expertise. Like other highly regulated arenas, HIV clinics contain dark corners that some want to explore and others want to protect. The regulatory activities of clinics offer two ways to conceal information without drawing attention. Elaborate paperwork presents opportunities for concealing awkward information while seeming to tell all. Elaborate divisions of labor likewise offer opportunities for obscuring meaning by isolating awkward facts from the other pieces of information that would allow outsiders to discern patterns. What outsiders do see, though, is staff members dutifully filing required regulatory documents and taking responsibility for their own assigned areas.

In this way of thinking, ignorance is not simply the opposite of knowledge. Knowledge and ignorance can be conceived as poles of a continuum that also includes partial, inexact, uncertain, provisional, and uneven knowledge. But ignorance and knowledge also have much in common. Like knowledge, ignorance can an important resource deployed strategically by organizations, though we should not assume that ignorance is always intentionally created and deployed. People may intentionally keep themselves or others in the dark, but they may instead simply forget to pass along information, not have time to collect it, or not see the implications of information that they already possess. And they may then discover advantages to not knowing and decide to perpetuate existing lacunae. Finally, even when one group decides to keep another ignorant, they may be unsuccessful. People sometimes discover things they are not intended to know, but they may not act on that knowledge. Sometimes people feign ignorance or tacitly agree not to act on information that others would have preferred to conceal.

Although the processes described in this chapter are, I argue, utterly mundane, they have not received much explicit attention from sociologists and organization theorists. And although there is no reason to expect knowledge-producing enterprises to be substantially different from other organizations, it is nevertheless unnerving to find these dark corners in organizations that claim they devote themselves to shedding light. The premium placed on information in these settings means that the concealment of information cannot be overt and often is not even understood by participants. Concealment and obfuscation may then allow people to deal with disagreements about information without confronting them head on. As in many organizations, the behavior of organizations and their members is shaped both by the capacity problems elucidated by March and Simon's

(1958) research on bounded rationality and the signaling imperatives illuminated by Feldman and March's (1981) work on symbolic uses of information. What is new is the extensive legalization of the entire system and its sometimes surprising effects on how information is gathered and hidden, used and carefully ignored.

The argument is developed by discussing how ignorance is created and strategically maintained in key organizational processes. Sites where rules have proliferated and become increasingly rigid, as they have in healthcare and clinical research, are fertile places for thinking about ignorance because legalization creates or modifies constraints, opportunities, rewards, and punishments for knowing and not knowing. With shifts in governance arrangements in medicine, new forms of governance often join rather than supplant previous forms. Thus professional, public, managerial, and market governance mechanisms are bewilderingly layered and interwoven (Scott et al. 2000, esp. 348–49). In medicine, as in other fields that have experienced ramped up pressures for accountability (Power 1997; Strathern 2000; Espeland and Vannebo 2007), new professions have arisen to write, revise, and track the rules themselves, to monitor work and records to ensure that rules are being followed, and to settle disputes, making divisions of labor ever more complex.

When Ignorance Really Is Bliss

The model of action that many subscribe to and that is surely part of the toolkit of HIV clinics assumes that action is grounded in knowledge. Problems are identified, solutions are proposed and debated, a workable (if not optimal) solution is chosen, and the solution is then implemented. But as we know from many years of organizational research (see esp. Cohen, March, and Olsen 1972), that is not always how it happens. Information is indeed collected, but it may have little bearing on decision making. What solution gets adopted is likely to depend heavily on who participates in decision making. Solutions often precede the identification of problems and wait in reserve until the right problem comes along to enable implementation (Feldman 1989). All this implies that ignorance often is bliss because knowledge can disrupt organizational activities. Under such circumstances, organizations may go to considerable trouble to remain ignorant.

Here I consider willful ignorance in the organizational life of HIV clinics. I ask what HIV clinics prefer not to know and show how they discreetly and subtly arrange for ignorance about research subjects, side effects of core technologies, effects of a division of labor between insiders and outsiders, and pressures to please funders. Given the cultural significance of knowledge, though, wise organizations carefully conceal their ignorance by collecting a lot of information and displaying their eagerness to learn. In organizations such as HIV clinics, documentation is a favored way of papering over ignorance.

Two distinct kinds of ignorance are present in organizations—sequestered knowledge and distributed ignorance. The first occurs when inconvenient facts simply do not fit with key rules that people are obliged to work with. Awkward facts can be sequestered and made inert through the creation of vast piles of paper that—ironically—suggest people know something that they actually do not (see, e.g., Rappert 2009). This kind of ignorance is consistent with neo-institutionalist discussions of decoupling and ceremonial forms of compliance (Meyer and Rowan 1977) and is especially likely to occur in the "thinner" institutionalization associated with regulatory systems (Scott 2008).

A second kind of ignorance arises when people focus so intently on one issue that they cannot—or will not—see other things. In such situations, people may know a great deal about some matters but lack a systemic perspective. They may have an inchoate understanding but not have produced the overview that brings things into sharp relief. Facts also may be inert because they are distributed across a group. When no one has all the facts, it is difficult to discern the relationships among facts. What is missing is something akin to the systematizing knowledge that anthropologists add to the local knowledge of "natives" who have had no reason to look for overall patterns (Dauber 1995). This kind of ignorance can be inadvertent or purposeful. Perhaps no one has bothered to bring disparate pieces of information together but perhaps information has been systematically decompiled. In principle, ignorance arising from the distributed character of knowledge can be overcome by putting the pieces together. But the pieces are not always brought into juxtaposition, and sometimes people are invested in preventing systematization, either because systemized knowledge makes their work more difficult or more costly or makes them look bad.

Constructing Proper Participants: Informed Consent, Ritual Surplus, and Sequestered Information

As they select participants for various roles and consider whether to reward, retain, or dismiss them, organizations gather information from and about those participants or potential participants. Some information is collected but apparently put to no further use; other information seems to be stored in case questions arise later. And some information does seem to guide decisions, although one can profitably ask whether alleged predictors of performance really have any bearing either on performance or on decisions about hiring and promotion.

In HIV clinics that do clinical research, much effort goes into locating, screening, and enrolling appropriate research subjects.[1] These are simultaneously scientific and regulatory tasks. In each of the HIV clinics I studied, at least one person was charged with the responsibility of keeping track of regulatory documents, including those pertaining to the recruitment of research subjects. Copies of submissions to institutional review boards (IRBs) and IRB approval letters were carefully stored. Deadlines for annual periodic reviews were charted on calendars and spreadsheets. Among the most sacred of the regulatory documents, though, were the signed forms indicating that research subjects had consented after being screened to verify that they met the protocol criteria, given information about the study, warned of possible side effects, and given an opportunity to ask questions. Those signed pieces of paper are taken as evidence of informed consent, and their existence in the file, along with the annual IRB approvals indicating that the forms met regulatory and legal requirements, acts as a shield for the organization should questions be raised later. When they check the work of a research team, research monitors routinely ask to see these consent forms. Staff members, including regulatory affairs specialists, are vigilant about this paperwork and quite upset when they discover a (rare) lapse.

Beyond the core features,[2] though, the ritual of informed consent, like other sacred rituals, varies somewhat from one locale to another. In the US, potential research subjects are typically handed a consent form to read. Sometimes the person "consenting [the subject]"[3] summarizes key points as the subject looks over the form, a practice that seems friendly but makes it more difficult for the subject to read the form. Sometimes the research worker (typically, a nurse) leaves the potential subject alone for a few minutes to read the form and then returns with an offer to answer questions. At Philly Lutaaya Clinic in Uganda, where literacy cannot be assumed, the staff member administering the consent procedure reads the form aloud to the potential research subject, often a pregnant woman, and then offers to answer questions. After some time, the form is read aloud a second time. Potential subjects may even be "tested" on the content to make sure they have understood. Only after potential research subjects "pass the test" are they allowed to sign the consent form. In training sessions, staff members discussed both the purpose of the gap between first and second readings of the consent form and the documentation that should accompany signed consent forms. For instance, if a woman said she needed to consult her husband, that information should be noted and the counselor doing the second reading should also verify that the woman had in fact consulted her husband about her participation in the study. Emphasizing the importance of making sure that consent was truly informed consent, the Ugandan regulatory affairs specialist elaborated: "You cannot play around with this important document. You need to fill in the gaps. Ask the woman what about her saying she had to talk it over with her husband. Ask the woman to come back if there are still issues that need to be clarified."

These differences are not simply innocuous or charming cultural variability. Rather, taken together, they offer us a convenient example with which to think about how facts are made inert and how and why they regain (unwelcome) vitality. Why, one might wonder, is the ritual enacted differently at Philly Lutaaya in Uganda than at Robert Rafsky or Bobbi Campbell, both in the US? Surely the understanding of the research subjects is as important to consent in the US as in Uganda, yet in one place it is seen as problematic and in the other it is almost taken for granted. The elaborated ritual did not arise because Ugandans particularly relish consent form read-alouds or examinations about clinical research or because Ugandan staff members especially enjoy documenting conversations about consent forms. Rather it arose because of the possibility that someone would ask embarrassing questions about whether research subjects had understood the consent form. Such scrutiny is more likely to occur when people have difficulty enacting the ritual in the conventional way. For instance, where the spelling of names is inexact or where people are not accustomed to writing their names, a name may easily be rendered in different ways on different occasions. Research monitors reviewing the record are trained to raise questions when they find such anomalies, and the "ritual surplus" backing up the signature helps allay their anxieties.

When things go awry in clinical trials—for instance, when a death occurs—a check on the adequacy of the consent process is a likely early step in any investigation. The death of Jesse Gelsinger, the eighteen-year-old participant in one US "gene therapy" trial, illustrates the issues that can arise. Three concerns were raised in the subsequent investigation: that researchers had not shared all relevant information (particularly information about monkey deaths in the research that preceded the human trials) with potential subjects and their families, that conflicts of interest were not divulged, and that affixing the label "therapy" to the trial was misleading and perhaps inappropriately quelled concern about the procedure.[4]

The Gelsinger case is extreme, of course. But the processes of recruiting research subjects and gaining their consent raise a host of points that are uncomfortable for researchers to acknowledge. First, risk is unavoidable in clinical research. There will always be uncertainty in clinical research—if there were not, there would be no reason to conduct the research. Although researchers are required to disclose information about potential harm, and mostly believe wholeheartedly in doing so, they also worry about discouraging potential participants. One consequence of this ambivalence is the difference in tone between the official forms (dry, thorough, often frightening) and the oral presentation (somewhat more sanguine about the risks). Discussing the informed consent process, Fisher (2009) suggests that research staff in nonacademic settings see themselves as correcting a false impression created by the written forms. "The forms are not conducive to providing a 'productive confidence-building interaction,'" one researcher said, explaining why he used different language than that used in the form when talking with potential subjects (Fisher 2009, 160). Although IRBs have been attentive to what information subjects are given, they have paid less attention to how it is conveyed, worrying mainly about complexity of vocabulary rather than about the framing of gains and losses.[5]

Some conflicts of interest are unavoidable in clinical research, although that may be uncomfortable for researchers to acknowledge. Researchers have an interest in securing the participation of research subjects—they cannot do their work without them. Although routines for disclosing and managing conflicts of interest are now thoroughly institutionalized, they cover only those instances where researchers have a substantial financial stake in the outcomes of research. Yet researchers always have some financial stake in research (that is, after all, how they earn their salaries) and even in research outcomes (important results raise the stature of both researchers and institutions).

Clinical research also has an unavoidable and perhaps irreducible coercive aspect. Research subjects have many motivations for participating in research, but their desperation sometimes blurs the line between coercion (which is prohibited) and consent. Researchers and IRBs seem to have worked out tacit understandings about what constitutes coercion. But these working agreements seem mostly to prohibit transferring large sums of money or consumer goods. Yet research suggests that many research subjects participate in clinical trials because they need the money they receive for participating in the early phases of clinical research, because they have no other way of securing treatment, because they have run out of other options and hope that an unproven therapy will work, or because they believe they get more attentive care from research staff than from "regular" doctors and nurses (Petryna and Kleinman 2006; Whyte et al. 2006; Fisher 2009). In short, research subjects see drug trials (at least after the initial phases checking safety and dosage) as therapy.

In the clinics where I did research, I heard similar explanations for why people wanted to be research subjects. These justifications came from both subjects themselves and researchers. Knowing that research subjects often had no other way to get drugs, researchers sometimes selected studies for the clinic with an eye to what their "patients" needed—a point discussed frequently in meetings of the research staff at Robert Rafsky Clinic. They also designed studies, particularly "observational studies," so they could secure drug supplies for their research subjects, keeping them tied to the clinic and therefore available for other projects. This was especially true at Cha-on Suesum Clinic and Robert Rafsky Clinic. Clinics and patients did not always see eye to eye with IRBs on the balance of costs and benefits. In the early days of anti-retroviral therapy (ART), Philly Lutaaya researchers and research subjects wanted to move forward with studies even though the drug companies were unwilling to supply patients with drugs for more than a year beyond the end of the study. For Ugandans living with HIV, that relatively brief period of treatment was the difference between leaving their children in the lurch and having time to make arrangements for their care after their own deaths. Sticking to its principles, the IRB would not give approval unless supplies were guaranteed for at least three years beyond study completion.[6]

Though much ink has been spilled on this subject, there is no bright line here. Some scholars contend that research subjects' difficult circumstances do not necessarily make research participation "exploitative" (see, e.g., Hawkins and Emanuel 2008), but this seems to be a distinction without a difference. Yet the "difficult circumstances" of prisoners led ethicists to conclude that researchers had to be careful not to coerce their participation (Halpern 2021). And it is the "difficult circumstances" of poor people, those without health insurance, and those living in poorer countries where treatment is unavailable that make clinical trials and the perks that come with them exceedingly attractive (Petryna, Lakoff, and Kleinman 2006; Petryna 2009; Crane 2013). Rather than bright lines, there are temporary, tacit agreements.

Furthermore, the consent process often follows rather than precedes the decision to participate. People who arrive at the point of being "consented" have already made a considerable investment in research participation. Often they (or their family members) have sought out a clinical trial, although a trusted physician may also have recommended research participation. In these instances, informed consent procedures may give people a last chance to change their minds or different reasons to do what they had already decided to do. Fisher (2009, 158–60), for instance, tells of a son's decision to enroll his mother in an Alzheimer's research project even though the researcher repeatedly told him that the study was to assess the safety of the drug and could not yield any therapeutic benefit. Once convinced that the study offered no therapeutic benefit, the son nevertheless decided to enroll his mother so she could get an extensive diagnostic examination. "It seemed that the son had made up his mind that his mother would participate in the study prior to hearing the details. What the informed consent visit achieved was to give him different reasons for justifying her participation," Fisher (2009, 159) concludes.

Informed consent procedures also sidestep a key question that most patients want answered: will I get the treatment or will I be in the control group? Discussing the experience of the informed consent procedure, one subject interviewed by Fisher (2009, 165) had only a vague recollection of the procedure, but added: "What I do remember is that I had only one question, which they could not answer: Was I on the placebo or the real thing?" In early AIDS studies, this uncertainty led some participants to ask chemists to examine their pills to determine whether they were in the experimental group; it led others to pool medications and redistribute them so that everyone got some treatment (Shilts 1987). HIV researchers told me that they found the early placebo studies agonizing—in the very early days when there were no alternative treatments to use as comparison points, control group members received only treatment for opportunistic infections.[7] Researchers were hugely relieved, according to one HIV nurse/clinical trials coordinator (not affiliated with the clinics I studied), when they were finally able to assure participants that all research subjects, whether they were in the experimental group or the control group, were getting something of therapeutic value rather than a placebo.

Biomedical information is complex, to be sure, and often patients do not have an adequate understanding at the time of the consent process, though they may gain a fuller understanding as they participate in the study. Although research staff members are selected for competence in scientific matters, research subjects are selected on quite different grounds—because of medical need rather than understanding or competence. Some patients, families, and research subjects come to have impressive mastery of relevant scientific information, but others clearly do not.[8] The different "selection criteria" for patients and research subjects as compared to clinical and research staff inevitably lead to difficulties in communication about complex scientific phenomena and surely contribute to some of the oversimplification and misunderstanding that follows.

To summarize, neither research subjects nor the recruitment and consent processes actually live up to the ethical ideals as embodied in the institutions of informed consent. This is not to say that research subjects have not, on net balance, decided that they wish to participate in clinical research, although it may mean that their reasons for participating would not meet with IRB approval. Researchers and IRBs have worked out a series of practices (mostly without the participation of research subjects) that they seem willing to live with. Elaborate procedures and considerable documentation paper over the cracks. "Ritualized acts of transparency"—such as the signing of consent forms or reporting on conflicts of interest—"often hide more than [they] reveal," Petryna and Kleinman (2006, 11) comment. In the case of informed consent, the rituals are necessary because the ideal is impossible to achieve in a world filled with inequality and uncertainty. The paper flow around informed consent and the ritual surplus where consent procedures are especially problematic help to deactivate questions about the adequacy of consent, at least as it is defined in the rules. Before questions about consent can be reactivated, someone would have to revise the accepted story that the flow of paper equals consent. In the meantime, sequestering doubts about consent and knowledge about the real reasons people wish to participate in research allows research to go forward. Thus, because we do lack adequate ways of talking about risk and harm and the uncomfortable choices people confront, allowing people to choose to remain ignorant about some things (the ambiguities of consent) allows them to reduce ignorance about others (which therapies work). In this regime, a proper research subject is one who has signed a consent form; that signed form papers over any ambiguities.

Constructing Credible Routines: Cross-National Translation, Layered Backstages, and Sequestered Information

Ignorance is never uniformly distributed; indeed the distribution of ignorance and knowledge often is structured by organizations that carefully pass information to some while keeping others in the dark. Clinic staff members may not want to dispel residual ambiguities about informed consent and surely have no interest in having others delve into these matters. Hoping all will go well, the parties tacitly agree on a working definition of consent. Sometimes, though, clinic workers are less worried about what they themselves know than about how to keep information from outsiders.

In HIV clinics, like most organizations, funds come with strings attached. Any information suggesting that clinic staff are violating (or not meeting) funders' requirements is likely to be sequestered. In HIV clinics, the most obvious such difficulty with compromising knowledge concerns PEPFAR (the US President's Emergency Plan for AIDS Relief). PEPFAR, for instance, required that some substantial portion of prevention funds be used for abstinence programs (a requirement retained in the 2008 reauthorization but later loosened), prohibited recipients from using funds to "promote or advocate the legalization or practice of prostitution or sex trafficking," and insisted that fund recipients certify that they have a "policy explicitly opposing prostitution and sex trafficking."[9] As PEPFAR WATCH (2006) explained,

> Current US law requires organizations receiving US global HIV/AIDS and anti-trafficking funds to adopt specific organization-wide positions opposing prostitution. Health and human rights organizations are deeply concerned that this restriction will preclude recipients of US funds from using the best practices at their disposal to prevent HIV/AIDS among these populations and to promote the fundamental human rights of all persons. In fact, evidence exists that these restrictions are already undermining promising interventions.[10]

Mindful of the US government stance, Philly Lutaaya Clinic staff members reminded each other when particular site visitors were known to be "A&B men."[11] It was not that clinic staff favored wanton sexual activity—in fact they tended to be rather prim about sex—but only that they had a pragmatic approach to the disease and an acute sensitivity to how US messages resonated locally. Local understandings were well illustrated at a national conference on HIV where a Ugandan government official discussed the ABC program. Declaring his support for abstinence, he added that although abstinence was a good idea, it did not work well after people reached eighteen or nineteen (when many people became sexually active). He also endorsed fidelity. But not everyone could manage abstinence or fidelity, he noted, so it was important to have condoms as a backup. He ended by reminding conference participants that sex was "an important life force," a surprising conclusion to a discussion of an ABC program. This would not have been the speech that clinic staff would have made to a visiting US government representative.

As they selected staff and patients to meet with visitors, clinic leaders were acutely aware that they needed to pick people who would reliably calibrate their message to the audience—not distorting information but also not revealing more than necessary about local adaptations. It is hard to explain to people unfamiliar with the local situation why local practices just do not fit the donors' category schemes. In Uganda and South Africa where polygynous relationships are not uncommon, clinic workers are never quite sure how to make their tallies. Does a husband with two wives count as one couple or two, and how should the admonition to "be faithful" be adapted to polygynous relationships? Clinic staff were unsure how to explain to site visitors that "transactional sex" was but one of many unequal exchange relationships and was not accurately described as prostitution (Swidler and Watkins 2007; Heimer 2013; Mojola 2014).

Clinics experienced a double bind when they were expected to demonstrate their expertise by sharing information about their policies, practices, standard operating procedures (SOPs), and coding rules in meetings with site visitors or in conference sessions on "best practices." They struggled over how to display their expertise or show off their patients without simultaneously revealing uncomfortable facts and compromising their access to funding. Because the agendas of donors, clinicians, scientists, and patients overlapped but did not align completely, clinic staff emphasized the areas of overlap rather than discrepancy. Yet in the daily work of many organizations, the difficult cases consume a disproportionate share of attention and resources. In academic settings, for instance, students who disrupt class, fail to turn in assignments, or plagiarize require much teacher time and ingenuity. Yet a well-oiled detention program is just not the inspiring success that will burnish a principal's reputation. Likewise, although Gugu Dlamini counselors spent many hours trying to persuade a poorly functioning family to allow their adolescent child to receive anti-retroviral drugs (ARVs) when community elders advocated treatment by a traditional healer, that difficult family was not likely to be poster material. Visitors or conference participants need to be shown the coding system but not the difficulty of fitting messy cases into the categories. They need to be shown the routines by which a clinic produces its product (testing programs, patients on treatment, uninfected babies of mothers with HIV, research projects and publications), but not the backstage where staff cope with the difficulties of following clinical guidelines when labs are not open 24/7 or implementing a protocol when electricity and water supplies fail repeatedly. Formality, as Stinchcombe (2001) reminds us, allows people to get on with the work in a surprising array of settings—courts, construction sites, financial transactions. We may want to know something about the routines, but once we are confident that someone has given attention to constructing them properly, we probably do not want to know about the myriad messy ways that reality and rule have been brought into alignment.

Kampala, Durban, and even Bangkok are simply not the same as major metropolitan areas in the US. But too honestly acknowledging repeated deviations from donor assumptions about how a "normal" clinic should function or what a "normal" patient is like risks the credibility of the clinic and staff. Vividly remembering the days when people from the global North seemed to believe that clinics in resource-constrained countries could not safely prescribe ARVs and their patients could not be trusted to adhere to complicated regimens, clinic staff would prefer to avoid explaining their work-arounds. Clinics walk a fine line, then, in translating local practice for foreign sponsors. Clinic routines display clinic expertise at overcoming obstacles. Yet when the challenges are too great or the gap between local practices and sponsor values is too large, translators may worry that sponsors will focus on the obstacles rather than clinic success in overcoming them. Almost inevitably clinics feel they must conceal some information. Site visitors expect to be taken backstage. Yet despite the hype, what they see is only the nice dressing room of lead actors, not the quarters where the rest of the cast prepares for the show.

Although translating to PEPFAR required unusual delicacy, US clinic staff faced similar conundrums about what and how to reveal as they juggled the requirements of insurers, state-level AIDS drugs assistance programs (ADAPs) and pharmaceutical company drug assistance programs, and so forth. Getting the translation right is absolutely crucial to the clinics' legitimacy and viability—but so is translating Western medical thinking to African patients and translating clinical trials to potential research subjects.

This problem of translation is similar to that of choosing and "consenting" research subjects. In both cases the well-being of the clinic must be protected by sequestering information about just how clinics comply with the rules. In the case of informed consent, an especially heavily regulated arena, clinics create an elaborate ritual, a paper trail to show that they have complied—indeed overcomplied—with the letter of the law and that research subjects meet all of the requirements and have fully and knowledgeably consented to participate. The reams of paper show the goodwill of the clinic and make further investigation extremely difficult. The focus is on outcomes from enacting a ritualized routine.

In contrast, in the case of translating the policies of donors into local routines, the local routines themselves are of great interest. Outsiders are interested in the clinic's expertise in translating funders' specifications into practices that will bring about compliance as a matter of course despite less-than-ideal local circumstances. In this instance, then, a clinic's written SOPs would be more convincing than documentation about any specific problem its staff encountered. Accustomed to frequent site visits, the clinics of poor countries know they need to be able to speak about "best practices" for clinics in countries with similar cultures and similar levels of development. A telling bit of evidence: it was Philly Lutaaya Clinic that could readily supply a complete set of SOPs in handy pdf files. There will always be gaps between categories and routines, on the one hand, and empirical realities, on the other. A convincing demonstration of sophistication about the rules and SOPs obscures the gap, sequesters information about anomalies, and forestalls many awkward questions.

As it turns out, backstages have more than one function. They provide a staging area where people can escape the public gaze while they carry out indelicate, unpleasant, or discrediting activities (Goffman 1959). But they also mark a boundary between those who prepare the show and those who watch it. Because boundaries both exclude and include, being invited to cross a boundary into a staging area signals a change in status, an increased intimacy. To preserve a backstage for discrediting work while simultaneously using the backstage to give an impression of intimacy and transparency thus requires layered backstages and some dissembling about the existence of the layers.

When Help Also Harms: Strategic Decompiling and Distributed Ignorance about Side Effects

But sequestering information is not the only way of managing uncomfortable knowledge. When we look at how clinics deal with uncomfortable facts about the possible side effects of their core technologies, we see that difficult knowledge can also be made inert by preventing facts from being put together to form the whole picture. With distributed ignorance or strategic decompiling, not officially having the information frees people from the necessity of acting.

Although organizations' core activities generally come with unanticipated costs and side effects, people and organizations tend to emphasize the benefits of core activities and discount or ignore the costs. The Hippocratic admonition to do no harm acknowledges that medical treatment may harm rather than help. Intervention can be futile and may bring considerable pain. In an intensive care unit studied by Zussman, medical staff referred to this suffering interchangeably as "torture" and "cheechee," referencing a joke about captured missionaries being offered the choice of cheechee or death (1992, 111–13). As they discover that cheechee is torture, the missionaries revise their initial decision, asking for death instead, only to be told "Yes, but first a little cheechee" (1992, 111). Zussman's point is that caregivers in intensive care units know that the help they offer comes with significant harm. Indeed, the obligation to carry on in the face of this knowledge means that caregivers too experience a type of cheechee.

The dilemma captured by Zussman is familiar to nearly everyone working in healthcare and clinical research and surely contributes to staff burnout. In infant intensive care, for instance, some evidence suggests that for those infants who ultimately succumb, one contribution of neonatology is to grossly extend the period of dying.[12] Pharmaceutical companies only reluctantly began to acknowledge that some antidepressants seem to increase suicide rates (McGoey 2007). Refusals to approve drugs, withdrawals of drugs after approval, and lawsuits over side effects that were not tracked properly are common and part of everyday discussion, with examples including thalidomide (birth defects), statins such as Baycol (rhabdomyolysis, a breakdown of muscle cells followed by kidney failure), cox-2 painkillers such as Vioxx (increased risk of cardiovascular problems), opioids such as Vicodin and OxyContin (overprescribing and addiction).[13]

In HIV clinics, testing and treatment may not bring the cheechee that comes with intensive care, but they do bring many troubles big and small. News that a person had HIV sometimes led to discrimination by employers or insurers or rejection by a spouse. Beyond the considerable discomforts of the early adjustment period, the treatment itself can bring liver failure; decreases in bone density; life-threatening lactic acidosis; drug resistance; and redistributions of fat resulting in sunken cheeks, buffalo humps, skinny legs and buttocks, and plump bellies and breasts (including on men), side effects that were not addressed as expeditiously or effectively as they are now. It was not always clear whether people knew about these possible side effects. As the examples below illustrate, areas of ignorance may be glossed over by a patina of knowledge. When more exact knowledge might interfere with getting on with the work, concerns are sometimes pushed aside, though not exactly covered up. Uncertainty can be a useful resource even if it has only a limited lifespan.

Knowing that people are intensely worried about how others will respond to the news that they are infected, clinics go to great lengths to protect patients' and research subjects' confidentiality. Bland clinic names may conceal a clinic's mission (as was the case at Robert Rafsky Clinic). Taking account of nosey neighbors and in-laws, Philly Lutaaya Clinic's drivers and health visitors were instructed to discreetly drop patients off near their homes. Such discretion was not the norm in the past, the health visitors' supervisor explained: "It used to be that people loved to have health visitors and they'd see you and ask when you were coming to their house. But now with HIV, there's a stigma attached because people assume that if there's a health visitor coming it's because someone is HIV positive."

Despite these protective routines, clinic staff rarely had a fix on just how serious the worries about stigma were. Observers like South African Justice

Cameron believed both that stigma often discouraged testing and that the exceptionalist approach to HIV had made stigma worse. Yes, some Ugandan women were thrown out by their husbands or partners when they were found to be infected, a point episodically discussed by Philly Lutaaya staff members, and some South African patients refused to be tested. But no one really knew how common these problems were, although some information could surely have been gleaned from files.

Researchers may also focus on the topics they are accustomed to studying (physiological aspects of disease), giving short shrift to matters more distant from their core expertise (such as the psychological aspects of disease). Redistribution of body fat—lipodystrophy—has long been known to be a correlate of HIV treatment. People receiving ARVs may experience fat loss (in the face, legs, or arms) or fat accumulation (in the belly, back of the neck, or breasts). Lipodystrophy is more common with some drugs (d4T and AZT) than others (tenofovir). Although newer drugs (3TC, tenofovir, and Sustiva, at the time of this research) less often led to lipodystrophy, some patients still experienced fat redistribution. Researchers have tried to figure out how best to measure lipodystrophy.[14] They have also done research on which drugs are especially likely to lead to lipodystrophy, which patients are most likely to experience lipodystrophy, and the relation between lipodystrophy and severity of disease. There is considerable variability in how these side effects are treated, with some facilities doing little or nothing, others switching patients to different drugs, and still others helping patients secure ameliorative treatments such as drug or hormone therapy, liposuction, or plastic surgery.

But although most caregivers are aware of facial wasting and other changes in patients' bodies, they seem to have known much less about the psychological effects that accompany these physical changes. Nelson Vergel, an AIDS activist, gathered data on patients' experience of lipodystrophy, finding that many patients altered their behavior because of distress about body changes and a substantial minority were so upset that they had contemplated suicide (Vergel 2008; Goldman 2009). Doctors apparently did not always understand the depth of their patients' despair.

Distributed ignorance also occurs in decisions about what drug regimen to give and whether to switch regimens. At the time of my research, the recommendation was for people living with HIV to begin therapy earlier in the disease than in the past,[15] to receive ART (a cocktail of drugs with different mechanisms for inhibiting viral reproduction), and to switch regimens only when clinically necessary (e.g., because of side effects or "failure"). The last of those recommendations sometimes created difficulties, making ignorance and ambiguity useful for researchers and policymakers, though the blind spots of researchers and policymakers seemed somewhat different.

Some parts of research and treatment programs may have consequences for future treatment options, but the staff of HIV clinics may be unaware of some of these contingencies, particularly in a rapidly evolving field such as HIV. They cannot realistically consider all possible contingencies and still proceed with their work. For the most part, this is not sinister but pragmatic ignorance. Early research raised concerns that single-dose nevirapine would induce resistance when mothers and babies were given that rudimentary (but affordable) therapy to reduce mother-to-child transmission.[16] In richer countries, the question was moot because no undue demands on resources were created by simply giving ART to the small numbers of pregnant women infected with HIV. In the very poorest countries, single-dose nevirapine was often the only feasible option.

As debate raged over how to reduce mother-to-child transmission, a parallel problem got much less coverage. When patients enroll in clinical trials, they get much of their care and many of their drugs gratis, but their treatment options are constrained by the research protocols. When studies end, patients may not be able to get drugs or may have difficulty paying for treatment, although drug companies now generally agree to continue to supply people with at least some of the drugs for long periods or even indefinitely. One concern has been that people serially enrolling in drug studies will "use up" options more quickly because of relatively frequent regimen changes. Yet this route to drug resistance and reduced options received little attention because researchers were focused on different questions and were making other comparisons.

Finally, ministries of health that are heavily invested in national HIV treatment programs may be slow to acknowledge that some patients cannot safely take the government's standard regimen. As discussed earlier, Gugu Dlamini doctors were quite worried that the South African government's first-line regimen did not take account of the likelihood of lactic acidosis, a life-threatening metabolic side effect of d4T that was more likely to occur in patients with high body mass indexes. The clinic had noted the danger, was careful about the regimens it used for heavier patients, and watched for this side effect. Clinic staff worried that joining the government rollout program would make it difficult for them to use a different regimen—one without d4T—for patients at risk for lactic acidosis. Given its investment in its first-line regimen and the public health advantages of putting all patients on the same first-line regimen, the government seemed not to want to know about lactic acidosis. Moreover, its program for reporting on adverse events (AEs) was weak.

In this instance, those who got a (temporary) strategic advantage from remaining ignorant (the government) were challenged repeatedly by others (Gugu Dlamini physicians) who were able to offer evidence about the frequency and severity of side effects or the costs of not modifying the national regimen. That there was an organizational boundary between these two parties facilitated this strategic decompiling, a point illustrated below with a different example.

As these examples from HIV clinics suggest, strategic ignorance is often temporary. Smithson (2008) argues that uncertainty has a positive side. Uncertainty creates occasions for discovery and creativity and can thus be an important resource.[17] In the world of HIV clinics where reputations are won and lost by doing research and creating innovative care programs, one party's strategic ignorance creates a strategic opportunity for someone else. Ignorance is thus likely to bring only temporary advantages, particularly if another clinic can secure additional resources to engage in low-cost "operational research" or "observational studies." The previously ignored problem of fat redistribution, for example, might then become an object of study and a boon rather than a threat to the research enterprise.

The question here is when an uncertainty is a threat and when it can instead be redeployed as a resource, making it a feature not a bug.[18] Myopia and denial are common responses to uncertainties about side effects. Thompson's (1967) work on organizations' penchant for buffering their technical core (e.g., by standardizing inputs rather than modifying core processes) suggests that organizations might prefer to ignore, conceal, obfuscate, and deny evidence that core activities are bringing unwanted by-products or side effects. In effect, these organizations are engaged in reputational buffering, allowing core activities to proceed until the evidence of unwanted side effects is truly overwhelming and very public. Reputational buffering, like any other kind of buffering, has its limits. As a general matter, organizations may be forced to adjust core activities when the stream of inputs or the market for outputs changes definitively and permanently. Clinics and research facilities may therefore become willing to adjust their work either when they see a way to transform a threatening uncertainty into an opportunity—an outcome that is especially likely in organizations specializing in research—or when the evidence of untoward and unexpected outcomes becomes so overwhelming that key constituencies (donors, patients, and research subjects) seem likely to move to a more reputable competitor. Without these pressures to compile information about what is really going on, organizations may wish to continue reaping the benefits from maintaining distributed ignorance.

Organizations focus on core activities to the exclusion of other things, ignoring or minimizing inconvenient facts that might make others less enthusiastic about their work, a tendency that is exaggerated when the uncomfortable, awkward facts lie partially or wholly outside an organization's boundaries. As I discuss below, when organizations' work is shared with others, the division of labor makes it easy not to acknowledge the import of facts that can be categorized as someone else's responsibility. Likewise, when resources come from a common pot, organizations may find it easier not to worry about the monetary costs of their activities. People may not want to know the true cost of their work, for instance, when budget constraints mean that the "pharmaceuticalization of health" (e.g., in HIV treatment) makes it impossible to provide even inexpensive basic public health for the rest of the population (Petryna 2009).

Shit Happens: Complex Divisions of Labor, Organizational Boundaries, and Distributed Ignorance

Because HIV is relatively new disease, treatment has usually been left to specialists. Yet even on the cutting edge of medicine, patients and their families play important roles. The chain of healthcare has many links; like any other chain, this chain is only as strong as its weakest link. Where complex care is provided by highly trained specialists working in well-equipped medical facilities, the weak link often seems to be the household. This may be especially true in poor countries where the gap between the resources available in hospitals and homes may be especially large and where biomedical workers (like biomedical workers everywhere) may not understand the perspectives and practices of patients and family members. The result is that the patients that hospitals have saved all too often go home to die of the common conditions associated with poverty. This is an old problem but may be especially common where medical matters and childcare overlap. Commenting on the futility of saving a tiny baby, one Brazilian neonatologist remarked that "when he reaches 2000 grams [4.4 lb.] he will go home and he will die" (Guillemin and Holmstrom 1990, 267). Yet even when they anticipated that some babies would succumb to common illnesses such as diarrhea once they left the special care nursery, doctors nevertheless did their best for them while they were hospitalized. Beyond offering basic instruction to parents, doctors seemed to believe that there was little they or the hospital could do to affect hygiene in the home.

In HIV care, the boundary between medical and lay responsibilities is especially fraught. It has been hard to ensure that patients take pills on an unusually tight schedule—missing or delaying doses was especially consequential when ART was first introduced, but problems with pill scheduling have diminished with simplified drug regimens. It is especially hard, though, to control a disease that is transmitted through bodily fluids because that means intervening in such intimate activities as sexuality and breastfeeding (and, of course, the use of intravenous drugs). Because discussion of variations in sexual practices is sensitive, racially charged, and stigmatizing (Schoofs 1999a; Heimer 2007), people may be uneasy about sharing information about what they are doing in bed, making it harder for health workers to supply targeted advice about how to reduce risk. Discussions of infant feeding practices may be somewhat easier, though parents are well aware that health workers may frown on some of their practices.

In rich countries, mother-to-child transmission is rare, both because women are less likely than men to be infected and because HIV-infected women receive ART during pregnancy and can bottle-feed their newborns. In poorer countries, more women are infected with HIV[19] and they often receive only minimal medical care during pregnancy. Until recently, many pregnant women did not get tested, and if they were tested and found to be infected, they received the less effective (but cheaper) forms of treatment.[20] Moreover, in countries such as South Africa and Uganda, bottle-feeding is really not an alternative.[21] Poor families cannot afford infant formula and are unable to feed formula safely given poor sanitation and lack of clean water. Babies who are not breastfed die often from diarrhea or malnutrition. Because it is mixed feeding (breastmilk combined with other things) that especially increases the likelihood of HIV transmission, the usual recommendation for poor countries has been exclusive breastfeeding for the first six months followed by abrupt weaning.[22]

Once mothers have been drilled on the importance of protecting their babies from HIV, though, they may find it excruciatingly difficult to follow a clinic's recommendation that they breastfeed. Knowing that their milk carried virus as well as nutrition, some Ugandan mothers with HIV spoke of being worried about "murdering" their babies by breastfeeding. Although there was some overlap between how clinic workers and mothers understood the situation, there were also substantial gaps, particularly in assessments of what was possible and morally appropriate. As is common in situations where professionals make recommendations about mothering (Hays 1996; Heimer and Staffen 1998), mothers likely felt judged by clinic workers, making them reluctant to reveal too much. With this complex division of labor, an organizational boundary, and divergent perspectives, distributed ignorance was almost inevitable.

One Philly Lutaaya program may inadvertently have made the problem worse. Babies were tested for HIV at several points, starting at six weeks of age. Because maternal antibodies can remain in infants' bodies for up to eighteen months, a positive HIV test result was not definitive. In contrast, a negative test result did mean that the baby was not infected. Despite being urged to continue exclusive breastfeeding until six months, mothers whose infants tested HIV negative often abruptly weaned their babies. These babies then sometimes died of diarrhea. Hard as it was for staff to believe, the clinic teaching about how HIV is transmitted, coupled with the early testing of babies, seemed to be undermining the clinic instruction on the wisdom of six months of exclusive breastfeeding.

Unpacking the social psychological features of this breastfeeding dilemma shows why the problem seemed so intractable. People died from HIV (at that time, a fatal disease), but everyone knew people who had survived diarrhea. It seemed implausible to mothers that their babies would die of diarrhea, but they were quite convinced that they would die if they became infected with HIV. Mothers had no illusion that they could prevent the transmission of HIV in breastmilk, but they believed they could provide safe alternative feedings with enough effort. In fact, for most poor Ugandan mothers, that was not actually possible.

Clinics have their hands full with responsibilities that clearly fall within their own domain. Given the difficulty of influencing what happens beyond their doors, staff members are tempted to adopt a working division of labor in which they worry only about what is strictly within their purview. Clinics treat HIV; mothers feed babies. Although the influence of the clinic surely wanes beyond its threshold, the division between household and clinic is always artificial. In this case, however, Philly Lutaaya's influence may have been both larger and somewhat different than its staff had anticipated. Although clinic guidelines urged exclusive breastfeeding for six months followed by abrupt weaning, some mothers apparently also heard two other messages: that their baby had been born uninfected and that an uninfected child could still become infected with tainted breastmilk. All three messages came from the clinic whether the clinic intended to transmit them or not. To be fair, once Philly Lutaaya staff became aware of the complexity and ambivalence of their message, they made efforts to get it right. But their first despairing response had essentially been that "shit happens." Although they understood that on net balance babies were more likely to survive by being breastfed (Coovadia and Coutsoudis 2001), clinic staff were nearly as worried as mothers about urging that uninfected babies receive "infected" milk. Some clinic staff admitted to finding it very difficult to tell mothers to continue breastfeeding when an early test indicated that the baby had been born uninfected.

For a time, clinic staff had chosen to remain essentially ignorant about infant feeding practices. Defining infant feeding as essentially beyond their purview made some patterns invisible to them. Only gradually did clinic staff put the pieces together, investigating their own ambivalence about feeding recommendations and uncovering inconsistencies in their recommendations. As they became more aware of the problem of distributed ignorance, clinic staff even designed and received funding for a research project to study breastfeeding practices, creating a new opportunity with the materials of distributed ignorance.

Although infant deaths from diarrhea are a particularly poignant instance of the effects of distributed ignorance, poor communication across the clinic-household boundary is not unusual. Distributed ignorance is an almost inevitable by-product of doing things in organizations. A complex division of labor necessarily means that people will not see the full round of organizational activities and so will be unaware of some effects of their own actions. Likewise, boundaries between organizations and their environments restrict the flow of information about consequences and decrease control over actions and events outside those boundaries. Organizational structures reflect the period and place of a field's founding rather than being simply a function of the kind of work the organization does (Stinchcombe 1965). Clinic boundaries are therefore likely to reflect conventions about what a clinic should look like and what tasks its staff should and should not shoulder rather than adapting boundaries and task assignments to local needs. "As standards travel, their social and economic embeddedness is revealed," note Petryna, Lakoff, and Kleinman (2006, 12).

With changes in location—say from the US to resource-constrained countries with different cultural traditions—mismatches become more likely. The clinic-household boundary can make issues like food scarcity seem like none of the clinic's business. Ex-pat clinic staff may be especially unable to imagine what life is like beyond the clinic threshold and how that might affect the outcomes of medical interventions. Discussing the global North's misplaced emphasis on anti-retrovirals when local populations lack necessities such as water, food, and basic medicines, journalist Mark Schoofs noted that even sophisticated clinicians who had spent years working in poorer countries could fail to grasp the urgency of local needs. Despite his years working in the Democratic Republic of Congo, UNAIDS director Peter Piot remarked that he had "only recently" become aware that hunger was the leading concern of rural Africans (Schoofs 1999b). The press of those needs shapes much about the HIV epidemic, including people's inability to eat the balanced diet necessary to sustain health during treatment, decisions to engage in sex work to secure food for children, and failure to purchase prescribed medicines. "They write you medicines, you fail to buy," observed one HIV patient in relatively prosperous Kampala (Schoofs 1999b). Even in the US, where the cultural divide is smaller, that failure to take medicines would often be coded as simple "noncompliance" by uncomprehending physicians rather than as something to be investigated.

Mismatches between inherited, customary organizational forms (including placement of boundaries and occupational divisions of labor) and local circumstances surely increase the likelihood of distributed ignorance. Because clinic workers are less aware of things that lie outside the clinic, the boundary between the clinic and the home may need to be in a different place in Uganda, where food and clean water are scarce and transportation is costly and difficult, than in the US. And Philly Lutaaya did make many adjustments to local circumstances. Health visitors went into the community to check on patients who failed to arrive for appointments. Staff members adjusted instructions on infant feeding. The clinic reconfigured its staff and space so meals could be provided to clinic patients. It supported "income-generation" projects (as did Gugu Dlamini Clinic in South Africa). And it worked with the World Food Program to secure food aid for its patients. But that required clinic counselors to gather more accurate and detailed information about patients' diets and food access rather than accepting at face value patients' first embarrassed responses to queries. Compiling information about what went on beyond the clinic boundary solved the problem of distributed ignorance and allowed the clinic and its patients to make stronger claims on assistance from the World Food Program.

Distributed ignorance can be reduced when people get glimmers of information about unexpected outcomes and disturbing side effects. Such reductions in ignorance may be more likely when there is an incentive to construct a fuller picture—for instance, when a researcher can build a reputation from making sense of the whole or an organization can claim additional resources after it gathers previously unavailable information. Sometimes, though, an organization (or individual) will bury its head in the sand and insist that there is no causal relationship between what the organization is doing and alleged side effects. And sometimes boundaries are reinforced and workers insist that some tasks are "not their job." When that happens, we should ask about strategic advantages that may flow from distributed ignorance and from ensuring that inconvenient facts remain inert.

Conclusion: The Mundanity of Ignorance

Discussing textbook revisions as an example of what people remember and what they forget, Mary Douglas observed that "when we look closely at the construction of past time, we find the process has very little to do with the past at all and everything to do with the present. Institutions create shadowed places in which nothing can be seen and no questions asked. They make other areas show finely discriminated detail, which is closely scrutinized and ordered" (1986, 69). What is remembered and what is forgotten, she argued, varies from one kind of social system to another—very hierarchical societies forget and remember different things than more egalitarian ones. This chapter carries forward Douglas's work by investigating how it becomes acceptable to overlook, ignore, discount, or disregard even in sites strongly organized around an imperative to gather information and create knowledge. Indeed, the evidence examined here suggests that biomedicine's rule-governed system for gathering and using information offers both incentives and tools for systematically creating ignorance as well as knowledge.

Summarized in table 7.1, the mechanisms I have uncovered for keeping information inert—sequestering facts and keeping information decompiled—are ones anticipated in the work of others. But the twist here is that these well-studied organizational phenomena—ritualism and decoupling, separations between back and frontstage, buffering of core processes, and transporting of organizational forms to new settings—all help to keep the dark corners dark. In this chapter's examples, a certain measure of ignorance allowed clinics to get on with their work. Creating mechanisms for maintaining ignorance then became just another part of clinic work.

The ritual surplus of informed consent processes, easily understood in institutionalist terms, papers over gaps in knowledge about the characteristics and motives of research subjects and allows people to overlook the uncomfortable fact that scientific research often does not and, almost certainly, cannot fully conform to ethical or scientific ideals. When clinic staff are admonished to "document, document, document," they are helping to create "finely discriminated detail" that simultaneously invites the scrutiny of regulatory workers and draws attention away from the "shadowed places" that Douglas alerts us to.

Bringing people backstage to show them how things are done may seem like a move to share information, and is often intended to convey that impression to research monitors and site visitors (Heimer and Gazley 2012). Yet shadowed places remain because the backstage is layered, making it possible for clinic staff to reveal some things while concealing others. Site

TABLE 7.1. Types of Ignorance: Examples, Strategies, and Consequences

CANONICAL EXAMPLE FROM HIV	TYPE OF IGNORANCE; HOW IGNORANCE AND AMBIGUITY MAINTAINED	WHO KNOWS AND WHO IS KEPT IGNORANT	CONSEQUENCE OF IGNORANCE
Establishing legitimacy of participants (or other key resource)— informed consent	**Sequestered knowledge** maintained through use of paper trail with ritualized elements and **ritual surplus**	Multilateral ambiguity or ignorance. Neither subjects nor researchers are entirely sure that subjects meet criteria; researchers are not entirely sure that consent is fully uncoerced. Unclear who should have right to decide	Capacity to secure key resource; permits action to occur once paper trail created and accepted; allows action despite ambiguity about core concept (here consent)
Translation, rules of correspondence— transactional sex is not sex work	**Sequestered knowledge** about details of how a routine works, the "fixes" that bring actual practices into "close enough" contact with routine, maintained through **layered backstages**	"Experts" who work with the routine know; outsiders kept ignorant	Too much information about backstage can jeopardize legitimacy of activity; too little information about routines themselves suggests that staff lack expertise
Side effects, externalities— lactic acidosis; lipodystrophy	**Distributed ignorance** maintained by **strategic decompiling**— narrow focus on core activities and collection of information only about those matters	No one knows for certain because information is distributed among multiple actors with no one possessing all of the relevant material	Core activity continues
Shared medical and lay responsibility— infant feeding and diarrhea	**Distributed ignorance** maintained by claims not to be responsible for actions of others, esp. with **complex divisions of labor** and across **organizational boundaries**	No one knows because ignorant about routines of distant interaction partners; some motivation to conceal ignorance because of desire to be seen as credible participant	All seems to be well until responsibility passes from expert to laypeople or to different environment

visitors get to see how clinics bridge cultural divides and translate donor requirements about such matters as encouraging abstinence and sexual fidelity into organizational routines. But they are not shown the more discrediting pushing and shoving, nipping and tucking, that is required to make things fit.

When core activities are discovered to have unfortunate, even devastating, side effects, a typical organizational reaction is to carry on, hoping the storm will pass. No one wants to believe that a side effect of treatment (such as redistribution of fat) might make people suicidal, that a national first-line regimen might prove deadly to some patients, or that enrolling people in one study after another might "use up" treatment options. When people believe wholeheartedly in their work, keeping distracting, disruptive information at bay helps them maintain their focus. Keeping bits of information separate and out of context—decompiled—buffers mission-central activities and allows people to get on with their work.

Finally, when standards and conventions travel from one place to another, cultural mismatches increase the likelihood that information will remain decompiled. Clinic practices, including conventions about the location of boundaries, the division of labor between clinics and households, and routines for HIV testing of infants were imported from places where infants were unlikely to die from diarrhea if they were weaned early. Yet the strength of these conventional boundaries and task assignments made it easy for clinic staff to remain ignorant about what was happening beyond the clinic threshold and how they might be increasing the pressure for mothers to (unsafely) wean babies. Because no PMTCT program would want to be blamed for increasing diarrhea deaths, there may have been some willful ignorance here.

People often come to believe in the values they profess, particularly when they create activities around those beliefs. Feldman and March (1981) sagely note that it is difficult to be a stable hypocrite. IRB personnel and regulatory specialists often seem to believe that a signature on a form reliably signals consent, a belief that others pragmatically decide not to contest. Believing in the importance of a simple, uniform first-line HIV regimen, staff from a ministry of health may not want to know that some patients are likely to experience life-threatening side effects on that regimen. Strategic ignorance helps protect the very important public health objective pursued by the ministry of health even as it jeopardizes some patients' lives. Yet when skeptics, pragmatists, and true believers must work together, strategic ignorance may suddenly create a strategic opportunity and inert facts sometimes quickly regain vitality. Information has many uses in organizational life. But so, it turns out, does ignorance.

[CHAPTER EIGHT]

"Wicked" Ethics

Compliance Work and the Practice of Ethics in HIV Clinics

In US hospitals, the office of research must review and approve all projects that involve hospital resources before they are submitted to the hospital's institutional review board (IRB) for ethics review. The hospital with which Robert Rafsky Clinic was affiliated offered a training session for principal investigators and research teams on research administration and the compliance process.

Training session handouts and slideshow images gave some historical background on regulatory compliance and stressed the increased intensity of regulation, emphasizing the updated rules, new occasions for regulatory interventions, and huge penalties for noncompliance. After discussing violations that had occurred in other sites, the presenter identified this institution's approach to regulatory compliance as the "right thing principle." He quoted the hospital code of ethics: "We will maintain the highest ethical standards in all medical research, clinical practice and business transactions." Going through a series of examples, he kept repeating that "you want to do the right thing." Much of the rest of the session focused on pricing of hospital services, including the importance of informing "patients" (actually research subjects) of costs that would not be borne by either the study or an insurer and so would be the patient's responsibility. Although patients sometimes incurred thousands of dollars of unanticipated costs as a result of participating in studies, the presenters were worried mainly about whether researchers had informed patients about these expenses. The office of research thus urged researchers to check with the largest insurers in advance and then to be completely clear with patients about what would not be covered either by the study or by insurers. If there was clarity about what would be covered (and by whom), then "when you are consenting the patient, you can have a good discussion about this and the patient will be fully informed."

One MD principal investigator (PI) chimed in on research costs borne by patients. What should researchers do if neither the study sponsor nor the insurer would pay for something that was part of a study, he asked. The research office staff seemed to think they had a great answer: the patient would have to pay only cost plus 5%. The researcher seemed troubled by this answer given the costliness of the services. But the research office continued to insist that its solution was a good one. If the patient had signed the consent form knowing what the costs would be, then it should be fine.

After being reminded of the hospital's pledge to maintain the "highest ethical standard" and being offered the "right thing principle" as a mantra, audience members might have been dismayed to find that those lofty statements translated only into an obligation to inform patients of expenses they would be expected to shoulder. The research office staff seemed not to notice that they had inserted an exceedingly thin conception of ethics— something akin to *caveat emptor*—into a setting where helping professionals such as doctors and nurses generally envisioned themselves as people who would go the extra mile to care for the desperate patients who came to them for help. In effect, the research office staff seemed to believe that the consent form should function as something like a commercial contract—a startling metamorphosis for a foundational element of the ethical practice of both healthcare and clinical research.

The words and actions of researchers contrast sharply with this official statement about what is owed to research subjects. Because research projects are designed to answer open scientific questions, they generally take account of the needs and interests of individual research subjects only in a rather abstract way. Research subjects may be cautioned that they might not get any personal benefit from participation in a study, and indeed, some research subjects specifically say their objective is to "give something back." Each clinic typically participates in many studies simultaneously and has some discretion about which studies to take on. In both parts of the matching process—choosing which studies to take on and which subjects to recruit—clinics have some discretion. Often they exercise that discretion to the benefit of their patients.

At Robert Rafsky's weekly research meetings, staff considered which studies would provide attractive possibilities for the clinic and its patients. Clinic researchers clearly articulated their view that studies were avenues to treatment for people who lacked other options or who might have trouble paying for care. For instance, one doctor talked about "putting the patient in studies as a way of helping cover the expenses of his treatment." Another staff member clarified that "study patients don't pay for a doctor's visit if they are seeing a study nurse at the same time. This was [the site PI's] decision. It is the benefit of participating in a study."

Even in a relatively privileged private clinic like Robert Rafsky, it was not easy to cover all of the costs of drugs, laboratory tests, and clinic visits. When pharmaceutical companies did agree to pay for drugs, payment sometimes was arranged as a reimbursement after patients had procured the drugs through primary care physicians, an uncomfortable situation for patients with slender resources. Some Robert Rafsky study participants who lacked insurance had to transfer to a publicly funded clinic to ensure that their expenses were covered either by the pharmaceutical company, the new study, or the public clinic's purse. Drug costs can be so exorbitant that patients without good insurance may elect to continue in studies even when they relocate, opting to pay an occasional plane fare to get the free drugs that come with study participation.

Implementation inevitably creates a gap between the designed system of legal or ethical regulation and what people actually experience. This gap between "law on the books" and "law in action" animates much sociolegal research. The disparate ways of thinking about and managing expenses incurred by research subjects illustrate the substantial gap between one version of "official ethics" and "ethics on the ground."

Here I show that this gap is not unique to financial matters but also exists in other areas of research, research administration, and even treatment. As a general matter, "official ethics" tends to be less generous than "ethics on the ground" and can even create impediments to protecting research subjects. Attempts to solve ethical problems often seem to make them more intractable, for instance, by delegitimating them, as occurred in the interchange between the ethics trainers and the MD principal investigator.

This tangled relation between ethical problems and solutions invites a comparison to "wicked problems" (Rittel and Webber 1973; Coyne 2005). In labeling problems as "wicked" (the contrast being "tame"), Rittel and Webber were reacting against attempts to rationalize planning and design and to tackle policy problems with the methods used in natural science and engineering. But problems of social policy cannot be solved that way, they argued, because our descriptions of problems strongly shape possible solutions, and attempted resolutions inevitably lead to unintended consequences. Solutions are only temporary at best. Ethics problems generally share the characteristics of wicked problems. Official ethics' attempts to produce universal solutions often make ethics problems more complicated. Official ethics defines problems narrowly and then diverts scarce attention and resources to compliance work, making dissent difficult. Ethics on the ground is, in part, a reaction to this "wickedness."

This comparison with wicked problems is meant to suggest that the ethical conundrums of HIV research and treatment cannot be fully solved by turning to the common strategies of invoking principles and creating new rules or fine-tuning old ones. Yes, ethics is about creating level playing fields and treating everyone fairly—about universalism, in short. But it is also about responding to individual needs and tailoring responses to specific circumstances. That is, ethics requires a sensitive and ever-changing mix of universalism tempered by particularism. To put it differently, formal rationality and proceduralism are ineffective and unpalatable solutions to ethical troubles. There is simply no way to avoid grappling with substance. Although the formally rational proceduralism of official ethics depicts itself as a general-purpose solution to the ethical conundrums encountered in HIV clinics, the ongoing adjustments made by clinic staff expose their visceral understanding of the substantive irrationality of these solutions. That tension between formal and substantive rationality—perhaps more accurately characterized as an antagonism between formal rationality and substantive irrationality—is hardly unique to HIV clinics, as sociological attention to these concepts makes clear (Weber 1968, 63–211; Kalberg 1980; Brubaker 1984). But that tension is especially acute in medical settings where "unrelieved pain and inexplicable suffering, joyful births and cruel deaths" (Bosk 2023) all are common and where medical workers' decisions and actions, based in part on their assessments of what is morally right, can tip the balance one way or the other. The objective of employing the language of "wickedness" is to draw attention to and label these failures of official ethics—failures created by a narrowed vision, formalistic approach, and refusal to acknowledge the yawning gap between the aspirations and promises of official ethics' legalistic edifice and what it generally delivers.

In this chapter I outline, and offer evidence for, a two-step process by which official ethics modifies our understanding of what is important, substituting official bureaucratic ethics for professional ethics or personal morality. After offering descriptions of official ethics and ethics on the ground, I tease out the core differences between ethics on the ground and official ethics and show how ethics on the ground is in part a response to official ethics. The chapter also fleshes out the comparison between official ethics and wicked problems and explains how official ethics has become "wicked."

Because some of the obligations of "official ethics" are tied to funding sources and external oversight, it is useful to remember that all of the clinics had hospital and university affiliations, and many of them received funds from the US government. All but the Thai clinic received US government support for treatment (and received funds from local sources), and all five clinics received some of their research funding (directly or indirectly) from the National Institutes of Health (NIH), necessitating adherence to US government rules about the ethical conduct of research. Because some research results would be used in drug approval processes, the clinics were also attentive to the rules of the US Food and Drug Administration.

Describing "Official Ethics" and "Ethics on the Ground"

A system of ethics generally has several components: (1) a set of more or less formal principles; (2) practices of citing such core principles; (3) a translation of principles into statutes, regulations, guidance, policies, and SOPs; and (4) methods for policing and enforcing adherence to the rules. Although both official ethics and ethics on the ground have these components, they are easier to identify in official ethics, partly because of the role official ethics plays in research bureaucracies and research administration. This tie to research administration makes official ethics both more formal and more uniform than ethics on the ground.

THE ELEMENTS OF OFFICIAL ETHICS

Accounts of the history of bioethics appear in many of the writings of bioethicists themselves and social scientists, as well as in materials disseminated by research administrators.[1] Even in these abbreviated historical treatments, it is *de rigueur* to cite a few core documents, such as the Nuremberg Code, the Belmont Report, and the Helsinki Declaration, and to explain that these treatises typically arose as responses to widely reported ethical abuses or attempts to fill gaps in existing statements of principles. They often emanated from official or semiofficial bodies, sometimes constituted specifically to propose reforms after research scandals.

Many citations to foundational treatises are quite brief, including only a mention of several documents and a listing of such key principles as autonomy, beneficence, nonmaleficence, and justice. Although these core treatises have been carefully analyzed by scholars (see, e.g., Emanuel, Wendler, and Grady 2000), they are also cited repeatedly and ritualistically in written and oral discussions of ethics. Copies of core documents are often handed out to clinic staff (as occurred in IRB-related training sessions at Philly Lutaaya Clinic and Robert Rafsky Clinic), included in edited volumes (see, e.g., Emanuel et al. 2003), and referenced on clinic, hospital, governmental, and regulatory websites.

More important, the core principles are translated into policy by governments and government agencies, healthcare organizations, and NGOs. Especially consequential is the US statute on research with human subjects

(45 C.F.R. 46), often referred to as the "Common Rule" because it must be adhered to by all US government agencies conducting human subjects research, and indeed by anyone receiving US government funds to conduct such research.[2] Although promulgated by the US government, these rules now apply well beyond US borders, including in all of the clinics I studied. The mechanism for disseminating these rules is the "federalwide assurance" (FWA), which lays out requirements for conducting ethics reviews, constituting ethics boards, and so forth.

The Office of Human Research Protections (OHRP) in the US Department of Health and Human Services (DHHS) is charged with monitoring and enforcement, but much of this work is delegated to research institutions that, by law, must have IRBs. Policing and enforcement have become more complex over time with local IRB policies carefully crafted to conform to OHRP "guidance"; training programs and certifications for researchers, research staff, and IRB workers and administrators; and even accreditation of research centers' and universities' human subjects protection programs. Because they are deeply worried that their research programs might be suspended for ethics violations, a point elaborated below, research institutions are careful to demonstrate compliance. Many new positions have been created for compliance workers—in the research administration offices of major research hospitals and universities, but also in dispersed sites such as hospital clinics and individual research projects.

The attentiveness of IRBs to OHRP invites comparison with the mutual orientation that occurs in other legal and regulatory systems, where definitions of compliance are worked out in the back and forth between courts, regulatory agencies, and regulated organizations. In EEO (equal economic opportunity) law, for instance, the meaning of rules is clarified as people who believe they have experienced discrimination file charges of discrimination, which are then reviewed by the Equal Economic Opportunity Commission. Plaintiffs whose cases survive this review may subsequently bring their cases to the federal district court, where defendant employers often argue that organizational grievance procedures and affirmative action policies should be seen as evidence of compliance with EEO law. Whether these procedures and policies actually address the core of workplace discrimination is another matter. Nevertheless, researchers have documented a process of mutual adaptation in which courts note and reference what employers are doing and uncritically accept their EEO policies and procedures as evidence that they are not discriminating (Edelman et al. 2011; Edelman 2016). The meaning of law has thus been worked out in the give and take between courts and employing organizations in a series of cases that have ultimately established precedents that accept organizations' own definitions of nondiscrimination.

Ethics regulation is somewhat unusual, though, because it is a prospective "licensing" system (Schneider 2015). This means enforcement occurs through prereviews of research projects rather than through retrospective court cases. In both prospective and retrospective regulatory systems, though, once the working definition of rules is settled, organizations focus on demonstrating compliance. The result is a system that requires organizations to demonstrate compliance with the rules, and this privileges formal rather than substantive rationality, form rather than content, and superficial rather than deep compliance. In this kind of ethics regulation, it is hardly surprising that a substantial portion of OHRP and IRB business is about adjusting the wording of consent forms or chastising researchers for missed deadlines (Gunsalus 2004; Burris and Welsh 2007).

OFFICIAL ETHICS IN THE CLINICS

Official ethics is a mundane part of university and research life and shows up in ethics training programs for research staff at all levels of a project. In the US, research staff typically are required to take computerized tests, with completion verified by project administrators and the local IRB. When requirements change, staff members must undergo a fresh round of training and testing, as occurred at Robert Rafsky Clinic during my fieldwork. At Philly Lutaaya Clinic in Uganda, I attended ethics training alongside new research staff. This training did not include the computerized test modules used at Robert Rafsky, but covered many of the same topics and cited the same touchstones of ethics scandals, commissions and reports, and principles of research ethics. If one looked only at the content of the training sessions and ignored skin color, linguistic variations, and differences in the opulence of the clinic furnishings and equipment, one would not have guessed that these sessions occurred in countries that differed so profoundly in wealth and cultural heritage.

Likewise, submissions to IRBs were quite similar across settings. Researchers were required to discuss risks faced by participants and how they would mitigate these risks, any benefits offered to participants, and arrangements for informing potential participants and seeking their consent. Although the key points remained the same, with mandated topics, wording, signatures, dates, and so forth, the ritual of seeking consent is enacted more elaborately in the clinics outside the US and, in Uganda, was often spread over several days with multiple readings of the consent form. A signed consent form for each research participant was carefully stored in project files, along with the annual approvals from the IRB verifying that the research met regulatory and legal requirements. These documents protect the organization should questions be raised and are always inspected when research monitors check on a research team's work.

Each of the HIV clinics I studied had several internal staff positions dedicated to tracking regulatory tasks and associated documentation and demonstrating compliance with ethics rules. These workers also tracked deadlines for annual reviews for the clinic's projects on a spreadsheet or calendar and sent reminders to researchers. The adoption of practices, forms, and structures that closely mimic those used in highly reputable peer organizations are part of the bid for legitimacy that drives institutionalization (DiMaggio and Powell 1991; Dobbin, Simmons, and Garrett 2007). Ethics compliance work is now a fully institutionalized, obligatory element of the work of reputable research enterprises.

But this uniformity of official ethics is accomplished with considerable awkwardness and at great cost. Because requirements were initially formulated for US sites, they often mesh awkwardly with the customs of other countries. Verification of age provides a good example. In US-sponsored clinical research, "adult" has generally been operationalized as "at least eighteen years." In Uganda, where social (though not legal) adulthood arrives earlier than in the US, this means women who already have several children can be barred from participation in clinical research on mother-to-child transmission of HIV because they do not meet the US definition of adult. In a triumph of form over content, biological age trumps social adulthood even though social adulthood is more easily verified than biological age, as this fieldnote from Philly Lutaaya shows:

> This question [on a recruitment form] asks "Is the mother 18 years or older?" How do they know if the woman is 18, [the trainer] asks. . . . Often women don't know their exact birthdate, and not even the year of their birth. [The counselors] talk about other ways of assessing age. If the woman is gravida 5 and says she is 20, someone says, then she is really not likely to be under 18. If she doesn't know her age, then they try to establish age with reference to historical events, such as when Museveni came to power [in 1986]. . . . [The trainer] contrasts the situation here with the US, where age is usually easy to establish since everyone has [drivers'] licenses, ID cards, birth certificates, etc. Here there is likely to be more ambiguity about age and it's important for regulatory [workers tasked with tracking regulatory matters] to know about those ambiguities and how they were resolved. . . . So, [the trainer] emphasizes, be sure to *document*. Not everyone can show an ID. You can't just say the participant doesn't know how old she is, but instead you have to add that you estimated her age by historical references.

When clinical trials were the only route to treatment, pregnant women who were unable to document their adulthood in a way that satisfied US-originated standards were more likely to give birth to HIV-infected babies. But this excessive proceduralism also had the potential to undermine some scientific objectives. Excluding young mothers made the study less representative of the Ugandan childbearing population and decreased the likelihood of learning about the peculiar real-world challenges young mothers might face in adhering to the prenatal appointment and medication regimen.

Researchers in all five clinics spoke frequently (and often unhappily) about the burden of compliance. But compliance was far more difficult to achieve in poor countries than rich ones, as one Philly Lutaaya quality assurance worker, quoted in chapter 5, explained when she pointed out the effects of not having recordkeeping supplies available on the wards where data were being gathered. Having experienced unusually frequent monitoring visits and monitors' skepticism about the capacities of clinics "in the boonies," one staff member at Cha-on Suesum Clinic explained, clinic workers in poorer countries like Thailand learned to do exactly what research protocols, good clinical practice, and the rules for ethical conduct of research required. As a proportion of available resources, compliance was far costlier in poor countries than in richer ones. To be absolutely clear, though, it was demonstrating compliance rather than conducting research ethically that was so costly. Where staff are thin on the ground and resources scarce, spending lavishly on demonstrating compliance can be justified only when the flow of resources to the clinic truly depends on it.

Official ethics emphasizes demonstrations of compliance with the standards for the ethical practice of research—the form, often literally, rather than the content. Official ethics is thus a universalizing system (Fox and Swazey 2005) that focuses on what will appear on the radar screen of research administrators and the research ethics bureaucracy. Research teams make sure that participants meet study criteria, are old enough to consent, and have signed consent forms. But this focus on what's on the radar screen means that much is also ignored. For instance, despite the attention to informed consent, no one paid much attention to the subtleties of translation, including, for instance, that there is no adequate way to translate Western medicine's understanding of risk into Luganda, the language used at Philly Lutaaya (Stewart and Sewankambo 2010). In contrast, ethics on the ground is much more about what is local and particular and, often, off the radar screen.

THE ELEMENTS OF ETHICS ON THE GROUND

Unlike official ethics, ethics on the ground, sometimes called "everyday bioethics" (Berlinguer 2004) or "bioethics from below" (Ryan 2004), is typically not marked by official statements of principles and may not even be explicitly identified as ethics. Without these markers, how can we tell that what we are seeing is truly ethics? Because uniformity in language is a way of marking turf, we expect more uniformity where people are making claims on resources and establishing routinized practices—in official systems, in short. And indeed in ethnographic studies of ethics in medical settings, people are not usually marking their ethical responses by labeling them explicitly as such.[3] Instead we see people troubled by a situation, circling back to the problem in conversation with colleagues, consulting others about what they did in similar circumstances—just what I observed in the HIV clinics. Rather than using the official language of principles and extensively citing the core documents of official ethics, the discourse of ethics on the ground instead focuses on what is fair and what is right, often tying the discussion to technical matters and sometimes giving accounts only later (Fassin 2008). Citations of autonomy, beneficence, and nonmaleficence are replaced with debates about what is fair or unfair, moral or immoral, right or just plain wrong. The emphasis is more on "doing ethics" than discussing ethics (Molyneux and Geissler 2008) and entails considerable boundary work that "signals both reflection and rectitude," by being prepared to engage in deeper discussion of troubling ethical questions and by continuing to reference standard formal legal and ethical frameworks, respectively (Wainwright et al. 2006, 744).

In addition to citing fairness or moral appropriateness, clinic workers troubled about ethical and moral issues also pointed to moral exemplars. At Robert Rafsky, for instance, the site PI was known for taking patient welfare especially seriously; when the interests of a study and the needs of a research participant conflicted, staff members sometimes asked each other what their PI would do. This doctor's impeccable scientific credentials made his concern for patient welfare especially noteworthy. Staff also cited clinic practices as precedent, particularly when gaps in official rules left them uncertain about how to proceed or when actions they believed to be ethically correct clearly violated official rules.

Although the principles of official ethics are transformed into policies, statutes, rules, and SOPs by working through official channels, the more inchoate moral sentiments of ethics on the ground get transformed into decisions and courses of action in discussions among colleagues troubled by the moral implications of their work. These on-the-spot decisions about particular instances often cumulate over time into routinized but not fully codified ways of doing things. Depending on how common or unusual a particular ethical problem is, though, some decisions have no further implications because comparable cases simply do not arise.

The policing and enforcement of the informal norms of ethics on the ground are quite different than the policing and enforcement of official ethics. There were no records kept, no schedules of submissions to official bodies, no visits by monitors asking to inspect forms. Nor were people worrying about threats to the organization, except when they felt compelled by ethics on the ground to do things that clearly did not comport with the law—for instance, when "extra" drugs returned by research subjects or patients[4] were illegally dispensed to fill gaps or to ensure that a person with a needlestick injury received prophylaxis immediately. In essence, enforcement occurred informally, perhaps especially through the gossiping of colleagues morally offended when a coworker's actions felt wrong to the group.

ETHICS ON THE GROUND IN THE CLINICS

Because ethics on the ground develops to fill the gaps opened up by official ethics, it tends to be less fully routinized than official ethics. Procedures for recruiting and retaining research subjects and for protecting confidentiality, two foci of official ethics, offer useful lenses for thinking about where the two systems of ethics diverge.

As they considered where to find potential research subjects, clinic staff understood and largely endorsed official definitions of "vulnerable groups" and the reasons studies generally should not draw research subjects from these populations. Official ethics uses the definition provided by official sources, for instance in 45 C.F.R. 46.[5] Ethics on the ground employs more contextually based definitions. One Robert Rafsky staff member put it this way: "For us, the issues of vulnerability are more about marginalized groups with an incurable or fatal disease rather than the kinds of vulnerability this module [in the ethics training materials] focuses on." Staff members were sensitive to the acute needs of potential research subjects, and understood that participation in a clinical trial was the only route to any sort of treatment, for some, or to new therapies as old ones ceased to work, for others.[6] Under these circumstances, coercion and vulnerability took on new meanings. Yet staff members also thought it unrealistic simply to define large groups of people as ineligible to participate in research.

In thinking about subject recruitment and retention, official ethics starts with research projects. Study protocols specify rules of inclusion and exclusion focused on scientific questions (the medical conditions, drugs, or therapies being studied) and matters of safety (pregnant women are excluded if a drug might harm fetuses). Official ethics supplements study protocols by alerting researchers to concerns about coercion—research subjects should freely consent rather than being pressured to participate in studies, for instance, by being offered reduced prison sentences, as sometimes happened in the past (Halpern 2021). In contrast, ethics on the ground starts with patients and asks which studies would be good for a particular patient or group of patients rather than which patient or group would be good for the study.[7]

A discussion among Robert Rafsky study staff illustrates the priority placed on patients' needs. Debra, one of the research nurses, was concerned about a female patient who was failing her last regimen. The woman was dying. If they could start her on new medications, they might save her life. Debra believed that Reverset, a new drug then being studied, might add twenty years to the woman's life. Debra reviewed the study criteria with Kay (whom we encountered earlier), the nurse assigned to the Reverset trial. To be eligible for this study, subjects had to have been on a stable regimen for sixty days. The woman had been on her regimen sixty days, Debra said, thinking out loud, but she was failing it. Kay explained that after subjects started the study, they had to continue on their previous regimen plus Reverset for sixty days. After having genotype and phenotype testing, they could then be switched to other drugs. Kay wasn't sure they could take someone who was failing their current regimen, but Debra asked Kay to check whether her patient could qualify. "We could save her, but we probably can't," Debra replied in frustration, acknowledging that they had only limited room for maneuver. They went on to discuss a second salvage regimen. Because the nurse responsible for that study was on leave, the clinic would probably need to train another study nurse. Offering to get the additional training, Debra made it clear how badly she wanted her patient enrolled in one of these salvage studies. "If she has any chance, this is it," she stressed. Although both Debra and Kay cared deeply about the integrity of their scientific work, they also felt morally obligated to do the best they could for the study patients who had come into their orbit.

In all five clinics, researchers worried about finding ways to meet the needs of existing patients—not the long-term needs of future patients, but the short-term needs of patients already attending their clinics. Rather than a search process (of finding patients for studies), then, ethics on the ground led clinics to engage in a complicated matching process (of linking existing patients to current or future studies or treatment programs) that took the needs of patients as seriously as the needs of studies. Would a new study ensure continuity in drug supply for a patient just completing a previous study? If a patient would have to find another way to pay for drugs, a new study might at least provide the laboratory tests needed to track the progress of HIV and adjust medications. If a regimen was no longer "working," perhaps enrolling the patient in an adherence or drug resistance study might help clinicians determine what had gone wrong and which drugs might preserve the patient's health.

In the long run, the practice of looking for ways to meet patients' needs once a study had ended became somewhat routinized, albeit in different ways in the four clinics with large numbers of post-trial patients. (Managing post-trial patients was not yet a concern in Gugu Dlamini Clinic's relatively young research program.) The practices of Robert Rafsky Clinic, whose patients were mostly insured, continued in the vein described above. At Bobbi Campbell Clinic, with mostly indigent patients, staff members also strategized about how to get free drugs through the state-level AIDS drug assistance program (ADAP) and drug company philanthropic programs, thinking carefully about sequencing of requests and funneling patients to particular programs. Cha-on Suesum Clinic created a follow-up observational study, although the inclusion criteria (only people who had already been Cha-on Suesum studies) betrayed that continuity in care was one of its main purposes.

At Philly Lutaaya Clinic, concerns about patient welfare pervaded clinic discussions. In one meeting, staff discussed how to assess need for infant formula. Many families needed formula, and errors in assessing need could result in babies being hospitalized for malnutrition. But because supplies were limited, a universal program was not possible. When breastfeeding is the norm, asking a father for money for formula was tantamount to disclosing HIV infection. Mothers, particularly in nonmarital unions, feared that fathers would then abandon them and the children. "This is a big issue," staff concluded. "Ethically, [we] cannot have a baby starving with the mother coming in week to week for study visits." In another meeting, the senior management team discussed how to balance treatment programs and research. "Our business is mainly research," one staff member asserted. The organization's leader retorted: "We can't do research unless we also have care." Discussing the deaths in one clinical trial, he added: "Those who died didn't die from the research but from the disease—because we didn't then have the capacity to treat them." In these discussions, no mention was made of the principles and policies of official ethics, which do not speak to these contingencies in any case.

Admittedly, though, an element of self-interest pervades these worries about research subjects' welfare. Like the beneficiaries in the humanitarian projects Krause (2014) studied, good research subjects are valuable commodities. At essentially every research meeting, staff strategized about how to locate and enroll appropriate research subjects. This is not simply about finding people with the right physical characteristics. Staff members especially value "professional research subjects"—people who both are serial research participants[8] and take their role seriously. They care about doing a good job, show up regularly for appointments, report honestly and in detail on symptoms, and adhere to the protocol as faithfully as possible. "You don't give up on a study patient until they are in the ground," one Robert Rafsky research nurse declared, meaning simultaneously that researchers endeavor to keep subjects enrolled in studies and make the studies mutually beneficial, that they try to track research subjects as they cycle on and off studies, and that they strive to provide them with good care. Clinic staff felt they owed research subjects, including people who were not especially good research subjects, much more than official ethics would suggest they were obligated to offer. Even in contract research organizations, not known for being "patient friendly," research coordinators felt they owed research subjects more than the bare minimum guaranteed by official ethics (Fisher 2006).

Ethics on the ground and official ethics also have different perspectives on how to implement the legal requirements for confidentiality. Especially influential are the HIPAA (Health Insurance Portability and Accountability Act of 1996) Privacy Rule[9] and rules about confidentiality of HIV testing and treatment, some emanating from the US, others enacted locally. US respondents were accustomed to working with HIPAA rules by the time of my fieldwork and interviews, but although clinic staff in other sites were bound by the rules by virtue of funding arrangements, they often found the rules cumbersome and counterintuitive. In understaffed clinics, patient identifiers sometimes crept onto file labels, a violation of the US rules but not of local practices.

Like the Malawian HIV counselors interviewed by Angotti (2010) and the Ugandan health workers studied by Whyte, Whyte, and Kyaddondo (2010), staff in the clinics I studied encountered situations where violating confidentiality seemed the lesser of two evils. What should they do about the many cases where HIV-infected patients had not disclosed to sexual partners and were not consistently practicing safe sex? At Robert Rafsky, for instance, one thirty-seven-year-old Latino man was having unprotected sex with the seventeen-year-old girlfriend he intended to marry. When the clinic worker urged him to tell her that he had HIV, the patient retorted: "You are denying my dream of getting married and having children." US clinics have no clear policy about how to handle this conundrum. This is the sort of patient "you want to hit or hide from," the staff member commented.

In South Africa, Gugu Dlamini staff members valiantly tried to master the legal requirements and to hammer out provisional policies. Yet the mind-boggling variety of scenarios they actually encountered made policymaking difficult. Could a mother be informed that her nondisclosing but very ill adult child had HIV and that she needed to use universal precautions in cleaning his sores? Could a pediatrician insist that a widowed father disclose the HIV status of his child to his girlfriend who cared for the child? Could a husband be informed of the results of an HIV test on his unconscious wife? What should a counselor do when a frightened patient, desperate to keep his job, asked her to create a false paper trail because his employer insisted on seeing his test result? Mulling over some of these scenarios with me, Mark, a member of the counseling staff who also had supervisory responsibilities, was especially troubled that one of the counselors had given a patient a slip falsely attesting that he had tested negative. It was against the law to provide false information—a "dismissible offense" that Mark was obliged to report to the hospital superintendent. Yet Mark thought it unlikely that anything would come of the incident. Because employers are legally prohibited from asking employees for information about their HIV status or firing those who are infected, the employer had no leg to stand on. Mark did hope, though, that the incident would bring home the importance of protecting patient confidentiality.

South African law does allow some bending of confidentiality rules for needlestick injuries and for people endangered by a nondisclosing, HIV-infected sexual partner. But entirely reasonable legal procedures can prove impractically cumbersome in clinic settings. An HIV infection can easily be transmitted before staff can complete the legal procedure. Patients were sometimes too ill, embarrassed, fearful, or selfish to do their part. That left staff torn between their own very real fears of getting themselves or the clinic into trouble and their equally real fears for the health and safety of innocent third parties. "It upsets [me] to have to teach about confidentiality—not that confidentiality isn't important," the psychologist confessed. "It makes [me] angry to have to put people at risk because others won't disclose," she added, before apologizing for her emotional outburst. At a training session on legal provisions for "silent tests" in cases of needlestick injury, the counselors laughed nervously, unsure whether the hospital's routine fully conformed to the law.

Many practices of ethics on the ground are largely off the regulatory radar screen both because they are evolving, situationally specific adjustments and because they have an uneasy relationship with official ethics and indeed with law. People struggle to follow the dictates of official ethics because they know they—and the clinic—can get into trouble if they do not. But if adherence to the dictates of official ethics is necessary for the welfare of the clinic, it is not ethically sufficient for the consciences of caregivers. That ever-present gap between necessary and sufficient makes official ethics "wicked" and ethics on the ground vitally important.

Comparing Official Ethics and Ethics on the Ground

What, then, are the core differences between these two approaches to ethics? Official ethics and ethics on the ground differ along four main dimensions. They differ, first, in how they conceive the social relationships of clinical research and medical care and whom they aim to protect. Second, they have divergent understandings of where ethics comes from and, third, who has ethical agency. Finally, they have different conceptions of how ethical obligations are to be met. These differences, summarized in table 8.1, are elucidated with more nuance below.

WHO IS THE FOCUS OF ETHICAL ATTENTION?

Ethics on the ground believes people's multiple roles create important context for clinic relationships. Research subjects are understood to be patients as well as research subjects because it is HIV that brought them to the clinic. Moreover, they are assumed to have partners, family members, and other important ties, and to face constraints associated with employment and other obligations. Likewise, clinic staff are not researchers or caregivers but both (Easter et al. 2006; Hedgecoe 2006); if they are researchers, they are always also caring professionals with all of the ethical obligations that come with those roles. Moreover, ethics on the ground suggests that researchers are better scientists and patients are better research subjects when this complexity is acknowledged. "This is not an assembly line—give me your data and get out the door," said one Robert Rafsky research nurse, explaining that making the environment comfortable encouraged people to be "good patients" and "good research subjects." In short, ethics on the ground conceives relationships as multistranded and social roles as overlapping and mutually supportive.

In contrast, official ethics abstracts out this complexity. Patients and research subjects are conceived more narrowly with details about their lives and relationships less likely to intrude into clinic interactions. Caregiving and research are seen as largely distinct activities that may conflict. Enthusiastic researchers might, for instance, compromise patient welfare

TABLE 8.1. Comparing Official Ethics and Ethics on the Ground

	OFFICIAL ETHICS	ETHICS ON THE GROUND
Who Is Focus of Ethics?	Ethics focuses on research subjects and patients conceived as individuals Ethics also considers organization's interests Distinctions between treatment and research seen as essential and protective	Ethics focuses on research subjects and patients seen as full people embedded in other social relationships Ethics also considers needs of family and close associates Overlap of treatment and research seen as necessary and good
Where Does Ethics Come From?	External sources (including beyond national borders) Ethics experts Top down Official agendas and decision points	Internal sources (indigenous) Lay and expert Collaborative Emerging from clinic discussions
Who Has Ethical Agency (and Who Doesn't)?	<u>Empowered</u> Ethics experts; IRB staff; regulatory affairs specialists Doctors and others high in medical hierarchy Organizations rather than individuals (because organizations create the constraining rules) <u>Disempowered</u> Individuals as compared to organizations Workers lower in medical hierarchy	<u>More empowered because sometimes able to disregard rules</u> Doctors and others high in medical hierarchy <u>Less empowered but sometimes able to maneuver around rules</u> Individuals as compared to organizations Workers lower in medical hierarchy
How Are Ethical Obligations Met?	Compliance with rules, procedures and guidelines, with some modest attention to when rules don't fit	Blending compliance with rules with obligations arising from professional norms and individual conscience

by pressuring patients to participate in research or keeping them on study drugs when lab values suggest those drugs might be causing harm. Compassionate caregivers might compromise the integrity of scientific investigations by making biased selections of candidates for research (e.g., by choosing patients who "need" the study). Indeed, some research practices such as carefully designed selection criteria, like those discussed by Debra and Kay, and double-blind procedures for randomizing research subjects to the arms of a study are designed, in part, to protect against biases introduced by the mixing of roles.

We should not overstate the uniformity of ethics on the ground, though. The near unanimous dissatisfaction with official ethics did not translate into an ethics on the ground that was consistent across sites. For instance, although clinic workers in all five sites acknowledged potential conflicts between research and treatment, many clinic workers seemed to assume that being mindful of such conflicts would enable them to guard against the exploitation of research subjects. Bobbi Campbell Clinic staff did not agree and assigned each research subject a primary care physician not involved in the research project. The clinic director carefully reminded research subjects that "researchers will have some loyalty to the study, and that they need a primary care provider to be the person who looks out for their own best interest." Because patients' needs vary so much from one clinic to the next, what is demanded by ethics on the ground also varies. But meeting those needs is almost always easier in clinics that have ample resources.

Official ethics usually focuses on individuals—the research participants—as the entities needing protection. In the clinics I studied, though, ethics on the ground expanded its focus to include the social circle surrounding research subjects and treatment program participants. This expanded understanding of who is the proper subject of ethical concern may be especially likely in HIV because staff worry about transmission to sexual partners and children. At both Gugu Dlamini and Philly Lutaaya, staff members argued that treatment was more likely to succeed when the whole family received care. People would then be more likely to disclose that they had HIV and to secure the support of "treatment buddies." Moreover, by caring for parents, clinic staff could increase the odds that someone would be alive to care for the HIV-infected youngsters. But this welcoming stance created fresh problems in environments of scarcity. In both Uganda and South Africa, staff struggled with how to define "family." As they crafted rules about who to include, one Ugandan doctor stressed that "'family members' must be kept within reason—it can't include every last cousin!"

Once the doors are opened to seeing people in the context of their relationships, firm boundaries are hard to establish, perhaps especially in Uganda and South Africa, where medical services were scarce and demand was very high. If patients' and research subjects' families were included, surely the families of staff members should also be included. And because good health depended on more than skilled medical care and reliable access to drugs, clinic boundaries in South Africa and Uganda expanded to include feeding programs, income-generation programs, and psychosocial counseling.

Beyond this inclusion of patients' partners and families in the circle of ethical concern, then, ethics on the ground was also more likely than official ethics to adopt a public health perspective that asked what is owed to groups, or even societies, as well as individuals. This perspective was especially common in the clinics of poorer countries. In the US clinics we studied, if a clinic's mandate did not specifically include caring for some particular group, clinic staff often were able to refer members of that group to other clinics. For instance, as a clinic associated with a private hospital, Robert Rafsky offered care only to insured patients and sent other patients to a local public clinic. Bobbi Campbell Clinic was a public facility, but its mandate included caring for people in a carefully demarcated geographical area. Because Bobbi Campbell received no reimbursement their care, patients residing outside that geographical area were referred to other public clinics. Because there are many organizations offering care, no single US clinic is likely to believe that patients truly have nowhere else to go, and clinic staff members often seem to experience the decreased sense of obligation noted in studies of diffused responsibility (Penner et al. 2005).

In poorer countries, though, there are likely to be fewer alternatives, and patients who do not "belong" to one clinic may not have anywhere else to go. Awareness of this dilemma can force clinics to adopt a public health perspective, further blurring the boundary between research and treatment. Focusing ethical attention exclusively on individuals and drawing boundaries between research and treatment may be luxuries more available in rich countries than poor ones.

Official ethics, working through government agencies and research administration offices in hospitals and research institutions, in fact seems as much focused on protecting organizations as protecting research subjects or patients. In the telling exchange with which this chapter opened, research administrators and researchers clashed over how to deal with expenses not covered by either the research project or some other payer. Focusing on the increased intensity of regulation and the huge penalties for noncompliance, research administrators adopted the line of official ethics. From their perspective, the key issue was the organizational responsibility to inform patients of such costs before consent forms were signed. For researchers, adopting the perspective of ethics on the ground, the issue was instead that many patients could not afford to absorb the expense of costly medical supplies and procedures. Official ethics made it nearly impossible for the research administrators to see what researchers were worried about.

Research dollars are now a substantial proportion of university budgets (Bledsoe et al. 2007). Ethics violations threaten the flow of funds. When research subjects are seriously harmed or die, ensuing investigations can shut down universities' entire research programs, as occurred with the deaths of Ellen Roche and Jesse Gelsinger (Steinbrook 2002). Rare though they are, these suspensions of university research programs have made universities exceedingly concerned about ensuring full compliance with human subjects regulations, whether individual researchers believe those rules focus on ethically significant matters or not. "If you wear the team colors long enough, you feel like part of the team," Elliott (2007, 43) observed, worrying about whose interests are served when bioethicists occupy positions in hospitals, pharmaceutical companies, and regulatory organizations.

WHERE DOES ETHICS COME FROM?

Because it was a response to perceived lapses in professional self-regulation, official ethics developed as a top-down regulatory enterprise in which governments created statutes, regulations, and guidance to establish ethical standards for human subjects research. These statutes, regulations, and guidance are then interpreted and implemented by government agencies and the university and research center offices that actually oversee the work of those conducting research. Although some room has been left for local discretion, the sphere of discretion has generally decreased over time as the machinery for licensing researchers and projects and for monitoring compliance has grown more elaborate (Babb 2020).

My distinction maps roughly onto Kleinman's distinction (1995, 45) between ethics—"the codified body of abstract knowledge held by experts about 'the good'"—and morality—"commitments of social participants in a local world about what is at stake in everyday experience"—though I place more emphasis on the bureaucratization of ethics. In contrast to official ethics, ethics on the ground is a more indigenous, local form of knowledge (Christakis 1992). Although it is necessarily in dialogue with official ethics, ethics on the ground is also in dialogue with other sources of ethical and moral thinking. Official ethics draws on "ethical experts," who serve on commissions, in agencies responsible for monitoring compliance with human subjects regulations, and on ethics panels in healthcare organizations. In the HIV clinics I studied, occupants of official positions handed down decisions about compliance with ethics regulations. Ethics on the ground was more likely to cite religious leaders (a local pastor was often cited at Gugu Dlamini Clinic), people regarded as moral exemplars in the clinics, and others who were not part of the regulatory hierarchy. In ethics on the ground, decisions about appropriate courses of action were made collectively in informal discussion and in regularly scheduled clinic meetings. Although "ethical issues" were not an official agenda item, talk about ethics grew from discussions of other agenda items such as adverse events (AEs) and serious adverse events (SAEs) or the recruitment of research subjects. Rather than being imposed from outside, then, ethics on the ground grew from local moral codes and talk among people who did not conceive themselves as having any particular ethics expertise beyond the expertise that arose from working in a helping profession and regularly encountering similar moral conundrums. With nearly everyone monitoring themselves and their colleagues, though, there may be little time left for an alternative agenda.

Official ethics has diffused around the globe, following the trail of research funding. Like other global rules, official ethics does not simply fill a vacuum but is mixed with or layered on top of preexisting indigenous rules and norms (Bartley 2011). Echoing this perspective, one Thai researcher ruefully noted that Americans forget Thailand conducted ethics reviews long before the imposition of the American IRB system. "Given the emphasis on US laws," one Philly Lutaaya staff member commented, "people might start to wonder if we have any laws here." Like the human rights ideas Merry (2006a, 2006b) studied, official ethics has not been fully indigenized. It often fails to acknowledge the preexisting layers, delegitimating those layers and leaving the work of translation and harmonization to others.

WHO HAS ETHICAL AGENCY—AND WHO DOESN'T?

Related to where ethics comes from is the question of who has ethical agency—whose moral reasoning can be the basis for action and who can take that action. Official ethics has brought an expanding staff of specialists to administer its rules and a growing distinction between those who are ethics experts and those who are not. These ethical specialists include trained bioethicists, who work in universities, write scholarly essays on bioethics, do ethics consults in medical settings, and serve on boards, commissions, and committees. Most of the work of ethics administration is not done by trained bioethicists, though, but instead by the certified IRB professionals or certified IRB managers who have a rather different kind of training (Heimer and Petty 2010; Babb 2020).

This cadre of ethics and regulatory specialists is central to the work of official ethics. In fact, they are also important for ethics on the ground because they create mandated practices to which ethics on the ground must respond and adjust. Crucial to both systems of ethics, though, is how ethical agency varies with whether a person is a high-ranked professional or a lower-ranked one. Doctors and nurses, to take two key professions, have very different relations to ethics, as Chambliss (1996) points out in explaining why nursing is a wonderful profession but a horrible job. Ethical dilemmas, he argues, are a luxury reserved for decision makers. Subordinate workers like nurses instead have ethical problems. Nurses are simultaneously professionals, trained to attend to their patients' welfare, subordinates required to follow doctors' orders, and employees obliged to adhere to their employers' rules. Because increasing proportions of medical professionals are employees of large medical organizations, more medical staff now have ethical problems. Both ethics on the ground and official ethics confront the effects of the hierarchy of medical professions and the bureaucracy of medical organizations. Yet for official ethics, hierarchy and bureaucracy are sometimes assets because they can lend authority to official ethics. This is especially likely, though, when high-status physicians accept the authority of official ethics. In the clinics I studied, though, physicians were often quite ambivalent about official ethics.

Finally, the specialization of ethics work can lead to ethics "deskilling." When there are official spokespeople for ethics, people learn to doubt their own ethical judgments and those of other ordinary people (Elliott 2007). Admittedly, official ethics has attempted to correct for this by including nonexperts on ethics review panels. Yet because these nonexperts are selected by the ethicists or IRB managers, they may not adequately represent the views of people in medical wards or research projects.

HOW ARE ETHICAL OBLIGATIONS MET?

In the realm of official ethics, many ethical obligations are met legalistically and procedurally. From the perspective of the Robert Rafsky–affiliated research administrators cited above, if research subjects have been informed of expenses they will incur and still sign consent forms, research costs pose no ethical issue. Ethical obligations are met by learning the principles, mastering the rules, and following correct procedures. To be safe, scrupulous organizations will augment, upgrade, and retrain their research ethics administrative staff and seek accreditation of their human subjects protection program. At lower levels in the institution, ethical obligations are met by avoiding vulnerable populations, designing consent forms meticulously, and filing appropriate forms. Ultra-careful regulatory specialists (like one staff member at Philly Lutaaya Clinic) may urge that treatment programs also adopt the stricter policies of research, a move that may seem to others a questionable use of scarce resources. There are, to be sure, some ethical obligations, such as the obligation to withdraw patients from studies if continued participation endangers their health, that cannot be met in a legalistic way, and we should be careful not to overstate the proceduralism of official ethics.

In contrast, the ethical problems faced by individual workers cannot be solved with proceduralism. Official ethics offers little help with the irreducible and inescapable personal obligations associated with caring professions. Ethics on the ground often counsels a different course of action, sometimes even (quiet) violation of the rules. When ethics becomes the property of organizations, it is ethics on the ground that accommodates individuals' concerns about meeting their personal and professional ethical obligations.

Conclusion: Why Might Ethics Be "Wicked"?

I have depicted official ethics and ethics on the ground as largely separate systems coexisting in healthcare organizations. But this overstates their independence. Considering the relation between these two systems of ethics returns us to the sense in which ethics can be "wicked."

Rather than sensitizing people to the full panoply of ethical questions, official ethics focuses attention on some questions and deflects attention from others. The compliance work associated with official ethics in fact consumes considerable time and attention, leaving less for ethics on the ground. Rather than helping us develop moral perception (Andre 2007), official ethics puts blinders on our eyes. Official ethics focuses primarily on individuals rather than groups, ignoring major structural inequalities. It is not exactly that systemic problems are completely overlooked, though. They are in fact sometimes present in codes of ethics. For instance, the AMA code of ethics states that "a physician shall support access to medical care for all people" (AMA n.d.). But principles not translated into rules and checklists may go unheeded when no demonstration of compliance is required or, alternatively, when the goal is beyond the reach of individual caregivers and researchers. Statements asserting that physicians must support universal access to healthcare thus have no meaningful consequence. The resulting thin conception of ethics seems to assume that ethical problems in research and caregiving alike are "located at the level of the individual doctor-patient [or researcher-research subject] relationship and consist of the inappropriate values operating within that relationship" (Bosk 1999, 55). In addition to putting blinders on our eyes, then, the embrace of official ethics by universities and the medical establishment has helped defang other critics.

Yet bioethicists are not always on the side of official ethics. Their trenchant critiques of bioethics' failings (Fox and Swazey 2005) point to the dangers of "wearing the team colors" (Elliott 2007), failing to listen (Andre

2007), neglecting inequalities (Turner 2005), overlooking the impact of social and economic factors on the spread of infectious diseases (Benatar 2002; Keenan 2005; Tausig et al. 2006), and ignoring common moral wisdom (Churchill and Schenck 2005). As long as the checklists and resources remain exclusively in the hands of official ethics, research ethics—and indeed medical ethics more generally—is likely to remain thin.

Official ethics' channeling of attention and resources is especially "wicked" where ethics rules have been exported to sites where compliance is difficult. The diversion of resources and attention from other ethical issues and indeed from healthcare to ethics compliance is especially consequential and damaging in resource-constrained countries. Insisting that an IRB be staffed as it would be in the US and meet on a similar schedule can mean a hospital has one less obstetrician available for complicated maternity cases. Staff shortages associated with compliance work were mentioned repeatedly during our fieldwork at Philly Lutaaya. At the same time, though, the pushback in poor countries may be stronger because medical organizations are less able to insulate themselves from ethical problems that arrive on their doorsteps. Where medical care is scarce and need is overwhelming, the divide between healthcare providers and researchers, on the one hand, and patients and research subjects, on the other, is obscured (Fassin 2008). When everyone has a close friend or relative who is affected, checklists to remind people to attend to structural inequalities may be unnecessary. Official ethics may siphon off resources in these situations, but it is less likely to succeed in putting blinders on people's ethical eyes.

So how did this happen? What mechanisms encouraged the growth of official ethics at the expense of indigenous ethical systems? The story of official ethics is in part a variant of the gap between official law on the books and law in action. Gaps between "law on the books" and "law in action" raise perennial questions about what rules mean and what actions count as compliance. Sometimes the meaning of rules gets settled through court cases or other forms of contestation. Relatively minor threats to organizations (e.g., to suspend research funding pending investigation of ethics violations) can lead to vast overreactions and the creation of extra positions and elaborate bureaucracies. Organizational rules are spelled out and checked carefully against government regulations and agency guidance. In short, organizations create positions and departments to ensure compliance and stave off threats to key resources. And within the new compliance bureaucracies, the interests of newly created compliance professions are married to the interests of the organizations. In this way, small threats are magnified.

In essence, via a two-step process, a compliance bureaucracy modifies understandings of what is important. First, it increases the sense of urgency by mandating a series of actions on a rigid timetable. Most violations in ethics compliance are violations of form, not substance—missed deadlines or minor documentation errors (Gunsalus 2004; Burris and Welsh 2007). But because organizational consequences can flow from them, such violations become important whether they are about the substance of ethics or not. With these two shifts—making things urgent and making them consequential for organizations—official ethics enlarges the gap between ethics on the books and ethics on the ground, reshapes understanding of what is important, and ultimately redefines what counts as ethical.

We must still ask why the growth of official ethics is so insidious. What official ethics does is substitute bureaucratic ethics for other systems of ethics—for professional ethics (Halpern 2004), industrial morality (Rees 1988), sociological citizenship (Silbey 2011), and other collective moral approaches that encourage responsiveness to the situation (Selznick 1992). It also displaces personal morality. What is lost is the distinction between law and morality and the critical edge that morality has traditionally brought to law (Heimer 2010, 2023). With the growth of official ethics, any distinction between law and ethics becomes wickedly difficult to make. Rules alone cannot get us the full distance to morality and may sometimes set us back.

"Sometimes" is an important word, though, signaling crucial variability in the good or ill that results from the legal turn in the ethics of healthcare and biomedical research. In concluding the book, I ask what the evidence suggests about special circumstances that sometimes shift the balance from compliance with the letter of the law to deeper attentiveness to the spirit and aspirations of the law.

[CHAPTER NINE]

Moral Worth and the Legal Turn in Medicine

From Scientific Claims to Moral Obligations

Medicine and medical science are supposed to improve the world. And every country in the world has signed one or more of the international declarations acknowledging the human right to health. Yet, in the history of clinical research and medical practice, inspiring stories of lives saved and health restored share space with horrifying tales of scientific and medical misconduct and more mundane accounts of discrimination and neglect.

Legal regulation has often been deployed to curb the abuses of scientists and medical practitioners and to redress inequalities. Despite scientists' and medical workers' insistence that they should be permitted to regulate themselves, then, a host of statutes, regulations, guidelines, protocols, and standard operating procedures (SOPs) have been introduced to govern medical settings both in the US and in other countries. Yet an examination of these newly legalized medical settings suggests that the effects of legal regulation are quite complex, sometimes extending protections and offering valued resources, but often simply reinscribing inequalities.

Despite the universalistic tenor of the legally inflected discourse of clinical science and medicine, my interviews and fieldwork show that the legal turn in healthcare smuggled in legal endowments that advantaged some groups while disadvantaging others.[1] Because the rules appear neutral—even fair—it can be hard to mount a challenge without appearing churlish. This chapter notes the marginalization experienced by some researchers (who might be included in projects as "hands" but not "heads"), populations (whose health problems might not be deemed worthy of investigation), and patients (who might receive inferior treatment). Working with rules that created an uneven playing field often brought extra work and sometimes considerable cynicism. But this chapter also draws attention to the special conditions, perhaps more common in HIV medicine than in other fields, where people embraced the rules and leveraged and expanded universalism to redress imbalances. In effect, I suggest, a globalized moral order emerged alongside the globalized scientific and biomedical order.

Contrasting Cases: Is the Universalism of the HIV World Anomalous?

Writing in *Lancet*, Attaran et al. (2004, 237) bemoaned the "medical malpractice in malaria treatment," specifically citing WHO and the Global Fund to Fight AIDS, Tuberculosis and Malaria (GFATM or Global Fund) as entities guilty of this malpractice. Mentioning treatment program funding applications from such countries as Senegal, Ethiopia, Kenya, and Uganda, the article charged that "WHO violates its own policy standard regularly" (Attaran et al. 2004, 238) by succumbing to pressure from countries such as the US that prefer to fund less expensive, suboptimal treatment.[2] Although the particular treatments being funded were listed in WHO guidelines as "not recommended" given local drug resistance profiles, WHO insisted that supporting such suboptimal treatment programs was "consistent with current treatment guidelines of WHO" (Attaran et al. 2004, 238). The authors concluded by noting that it would be medical malpractice if a doctor or pharmacist provided treatment known to fail something like 80% of the time, withholding effective treatments as "too expensive" (Attaran et al. 2004, 238).

The contrasting case here is HIV where, shortly after the 1996 announcement that HIV could be effectively treated with carefully designed antiretroviral cocktails, no one prescribed suboptimal mono- or dual-therapy. No one continued to fund suboptimal treatment for HIV. In contrast, funding suboptimal treatment for malaria seems to have been common despite equally compelling scientific evidence about efficacy.

What accounts for this difference between malaria and HIV policy? Why did optimal treatment become "standard of care" for HIV, with everyone from Médecins sans Frontières (MSF) to WHO, the Global Fund, PEPFAR (President's Emergency Plan for AIDS Relief), and even the country programs of resource-constrained nations signing on? Here I develop an argument about how a norm of universal optimal HIV treatment gradually developed over the years between the first official recognition of HIV as a distinctive disease in 1981 through the time of my research and continuing on up to the present. But I also note the precariousness of such a norm.

I begin by using the case of HIV/AIDS and access to anti-retroviral therapy (ART) to show how consensus about the efficacy of ART, embodied in clinical guidelines, added support to claims that the poor should have equal access to treatment. I trace the evolution of the debate on access, showing the intertwined paths of guideline development, discussions of clinical research ethics, and discourse on drug access. In essence, clinical guidelines were used strategically as a legal resource, a legislative endowment

(Lempert and Sanders 1986) that could be deployed on behalf of the disadvantaged. I show both how the endowment was created and how it came to be used, including how the international system of clinical trials created an opening for early claims about fairness in drug access. But however universalistic they sound, rules do not always lead to increased equality. The legalism of the World Trade Organization (WTO) thus offers an instructive counterpoint to the legalism of clinical guidelines—a second way that the "rule of law" has penetrated the medical world and shaped access to healthcare. I then consider the effects of institutional review board (IRB) rules on the treatment of research subjects. And finally I look at how the rules have shaped the experiences of researchers and their sense of themselves as morally worthy (or unworthy) participants in the global research enterprise.

Some of the inequalities examined in this chapter have been thoroughly documented already by social scientists. People from different social strata arrive for healthcare with different medical conditions—the diseases of the poor (and poor countries) versus the diseases of the rich (and rich countries)—and experience different outcomes (Benatar 2015; Truesdale and Jencks 2016). But even when they have identical problems, patients with different characteristics do not fare equally, and some of those "health disparities" arise in the healthcare encounter itself (Lutfey Spencer and Grace 2016). We also know that there are inequities in clinical research, with some groups excluded from research participation (Epstein 2007), others overrepresented in the early nontherapeutic stages of clinical research (Fisher 2009, 2020), and still others exploited by researchers who site studies in poorer countries where costs are low and "treatment-naïve" subjects plentiful (Lusgarten 2005; Petryna 2009). We know somewhat less, though, about the experiences of inequality of people on the other side of the examining table, namely the clinicians and researchers.

One element shaping these encounters, as I have argued throughout this book, is the rules—statutes and regulations, clinical guidelines, research protocols, professional norms, organizational policies, and SOPs. Generally speaking, these rules are intended to increase uniformity in the work of clinicians and researchers. Like cases should be treated alike. Clinical guidelines are meant to reduce "practice variations." IRB and GCP (Good Clinical Practice) rules are expected to ensure that vulnerable research subjects are not exploited by researchers. Research protocols and SOPs should ensure that data collected in multiple sites are comparable enough to be treated as part of a single study.

These rules also bring with them expectations—often unarticulated—about the essential parity of the participants in this social world. In that sense, these legal forms serve as mechanisms for closing "recognition gaps" and decreasing disparities in people's experience of moral worth and cultural membership (Lamont 2018, 2023). Expectations of essential equality are especially likely to be explicit for those involved as patients or research subjects. For medical caregivers and clinical researchers, in contrast, expectations of parity are less fully articulated, yet the clear implication is that if people have received the professional training to work as physicians, researchers, nurses, or lab techs and have received the additional training required to perform specific tasks—a newly developed medical procedure, a data collection technique for a particular clinical trial—they should be treated as essentially equal to others in similar roles.

The assumption of moral worthiness, whether it takes the form of universalistic treatment of patients and research subjects or respect for professional peers, has been an essential element of medicine's self-conception.[3] These expectations of moral parity have been articulated in especially strong terms in the world of HIV treatment and research. New programs to test for HIV, put people on treatment, and end the epidemic are announced with great fanfare at the biannual International AIDS Conference (IAC). These conferences are explicitly billed as global events, and the announced plans and programs are equally explicit about making testing, treatment, and prevention available to everyone. Likewise, research programs are intended to be inclusive, bringing researchers from developing countries into the community of researchers as co-PIs and co-researchers in multisited studies, and these inclusive policies are showcased at the conferences. Indeed, the frequent protests at these conferences reinforce the egalitarian sentiment. Protesters loudly object to programs and policies that exclude or disadvantage particular groups. The otherwise laudable US treatment program PEPFAR, for instance, was widely criticized for its anti-prostitution pledge requirement.[4] Protesters have also targeted pharmaceutical companies and governments whose policies complicate or jeopardize treatment access. And conference locations are chosen or excluded to reinforce these messages about moral parity and inclusion.

Despite the universalistic thrust of the governing rules and the inclusive culture of the HIV treatment and research environment, old inequalities persist and new inequalities arise. This chapter looks at the gap between promises and reality, asking what it is about the rules themselves and how they are administered that supports the continued existence or reemergence of inequalities. Although many participants in this field seemed to feel little sense of disappointment—in some instances because they never actually expected anything like parity, in others because they were among the already privileged—other participants felt betrayed and demeaned. That said, it is also important to think about the very special circumstances when the rules truly encourage people to think deeply about what they owe each other and to see each other as morally worthy. My task, then, is to re-examine variations in the experience of being a patient, a research subject, a clinician, or a researcher in the light of rules intended to level the playing field, make access to treatment more equal, or ensure the uniformity of data. Here I consider what these attempts to increase uniformity actually do and ask about the very special conditions that may move forward the goal of increased equity in treatment and research, for patients, research subjects, clinicians, and researchers.

From Death Sentence to Chronic Disease—But for Whom?

For many years, HIV was considered a death sentence. Now in many parts of the world, it is considered a treatable chronic disease.[5] HIV began as a mysterious disease, hard to pin down partly because HIV did its damage by destroying the immune system so people died of other diseases rather than of HIV itself. In 1981 scientists at the US Centers for Disease Control (CDC) began seeing cases of the disease that became known as AIDS, but the virus wasn't isolated until 1983. Antibody tests became commercially available in 1985, but treatment, cure, and prevention proved much more elusive, partly because a virus that mutates rapidly is a moving target.

Until 1987, doctors could treat the opportunistic infections (OIs) that followed HIV infection but not the disease itself. That changed in 1987 with Food and Drug Administration (FDA) approval of AZT, the first anti-retroviral drug (ARV). Although other ARVs followed, treatment was only a modest improvement: some viral suppression for a year or two, side effects that were sometimes so severe that patients abandoned therapy, regimens with huge numbers of pills and strict rules about when and how pills must be taken, and astronomical prices.

In 1996, a major breakthrough came when scientists demonstrated that patients fared significantly better when treated with three or more ARVs simultaneously. Although highly active anti-retroviral therapy (HAART), as it was then called,[6] was still not a "cure," it worked better (reducing viral load further) and longer than mono- or even dual-therapy. HAART diffused rapidly, although the conventional story may be somewhat deceptive. Popular accounts suggest an abrupt shift, but the historical record suggests a somewhat more gradual change. Although the study results were announced at the Vancouver AIDS Conference in July 1996, they had already been published in scientific journals. Figures on adoption of triple-therapy may lump together patients already on triple-therapy before the Vancouver meetings with those who started after the official announcement. Nevertheless, it is clear that adoption was swift. By one account, "within a week of its announcement at the 1996 Vancouver AIDS conference, over 75,000 AIDS patients in North America had already been placed on the regimen" (Engel 2006, 246). A decade or so after HAART became the norm, patients began to grumble that the cure might be worse than the disease (Gross 2008), but that complaint usually arose only after some substantial period of improved health and did not, in any case, generally lead people to quit therapy.

Thus far, this remarkable story is largely about scientific progress and the treatment of a dreadful new disease in rich countries. In fact it should also be told as a story about the creation of a new norm as a consensus developed that treatment should be made available to all. The new norm was not a medical norm but a moral one. This account of the transformation of scientific knowledge into moral claims is even more striking when it includes what happened in poorer countries.

The large, generalized epidemics of sub-Saharan Africa have wrought havoc, not least because the healthcare systems of poorer countries lack the resources to pay for ART. For poor countries, the relevant parts of the HIV story include the milestones noted above, but they also include a modest number of other advances. Brazil's program of universal treatment made ART much more widely available in that country. The development of a short-course treatment for preventing mother-to-child transmission (PMTCT) made PMTCT affordable even in poor countries. The South African suit against pharmaceutical companies not only raised awareness about how pharmaceutical companies use legal mechanisms to protect profits at the expense of public health but also increased drug access in South Africa. By issuing treatment guidelines for resource-limited countries, WHO facilitated testing and treatment in poorer countries and acknowledged that adjusting guidelines is a task that should not be left to overworked individual practitioners. The creation of UNAIDS (Joint United Nations Programme on HIV/AIDS), the Global Fund, TASO (The AIDS Support Organization), TAC (Treatment Action Campaign), and PEPFAR helped focus attention on HIV/AIDS and shift resources to the places where they were most needed. The Doha Declaration eased WTO restrictions on the production of generic drugs in cases of national emergency, legitimating poor country complaints about the unfairness of a trade regime that favored the interests of richer countries and put profits ahead of public health. The 3 by 5 plan[7] and its successors, the

90-90-90 and 95-95-95 programs[8] set timetables for testing and treatment in poor countries as well as rich ones and created mechanisms for tracking progress. Keeping their eye on the aim universal access, these programs kept the pressure on by episodically ratcheting up goals and adding new slogans.

What is notable about these milestones is that they are not primarily about new scientific findings but about claims that the science of richer countries has some relevance for poorer ones. These are, then, milestones that mark moral claims more than scientific ones, with aspirational slogans encouraging the metamorphosis of hard science and soft law into moral obligations.

This observation suggests that similar milestones must be marked in the rich world, that the moral meaning of scientific conclusions in the US and Europe also had to be constructed and disseminated by key social movement actors there. Without the targeted interventions of ACT UP (AIDS Coalition to Unleash Power) or GMHC (Gay Men's Health Crisis), for instance, the moral implications of existing practices might have remained invisible and the approvals process of the FDA would be different than it is now.

How, then, were these moral claims constructed from scientific ones? The crafting of moral claims required many steps, with the cultural materials from which claims were fashioned coming largely from rules and guidelines, sources that had been present in the environment all along. What has been distinctive about HIV, though, is that the structuring of the day-to-day activities of research and treatment and the more episodic large gatherings for conferences have kept up a steady dialogue in which one group after another pushed for expanded understandings of patient and research subject rights. As people grappled with how rules should be applied, they concretized their previously abstract understandings of universalism. Because the principles were widely endorsed, the general effect was a ratcheting up of patient and research subject rights and a corresponding creation of obligations for researchers, caregivers, and funders. The core elements, then, are these: the hard science (repeated scientific discoveries, widely publicized), the "soft laws" (governing both research and treatment), and the social arrangements that helped create social movement actors and have brought activists, scientists, doctors and other caregivers, philanthropists, NGOs, government aid programs, and even pharmaceutical companies into sustained, repeated, and intense dialogue. Taken together, these elements began to produce a globalized moral order. Rules and guidelines—the dry stuff of bureaucratic regulation—were gradually transmuted into moral claims.

Clinical Guidelines and Pressures for Treatment Equity

Of fundamental importance were clinical guidelines themselves. These guidelines have been discussed extensively throughout the book as I investigated their origins in the legalization of healthcare, examined the paradoxical variability in how the clinics worked with these universal prescriptions, and asked about the effects of the "hardening" of clinical guidelines. Here I ask a somewhat different question: namely, how essentially scientific claims about the efficacy of particular treatment regimens are (sometimes) transformed into moral claims about rights to particular kinds of care.

Clinical guidelines are universalistic, prescriptive statements. Although they are intended to be used flexibly—what a physician should do depends on details about a patient's condition and history—guidelines do not offer the option of ignoring or turning away people who need medical care. In the case of HIV, for instance, the guidelines tell doctors how to assess disease progress; when to start the patient on ART; which regimen to use depending, for instance, on whether the patient is a child or an adult, pregnant, or coinfected with TB; and what to do about side effects. Although some guidelines (such as those issued by the CDC) assume doctors will be able to use sophisticated lab tests in making their assessments, others (such as those issued by WHO or MSF) tell doctors how to adjust decision procedures when they are unable to get CD4 counts or viral loads or maybe even measures of changes in weight. However doctors go about "staging" the disease, the final recommendations have been quite similar: as patients' immune systems deteriorate, put them on ART and make it multidrug ART.[9] What the guidelines do not say is this: when people live in poorer countries or are themselves poor, they can forgo treatment or receive mono- or dual-therapy rather than the multidrug regimen that makes viral replication impossible. Because the guidelines remain universal, treatment disparities become glaringly obvious.

As they work with clinical guidelines, caregivers cannot help but notice when—for whatever reason—they are unable to give their patients the care recommended by the guidelines. Both the nature and frequency of the difficulties caregivers encounter in following guidelines vary from one clinic to another. Although caregivers at Robert Rafsky occasionally had difficulty locating a study, insurer, or philanthropic program to pay for care, these were experienced as troubles for individual patients, not systemic problems for large groups of patients. In part this was because problems that might have been experienced as collective were externalized—patients with no identifiable payer were sent to the local public hospital.

Bobbi Campbell, a public facility, faced somewhat greater resource challenges. On the one hand, they were prohibited from treating patients who were not part of their geographical catchment area. On the other, available resources were not always adequate, in part because the high cost of ART (and particularly second-line and newly available drugs). Patients' care was largely covered by the Ryan White Care Program and the Ryan White ADAP (AIDS drugs assistance program). But because Ryan White is a discretionary program that gives limited funds to clinics rather than an entitlement program for affected individuals, funding for care and for drugs is not guaranteed, and shortfalls sometimes occur (Smith and Buchanan 2001). Bobbi Campbell caregivers therefore carefully juggled their patients' needs, "cobbling together" resources. Some slots went to patients who needed to start treatment immediately. Caregivers carefully considered whose medications should be covered by ADAP and who should be put on waiting lists for pharmaceutical company philanthropic program slots. These decisions were made in dialogue with the guidelines. The guidelines thus created pressures that caregivers did their best to respond to.

At Cha-on Suesum, which came into existence as a research facility, the effect of universalistic rules and expanding understandings of moral obligations took a distinctive form. Noting that their research subjects would no longer have access to treatment once a study ended, caregivers sought ways to continue to treat people who had now become their patients as well as their research subjects. Finding care for "professional research subjects" was a common dilemma, but Cha-on Suesum was unusual in the systematic approach and moral conviction with which it pursued a solution. The research subjects needed ongoing treatment, and the staff members who had enrolled them in research projects and started them on treatment felt a moral obligation to ensure continuity in care. Whereas Robert Rafsky staff searched for studies for which their patients would be eligible as they cycled off completed studies, Cha-on Suesum instead sought a group-level solution. Cha-on Suesum initially "taxed" externally funded research projects so they could transition from stopgap measures to a more reliable, equitable means of providing care. Eventually, they created a post-trial research program that institutionalized a group-level entitlement to treatment and ongoing access to drugs. The use of the Thai generic GPO-VIR as the backbone of the treatment program made the whole scheme affordable. In the Thai "observational studies," data were gathered regularly from patients so that physician researchers could accumulate knowledge about what happened as patients continued taking anti-retroviral drugs. Because this was the first generation of patients to take these drugs, the information from these observational studies would be invaluable. But it was nevertheless important to understand that the studies arose as much from humanitarian as scientific impulses.

Like Thailand's Cha-on Suesum Clinic, Uganda's Philly Lutaaya Clinic originated as a strictly research facility but grew into a research-and-treatment facility as researchers became committed to providing ongoing care for their research subjects. Although Cha-on Suesum Clinic provided ongoing care by creating a long-term observational study, Philly Lutaaya Clinic created and sought donor funds for treatment programs. Many of these funds came from US sources, including PEPFAR, and were sometimes administered by philanthropies such as the Elizabeth Glaser Pediatric AIDS Foundation (EGPAF). Philly Lutaaya's growing commitment to providing treatment was about more than funding for drugs. In addition, staff members committed to unreasonably long work hours to care for the patients receiving the donor- or government-provided drugs. As discussed earlier, caregivers struggled with their desire to make their family treatment programs inclusive, even though they worried that including "every last cousin" would break the clinic. Yet if patients stretched and accepted uncomfortable obligations—such as disclosing their HIV status or spending time and money traveling to the clinic—caregivers felt that these "good HIV patients" deserved a corresponding level of uncomfortable stretching and commitment from caregivers.

Staff members at Gugu Dlamini likewise described themselves as having a "moral responsibility to do HIV care" as the people arriving at their clinic embraced the patient role. Once patients and their "treatment buddies" had completed their pretreatment training, staff members were exceedingly reluctant to terminate treatment even when patients missed appointments, were unable to pay required fees, or moved (perhaps temporarily) out of the clinic's catchment area. In effect, a relationship had been formed, and treatment contracts that had once bound only patients had become bilateral contracts that (informally) bound both caregivers and patients.

In all five clinics, then, treatment decisions were made in dialogue with guidelines. The nature of that dialogue varied, though, with guidelines serving mostly as a reference point in one clinic (Robert Rafsky) and as a standard to which clinicians were expected to adhere as closely as possible in all of the others. In some clinics where guidelines were treated as a standard, clinicians had to account to fellow practitioners for deviations; in others, they had to explain themselves to outsiders. In no clinic were clinicians expected to adhere rigidly to guidelines. Beyond shaping treatment decisions, guidelines also helped clinicians claim resources for their patients. Both Bobbi Campbell Clinic and Gugu Dlamini Clinic, for instance, were required to follow guidelines to access government funding—Ryan White funds in the US and ARV rollout funds in South Africa.

The role of guidelines was much deeper, though, because the universalism of guidelines fostered a universalistic clinic culture and a view that rights to health were part of the fundamental package of human rights, even when staff members did not explicitly use the language of rights (Heimer and Tolman 2021).[10] This development seems not to have been anticipated by those advocating for evidence-based medicine (EBM) or pushing to reduce practice variations. Those reformers were more concerned with putting medicine on a firmer footing than protecting the rights of patients. That shift in focus came largely from outside, as rights to health were incorporated into constitutions and as patients and activists used the increased legalism of healthcare as a wedge to push for treatment equity. Although patients' rights were part of the cultural lexicon considerably before the advent of HIV, such rights were generally understood more narrowly as a right to be informed and consulted rather than as a human right to medical care that could support claims on the resources of healthcare organizations or governments. Within a cultural context reshaped by HIV, though, healthcare staff, like the Gugu Dlamini workers cited above, came to see providing care as a "moral responsibility." The changed cultural context shaped how clinic workers thought about and worked with guidelines.

Taken together, though, HIV clinical guidelines provide traces of new pressures on medical caregivers: some explicit, others more subtle. First, guidelines are both evidence of new constraints on the activities of caregivers and the vehicle for those constraints. As a general matter, the guidelines issued by bodies such as WHO and DHHS (Department of Health and Human Services) are "guidance." But as guidelines are adopted by other bodies, they become more explicit and more constraining. When those issuing guidelines must also ensure that resources are available to do what the guidelines recommend, they are more likely to insist that caregivers actually adhere to guidelines. Thus, Gugu Dlamini Clinic and other health facilities participating in government treatment programs are required to prescribe government-approved regimens and to account for (though perhaps not quite "ask permission" for) any deviations. Likewise, when clinics adopt guidelines, their claims on streams of resources—from governments, insurers, or hospital funds—often depend on following their own guidelines.

Guidelines also signal increasing inclusiveness. The DHHS guidelines, focused on the needs of the US population, often did not say much about how they should be used in resource-constrained settings where, for instance, lab tests could not be performed. Decisions about when to start treatment are based on the staging of the disease. The CDC staging system relied heavily on assessments (CD4 counts, measures of viral load, confirmations of diagnoses of OIs) that were simply impossible in poorer countries. The WHO guidelines, developed somewhat later, substituted a staging system that employed clinical assessments in place of laboratory assessments and so could be used in poorer countries. Moreover, over time the symptom patterns included in the staging tables began to include not only symptoms most common in adult men, but also the symptoms more common for women and children. This was important both for getting other groups into treatment and in garnering resources for them. In the US, for instance, the early definition of full-blown AIDS, a classification that could help secure access to financial resources, was biased in favor of men (Patton 1994). Women were thus less likely to receive either the treatment they needed or financial support such as disability payments.

Finally, embedded in the guidelines is a third, more subtle story, about how the clarity of treatment guidelines creates novel obligations both for patients and for caregivers. From the beginning, HIV has been "institutionally rich," with voluntary counseling and testing (VCT) routines, pretreatment training programs, and treatment contracts. Although these "contracts" are intended to bind patients, they also create moral obligations for clinics and their staff members. Poor patients cannot be asked to promise to adhere to drug regimens faithfully for life unless they have access to the drugs. Recognizing that patients cannot live up to their promises without the intervention of clinics and caregivers, caregivers then take on the obligation of finding resources for their patients. It is they who write grant proposals for treatment programs, create studies that will provide medicines for research subjects, and refer patients to treatment programs in other places when they are unable provide adequate care in their own clinic. In the early days, Thai researchers sometimes dug into their own pockets to pay for patients' drugs; Ugandan and South African clinic staff sometimes passed the hat to pay for exceptional expenses for patients or patients' children. And, particularly in Uganda, they worked brutally long hours to ensure that their patients received care.

Treatment guidelines are not the only rules with which clinic staff work, though. When clinics are also research facilities, as these five clinics were, staff members' work is also shaped by rules governing the conduct of research as well as by the general administrative rules (clinic SOPs, accounting regulations, and so forth) of healthcare organizations.

Rules about the Conduct of Research
and Debates about Ethics

Rules about research, including both project-specific and general rules, are especially important in molding thinking about ethical treatment of patients and research subjects, sometimes working in tandem with clinical guidelines to transform scientific conclusions into moral mandates. Earlier discussions pegged the origin of research rules to the legal turn in health-care and the research scandals that preceded the introduction of more formal regulation, examined the relationship between research rules and the priority placed on creating trustworthy data in multisited clinical trials, and explored some of the side effects of more rigid systems of rules. Here I ask about the conditions that may increase the likelihood that research regulation will live up to its ethical commitments and foster research that provides both short- and long-term benefits to participants and the larger community. That requires thinking about how the rules about the ethical conduct of research and other research rules sometimes work together, but sometimes undermine each other.

Rules about the ethical conduct of research speak clearly and forcefully to moral issues. Yet project-specific research protocols and the accompanying more general SOPs also speak, though less directly, to questions of ethics and moral worth. Differences in how the endemic diseases of richer and poorer countries are treated in research protocols, for instance, illustrate how questions of worth creep into apparently neutral documents. Because protocols treat richer countries as the norm, researchers in poorer countries spend considerable time documenting "adverse events" (AEs) that are in fact "normal" endemic diseases in their locales. This documentation "tax" suggests a differential—albeit inadvertent—valuation of the time and trouble of research staff in rich versus poor countries.

Matters of worth have long received attention in the rules about research ethics. Debates about the ethics of clinical research have been vigorous and well analyzed by others (see, e.g., Emanuel, Wendler, and Grady 2000; Rothman 2000; Benatar 2002; Halpern 2004). Clinical researchers, including both academic and pharmaceutical company researchers (a line that is less clear than one might expect), have found developing countries to be attractive sites for their studies (Petryna 2009). The advantages are obvious—research can be conducted in poor countries more cheaply than in richer ones. Treatment-naïve subjects, whose responses to drugs will not be distorted by previous therapies, are also more plentiful. And if a local standard of care (rather than a universal one) is used to determine what the control group will receive, then countries that provide little care for their citizens become especially attractive locations for studies. As the professional staffs and lab facilities of poor countries improve and as it becomes progressively easier to transport samples and to move data electronically, the challenges of doing research in underresourced countries have diminished markedly, making such countries even more attractive as research sites than they have been in the past.

Debates over research ethics have also grown more intense, though, and studies sited in poorer countries have received special scrutiny, although this scrutiny sometimes misses the point or adds unhelpful complexity to research. Some of the most vexing questions concern appropriate and inappropriate "incentives" for study participation and what constitutes "coercion," whose "standard of care" should be used to determine what treatments a control group receives, and what obligations researchers have to research subjects after a study ends. As the wrangling over revisions of the Declaration of Helsinki made clear (Rothman 2000; Carlson, Boyd, and Webb 2004), these are hard questions. Designed to curb exploitation of people in poor countries, these rules have nevertheless proven controversial, often seeming to sacrifice the better to the best. Any temporary consensus can easily unravel as principles confront the practical realities of each new research project.

These challenges were poignantly illustrated in discussions about the ethics of research on short-course ARV regimens to prevent the transmission of HIV during pregnancy. Giving control groups in rich and poor countries alike the "best proven" regimen seemed, at first glance, to be the ethically appropriate design. How could anyone justify giving expectant mothers in poor countries' control groups the (inferior) local standard treatment[11] when their counterparts in rich countries were receiving the best proven regimen? But here two ethical principles conflicted. On the one hand, parity among control groups seemed appropriate. Yet the results from that research design would be useful only in the locations where that particular control group/experimental group contrast was meaningful. A finding that the short-course regimen was inferior to standard ART offered guidance only where putting all HIV-infected pregnant women on ART was a viable option—a useful finding for rich countries but not for poorer ones. It did not answer the most pressing questions for poorer countries where starting all HIV-infected pregnant women on ART was simply not feasible. In those countries, it would be far more useful to know how the short-course regimen (perhaps just in reach given local resource constraints) compared with the current local standard. Moreover, no health ministry would be happy to be accused of giving its citizen second-rate treatments, even if that was all it could afford and even if the alternative was no treatment at all. Whether this was complacency or realism is an important question, raised especially by social movement actors, a point taken up below.

The question of what researchers and research sponsors owe research subjects once a study has ended has been raised repeatedly in debates about ethical principles (see Carlson, Boyd, and Webb 2004). Studies of ARVs raise these questions in particularly agonizing ways. On the one hand, ART is the only effective treatment for HIV/AIDS, so especially for people in poor countries, access to ART is valuable even if it is fleeting. For some people, ART for the duration of a study may mean having just enough time to make arrangements for their children's futures. In one Ugandan interview, I heard about children who had been orphaned repeatedly as first their parents and then their foster parents died. In those days, Ugandans were eager to participate in studies that offered ART for any period of time. But US IRBs sometimes declined to approve these studies, one researcher informed me, because drug companies were unwilling to provide study drugs to research subjects after research projects ended. Early compromises required that ART be continued for some modest time after the end of a study—three years, say—but not "forever." Medical guidelines for ART are quite clear, though: when people start therapy, it should be with the assumption that they will take the drugs for the rest of their lives. Cycling on and off therapy is bad for individual patients and bad for public health because it increases the likelihood that resistant strains will develop.[12]

In insisting that Ugandan research subjects be given at least some continuing ART after a study ended, US IRBs annoyed many parties, including local research participants. In clinics where other payers might step in to cover ongoing costs of ART for patients who had begun treatment as research subjects, IRBs had less need to worry about researcher, sponsor, or drug company guarantees. At Robert Rafsky Clinic, for instance, physician researchers and other staff were adept at securing ARVs for patients who had no other way to cover the cost of drugs. In Uganda and other poor countries, the IRB requirement that research subjects receive drugs when studies ended increased the cost of doing research, though research costs probably remained well below what they would have been in richer countries. In effect, the IRBs answered the "complacency or realism?" question mentioned above by concluding that stingy post-trial provision of drugs was unacceptable complacency. The clarity of treatment guidelines and the vigorous international discussion of what research owes participants made anything but universal access to treatment increasingly unpalatable.

Hardening the Soft Law of Research and Treatment

The hardening of the soft law of treatment and research has often brought with it an unpleasantly rigid compliance regime. At the same time, though, the complex regulations surrounding treatment and research have also often pushed the envelope on universal rights of human research subjects and human rights to healthcare.

It is hard to assess the net effect of these rules about the conduct of research, especially as embodied in the IRB system. In the social sciences, where AEs are relatively rare, IRB oversight has surely done more to suppress research than to protect human subjects (Bledsoe et al. 2007). In clinical research, the delays and irritations have likewise been very costly (Schneider 2015; Whitney 2023). Yet in some instances, IRBs have pushed researchers and pharmaceutical companies to think harder about what they owe research subjects. And by refusing to approve studies until more adequate resources were provided—extending patients' post-study access to ARVs, for instance—IRBs stiffened researchers' resolve to do the right thing and both clarified and enlarged pharmaceutical company obligations. IRBs have not always been on the side of the angels, but nevertheless a dialogue organized around universalistically stated declarations of human rights has tended to ratchet up rights. Rights are extended to more groups in more places; loopholes are closed when inconsistencies or abuses are pointed out; enforcement mechanisms are put in place; resources are made available because basic research is not permitted to go forward until provisions are made to give research subjects decent care.

Thus far I have identified two ways that rules increased the pressure to treat people living with HIV in poorer countries the same way that people in richer countries were treated. Written to apply universally, clinical guidelines may offer different methods for staging in poor countries where lab tests are less available. But they do not suggest that people in poorer countries receive different treatment than people in richer ones when ART is indicated. At the time of my research, no one recommended mono-therapy for Ugandans when multidrug therapy would be given in the US.[13] By leaving no room for quibbling, these guidelines pressured clinicians—and donors, as I argue below—to offer the same treatment everywhere. The bright line of clinical guidelines made it wrong to do otherwise. Likewise, when IRBs refused to approve projects that did not offer some continuing therapy after a study's end, researchers and research sponsors had no choice but to fund ongoing treatment if they hoped to conduct the research.

To be sure, these lines in the sand were not drawn overnight. Clinical practice guidelines have been a work in progress for many years. Often the EBM movement seems more intent on ensuring that treatment be solidly built on a foundation of scientific research than that people everywhere have a right to the same treatment. But where there are few alternatives and where scientific research reaches a clear answer and that answer is then incorporated into guidelines, the pressure for universalism increases. And physicians who have been taught that they are obliged to follow guidelines just may come to believe that guidelines apply universally.

Likewise, the dialogue between IRBs and researchers has unfolded over many years. Often researchers find ways to compromise with IRBs, meeting the letter if not the spirit of the law.[14] In the case of ART, though, researchers and IRBs both agreed that the IRB position was right in principle. The only question was whether it was achievable. Once the IRB drew the line in the sand, though, researchers had little choice but to find some way to rise to the occasion.

Social Movements and the Moral Imperative of Universal Treatment

Activists also have played key roles in creating moral obligations out of the cultural materials of science and medicine. The early history of AIDS activism in the US is well known, with GMHC (founded in 1981) and ACT UP (founded in 1987) playing especially prominent roles (Shilts 1987; Epstein 1996; Schulman 2021). For my argument here, it was important that AIDS activists insisted they have a voice in professional arenas where decisions were made about research direction and funding, policies on approval and availability of drugs, and financial support for treatment for people who were ineligible for Medicaid and uninsured (e.g., because they had lost their jobs and their COBRA[15] eligibility had expired).

The encounter between activists, scientists, and government bureaucrats changed the perspectives of all three. Activists gained an appreciation of the importance of research in demonstrating the efficacy of drugs and uncovering side effects. Many experimental treatments in fact proved ineffective or even dangerous. More important, though, activists kept scientists and bureaucrats focused on the human implications of their work. Pressure from activists led to adjustments of FDA rules, including the introduction of an "accelerated approval" (interim licensing) program by the FDA in 1992, modifications of regular procedures so that drugs were less likely to languish because of bureaucratic red tape,[16] and increased willingness to permit "compassionate use"[17] of unapproved drugs. With the representation of HIV-infected people and the involvement of activists in arenas from which they had previously been excluded, moral implications of decisions were more likely to be addressed. Movement activists increased the saliency of the moral implications of guidelines.

One might wonder whether this was just a peculiarity of the US scene, where HIV was primarily a disease of gay men. For instance, activists might play a smaller role in countries with generalized epidemics or where HIV was somewhat more likely to be a disease of the poor. In each of the countries where I carried out my research, though, AIDS activists played a significant role in setting AIDS policy. Uganda's TASO, founded in 1987, was the first "community-based" AIDS support organization in sub-Saharan Africa. In Thailand, AIDS Access Foundation, whose Bangkok office opened in 1991, joined MSF and other organizations to protest the policies of pharmaceutical companies (Ford et al. 2004; 't Hoen et al. 2011).[18] In South Africa, it would be hard to overstate the role of TAC and ALP (the AIDS Law Project) in legal disputes over access to drugs[19] and government treatment policies. Attempting to force the government to meet its constitutional obligations, TAC went to court on a series of HIV-related programs, including preventing mother-to-child transmission of HIV, the national anti-retroviral rollout, treatment for prisoners in KwaZulu-Natal, challenges to pharmaceutical company policies, and supporting the Medicines Act against individuals who denounced ART and pushed ineffective alternative treatments (Heywood 2009). TAC's remarkable success in shaping South African AIDS policy seems to have arisen from how it combined negotiation, litigation, and mobilization (Heywood 2009, 22). These examples clearly show that AIDS activism is neither a strictly US phenomenon nor a US export. What may be less clear is whether AIDS activists in other countries have been as successful as their US counterparts in securing spots at decision-making tables.

The biannual IAC,[20] a big-tent meeting in many senses, increased and supported the spread of AIDS activism. Its official program includes presentations of papers in a wide variety of disciplines, workshops, press releases about important findings, and even a "Global Village" (more like a bazaar than a professional meeting) in tandem with many satellite meetings (often sponsored by pharmaceutical companies). While it is possible for people to keep to their own groups, the conference also makes it easy for activists to talk to scientists and policymakers as well as to each other. Dominant scientific culture jostles up against countercultural elements more frequently and perhaps more comfortably at these meetings than at the functions of most other professional societies.

Comfort and civility do not always prevail, though. Vigorous demonstrations are common and have sometimes closed down drug company exhibits. Government officials are called to task and even urged to resign (as South Africa's minister of health was at the 2006 Toronto conference). But these frank challenges to the status quo are mixed with celebration of successes and community as celebrities and leaders urge attendees to contribute to the GFATM (Nelson Mandela at the 2004 Bangkok conference) or exhort men to consider circumcision (Bill Clinton at the 2006 Toronto conference) or remind women that "condoms are a girl's best friend" (Thai Senator Mechai Viravaidya at the 2004 Bangkok conference). It would be completely counter to the spirit of these meetings to suggest that people in poor countries should receive treatment that was inferior to that given in rich countries. Rather, the revival-meeting spirit of these conferences would instead inspire participants to try to increase the pot of resources so that everyone could be treated.

If the AIDS conferences are the forum that creates a collective, can-do spirit, it is probably the WTO that exemplifies what activists are fighting against. It is hard for activists to be completely opposed to pharmaceutical companies, who do, after all, produce the drugs even if they charge exorbitant prices. Some companies are easier to hate than others, though, and Abbott drew a large share of the fire both when it raised the price of Norvir in 2003[21] and when it withheld drugs from Thailand in 2007 in retaliation after the Thai government issued a compulsory license permitting local manufacture of a generic version of Kaletra (a "boosted" ARV).[22] Many in the HIV world see the WTO as a rich country forum that especially favors US interests and has few redeeming qualities (see, e.g., Mugyenyi 2008). Focused on protecting the rights of patent holders, WTO rules have restricted middle-income and poor countries' rights to produce generic versions of patented drugs for domestic use and for export to poor neighbors. Although the Doha Declaration eased these restrictions, the US threatened retaliation against countries that exercised their new rights.

For our analytical purposes, the WTO is a useful example to think with for a couple of reasons. First, political responses to the WTO counter any inclination to Pollyannaism about whether solidarity is always "solidarity with." Responses to the WTO show that "solidarity against" also can advance moral claims. But more important, an examination of the WTO case shows that the (relative) success of the push for universalism in HIV treatment has not come because of cooperation from drug companies or the

WTO. Rather, this (perhaps temporary) success occurred because many other actors, including especially the health professionals studied by Harris (2017a, 2017b), came to believe that scientific findings implied strong moral claims. Although the goal of universal access to treatment has not yet been reached, the substantial achievements of UNAIDS's 3 by 5, 90-90-90, and 95-95-95 programs; PEPFAR; and other treatment programs should not be understated.

Clinical Guidelines and Research Rules as Legitimation for Social Movement Objectives

Clinical guidelines and research protocols are the apparently neutral language medical people use to discuss what they should be doing. Yet moral questions are smuggled into the discussion along with the scientific issues. In the case of HIV treatment, making scientific conclusions clearer made it harder to avoid the moral implications of new biomedical knowledge, particularly in a community that had constituted itself so that those most interested in the results now actually had a voice. To use the language of the sociology of law, clinical guidelines and rules about the conduct of research were a legal endowment (Lempert and Sanders 1986) that could be deployed on behalf of patients and research subjects. Such a deployment is far more likely to happen when someone is on hand to represent the interests of those who are living with HIV.

Key elements of the causal story now need to be brought into the foreground. First, it surely mattered that many of the elements were in place before the definitive scientific breakthrough demonstrating that HIV could be kept in check with an ARV cocktail composed of drugs from different classes with different mechanisms for inhibiting viral replication. Research programs existed, as did an international umbrella organization with a history (admittedly short, but long enough) of bringing groups of stakeholders together. When a definitive result became available, then, an audience was there to receive it. By the time research results on triple-therapy were announced, the HIV research and treatment community had already begun to create and use treatment guidelines. In the research world, concerns about protecting poor-country research subjects had already been raised, with a series of reports (Nuremberg, Belmont, Helsinki) gradually solidifying opinion about what the core issues were. Strong social movement actors had coalesced in many countries and were in regular contact with each other at the IAC. And finally, the existence of a clear but legalistic Darth Vader in the WTO gave activists a common enemy and suggested that the fight should be at least partly a legal one focused on circumventing the patent regime.

Researchers announced the clinical trial results on triple-therapy with great fanfare and presented them as having broad applicability. The results were quickly translated into guidelines. But these new universal guidelines confronted physicians with new challenges. In the past, physicians had been resigned to having little if anything to offer their patients beyond treatment for OIs. But in this radically transformed treatment environment, physicians now actually knew what worked. Although the drugs were prohibitively expensive, the lucid treatment guidelines were *universal* guidelines, suggesting what treatment should be given to all HIV patients, poor and rich alike, as their illness reached the stage where treatment became clinically necessary. The irrefutable evidence of the efficacy of the new regimens, restated in universal guidelines, created moral obligations for physicians and researchers to provide ART on a continuing basis for their patients and research subjects.

But once they accepted this moral obligation—for their clinics as well as themselves—they were strongly motivated to find payers to share the financial burden. Social movement actors, including individual activists, community support organizations, and NGOs, did their best to help, dispensing shame and honor, threats and rewards as they talked the language of human rights. Suggesting that the implication of the guidelines was completely obvious—guidelines were a mandate, after all—one MSF worker in Thailand gave patients copies of guidelines for prophylaxis to carry with them as a way to force hospitals to provide treatment in the period before they needed ART. One of the most prominent proponents of universal access to treatment, Peter Mugyenyi, founding director of the Joint Clinical Research Center in Uganda, insisted that his patients should have treatment. Defying import laws, he found inexpensive sources of drugs, created satellite clinics in rural areas, and put thousands of patients on ART (Waldholz 2002; Mugyenyi 2008). Not mincing words, Mugyenyi wrote of "genocide by denial" (the title of his 2008 book) and argued that pharmaceutical company pricing that put recommended treatments out of reach for the world's poor amounted to gross human rights violations against the poor simply because they were poor. Over time, then, scientific findings, research rules, clinical guidelines, state and national regulations, national constitutions, and international treaties were woven into a seamless web transforming scientific findings into moral mandates.

Rules generally bind those lower in the social world more than those nearer the top (Black 1976). They tend to be created by the powerful to govern the weak. Even when the laws also apply to them, more powerful people often have resources needed to fight back and evade the full force of the law. Illustrating the imposition of law on weaker groups, Peter Evans (2004) notes that the "institutional monocropping" common in development programs often entails more powerful groups creating and imposing uniform institutional blueprints on those with less power. And although the "deliberative democracy" Amartya Sen (1999) advocates is explicitly intended to empower influential activists at the bottom, one can easily imagine implementations of such programs that would be just as top-down as other grafted institutions.

And so it was in the early days of HIV. Activists insisted on being included, but often ended up in circumscribed roles because they lacked the insider knowledge needed to insert themselves effectively. But universalistic guidelines and protocols were tools they could use to get institutions to listen. Even early US activists might not have known what to do as members of a "community advisory board," and, transplanted to other countries, these democratic institutions did not work very well, particularly at the outset. The participatory element either became a forum for proposing minor modifications to existing programs and protocols or a place to admonish patients and research subjects to "get with the program," adhere to their regimens, bring family members in for testing, and so forth.

Over time, though, even grafted institutions can become "inhabited institutions" (to borrow terminology from Hallett and Ventresca [2006]) as meanings are reconstructed through interaction. In the HIV world, people were kept in dialogue for years on end. Initially it was patients and their caregivers who encountered each other repeatedly. (As Richard, the Robert Rafsky physician, explained, physicians' long-term ties with their patients meant that HIV care was not as impersonal as I seemed to think.) But because of the interdependence of researchers, administrators, IRB review panels, "professional research subjects," sponsors, research monitors, pharmaceutical companies, NGOs, WHO and other supra-national bodies, and government entities such as ministries of health, gradually groups reshaped the institutions so they fit and were meaningful. Community advisory boards, for instance, moved from being one-shot bodies assembled to review particular studies to being continuously existing review entities that really could help shape research agendas.

In many situations, it is the powerful who are the "repeat players." In the world of HIV research and treatment, though, repeat players are much more diverse. That means activists have a chance to develop some sympathy for the conventions of science (Epstein 1996). It also means that when the weak "speak truth to power," to employ the Quaker maxim, they may eventually be heard because those in power depend on them. It simply is not possible to do clinical research without research subjects, and no treatment program can claim to be successful without adherent patients. That dependence of clinical research on research subjects gives research participants some leverage, though they have rarely recognized, coalesced around, or used that leverage.[23] Repeated encounters also mean that the weaker participants have many opportunities to reiterate their message during the life of a research project or over the years they receive treatment.

Much has been learned since 1981 when HIV was officially recognized as a disease, and not all of it has been about the biological aspects of diseases and drugs. In addition, the field has experienced a shift in legal consciousness as a loose legalistic system with strongly articulated principles encouraged people to think proactively about what is the right thing to do. When people are placed in structures that allow them to exhort others to provide the drugs, salaries, laboratories, and appropriate scientific and legal support, then universalistically stated guidelines and rules about the conduct of research can actually make a difference. But what can be achieved depends as well on incorporating clinicians and researchers from poorer countries into the global medical and scientific community, as I illustrate below.

Caring for Patients and Conducting Research in the "Boonies"

Social recognition and assessments of moral worth also affect the experience of healthcare workers and clinical researchers. In principle, the "recipes" of clinical guidelines and research protocols can be followed by anyone with the requisite training, yet clinic workers in poorer countries sometimes felt demeaned by colleagues from richer countries. These experiences of inequality were felt especially keenly by researchers from poorer countries. Philly Lutaaya's and Cha-on Suesum's research teams included well-trained, skilled, experienced clinical researchers deeply engaged in global HIV research. (Gugu Dlamini's staff was just beginning to do research.) They participated in multisited projects, presented their work at conferences, published in top journals, and sat on guideline-writing committees. Yet they also spoke about feeling disadvantaged. All too often, they said, their skills were not fully appreciated. They described being incorporated as "hands" (technicians) carrying out research tasks but excluded from positions as "heads" (scientists) conceiving new lines of investigation and serving on the protocol teams that designed projects, a pattern observed by other scholars as well (Gazley 2011, 47; see also Doing 2004, 2009).

Moments of inclusion—such as the showcasing of work by Cha-on Sue-sum researchers during the Bangkok AIDS conference—were more than balanced by the experiences of exclusion. Philly Lutaaya researchers complained about being unable to publish key findings because clinics like theirs lacked the equipment to produce "gold standard" indicators. Because they were among the small group of researchers studying pediatric AIDS, this meant that some findings about children's experiences with HIV remained unavailable to other researchers and clinicians. These researchers' reputations suffered as a result, but the journals' reluctance to publish their work also signaled an indifference to issues that seemed pressing to them and their compatriots. Thai researchers similarly felt that Western researchers were unwilling to add their topics (lower dosages for patients with smaller bodies, side effect profiles common in Thailand) to the global research agenda (Gazley 2011).

The experience of marginalization was particularly disappointing because it occurred in the context of a research and treatment culture that promised inclusion. But as Thai and Ugandan (and to a lesser extent South African) researchers took up invitations to join research teams, they were chagrined and embarrassed when their attempts to participate were rebuffed. These humiliating snubs arose in a variety of ways: lack of enthusiasm for their research topics, insufficient help in securing resources to produce the kind of data required by top journals, too ready acceptance of rules and practices that created disadvantages for people like them. The rules did not generally aim to disadvantage foreign researchers. Rather, the disadvantage was an inadvertent side effect of superficially neutral rules created to solve other problems. The interests of foreign researchers were simply overlooked, left off the agenda as rules were being crafted, and not seen as important enough to merit amendments after the fact. One seemingly neutral rule after another posed no special difficulty for US researchers but created roadblocks for researchers in other countries. Although each impediment could be explained away, the cumulative effect was to make foreign researchers look inefficient or incompetent.

Restrictions on which drugs could be used in research illustrate some of these points. Much of the funding for research (as well as for treatment), both in the US and other countries, came from the US government. But that generous research funding came with restrictions on which drugs could be used as comparison points in research. When Thai researchers proposed to use GPO-VIR (the locally produced fixed-dose combination) in research, they discovered that US funding rules prohibited this. Another challenge occurred when funds that enabled Thai researchers to travel to conferences suddenly dried up. Because pharmaceutical companies had generously sponsored conference travel, travel expenses were not written into research grants. But when the Thai government issued compulsory licenses, undermining patent rights, pharmaceutical companies abruptly retaliated by withdrawing researchers' travel funds, even though the compulsory licenses were legally permissible after the Doha Declaration adjustments to TRIPS (WTO Agreement on Trade Related Aspects of Intellectual Property Rights) and were the result of government, not researcher, action.

These experiences of marginalization were reinforced during regulatory encounters. No one enjoys regulatory encounters; in that regard at least, everyone is equal. In all five clinics, primary care physicians and nurses, project principal investigators and research nurses, clinic managers, project coordinators, administrators, and quality assurance specialists all complained about the cumbersome process of preparing reports and dreaded the arrival of site visitors, research monitors, and other regulators. Although they uniformly endorsed the objectives of oversight, staff members generally felt that compliance work took them away from other important duties. My data from the five clinics suggest that, although the rules are uniform, regulatory encounters do not unfold in the same way in all locations. The pattern I observed resembles observations from other situations where some categories of people are esteemed and others disvalued. Obviously not as extreme as the social death of slavery where enslaved people are not considered fully human (Patterson 1982), the experience was more like the discounting and skepticism that women and minorities encounter in many social situations. And as in those other cases, the effects of this discounting and skepticism often are compounded over time.

Despite the ubiquity of complaints about regulatory encounters, the accounts of clinic staff in Thailand, South Africa, and Uganda were distinctive in several ways. First, clinics in these countries simply got more intensive monitoring than US clinics did.[24] Monitors came more often, spent more time at each visit, and looked more closely at records. For instance, Cha-on Suesum staff reported that one monitor "spent weeks and weeks here, taking up loads of time." In contrast, a monitoring visit would typically take only a day or two in the US clinics. Moreover, the Cha-on Suesum informant noted, the clinic had been audited twice in a five-year period when monitors were supposed to come only once. The researcher (an Australian ex-pat) was clearly frustrated, reporting that he had to spend a lot of time sorting things out. He felt that Cha-on Suesum got extra scrutiny from US regulators because of "being in the boonies." At Gugu Dlamini, staff members complained that clinic work was disrupted nearly every day by the arrival of site visitors. Philly Lutaaya Clinic received especially intensive scrutiny. One multilayered investigation dragged on for well over a year before investigators issued a final report conceding that the criticisms were almost entirely without merit.[25] During that period, clinic staff were obliged to provide endless documentation to rebut the charges. In some instances, they also had to delicately point out errors in investigators' reading of the records or understanding of the local situation.

Given the outcomes, one could take a benign view of these costly and unpleasant regulatory encounters. Cha-on Suesum's staff members did manage to get things sorted out with the monitor, and its researchers were given those plum speaking slots when the IAC met in Bangkok. Gugu Dlamini's staff got along amicably enough with its site visitors, and its practices were praised as examples for others to emulate during an NGO's user group meeting. Philly Lutaaya's researchers were vindicated in the long run, and the clinic's regulatory affairs specialist received an international award, suggesting that some outsiders recognized her exemplary work.

But these successes came at a steep cost—a cost that the US clinics did not incur. For the most part, the rules for the conduct of research and the provision of HIV treatment are intended to be fair.[26] Yet the rules, designed initially by people accustomed to working in the hospitals and clinics of rich countries, were often ill suited for use in other settings. The challenges could seem trivial, but they quickly mounted up, as the next examples show. Clinical research requires that serious adverse events (SAEs) be carefully tracked and promptly reported. But because background health conditions vary from one country or population group to another, uniform reporting requirements can have varying effects on clinic workloads, as noted earlier. Ugandan staff spent endless hours reporting on endemic conditions often clearly unrelated to study drugs. Had the rules been designed with the Ugandan context in mind, much of this reporting would not have been mandated. In addition, rules about timelines for reporting SAEs did not take into account time zone differences, difficulties with internet access, unreliable electricity, and scarce computers and photocopy machines, all of which made adherence challenging. Moreover, Ugandan researchers often lacked basic materials needed to create and store the data and documents in the first place. Pointing out just how large the gap can be, one staff member admonished her colleagues to "think not just about whether people have followed the rules" but to consider "what it is about the rules that might make them hard to follow" and then to continue their thought process by looking at "things like working conditions."

Because they felt that others doubted their competence, people often overcompensated. Like the Cha-on Suesum staff member who sharply scolded subordinates over how they were packing samples, clinic workers often rigidly insisted that there was only one correct way to do things because they wanted to "look as good as possible" and worried that they might "look stupid" to outsiders.

This concern with looking good was especially intense after regulatory encounters (Heimer and Gazley 2012). Although the regulatory affairs specialists (exact titles vary) who track and file consent forms, IRB approvals, and other documents are generally meticulous in their work, they are especially careful in clinics that have received more than their share of scrutiny. In Uganda, for instance, I was required to show documents verifying that I had jumped through all of the relevant US and Ugandan regulatory hoops every time I reappeared in the clinic after some months away. In fact, because the clinics were my research subjects rather than the sponsors of my research, the clinic had no reason to request my documentation. (Obviously I dutifully supplied it anyway.) Likewise, non-US research monitors, eager to demonstrate their even-handedness, competence, and rigor, monitored more strictly and thoroughly than US research monitors, who were already meticulous. African research monitors, like the research staff, anticipated that people at the next level would expect them to perform less well than their US counterparts. In each of these cases, the putatively level playing field was anything but level.

Conclusion: Moral Worth and the Promise of Law

Introducing new rules and legalistic ways of doing things is not as efficacious as many had hoped, a finding that may disappoint legal and regulatory specialists. Clinical guidelines do not automatically raise the floor of treatment or eliminate practice variations. And they may decrease willingness to use discretion at the bedside if caregivers become excessively fearful of the heavy hand of courts and regulators. We want physicians to provide the best care they can. When early indications suggest patients' health is endangered by recommended treatments, caregivers may need to override governments' rules (as occurred with d4T in South Africa's first-line regimen). In the rare instances when supplementary resources make superior care possible, we want physicians to use those resources for the benefit of their patients (as Dr. Pfaff did in KwaZulu-Natal) even if that means (apparently) violating government guidelines.

Likewise, despite the good intentions of those who crafted legal frameworks to ensure that clinical research would be conducted ethically, those rules have often deflected attention from other pressing ethical issues or led to enforcement that was insensitive to context. Noting abuses—such as the Nazi, Japanese, and even US wartime experiments on human subjects—legislators, regulators, international organizations, and professional bodies have hastened to put in place rules that signaled their horror and their determination to prevent recurrences. Although the rules have surely reduced (but not eliminated) the specifically prohibited abuses, other forms of abuse have come to light in subsequent years. New policies attempt to curb such ethically questionable practices as moving research from richer countries to poorer ones to reduce costs or offering different care to members of control groups in poor and rich countries. In fact, it is not easy to anticipate when increased universalism will prove beneficial and when it will instead lead to fresh, perhaps even more tangled layers of rules and principles without providing tangible improvements. What is clear, though, is that equity is hard to secure as long as the gross inequalities among and within societies continue to exist. Concerns about what control groups receive in different locales matter primarily because of the huge discrepancies between the healthcare available to ordinary people in poor countries such as Uganda and what is available to people in richer countries.

This balancing of local needs and universal principles has not been easy, and research subjects and researchers in poorer countries have agonized over the very real-life (and death) consequences that unfolded as colleagues in richer countries argued over how the Helsinki Declaration or the Belmont principles applied to their case. In Uganda, for instance, researchers worried that more babies would be born HIV infected because the start of a clinical trial was delayed over an ethics dispute and, in another instance, that parents who already had AIDS would not get the year or two of ARVs they urgently needed because the US IRB and the pharmaceutical company were at loggerheads over how many years of treatment should be provided after the clinical trial had ended.

Important as it is to remember that legalism is not a panacea, particularly when rules are ill adapted to local conditions, it is also imperative to acknowledge the very real promise of law and legally inflected frameworks. My argument in this last chapter has been that the legal turn has brought more than just a set of rules. As important as the rules themselves have been, the articulation of principles also establishes the fundamental moral parity of participants and provides grounds for enlarging the rights of those who have not previously been treated fairly. But legal frameworks fulfill their moral promise only under special conditions. And it is those conditions that I have tried to spell out here. Without them, legal frameworks may not be entirely empty, but the protections they offer all too often introduce a different set of costs, namely those associated with compliance regimes. The work of this conclusion, then, has been to highlight the moral promise of rules themselves while showing what else has to be in place for the rules to have their full moral effect.

Rules that are purportedly about such mundane matters as when to prescribe ARVs and what drug regimens to use, or how to report SAEs in clinical research, have effects that extend well beyond the governance of these specific tasks. In particular, the universalistic language of these rules suggests that all people with a particular health condition should receive equal treatment or that anyone who is trained and follows the research rules properly can produce good research. In addition to regulating medical work, the rules also help construct participants (patients, research subjects, clinicians, researchers) as worthy participants, people whose needs for care merit the same attention and resources as anyone else's and whose contributions as caregivers, researchers, or stakeholders in the HIV world merit respect.

That bald statement is too simple, of course. In particular, this universalizing effect is magnified under particular, somewhat unusual, conditions. Ample funding helps. But so, too, does bringing a wide variety of actors into the forums where rules are discussed and reworked. Big-tent HIV conferences and AIDS activism both helped create those unique circumstance and were both important—at least for a while—in fostering a culture that supported universalizing interpretations of rules. Moreover, over time, key actors grew into their roles. Physicians began to see themselves as advocates; researchers came to understand that they could push back against pharmaceutical companies; researchers in poorer countries began to advocate for themselves as researchers as well as for their patients, research subjects, and clinics; research subjects around the world learned that they could help set the research agenda.

But even facially neutral rules that are intended to level the playing field are shot through with assumptions and details that sometimes inadvertently, sometimes purposefully, favor already advantaged groups. Even when a field's culture supports inclusion and access, the seemingly endless struggle to overcome the obstacles built into rules and the challenges of working with inadequate resources can easily make all participants (patients, research subjects, clinicians, researchers) look and feel inadequate and unworthy. The supports for inclusion and fairness cannot be taken for granted. Yet whether it is the hard law of statutes, the soft law of regulations and guidelines, the principles articulated in declarations, or the policies outlined by clinics, law can offer hope by reminding us to ask what we owe each other. That deep inclusion is the most important promise of law.

Acknowledgments

Although the focus of this book is the legal and regulatory systems that support HIV research and treatment, it is also inescapably about a global pandemic, a dread disease now somewhat tamed, whose ravages created a need not only for diagnostic tests and therapies but also for well-run clinics to conduct research and provide treatment. I have been saddened, moved, and inspired by the experiences of the people I spoke with, observed, and read about during the years I gathered data and wrote. Although HIV continues to be stigmatizing and isolating, it has also been a shared experience as people came together to give and receive care, to learn more about the disease and how to combat it, to protest the social and political arrangements that complicated the battle and to pledge to do better, to celebrate successes, and to remember and mourn those who died.

Given that my research was sited in clinics, I heard many stories about the plight of patients and research subjects and about staff members' anguish when they couldn't do much to relieve suffering, prolong life, or restore health. The accounts of the people I met beyond these clinic—activists, NGO staffers, government employees, people working in regulatory agencies, infectious disease researchers in universities—were not appreciably different. Wherever they worked, the people I encountered thought and cared deeply, and not just abstractly, worrying about collective problems while keeping their eyes on the needs of the individual men, women, and children who were living with HIV. I do not mean to suggest, though, that they were a uniformly grim lot. Indeed, I admired and appreciated the moments of levity and shared pleasures, sweetness that helped us see the stakes from a different perspective: rambunctious children on tricycles in Uganda, a tray of delicious fruit shared during a late-afternoon interview in Thailand, celebratory dinners honoring colleagues' work, singing together in South Africa. I am prohibited from thanking them by name, but my first and deepest debt is to these HIV workers from whom I learned so much.

Although scholarship is another one of those reputedly lonely enterprises, it, too, depends heavily on the support of institutions and individuals, and I have received an abundance of support. The American Bar Foundation and the Department of Sociology at Northwestern University, my institutional homes during the "book years," provided congenial work environments, considerable research support, and stimulating colleagues. The American Bar Foundation is one of the rare organizations whose board, directors, and staff believe in supporting research in all phases, from early project development, through data collection, analysis, writing, revision, and dissemination of findings. There is no adequate way to express my gratitude for the financial, intellectual, and personal support of the American Bar Foundation, Northwestern University, and my colleagues in those two institutions.

The research expenses for multisited studies are not trivial, and the fieldwork and interviews for this project simply would not have been possible without a generous research grant from the National Science Foundation (NSF SES-0319560). Supplementary funds from the Russell Sage Foundation helped support the portion of my research focused on trust.

Those monies helped pay the salaries of my invaluable research assistants, most of whom I found through my affiliation with Northwestern. In the main data collection phases, three Northwestern graduate students and I worked together doing interviews and fieldwork, gathering data for their dissertations as well as my book and articles. At the outset, Rebecca Culyba reminded me sharply that if I wanted her to work with me, I had to tell her what I was going to be doing. JuLeigh Petty and I often wrote tag-team fieldnotes, and I would never have mastered the names of HIV drugs without her charts. Lynn Gazley and I struggled over transliterations of Thai words and names, sharing our chagrin at being completely unable to read the consent form we were handing out. They, and Alan Czaplicki, made my research trips outside the US both more productive and more fun. In the long life of this project, I also had help from Jaimie Morse, Diana Rodriguez-Franco, Savina Balasubramanian, Alka Menon, and Lilly Dagdigian, who joined the team as we began the massive task of coding the data. Arielle Tolman and Elsinore Kuo worked with me primarily in the post-coding phases, including reading the book manuscript. In Uganda, Enid Wamani joined me for fieldwork and interviewing, filling me in on Ugandan culture and sharing her lovely family with me. In Thailand, Dusita Pheungsamran helped with interviewing, fieldwork, and both linguistic and cultural translation. At different times, two Northwestern undergraduates, Katherine Lin and Shreya Verma, joined the team briefly before heading off to graduate school and medical school, respectively. As much as I valued the sheer labor of my research assistants and graduate students, I even more deeply appreciated their intellectual contributions, including their willingness to mull over ideas and even occasionally to write articles with me.

Time is, of course, a primary resource required for research and writing, and fellowships at Princeton University's Program in Law and Public Affairs and at the Center for Advanced Study in Behavioral Sciences, where I held the Lenore Annenberg and Wallis Annenberg Fellowship in Communication, provided concentrated periods for analysis and writing and wonderful colleagues to think with. During my data collection foray in South Africa, I enjoyed the colleagueship of scholars at the Centre for HIV/AIDS Networking (HIVAN) and was hosted by the Department of Sociology, University of KwaZulu-Natal, where I had a visiting lectureship. In Uganda, I was hosted by Makerere Institute of Social Research, which facilitated access to Ugandan colleagues and provided both practical research support and housing. A quick trip to Malawi for what I can't resist calling Sociology Summer Camp with Ann Swidler, Susan Watkins, Adam Ashforth, and their students was a high point in the research process. I also spent several productive weeks as a visitor at the Centre de Sociologie des Organisations, Institut d'Études Politiques (Sciences Po) in Paris. As the book neared completion, a writing retreat on Vancouver Island with regulation scholars Cristie Ford (our host), Nancy Reichman, Tanina Rostain, Jodi Short, and Susan Silbey reminded me just how pleasant it can be to share ideas, food, and even the chores of daily living with like-minded colleagues.

Academic life is filled with conference presentations, seminars, classes, meetings, and hallway conversations where thoughts grow and change. Impossible as it is to trace which idea, phrase, or reference came from which conversation, I am deeply grateful to the colleagues, students, and friends who listened and responded, read a chapter or paper, invited me to join a panel or present a paper, asked a provocative question, cast doubt on my arguments, or gave quick feedback on a problematic paragraph: Gabriel Abend, Catherine Albiston, Elizabeth Armstrong, Sarah Babb, João Biehl, Caroline Bledsoe, John Braithwaite, Valerie Braithwaite, Scott Burris, Elizabeth Chiarello, Nitsan Chorev, Elisabeth Clemens, Jean Comaroff, John Comaroff, Clay Davis, Claire Decoteau, Paul DiMaggio, Robert Dingwall, Frank Dobbin, the late Lauren Edelman, Jill Fisher, Bryant Garth, John Hagan, Terence Halliday, Sydney Halpern, Joseph Harris, Richard Healey, Steve Hoffman, Wassana Im-Em, Robert Kagan, Katherine Kellogg, Anna Kirkland, Barbara Kiviat, Heinz Klug, John Knodel, Martin Krygier, Michèle Lamont, Armando Lara-Milan, Richard Lempert, Margaret Levi, Ron Levi, Sandra Levitsky, Donald Light, Jane Mansbridge, Michael McCann, Linsey McGoey, Ajay Mehrotra, Daniel Menchik, the late Sally Merry, Sanya

Mojola, Robert Nelson, Laura Beth Nielsen, Ann Orloff, Adriana Petryna, Jane Pryma, Victor Quintanilla, Michael Sauder, Carl Schneider, Susan Shapiro, Talia Shiff, Laura Stark, Kearsley Stewart, Mark Suchman, Helen Tilley, Stefan Timmermans, Yordanos Tiruneh, Benjamin van Rooij, Marc Ventresca, Stephen Warner, and Viviana Zelizer. To offer these thanks in list form suggests a uniformity and flatness that grossly misrepresents the nature of the encounters. It may also suggest that academic life is nonstop talking (almost true) and that the list is exhaustive (by no means true).

As the book neared completion, I received the best gift a scholar can hope for: comments on the full manuscript. I was lucky that my readers brought insights from different subfields and perhaps even more lucky that they approached the manuscript with such generosity of spirit. Mary Jo Neitz, a friend and colleague whose views and good sense I have trusted since graduate school days, read the manuscript in its entirety and has been my most reliable sounding board, offering insights into my project, my character (yes, Protestant ethic), and how the two intersected. Charles Camic, another friend and colleague from graduate school, brought expertise in the history of science and social theory to his reading of the manuscript. In my moments of discouragement as revisions dragged miserably on, I was consoled by my recollections of his final days revising his wonderful book on Veblen. Jennifer Earl, who first arrived in my life as a hard-working, insatiably curious undergraduate, brought expertise in sociolegal studies and provided detailed commentary on the entire manuscript, following up later to make sure I was tracking both her praise and her critique. Steve Epstein, my colleague at Northwestern, with his deep knowledge of fields central to the book and fine sense of language, carefully calibrated his critiques so that they would land. Ann Swidler's reading of the manuscript was informed by her considerable knowledge of Africa and international AIDS work and breadth as a sociologist, as well as her sharp eye for detail that might sidetrack readers. Each of these people was on my secret list of scholars whose assessments I most wanted. An additional perceptive review was supplied by an anonymous reader (perhaps also on my "secret list"?) selected by my publisher. Bill Mullen gave invaluable eleventh-hour advice about how to trim the manuscript, somehow managing to be both gentle enough to make the process almost bearable and ruthless enough to get the job done. Although the book was near completion when they saw the manuscript, it has been quite transformed by their sage advice. Also on my list was Charles Bosk, who, sadly, passed away before the book was completed. I was fortunate, though, that he accepted an invitation to be the main act in a seminar on several draft chapters during my year at Princeton. It is this group of incisive and thorough readers that come to mind as I offer the standard acknowledgment that I accept responsibility for remaining errors and gaps. With them in mind, though, my acceptance of responsibility is visceral. I wince thinking about the critiques I didn't fully respond to and fear that I have still buried the best sentences in obscure places.

At the University of Chicago Press, I much appreciated the efforts of Charles Myers, Sara Doskow, and Rosemary Frehe as they shepherded the book through the production process, mixing realism with kind respect for my preferences. Without sacrificing meticulousness, Lisa Wehrle brought a welcome human touch to her copyediting. An early version of chapter 7 was published in *Economy and Society*.[1] Likewise, a version of chapter 8 was published in *Social Science and Medicine*.[2] Portions of appendix A on research methods, available online at this book's page at the University of Chicago Press website, appeared in *Sociological Methods and Research*.[3] These pieces appear in the book with the permission of Taylor and Francis, Elsevier, and Sage Publications, respectively.

People don't fall into neat categories, fortunately, and I am profoundly grateful for the colleagues and friends who moved so gracefully between categories, talking shop and sharing joys, sorrows, books, food, flowers, and more: Charles Camic and Elizabeth Mertz, Jothie Rajah, Kim Scheppele, Phyllis Moen, Mitchell Stevens, Jennifer Earl, Mary Jo Neitz, Wendy Espeland and Bruce Carruthers, and Bruce Enenbach. In the time of COVID, we learned new ways to be friends, with fewer in-person visits and more Zooms and phone calls. When we were suddenly trapped in our homes during the early days of COVID, I was lucky to share a two-flat with Wendy Espeland and Bruce Carruthers, cofounders of the long-running Lochinvar Society, who became my lock-down multipurpose family and office mates. As I was trying to pretend that COVID was just a strange writing retreat, I was fortunate that Beth Mertz accommodated my desire for daily Zoom study dates. Later Mary Jo Neitz gamely began thrice-weekly Zoom work sessions, which continue to the present, with an occasional Zoom cooking spree thrown in. Though he was perhaps baffled by my devotion to this project and completely in the dark about how long it would go on (as was I, honestly), Bruce Enenbach brought support, comfort, delight, and distraction to the last couple of years of writing and revision. Attentive to the ups and downs of the work and my mood, he was also remarkably tolerant of my philistinic inclination to enjoy music especially for keeping my mind from wandering too far from writing.

My children and stepchildren and assorted family members—Max, Beth, and Rigo; Amy, Masoud, Roshan, and Farah; Adam and Maureen; Kirk; Kai and Julia; and Clare, Mika, Shai, and Tavi—have been with me, sometimes happily, sometimes grudgingly, on this too-long journey. Kai and

Clare each joined me briefly in Uganda, bringing them face to face with the world I was experiencing and writing about. My brothers felt rather free to poke and prod, but more kindly than was their custom when we were younger. As I first headed off to Uganda, my brother Haldor, remembering the aroma of cooking fires, urged me to inhale deeply as I stepped off the plane. My brother David, touching base with me almost daily since the start of COVID, understood and supported my need to get something accomplished, but reminded me that each day should include some fun. Early in my research, my late mother, Ruth, enthusiastically arranged a gathering of her octogenarian friends to hear about my adventures in the field. I generally tried, but sometimes failed, to insulate my family from book-related trials and tribulations as the work progressed, and they generally strove to show interest and concern without diving too deeply into the messy details and without asking when I would be finished. Above all, my family did not express doubt that I would complete the book. The desire to spend more time with family surely nudges many academic projects across the finish line, and this is book is no exception. One of the pleasures of finishing this one is the prospect of more time with my far-flung children and grandchildren, including one small person who sat patiently—ok, not so patiently— reading a book on the stairs waiting for their Granny to come hang out. I have joyously sent an all-points bulletin informing them that the finish line has been crossed.

The biggest sadness for me is that my husband Art Stinchcombe, for decades my closest intellectual companion, began to lose his intellectual acuity partway through the project. In the early period of my fieldwork, Art occasionally accompanied me on research trips, pursuing projects of his own wherever we happened to be. When I packed a summer with revisits to fieldsites, he commented—not happily—that my periods at home were "more administrative visits than conjugal visits." Over the years, as he transitioned to being a tether whose need for care curtailed my research forays and conference attendance and truncated my workdays, he nevertheless remained enthusiastic about my work. How fortunate I was to have had so many years with someone eager to discuss ideas, willing to drop everything to read a draft, and good humored when his advice was blithely ignored! I am all too aware that the final book would have been enriched and improved by Art's scribbles in the margins of my drafts. He would have been delighted to see the finished product and would have spent hours rereading the printed pages. Obviously, it is to him that I lovingly dedicate this book.

Appendixes

Both appendixes for this book, Appendix A: Some Funny Things Happened on the Way to the Clinics: Data and Methods and Appendix B: Timeline of HIV/AIDS Disease and Responses, can be accessed online at the University of Chicago Press website (https://press.uchicago.edu/dam/ucp/books/pdf/Heimer_Appendices.pdf).

Notes

CHAPTER ONE

1. I am grateful to Ann Swidler for suggesting this term.

2. The prevalence of anti-discrimination laws should not be overstated, though. According to the 2008 UNAIDS report on the global pandemic, "In the epidemic's third decade, one third of countries lack laws protecting people living with HIV from discrimination" (UNAIDS 2008, 12). By 2010, 92% of countries had passed protective laws (UNAIDS 2010, 10), though they were not always enforced. Reviewing HIV-related legal provisions in sub-Saharan Africa, Eba (2015) concludes that, when they are in place, legal provisions are not generally strong enough to offer much protection against discrimination.

3. The toolkit specifically mentions three international legal instruments that govern RCT: (1) UNAIDS/OCHR, "Advancing Care, Treatment and Support for People Living with HIV/AIDS: Updating Guideline 6 of the HIV/AIDS and Human Rights: International Guidelines; Report of the 3rd International Consultation on HIV/AIDS and Human Rights," July 2002; (2) UNGASS (UN General Assembly Special Session on HIV/AIDS), "Declaration of Commitment on HIV/AIDS," 2001; (3) UNGASS (UN General Assembly Special Session on HIV/AIDS), "Update on the Declaration of Commitment on HIV/AIDS," 2002.

4. There is some evidence that the move to RCT did sometimes decrease attention to rights. An exploratory study in rural Uganda, for instance, found that as VCT was replaced by RCT, staff members sometimes began to treat testing as mandatory rather than voluntary (Vernooij and Hardon 2013).

5. De-implementation is the process by which interventions, programs, or policies are discontinued or used less frequently (McKay, Combs, Dolcini et al. 2020; McKay, Tetteh, Reid et al. 2020), for instance, because the interventions are ineffective or harmful, inefficient or not cost-effective, or simply no longer needed (McKay, Tetteh, Reid et al. 2020). But de-implementation is no more straightforward than implementation, and many organizations fail to de-implement interventions and policies that do not serve their intended purposes, as the case of de-implementing VCT shows.

6. Launched in December 2003, the 3 by 5 campaign's objective was to get 3 million people living with HIV in developing countries on anti-retroviral therapy (ART), a cocktail of drugs with different mechanisms for inhibiting viral replication, by the end of 2005. Announced in 2014, the 90-90-90 campaign's objective was to have 90% of people living with HIV know their HIV status, 90% of people diagnosed with HIV receiving ART, and 90% of those receiving ART achieving viral suppression by 2020.

The targets were later raised to 95-95-95 by 2030. Meeting the 2020 and 2030 targets would mean that, respectively, 73% and 86% of people living with HIV would be virally suppressed and therefore very unlikely to transmit the virus to others.

7. In the US in 2009, the estimated transmission rates per 100 person years were 6.6 for people living with HIV who had not been diagnosed, 5.3 for people who had tested positive but had not been retained in care, 2.6 for people retained in care but not on ART, 1.8 for people receiving ART but not virally suppressed, and 0.5 for those who had achieved viral suppression (Skarbinski et al. 2015, 591).

8. CD4 cells are a type of white blood cell that helps the body fight infection. HIV damages the immune system by targeting CD4 cells. Physicians therefore track the progression of HIV by measuring patients' CD4 levels. CD4 levels rebound with ART.

9. The World Trade Organization (WTO) Agreement on Trade-Related Aspects of Intellectual Property Rights (TRIPS) was signed in 1994 and went into effect in 1995. TRIPS establishes minimum standards for national governments' regulation of intellectual property rights. Included among these intellectual property rights are patents on pharmaceutical products. TRIPS is important for HIV because of its restrictions on the production and sale of patented medications, including medications used in the treatment of HIV/AIDS. These restrictions were eased somewhat in the 2001 Doha Declaration.

10. Pneumocystis carinii pneumonia (PCP), now called pneumocystis jiroveci pneumonia, is an opportunistic fungal lung infection commonly experienced by people with HIV. The increased demand for pentamidine to treat PCP drew the attention of CDC scientists in 1981. Because PCP is rare in people with healthy immune systems, the increase in the number of PCP cases suggested that the new disease had something to do with compromised immune systems. A spike in cases of Kaposi sarcoma (KS), which usually occurs in older people, among young gay men also drew CDC's attention. In mid-1981, the CDC formed the Task Force on Kaposi's Sarcoma and Opportunistic Infections.

11. Unlike the CDC staging system, the WHO staging system, created in 1990, did not require a CD4 count. Both staging systems note whether patients have experienced a variety of "symptomatic" conditions (such as shingles) or "AIDS-indicator conditions" (such as KS and PCP). Although severe weight loss figures into both staging systems, the WHO's reference point is "presumed or measured body weight," while the CDC's is "baseline body weight."

12. Scholars of regulation have noted the decentralization (or "decentering") of regulation has brought with it an increase in the number of entities involved in regulatory activity (Black 2001; Jordana and Levi-Faur 2004; Parker and Nielsen 2009).

13. See UNAIDS (2024) and the associated spreadsheet with some estimates from 1990 to 2023.

14. But see Tilley (2010, 2011) on medical and scientific discoveries in the context of British colonization of Africa. Tilley argues that both colonizer and colonized were transformed by these interactions.

CHAPTER TWO

1. See Goffman (1967) on fatefulness and other features of places experienced as "where the action is."

2. Assessing the preparedness of the 195 countries that are States Parties to the 2005 International Health Regulations, the Global Health Security (GHS) Index arrived at

a mean score of 40.2% and concluded that "national health security is fundamentally weak around the world" (Johns Hopkins University 2020, 11).

3. See especially UN (1948) (article 25 speaks to the right to health); UNOHCHR (1966); WHO (1978); and UNOHCHR (2008).

4. Established by Health Canada in collaboration with the WHO, GPHIN is a multilingual electronic early warning system that monitors a wide swath of online sources, including news outlets and websites. It "read[s] between the lines" for information suggesting unusual disease patterns (Morse 2012). The WHO started using GPHIN in 1997.

Set up in 1997 by the WHO and formally launched in 2000, GOARN is a collaboration of other networks that links a wide variety of experts and combines surveillance and response (Fidler 2004; Heymann et al. 2001).

5. Information about publicly and privately funded clinical trials is available at ClinicalTrials.gov. Viewed July 4, 2024. At last viewing, the list included 500,328 research studies in all 50 US states and in 222 countries.

6. The European Medicines Agency provides similar access to the large EU market. Swanson (2015) compares the top five markets (France, Germany, China, Japan, and the US).

7. On Reagan's essential silence on AIDS and his failure to support the scientific and medical consensus on key points—policies of "AIDS denialism" not so different from the denialism of South African President Mbeki—see Boffey (1985); Boyd (1987); White (2004); Plante (2011).

8. Bob Rafsky (1945–93), a prominent AIDS activist, was a senior vice president of a New York public relations firm when he learned that he had become infected with HIV. He left that career to work full time with ACT UP (AIDS Coalition to Unleash Power), functioning as the group's media coordinator. An impassioned, blunt speaker, Rafsky worked hard to make AIDS a national political issue and to secure treatment for those who were infected. "I'm dying from AIDS, while you're dying of ambition," Rafsky charged, pressing then presidential candidate Bill Clinton about his AIDS agenda (Mathews 1993; Howe 1993; see also *How to Survive a Plague*, directed by David France [New York: Public Square Films, in association with Ninety Thousand Words, 2012], at 01:15:24).

Rafsky was a strong advocate for scientific research on HIV/AIDS and worked with TAG (the Treatment Action Group, initially the scientific wing of ACT UP and later a separate organization) to speed up the approval of new drugs, reduce drug prices, and make HIV drugs more accessible.

9. In many places in the US, reporting HIV infections is not mandated, and therefore good estimates are not readily available. The CDC has better information on new AIDS diagnoses, and I therefore report those figures, even though it might be preferable to use statistics that more closely matched the information available about the sites outside the US.

10. Formed in 1986, the Division of AIDS (DAIDS) is a subpart of the National Institute of Allergies and Infectious Diseases (NIAID), itself one of the institutes and centers that make up the National Institutes of Health (NIH). NIAID-sponsored HIV research networks currently include ACTG (Advancing Clinical Therapeutics Globally for HIV/AIDS and Other Infections, previously the AIDS Clinical Trials Group), HPTN (HIV Prevention Trials Network), HVTN (HIV Vaccine Trials Network), and IMPAACT (International Maternal Pediatric Adolescent AIDS Clinical Trials) (https://www.niaid.nih.gov/research/hivaids-clinical-trials-networks; accessed July 5, 2024).

328 ‹ NOTES TO PAGES 47–60

11. For a general treatment of the tension between treatment and research, see Weisz (2014).

12. Bobbi Campbell (1952–84) was the sixteenth person to be diagnosed with Kaposi sarcoma (KS) at the start of the AIDS epidemic and the first to openly acknowledge his AIDS diagnosis. Campbell strongly believed that people living with HIV should be heard and included in policymaking. Because of his conviction that confronting stigma was a first step in empowering such participation, he allowed photographs of his KS lesions to be used for instructional materials. He was the "AIDS Poster Boy" (as proclaimed on the T-shirt he wore to the 1983 San Francisco Gay Pride Parade).

Perhaps most important, Campbell coauthored the foundational Denver Principles, a key document of the PWA (People With AIDS) self-empowerment movement. The San Francisco Model of AIDS care that he helped shape is credited as a forerunner of the Ryan White HIV/AIDS Program, which provides public funding for AIDS care in the US, including at the Bobbi Campbell Clinic. Recognizing Campbell's contributions, the San Francisco Pride Parade of 1985 was dedicated to him. See SF Pride (1985); Callan and Turner (1997); Inglis (2004); Wright (2013). Images and video clips are widely available on the internet.

13. This has become less true since the passage of the Affordable Care Act (Obamacare) in 2010. Discussing the relationship between law and health policy, Levitsky (2013) suggests that the ACA might alter how Americans think about the state's responsibility to safeguard citizens' health.

14. The Universal Coverage Scheme, covering about three-fourths of Thais, was introduced in October 2001 with a copay of 30 Baht (then about 0.66 USD) for each medical visit; universal access to anti-retrovirals was added in 2003 (Coronini-Cronberg, Laohasiriwong, and Gericke 2007; Hughes and Leethongdee 2007).

15. See Sirivichayakul et al. (2008) on the history of ART in Thailand, including the introduction of GPO-VIR.

16. One early program, the "100% Condom Programme" initiated in Ratchaburi province in 1989, mandated that sex workers use condoms in every sex act (UNAIDS and MOPH 2000).

17. Cha-on Suesum, who worked as a factory guard, contracted HIV from a blood transfusion in 1986 and was diagnosed in 1987. He was fired from his job because of his infection. His wife, employed at the same factory, was also fired.

Suesum agreed to have his case publicized and his identity revealed. After the Population and Community Development Association, a Thai NGO, hired Suesum as an AIDS educator, he appeared on popular television shows, received front-page news coverage, and visited offices and worksites. His openness is credited with bringing HIV into public discussion and convincing Thais that HIV and discrimination against people with AIDS were real problems. His rapid decline and death were vivid evidence that the disease was serious and deadly. The injustice of his firing legitimized and gave urgency to the rights claims of people with HIV.

Despite the importance of Cha-on Suesum's case, little information is available about him outside Thailand. Although many HIV websites mention him, they tend to use the same two or three fixed phrases and cite the same source (Porapakkham et al., 1995, 28, 38–39), when they offer any citation at all. See also Singhal and Rogers (2003).

18. Citation omitted to protect confidentiality.

19. AIDS denialism shaped South African HIV/AIDS policy from 1999–2007 (Decoteau 2013, 83). Chigwedere et al. (2008) estimate the immediate effect of denialism as

NOTES TO PAGES 61–66 › 329

330,000 excess deaths from the failure to implement an appropriate ART treatment program and 35,500 excess infant infections from the failure to implement an adequate program to prevent mother-to-child transmission. See also Specter (2007); Dugger (2008a, 2008b); Harris (2017a).

20. Gugu Dlamini (1962–98) was an HIV+ activist who was beaten, stabbed, stoned, and pushed down a cliff in KwaMashu, the township near Durban where she lived with her thirteen-year old daughter (McNeil 1998; IRIN 2011). Her killers were men from her township. Dlamini had joined a support group and become active in campaigns to raise awareness about HIV. Her murder followed her disclosure of her HIV status, first on a radio program and then in the KwaMashu stadium. Dlamini is seen as a figure who stood against AIDS stigma and AIDS denialism. A foundation and a Durban park bear her name. In response to Dlamini's death, the recently formed Treatment Action Campaign (TAC) created T-shirts with Dlamini's photo and the words "never again" on the back and the slogan "HIV positive" emblazoned in capital letters on the front (Nattrass 2007, 46–46; Grükenmeier 2013, 85–86). The HIV positive T-shirt has since become an important symbol of solidarity around HIV.

21. As I began fieldwork, Gugu Dlamini was about to sign a contract to provide treatment for research participants from a neighboring research clinic.

22. This is for adolescents and adults. A percentage rather than a raw number is used for children.

23. People with HIV are twenty-five times as likely as other people to get TB, and this perhaps helps explain the exceptionally high rate of TB in South Africa, where the first cases of XDR-TB (extensively drug resistant tuberculosis) were discovered in 2006. An effective new treatment regimen for XDR-TB was approved by the FDA in 2019 (McNeil 2019).

24. See Heimer (2013) for an analysis of this down-referral program.

25. One could make a case for measuring economic differences (among countries, cities, or individuals) by using as an indicator the units in which cigarettes are bought and sold. The cigarette-unit indicator would (correctly) place Uganda among the world's very poorest countries.

26. Philly Bongoley Lutaaya (1961–89), the AfroPop star famous for *Born in Africa*, was the first prominent Ugandan to openly acknowledge his HIV status. Although he was living in Sweden at the time, Lutaaya made his announcement at the Kampala Sheraton Hotel. At that time, people believed to be HIV infected were ostracized. Treatment was not yet available. As his brother Abbey observed, AIDS was considered a "harsh matter," and those who were infected were expected to "withdraw from public eyes" and to "die quietly in some remote corner of some village place" (*Born in Africa*, written and directed by John Zaritsky, originally aired on PBS, *Frontline* [Alexandria, VA: PBS Video, 1990], at 00:06:17–00:06:41). Lutaaya spent the remaining eight months of his life writing songs about AIDS and touring Ugandan churches, mosques, and schools to spread the message about HIV. Ultimately, his announcement came to be seen as courageous and patriotic. In Uganda, October 17 is celebrated as Philly Lutaaya Day. Lutaaya's song "Alone" is the unofficial anthem of TASO (The AIDS Support Organization), one of Uganda's AIDS groups. See also New Vision (2007); Nsimbe (2010).

27. Readers may be skeptical about this assertion, but the "Site Security" SOP notes that "[clinic name] guards are armed with a bow and arrow only."

28. These are metal shipping containers, originally used to transport goods by rail or boat, now recycled as poor-country substitutes for mobile offices. Such containers may also serve as stores, restaurants, or beauty parlors.

29. This tension over data collection by treatment-focused staff also occurred in other sites.

30. Because the world of HIV research is rather small in some countries, I have omitted details about funding to conceal clinic identities.

31. Research subjects are an important constituency. Their demand for treatment, when it is not available elsewhere, creates an additional pressure for research clinics to adopt the results of clinical trials.

32. One could see the availability of condoms in Gugu Dlamini's bathrooms and the provision of food at Philly Lutaaya as attempts to make their clinic patients' experience more comparable to the experience of patients in rich countries. If condoms are unavailable, people living with HIV cannot comply with the dictates of the ABC (Abstinence, Be faithful, use Condoms) program. And if food is scarce, people living with HIV may be unable to take their medications as prescribed.

CHAPTER THREE

1. On the distinction between hard and soft law, which comes originally from international law but has now been used in other arenas, see Abbott and Snidal (2000); Trubek, Cottrell, and Nance (2006).

2. See, e.g., Rosenthal (2017, 2020).

3. These arguments about clinical guidelines as a key element of the legalization of medicine are developed more fully in Heimer, Petty, and Culyba (2005).

4. See https://www.dartmouthatlas.org (viewed July 6, 2024).

5. In 1993, the Agency for Health Care Policy and Research (later renamed Agency for Healthcare Research and Quality) launched a program to prepare clinical guidelines. NGC was ultimately created in partnership with the AMA and the American Association of Health Plans (now America's Health Insurance Plans).

6. For more on this transition, see Smith (2020). Gerberich, Spencer, and Ipema (2019) discuss practitioners' adjustments to the loss of NGC. In a posting about the closing of NGC, the Agency for Healthcare Quality and Research (AHRQ) shares that it has "decided to launch a reimagined NGC and secured funding to do so." https://www.ahrq.gov/gam/updates/index.html (accessed July 14, 2024).

7. Bosk (2003/1979), in discussing the training of surgery residents, distinguishes internal from external and informal from formal regulation.

8. The US does have a public pay/public provision segment, namely veterans' healthcare paid for by the Veterans Administration and provided by VA employees in dedicated VA facilities.

9. For a brief discussion of Medicaid's role in US healthcare, see Rudowitz et al. (2023).

10. See Williams, Rudowitz, and Burns (2023).

11. The statutory minimum and maximum federal contributions are 50% and 83%, respectively (Congressional Research Service, *Medicaid's Federal Medical Assistance Percentage (FMAP)*, updated July 29, 2020, https://fas.org/sgp/crs/misc/R43847.pdf). In FY 2025, federal contributions ranged from 50% (ten states) to 76.9% (Mississippi). Special provisions have been made for Puerto Rico (reimbursement rate set at 76%

through 2027) and the American territories (reimbursement rate permanently set at 83%). For the Federal Assistance Percentage (FMAP) multiplier for states, including historical data between and FY2004 and FY2025, see "State Health Facts," Kaiser Family Foundation, accessed July 6, 2024, https://www.kff.org/medicaid/state-indicator/federal-matching-rate-and-multiplier/?currentTimeframe=0&sortModel=%7B%22colId%22:%22FMAP%20Percentage%22,%22sort%22:%22desc%22%7D.

12. On funding for HIV research, see "U.S. Federal Funding for HIV/AIDS: Trends over Time," Kaiser Family Foundation, March 26, 2024, https://www.kff.org/hivaids/fact-sheet/u-s-federal-funding-for-hivaids-trends-over-time/#.

13. The Division of AIDS (DAIDS), founded in 1986, is part of the National Institute of Allergy and Infectious Diseases, itself part of the National Institutes of Health, under the umbrella of the Department of Health and Human Services. Within DAIDS, the research networks such as ACTG (AIDS Clinical Trials Group) and HPTN (HIV Prevention Trials Network) funded much of the research conducted in the clinics discussed in this book.

14. The 1902 Biologics Control Act assigned this responsibility to the Hygienic Lab. Only in 1972 was responsibility for regulating biologics transferred to the FDA.

15. Because the Bureau of the Budget was reluctant to fund medical research, the NIH was unable to begin offering extramural research grants until the following year when it secured adequate funds (Swain 1962).

16. In 2012, an estimated 21% to 47% of the US healthcare budget was wasted, often because of administrative complexity (Berwick and Hackbarth 2012; Kaiser Family Foundation 2012).

17. Faculty practice plans are organizations that provide assistance with credentialing, billing, collections, revenue distribution, and financial services to the full-time teaching faculty associated with a medical school and/or healthcare organization. Other clinical staff (such as dentists or nurses) may also have practice plans.

18. The NIH-level Office of Protection from Research Risks was elevated in 2000 to become the DHHS-level Office for Human Research Protections.

19. Confusingly, the Joint Commission changed names several times, including dropping "on the Accreditation of Health Care Organizations" from its title in 2007. Its affiliate for international accreditation, consultation, and education, the Joint Commission International, was created in 1998.

20. The capacity to accredit for purposes of Medicare and Medicaid reimbursement is then called "deeming authority."

21. In 2018, about 88% of accredited US hospitals were reviewed by the Joint Commission (Jha 2018). The Joint Commission's reach increased dramatically, with growth in the number of organizations and programs accredited (over 22,000 in 2024), expansion of the types of organizations accredited (laboratories, nursing homes, and rehabilitation centers, as well as hospitals), and the development of programs to certify organizations for disease-specific care and write standards. See "Facts about the Joint Commission," Joint Commission, accessed July 6, 2024, http://www.jointcommission.org/who-we-are/facts-about-the-joint-commission/.

JCI, the Joint Commission's international affiliate, "partners with hospitals, clinics, and academic medical centers, health systems and agencies, government ministries, academia, and international advocates" in more than 70 countries. See "Who We Are," Joint Commission International, accessed July 6, 2024, https://www.jointcommission international.org/who-we-are/.

332 ‹ NOTES TO PAGES 98–118

22. A list of organizations with deeming authority can be found at "Joint Commission," Wikipedia, last modified June 11, 2024, https://en.wikipedia.org/wiki/Joint_Commission.

23. Only in 1930 did the FDA acquire its current name. Originating as a subunit of the US Department of Agriculture, it was initially the USDA's Division/Bureau of Chemistry.

24. Some observers have been worried that approvals processes may be influenced by the FDA's dependence on user fees. Carpenter et al. (2003) conclude that review time for new drug applications is more influenced by the amount of funding available for FDA staff than the funding source.

25. See Hall (2006) for one list of such principles. Jost (2004) discusses important scholarly influences on the development of health law. Rosoff's (2004) discussion of the evolution of health law notes scholarly influences but also includes commentary on changes in the organization of healthcare and the effects of social movements.

26. The International Antiviral Society–USA (IAS–USA) is a not-for-profit professional education organization that sponsors continuing medical education programs and prepares clinical guidelines. Its website notes that is not affiliated with the International AIDS Society (IAS), which is an international organization of members working in HIV/AIDS and the organizer of the major HIV/AIDS conferences. See "Mission," International Antiviral Society–USA, accessed July 6, 2024, https://www.iasusa.org/about/mission/.

27. According to Valenti (2004), the first HIV treatment guidelines were produced by the DHHS in 1995.

28. A=strong, should always be offered; B=moderate, should usually be offered; C=optional; D=should usually not be offered; E=should never be offered.

29. I: at least one randomized trial with clinical results; II: clinical trials with laboratory results; III: expert opinion.

30. As a general matter, there is wide consensus about the appropriateness of these rating schemes. Nevertheless, two caveats are needed. First, medical researchers in several of the developing-country sites complained about the first-world lock on publication outlets and the difficulty of getting research published when researchers lacked access to laboratory facilities capable of producing "gold standard" indicators. This has meant that research results on such matters as pediatric HIV and pregnancy have been disseminated more slowly than results about population groups and conditions that are of more interest to rich countries. Second, the consensus about what kind of evidence should support guidelines and "best practices" seems stronger for strictly medical matters than for other kinds of guidelines, where definitions of what constitutes a "best practice" might surprise readers.

31. Good Clinical Practice rules, discussed more fully below, are guidelines and training regimens under the aegis of the ICH.

32. AEs are untoward events associated with a medical product; SAEs are AEs that result in death, life-threatening illness, hospitalization (initial or prolonged), disability, congenital anomaly, or require treatment to prevent permanent damage (21 C.F.R. § 312.32). SAEs are tracked by funding agencies and IRBs.

33. Both the current version and previous iterations of the Declaration of Helsinki can be found at "WMA Declaration of Helsinki—Medical Principles for Medical Research Involving Human Subjects," WMA, accessed July 6, 2024, https://www.wma.net/policies-post/wma-declaration-of-helsinki-ethical-principles-for-medical

-research-involving-human-subjects/. Another revision was in process in 2023 and 2024, with the expectation that it would be considered by the Council and General Assembly of the World Medical Association in October 2024, accessed July 6, 2024, https://www.wma.net/what-we-do/medical-ethics/declaration-of-helsinki/.

34. Much has been written about these debates. See Angell (1997), Lurie and Wolf (1997), Varmus and Satcher (1997), Rothman (2000), and Benatar (2002).

35. Rothman (2000) notes that leaders of poorer countries might sometimes be reluctant to offer local control groups the treatment they would receive in richer countries. In the case of the clinical trials of mother-to-child transmission, demonstrating that the short-course AZT regimen was effective but not as effective as the long-course was tantamount to asking political leaders to offer their citizens a treatment shown to be "second class."

36. See "Efficacy Guidelines," ICH, accessed July 6, 2024, https://www.ich.org/page/efficacy-guidelines.

37. See "Good Clinical Practice," Research Office, Imperial College, accessed July 6, 2024, https://www.imperial.ac.uk/research-and-innovation/research-office/research-governance-and-integrity/what-is-research-governance/regulatory-frameworks/good-clinical-practice/.

38. Despite the US government's stance on GCP versus the Declaration of Helsinki, other US entities such as the AMA continue to belong to the WMA.

39. See "Regulations: Good Clinical Practice and Clinical Trials," US Food & Drug Administration, accessed July 6, 2024, https://www.fda.gov/science-research/clinical-trials-and-human-subject-protection/regulations-good-clinical-practice-and-clinical-trials.

40. Another US government agency concerned with research ethics, the Office of Research Integrity, focuses on the responsible conduct of research and on detection, investigation, and prevention of research misconduct.

CHAPTER FOUR

1. "Who We Are: 25 Year Timeline of the IAS," International AIDS Society, archived at the Wayback Machine, https://web.archive.org/web/20150911230940/http://www.iasociety.org/Who-we-are/About-the-IAS/25th-anniversary-of-the-IAS/Timeline.

2. "25 Year Timeline of the IAS."

3. Congolese President Mobutu did not want Kapita to acknowledge that Africa had an AIDS epidemic. "Who We Are: 25th Anniversary of the IAS: History of the IAS: Episode 1: International AIDS Conferences 1985-1988: Struggling for Knowledge," International AIDS Society, archived at the Wayback Machine, https://web.archive.org/web/20150910171403/http://www.iasociety.org/Who-we-are/About-the-IAS/25th-anniversary-of-the-IAS/Episode-1. According to Kapita, chief of internal medicine at Hôpital Mama Yemo in Kinshasa, he and other clinicians working in central Africa had been seeing cases that were likely to have been HIV/AIDS since the mid-1970s (Pepin 2011, 32). However, because of official prohibitions on discussion of the disease, patients could not be told they had AIDS (Timberg and Halperin 2012, 93).

4. The first demonstrations occurred at the 1987 conference in Washington, DC, and have been a prominent feature of the conferences ever since. At the 2004 Bangkok conference, treatment activist demonstrations interrupted the presentations of Pfizer's CEO and French President Chirac's representative. By the middle of the conference,

most pharmaceutical companies had closed their lavish exhibits to avoid increasingly hostile demonstrators.

5. For example, at the 2016 IAC held (a second time) in Durban, South Africa, the Global Village, free and open to the public, was described in program materials as "a diverse and vibrant space where communities gather from all over the world to meet, share and learn from each other." "Global Village & Youth Programme," AIDS 2016, archived at the Wayback Machine, https://web.archive.org/web/20151223025747/http://www.aids2016.org:80/Programme/Global-Village-Youth-Programme.

6. Other conferences also advanced this goal and addressed the relationship between scientific evidence and guidelines (and law). For example, the Vienna Declaration (2010) advocated science-based drug policies (such as needle-exchange programs) and pushed for an end to draconian drug laws that have hampered attempts to fight HIV. "The Vienna Declaration," archived at the Wayback Machine, https://web .archive.org/web/20150909090706/http://www.viennadeclaration.com/wordpress/ wp-content/uploads/2011/04/Vienna-Declaration-Download.pdf.

7. "25 Year Timeline of the IAS."

8. "Overview: History: A Timeline of HIV and AIDS," HIV.gov, accessed July 7, 2024, https://www.hiv.gov/hiv-basics/overview/history/hiv-and-aids-timeline.

9. The explosion of clinical practice guidelines is one element of a broader trend toward evidence-based medicine that has shaped the medical field worldwide since the 1970s. See Timmermans and Kolker (2004, esp. 182–84). Guideline proliferation took off in the 1980s, and as of 2006, more than 2,000 clinical practice guidelines were available at the US National Guideline Clearinghouse's website (Weisz et al. 2007, 691–92).

10. Limitations to the adoption of guidelines had begun to be recognized by the late 1980s. See Cabana et al. (1999, 1458, 1463nn4–5).

11. The themes of the International AIDS Conferences support this point. Information about IAS conferences held between 1985 and 2012 can be found in "25 Year Timeline of the IAS." Information about the 2002–22 IAS conferences can be found "Past Conferences," International AIDS Society, accessed July 7, 2024, https://www .iasociety.org/past-conferences.

12. UNAIDS and WHO launched the 3 by 5 Initiative in 2003, with the goal of providing anti-retroviral treatment for 3 million people living with HIV/AIDS around the world by the end of 2005. See "The 3 by 5 Initiative," World Health Organization, archived at the Wayback Machine, https://web.archive.org/web/20031203024142/ https://www.who.int/3by5/en/.

13. Three bodies provide useful information on variability in medical education: World Federation for Medical Education (WFME; see https://wfme.org/), the Educational Commission for Foreign Medical Graduates (ECFMG; see https://www.ecfmg .org/), and the Foundation for the Advancement of International Medical Education and Research (FAIMER; see https://faimer.org/).

14. WHO endorses such task shifting as a promising way to address shortages of healthcare workers, especially in countries with high HIV burdens. See World Health Organization, *Task Shifting: Rational Redistribution of Tasks Among Health Workforce Teams: Global Recommendations and Guidelines* (2008), archived at the Wayback Machine, https://web.archive.org/web/20151020080116/http://www.who.int/healthsys tems/TTR-TaskShifting.pdf?ua=1.

15. But Grimshaw and Russell's (1993) systematic review found that clinical practice had changed significantly to comport with guidelines in fifty-five of fifty-nine evaluations of clinical guidelines.

16. A similar case, discussed more fully in chapter 6, occurred in South Africa when a physician provided care that exceeded the standard specified in provincial and national guidelines (Dugger 2008a; TAC 2008a).

17. This failure to include generics was partly attributable to a restriction associated with international PEPFAR funding. PEPFAR gradually, haltingly altered its stance (Dietrich 2007). Although PEPFAR has come to rely heavily on generic anti-retrovirals, observers remain concerned about access to newer generations of generic anti-retrovirals (Holmes et al. 2010; Venkatesh, Mayer, and Carpenter 2012).

18. On the use of FDCs in resource-limited countries and the efficacy and toxicities of GPO-VIR specifically, see Ramautarsing and Ananworanich (2010); Desakorn et al. (2011).

19. An informant at the AIDS Law Project supplied an example of how not to use guidelines. Prisons follow guidelines exactly, he said. When the guidelines said to start anti-retrovirals when a patient's CD4 count dropped to 200, prison doctors would not initiate therapy if a prisoner had a CD4 count of 203 and would not check the CD4 count again until a year later. Guidelines must be written to take account of the inflexibility of some of the institutions in which they will be used, he suggested.

20. Few new ARVs that were eligible to be incorporated into international guidelines met the budgetary constraints of South Africa's Medicines Control Council (MCC).

21. For instance, the TB guidelines said that patients infected with TB should be isolated in negative pressure rooms. But the hospital had no negative pressure rooms. The existing isolation rooms were so poorly ventilated that they could not be used for TB patients.

22. All of the clinics also received oversight by domestic regulatory bodies, of course. Although it is difficult to compare the intensity of domestic oversight in these four countries, my sense is that it is more intense in the US than in the other three.

23. These training activities were less an official clinic activity than an activity of individual staff members who served as faculty for other programs. A staff member affiliated with one of these training programs (but not with Philly Lutaaya) noted that Uganda has its own guidelines, which are "disseminated but not enforced." Clinical teaching was consistent with that approach: clinicians should "practice ethically based on guidelines."

24. Clinicians often report that they are unaware of the clinical guidelines in their field or do not adhere to them (Cabana et al. 1999). Even when guidelines are referenced, they do not shape decisions and actions as fully as might have been expected. At best, they lead to "local universality" (Timmermans and Berg 1997). Many researchers have asked how clinicians might be induced to adhere more closely to guidelines. Others have considered whether properties of the guidelines themselves affect implementation. And a few researchers have asked whether features of the organizations in which clinicians work might affect whether and how clinical guidelines are used (Davis and Taylor-Vaisey 1997; Grol and Grimshaw 2003).

25. See Scott et al. (2000, esp. 20–22) on the institutional environment of (US) healthcare organizations.

26. Readers may notice the implicit comparison to the age, period, and cohort effects discussed by demographers, sociologists, and political scientists. Cohort effects do not have a ready comparison point in discussions of fields of practice, although, of course, there are cohorts of practitioners, and some of the caregivers and researchers I talked with did point out differences between practitioners who were there "at the beginning" and those who came into the field later.

27. In August 1987, the CDC published "Recommendations for Prevention of HIV Transmission in Health-Care Settings," specifying that blood and fluid precautions be used regardless of infection status (clarified and supplemented in CDC 1988). The guidelines for universal precautions are often cited as an important innovation brought by HIV care, with impacts that extend well beyond this single disease. Yet the literature suggests that these rules are often ignored. See, e.g., Ferguson et al. (2004).

28. During this period, the public hospital with which Bobbi Campbell was affiliated was in such dire financial straits that vendors cut off supplies because of unpaid bills and the hospital began requiring patient copays.

29. In a fixed-dose combination, multiple ARVs are contained in a single dosage form such as a capsule or tablet. Fixed-dose combinations reduce the pill burden and facilitate patient adherence to drug regimens.

30. Conventions on publication also slowed the accumulation and transmission of information about the management of pediatric HIV/AIDS. Although pediatric patients and research subjects were mostly concentrated in poorer countries, high-prestige journals were disproportionately located in richer ones. The most prominent general and specialty medical journals insisted on the use of established indicators, such as sophisticated clinical measurements and laboratory tests. Although such requirements surely made for more reliable, comparable research, when evidence was sparse and largely being collected in the clinics of poor countries, these stringent requirements could not be met, and thus evidence from these clinics was not widely disseminated and did not have the legitimacy that came with publication in first- or second-tier journals. Insofar as the topics studied in poorer clinics differ from those studied in richer ones, the result has been that some topics simply do not get much coverage in international forums.

31. Boarding schools posed special problems because children often required help with their medications while away from home.

32. On the gravity of the lactic acidosis/d4T connection, see Alcorn (2006, 2009) and Clayden (2008). Lactic acidosis sometimes went unheeded in other settings as well. Pallasch (2007) discusses a Chicago woman whose doctors overlooked this serious side effect.

CHAPTER FIVE

1. Such conflicts between patient interests and drug company profits continue to appear in accounts of pharmaceutical companies' attempts to increase profits by gaming the US patent system. See Robbins and Stolberg (2023) on Gilead's alleged delay in releasing a promising HIV treatment that reduced such side effects as kidney and bone damage.

2. For accounts of the dispute and subsequent investigations, see Crewdson (1989); Gorman (1993); Hilts (1993); Epstein (1996); Weil and Arzbaecher (1996); Cohen and Enserink (2008).

3. ORI, part of the US Department of Health and Human Services, was created by the merger of two other agencies, one being OSI.

4. Has distrust of science actually increased in recent decades as theorists like Niklas Luhman seem to believe? Survey evidence suggests that although confidence in other institutions had fallen, confidence in science had remained quite stable (Smith and Son 2013). Confidence in science tends to be higher in "advanced" societies where education levels are high than in societies with less educated citizens (Gauchat 2012).

It also varies with political ideology; although conservatives and moderates have lost confidence in science, liberals have not (Gauchat 2012). See also Jasanoff (2017) on invocations of science to shore up trust.

5. See Fujimura and Chou's (1994) illuminating analysis of how Duesberg supported his argument by selecting, juxtaposing, and transforming other scientists' evidence in ways that felt inappropriate to them.

6. The AIDS self-empowerment movement (Callan and Turner 1997) and, somewhat later, the advent of community-based participatory research (Rhodes, Malow, and Jolly 2010) were important steps on the path to deeper involvement of people with HIV/AIDS in shaping both research and treatment programs.

7. In an attempt to demonstrate their openness to complementary and alternative therapies, practitioners sympathetic to Western medicine sometimes turned to a rule-guided approach, subjecting "traditional" cures to rudimentary clinical trials. The results uniformly showed traditional medicines to be ineffective against HIV, though it is not clear that traditional healers would have regarded these testing procedures as appropriate or dispositive. It bears noting that "traditional" therapies for HIV/AIDS do not have a long track record. Created specifically to treat HIV, these preparations were traditional only in the sense that they were developed by traditional healers, not in the sense that they had been part of some long-standing therapeutic tradition.

8. See, for example, the case of Nigerian children who died in Pfizer's 1996 meningitis drug trial (Shah 2003; Stephens 2006; McNeil 2011). Many anomalies have been uncovered in investigations of this study, which a Nigerian panel labeled "an illegal trial of an unregistered drug" and a "clear case of exploitation of the ignorant" (Stephens 2006). In the same hospital where Pfizer conducted this trial, Doctors Without Borders was offering a safe, effective antibiotic for meningitis. The families of children receiving Pfizer's drug seem not to have known that it was an experimental treatment. See also Kalb and Koehler (2002) on a variety of legal and ethical infractions in research.

9. Both graduate medical education and medical research are heavily subsidized in the US. Until recently, the US government was the major funder of biomedical research. According to Light and Lexchin (2012), "More than four-fifths of all funds for basic research to discover new drugs and vaccines come from public sources." But the government share of the research budget has declined over time because of decreases in government funding for research generally and increases in funds coming from corporations (particularly pharmaceutical companies and philanthropists). See Mervis (2017); Bluestone, Beier, and Glimcher (2018); Sargent (2022); Greenwood (2023). In addition, because R&D expenditures have grown faster in other countries, the US share of the global R&D budget also has declined (Sargent 2022).

10. But, unlike the child remarking on the emperor's new clothes, most people do not comment on this absence of evidence. Such politeness likely facilitates the proliferation of rules by reducing the threshold for claiming the legitimacy of a "best practice."

11. For instance, many researchers, including those who study regulation and those who are subject to it, argue that the regulation of human subjects research is heavy handed and often misdirected (Bledsoe et al. 2007; Heimer and Petty 2010; Babb 2020), even causing considerable harm by delaying or preventing important research (Schneider 2015; see also Whitney and Schneider 2011; Whitney 2016, 2023). That insiders are aware of the problems is suggested by reports from the Office of the Inspector General (DHHS 1998, 2000a, 2000b, 2000c) as well as testimony to the US House of Representatives (Yessian 1999).

12. Although it may be desirable to have all of these forms of accountability, Emanuel and Emanuel (1996) note the importance of insulating them from each other, for example, by ensuring that research centers do not insert economic considerations into the relationship between clinical researchers and their research subjects.

13. Robert Rafsky was the lead clinic in a CTU that included two other clinics. Lead clinics cannot fully control the actions of their subsites, and Robert Rafsky staff members often expressed frustration with their subsites.

14. At the time of this research, the AIDS Clinical Trials Group (ACTG) had thirty-four CTUs. Both Robert Rafsky and Bobbi Campbell Clinics worked through the ACTG. Philly Lutaaya Clinic worked with HIV Prevention Trials Network (HPTN).

15. The remainder assessed lost-to-follow-up rates; voluntary discontinuation rates; data management performance; monitoring of initial informed consent, entry criteria, clinical endpoint determination, and adequacy of source documentation; timeliness of SAE reporting and protocol registration; scientific contributions; laboratory shipments; and existence of a community advisory board.

16. Variants of this bind occur in many professions and have been noted in the work of street-level bureaucrats (Lipsky 2010), nurses (Chambliss 1996), pharmacists (Chiarello 2014), and teachers (Taylor 2007), to mention only a few. Although members of elite professions often have considerable discretion, recent changes in US law, and particularly abortion law, have eroded the discretion of physicians (Bardhi and Rizk 2022; Bazelon 2022; Heimer 2023).

17. Briefly, Good Clinical Practice (GCP) is an international quality standard that governs all research with human subjects. Its rules are intended to ensure that the data and reported results of clinical research are credible and accurate and that the rights, safety, and confidentiality of research participants have been protected.

18. Source documents are not always under the control of the research organization. For instance, if a research subject is hospitalized while enrolled in a study, researchers will need to get information about that episode from the hospital's records. This transfer of information is usually relatively straightforward in richer countries, but it can be problematic in poorer ones where transmitting information either electronically or by photocopy can be challenging.

19. Fujimura (1992, 169–70) discusses how "standardized packages"—"gray boxes" that combine several boundary objects—narrow and restrict how the objects are defined and used, enabling interaction and cooperative work among people from different social worlds. The "evidentiary packages" of clinical research are likewise gray boxes that combine data, conventions about collection and manipulation of data, and rules for assessing the appropriateness of what has been done.

20. In other settings where credibility is being assessed, reviewers look for inconsistencies either in accounts themselves or between accounts and publicly available information. See, e.g., Shiff (2021) on asylum applications and Rissing and Castilla (2016) on immigrant work authorizations.

21. Differences in training are acknowledged in several ways: titles (some medical staff in Uganda are "medical officers" rather than doctors), in desirability of advanced training (many Ugandan and South African physicians seek additional training in the UK or US), and in comments suggesting that US nurses' training is essentially comparable to training received by physicians in some other countries.

22. Often, training was of relatively short duration—a few days to get certified for some research-related task, a day tacked onto a professional conference, or even briefer sessions to learn project-specific routines and skills.

NOTES TO PAGES 190–207 › 339

23. When my team and I visited a TB clinic in South Africa, the head doctor gave a similar account of the impossibility of implementing training without appropriate resources. Nurses could not do the pap smears they had just been trained to perform, she noted, when the clinic had no examining tables, no way to ensure privacy in examining rooms, and either no speculums or only speculums that were the wrong size.

24. The monitors uncovered serious departures from GCP. Rather than terminating its relationship with the clinic, the pharmaceutical company sponsoring the research hired a full-time monitor to coach clinic staff and provide ongoing training to bring them up to speed (Heimer and Gazley 2012).

25. In this case, staff members had noted their failure to perform a required procedure and explained why performing the procedure had been impossible. They were annoyed that the monitor "dinged" them anyway.

26. "Notice of Initiation of Disqualification Proceedings and Opportunity to Explain: Daniel S. Berger, MD," DHHS, November 27, 2009, https://www.fda .gov/regulatory-information/electronic-reading-room/cder-notice-initiation -disqualification-proceeding-and-opportunity-explain-nidpoe-date-issued-10.

27. "Clinical Investigators—Disqualification Proceedings—Detail: Daniel S. Berger, MD," FDA, last updated May 5, 2020, https://www.accessdata.fda.gov/scripts/sda/ sdDetailNavigation.cfm?sd=clinicalinvestigatorsdisqualificationproceedings&id =CD5EDDB44C9EAA37E040A8C0754D57E1&rownum=19.

28. A similar use of sticky notes occurred in Thailand. The internal monitor noted that when he found errors he generally tried to get the person who made the mistake to correct it. He would return the CRF to the research nurse with a sticky note spelling out the needed corrections.

CHAPTER SIX

1. The two-drug regimen provided a short course of AZT coupled with a single dose of nevirapine at the onset of labor and a dose of nevirapine for the child shortly after birth. South Africa's single-dose regimen provided nevirapine but no AZT.

2. See Marseille et al. (1999); Sweat et al. (2004); Dao et al. (2007) on the efficacy and cost-effectiveness of various PMTCT regimens during this time period.

3. Participants in an EGPAF (Elizabeth Glaser Pediatric AIDS Foundation) users group meeting bluntly assessed government PMTCT programs as "not good in KwaZulu-Natal or generally in South Africa, actually overall a disaster." In their view, the KZN provincial government was "rule-bound and inefficient" but "improving and making a serious effort," while the national government was "throwing a monkey wrench in AIDS programs."

4. Although Gil Eyal's (2013a) important work has shifted how sociologists think about the relationship between professions and expertise, this chapter suggests that professions and the boundaries between them remain important, particularly when reinforced by law.

5. See Rosenbaum (2003) for an assessment of how the engagement between law and medicine has affected the US medical profession.

6. The 1984 Baby Doe Law aimed to prevent medical neglect of disabled newborns, a problem later shown not to exist, by mandating that states receiving federal funds for child abuse programs report on such medical neglect. Neonatologists worried that overzealous regulators had little understanding of the medical complexity of their work. See Heimer and Staffen (1998, 165–66).

7. At the time of this research, the UNAIDS guide to developing HIV/AIDS treatment guidelines provided a table that categorized evidence into six "levels" (UNAIDS 1999, 14). A second table explained the "grading" of recommendations and how their link to the "level" of the evidence, suggesting, for instance, that evidence from at least one randomized clinical trial would be required for a "Grade A recommendation" (UNAIDS 1999, 16). Guidelines then generally explain how they have ranked evidence and graded recommendations. See, e.g., WHO (2006, 8); DHHS (2008, 57).

8. Heimer, Petty, and Culyba (2005) review the literature on the use of guidelines as "shields" by practitioners and "swords" by plaintiffs and discuss guidelines as professional and organizational risk management.

9. The most recent US government guidelines are available at https://clinicalinfo .hiv.gov/en/guidelines (accessed July 14, 2024).

The most recent guidelines of WHO are available at https://www.who.int/publi cations/i/item/9789240031593 (accessed July 8, 2024). WHO also episodically issues amendments to elements of these consolidated guidelines.

IAS-USA develops treatment guidelines and offers educational programs. Its most recent guidelines, issued in 2022 and also published in *JAMA* (Gandhi et al. 2022), are available at https://www.iasusa.org/resources/guidelines/ (accessed July 8, 2024).

10. Current state testing guidelines and other state law governing HIV care can be found on the CDC website: https://www.cdc.gov/hiv/policies/law/states/index.html (last reviewed March 17, 2022).

11. This comment was made in an antenatal clinic staff meeting. Arguing that all hospital workers should get tested, he asked staff to raise their hands if they had been tested.

12. The clinic director noted the considerable anxiety of doctors and other clinic workers about forgoing pretest counseling even in healthcare settings. Among other things, they were uncertain about the legal status of testing regimens and worried about the possibility of being sued. But as Cameron explained, pretest counseling is not inscribed in law in South Africa. Pretest counseling was a policy of the Medical Council, with the courts following the Medical Council's recommendations. To change the policy—which the courts would then enforce—required only that the Medical Council reconvene and issue a new recommendation. Most HIV workers would not have had the benefit of Cameron's lucid explanation of the law.

13. This was discussed at length in a training session for Gugu Dlamini Clinic counselors.

14. Under VCT, 60–65% of women coming to Philly Lutaaya followed through with testing; virtually 100% tested under RCT. A study in rural Uganda suggested that testing was a key bottleneck and estimated that increased testing would reduce mother-to-child transmission more than increased availability of ART (Larsson et al. 2015).

15. See Grol-Prokopczyk (2013); Kojima et al. (2005) on Thailand's ethics guidelines for biomedical research.

16. For instance, the Ugandan Ministry of Health began to recommend triple therapy for PMTCT starting in 2012 (Namara-Lugolobi et al. 2022; Dirlikov et al. 2023). According to the CDC, Uganda now has 99% anti-retroviral coverage for pregnant women identified as having HIV (CDC 2024), well above the global average of 81% coverage for this group (USAID 2023).

17. In the US, there is also a corresponding, subterranean discussion about the toxicity of ART and attempts to evade physicians and state officials who may try to prevent an HIV positive mother from breastfeeding (Wolf et al. 2001).

18. In a lengthy interview, one pediatrician compared Gugu Dlamini's pediatric and adult treatment programs and discussed the urgency of codifying the practices of the pediatricians. The adult program was very protocol driven, while the pediatric treatment program "has got sort of vague protocols that we change all the time." Those extensive changes had been worked out over time as the team gained experience and adjusted to the particular problems of their patient population. Now they were hastily codifying their practices because both pediatricians were about to go on maternity leave. But she also worried that a more guideline-driven, collective program might mean losing the capacity to see patients repeatedly, track individual patients, and radically adjust to both medical and social circumstances. She also noted that the guidelines for adolescent HIV care were even further behind than pediatric guidelines because so few HIV-infected children had survived until adolescence.

19. At the time of my research, the Ugandan Ministry of Health was also considering allowing children to give consent for HIV testing at age twelve.

20. A study of cardiac units confirms this point. Majumdar et al. (2008) found that hospitals involved in clinical trials were more likely to use guidelines and had lower in-hospital mortality rates than hospitals that were not participating in clinical trials. In the research discussed in this book, a team member and I also found that clinics were changed by their clinical trials participation (Petty and Heimer 2011). Clinical trials participation changed skills, practices, and orientations, but it also modified clinics' material environments. Especially in poorer countries, the additional tools and supplies made all the difference in whether clinics could align their practice with the results of clinical trials.

21. On the contrast between schematic activity, where scripts attempt to radically reduce the need for thought, and deliberative activity, where scripting is intended more to channel than eliminate thought, see Dewey (1930); DiMaggio (1997); Heimer (2001, 2008); Sabel (2007); Weick and Sutcliffe (2007).

22. Responses to recent changes in US abortion law show how this process works (Heimer 2023; Press 2023). Press (2023) suggests that larger organizations such as Planned Parenthood are less willing than smaller, independent clinics to take legal risks.

CHAPTER SEVEN

1. Lusgarten (2005) cites estimates that 40% of clinical trial budgets is spent on recruitment of research subjects.

2. Consent forms are carefully scripted documents. IRB rules mandate inclusion of specific elements, often specifying exact language to be used. Revisions of consent forms are the most common revision requested by IRBs as projects go through initial reviews (Bell, Whiton, and Connelly 1998; Heimer and Petty 2010).

3. This is the phrase used, although some instructional documents remind clinic staff that they "seek consent from" rather than "consent" the research subjects.

4. See Gelsinger (2008); Milstein (2008). Paul Gelsinger (Jesse's father) contends that researchers downplayed risks and overstated potential benefits of the research. Robert Dingwall's (2001) insightful analysis of this case juxtaposes the competing narratives of federal and university regulators and argues that more elaborate rules are unlikely to help much in curbing misconduct in the quasi-economic enterprise of clinical trials.

5. This omission is particularly odd given that early research on heuristics and biases (such as Tversky and Kahneman 1974) often used medical examples. Moreover, this

research has received considerable popular attention, so it should be accessible to those crafting IRB rules.

6. The drug companies eventually relented. This episode and its contribution to creating a moral commitment to universal access receive more attention in chapter 9.

7. That the trials were fully blind may have made things somewhat easier for researchers. One research coordinator (not in my study sites) confided that "it would be sad to know that patients, people you like, are not getting medication—so it is better not to know."

8. Heimer and Staffen (1998) studied variability in mastery of medical matters among parents of hospitalized newborns, a similar problem.

9. Quotations from the legislation: United States Leadership against HIV/AIDS, Tuberculosis and Malaria Act of 2003, 22 U.S.C. §§ 7601(23), 7631e, 7631f, respectively. Moss and Kates (2022) review provisions of the PEPFAR reauthorizations, noting some loosening of the more restrictive provisions over time. The initial requirement that a third of prevention funds go to abstinence programs has been replaced with a requirement for "balanced programs" with mandated reporting. The anti-prostitution provisions were put in place in 2003 and have remained in all of the reauthorizations for funding through 2023.

10. Three issues raised by the anti-prostitution portion of the legislation have been discussed extensively: potential violations of recipient organizations' First Amendment rights (Middleberg 2006; Barnes 2013, 2020; Howe 2020); ambiguities in how anti-prostitution policies map onto potential actions of recipients (Middleberg 2006; CHANGE 2008); and conflicts between anti-prostitution policies and PEPFAR's policy of working with "key populations" (Beard 2018).

11. The reference is to ABC programs that urge abstinence (A), being faithful (B), and (as a fallback) using condoms (C).

12. Comparing the mid-1980s with the late 1980s, Hodgman reported "an increase in the mean age at death from 73 hours to 880 hours [or 37 days]" (1990, 2657; see also Heimer and Staffen 1998, 41).

13. The problem that harm seems to "come with the territory" of some activities is clearly not limited to medicine. Tradeoffs between costs and benefits may be particularly apparent in sports and other activities that place a premium on peak performances. Concussions, broken bones, long-term consequences of performance-enhancing drugs and supplements are old news in the world of sports. What is remarkable is only the capacity for denial. Illustrating a startling ability to ignore what has seemed obvious to many, the American NFL (National Football League) only in 2009 acknowledged that cognitive problems are vastly higher in former NFL players than in other groups—five times the national average for people over fifty and nineteen times the average rate for people aged thirty to forty-nine (Schwarz 2009; see also Kain 2009, comparing the NFL's denials with the tobacco industry's denial of a link between tobacco use and cancer; Greenhow and East 2015).

14. The alternatives are visual inspection, skinfold measurements done with calipers, BIA (bio-electrical impedance analysis), and full-body DEXA (dual energy X-ray absorptiometry) scans.

15. Over time, guidelines have recommended progressively earlier initiation of ART. HIV treatment guidelines initially pegged ART initiation to dropping CD4 counts, first setting the cut-off at a CD4 count of 200 (corresponding to the onset of full-blown AIDS). Because patients benefit from initiation of treatment before their immune

NOTES TO PAGES 252–272 › 343

systems are compromised by the virus, guidelines now recommend that ART begin as soon as possible after diagnosis regardless of viral load or CD4 count. In practice, because resources are scarce and patients come in only when they are quite ill, clinics in poorer countries have always started treatment later.

16. The conclusion in that case was that resistance did occur but disappeared over time (Eshleman and Jackson 2002).

17. Indeed, Horgan (1996) and some of the scientists he interviewed worried about a shortage of this key resource—uncertainty—on which scientific activity depends. Too little ignorance and uncertainty, they suggested, might lead to science focused on trivial refinements of existing theories.

18. One very common but underanalyzed example of willful ignorance maintained by strategic decompiling: double-blinding in clinical research.

19. In 2007, the end of the period of our clinic observations, 61% of the adults living with HIV in sub-Saharan Africa were women (UNAIDS 2007, 8). In 2021, women and girls accounted for 63% of all new HIV infections in sub-Saharan Africa (UNAIDS 2022a, 2).

20. By 2007, only 33% of pregnant women with HIV in low- and middle-income countries were receiving anti-retroviral medicines to prevent mother-to-child transmission of HIV (UNAIDS 2008, 15). This is an improvement over previous years, but it is unclear whether the women were receiving the cocktail of drugs (used in richer countries) or a single- or dual-drug regimen either toward the end of pregnancy or at delivery. By 2021, far more pregnant women were receiving ART—82% globally. Rates were particularly high (90%) in eastern and southern Africa, but lower (60%) in western and central Africa (UNAIDS 2022b, 55).

21. On infant feeding and HIV transmission, see Coovadia and Coutsoudis (2001); Heimer (2007, 567–69).

22. Both parts of this recommendation are hard to follow. In cultures where most mothers breastfeed, women who do not nurse their babies (e.g., after the recommended abrupt weaning) will be suspected of having HIV. In the first six months of exclusive breastfeeding, mothers may find it difficult to resist pressure to follow traditional practices that call for feeding small quantities of other foods, particularly when the baby is temporarily in the care of other family members.

CHAPTER EIGHT

1. For historical treatments of bioethics and ethics regulation, see Rothman (1991), De Vries, Dingwall, and Ofrali (2009); Evans (2011); Stark (2012); Babb (2020); Halpern (2004, 2021). For a review of scholarship on IRBs and the regulation of human subjects research, see Heimer and Petty (2010).

2. Subpart A is the Common Rule; subparts B, C, and D discuss additional protections for special groups such as pregnant women, fetuses, and neonates (B), prisoners (C), and children (D).

3. Discussions of morality and ethics in medicine can be found in the ethnographic work of Bosk (1992, 1999, 2003 [1979]); Fox and Swazey (1992); Zussman (1992); Anspach (1993); Chambliss (1996); Heimer and Staffen (1998); Wendland (2010); Kellogg (2011); and Timmermans and Buchbinder (2012), among others.

4. Patients or research subjects might have extras because they had missed some doses, been given extras to ensure that they did not run out before their next clinic visit, or had switched medications.

5. These definitions and rules focus on groups especially vulnerable to coercion (such as prisoners) or incapable of giving full informed consent (e.g., because of immaturity or cognitive impairments).

6. Ethicists have worried about "therapeutic misconception," the assumption of patients that clinical researchers share the therapeutic commitments of physicians when in fact their primary commitment is to the research protocol. As Stewart and Sewankambo (2010) note, the details of therapeutic misconceptions vary over time and place. Well-funded research clinics may be able to provide better care than other facilities even if the researchers' primary focus is not the welfare of the study subjects.

7. Krause's (2014) analysis of humanitarian projects finds a similar disjuncture between the articulated objective of helping those most in need and the organizational requirement to produce successful projects, which instead leads to helping those easiest to help.

8. Elliott (2008) writes of professional guinea pigs, who make their living by participating in medical research. His view is somewhat different than that of Fisher (2006). Her interviews and observations in contract research centers (CRC), where early stage studies establish drug safety, suggest that participants make savvy choices about which studies to participate in. Because they are required to live in the CRC, research subjects have ample opportunity to compare notes.

9. For an explanation of the elements of this rule, see "HIPAA for Professionals," DHHS, last reviewed July 10, 2024, https://www.hhs.gov/hipaa/for-professionals/index.html.

CHAPTER NINE

1. Law is often described as being a neutral set of tools that, in principle, can be used by anyone. At every turn, though, scholars find that people who are already well off are likely to come out ahead in legally mediated encounters. Lempert and Sanders (1986, 430–61) show how these advantages can originate in the crafting of legislation ("legal endowments") and cumulate over time as laws are implemented and then sometimes reassessed by judiciaries. See also Minow (1990).

2. Bortolotti (2010) makes similar claims about malaria policy. Likewise, only in 2018 did WHO recommend guidelines that would treat TB outbreaks in poor and rich countries the same way (*New York Times* 2018).

3. Obviously, there is no shortage of examples that do not align with this general trend. Moreover, these examples, both of gross abuses of patients and research subjects and of more mundane disparate treatment, are not just from the distant past.

4. For an update (September 2018) on changes in enforcement of this policy, see Jennifer Beard, "What's Up With PEPFAR's Anti-prostitution Pledge?," Public Health Post, September 5, 2018, https://www.publichealthpost.org/viewpoints/whats-up-with-pepfars-anti-prostitution-pledge/. According to the author, the policy is still on the books, but "for now, evidence seems to be winning the tug of war with ideology."

5. Recent innovations have facilitated adherence to treatment by reducing pill burdens (with fixed-dose combination pills), offering long-acting injectables, and changing formulations to reduce side effects. Equally important, HIV is becoming preventable because of the availability of preexposure prophylaxis (PrEP, for people at risk of infection) and because viral suppression (in people living with HIV) makes transmission to uninfected sexual partners extremely unlikely. A recent UNAIDS slogan—U=U—is attempting to spread the message that "undetectable equals untransmittable." See

"Undetectable Equals Untransmittable," UNAIDS, July 20, 2018, https://www.unaids.org/en/resources/presscentre/featurestories/2018/july/undetectable-untransmittable.

6. As HAART became the norm, it began to be referred to simply as ART. The distinction indicated by the first two letters of the abbreviation became less relevant as physicians stopped prescribing mono- and dual-therapy.

7. The program's goal was to put 3 million people on ART by 2005.

8. The 90-90-90 campaign's objective was for 90% of people living with HIV to know their HIV status, 90% of people diagnosed with HIV to receive ART, and 90% of those receiving ART to achieve viral suppression by 2020. The targets were later raised to 95-95-95 by 2030.

9. Over the years, advice about when to start ART has changed as evidence confirmed that starting therapy early brought significant therapeutic benefits. By now, the recommendation is to start ARVs as soon as possible after HIV diagnosis. Recent recommendations with explanations aimed at a lay audience can be found at "How HIV Treatment Works," Be in the Know, last updated October 16, 2023, https://www.beintheknow.org/living-hiv/hiv-treatment/how-hiv-treatment-works. See also "HIV Treatment: The Basics," HIVinfo.NIH.gov, last reviewed August 16, 2021, https://hivinfo.nih.gov/understanding-hiv/fact-sheets/hiv-treatment-basics. Formal US guidelines with the recommendation to start ART immediately can be found at "Clinical Guidelines," HIV.gov, accessed July 11, 2024, https://clinicalinfo.hiv.gov/en/guidelines. WHO guidelines with the same recommendation can be found at WHO, *Consolidated Guidelines on HIV Prevention, Testing, Treatment, Service Delivery and Monitoring: Recommendations for a Public Health Approach*, https://www.who.int/publications/i/item/9789240031593.

10. Discussing the role of activists in expanding access to healthcare, Harris (2017b) argues that progressive physicians played central roles in reforming Thailand's healthcare system.

11. In many poor countries, the local standard was, at best, nevirapine for the mother when labor began and a dose of nevirapine for the baby shortly after birth.

12. HIV researchers had hoped that "structured treatment interruptions" might economize on expensive medications and reduce side effects without adversely affecting health (Stecher al. 2016).

13. This is true for treatment of HIV-infected adults, but less true for treatment of other groups. Recommendations for PMTCT did differ somewhat from one country to the next. Also, the guidelines of resource-constrained countries have not always kept pace with the latest international recommendations that costly ART begin sooner.

14. It is not that IRBs believe in research ethics and researchers do not. Often researchers believe the spirit of the law requires something quite different, and perhaps more expansive, than what the IRB stipulates.

15. COBRA (the Consolidated Omnibus Budget Reconciliation Act of 1985) requires that employer-sponsored group health insurance plans offer US employees and their families a temporary extension of health insurance coverage when they lose their jobs or suffer certain other disruptive life events.

16. In 1995, for example, Saquinavir received FDA approval in just 97 days (Hilts 1995), "virtually a nanosecond on a typical drug approval timeline." See "First Protease Inhibitor Becomes Available," Health Resources and Services Administration, Ryan White HIV/AIDS Program, accessed July 11, 2024, https://ryanwhite.hrsa.gov/livinghistory/1995.

17. This is the language used by physicians and patients. The FDA instead uses the term "expanded access" for this carefully regulated pathway. See "Expanded Access," FDA, accessed July 11, 2024, https://www.fda.gov/news-events/public-health-focus/expanded-access.

18. Among the Thai accomplishments: bringing the first antitrust suit in which a patient—rather than another pharmaceutical company—was recognized as an aggrieved party (Harris 2017a, 137).

19. In 1998, forty-one pharmaceutical companies filed a suit against the South African government over amendments to the South African Medicines Act designed to make low-cost medicines more available. In 2001, as the case was progressing, ALP filed an *amicus* brief on behalf of TAC focusing on access to ARVs. A few months later, after international outcry, the pharmaceutical companies dropped their suit. See Swarns (2001); Fisher and Rigamonti (2005); Heywood (2009); 't Hoen et al. (2011).

20. The International AIDS Society also organizes the IAS Conference on HIV Science and the HIV Research for Prevention Conference.

21. This action enraged even other pharmaceutical companies. GlaxoSmithKline threatened to sue because the Abbott anti-retroviral Norvir was a component in some regimens that included GSK drugs.

22. It was this dispute over compulsory licenses that inspired some Thai taxi drivers to refuse to take passengers to the US embassy in the summer of 2007.

23. Braithwaite (2004) discusses parallel opportunities for the weak to exert power at the level of nation-states. Noting that the magnitude of poor countries' debt means that, in effect, poor countries as a group own rich countries' banks, Braithwaite spells out what that means for the methods of power available to poorer countries.

24. One study being conducted at Robert Rafsky Clinic had paired a monitoring visit with every research visit, a situation the study's experienced and confident research nurse found humorous.

25. Details about this controversy have been omitted to conceal the clinic's identity.

26. The notable exception concerns requirements that treatment programs and clinical research use brand-name drugs produced by US-based pharmaceutical companies. (It was this provision that prohibited Cha-on Suesum's proposed use GPO-VIR in clinical trials.) But when PEPFAR required the use of brand-name drugs, the Congressional Budget Office (CBO) objected, pointing out that cheaper alternatives were available. Rules mandating the use of brand-name drugs were accompanied by elaborate claims about quality and safety, claims that failed to convince caregivers and researchers—and, as it turned out, the CBO.

ACKNOWLEDGMENTS

1. Chapter 7 is derived, in part, from Carol A. Heimer, "Inert Facts and the Illusion of Knowledge: Strategic Uses of Ignorance in HIV Clinics," *Economy and Society* 41, 1 (2012): 17–41, https://www.tandfonline.com/doi/full/10.1080/03085147.2011.637332.

2. Chapter 8 is derived, in part, from Carol A. Heimer, "'Wicked' Ethics: Compliance Work and the Practice of Ethics in HIV Research," *Social Science and Medicine* 98 (2013): 371–78, https://doi.org/10.1016/j.socscimed.2012.10.030.

3. Appendix A is derived, in part, from Carol A. Heimer, "What Is a Clinic: Relationships and the Practice of Organizational Ethnography," *Sociological Methods and Research* 48, 4 (2019): 763–800, https://doi.org/10.1177/0049124117746426.

References

Abbott, Kenneth W., Robert O. Keohane, Andrew Moravcsik, Anne-Marie Slaughter, and Duncan Snidal. 2000. "The Concept of Legalization." *International Organization* 54:401–19.

Abbott, Kenneth W., and Duncan Snidal. 2000. "Hard and Soft Law in International Governance." *International Organization* 54:421–56.

Abdool Karim, Quarraisha, and Salim S. Abdool Karim. 2002. "The Evolving HIV Epidemic in South Africa." *International Journal of Epidemiology* 31 (1): 37–40.

ACOG (American College of Obstetricians and Gynecologists). 2001. "ACOG Committee Opinion—Scheduled Cesarean Delivery and the Prevention of Vertical Transmission of HIV Infection." *International Journal of Gynecology and Obstetrics* 73 (3): 279–81. ACOG *Committee Opinion* No. 234 from 2020, reaffirming 2017 opinion. https://pubmed.ncbi.nlm.nih.gov/11424912/.

Alcorn, Keith. 2006. "70% Still on First Regimen after Three Years in Khayelitsha, but Lactic Acidosis a Major Challenge." *Aidsmap*, February 7, 2006. https://www.aidsmap.com/news/feb-2006/croi-70-still-first-regimen-after-three-years-khayelitsha-lactic-acidosis-major.

———. 2009. "d4T Dose Reduction Does Not Result in Poorer Treatment Outcomes in South African Patients." *Aidsmap*, September 4, 2009. https://www.aidsmap.com/news/sep-2009/d4t-dose-reduction-does-not-result-poorer-treatment-outcomes-south-african-patients.

AMA (American Medical Association). n.d. "AMA Principles of Medical Ethics." (Adopted June 1957; revised June 1980, June 2001.) Accessed July 13, 2024. https://code-medical-ethics.ama-assn.org/principles.

Andre, Judith. 2007. "Learning to Listen: Second-Order Moral Perception and the Work of Bioethics." In *The Ethics of Bioethics*, edited by Lisa A. Eckenwiler and Felicia G. Cohn, 220–28. Baltimore: Johns Hopkins University Press.

Angell, Marcia. 1997. "The Ethics of Clinical Research in the Third World." *New England Journal of Medicine* 337:847–49.

———. 2005. *The Truth About the Drug Companies: How They Deceive Us and What to Do About It*. New York: Random House.

Angotti, Nicole. 2010. "Working Outside of the Box: How HIV Counselors in Sub-Saharan Africa Adapt to Western HIV Testing Norms." *Social Science and Medicine* 71:986–93.

———. 2012. "Testing Differences: The Implementation of Western HIV Testing Norms in Sub-Saharan Africa." *Culture Health, and Sexuality* 14 (4): 365–78.

Annas, George J. 1989. "Health Law at the Turn of the Century: From White Dwarf to Red Giant." *University of Connecticut Law Review* 21:551–69.

Anspach, Renée R. 1993. *Deciding Who Lives: Fateful Choices in the Intensive Care Nursery*. Berkeley: University of California Press.

Attaran, Amir, Karen I. Barnes, Christopher Curtis, Umberto d'Alessandro, Caterina I. Fanello, Mary R. Galinski, Gilbert Kokwaro, Sornchai Looareesuwan, Michael Makanga, Theonest K. Mutabingwa, Ambrose Talisuna, Jean François Trape, and William M. Watkins. 2004. "WHO, the Global Fund, and Medical Malpractice in Malaria Treatment." *Lancet* 363 (January 17): 237–40.

Attewell, Paul. 1987. "The Deskilling Controversy." *Work and Occupations* 14 (3): 323–46.

Ayres, John D. 1994. "The Use and Abuse of Medical Practice Guidelines." *Journal of Legal Medicine* 15:421–43.

Babb, Sarah. 2020. *Regulating Human Research: IRBs from Peer Review to Compliance Bureaucracy*. Palo Alto, CA: Stanford University Press.

Baggaley, R., B. Hensen, O. Ajose, K. L. Grabbe, V. J. Wong, A. Schilsky, Y.-R. Lo, F. Lule, R. Granich, and J. Hargreaves. 2012. "From Caution to Urgency: The Evolution of HIV Testing and Counselling in Africa." *Bulletin of the World Health Organization* 90:652–658B.

Bardhi, Olgert, and Patrick E. Rizk. 2022. "The Future of Medical Abortion Care: An Internal Medicine Obligation." *Journal of General Internal Medicine* 37 (16): 4268–69.

Barnes, Robert. 2013. "Supreme Court Says Law Can't Dictate Anti-Abortion AIDS Groups' Speech." *Washington Post*, June 20, 2013.

———. 2020. "Supreme Court Again Reconsiders Requirements for Groups Fighting AIDS." *Washington Post*, May 5, 2020.

Barrett, Ronald, Christopher W. Kuzawa, Thomas McDade, and George J. Armelagos. 1998. "Emerging and Re-emerging Infectious Diseases: The Third Epidemiologic Transition." *Annual Review of Anthropology* 27:247–71.

Bartlett, John G., Bernard M. Branson, Kevin Fenton, Benjamin C. Hauschild, Veronica Miller, Kenneth H. Mayer. 2008. "Opt-Out Testing for Human Immunodeficiency Virus in the United States: Progress and Challenges." *Journal of the American Medical Association* 300 (8): 945–51.

Bartley, Tim. 2011. "Transnational Governance as the Layering of Rules: Intersections of Public and Private Standards." *Theoretical Inquiries in Law* 12:517–42.

Bayer, Ronald. 1991. "Public Health Policy and the AIDS Epidemic: An End to HIV Exceptionalism?" *New England Journal of Medicine* 324 (21): 1500–1504.

Bayer, Ronald, and Claire Edington. 2009. "HIV Testing, Human Rights, and Global AIDS Policy: Exceptionalism and Its Discontents." *Journal of Health Politics, Policy and Law* 34 (1): 301–23.

Bayer, Ronald, Morgan Philbin, and Robert H. Remien. 2017. "The End of Informed Consent for HIV Testing: Not with a Bang but a Whimper." *American Journal of Public Health* 207:1259–65.

Bazelon, Emily. 2022. "Risking Everything to Offer Abortions Across State Lines." *New York Times Magazine*, October 4, 2022.

BBC. 2006. "AIDS Experts Condemn SA Minister." BBC News, September 6, 2006. http://news.bbc.co.uk/go/pr/fr/-/2/hi/africa/5319680.stm.

Beard, Jennifer. 2018. "What's Up with PEPFAR's Anti-Prostitution Pledge?" Public Health Post. https://www.publichealthpost.org/viewpoints/whats-up-with-pepfars-anti-prostitution-pledge/.

Beauchamp, Tom L. 2011. "Informed Consent: Its History, Meaning, and Present Challenges." *Cambridge Quarterly of Healthcare Ethics* 20:513–23.

Becker, Howard S., Blanche Geer, Everett C. Hughes, and Anselm L. Strauss. 1961. *Boys in White: Student Culture in Medical School*. Chicago: University of Chicago Press.

Bell, James, John Whiton, and Sharon Connelly. 1998. *Evaluation of NIH Implementation of Section 491 of the Public Health Service Act, Mandating a Program of Protection for Research Subjects*. Prepared for the Office of Extramural Research National Institutes of Health.

Benatar, Solomon R. 2002. "Reflections and Recommendations on Research Ethics in Developing Countries." *Social Science and Medicine* 54:1131–41.

———. 2015. "Health in Low-Income Countries." In *International Encyclopedia of the Social and Behavioral Sciences*, 2nd ed., 10:633–39. http://dx.doi.org/10.1016/B978-0-08-097086-8.64019-9.

Bendavid, Eran, Margaret L. Brandeau, Robin Wood, and Douglas K. Owens. 2010. "Comparative Effectiveness of HIV Testing and Treatment in Highly Endemic Regions." *Archives of Internal Medicine* 170 (15): 1347–54.

Berlinguer, Giovanni. 2004. "Bioethics, Health and Inequality." *Lancet* 36 (4): 1086–91.

Berwick, Donald M., and Andrew D. Hackbarth. 2012. "Eliminating Waste in US Health Care." *JAMA* 307 (14): 1513–16.

Best, Rachel Kahn. 2019. *Common Enemies: Disease Campaigns in America*. New York: Oxford University Press.

Biehl, João. 2009. "The Brazilian Response to AIDS and the Pharmaceuticalization of Global Health." In *Anthropology and Public Health: Bridging Differences in Culture and Society*, 2nd ed., edited by Robert A. Hahn and Marcia C. Inhorn, 480–511. New York: Oxford University Press.

Black, Donald J. 1976. *The Behavior of Law*. New York: Academic Press.

Black, Julia. 2001. "Decentring Regulation: Understanding the Role of Regulation and Self Regulation in a 'Post-Regulatory' World." *Current Legal Problems* 54:103–46.

Blandy, Fran. 2006. "S.A. Govt. Under Fire at AIDS Conference." *Mail and Guardian*, August 19, 2006. https://mg.co.za/article /2006-08-19-sa-govt-under-fire-at-aids-conference/.

Bledsoe, Caroline H., Bruce Sherin, Adam G. Galinsky, Nathalia M. Headley, Carol A. Heimer, Erik Kjeldgaard, James Lindgren, Jon D. Miller, Michael E. Roloff, and David H. Uttal. 2007. "Regulating Creativity: Research and Survival in the IRB Iron Cage." *Northwestern University Law Review* 101 (2): 593–641.

Bluestone, Jeffrey A., David Beier, and Laurie H. Glimcher. 2018. "The NIH is in Danger of Losing Its Edge in Creating Biomedical Innovations." *Stat*, January 3, 2018. https://www.statnews.com/2018/01/03/nih-biomedical-research-funding/.

Boffey, Philip. 1985. "Reagan Defends Financing for AIDS." *New York Times*. September 19, 1985.

Bortolotti, Dan. 2010. *Hope in Hell: Inside the World of Doctors Without Borders*. Buffalo: Firefly Books.

Bosk, Charles L. 1992. *All God's Mistakes: Genetic Counseling in a Pediatric Hospital*. Chicago: University of Chicago Press.

————. 1999. "Professional Ethicist Available: Logical, Secular, Friendly." *Daedalus* 128 (4): 47–68.

————. 2003 (1979). *Forgive and Remember: Managing Medical Failure*, 2nd ed. Chicago: University of Chicago Press.

————. 2023. "The Price of Perfection: The Cost of Error." *Sociological Forum* 38 (4): 1497–1506.

Boyd, Gerald M. 1987. "Reagan Urges Abstinence for Young to Avoid AIDS." *New York Times*, April 2, 1987.

Braithwaite, John. 2004 "Methods of Power for Development: Weapons of the Weak, Weapons of the Strong." *Michigan Journal of International Law* 26 (1): 297–330.

Braithwaite, John, and Peter Drahos. 2000. *Global Business Regulation*. Cambridge, UK: Cambridge University Press.

Branson, Bernard. 2007. "Current HIV Epidemiology and Revised Recommendations for HIV Testing in Health-Care Settings." *Journal of Medical Virology* 79, suppl. 1: S6–10.

Braverman, Harry. 1974. *Labor and Monopoly Capital: The Degradation of Work in the Twentieth Century*. New York: Monthly Review Press.

Brier, Jennifer. 2009. *Infectious Ideas: US Political Responses to the AIDS Crisis*. Chapel Hill: University of North Carolina Press.

Brodkin, Evelyn Z. 2012. "Reflections on Street-Level Bureaucracy: Past, Present, and Future." *Public Administration Review* 72 (6): 940–49.

Brown, Phil, Stephen Zavestoski, Sabrina McCormick, Brian Mayer, Rachel Morello-Frosch, and Rebecca Gasior Altman. 2004. "Embodied Health Movements: New Approaches to Social Movements in Health." *Sociology of Health and Illness* 26 (1): 50–80.

Brown, Theodore M., and Elizabeth Fee. 2014. "Social Movements in Health." *Annual Review of Public Health* 35:385–98.

Brown, Theresa, and Stephen Bergman. 2019. "Doctors, Nurses, and the Paperwork Crisis That Could Unite Them." *New York Times*, December 31, 2019.

Brubaker, Rogers. 1984. *The Limits of Rationality: An Essay on the Social and Moral Thought of Max Weber*. London: Routledge.

Burris, Scott, and Jen Welsh. 2007. "Regulatory Paradox: A Review of Enforcement Letters Issued by the Office for Human Research Protection." *Northwestern University Law Review* 101:643–85.

Cabana, Michael D., Cynthia S. Rand, Neil R. Powe, Albert W. Wu, Modena H. Wilson, Paul-André C. Abboud, and Haya R. Rubin. 1999. "Why Don't Physicians Follow Clinical Practice Guidelines? A Framework for Improvement." *Journal of the American Medical Association* 282 (15): 1458–65.

Callaghan, Mike, Nathan Ford, and Helen Schneider. 2010. "A Systematic Review of Task- Shifting for HIV Treatment and Care in Africa." *Human Resources for Health* 8 (1): 8. http://www.human-resources-health.com/content/8/1/8.

Callahan, Patricia. 2010. "FDA Won't Disqualify HIV Doctor Dr. Daniel Berger from Drug Studies." *Chicago Tribune*, September 9, 2010.

Callan, Michael, and Dan Turner. 1997. "A History of the People with AIDS Self-Empowerment Movement." *TheBody*. https://www.thebody.com/article/a-history-of-the-people-with-aids-self-empowerment.

Cameron, Edwin. 2005. *Witness to AIDS*. London: I. B. Tauris.

————. 2007. "Normalizing Testing—Normalizing AIDS." *Theoria* 54 (112): 99–108.

Canales, Rodrigo. 2011. "Rule Bending, Sociological Citizenship, and Organizational Contestation in Microfinance." *Regulation and Governance* 5:90–117.

Carlson, Robert V., Kenneth M. Boyd, and David J. Webb. 2004. "The Revision of the Declaration of Helsinki: Past, Present, and Future." *British Journal of Clinical Pharmacology* 57 (6): 695–713.

Carpenter, Daniel. 2010. *Reputation and Power: Organizational Image and Pharmaceutical Regulation at the FDA.* Princeton, NJ: Princeton University Press.

Carpenter, Daniel, Michael Chernew, Dean G. Smith, and A. Mark Fendrick. 2003. "Approval Times for New Drugs: Does the Source of Funding for FDA Staff Matter?" *Health Affairs* 22, suppl. 1 (web exclusive). https://doi.org/10.1377/hlthaff.W3.618.

Carvalho, Simon, and Mark Zacher. 2001. "The International Health Regulations in Historical Perspective." In *Plagues and Politics: Infectious Disease and International Policy,* edited by Andrew T. Price-Smith, 235–61. New York: Palgrave Macmillan.

CDC (Centers for Disease Control and Prevention). 1988. "Perspectives in Disease Prevention and Health Promotion Update/Universal Precautions for Prevention of Transmission of Human Immunodeficiency Virus, Hepatitis B Virus, and Other Bloodborne Pathogens in Health-Care Settings." *Morbidity and Mortality Weekly Report* 37 (24): 377–88. http://www.cdc.gov/mmwr/preview/mmwrhtml/00000039.htm.

———. 2006. *Revised Recommendations for HIV Testing of Adults, Adolescents and Pregnant Women in Health-Care Settings. Morbidity and Mortality Weekly Report* 55 (RR-14): 1–17. http://www.cdc.gov/mmwr/pdf/rr/rr5514.pdf.

———. 2024. "Uganda Reduces Rates of Mother-to-Child Transmission of HIV." https://www.cdc.gov/global-hiv-tb/php/success-stories/uganda-pmtct.html.

Chalmers, Iain, Kay Dickersin, and Thomas C. Chalmers. 1992. "Getting to Grips with Archie Cochrane's Agenda." *British Medical Journal* 305:786–88.

Chalmers, Iain, Larry V. Hedges, and Harris Cooper. 2002. "A Brief History of Research Synthesis." *Evaluation and the Health Professions* 25 (1): 12–37.

Chambliss, Daniel F. 1996. *Beyond Caring: Hospitals, Nurses, and the Social Organization of Ethics.* Chicago: University of Chicago Press.

CHANGE (Center for Health and Gender Equity). 2008. "Implications of US Policy Restrictions for HIV Programs Aimed at Commercial Sex Workers." Archived at the Wayback Machine, https://web.archive.org/web/20110531140512/http://www.genderhealth.org/files/uploads/change/publications/aplobrief.pdf.

Chiarello, Elizabeth. 2014. "Medical Versus Fiscal Gatekeeping: Navigating Professional Contingencies at the Pharmacy Counter." *Journal of Law and Medical Ethics* 42 (4): 518–34.

Chigwedere, Pride, George R. Seage III, Sofia Gruskin, Tun-Hou Lee, and M. Essex. 2008. "Estimating the Lost Benefits of Antiretroviral Drug Use in South Africa." *Journal of Acquired Immune Deficiency Syndrome* 49 (4): 410–15.

Chorev, Nitsan, and Andrew Schrank. 2017. "Professionals and Professions in the Global South: An Introduction." *Sociology of Development* 3 (3): 197–210.

Christakis, Nicholas A. 1992. "Ethics Are Local: Engaging Cross-Cultural Variation in the Ethics for Clinical Research." *Social Science and Medicine* 35:1079–91.

Churchill, Larry R., and David Schenck. 2005. "One Cheer for Bioethics: Engaging the Moral Experiences of Patients and Practitioners Beyond the Big Decisions." *Cambridge Quarterly of Healthcare Ethics* 14:389–403.

Clayden, Polly. 2008. "The Estimated Cost of Switching from d4T to TDF in South Africa." *i-Base.* https://i-base.info/htb/750.

Cochrane, Archie L. 1972. *Effectiveness and Efficiency: Random Reflections on Health Services*. London: Nuffield Hospitals Trust.

Cockerham, Geoffrey B., and William C. Cockerham. 2010. *Health and Globalization*. Malden, MA: Polity Press.

Cohen, Jon. 1991. "John Crewdson: Science Journalist as Investigator." *Science* 254 (5034): 946–49.

———. 1994. "The Duesberg Phenomenon." *Science* 266 (5191): 1642–44.

Cohen, Jon, and Martin Enserink. 2008. "HIV, HPV Scientists Honored, But One Scientist Is Left Out." *Science* 322 (5899) (October 10): 174–75.

Cohen, Michael D., and P. Brian Hilligoss. 2010. "The Published Literature on Handoffs in Hospitals: Deficiencies Identified in an Extensive Review." *Quality and Safety in Healthcare* 19:493–97.

Cohen, Michael D., James G. March, and Johan P. Olsen. 1972. "A Garbage Can Model of Organizational Choice." *Administrative Science Quarterly* 17:1–25.

Collins, Chris, Thomas Coates, and Greg Szekeres. 2008. "Accountability in the Global Response to HIV: Measuring Progress, Driving Change." *AIDS* 22, suppl. 2: S105–11.

Collins, H. M. 1974. "The TEA Set: Tacit Knowledge and Scientific Networks." *Science Studies* 4 (2): 165–86.

———. 2001. "Tacit Knowledge, Trust and the Q of Sapphire." *Social Studies of Science* 31 (1): 71–85.

Coovadia, Hoosen M., and Anna Coutsoudis. 2001 "Problems and Advances in Reducing Transmission of HIV-1 Through Breast-Feeding in Developing Countries." *AIDScience* 1 (4). http://aidscience.org/Articles/aidscience004.asp.

Coronini-Cronberg, Sophie, Wongsa Laohasiriwong, and Christian A. Gericke. 2007. "Health Care Utilisation Under the 30-Baht Scheme Among the Urban Poor in Mitrapap Slum, Khon Kaen, Thailand: A Cross-Sectional Study." *International Journal for Equity in Health* 6:11. http://www.equityhealthj.com/content/6/1/11.

Coslovsky, Salo V. 2011. "Relational Regulation in the Brazilian Ministério Publico: The Organizational Basis of Regulatory Responsiveness." *Regulation and Governance* 5:70–89.

Coyne, Richard. 2005. "Wicked Problems Revisited." *Design Studies* 26:5–17.

Crane, Johanna Tayloe. 2013. *Scrambling for Africa: AIDS, Expertise, and the Rise of American Global Health Science*. Ithaca, NY: Cornell University Press.

Crewdson, John. 1989. "The Great AIDS Quest." *Chicago Tribune*, November 19, 1989.

Cubanski, Juliette, Tricia Newman, Sarah True, and Meredith Freed. 2019. "What's the Latest on Medicare Drug Price Negotiations?" Kaiser Family Foundation. http://www.kff.org/medicare/issue-brief/whats-the-latest-on-medicare-drug-price-negotiations/.

Curran, William J., and E. Donald Shapiro. 1970. *Law, Medicine, and Forensic Science*, 2nd ed. Boston: Little, Brown.

Dao, Halima, Lynne M. Mofenson, Rene Ekpini, Charles F. Gilks, Matthew Barnhart, Omotayo Bolu, and Nathan Shaffer. 2007. "International Recommendations on Antiretroviral Drugs for Treatment of HIV-Infected Women and Prevention of Mother-to-Child HIV Transmission in Resource-Limited Settings: 2006 Update." *American Journal of Obstetrics and Gynecology* (Supplement to September 2007): S42–55.

Darrow, William. 2021. "The First 40 Years of AIDS: Promising Programs, Limited Success." *AIDS and Behavior* 25:3449–71.

Dauber, Kenneth. 1995. "Bureaucratizing the Ethnographer's Magic." *Current Anthropology* 36:75–95.

Davis, David A., and Anne Taylor-Vaisey. 1997. "Translating Guidelines into Practice: A Systematic Review of Theoretic Concepts, Practical Experience and Research Evidence in the Adoption of Clinical Practice Guidelines." *Canadian Medical Association Journal* 157:408–16.

Decoteau, Claire Laurier. 2013. *Ancestors and Antiretrovirals: The Biopolitics of HIV/AIDS in Post-Apartheid South Africa*. Chicago: University of Chicago Press.

DeParle, Jason. 2006. "District of Columbia Urges Routine H.I.V. Testing." *New York Times*, June 25, 2006.

Department of Health, South Africa. 2002. "Circular Minute on Prevention of Mother-to-Child Transmission of HIV." Western Cape Government, April 16, 2002. https://www.westerncape.gov.za/text/2003/circular_minute_prevention_mtc_hiv.pdf.

———. 2005. *Guidelines for the Management of HIV-Infected Children*. Archived at the Wayback Machine, https://web.archive.org/web/20060923110107/http://www.doh.gov.za/docs/factsheets/guidelines/hiv/index.html.

———. 2008a. "Prevention of Mother to Child Transmission of HIV." January 25, 2008. Archived at the Wayback Machine, https://web.archive.org/web/20130509144403/http://www.doh.gov.za/docs/pr/2008/pro125.html.

———. 2008b. *Policy and Guidelines for the Implementation of the PMTCT Programme*. February 11, 2008. Archived at the Wayback Machine, https://web.archive.org/web/20080908120144/www.doh.gov.za/docs/policy/pmtct-f.html. [Pages not numbered, so count starts with title page.]

Department of Health and Human Services, Office of Inspector General. 1998. Institutional Review Boards: A Time for Reform. Washington, DC: Department of Health and Human Services, Office of Inspector General. Publication OEI-01-97-00193.

———. Department of Health and Human Services, Office of Inspector General. 2000a. Protecting Human Research Subjects: Status of Recommendations. Washington, DC: Department of Health and Human Services, Office of Inspector General. Publication OEI-01-97-00197.

———. Department of Health and Human Services, Office of Inspector General. 2000b. FDA Oversight of Clinical Investigators. Washington, DC: Department of Health and Human Services, Office of Inspector General. Publication OEI-05-99-00350.

———. Department of Health and Human Services, Office of Inspector General. 2000c. Recruiting Human Subjects: Pressures in Industry-Sponsored Clinical Research. Washington, DC: Department of Health and Human Services, Office of Inspector General. Publication OEI-01-97-00195.

Desakorn, Varunee, Biraj Man Karmacharya, Vipa Thanachartwet, Nyan Lin Kyaw, Somsit Tansuphaswadiku, Duangjai Sahassananda, Jittima Dhitavat, Wirach Maek-a-nantawat, and Punnee Pitisuttithum. 2011. "Effectiveness of Fixed-Dose Combination Stavudine, Lamivudine and Nevirapine (GPO-VIR) for Treatment of Naïve HIV Patients in Thailand: A 3-Year Follow-Up." *Southeast Asian Journal of Tropical Medicine and Public Health* 42 (6): 1414–22.

Detels, R., L. Jacobson, L. Margolick, O. Martinez-Maza, A. Muñoz, J. Phair, C. Rinaldo, and S. Wolinsky. 2012. "The Multicenter AIDS Cohort Study, 1983 to . . ." *Public Health* 126 (3): 196–98.

De Vries, Raymond, Robert Dingwall, and Kristina Orfali. 2009. "The Moral Organization of the Professions: Bioethics in the United States and France." *Current Sociology* 57:555–79.

Dewey, John. 1930. *Human Nature and Conduct*. New York: Henry Holt.

Dezalay, Yves, and Bryant Garth. 1996. *Dealing in Virtue: International Commercial Arbitration and the Construction of a Transnational Legal Order*. Chicago: University of Chicago Press.

———. 2002. *The Internationalization of Palace Wars: Lawyers, Economists, and the Contest to Transform Latin American States*. Chicago: University of Chicago Press.

———. 2010. *Asian Legal Revivals: Lawyers in the Shadow of Empire*. Chicago: University of Chicago Press.

DHHS (US Department of Health and Human Services), Panel on Treatment of HIV-Infected Women and Prevention of Perinatal Transmission. 2007. *Public Health Service Task Force Recommendations for Use of Antiretroviral Drugs in Pregnant HIV-Infected Women for Maternal Health* and *Interventions to Reduce Perinatal HIV Transmission in the United States*. November 2, 2007; pp. iv, 96. https://clinicalinfo.hiv.gov/sites/default/files/guidelines/archive/PerinatalGL02112007901.pdf.

———. Panel on Antiretroviral Guidelines for Adults and Adolescents. 2008. *Guidelines for the Use of Antiretroviral Agents in HIV-1 Infected Adults and Adolescents*. January 29, 2008, 1–128. Archived at the Wayback Machine, https://web.archive.org/web/20060410113146/http://www.aidsinfo.nih.gov/ContentFiles/AdultandAdolescentGL.pdf.

Dietrich, John W. 2007. "The Politics of PEPFAR: The President's Emergency Plan for AIDS Relief." *Ethics and International Affairs* 21 (3): 277–92.

DiMaggio, Paul. 1997. "Culture and Cognition." *Annual Review of Sociology* 23:263–87.

DiMaggio, Paul J., and Walter W. Powell, eds. 1991. *The New Institutionalism in Organizational Analysis*. Chicago: University of Chicago Press.

Dingwall, Robert. 2001. "Scientific Misconduct as Organisational Deviance." *Zeitschrift für Rechtssoziologie* 22 (2): 245–58.

Dirlikov, Emilio, Joseph Kamoga, Stella Alamo Talisuna, Jennifer Namusobya, Daniel E. Kasozi, Juliet Akao, Estella Birabwa, Jennifer A. Ward, Bill Elur, Ray W. Shiraishi, Carl Corcoran, Vamsi Vasireddy, Richard Nelson, Lisa J. Nelson, Mary Borgman, Eleanor Namusoke Magongo, Linda Nabitaka Kisaakye, Cordelia Katureebe, Wilford Kirungi, Joshua Musinguzi, and PEPFAR Uganda. 2023. "Scale-Up of HIV Antiretroviral Therapy and Estimation of Averted Infections and HIV-Related Deaths—Uganda, 2004–2022." *Morbidity and Mortality Weekly Report* 72 (4): 90–94.

Djulbegovic, Benjamin, and Gordon H. Guyatt. 2017. "Progress in Evidence-Based Medicine: A Quarter Century On." *Lancet* 390:415–23.

Dobbin, Frank, Beth Simmons, and Geoffrey Garrett. 2007. "The Global Diffusion of Public Policies: Social Construction, Coercion, Competition, or Learning?" *Annual Review of Sociology* 33:449–72.

Doing, Park. 2004. "'Lab Hands' and the 'Scarlet O': Epistemic Politics and (Scientific) Labor." *Social Studies of Science* 34 (3): 299–323.

———. 2009. *Velvet Revolution at the Synchrotron: Biology, Physics and Change in Science*. Cambridge, MA: MIT Press.

Douglas, Mary. 1986. *How Institutions Think*. Syracuse, NY: Syracuse University Press.

Duesberg, Peter. 1989. "Human Immunodeficiency Virus and Acquired Immunodeficiency Syndrome: Correlation But Not Causation." *Proceedings of the National Academy of Sciences* 86:755–64.

———. 1998. *Inventing the AIDS Virus*. Washington, DC: Regnery.

Dugger, Celia W. 2008a. "Rift over AIDS Treatment Lingers in South Africa." *New York Times*, March 9, 2008.

———. 2008b. "Study Cites Toll of AIDS Policy in South Africa." *New York Times*, November 26, 2008.

Easter, Michele M., Gail E. Henderson, Arlene M. Davis, Larry R. Churchill, and Nancy M. P. King. 2006. "The Many Meanings of Care in Clinical Research." *Sociology of Health and Illness* 28:695–712.

Eba, Patrick M. 2015. "HIV-Specific Legislation in Sub-Saharan Africa: A Comprehensive Human Rights Analysis." *African Human Rights Law Journal* 15:224–62.

Eddy, David M. 1996. *Clinical Decision Making: From Theory to Practice*. Sudbury, MA: Jones and Bartlett.

———. 2005. "Evidence-Based Medicine: A Unified Approach." *Health Affairs* 24 (1): 9–17.

———. 2011. "The Origins of Evidence-Based Medicine—A Personal Perspective." *American Medical Association Journal of Ethics* 13 (1): 55–60.

Edelman, Lauren B. 2016. *Working Law: Courts, Corporations, and Symbolic Civil Rights*. Chicago: University of Chicago Press.

Edelman, Lauren B., Linda H. Krieger, Scott R. Eliason, Catherine R. Albiston, and Virginia Mellema. 2011. "When Organizations Rule: Judicial Deference to Institutionalized Employment Structures." *American Journal of Sociology* 117:888–954.

Edelman, Lauren B., and Mark C. Suchman. 1999. "When the 'Haves' Hold Court: Speculations on the Organizational Internalization of Law." *Law and Society Review* 33 (4): 941–91.

Eimer, Thomas, and Susanne Lütz. 2010. "Developmental States, Civil Society, and Public Health: Patent Regulation for HIV/AIDS Pharmaceuticals in India and Brazil." *Regulation and Governance* 4:135–53.

Elliott, Carl. 2007. "The Tyranny of Expertise." In *The Ethics of Bioethics: Mapping the Moral Landscape*, edited by Lisa A. Eckenwiler and Felicia G. Cohn, 43–46. Baltimore: Johns Hopkins University Press.

———. 2008. "Guinea-Pigging." *New Yorker*, January 7, 2008, 36–41.

Emanuel, Ezekiel J., Robert A. Crouch, John D. Arras, Jonathan D. Moreno, and Christine Grady, eds. 2003. *Ethical and Regulatory Aspects of Clinical Research*. Baltimore: Johns Hopkins University Press.

Emanuel, Ezekiel J., and Linda L. Emanuel. 1996. "What Is Accountability in Health Care?" *Annals of Internal Medicine* 124:229–39.

Emanuel, Ezekiel J., David Wendler, and Christine Grady. 2000. "What Makes Clinical Research Ethical?" *Journal of the American Medical Association* 283 (20): 2701–11.

Engel, Jonathan. 2006. *The Epidemic: A Global History of AIDS*. New York: Smithsonian Books and HarperCollins.

Englund, Harri. 2006. *Prisoners of Freedom: Human Rights and the African Poor*. Berkeley: University of California Press.

Epstein, Steven. 1996. *Impure Science: AIDS, Activism, and the Politics of Knowledge*. Berkeley: University of California Press.

———. 2007. *Inclusion: The Politics of Difference in Medical Research*. Chicago: University of Chicago Press.

———. 2016. "The Politics of Health Mobilization in the United States: The Promise and Pitfalls of 'Disease Constituencies.'" *Social Science and Medicine* 165:246–54.

Eshleman, S. H., and J. B. Jackson. 2002. "Nevirapine Resistance After Single Dose Prophylaxis." *AIDS Reviews* 4:59–63.

Eskridge, William N., Jr., and John Ferejohn. 2010. *A Republic of Statutes: The New American Constitution*. New Haven, CT: Yale University Press.

Espeland, Wendy Nelson, and Michael Sauder. 2009. "Rankings and Reactivity: How Public Measures Recreate Social Worlds." *American Journal of Sociology* 113:1–40.

———. 2016. *Engines of Anxiety: Academic Rankings, Reputation, and Accountability*. New York: Russell Sage Foundation.

Espeland, Wendy Nelson, and Berit Irene Vannebo. 2007. "Accountability, Quantification, and Law." *Annual Review of Law and Social Science* 3:21–43.

Evans, David. 2009. "MACS Turns 25: The Influential HIV Study Continues." POZ: Health, Life, and HIV, May 12, 2009. http://www.poz.com/articles/hiv_macs _anniversary_401_16589.shtml.

Evans, John H. 2011. *The History and Future of Bioethics: A Sociological View*. New York: Oxford University Press.

Evans, Peter. 2004. "Development as Institutional Change: The Pitfalls of Monocropping and the Potentials of Deliberation." *Studies in Comparative International Development* 38 (4): 30–52.

Evidence-Based Medicine Working Group. 1992. "Evidence-Based Medicine: A New Approach to Teaching the Practice of Medicine." *Journal of the American Medical Association* 268 (17): 2420–25.

Ewick, Patricia, and Susan S. Silbey. 1998. *The Common Place of Law: Stories from Everyday Life*. Chicago: University of Chicago Press.

Eyal, Gil. 2013a. "For a Sociology of Expertise: The Social Origins of the Autism Epidemic." *American Journal of Sociology* 118 (4): 863–907.

———. 2013b. "Spaces Between Fields." In *Bourdieu and Historical Analysis*, edited by Philip S. Gorski, 158–82. Durham, NC: Duke University Press.

Fassin, Didier. 2007. *When Bodies Remember: Experiences and Politics of AIDS in South Africa*. Berkeley: University of California Press.

———. 2008. "The Elementary Forms of Care: An Empirical Approach to Ethics in a South African Hospital." *Social Science and Medicine* 67:262–70.

Feldman, Martha S. 1989. *Order Without Design: Information Production and Policy Making*. Stanford, CA: Stanford University Press.

Feldman, Martha S., and James G. March. 1981. "Information in Organizations as Signal and Symbol." *Administrative Science Quarterly* 26:171–86.

Feldman, Martha S., and Brian T. Pentland. 2003. "Reconceptualizing Organizational Routines as a Source of Flexibility and Change." *Administrative Science Quarterly* 48 (1): 94–118.

Ferejohn, John. 2012. Review of *Reputation and Power: Organizational Image and Pharmaceutical Regulation at the FDA*, by Daniel Carpenter. *Perspectives on Politics* 10 (3): 797–800.

Ferguson, Kristi J., Howard Waitzkin, Susan E. Beekmann, and Bradley N. Doebbeling. 2004. "Critical Incidents of Nonadherence with Standard Precautions Guidelines

Among Community-Based Health Care Workers." *Journal of General Internal Medicine* 19:726–31.

Fidler, David P. 2001. "The Globalization of Public Health: The First 100 Years of International Health Diplomacy." *Bulletin of the World Health Organization* 79 (9): 842–49.

———. 2004. *SARS, Governance and the Globalization of Disease.* New York: Palgrave Macmillan.

Fincher-Mergi, Melissa, Kathy Jo Cartone, Jean Mischler, Patricia Pasieka, E. Brooke Lerner, and Anthony J. Billittier IV. 2002. "Assessment of Emergency Department Healthcare Professionals' Behaviors Regarding HIV Testing and Referral for Patients with STDs." *AIDS Patient Care STDs* 16 (11): 549–53.

Fisher, Jill A. 2006. "Co-ordinating 'Ethical' Clinical Trials: The Role of Research Coordinators in the Contract Research Industry." *Sociology of Health and Illness* 28:678–94.

———. 2009. *Medical Research for Hire: The Political Economy of Pharmaceutical Clinical Trials.* New Brunswick, NJ: Rutgers University Press.

———. 2020. *Adverse Events: Race, Inequality, and the Testing of New Pharmaceutical Products.* New York: New York University Press.

Fisher, William W., III, and Cyrill P. Rigamonti. 2005. "The South Africa AIDS Controversy: A Case Study in Patent Law and Policy." Harvard Law School. https://cyber.harvard.edu/people/tfisher/South%20Africa.pdf.

Flood, Ann Barry, and Mary L. Fennell. 1995. "Through the Lenses of Organizational Sociology: The Role of Organizational Theory and Research in Conceptualizing and Examining Our Health Care System." *Journal of Health and Social Behavior* 35:154–69.

Ford, Nathan, David Wilson, Onanong Bunjumnong, and Tido von Schoen Angerer. 2004. "The Role of Civil Society in Protecting Public Health over Commercial Interests: Lessons from Thailand." *Lancet* 363:560–63.

Fox, Renée C., and Judith P. Swazey. 1992. *Spare Parts: Organ Replacement in American Society.* New York: Oxford University Press.

———. 2005. "Examining American Bioethics: Its Problems and Prospects." *Cambridge Quarterly of Healthcare Ethics* 14:361–73.

Freese, Jeremy, and David Peterson. 2017. "Replication in Social Science." *Annual Review of Sociology* 43:147–65.

Fujimura, Joan H. 1992. "Crafting Science: Standardized Packages, Boundary Objects, and Translation." In *Science as Practice and Culture,* edited by Andrew Pickering, 168–211. Chicago: University of Chicago Press.

Fujimura, Joan H., and Danny Y. Chou. 1994. "Dissent in Science: Styles of Scientific Practice and the Controversy over the Cause of AIDS." *Social Science and Medicine* 38 (8): 1017–36.

Galanter, Marc. 1974. "Why the 'Haves' Come Out Ahead: Speculations on the Limits of Legal Change." *Law and Society Review* 9 (1): 95–160.

Gandhi, Rajesh T., Roger J. Bedimo, Jennifer Hoy, Raphael J. Landovitz, Davey M. Smith, Ellen F. Eaton, Clara Lehmann, Sandra A. Springer, Paul E. Sax, Melanie A. Thompson, Constance A. Benson, Susan P. Buchbinder, Carlos del Rio, Joseph J. Enron Jr., Huldrych F. Günthard, Jean-Michel Molina, Donna M. Jacobsen, and Michael S. Saag. 2022. "Antiretroviral Drugs for Treatment and Prevention of HIV Infection in Adults: 2022 Recommendations of the International Antiviral Society–USA Panel." *Journal of the American Medical Association*. doi:10.1001/jama.2022.22246.

Gauchat, Gordon. 2012. "Politicization of Science in the Public Sphere: A Study of Public Trust in the United States, 1974 to 2010." *American Sociological Review* 77:167–87.

Gawande, Atul. 2009. *The Checklist Manifesto: How to Get Things Right*. New York: Henry Holt.

Gazley, J. Lynn. 2011. "Our Particular Patients: Local Relevance in Clinical Research." PhD diss., Northwestern University.

Gelsinger, Paul. 2008. "Comment." Posted January 31, 2008. Archived at the Wayback Machine, https://web.archive.org/web/20140817192630/http://www.bioethics.net/2008/01/a-comment-from-paul-gelsinger-on-gene-therapy-and/.

Gerberich, Amanda, Samantha Spencer, and Heather Ipema. 2019. "National Guideline Clearinghouse Is No More: Keep Calm and Search On." *Annals of Pharmacotherapy* 53 (4): 434–36.

Gieryn, Thomas F. 1999. *Cultural Boundaries of Science: Credibility on the Line*. Chicago: University of Chicago Press.

Goffman, Erving. 1959. *The Presentation of Self in Everyday Life*, Garden City, NY: Doubleday.

———. 1967. *"Where the Action Is."* In *Interaction Ritual: Essays on Face-to-Face Behavior*, 149–270. Garden City, NY: Anchor Books.

———. 1969. *Strategic Interaction*. Philadelphia: University of Pennsylvania Press.

Goldman, Bonnie. 2009. "Body Shape Changes Dramatically Impact the Self-Esteem of HIV-Positive People: An Interview with Nelson Vergel." *TheBody*, April 15, 2009. https://www.thebody.com/article/body-shape-changes-dramatically-impact-self-esteem-hiv-positive-p.

Gorman, Christine. 1993. "Victory at Last for a Besieged Virus Hunter." *Time*, November 22, 1993, 61.

Gostin, Lawrence O. 2006. "HIV Screening in Health Care Settings: Public Health and Civil Liberties in Conflict?" *Journal of the American Medical Association* 296:2023–25.

Gostin, Lawrence O., and Rebecca Katz. 2016. "The International Health Regulations: The Governing Framework for Global Health Security." *Milbank Quarterly* 94 (2): 264–313.

Gostin, Lawrence O., and Devi Sridhar. 2014. "Global Health and the Law." *New England Journal of Medicine* 370:1732–40.

Greenhow, Annette, and Jocelyn East. 2015. "Custodians of the Game: Ethical Considerations for Football Governing Bodies in Regulating Concussion Management." *Neuroethics* 8:65–82.

Greenwood, Michael. 2023. "Who Funds Clinical Trials?" *News Medical*. https://www.news-medical.net/life-sciences/Who-Funds-Clinical-Trials.aspx.

Grimes, David A., David Hubacher, Kavita Nanda, Kenneth F. Schulz, David Moher, and Douglas G. Altman. 2005. "The Good Clinical Practice Guideline: A Bronze Standard for Clinical Research." *Lancet* 366:172–74.

Grimshaw, Jeremy M., and Ian T. Russell. 1993. "Effect of Clinical Guidelines on Medical Practice: A Systematic Review of Rigorous Evaluations." *Lancet* 342:1317–22.

Griswold, Wendy. 1987. "A Methodological Framework for the Sociology of Culture." *Sociological Methodology* 17:1–35.

Grol, Richard, and Jeremy Grimshaw. 2003. "From Best Evidence to Best Practice: Effective Implementation of Change in Patients' Care." *Lancet* 362:1225–30.

Grol-Prokopczyk, Hannah. 2013. "Thai and American Doctors on Medical Ethics: Religion, Regulation, and Moral Reasoning Across Borders." *Social Science and Medicine* 76:92–100.

Gross, Jane. 2008. "AIDS Patients Face Downside of Living Longer." *New York Times*, January 6, 2008.

Grükenmeier, Ellen. 2013. *Breaking the Silence: South African Representations of HIV/AIDS*. Rochester, NY: Boydell and Brewer.

Guillemin, Jeanne Harley, and Lynda Lytle Holmstrom. 1990. *Mixed Blessings: Intensive Care for Newborns*. New York: Oxford University Press.

Gunsalus, C. K. 2004. "The Nanny State Meets the Inner Lawyer: Overregulating While Underprotecting Human Participants in Research." *Ethics and Behavior* 14 (4): 369–82.

Hall, H. Irene, Qian An, Tian Tang, Ruiguang Song, Mi Chen, Timothy Green, and Jian Kang. 2015. "Prevalence of Diagnosed and Undiagnosed HIV Infection—United States, 2008–2012." *Morbidity and Mortality Weekly Report* 64 (240): 657–62.

Hall, Mark A. 2006. "The History and Future of Health Care Law: An Essentialist View." *Wake Forest Law Review* 41:347–64.

Hallett, Tim, and Marc J. Ventresca. 2006. "Inhabited Institutions: Social Interactions and Organizational Forms in Gouldner's Patterns of Industrial Bureaucracy." *Theory and Society* 35:213–36.

Halliday, Terence C., and Bruce G. Carruthers. 2007. "The Recursivity of Law: Global Norm Making and National Lawmaking in the Globalization of Corporate Insolvency Regimes." *American Journal of Sociology* 112:1135–1202.

Halliday, Terence C., and Pavel Osinsky. 2006. "Globalization and Law." *Annual Review of Sociology* 32:447–70.

Hallonsten, Olof. 2022. "On the Essential Role of Organized Skepticism in Science's 'Internal and Lawful Autonomy' (*Eigengesetzlichkeit*)." *Journal of Classical Sociology* 22 (3): 282–303.

Halpern, Sydney A. 2004. *Lesser Harms: The Morality of Risk in Medical Research*. Chicago: University of Chicago Press.

———. 2021. *Dangerous Medicine: The Story Behind Human Experiments with Hepatitis*. New Haven, CT: Yale University Press.

Harden, Victoria A. n.d. "A Short History of the National Institutes of Health: The Move to Washington." Archived at the Wayback Machine, https://web.archive.org/web/20041027151640/http://www.history.nih.gov/exhibits/history/docs/page_02.html.

Harris, Joseph. 2017a. *Achieving Access: Professional Movements and the Politics of Health Universalism*. Ithaca, NY: Cornell University Press.

———. 2017b. "'Professional Movements' and the Expansion of Access to Healthcare in the Industrializing World." *Sociology of Development* 3 (3): 252–72.

Hawkins, Jennifer S., and Ezekiel J. Emanuel, eds. 2008. *Exploitation and Developing Countries: The Ethics of Clinical Research*. Princeton, NJ: Princeton University Press.

Hays, Sharon. 1996. *The Cultural Contradictions of Motherhood*. New Haven, CT: Yale University Press.

Hayward, Robert S. A. 1997. "Clinical Practice Guidelines on Trial." *Canadian Medical Association Journal* 156 (12): 1725–27.

Hedgecoe, Adam M. 2006. "It's Money that Matters: The Financial Context of Ethical Decision-Making in Modern Biomedicine." *Sociology of Health and Illness* 28:768–84.

Heimer, Carol A. 1999. "Competing Institutions: Law, Medicine, and Family in Neonatal Intensive Care." *Law and Society Review* 33:17–66.

———. 2001. "Cases and Biographies: An Essay on Routinization and the Nature of Comparison." Annual Review of Sociology 27:47–76.

———. 2006. "Responsibility in Health Care: Spanning the Boundary Between Law and Medicine." *Wake Forest Law Review* 41 (2): 465–507.

———. 2007. "Old Inequalities, New Disease: HIV/AIDS in Sub-Saharan Africa." *Annual Review of Sociology* 33:551–77.

———. 2008. "Thinking about How to Avoid Thought: Deep Norms, Shallow Rules, and the Structure of Attention." *Regulation and Governance* 2 (1): 30–47.

———. 2010. "The Unstable Alliance of Law and Morality." In *Handbook of the Sociology of Morality*, edited by Steven Hitlin and Stephen Vaisey, 179–202. New York: Springer.

———. 2013. "Resilience in the Middle: Contributions of Regulated Organizations to Regulatory Success." *Annals of the American Academy of Political and Social Science* 649:139–56.

———. 2018. "We're Advancing to a Cure After 30 Years of HIV/AIDS Treatment." *The Hill*, November 30, 2018. https://thehill.com/opinion/healthcare /419073-were-advancing-to-a-cure-after-30-years-of-hiv-aids-treatment.

———. 2023. "Where Law and Morality Meet: Moral Agency and Moral Deskilling in Organizations." In *Second Handbook of the Sociology of Morality*, edited by Steven Hitlin, Aliza Luft, and Shai M. Dromi, 43–57. New York: Springer.

Heimer, Carol A., and Wendy Nelson Espeland. n.d. "Side Effects: Accountability in International HIV/AIDS Programs." Unpublished manuscript.

Heimer, Carol A., and J. Lynn Gazley. 2012. "Performing Regulation: Transcending Regulatory Ritualism in HIV Clinics." *Law and Society Review* 46:853–87.

Heimer, Carol A, and Jaimie Morse. 2016. "Colonizing the Clinic: The Adventures of Law in HIV Treatment and Research." In *The New Legal Realism, Volume II: Studying Law Globally*, edited by Heinz Klug and Sally E. Merry, 69–95. Cambridge, UK: Cambridge University Press.

Heimer, Carol A., and JuLeigh Petty. 2010. "Bureaucratic Ethics: IRBs and the Legal Regulation of Human Subjects Research." *Annual Review of Law and Social Science* 6:601–26.

Heimer, Carol A., JuLeigh Coleman Petty, and Rebecca J. Culyba. 2005. "Risk and Rules: The 'Legalization' of Medicine." In *Organizational Encounters with Risk*, edited by Bridget Hutter and Michael Power, 92–131. Cambridge, UK: Cambridge University Press.

Heimer, Carol A., and Lisa R. Staffen. 1998. *For the Sake of the Children: The Social Organization of Responsibility in the Hospital and the Home*. Chicago: University of Chicago Press.

Heimer, Carol A., and Arielle W. Tolman. 2021. "Between the Constitution and the Clinic: Formal and De Facto Rights to Health." *Law and Society Review* 55:563–86.

Heymann, David L., Guénaël R. Rodier, and the WHO Operation Support Team to the Global Alert and Response Network. 2001. "Hot Spots in a Wired World: WHO Surveillance of Emerging and Re-emerging Infectious Diseases." *Lancet Infectious Diseases* 1:345–53.

Heywood, Mark. 2009. "South Africa's Treatment Action Campaign: Combining Law and Social Mobilization to Realize the Right to Health." *Journal of Human Rights Practice* 1 (1): 14–36.

Heywood, Mark, and Morna Cornell. 1998. "Human Rights and AIDS in South Africa: From Right Margin to Left Margin." *Health and Human Rights* 2 (4): 61–82.

Hilts, Philip J. 1993. "US Drops Misconduct Case Against an AIDS Researcher." *New York Times*, November 13, 1993.

———. 1995. "FDA Backs a New Drug to Fight AIDS." *New York Times*, December 8, 1995.

Hodgman, Joan E. 1990. "Neonatology." *Journal of the American Medical Association* 263:2656–57.

Holmes, Charles B., William Coggin, David Jamieson, Heidi Mihm, Reuben Granich, Phillip Savio, Michael Hope, Caroline Ryan, Michele Moloney-Kitts, Eric P. Goosby, and Mark Dybul. 2010. "Use of Generic Antiretroviral Agents and Cost Savings in PEPFAR Treatment Programs." *Journal of the American Medical Association* 304 (3): 313–20.

Horgan, John. 1996. *The End of Science: Facing the Limits of Knowledge in the Twilight of the Scientific Age*. Reading, MA: Addison-Wesley.

Horowitz, Ruth. 2013. *In the Public Interest: Medical Licensing and the Disciplinary Process*. New Brunswick, NJ: Rutgers University Press.

Howe, Amy. 2020. "Opinion Analysis: Justices Uphold Condition for HIV/AIDS Funding." *SCOTUSblog*, June 29, 2020. https://www.scotusblog.com/2020/06/opinion-analysis-justices-uphold-condition-for-hiv-aids-funding/.

Howe, Marvine. 1993. "Robert Rafsky, 47, Media Coordinator for AIDS Protesters." *New York Times*, February 23, 1993.

Hughes, David, and Songkramchai Leethongdee. 2007. "Universal Coverage in the Land of Smiles: Lessons from Thailand's 30 Baht Health Reforms." *Health Affairs* 26 (4): 999–1008.

Huising, Ruthanne, and Susan S. Silbey. 2011. "Governing the Gap: Forging Safe Science Through Relational Regulation." *Regulation and Governance* 5:14–42.

Hupe, Peter, ed. 2019. *Research Handbook on Street-Level Bureaucracy: The Ground Floor of Government in Context*. Cheltenham, UK: Edward Elgar.

Hurwitz, Brian. 1999. "Legal and Political Considerations of Clinical Practice Guidelines." *British Medical Journal* (International) 318 (7184): 661–64.

Inglis, Alexander. 2004. "The Exhumation of Bobbi Campbell (28 Jan 1952-15 August 1984)." *Sensual Poet*. http://sensualpoet.blogspot.com/2004_02_22_archive.html.

Institute of Medicine, Committee on Standards for Developing Trustworthy Clinical Practice Guidelines. 2011. *Clinical Practice Guidelines We Can Trust*, edited by Robin Graham, Michelle Mancher, Dianne Miller Wolman, Sheldon Greenfield, and Earl Steinberg. Washington, DC: National Academies Press.

Institute of Medicine, Committee to Advise the Public Health Service on Clinical Practice Guidelines. 1990. *Clinical Practice Guidelines: Directions for a New Agency*, edited by Marilyn J. Field and Kathleen N. Lohr. Washington, DC: National Academies Press.

Institute of Medicine, National Research Council. 1999. *Reducing the Odds: Preventing Perinatal Transmission of HIV in the United States*. Washington, DC: National Academies Press.

IRIN. 2011. "Mandisa Dlamini, 'You Don't Know the Real Gugu Dlamini.'" *IRIN*, June 8, 2011. Archived at the Wayback Machine, https://web .archive.org/web/20150504092050/http://www.irinnews.org/hov/92929/ south-africa-mandisa-dlamini-you-don-t-know-the-real-gugu-dlamini.

Iskander, Natasha. 2021. *Does Skill Make Us Human? Migrant Workers in 21st Century Qatar and Beyond*. Princeton, NJ: Princeton University Press.

Jasanoff, Sheila. 2017. "Back from the Brink: Truth and Trust in the Public Sphere." *Issues in Science and Technology* 33 (4): 25–28.

Jha, Ashish K. 2018. "Accreditation, Quality, and Making Hospitals Better." *Journal of the American Medical Association* 320 (23): 2410–11.

Johns, David Merritt, Ronald Bayer, and Amy L. Fairchild. 2016. "Evidence and the Politics of Deimplementation: The Rise and Decline of the 'Counseling and Testing' Paradigm for HIV Prevention at the US Centers for Disease Control and Prevention." *Milbank Quarterly* 94 (1): 126–62.

Johns Hopkins University. 2020. *Global Health Security Index: Building Collective Action and Accountability*. Baltimore: Johns Hopkins University. https://www.ghsindex .org/wp-content/uploads/2020/04/2019-Global-Health-Security-Index.pdf.

Jordana, Jacint, and David Levi-Faur. 2004. "The Politics of Regulation in the Age of Governance." In *The Politics of Regulation: Institutions and Regulatory Reforms for the Age of Governance*, edited by Jacint Jordana and David Levi-Faur, 1–28. Cheltenham, UK: Edward Elgar.

Jost, Timothy Stoltzfus. 2004. "The Uses of *The Social Transformation of American Medicine*: The Case of Law." *Journal of Health Politics, Policy and Law* 29 (4–5): 799–814.

———. 2009. "The Regulation of Private Health Insurance." National Academy of Social Insurance. Archived at the Wayback Machine, https://web.archive.org/ web/20100707143046/https://www.nasi.org/usr_doc/The_Regulation_of _Private_Health_Insurance.pdf.

Kain, Daniel J. 2009. "It's Just a Concussion: The National Football League's Denial of a Casual Link between Multiple Concussions and Later-Life Cognitive Decline." *Rutgers Law Journal* 40 (3): 697–736.

Kaiser Family Foundation. 2006. "High Approval by Americans of Routine Testing: Kaiser Family Foundation. Survey of Americans on HIV/AIDS." Kaiser Family Foundation. https://www.kff.org/wp-content/uploads/2013/01/7521.pdf.

———. 2012. "Health Care Costs: A Primer." http://www.kff.org/report-section/ health-care-costs-a-primer-2012-report/.

Kalb, Paul E., and Kristin Graham Koehler. 2002. "Legal Issues in Scientific Research." *Journal of the American Medical Association* 287 (1): 85–91.

Kalberg, Stephen. 1980. "Max Weber's Types of Rationality." *American Journal of Sociology* 85 (5): 1145–79.

Katz, Rebecca, Vibhuti Haté, Sarah Kornblet, and Julie E. Fischer. 2012. "Costing Framework for International Health Regulations (2005)." *Emerging Infectious Diseases* 18 (7): 1121–27.

Kay, Emma Sophia, D. Scott Batey, and Michael J. Mugavero. 2016. "The HIV Treatment Cascade and Care Continuum: Updates, Goals, and Recommendations for the Future." *AIDS Research and Therapy* 13, article no. 35. doi: 10.1186/ s12981-016-0120-0.

Kay, Tamara. 2011. "Legal Transnationalism: The Relationship between Transnational Social Movement Building and International Law." *Law and Social Inquiry* 36:419–54.

Keenan, James F. 2005. "Developments in Bioethics from the Perspective of HIV/AIDS." *Cambridge Quarterly of Healthcare Ethics* 14:416–23.

Kellogg, Katherine C. 2011. *Challenging Operations: Medical Reform and Resistance in Surgery.* Chicago: University of Chicago Press.

Keohane, Robert O., and Joseph S. Nye. 2000. "Introduction." In *Governance in a Globalizing World*, edited by Joseph S. Nye and John D. Donahue, 1–41. Cambridge, MA: Brookings Institution.

Kim, Jim Yong. 2004. "Scaling Up Access to Care in Resource Constrained Settings: What Is Needed?" Plenary Address at the Fifteenth International AIDS Conference, Bangkok. July 13. Archived at the Wayback Machine, https://web.archive.org/web/20040714125854/http://www.who.int/3by5/plenaryspeech/en/.

King, Nicholas B. 2002. "Security, Disease, and Commerce: Ideologies of Postcolonial Global Health." *Social Studies of Science* 32:763–89.

Kleinman, Arthur. 1995. *Writing at the Margin.* Berkeley: University of California Press.

Klug, Heinz. 2000. *Constituting Democracy: Law, Globalization, and South Africa's Political Reconstruction.* New York: Cambridge University Press.

———. 2002. "Hybrid(ity) Rules: Creating Local Law in a Globalized World." In *Global Prescriptions: The Production, Exportation, and Importation of a New Legal Orthodoxy*, edited by Yves Dezalay and Bryant G. Garth, 276–305. Ann Arbor: University of Michigan Press.

———. 2008. "Law, Politics, and Access to Essential Medicines in Developing Countries." *Politics and Society* 36 (2): 207–46.

———. 2012. "Access to Medicines and the Transformation of the South African State: Exploring the Interactions of Legal and Policy Changes in Health, Intellectual Property, Trade, and Competition Law in the Context of South Africa's HIV/AIDS Pandemic." *Law and Social Inquiry* 37:297–329.

Knorr Cetina, Karin. 1981. *The Manufacture of Knowledge: An Essay on the Constructivist and Contextual Nature of Science.* Oxford, UK: Pergamon Press.

———. 1999. *Epistemic Cultures: How the Sciences Make Knowledge.* Cambridge, MA: Harvard University Press.

Kojima, Somei, Jitra Waikagul, Wichit Rojekittikhun, and Naoto Keicho. 2005. "The Current Situation Regarding the Establishment of National Ethical Guidelines for Biomedical Research in Thailand and Its Neighboring Countries." *Southeast Asian Journal of Tropical Medicine and Public Health* 36 (3): 728–32.

Krause, Monika. 2014. *The Good Project: Humanitarian Relief NGOs and the Fragmentation of Reason.* Chicago: University of Chicago Press.

Lallemant, Marc, Gonzague Jourdain, Sophie Le Coeur, Jean Yves Mary, Nicole Ngo-Giang-Huong, Suporn Koetsawang, Siriporn Kanshana, Kenneth MacIntosh, and Vallop Thaineua. 2004. "Single-Dose Perinatal Nevirapine plus Standard Zidovudine to Prevent Mother-to-Child Transmission of HIV-1 in Thailand." *New England Journal of Medicine* 351 (3): 217–28.

Lamont, Michèle. 2018. "Addressing Recognition Gaps: Destigmatization and the Reduction of Inequality." *American Sociological Review* 83 (3): 419–44.

———. 2023. *Seeing Others: How Recognition Works—And How It Can Heal a Divided World.* New York: Atria/One Signal.

Larsson, Elin C., Anna Mia Ekström, George Pariyo, Göran Tomson, Mohammad Sarowar, Rose Baluka, Edward Galiwango, and Anna Ekéus Thorson. 2015. "Prevention of Mother-to-Child Transmission of HIV in Rural Uganda: Modelling Effectiveness and Impact of Scaling-Up PMTCT Services." *Global Health Action* 8 (1): 26308. http://dx.doi.org/10.3402/gha.v8.26308.

Latour, Bruno. 1987. *Science in Action.* Cambridge, MA: Harvard University Press.

Latour, Bruno, and Steve Woolgar. 1979. *Laboratory Life: The Social Construction of Scientific Facts.* London: Sage.

Leidner, Robin L. 1993. *Fast Food, Fast Talk: Service Work and the Routinization of Everyday Life.* Berkeley: University of California Press.

Lempert, Richard, and Joseph Sanders. 1986. *An Invitation to Law and Social Science: Desert, Disputes, and Distribution.* Philadelphia: University of Pennsylvania Press.

Levi, Jacob, Alice Raymond, Anton Pozniak, Pietro Vermazza, Philipp Kohler, and Andrew Hill. 2016. "Can the UNAIDS 90-90-90 Target Be Achieved? A Systematic Analysis of National HIV Treatment Cascades." *British Medical Journal Global Health* 16 (1): e000010. doi:10.1136/ bmjgh-2015-000010.

Levitsky, Sandra R. 2013. "Integrating Law and Health Policy." *Annual Review of Law and Social Science* 9:33–50.

Levitsky, Sandra R., and Jane C. Banaszak-Holl. 2010. "Social Movements and the Transformation of American Health Care: Introduction." In *Social Movements and the Transformation of American Health Care,* edited by Jane C. Banaszak-Holl, Sandra R. Levitsky, and Mayer N. Zald, 3–18. New York: Oxford University Press.

Light, Donald W. 1994. "Countervailing Power: The Changing Character of the Medical Profession in the United States." In *The Changing Character of the Medical Profession: An International Perspective,* edited by Frederic W. Hafferty and John B. McKinlay, 69–79. New York: Oxford University Press.

Light, Donald W., and Joel R. Lexchin. 2012. "Pharmaceutical Research and Development: What Do We Get for All That Money?" *British Medical Journal* 345:e348.

Lipsky, Michael. 2010. *Street-Level Bureaucracy: Dilemmas of the Individual in Public Services,* 30th ann. expanded ed. New York: Russell Sage Foundation.

Llewellyn, Karl N. 1960. *The Common Law Tradition: Deciding Appeals.* Boston: Little, Brown.

Louw, Marius. 2006. "Please Fire Manto Now." *News 24,* September 6, 2006. Archived at the Wayback Machine, https://web.archive.org/web/20061128154116/http://www.news24.com/News24/South_Africa/Aids_Focus/0%2C%2C2-7-659_1993915%2C00.html.

Lurie, Peter, and Sidney Wolfe. 1997. "Unethical Trials of Interventions to Reduce Perinatal Transmission of the Human Immunodeficiency Virus in Developing Countries." *New England Journal of Medicine* 337:853–56.

Lusgarten, Abrahm. 2005. "Drug Testing Goes Offshore." *Fortune* 152 (3): 66–72.

Lutfey Spencer, Karen, and Matthew Grace. 2016. "Social Foundations of Health Care Inequality and Treatment Bias." *Annual Review of Sociology* 42:101–20.

Lynch, Michael. 1985. *Art and Artifact in Laboratory Science: A Study of Shop Work and Shop Talk in a Research Laboratory.* London: Routledge and Kegan Paul.

Majumdar, Sumit R., Matthew T. Roe, Eric D. Peterson, Anita Y. Chen, W. Brian Gibler, and Paul W. Armstrong. 2008. "Better Outcomes for Patients Treated at Hospitals that Participate in Clinical Trials." *Archives of Internal Medicine* 168 (6): 657–62. https://pubmed.ncbi.nlm.nih.gov/18362259/.

March, James G., and Herbert A. Simon. 1958. *Organizations*. New York: Wiley.

Marseille, Elliot, James G. Kahn, Francis Mmiro, Laura Guay, Philippa Musoke, Mary Glenn Fowler, and J. Brooks Jackson. 1999. "Cost Effectiveness of Single-Dose Nevirapine Regimen for Mothers and Babies to Decrease Vertical HIV-1 Transmission in Sub-Saharan Africa." *Lancet* 354:803–9.

Mathews, Jay. 1993. "Robert Rafsky, Writer and Activist in AIDS Fight, Dies." *Washington Post*, February 23, 1993.

Mbali, Mandisa. 2004. "AIDS Discourses and the South African State: Government Denialism and Post-Apartheid AIDS Policy-Making." *Transformation: Critical Perspectives on Southern Africa* 54:104–22.

McGoey, Linsey. 2007. "On the Will to Ignorance in Bureaucracy." *Economy and Society* 36:212–35.

McKay, Virginia R., Todd B. Combs, M. Margaret Dolcini, and Ross C. Brownson. 2020. "The De-implementation and Persistence of Low-value HIV Prevention Interventions in the United States: A Cross-sectional Study." *Implementation Science Communications* 1 (60). https://doi.org/10.1186/s43058-020-00040-6.

McKay, Virginia R., Emmanuel K. Tetteh, Miranda J. Reid, and Lucy M. Ingaiza. 2020. "Better Service by Doing Less: Introducing De-implementation Research in HIV." *Current HIV/AIDS Reports* 17:431–7.

McNeil, Donald G., Jr. 1998. "Neighbors Kill an H.I.V.-Positive AIDS Activist in South Africa." *New York Times*, December 28, 1998.

———. 2011. "Nigerians Receive First Payments for Children Who Died in 1996 Meningitis Drug Trial." *New York Times*, August 11, 2011.

———. 2019. "Scientists Discover New Cure for Deadliest Strain of Tuberculosis." *New York Times*, August 14, 2019.

McNeill, William H. 1976. *Plagues and Peoples*. Garden City, NY: Anchor Doubleday.

Mei, Aihong, Dingwei Gao, Jinxia Jiang, Tinting Qiao, Fang Wang, and Dan Li. 2022. "The Medical Education Systems in China and Thailand: A Comparative Study." *Health Science Reports* 2022 (5):e826. doi:10.1002/hsr2.826.

Mello, Michelle M. 2001. "Of Swords and Shields: The Role of Clinical Practice Guidelines in Medical Malpractice Litigation." *University of Pennsylvania Law Review* 149 (3): 645–710.

Merenstein, Daniel. 2004. "Winners and Losers [A Piece of My Mind]." *Journal of the American Medical Association* 291 (1): 15–16.

Merry, Sally E. 1990. *Getting Justice and Getting Even: Legal Consciousness among Working-Class Americans*. Chicago: University of Chicago Press.

———. 2006a. "Transnational Human Rights and Local Activism: Mapping the Middle." *American Anthropologist* 108:38–51.

———. 2006b. *Human Rights and Gender Violence: Translating International Law into Local Justice*. Chicago: University of Chicago Press.

Merton, Robert K. 1973. "The Normative Structure of Science." In *The Sociology of Science: Theoretical and Empirical Investigations*, by Robert K. Merton, 267–78. Chicago: University of Chicago Press.

———. 1949/1968. "Science and the Social Order" and "Science and Democratic Social Structure." In *Social Theory and Social Structure*, by Robert K. Merton, 591–603, 604–15 (respectively). New York: Free Press.

Mervis, Jeffrey. 2017. "Data Check: US Government Share of Basic Research Funding Falls below 50%." *Science*, March 9, 2017. doi: 10.1126/science. aal0890. https://www.science.org/content/article/data-check- us-government-share-basic -research-funding-falls-below-50.

Merz, S. M. 1993. "Clinical Practice Guidelines: Policy Issues and Legal Implications." *Joint Commission Journal of Quality Improvement* 19 (8): 306–12.

Meyer, John W., and Brian Rowan. 1977. "Institutionalized Organizations: Formal Structure as Myth and Ceremony." *American Journal of Sociology* 83:340–63.

Middleberg, Maurice J. 2006. "The Anti-Prostitution Policy in the US HIV/AIDS Program." *Health and Human Rights* 9 (1): 3–15.

Millenson, Michael L. 1997. *Demanding Medical Excellence: Doctors and Accountability in the Information Age*. Chicago: University of Chicago Press.

Milstein, Alan. 2008. "On Gene Therapy and Informed Consent." Posted January 29, 2008. https://bioethicstoday.org/blog/on-gene-therapy-and-informed-consent/.

Minow, Martha. 1990. *Making All the Difference: Inclusion, Exclusion, and American Law*. Ithaca, NY: Cornell University Press.

Mojola, Sanyu A. 2104. *Love, Money, and HIV: Becoming a Modern African Woman in the Age of AIDS*. Berkeley: University of California Press.

Mol, Annemarie, and Marc Berg. 1998. "Differences in Medicine: An Introduction." In *Differences in Medicine: Unraveling Practices, Techniques, and Bodies*, edited by Marc Berg and Annemarie Mol, 1–12. Durham, NC: Duke University Press.

Molyneux, Sassy, and P. Wenzel Geissler. 2008. "Ethics and the Ethnography of Medical Research in Africa." *Social Science and Medicine* 67:685–95.

Monette, Paul. 1988. *Borrowed Time: An AIDS Memoir*. New York: Harcourt Brace.

Morse, Stephen S. 2012. "Public Health Surveillance and Infectious Disease Detection." *Biosecurity and Bioterrorism- Biodefense Strategy Practice and Science* 10 (1): 6–16.

Moss, Kellie, and Jennifer Kates. 2022. "PEPFAR Reauthorization: Side-by-Side of Legislation Over Time." Kaiser Family Foundation. https://www.kff.org/global -health-policy/issue-brief/pepfar-reauthorization -side-by-side-of-existing-and-pro posed-legislation/.

Mugyenyi, Peter. 2008. *Genocide by Denial: How Profiteering from HIV/AIDS Killed Millions*. Kampala: Fountain.

Mulkay, Michael. 1984. "The Scientist Talks Back: A One-Act Play, with a Moral, about Replication and Reflexivity in Sociology." *Social Studies of Science* 14 (2): 265–82.

Munger, Frank. 2008–9. "Globalization, Investing in Law, and the Careers of Lawyers for Social Causes—Taking on Rights in Thailand." *New York Law Review* 53:745–804.

———. 2012. "Globalization through the Lens of Palace Wars: What Elite Lawyers' Careers Can and Cannot Tell Us about Globalization of Law." *Law and Social Inquiry* 37:476–99.

Namara-Lugolobi, Emily, Zikulah Namukwaya, Maxensia Owor, Joseph Ouma, Joyce Namale-Matovu, Clemensia Nakabiito, Christopher Ndugwa, Mary Glenn Fowler, and Phillipa Musoke. 2022. "Twenty Years of Prevention of Mother to Child HIV Transmission: Research to Implementation at a National Referral Hospital in Uganda." *African Health Sciences Special Issue* 22:23–33.

National HIV/AIDS Clinicians' Consultation Center. 2011. "Compendium of State HIV Testing Laws: Quick Reference Guide for Clinicians." September 19, 2011. https://www.hivlawandpolicy.org/resources/compendium-state- hiv-testing-laws-quick-reference-guide-clinicians-national-hivaids.

Nattrass, Nicoli. 2007. *Mortal Combat: AIDS Denialism and the Struggle for Antiretrovirals in South Africa*. Scottsville, South Africa: University of KwaZulu-Natal Press.

New Vision. 2007. "Philly Lutaaya: The Legend Lives On." *New Vision*, November 29, 2007. http://www.newvision.co.ug/new_vision/news/1214296/philly-lutaaya -legend-lives.

New York Times. 1993. "Doctor Cleared of Misconduct in AIDS Study." *New York Times*, November 5, 1993.

———. 2006. "Editorial: Modifying the AIDS Laws." *New York Times*, February 6, 2006.

New York Times (Editorial Board). 2018. "We Know How to Conquer Tuberculosis." *New York Times*, September 26, 2018.

Nolen, Stephanie. 2023. "Global Push to Treat H.I.V. Leaves Children Behind." *New York Times*, January 17, 2023.

Nsimbe, John Vianney. 2010. "Philly Lutaaya's Daughter Breaks Silence." *Observer*, January 6, 2010.

O'Brien, Judith A., Lenworth M. Jacobs Jr., and Danielle Pierce. 2000. "Clinical Practice Guidelines and the Cost of Care: A Growing Alliance." *International Journal of Technology Assessment in Health Care* 16:1077–91.

Office for Human Research Protections (OHRP). 2019. *International Compilation of Human Subject Research Protections*. www.hhs.gov/ohrp/international/compilation- human-research-standards/index.html.

Ofri, Danielle. 2017. "The Patients vs. Paperwork Problem for Doctors." *New York Times*, November 14, 2017.

Ohnesorge, John K. M. 2007. "The Rule of Law." *Annual Review of Law and Social Science* 3:99–114.

Open Vision Youth Club. 2004. "Philly Bongole Lutaaya." https://myhero.com/ PHILLY.

O'Reilly, James T., and Melissa D. Berry. 2011. "The Tsunami of Health Care Rulemaking: Strategies for Survival and Success." *Administrative Law Review* 63 (2): 245–81.

Ostrom, Elinor. 1990. *Governing the Commons: The Evolution of Institutions for Collective Action*. New York: Cambridge University Press.

Packard, Randall M. 2016. *A History of Global Health: Interventions into the Lives of Other People*. Baltimore: Johns Hopkins University Press.

Pallasch, Abdon M. 2007. "Fled Africa Horror Only to Die from Medicine; Clinic Didn't Notice Woman's Bad Reaction to Drugs." *Chicago Sun Times*, July 18, 2007.

Parker, Christine, and Vibeke Nielsen. 2009. "The Challenge of Empirical Research on Business Compliance in Regulatory Capitalism." *Annual Review of Law and Social Science* 5:45–70.

Patterson, Orlando. 1982. *Slavery and Social Death: A Comparative Study*. Cambridge, MA: Harvard University Press.

Patton, Cindy. 1994. *Last Served: Gendering the HIV Pandemic*. London: Taylor and Francis.

Peckham, Carol. 2015. "Physician Burnout: It Just Keeps Getting Worse." Medscape Family Medicine, January 26, 2015. https://www.medscape.com/ viewarticle/838437.

Penner, Louis A., John F. Dovidio, Jane A. Piliavin, and David A. Schroeder. 2005. "Prosocial Behavior: Multilevel Perspectives." *Annual Review of Psychology* 56:365–92.

PEPFAR WATCH. 2006. "Sex Workers." Archived at the Wayback Machine, https://web.archive.org/web/20070716181822/www.pepfarwatch.org/index.php?option=com_content&task=view&id=23&Itemid=37.

Pepin, Jaques. 2011. *The Origins of AIDS*. Cambridge, UK: Cambridge University Press.

Petersen, Alan, and Deborah Lupton. 1996. *The New Public Health: Health and Self in the Age of Risk*. Thousand Oaks, CA: Sage.

Petryna, Adriana. 2009. *When Experiments Travel: Clinical Trials and the Global Search for Human Subjects*. Princeton, NJ: Princeton University Press.

Petryna, Adriana, and Arthur Kleinman. 2006. "The Pharmaceutical Nexus." In *Global Pharmaceuticals: Ethics, Markets, Practices*, edited by Adriana Petryna, Andrew Lakoff, and Arthur Kleinman, 1–32. Durham, NC: Duke University Press.

Petryna, Adriana, Andrew Lakoff, and Arthur Kleinman, eds. 2006. *Global Pharmaceuticals: Ethics, Markets, Practices*. Durham, NC: Duke University Press.

Petty, JuLeigh. 2008. "Science in the Clinic: HIV Research in the Era of Evidence-Based Medicine." PhD diss., Northwestern University.

Petty, JuLeigh, and Carol A. Heimer. 2011. "Extending the Rails: How Research Reshapes Clinics." *Social Studies of Science* 41:337–60.

Philips, Mit, Rony Zachariah, and Sarah Venis. 2008. "Task Shifting for Antiretroviral Treatment Delivery in Sub-Saharan Africa: Not a Panacea." *Lancet* 371:682–84.

Plante, Hank. 2011. "Reagan's Legacy." San Francisco AIDS Foundation. http://sfaf.org/hiv-info/hot-topics/from-the-experts/2011-02-reagans-legacy.html.

Porapakkham, Yaowarat, Somjai Pramarnpol, Supatra Athibhoddhi, and Richard Bernhard. 1995. "The Evolution of HIV/AIDS Policy in Thailand: 1984–1994." http://pdf.usaid.gov/pdf_docs/PNACG546.pdf.

Porter, Theodore M. 1986. *The Rise of Statistical Thinking, 1820–1900*. Princeton, NJ: Princeton University Press.

———. 1995. *Trust in Numbers: The Pursuit of Objectivity in Science and Public Life*. Princeton, NJ: Princeton University Press.

Powell, Walter W., and Paul J. DiMaggio, eds. 1991. *The New Institutionalism in Organizational Analysis*. Chicago: University of Chicago Press.

Power, Michael. 1997. *The Audit Society: Rituals of Verification*. New York: Oxford University Press.

———. 2003. "Evaluating the Audit Explosion." *Law and Policy* 25:185–202.

Press, Eyal. 2023. "The Problem with Planned Parenthood." *New Yorker*, May 15, 2023.

Pronovost, Peter, and Eric Vohr. 2011. *Safe Patients, Smart Hospitals: How One Doctor's Checklist Can Help Us Change Health Care from the Inside Out*. New York: Penguin.

Pryma, Jane. 2020. "The Politics of Pain Relief: Managing Suffering in the United States and France." PhD diss., Northwestern University.

Rae, Matthew, Rebecca Copeland, and Cynthia Cox. 2019. "Tracking the Rise in Premium Contributions and Cost-Sharing for Families with Large Employer Coverage." Peterson-KFF Health System Tracker. August 19, 2019. http://www.healthsystemtracker.org/brief/tracking-the-rise-in-premium-contributions-and-cost-sharing-for-families-with-large-employer-coverage/.

Ramautarsing, Reshmie, and Jintanat Ananworanich. 2010. "Generic and Low Dose Antiretroviral Therapy in Adults and Children: Implication for Scaling Up Treatment in Resource Limited Settings." *AIDS Research and Therapy* 7, article 18. https://doi.org/10.1186/1742-6405-7-18.

Rappert, Brian. 2009. "Ignorance and Statecraft: Strategies for Maintaining and Challenging Doubt about the Costs of War." Presented at conference on "Strategic Unknowns," University of Oxford.

Rees, Joseph V. 1988. *Reforming the Workplace: A Study of Self-Regulation in Occupational Safety*. Philadelphia: University of Pennsylvania Press.

Reich, Robert B. 2010. "Bust the Health Care Trusts." *New York Times*, February 23, 2010.

Relman, Arnold. 1980. "The New Medical-Industrial Complex." *New England Journal of Medicine* 303 (17): 963–70.

———. 2010. "Health Care: The Disquieting Truth." *New York Review of Books*, September 30, 2010.

Rhodes, Scott D., Robert M. Malow, and Christine Jolly. 2010. "Community-Based Participatory Research (CBPR): A New and Not-So-New Approach to HIV/AIDS Prevention, Care, and Treatment." *AIDS Education and Prevention* 22 (3): 173–83.

Rissing, Ben A., and Emilio J. Castilla. 2016. "Testing Attestations: US Employment and Immigrant Work Authorizations." *ILR Review* 69 (5): 1081–113.

Rittel, Horst, and Melvin Webber. 1973. "Dilemmas in a General Theory of Planning." *Policy Sciences* 4:155–69.

Robbins, Rebecca, and Sheryl Gay Stolberg. 2023. "How a Drug Maker Profited by Slow-Walking a Promising H.I.V. Therapy." *New York Times*, July 22, 2023.

Rosenbaum, Sara. 2003. "The Impact of United States Law on Medicine as a Profession." *Journal of the American Medical Association* 289: 1546–56.

Rosenthal, Elisabeth. 2017, 2018. *An American Sickness: How Healthcare Became Big Business and How You Can Take It Back*. New York: Penguin Books.

———. 2020. "Who's Profiting from Your Outrageous Medical Bills?" *New York Times*. February 14, 2020.

Rosoff, Arnold J. 2001. "Evidence-Based Medicine and the Law: The Courts Confront Clinical Practice Guidelines." *Journal of Health Politics, Policy and Law* 26 (2): 327–68.

———. 2004. "Health Law at Fifty Years: A Look Back." *Health Matrix: Journal of Law-Medicine* 14 (1): 197–211.

———. 2012. "The Role of Clinical Practice Guidelines in Healthcare Reform: An Update." *Annals of Health Law* 21 (1): 21–33.

Rothman, David J. 1991. *Strangers at the Bedside: A History of How Law and Bioethics Transformed Medical Decision Making*. New York: Basic Books.

———. 2000. "The Shame of Medical Research." *New York Review of Books*, November 30, 2000, 60–64.

———. 2001. "The Origins and Consequences of Patient Autonomy: A 25-Year Retrospective." *Health Care Analysis* 9:255–64.

Rothman, David J., and Sheila M. Rothman. 1984. *The Willowbrook Wars: Bringing the Mentally Disabled into the Community*. New York: Harper and Row.

Rudowitz, Robin, Alice Burns, Elizabeth Hinton, and Maiss Mohamed. 2023. "10 Things to Know about Medicaid." Kaiser Family Foundation. https://www.kff.org/mental-health/issue-brief/10-things-to-know-about-medicaid/.

Ruggie, Mary. 1992. "The Paradox of Liberal Intervention: Health Policy and the American Welfare State." *American Journal of Sociology* 97 (4): 919–44.

Ryan, Maura. 2004. "Beyond a Western Bioethics?" *Theological Studies* 65:1058–77.

Sabel, Charles F. 2007. "A Real-Time Revolution in Routines." In *The Corporation as a Collaborative Community: Reconstructing Trust in the Knowledge Economy*, edited by Charles Heckscher and Paul S. Adler, 106–56. New York: Oxford University Press.

Sackett, David L., William M. C. Rosenberg, J. A. Muir Gray, R. Brian Haynes, and W. Scott Richardson. 1996. "Evidence Based Medicine: What It Is and What It Isn't." *British Medical Journal* 312 (7023): 71–72.

Sandefur, Rebecca L. 2008. "Access to Civil Justice and Race, Class, and Gender Inequality." *Annual Review of Sociology* 34:339–58.

———. 2009. "The Fulcrum Point of Equal Access to Justice: Legal and Nonlegal Institutions of Remedy." *Loyola of Los Angeles Law Review* 42:949–78.

Santos, Boaventura de Sousa. 1995. *Toward a New Common Sense: Law, Science and Politics in the Paradigmatic Transition*. New York: Routledge.

Sargent, John F., Jr. 2022. "US Research and Development Funding and Performance: Fact Sheet." CRS Report R44307. Washington, DC: Congressional Research Service.

Schneider, Carl. 2015. *The Censor's Hand: The Misregulation of Human Subjects Research*. Cambridge, MA: MIT Press.

Schoofs, Mark. 1999a. "AIDS: The Agony of Africa. Part Five: Death and the Second Sex. How Women's Powerlessness Spreads HIV." *Village Voice* 44 (48): 67–68, 71, 73.

———. 1999b. "AIDS: The Agony of Africa. Concluding Part: Use What You Have." *Village Voice* 44 (52): 53–56.

Schulman, Sarah. 2021. *Let the Record Show: A Political History of ACT UP New York, 1987–1993*. New York: Farrar, Straus and Giroux.

Schwarz, Alan. 2009. "Dementia Risk Seen in Players in N.F.L. Study." *New York Times*, September 30, 2009.

Scott, W. Richard. 2008. "Approaching Adulthood: The Maturing of Institutional Theory." *Theory and Society* 37:427–42.

Scott, W. Richard, Martin Ruef, Peter J. Mendel, and Carol A. Caronna. 2000. *Institutional Change and Healthcare Organizations: From Professional Dominance to Managed Care*. Chicago: University of Chicago Press.

Selznick, Philip. 1992. *The Moral Commonwealth*. Berkeley: University of California Press.

Sen, Amartya. 1999. *Development as Freedom*. New York: Alfred A. Knopf.

SF Pride. 1985. "A Dedication to Bobbi Campbell." Archived at the Wayback Machine, https://web.archive.org/web/20140703121904/http://sfpride.org/heritage/1985.html.

Shaffer, Gregory. 2012. "Transnational Legal Process and State Change." *Law and Social Inquiry* 37:229–64.

Shah, Sonia. 2003. "Globalization of Clinical Research by the Pharmaceutical Industry." *International Journal of Health Services* 33 (1): 29–36.

Sheetz, Megan L. 1997. "Toward Controlled Clinical Care through Clinical Practice Guidelines: The Legal Liability for Developers and Issuers of Clinical Pathways." *Brooklyn Law Review* 63:1341–80.

Sheon, Nicolas Maurice. 1999. "Sacraments of Surveillance: Ethnography of an HIV Test Clinic." PhD diss., University of California, Berkeley.

Shiff, Talia. 2021. "A Sociology of Discordance: Negotiating Schemas of Deservingness and Codified Law in US Asylum Status Determinations." *American Journal of Sociology* 127 (2): 337–75.

Shilts, Randy. 1987 *And the Band Played On: Politics, People, and the AIDS Epidemic.* New York: St. Martin's Press.

Silbey, Susan S. 1997. "Let Them Eat Cake: Globalization, Postmodern Colonialism, and the Possibilities of Justice." *Law and Society Review* 31:207–36.

———. 2011. "The Sociological Citizen: Pragmatic and Relational Regulation in Law and Organizations." *Regulation and Governance* 5:1–13.

Singhal, Arvind, and Everett M. Rogers. 2003. *Combating AIDS: Communication Strategies in Action.* Thousand Oaks, CA: Sage.

Sinsky, Christine, Lacey Colligan, Ling Li, Mirela Prgomet, Sam Reynolds, Lindsey Goeders, Johanna Westbrook, Michael Tutty, and George Blike. 2016. "Allocation of Physician Time in Ambulatory Practice: A Time and Motion Study in 4 Specialties." *Annals of Internal Medicine* 165 (11): 753–60.

Sirivichayakul, Sunee, Praphan Phanuphak, Tippawan Pankam, Rachanee O-Charoen, Donald Sutherland, and Kiat Ruxrungtham. 2008. "HIV Drug Resistance Transmission Threshold Survey in Bangkok, Thailand." *Antiviral Therapy* 13, suppl. 2:109–13.

Skarbinski, Jacek, Eli Rosenberg, Gabriela Paz-Bailey, H. Irene Hall, Charles E. Rose, Abigail H. Viall, Jennifer L. Fagan, Amy Lansky, and Jonathan H. Mermin. 2015. "Human Immunodeficiency Virus Transmission at Each Step of the Care Continuum in the United States." *Journal of the American Medical Association Internal Medicine* 175 (4): 588–96.

Smith, Catherine R. Hogan. 2020. "Information Services: Where to Find Evidence-Based Guidelines Post-National Guidelines Clearinghouse." Medical Library Association, September 3. https://assets.ecri.org/PDF/In-the-News/MLA-Information-Services-Find-Evidence-Based-Clinical-Practice-Guidelines-ECRI.pdf.

Smith, Daniel J. 2003. "Patronage, Per Diems and the 'Workshop Mentality': The Practice of Family Planning Programs in Southeastern Nigeria." *World Development* 31:703–15.

Smith, Scott R., and Robert J. Buchanan. 2001. "The AIDS Drug Assistance Programs and Coverage of HIV-Related Medications." *Annals of Pharmacotherapy* 35:155–66.

Smith, Tom W., and Jaesok Son. 2013. *Trends in Public Attitudes about Confidence in Institutions.* Chicago: National Opinion Research Center.

Smithson, Michael. 2008. "The Many Faces and Masks of Uncertainty." In *Uncertainty and Risk: Multidisciplinary Perspectives*, edited by Gabrielle Bammer and Michael Smithson, 13–25. London: Earthscan.

Specter, Michael. 2007. "The AIDS Denialists." *New Yorker*, March 12, 2007. https://www.newyorker.com/magazine/2007/03/12/the-denialists.

Squires, James D. 1989. "Editor's Note." *Chicago Tribune*, November 19, 1989.

Stark, Laura. 2012. *Behind Closed Doors: IRBs and the Making of Ethical Research.* Chicago: University of Chicago Press.

Starr, Paul. 1982. *The Social Transformation of American Medicine.* New York: Basic Books.

Stecher, Melanie, Florian Klein, Clara Lehmann, Martin Platten, Daniel Gillor, Georg Behrens, Gerd Fätkenheuer, and Joerg Janne Vehreschild. 2016. "Systematic Review of the Current Literature on Structured Treatment Interruptions in HIV-infected Patients Receiving Antiretroviral Therapy—Implications for Future HIV Cure Trials." *Open Forum Infectious Diseases* 3, suppl. 1: 1537.

Steinbrook, Robert. 2002. "Protecting Research Subjects: The Crisis at Johns Hopkins." *New England Journal of Medicine* 346:716–20.

Stephens, Joe. 2006. "Panel Faults Pfizer in '96 Clinical Trial in Nigeria: Unapproved Drug Tested on Children." *Washington Post*, May 7, 2006.

Stewart, Kearsley, and Nelson Sewankambo. 2010. "Okukkera Ng'omuzungu (Lost in Translation): Understanding the Social Value of Global Health Research for HIV/AIDS Research Participants in Uganda." *Global Public Health* 5 (2): 164–80.

Stinchcombe, Arthur L. 1965. "Social Structure and Organizations." In *Handbook of Organizations*, edited by James G. March, 142–93. Chicago: Rand McNally.

———. 2001. *When Formality Works: Authority and Abstraction in Law and Organizations*. Chicago: University of Chicago Press.

Strathern, Marilyn, ed. 2000. *Audit Cultures: Anthropological Studies in Accountability, Ethics and the Academy*. London: Routledge.

Sullivan, Noelle. 2016. "Global Poor's Medical Care Would be Unethical in US." *Orlando Sentinel*, February 25, 2016.

Swain, Donald C. 1962. "The Rise of a Research Empire: NIH, 1930 to 1950." *Science* 138 (n.s.) (3546): 1233–37.

Swanson, Cheryl. 2015. "5 Largest Markets for Pharmaceuticals." Motley Fool, May 12, 2015. https://www.fool.com/investing/general/2015/05/12/5-largest-markets-for -pharmaceuticals.aspx.

Swarns, Rachel L. 2001. "Drug Makers Drop South Africa Suit over AIDS Medicine." *New York Times*, April 20, 2001.

Sweat, Michael D., Kevin R. O'Reilly, George P. Schmid, Julie Denison, and Isabelle de Zoysa. 2004. "Cost-Effectiveness of Nevirapine to Prevent Mother-to-Child HIV Transmission in Eight African Countries." *AIDS* 18 (12): 1661–71.

Swidler, Ann, and Susan Cotts Watkins. 2007. "Ties of Dependence: AIDS and Transactional Sex in Rural Malawi." *Studies in Family Planning* 38:147–62.

———. 2008. "'Teach a Man to Fish': The Sustainability Doctrine and Its Social Consequences." *World Development* 37:1182–96.

———. 2017. *A Fraught Embrace: The Romance and Reality of AIDS Altruism in Africa*. Princeton, NJ: Princeton University Press.

Szymczak, Julia E., and Charles L. Bosk. 2012. "Training for Efficiency: Work, Time, and Systems-Based Practice in Medical Residency." *Journal of Health and Social Behavior* 53 (3): 344–58.

TAC (Treatment Action Campaign). 2001. "Judgment to be Handed Down in Mother-to-Child Transmission Case by the Pretoria High Court on Friday 14 December at 10h00." TAC Press Release, December 13, 2001. Archived at the Wayback Machine, https://web.archive.org/web/20030510080503/http://www.tac.org.za /newsletter/2001/ns14_12_2001.txt.

———. 2007. "A Response to Minister of Health on Improved Treatment Regimen to Prevent Mother to Child Transmission of HIV." *TAC Electronic Newsletter*. Archived at the Wayback Machine, https://web.archive.org/web/20071111060858/www.tac .org.za/nl20070911.html.

———. 2008a. "Statement on Disciplinary Action against Dr. Colin Pfaff." February 18, 2008. Archived at the Wayback Machine, https://web.archive.org/ web/20081122000333/http://www.tac.org.za/community/node/26.

———. 2008b. "Disciplinary Action Withdrawn against Dr. Colin Pfaff." February 23, 2008. Archived at the Wayback Machine, https://web.archive.org/ web/20081122003830/www.tac.org.za/community/node/1946.

Tausig, Mark, Michael J. Selgelid, Sree Subedi, and Janaran Subedi. 2006. "Taking Sociology Seriously: A New Approach to the Bioethical Problems of Infectious Disease." *Sociology of Health and Illness* 28:838–49.

Taylor, Ian. 2007. "Discretion and Control in Education: The Teacher as Street-Level Bureaucrat." *Educational Management Administration and Leadership* 35 (4): 555–72.

't Hoen, Ellen F. M. 2009. *The Global Politics of Pharmaceutical Monopoly Power: Drug Patents, Access, Innovation and the Application of the WTO Doha Declaration on TRIPS and Public Health.* Diemen, Neth.: AMB.

't Hoen, Ellen, Jonathan Berger, Alexandra Calmy, and Suerie Moon. 2011. "Driving a Decade of Change: HIV/AIDS, Patents and Access to Medicines for All." *Journal of the International AIDS Society* 14 (1). https://onlinelibrary.wiley.com/doi/10.1186/1758-2652-14-15.

Thompson, James D. 1967. *Organizations in Action: Social Science Bases of Administrative Theory.* New York: McGraw-Hill.

Tilley, Helen. 2010. "Global Histories, Vernacular Science, and African Genealogies: Or, Is the History of Science Ready for the World?" *Isis* 101 (1): 110–19.

———. 2011. *Africa as a Living Laboratory: Empire, Development, and the Problem of Scientific Knowledge, 1870–1950.* Chicago: University of Chicago Press.

Tilly, Chris, and Charles Tilly. 1997. *Work Under Capitalism.* Boulder, CO: Westview Press.

Timberg, Craig, and Daniel Halperin. 2012. *Tinderbox: How the West Sparked the AIDS Epidemic and How the World Can Finally Overcome It.* New York: Penguin Press.

Timmermans, Stefan. 2005. "From Autonomy to Accountability: The Role of Clinical Practice Guidelines in Professional Power." *Perspectives in Biology and Medicine* 48 (4): 490–501.

Timmermans, Stefan, and Marc Berg. 1997. "Standardization in Action: Achieving Local Universality through Medical Protocols." *Social Studies of Science* 27 (2): 273–305.

———. 2003. *The Gold Standard: The Challenge of Evidence Based Medicine and Standardization in Healthcare.* Philadelphia: University of Pennsylvania Press.

Timmermans, Stefan, and Mara Buchbinder. 2012. *Saving Babies Through Screening? The Consequences of Expanding Genetic Newborn Screening in the United States.* Chicago: University of Chicago Press.

Timmermans, Stefan, and Steven Epstein. 2010. "A World of Standards but not a Standard World: Towards a Sociology of Standards and Standardization." *Annual Review of Sociology* 36:69–89.

Timmermans, Stefan, and Emily S. Kolker. 2004. "Evidence-Based Medicine and the Reconfiguration of Medical Knowledge." *Journal of Health and Social Behavior* 45:177–93.

Trubek, David M., Patrick Cottrell, and Mark Nance. 2006. "'Soft Law,' 'Hard Law,' and EU Integration." In *Law and New Governance in the EU and US*, edited by Gráinne de Búrca and Joanne Scott, 65–94. Oxford, UK: Hart.

Truesdale, Beth C., and Christopher Jencks. 2016. "The Health Effects of Income Inequality: Averages and Disparities." *Annual Review of Public Health* 37:413–30.

Turner, Leigh. 2005. "Bioethics, Social Class, and the Sociological Imagination." *Cambridge Quarterly of Healthcare Ethics* 14:374–78.

Tversky, Amos, and Daniel Kahneman. 1974. "Judgment Under Uncertainty: Heuristics and Biases." *Science* 185:1124–31.

Uganda, Ministry of Health. 2005. *Uganda National Policy Guidelines for HIV Counselling and Testing*. http://library.health.go.ug/sites/default/files/resources/HIV%20Counseling%20and%20Testing%20policy.pdf.

UN (United Nations). 1948. "Universal Declaration of Human Rights." https://www.un.org/sites/un2.un.org/files/2021/03/udhr.pdf.

UNAIDS (Joint United Nations Programme on HIV/AIDS). 1999. *Developing HIV/AIDS Treatment Guidelines*. Geneva, Switz.: UNAIDS. https://data.unaids.org/publications/irc-pub03/developingkm_en.pdf.

———. 2006. *2006 Report on the Global AIDS Epidemic*. https://data.unaids.org/pub/report/2006/2006_gr_en.pdf.

———. 2007. *AIDS Epidemic Update*. https://data.unaids.org/pub/epislides/2007/2007_epiupdate_en.pdf.

———. 2008. *2008 Report on the Global AIDS Epidemic*, Executive Summary. https://data.unaids.org/pub/globalreport/2008/jc1511_gr08_executivesummary_en.pdf.

———. 2010. *2010 Report on the Global AIDS Epidemic*. https://www.unaids.org/globalreport/documents/20101123_GlobalReport_full_en.pdf.

———. 2014. *90-90-90: An Ambitious Treatment Target to End the AIDS Epidemic*. https://www.unaids.org/sites/default/files/media_asset/90-90-90_en.pdf.

———. 2022a. *Fact Sheet 2022*. https://www.unaids.org/en/resources/fact-sheet.

———. 2022b. *In Danger: UNAIDS Global AIDS Update 2022*. https://www.unaids.org/sites/default/files/media_asset/2022-global-aids-update_en.pdf.

———. 2024. *Global HIV & AIDS Statistics—Fact Sheet*. https://www.unaids.org/en/resources/fact-sheet.

UNAIDS (Joint United Nations Programme on HIV/AIDS) and MOPH (AIDS Division, Ministry of Public Health, Thailand). 2000. "Evaluation of the 100 Percent Condom Programme in Thailand." https://data.unaids.org/publications/irc-pub01/jc275-100pcondom_en.pdf.

UNAIDS (Joint United Nations Programme on HIV/AIDS) and WHO (World Health Organization). 2004. "UNAIDS/WHO Policy Statement on HIV Testing." https://data.unaids.org/una-docs/hivtestingpolicy_en.pdf.

UNOHCHR (United Nations Office of the High Commissioner for Human Rights). 1966. "The International Covenant on Economic, Social and Cultural Rights." https://www.ohchr.org/en/instruments-mechanisms/instruments/international-covenant-economic-social-and-cultural-rights.

———. 2008. *Fact Sheet No. 31: The Right to Health*. https://www.ohchr.org/en/publications/fact-sheets/fact-sheet-no-31-right-health.

USAID (US Agency for International Development). 2023. "Prevention of Mother to Child Transmission (PMTCT)." https://www.usaid.gov/global-health/health-areas/hiv-and-aids/technical-areas/pmtct.

Valenti, William M. 2004. "Using Treatment Guidelines and Consensus Statements in HIV Care." *AIDS Read* 14 (2): 78–81.

Varmus, Harold, and David Satcher. 1997. "Ethical Complexities of Conducting Research in Developing Countries." *New England Journal of Medicine* 337:1003–5.

Venkatesh, Kartik K., Kenneth H. Mayer, and Charles C. J. Carpenter. 2012. "Low-Cost Generic Drugs Under the President's Emergency Plan for AIDS Relief Drove Down Treatment Cost; More Are Needed." *Health Affairs* 31 (7): 1429–38.

Vergel, N. 2008. "Impact of Body Changes on the Quality of Life of HIV-Positive Treatment-Experienced Patients—An Online Community-Based Survey." *Program and Abstracts of the 10th International Workshop on Adverse Drug Reactions and Lipodystrophy in HIV*, Abstract P-67, November 6–8, 2008. London.

Vernooij, Eva, and Anita Hardon. 2013. "'What Mother Wouldn't Want to Save Her Baby?' HIV Testing and Counselling Practices in a Rural Ugandan Antenatal Clinic." *Culture, Health and Sexuality* 15 (S4): S553–66.

Vijayananthan, Anushya, and Ouzreiah Nawawi. 2008. "The Importance of Good Clinical Practice Guidelines and Its Role in Clinical Trials." *Biomedical Imaging and Intervention Journal* 4 (1): e5. doi:10.2349/biij.4.1.e5.

Wainwright, Steven P., Clare Williams, Mike Michael, Bobbie Farsides, and Alan Cribb. 2006. "Ethical Boundary-Work in the Embryonic Stem Cell Laboratory." *Sociology of Health and Illness* 28:732–48.

Waldholz, Michael. 2002. "African Crusaders Savor Wins in AIDS War but Need Funds." *Wall Street Journal*, June 13, 2002.

Walker, R. Dale, Matthew Owen Howard, M. Dow Lampert, and Richard Suchinsky. 1994. "Medical Malpractice Guidelines." *Western Journal of Medicine* 161:39–44.

Watkins, Susan Cotts, and Ann Swidler. 2013. "Working Misunderstandings: Donors, Brokers, and Villagers in Africa's AIDS Industry." *Population Development Review* 38, suppl.: 197–218.

Weber, Max. 1968. *Economy and Society: An Outline of Interpretive Sociology*. Edited by Guenther Roth and Claus Wittich. New York: Bedminster Press.

Weick, Karl E., and K. M. Sutcliffe. 2007. *Managing the Unexpected: Resilient Performance in an Age of Uncertainty*, 2nd ed. San Francisco: Jossey-Bass.

Weil, Vivian, and Robert Arzbaecher. 1996. "Ethics and Relationships in Laboratories and Research Communities." *Professional Ethics* 4 (3–4): 83–125.

Weisz, George. 2014. "The Ongoing Tension: Clinical Practice and Clinical Research." In *The Institution of Science and the Science of Institutions: The Legacy of Joseph Ben-David*, edited by Marcel Herbst, 63–79. New York: Springer.

Weisz, George, Alberto Cambrosio, Peter Keating, Loes Knaapen, Thomas Schlich, and Virginie J. Tournay. 2007. "The Emergence of Clinical Practice Guidelines." *Milbank Quarterly* 85 (4): 691–727.

Wendland, Claire L. 2010. *A Heart for the Work: Journeys Through an African Medical School*. Chicago: University of Chicago Press.

———. 2012. "Moral Maps and Medical Imaginaries: Clinical Tourism at Malawi's College of Medicine." *American Anthropologist* 114 (1): 108–22.

Wennberg, John E. 2010. *Tracking Medicine: A Researcher's Quest to Understand Health Care*. New York: Oxford University Press.

———. 2011. "Time to Tackle Unwarranted Variations in Practice." *British Medical Journal* 342:687–92.

Wennberg, John, and Alan Gittelsohn. 1973. "Small Area Variations in Health Care Delivery: A Population-Based Health Information System Can Guide Planning and Regulatory Decision-Making." *Science* 182 (4117): 1102–8.

Werner, Rachel M., G. Caleb Alexander, Angela Fagerlin, and Peter A. Ubel. 2002. "The 'Hassle Factor': What Motivates Physicians to Manipulate Reimbursement Rules?" *Archives of Internal Medicine* 162:1134–39.

White, Allen. 2004. "Reagan's AIDS Legacy/Silence Equals Death." *SFGate*, June 8, 2004. https://www.sfgate.com/opinion/openforum/article/Reagan-s-AIDS-Legacy-Silence-equals-death-2751030.php.

Whitney, Simon N. 2016. "Institutional Review Boards: A Flawed System of Risk Management." *Research Ethics* 12 (4): 182–200.

———. 2023. *From Oversight to Overkill: Inside the Broken System that Blocks Medical Breakthroughs—And How We Can Fix It.* Irvington, NY: Rivertowns Books.

Whitney, Simon N., and Carl E. Schneider. 2011. "A Method to Estimate the Cost in Lives of Ethics Board Review of Biomedical Research." *Journal of Internal Medicine* 269:392–406.

WHO (World Health Organization). 1978. "Declaration of Alma-Ata." https://cdn .who.int/media/docs/default-source/documents/almaata-declaration-en .pdf?sfvrsn=7b3c2167_2.

———. 2002. "Increasing Access to Knowledge of HIV Status: Conclusions of a WHO Consultation, 3–4 December 2001." https://apps.who.int/iris/bitstream /handle/10665/67362/WHO_HIV_2002.09.pdf?sequence=1&isAllowed=y.

———. 2006. *Antiretroviral Therapy for HIV Infection in Adults and Adolescents: Recommendations for a Public Health Approach*, 2006 revision. Geneva, Switz.: WHO. https://apps.who.int/iris/handle/10665/43554.

WHO (World Health Organization), PEPFAR (US President's Emergency Fund for AIDS Relief), and UNAIDS (Joint United Nations Programme on HIV/AIDS). 2008. "Task Shifting: Rational Redistribution of Tasks among Health Workforce Teams: Global Recommendations and Guidelines." https://apps.who.int/iris/bitstream /handle/10665/43821/9789241596312_eng.pdf?sequence=1&isAllowed=y.

WHO (World Health Organization) and UNAIDS (Joint United Nations Programme on HIV/AIDS). 2005. *Scaling-Up HIV Testing and Counselling Services: A Toolkit for Programme Managers.* Archived at the Wayback Machine, https://web.archive.org /web/20060826102427/http://www.who.int/hiv/pub/vct/counsellingtestingtool kit.pdf.

———. 2007a. "WHO and UNAIDS Issue New Guidance on HIV Testing and Counselling in Health Facilities." https://apps.who.int/iris/bitstream/handle/10665/73959 /PR_24_eng.pdf?sequence=1&isAllowed=y.

———. 2007b. *Guidance on Provider-Initiated HIV Testing and Counselling in Health Facilities.* Geneva, Switz.: WHO. https://apps.who.int/iris/bitstream /handle/10665/43688/9789241595568_eng.pdf?sequence=1&isAllowed=y.

———. 2017. "WHO, UNAIDS Statement on HIV Testing Services: New Opportunities and Ongoing Challenges." https://www.unaids.org/sites/default/files/ media_asset/2017_WHO-UNAIDS_statement_HIV-testing-services_en.pdf.

Whyte, Susan R., Michael A. Whyte, and David Kyaddondo. 2010. "Health Workers Entangled: Confidentiality and Certification." In *Morality, Hope and Grief: Anthropologies of AIDS in Africa*, edited by Hansjörg Dilger and Ute Luig, 80–103. New York: Berghahn Books.

Whyte, Susan Reynolds, Michael A. Whyte, Lotte Meinert, and Betty Kyaddondo. 2006. "Treating AIDS: Dilemmas of Unequal Access in Uganda." In *Global Pharmaceuticals: Ethics, Markets, Practices*, edited by Adriana Petryna, Andrew Lakoff, and Arthur Kleinman, 240–62. Durham, NC: Duke University Press.

Williams, Elizabeth, Robin Rudowitz, and Alice Burns. 2023. "Medicaid Financing: The Basics." Kaiser Family Foundation. https://www.kff.org/medicaid/issue-brief /medicaid-financing-the-basics/.

Wolf, Leslie E., Alexis Donoghoe, and Tim Lane. 2007. "Implementing Routine HIV Testing: The Role of State Law." *PloS ONE* 2 (10): e1005. doi:10.1371/journal. pone.0001005.

Wolf, Leslie E., Bernard Lo, Karen Beckerman, Alejandro Dorenbaum, Sarah J. Kilpatrick, and Peggy S. Weintrub. 2001. "When Parents Reject Interventions to Reduce Postnatal Human Immunodeficiency Virus Transmission." *Archives of Pediatrics and Adolescent Medicine* 155 (8): 927–33.

Wolinsky, Howard. 2006. "The Battle of Helsinki." *European Molecular Biology Organization Reports* 7 (7): 670–72.

Wright, Joe. 2013. "Only Your Calamity." *American Journal of Public Health* 2013 (3): 1788–98.

Wynia, Matthew K., Deborah S. Cummins, Jonathan B. Van Geest, and Ira B. Wilson. 2000. "Physician Manipulation of Reimbursement Rules for Patients: Between a Rock and a Hard Place" *Journal of the American Medical Association* 283:1858–65.

Yamwong, Preyanuj. 2006. "The Medical Education System in Thailand." *Asia-Pacific Biotech News* 10 (15): 815–17.

Yessian, Mark. 1999. *Institutional Review Boards: A System of Protections Still in Need of Reform: Hearing Before the Subcomm. on Criminal Justice, Drug Policy and Human Resources of the H. Comm. on Gov't Reform*, 106th Cong., December 9, 1999 (statement of Mark Yessian, Regional Inspector General of Evaluations and Inspections).

Zimerman, Ariel. 2013. "Evidence-Based Medicine: A Short History of a Modern Medical Movement." *AMA Journal of Ethics* 15 (1): 71–76.

Zussman, Robert. 1992. *Intensive Care: Medical Ethics and the Medical Profession*. Chicago: University of Chicago Press.

Index

Page numbers in italics refer to tables.

A&B men, 246
Abbott Laboratories, 3, 305, 346n21
abstinence: ignorance and, 246, 261, 342n9,
  342n11; standards and, 44, 330n32
Abstinence, Be faithful, use Condoms
  (ABC) program, 246, 330n32, 342n11
access to justice, 26–27
accountability: disciplining and, 216;
  efficiency and, *84*; ethics and, 275;
  healthcare and, 91–94; ignorance and,
  238; increased pressures of, 16, 91–94,
  97, 131, 165; monitoring regimes and,
  173–79; research, 16, *84*, 144, 149, 155–
  57, 161, 165, 173–78, 183, 204, 216, 238,
  338n12; trustworthy data and, 165, 173–
  79, 181, 183, 204, 338n12; universals and,
  129, 131, 144, 146, *149*, 150, 155–61
activists: California and, 3–4; disciplining
  and, 213, 215, 221; guidelines and, 2–4,
  8, 13, 18, 23, 31, 33; ignorance and, 251;
  moral issues and, 293, 297, 303–8, 315,
  345n10; New York and, 3–4; Rafsky,
  327n8; rule proliferation and, *82*, 85,
  101–2, 122, 333n4; standards and, 41,
  44, 46, 327n8, 329n20; testing and, 4;
  trustworthy data and, 168; universals
  and, 127–28
addictions, 101, 250
Advancing Clinical Therapeutics Globally
  for HIV/AIDS. *See* AIDS Clinical
  Trials Group (ACTG)
adverse event (AE): ethics and, 252,
  282; moral issues and, 299, 302, 312,

315; rule proliferation and, 114, *117*,
  332n32; serious adverse event (SAE),
  186, 198–99, 338n15; training and, 188;
  trustworthy data and, *182*, 186, 188,
  198–201
Affordable Care Act (Obamacare),
  328n13
African Americans, 40, 42, 47, 50, 52
AIDS: altruism, 7; blood and, 3, 22, 166,
  218; denialism and, 13, 44, 60, 167–70,
  327n7, 328n19, 329n20; disciplining and,
  214–15, 218–25, 340n7; as epidemic, 1–3,
  5, 10–11, 18, 21–23, 30, 41–47, 56, 60–61,
  90, 122, 127, 163, 165, 168, 213, 220, 225,
  258, 290, 292, 304, 325n2, 328n12, 333n3;
  ethics and, 274; Fifteenth International
  AIDS Conference, 60; guidelines and,
  1–7, 10–13, 16–24, 325n3, 326n9, 326n11;
  ignorance and, 244–48, 251, 342n9,
  342n15; moral issues and, 288–98, 301–
  5, 310, 314–15; rule proliferation and,
  80–87, 92–93, 106–7, *108*, 111, 332n26;
  Ryan White HIV/AIDS Program,
  52–53, *82*, *84*, 92, 94, 96, 102, *109*, 111,
  113, 133, *148–49*, 155, 295, 328n12, 345n16;
  standards and, 34, 41–49, 52, 55, 57, 60,
  63, 68, 72, 327nn7–10, 328n12, 328n17,
  328n19, 329n20, 329n26; stigma of, 4–5,
  12, 215, 328n12, 329n20; trustworthy
  data and, 164–70, 176, 337nn6–7;
  UNGASS and, 8, 325n3; universals and,
  127–29, 132–33, 137, 143–47, 150–54,
  157–63, 333n3, 335n19, 336n30

AIDS Clinical Trials Group (ACTG): as Advancing Clinical Therapeutics Globally for HIV/AIDS, 327n10; rule proliferation and, 331n13; standards and, 327n10; trustworthy data and, 176, 185, 193, 327n10, 338n14
AIDS Coalition to Unleash Power (ACT UP), 293, 303, 327n8
AIDS drugs assistance program (ADAP), 92, 96, 248, 274, 295
AIDS Education and Training Centers (AETC), *109*, 111–13, 141
AIDS Law Project (ALP), 304, 335n19, 346n19
Alzheimer's disease, 243–44
American Medical Association (AMA), *85*, 89, 284, 330n5, 333n38
America's Health Insurance Plans, 330n5
anemia, 199
Angotti, Nicole, 275
anonymity, 4, *212*
antibiotics, 37, 63, 337n8
antibodies: blood and, 213, 304; commercial tests for, 3–4, 291; HIV and, 3–4, 213, 256, 291; mucosal swabs and, 213; urine and, 213
anti-prostitution policies, 290, 342nn9–10, 344n4
anti-retroviral drugs (ARV): Bobbi Campbell Clinic and, 56; Cha-on Suesum Clinic and, 56–57; disciplining and, *212*; GPO-VIR and, 56, 71, 135, 151, 295, 310, 328n15, 335n18, 346n26; Gugu Dlamini Clinic and, 62, 136–37, 247; moral issues and, 291, 297, 300, 305–6; Philly Lutaaya Clinic and, 67, 69, 139; Robert Rafsky Clinic and, 132–33; standards and, 67; universals and, 125, 139, 152
anti-retroviral therapy (ART): Bobbi Campbell Clinic and, 55; in Brazil, 292; disciplining and, 211, 219–20, 223–27, 340n17; ethics and, 345nn6–9, 345n13; Gugu Dlamini Clinic and, 62–64, 154; guidelines and, 10–11, 325n6, 326n7; ignorance and, 243, 251–52, 255, 342n15, 343n20; moral issues and, 288, 292–95, 300–304, 307; Philly

Lutaaya Clinic and, 137; Robert Rafsky Clinic and, 47; side effects and, 48; standards and, 41, 47–48, 55, 62–64, 71, 328n19; universals and, 124–25, 137, 142, 153–54
antitrust issues, *80*, *84*, 95, 346n18
Aspen, 40
Attaran, Amir, 288
Avian flu, 36
AZT (azidothymidine), 118, 167, 205, 211, 251, 291, 333n35, 339n1

Baby Doe Law, 207, 339n6
Bactrim, 63, 125
Barré-Sinoussi, Simone, 166–67, 170
Bauer, Gary, 44
Belmont Report, *115*, 118, 120, 266, 306, 314
Berger, Daniel, 194
Berry, Melissa D., 76
Biologics Control Act, 331n14
biology: disease and, 1; ethics and, 269; guidelines and, 14, 18, 22, 31; moral issues and, 309; rule proliferation and, 93; universals and, 123, 161–62, 167
blood: AIDS and, 3, 22, 166, 218; antibodies and, 213, 304; hemophilia and, 42, 61, 151; HIV and, 3–4, 21–22, 144, 166, *212*, 213, 326n8, 328n17, 336n27; transfusions of, 3, 138–39, 207, 328n17; transmission via, 21, 336n27
Bobbi Campbell Clinic: ART and, 55; ARV and, 56; description of, 53; "double billing" at, 54; ethics and, 274, 279–80; funding, 52–55, 133–34; ignorance and, 241; IRBs and, 53, 55; Medicaid and, 52, 54; Medicare and, 52, 54; moral issues and, 295–96; research and, 52–55, 71–72, 141, 146, 151, 155, 159, 176, 197, 241, 274, 279, 338n14; rule proliferation and, *109–10*, 112–13, 121; Ryan White HIV/AIDS Program and, 52–53; standards and, 52–55, 71–72, 328n12; statistics of, 52; trustworthy data and, 176, 197, 201, 338n14; universals and, 133–36, 139–42, 146–63, 336n28

Bosk, Charles, 24, 227, 230, 265, 284, 343n3
Boston University, 103
Braverman, Harry, 229
breakpoints, 11
breastfeeding/breastmilk, 68, 211, 219, 255–57, 274, 340n17, 343nn21–22
Bush, George W., 92

Cabana, Michael D., 129
California Department of Public Health, 4
Cambodia, 136, 188
Cameron, Edwin, 6, 215, 250–51, 340n12
Campbell, Bobbi, 328n12
cancer, 59, 342n13
Candida auris, 37
Canterbury v. Spence, 102
Carpenter, Daniel, 99
Carrie, Corrine, 9
case report form (CRF), 339n28; confidentiality of, 217; preparing, 114, 180, 192, 195, 197; trustworthy data and, 194; as work of research nurses, 49, 179
Case Western Reserve University, 103
causal factors, 13–14, 106, 143–45, 258, 306
CD4: disciplining and, 211, 228; guidelines and, 326n8, 326n11; ignorance and, 342n15; moral issues and, 294, 298; standards and, 55, 63; universals and, 124–26, 136–37, 151, 335n19
Centers for Disease Control and Prevention (CDC): disciplining and, 209–10, 212, 214, 340n10, 340n16; fiscal responsibility and, 92; gay men and, 326n10; guidelines and, 6–12, 22, 326nn10–11; moral issues and, 291, 294, 298; rule proliferation and, 92, 108–9, 111; staging system, 326n11; standards and, 68, 327n9; universals and, 141–42, 336nn26–27
Centers for Medicare and Medicaid Services (CMS), 86, 92, 98
certification, 29, 41, 112, 181, 188–89, 192, 267
certified IRB professionals/managers, 203–4, 282
Chambliss, Daniel F., 230, 282–83
Cha-on Suesum Clinic: ARV and, 56–57; description of, 56; ethics and, 270,

274; *farang* rules and, 217; Fifteenth International AIDS Conference and, 60; founding of, 56–57; Kowit and, 135–36; MACS and, 57; moral issues and, 295–96, 309–12, 346n26; NIH and, 57–60; research and, 56–60, 71–72, 121, 136, 141, 146, 156, 159–61, 173, 176, 188, 191–97, 217, 243, 270, 295–96, 309–12, 346n26; rule proliferation and, 110, 121; staff education, 57–59; standards and, 56–60, 71–72, 328n17; subsidies and, 56; trustworthy data and, 173, 176, 188, 191–97; Universal Coverage Scheme and, 56, 328n14; universals and, 135–36, 139–42, 146–63; WHO and, 135–36
charity, 77
Chicago Tribune, 166
Chirac, Jacques, 166, 333n4
CIA, 44
Clinical Evidence (journal), 89
clinical trials unit (CTU), 175–76, 338n13
clinics: certification and, 29, 41, 112, 181, 188–89, 192, 203, 267; comparison of, 70–73; coordination effects and, 144, 146, 152, 155; disciplining and, 205–35; disease-novelty effects and, 143–44, 146, 150; divisions of labor in, 64, 143, 154, 237–38, 254–58, 261; ethics and, 262–86; guidelines and, 1–33 (*see also* guidelines); ignorance and, 236–61; institutionalization effects and, 143, 146, 148; legal issues and, 23–29; legitimacy and, 140, 141, 145–46, 149, 158–61, 336n30; medicine and, 23–29; moral issues and, 387–95; orderly flexibility in, 197–202; overworked conditions in, 35, 292; ownership effects and, 145–46, 149, 158; practice variations and, 28; research administration and, 106–20; rule proliferation and, 75–122; satellite, 130, 146, 154, 304, 307; standards and, 34–74 (*see also* standards); task shifting and, 226–30; treatment equity and, 294–98; trustworthy data and, 154 (*see also* trustworthy data); universals and, 22–23, 94, 132–45, 152, 336n27. *See also specific clinics*

Clinton, Bill, 305
COBRA, 303
Cochrane, Archie, 88
coercion: disciplining and, 220; ethics
and, 190, 220, 242–43, *260*, 272–73,
300, 344n5; moral issues and, 300;
trustworthy data and, 190
cohort effects, 335n26
Common Rule, 94, *116*, 120, 267, 343n2
compliance work: bureaucracies and,
98–101; ethics and, 264, 267, 269,
284–85; moral issues and, 311; rule
proliferation and, 105–6; trustworthy
data and, 177–78, 204
condoms, 62, 246, 305, 328n16, 330n32,
342n11
confidentiality: anonymity and, 4, *212*;
disciplining and, 213–21; discretion
limits and, 230–33; ethics and, 272,
275–76; guidelines and, 4–5, 8–9, 14–
15, 216–19; ignorance and, 250; rule
proliferation and, 119, 122; standards
and, 46, 71, 328n18; testing guidelines
and, 216–19; trustworthy data and,
338n17; universals and, 151
Congo (DRC), 21, 127, 257, 333n3
consent: disciplining and, *212*, 214–15, 221,
223, 229, 341n19; ethics and, 262–63,
268, 270, 273, 280, 283; guidelines
and, 4–5, 8–9, 12, 20, 33; ignorance
and, 239–45, 248, 259–61, 341nn2–3,
344n5; informed, *82*, *86*, 102, 122, 180,
188, *212*, 229, 239–45, 248, 259, *260*,
270, 338n15, 344n5; moral issues and,
313; passive approval and, 5; by proxy,
5; recruiting research subjects, 32, 38,
117, 175–76, 183, 190, 240–44, 263, 269,
272, 282, 341n1; rule proliferation and,
82, *86*, 101–2, 105, 114, 122; standards
and, 67; trustworthy data and, 180,
188, 194–95, 338n15
contract research center (CRC), 344n8
coordination effects, 144, 146, 152, 155
Corporation for Public Broadcasting, 44
counseling: disciplining and, 213–15, 221,
224, 231, *232*, 340n12; ethics and, 276,
279; guidelines and, 2–10, 14, 30;
moral issues and, 298; PICT, 6–7, 11;

RCT, 6–12, 213–14, 325nn3–4, 340n14;
rule proliferation and, 107, *110*, 113;
standards and, 47, 62–63; VCT, 4–12,
15, 22, 213–14, 298, 325nn4–5, 340n14
COVID-19 pandemic, 36–37
CPR, 24
credibility: clinical trials and, 170–
73; disciplining and, 217, 227;
downstream effects and, 166–70; early
research controversies and, 166–70;
evidentiary packages and, 179–202;
ignorance and, 243; monitoring
regimes and, 173–79; norms and, 197–
202; records and, 192–97; scientific
reputations and, 166–70; skepticism
and, 165–69, 174–202; training and,
187–92; trustworthy data and, 164–
205; uniform work plans and, 182–87
C-sections, 152
Curran, William, 103

d4T, 157, 160, 228, 251–52, 313, 336n32
DAIDS (NIH Division of AIDS), 68,
327n10, 331n13
Dartmouth Atlas Project, 88
decentralization, 89, 120, 326n12
Declaration of Helsinki, *115–16*, 118–19,
300, 332n33, 333n38
De Cock, Kevin, 7–8
denialism: AIDS and, 13, 44, 60, 167–70,
327n7, 328n19, 329n20; guidelines and,
13; South Africa and, 13, 44, 60, 168,
327n7, 328n19; standards and, 44, 60,
327n7; trustworthy data and, 167–70;
Uganda and, 44
Denver Principles, 328n12
Department of Health and Human
Services (DHHS): compliance
bureaucracies and, 99; disciplining
and, 209–10, 221–22; ethics and,
267; moral issues and, 297; rule
proliferation and, *108–10*, 111–12,
116, 120; trustworthy data and, 166;
universals and, 134, 141–42
Department of Veteran Affairs (VA), 92,
96, 329n26, 330n8
diarrhea, 199, 254–57, *260*, 261
Dingell, John, 166

INDEX › 383

Directory of Practice Parameters (AMA), 89

disciplining: accountability and, 216; activists and, 213, 215, 221; AIDS and, 214–15, 218–25, 340n7; ART and, 211, 219–20, 223–27, 340n17; ARV and, *212*; CD4 and, 211, 228; CDC and, 209–10, *212*, 214, 340n10, 340n16; clinics and, 205–35; confidentiality and, 213–21; consent and, *212*, 214–15, 221, 223, 229, 341n19; counseling and, 213–15, 221, 224, 231, *232*, 340n12; credibility and, 217, 227; DHHS and, 209–10, 221–22; discretion and, 206–7, *212*, 226, 230–34; disease and, 213–14, *232*; doctors and, 205, 208, 211, *212–13*, 217, 219, 224–35, 340n12; drugs and, 205–6, 211, *212–13*, 219–28, *232*, 339n1, 342n6, 342n13, 343n20; education and, 216, 340n9; empowerment and, 207, 211, 224, *232*; epidemics and, 213, 220, 225; ethics and, 205–7, 215, 217, 222, 340n15; expert work and, 226–30; Good Clinical Practice (GCP) and, 217; governance and, 234; Gugu Dlamini Clinic and, 215, 218–28, 231, 340n13, 341n18; hardened guidelines and, 205–35; healthcare and, 206–7, 214, 226, 229–34, 340n12; hospitals and, 206, 221, 228–32, 235, 340n11, 341n20; IAS and, 209–10, 340n9; infection and, 211, *212*, 213–14, 218–24, 228–30, *232*; informed consent and, *212*, 229; insurance and, 213, 216, 229; IRBs and, 217; legal issues and, 206–35, 340n12, 341n22; malpractice and, 207, 209; managing uncertainty and, 208–10; medicine and, 205–35; new anxieties for, 207–8; NIH and, 209; norms and, 230; nurses and, 211, *212*, 216–17, 221, 230–33; official rigidity and, 224–26; pediatricians and, *212*, 219, 222–24, 228, *232*, 339n3, 341n18; PEPFAR and, 229; pharmaceutical companies and, 210; Philly Lutaaya Clinic and, 214, 218, 222, 227–28, 340n14; physicians and, 211, 226–33, 340n17; PMTCT and, 205, 210–12, 215–16, 219–21, 339nn2–3, 340n16; poorer countries and, 219, 222, 341n20; pregnancy and, 206, 211, *212*, 213–14, 219–21, 228; protocols and, 207–8, 226, 229, 341n18; RCT and, 213–14, 340n14; regulations and, 207–8, 211, 213–16, 221–22, 226, 230, 234, 339n6; richer countries and, *212*, 220, 222, 231; Robert Rafsky Clinic and, 216; rules and, 205–35; side effects and, 211, 225–26, 228; social issues and, 213, 223, 234, 341n18; South Africa and, 205–6, 211, *212*, 215–16, 218, 219–29, 339n1, 339n3, 340n12; specialists and, *232*, *233*; standard operating procedure (SOP) and, 207, 211; TAC and, 206, 220; task shifting and, 226–30; testing and, 210–23, *232*, 340n10, 340n12, 340n14, 341n19; Thailand and, 217, 219, 225; therapy initiation and, 224–26; training and, 207, 210–13, 217–18, 221, 225–26, 231, *232*, 235, 340n13; transmission and, 205, 211, 215, 219–22, 226, 233, 340n14; tuberculosis and, 227–28; Uganda and, 214–15, 218–19, 222–27, 340n14, 340n16, 341n19; UNAIDS and, 209, 211, 229, 340n7; uncharted medical territory and, 222–24; VCT and, 213–14; WHO and, 205, 209–10, 222, 229, 340n9

discretion: disciplining and, 206–7, *212*, 226, 230–34; ethics and, 263, 281; guidelines and, 26–28; ignorance and, 250; legal issues and, 233–34; limits on, 230–33; moral issues and, 295, 313; privacy and, 7 (*see also* privacy); rule proliferation and, *80*, 97, 114; trustworthy data and, 177, 199–202, 338n16; universals and, *149*

discrimination: anti-discrimination laws, 6, 325n2; ethics and, 267; guidelines and, 3–7, 12, 325n2; ignorance and, 250, 259; moral issues and, 287; standards and, 328n17; stigma and, 3–7, 12, 250, 259, 267, 287, 325n2, 328n17 disease: biology and, 1; constituency activism and, *86*; disciplining and, 213–14, *232*; ethics and, 272, 274, 285; guidelines and, 1, 4–6, 12–15, 18, 21–22, 30, 326n10; ignorance and, 246, 251, 254, 256; infection and, 4 (*see also* infection); moral issues and, 288–94, 298–99, 304, 309; rule proliferation and, 91–93, 101, 107, 122, 331n21; standards and, 44–50, 55–56, 63, 67–73, 327n4, 327n10, 328n17; trustworthy data and, 164–68; universals and, 123, 126–33, 141–52, 161, 163, 333n3, 336n27. *See also specific diseases*

disease-novelty effects, 143–44, 146, 150

division of labor: clinics and, 64, 143, 154, 237–38, 254–58, 261; complex, 254–57, *260*; at Gugu Dlamini Clinic, 64, 154; ignorance and, 237–38, 254–58, 261; Stinchcombe on, 143

Dlamini, Gugu, 329n20

doctors: disciplining and, 205, 208, 211, *212–13*, 217, 219, 224–35, 340n12; ethics and, 263, 271, *278*, 279, 282–84; general practitioners, 38; guidelines and, 13, 15, 25; Hippocratic Oath and, 249; hospitals and, 48, 69, 111, 124, 152–53, 198, 228–32, 254, 263, 337n8; ignorance and, 242, 251–52, 254; legal issues and, 13; moral issues and, 288, 291–94; qualifications of, 130; rule proliferation and, 90, 97, 104, 111, 114; specialists, 38, 103–7, 130, 137, 145, 171, 181, 191, 201, *232*, 233, 240–41, 254, 261, *278*, 282–83, 311–13; standards and, 35, 38–39, 48–50, 54, 59, 66, 69; trustworthy data and, 160, 164, 180, 195, 198, 338n21, 339n23; universals and, 123–25, 130, 135–36, *149*, 152–53, 157, 335n19, 336n32

Doctors Without Borders (Médecins sans Frontières (MSF)), *109*, 111, 288, 294, 304, 307, 337n8

Doha Declaration, 22, 41, 56, 292, 305, 311, 326n9

"double billing," 51, 54

Douglas, Mary, 259

downstream effects, 166–70

drugs: access to, 2, 22–23, 34, 57, 129, 162, 219, 247, 279, 288–89, 292, 295, 298, 301, 304, 307, 312, 327n8, 342n6; addictions and, 101, 250; assistance programs and, 52, 92, 248, 274, 295; cocktails of, 14, 127, 150–52, 251, 288, 306, 325n6, 343n20; combination pills, 344n5; disciplining and, 205–6, 211, *212*, 219–28, *232*, 339n1, 342n6, 342n13, 343n20; ethics and, 264, 266, 272–74, 278, 279, 344n8; FDA and, 3, 22, 40, *85–86*, 98–99, 164, 168, 172, 177, 179, *182*, 193–94, 291, 303, 329n23, 332n24; generic, 40, 45, 71, 135, 292, 295, 305, 335n17; Gieryn on, 171–72; guidelines and, 1–5, 14–17, 22–23, 29, 31, 325n6; ignorance and, 242–44, 247–52, 255; injectable, 344n5; Kefauver-Harris Amendment and, 99; moral issues and, 288–312, 315, 345n16, 346n21; pharmaceutical companies and, 14 (*see also* pharmaceutical companies); price of, *82*, *84*, 96, 163, 205, 291, 305, 327n8; procurement of, 14, 264; rule proliferation and, *80–86*, 88, 92, 96–99, 111, 114, 118, 332n24; side effects and, 4–8, 15 (*see also* side effects); South Africa and, 14, 40, 42, 45, 52, 71, 111, 136, 158, 169, 205–6, 211, 219–23, 279, 292, 298, 304–5; standards and, 34, 37, 40–45, 48–52, 55–57, 64–68, 71, 327n8, 329n23; Thailand and, 14, 42, 45, 57, 111, 135–36, 219, 296, 304–7; toxicity and, 15, 118, 135, 158, 335n18, 340n17; trustworthy data and, 164, 167–72, 177–79, *182*, 183, 190, 193–94, 198, 336n1, 337nn8–9; two-drug standard and, 205, 211, 220, 339n1; Uganda and, 14, 42, 45, 64–65, 68, 71, 111, 124–25, 147, 219, 223, 227, 243, 279, 288, 296–304, 307, 312; universals and, 124–31, 134–37, 141, 147, 150–51, 153, 157–58, 163, 334n6, 336n29; Vienna Declaration and, 334n6

drug users, 4–5, 56, 61

Duesberg, Peter, 167–68, 170, 337n5

Ebola, 36
ECRI Guidelines Trust, 89
Eddy, David, 89
education: AETC and, 111; certification and, 29, 41, 112, 181, 188–89, 192, 203, 267; Cha-on Suesum Clinic and, 57–59; disciplining and, 216, 340n9; guidelines and, 21–22, 27, 112; Haiti and, 21; hygiene and, 22, *84*, 93, 254, 331n14; investment in, 22; literacy and, 56, 240; professional providers and, 55; richer people and, 22, 27, 56; rule proliferation and, 100, 112, 122, 331n19, 332n26; science and, 336n4; South Africa and, 62; specialists and, 38, 103, 105, 107, 130, 137, 145, 171, 181, 191, 201, *232*, 233, 240–41, 254, 261, *278*, 282–83, 311–13; standards and, 55–56, 62; Suesum and, 328n17; Thailand and, 56, 328n17; trustworthy data and, *182*, 188, 336n4, 337n9; universals and, 137, 139, 162, 334n13; US healthcare and, 100
Effectiveness and Efficiency (Cochrane), 88
efficiency: accountability and, *84*; guidelines and, 25–26; rule proliferation and, *83–84*, 88, 104; standards and, 53, 60; trustworthy data and, 168, 173; universals and, 131, 143–44
Eimer, Thomas, 41
Elixir Sulfanilamide, 99
Elizabeth Glaser Pediatric AIDS Foundation (EGPAF), 296, 339n3
Elliott, Carl, 105–6
empowerment: disciplining and, 207, 211, 224, *232*; ethics and, *278*; guidelines and, 25; moral issues and, 308; rule proliferation and, 113; standards and, 65, 328n12; trustworthy data and, 337n6; universals and, 145, 162
epidemics: disciplining and, 213, 220, 225; gay men and, 5, 30, 42, 47, 151, 304; guidelines and, 2–5, 10–11, 18, 21–23, 30, 325n2; HIV/AIDS, 1–3, 5, 10–11, 18, 21–23, 30, 41–47, 56, 60–61, 90, 122, 127, 163, 165, 168, 213, 220, 258, 290, 292, 304, 325n2, 333n3; ignorance and,

258; moral issues and, 30–34, 290, 292; rule proliferation and, 90, 122, 127, 333n3; standards and, 41–47, 55–56, 60–61, 328n12; trustworthy data and, 165, 168; UNAIDS and, 325n2; universals and, 151, 163
Equal Economic Opportunity Commission (EEOC), 267–68
Eskridge, William N., Jr., 99
Espeland, Wendy Nelson, 174
ethics: accountability and, 275; agency and, *278*, 282–83; AIDS and, 274; ART and, 345nn6–9, 345n13; attention and, 277–81; biology and, 269; Bobbi Campbell Clinic and, 274, 279–80; Cha-on Suesum Clinic and, 270, 274; compliance work and, 264, 267, 269, 284–85; confidentiality and, 272, 275–76; consent and, 262–63, 268, 270, 273, 280, 283; counseling and, 276, 279; debates over, 299–301; Declaration of Helsinki and, *115–16*, 118–19, 300, 332n33, 333n38; DHHS and, 267; disciplining and, 205–7, 215, 217, 222, 340n15; discretion and, 263, 281; discrimination and, 267; disease and, 272, 274, 285; doctors and, 263, 271, *278*, 279, 282–84; drugs and, 264, 266, 272–74, 278, 279, 344n8; EEO law and, 267–68; empowerment and, *278*; Gugu Dlamini Clinic and, 274, 276, 279, 281; guidelines and, 2, 5–6, 23, 29, 32–33; healthcare and, 263, 266, 281, 284; Hippocratic Oath and, 249; hospitals and, 262–67, 274, 276, 280–81, 285; human rights and, 282; ignorance and, 243–44, 259; infection and, 270, 274–76, 279, 285; informed consent and, 270, 344n5; insurance and, 264, 275; IRBs and, 23, 262, 266–68, *278*, 282–85, 343n1; lapses in, 2, 120; legal issues and, 264–72, 275–76, 283, 286; legitimacy and, 269; medicine and, 270, 343n3; moral issues and, 288, 299–301, 313–14, 345n14; NIH and, 265; norms and, 272, *278*, 282; nurses and, 263, 273–75, 277, 282–83; obligations, 283–84;

ethics (*continued*)
official, 33, 264–86; OHRP and, 267–68; on the ground, 33, 264–86; pediatricians and, 276; pharmaceutical companies and, 264, 281; Philly Lutaaya Clinic and, 266–70, 274, 279, 282–85; physicians and, 264, 279, 283–84, 344n6; poorer countries and, 270, 280, 285; pregnancy and, 270, 273, 343n2; privacy and, 275; protocols and, 270–75; recruiting research subjects, 32, 38, 117, 175–76, 183, 190, 240–44, 263, 269, 272, 282, 341n1; regulations and, 264–69, 276, *278*, 280–85, 343n1; richer countries and, 270, 280, 343n20; Robert Rafsky Clinic and, 262–68, 271–75, 277, 280, 283; rule proliferation and, 78, *87*, 93–94, 100, 105, 107, 113–20, 333n40; rules and, 262–86; skepticism and, 270; social issues and, 264–66, 269, 277–81, *278*, 285; source of, 281–82; South Africa and, 279; specialists and, *278*, 282–83; standard operating procedure (SOP) and, 266, 271; testing and, 268, 273, 275–76; Thailand and, 270, 282, 340n15, 345n10; therapeutic misconception and, 344n6; training and, 262, 266–68, 272–73, 276, 282; transmission and, 269, 276, 279; trustworthy data and, 168, 172–73, 189–90, 337n8; Uganda and, 268–70, 275, 279; universals and, 335n23; wicked problems and, 264–65, *278*, 284–86
Ethiopia, 288
ethnicity, 27
ethnographic methods, 24, 45, 271, 323, 343n3, 346n3
European Medicines Agency, 327n6
evaluations, 63, *83*, *148*, 176–77, 334n15
evidence-based medicine (EBM): guidelines and, 26, 79, 88–91; moral issues and, 297, 303; rule proliferation and, *80–83*, 89–90; universals and, 131–32, 141–44, 146, 155, 158, 334n9
Evidence-Based Medicine Working Group, 88–89

evidentiary packages, 179–81; as "gray boxes," 338n19
exposure, 3, 7, *110*, 111, 344n5

Federal Medical Assistance Percentage (FMAP) multiplier, 330n11
Federalwide Assurance (FWA), *116*, 120, 267
Feldman, Martha S., 238
Ferejohn, John, 99
fever, 199
Fifteenth International AIDS Conference, 60
fiscal responsibility, 91–94
Fisher, Jill, 242–44
fixed-dose combination (FDC), 151
Food, Drug, and Cosmetics Act, 99
Food and Drug Administration (FDA): as compliance bureaucracy, 98–99; drugs and, 3, 22, 40, *85–86*, 98–99, 164, 168, 172, 177, 179, *182*, 193–94, 291, 303, 329n23, 332n24; guidelines and, 3, 19, 22; Kefauver-Harris Amendment and, 99; moral issues and, 291, 293, 303, 345n16, 346n17; rule proliferation and, *80–81*, *85–86*, 98–99, 119, 331n14, 332nn23–24; standards and, 40, 329n23; trustworthy data and, 164, 168, 172, 177, 179–80, *182*, 193–94, 339n27; as USDA Division/Bureau of Chemistry, 332n23; user fees and, 332n24
formality/informality: of codes, 6; of ethics principles, 266, 271; of laws and legal systems, 16–20, 29, 77, 79, 104, 129, 206, 207, 231, 234, 271, 330n7; of procedures, 138, 203, 223, 247; of rules, 14–20, 27, 29, 90, 95, 172, 177; of treatment contracts, 296

Gallo, Robert, 166–67, 170
gangrene, 169
gay men: AIDS and, 4–5, 12, 215, 328n12, 329n20; CDC and, 326n19; drug users and, 4–5, 56, 61; epidemic issues and, 5, 30, 42, 47, 151, 304; HIV and, 3–5, 12, 20, 22, 35, 42, 47, 304, 328n12; infections and, 3–4, 22, 42, 47, 326n10;

stigma and, 4–5, 12, 215, 328n12, 329n20

Gay Men's Health Crisis (GMHC), 293, 303

gay rights, 3

Gazley, J. Lynn, 176

Gelsinger, Jesse, 241, 341n4

general practitioners, 38

gene therapy, 241

Gieryn, Thomas F., 166, 171–72

Gini coefficient, 42, 60

GlaxoSmithKline, 346n21

Global Fund to Fight AIDS, Tuberculosis and Malaria (GFATM), 288, 292, 305

Global Health Workforce Alliance, 38

globalization: drivers of, 36–37; effects of, 36–37; global North, 5, 19, 29, 32, 39, 42, 161, 248, 257; global South, 5, 19, 29, 32, 147; guidelines and, 1, 16, 18–20, 30; healthcare and, 34–41; human rights and, 37–38; Klug on, 18–19; legal issues and, 1, 16–20, 30, 287; localizing phenomena of, 41–46; of medicine, 1, 16–20, 36, 287; moral issues and, 287, 293; norms and, 18; poorer countries and, 36–37; richer countries and, 36–37; site selection and, 41–46; standards and, 35–41; transnational diffusion and, 18

Global Public Health Intelligence Network (GPHIN), 38, 327n4

"gold standard" indicators, 310, 332n30

Good Clinical Practice (GCP): disciplining and, 217; moral issues and, 289; rule proliferation and, 113, 116, 119–20, 333n38; trustworthy data and, 172, 179, 182, 188, 338n17, 339n24

Gostin, Lawrence O., 9

governance: codes and, 1, 6, 23, 53–54, 114–18, 121, 217, 258, 262, 266, 282, 284; compliance bureaucracies and, 98–101; disciplining and, 234; divisions of labor and, 64, 143, 154, 237–38, 254–58, 261; external control and, 79, 88–91; guidelines and, 2, 13, 15–20, 23–30; healthcare and, 2, 13, 16–17, 23, 25, 30, 36, 41, 42, 76–77, 103, 238; ignorance and, 238;

micromanagement and, 26–27; moral issues and, 315; policing and, 19–20, 145; reform and, 18–19, 26, 85, 266, 297, 345n10; research administration and, 106–20; rule proliferation and, 75–77, 103, 113, 121; standards and, 36, 41; surveillance and, 18, 20, 327n4; trustworthy data and, 177, 202

Government Pharmaceutical Organization (GPO): moral issues and, 295, 310, 346n26; standards and, 56, 71, 328n15; universals and, 135, 151, 335n18

Griswold v. Connecticut, 102

Gugu Dlamini Clinic: ART and, 62–64, 154; ARV and, 62, 136–37, 247; description of, 61–62; disciplining and, 215, 218–28, 231, 340n13, 341n18; division of labor at, 64, 154; ethics and, 274, 276, 279, 281; funding, 62–65; ignorance and, 247, 252–53, 258; medical records and, 64; moral issues and, 296–97, 309–12; PEPFAR and, 63–64; PMTCT and, 220–22; research and, 60–65, 71–72, 141, 156–61, 176, 247, 274, 309–12, 329n21; rule proliferation and, 110, 112–13, 121; staff concerns at, 64–65; staging at, 63; standards and, 60–65, 71–72, 329nn20–21, 330n32; trustworthy data and, 169, 176; universals and, 136–42, 146–63

guidelines: activists and, 2–4, 8, 13, 18, 23, 31, 33; AIDS and, 1–7, 10–13, 16–24, 325n3, 326n9, 326n11; ART and, 10–11, 325n6, 326n7; binding versus nonbinding, 1–2, 77, 104, 109, 115, 119; biology and, 14, 18, 22, 31; CD4 and, 326n8, 326n11; CDC and, 6–12, 22, 326nn10–11; clinics and, 1–33; codes and, 1, 6, 23, 53–54, 114–18, 121, 217, 258, 262, 266, 282, 284; confidentiality and, 4–5, 8–9, 14–15, 216–19; consent and, 4–5, 8–9, 12, 20, 33; counseling and, 2–10, 14, 30; denialism and, 13; disciplining and, 205–35; discretion and, 26–28; discrimination and, 3–7, 12, 325n2; disease, 1, 4–6, 12–15, 18,

guidelines (*continued*)
21–22, 30, 326n10; doctors and, 13, 15, 25; drugs and, 1–5, 14–17, 22–23, 29, 31, 325n6; education and, 21–22, 27, 112; efficiency and, 25–26; empowerment and, 25; epidemics and, 2–5, 10–11, 18, 21–23, 30, 325n2; ethics and, 2, 5–6, 23, 29, 32–33; evidence-based medicine (EBM) and, 26, 79, 88–91; expert work and, 226–30; external control and, 79, 88–91; FDA and, 3, 19, 22; globalization and, 1, 16, 18–20, 30; governance and, 2, 13, 15–20, 23–30; hardened, 17, 19, 77, *85*, 91, 112, *116–17*, 120, 205–35, 302–3, 315; healthcare and, 1–5, 8–10, 13–26, 30–33, 76–87; hospitals and, 24; human rights and, 4–9, 12, 26, 325n3; infection and, 1, 3–4, 7, 10–15, 18–22, 32, 326n8, 326n10; insurance and, 14, 22; Joint Commission and, 16, *81*, *85–86*, 92, 94, 98–99, 208, 331n19, 331n21, 332n22; legal issues and, 210–22 (*see also* law and legal issues); malaria and, 15; managing uncertainty and, 208–10; Medicaid and, 9; medical malpractice and, 20; Medicare and, 9; medicine and, 1–2, 7, 9, 13, 16–33; NIH and, 23; norms and, 5, 12, 18–19, 27, 29; Nuremberg Code, 114, *115*, 118, 266; opportunistic infection (OI) and, 10, 13–15; PEPFAR and, 45, 50, 63–64; pharmaceutical companies and, 14, 22–23, 33; physicians and, 12, 22, 24–25, 31, 326n8; PICT and, 6–7, 11; poorer countries and, 1, 14–15, 20, 22, 26, 28, 31, 309–13; practice variations and, 28; pregnancy and, 7, 14–15; privacy and, 7; protocols and, 1, 4–6, 14, 15, 22, 24, 30, 32; RCT and, 6–12, 325nn3–4; regulations and, 1–3, 10, 13–18, 22–33, 326n9, 326n12; research administration and, 106–20; richer countries and, 1–2, 5–6, 15, 22, 26–28, 32; rules and, 1–33 (*see also* rules); skill and, 226–30; social issues and, 2–5, 11–18, 21–22, 27–32, 303–9; soft law, 19–20, 77, *80*, 112, *117*, 120, 172,

173, 202, 234, 293, 302–3, 315, 330n1; South Africa and, 1–2, 5–6, 13–14, 30; standards and, 34–74 (*see also* standards); testing, 2–14, 22, 30, 213–16; training and, 6, 17–18, 20, 24, 29, 31–32; treatment equity and, 127–32, 294–98; TRIPS and, 14, 22, 326n9; tuberculosis and, 15; Uganda and, 1–2, 14, 30, 325n4; UNAIDS and, 6–12, 325nn2–3, 326n13; universals and, 123–63 (*see also* universals); VCT and, 4–12, 15, 22, 325nn4–5; WHO and, 6–11, 19, 326n11; WTO and, 326n9
Guyatt, Gordon, 89

Haiti, 21–22
Harden, Victoria, 93
healthcare: accountability and, 91–94; compliance bureaucracies and, 98–101; disciplining and, 206–7, 214, 226, 229–34, 340n12; employer-sponsored, 96; ethics and, 263, 266, 281, 284; experts and, 230–33; faculty practice plans and, 96–97; fiscal responsibility and, 91–94; globalism and, 16–20, 34–41; governance and, 2, 13, 16–17, 23, 25, 30, 36, 41–42, 76–77, 103, 238; guidelines and, 1–5, 8–10, 13–26, 30–33; ignorance and, 236, 238, 250, 254; increasing profits in, 95–98; legal issues and, 4, 76–87, 102–4, 122; moral issues and, 287–89, 292, 294, 297–98, 302, 309, 314, 345n10; public payment for, 91–94; research administration and, 106–20; rule proliferation and, 76–78, *80–87*, 89–106, 112–13, 121–22, 330nn5–9, 331nn16–17, 332n25; standards and, 34–41, 52, 56, 73; trustworthy data and, 174, 202; Universal Coverage Scheme and, 56, 328n14; universals and, 123, 131, 133, 137, 142, 143, 152, 162–63, 334n14, 335n25
health disparities, 73, 289, 294
Health Insurance Portability and Accountability Act (HIPAA), 216–17, 275, 344n9
Helsinki Rules: ethics and, 266; moral issues and, 300, 306, 314; rule

proliferation and, *115–16*, 118–20, 332n33, 333n38

hemophilia, 42, 61, 151

hepatitis, 15, *110*

heterosexuals: HIV and, 5, 35, 42, 47, 61, 220; standards and, 35, 42–43, 47, 61; Uganda and, 1

highly active anti-retroviral therapy (HAART), 125, 291–92, 345n6

Hippocratic Oath, 249

HIV: annual global deaths of, 20–21; antibodies and, 3–4, 213, 256, 291; blood and, 3–4, 21–22, 144, 166, *212*, 213, 326n8, 328n17, 336n27; causal factors and, 13–14, 143–45, 306; commercial tests for, 3–4, 291; as death sentence, 291–93; disciplining medicine and, 205–35; downstream effects and, 166–70; early research controversies and, 166–70; as epidemic, 1–5, 10–11, 18, 21–23, 30, 41–47, 56, 60–61, 90, 122, 127, 163, 165, 168, 213, 220, 258, 290, 292, 304, 325n2, 333n3; ethics and, 262–86; exposure and, 3, 7, *110*, 111, 344n5; first case of, 20; as first global disease, 34–35; gay men and, 3–5, 12, 20, 22, 35, 42, 47, 304, 328n12; guidelines and, 1–33; heterosexuals and, 5, 35, 42, 47, 61, 220; history of, 13–16; moral issues and, 387–95; origins of, 20–21; as pandemic, 12, 20, 34; as preventable disease, 131; rule proliferation and, 75 (*see also* rule proliferation); Ryan White HIV/AIDS Program and, 52–53, *82*, *84*, 92, 94, 96, 102, *109*, 111, 113, 133, *148–49*, 155, 295, 328n12, 345n16; screening, 5, 7, 9, *83*, 175, 188, 214, 240; South Africa and, 1–2, 5–6, 13–14, 30, 34, 44–45, 52, 60–61, 71–72, 111, 113, 130, 152, 157–58, 168, 205–6, *212*, 215, 218–22, 226–29, 251–52, 255, 276, 279, 292, 298, 328n19, 329n23, 340n12; standards and, 34–74; strategic use of ignorance in clinics and, 236–61; testing, 3–13 (*see also* testing); Thailand and, 2, 14, 30, 34, 42, 45, 56–57, 59, 111, 130, 219, 304–5, 310,

317–18, 328n17; trustworthy data and, 165–74, 194, 202; Uganda and, 1–2, 14, 30, 34, 44–45, 60, 67–68, 71, 111, 124, 130, 141, 152, 214–15, 219, 222, 227, 243, 246, 251, 255–56, 269, 275, 279, 298, 301–4, 312, 317–19, 329n26, 340n16, 341n19; UNGASS and, 8, 325n3; universals and, 143–63

HIV Prevention Trials Network (HPTN), 327n10, 331n13, 338n14

HIV Vaccine Trials Network (HVTN), 327n10

homosexuals. *See* gay men

hospitals: as charitable institutions, 77; disciplining and, 206, 221, 228–32, 235, 340n11, 341n20; doctors and, 48, 69, 111, 124, 152–53, 198, 228–32, 254, 263, 337n8; ethics and, 262–67, 274, 276, 280–81, 285; guidelines and, 24; ignorance and, 254, 342n8; moral issues and, 294, 297, 307, 312; nurses and, 282 (*see also* nurses); patients' rights and, 6, 8, 78, *86*, 101, 177, 207, 297; physicians and, 279 (*see also* physicians); rule proliferation and, 75, 77, *84–85*, 93–96, 105–11, 122, 331n21, 332n32; shortened stays in, 131; standards and, 34, 38, 42, 48, 51–53, 56, 61–72; trustworthy data and, 169, 184, 191, 196, 198, 337n8, 338n18; universals and, 124, 131, 133, 137, 143, *148*, 149–55, 335n21, 336n28

human rights: ethics and, 282; globalization and, 37–38; guidelines and, 4–9, 12, 26, 325n3; ignorance and, 246; moral issues and, 287, 297, 302, 307; patients' rights and, 6, 8, 78, *86*, 101, 177, 207, 297; right to health and, 37–38, 129, 297, 387n3; rule proliferation and, 113–14, *115*; standards and, 37; testing and, 4, 6, 9

hygiene, 22, *84*, 93, 254, 331n14

ignorance: absence of information, 236–61; abstinence and, 246, 261, 342n9, 342n11; accountability and, 238; activists and, 251; AIDS and, 244–48, 251, 341n9, 342n15; ART

ignorance (*continued*)
and, 243, 251–52, 255, 342n15, 343n20; as bliss, 238–39; Bobbi Campbell Clinic and, 241; CD4 and, 342n15; confidentiality and, 250; consent and, 239–45, 248, 259–61, 341nn2–3, 344n5; credibility and, 243–49; cross-national translation and, 245–49; discretion and, 250; discrimination and, 250, 259; disease and, 246, 251, 254, 256; distributed, 239, 244–45, 249–61; division of labor and, 237–38, 254–58, 261; doctors and, 242, 251–52, 254; drugs and, 242–44, 247–52, 255; epidemics and, 258; ethics and, 243–44, 259; governance and, 238; Gugu Dlamini Clinic and, 247, 252–53, 258; healthcare and, 236, 238, 250, 254; hospitals and, 254, 342n8; human rights and, 246; infection and, 244, 247, 250–52, 255–57, 343n19; informed consent and, 239–45, 248, 259, *260*; insurance and, 243; IRBs and, 240–45, 261, 341n2, 341n5; layered backstages and, 245–49, *260*; legal issues and, 236–40, 246; legitimacy and, 248, *260*; malaria and, 342n9; medicine and, 238, 254, 257–59, 342n13, 343n20; mundanity of, 259–61; nurses and, 240–44, 254; organizational boundaries and, 254–58, *260*; participant construction and, 239–45; PEPFAR and, 246, 248, 342nn9–10; pharmaceutical companies and, 248, 250; Philly Lutaaya Clinic and, 240–41, 243, 246–51, 256–58; physicians and, 243, 253, 258; PMTCT and, 261; poorer countries and, 243, 247–48, 252–57, 342n14; pregnancy and, 240, 252, 255, 343n20; protocols and, 240, 247, 252; regulations and, 236–41, 248, 259–61, 341n4; richer countries and, 252, 255; ritual surplus and, 239–45, 259, *260*; Robert Rafsky Clinic and, 241, 243, 250; rules and, 236, 239, 245, 247–49, *260*; sequestered knowledge and, 236–49, 259, *260*; side effects and, 238, 240, 249–54, 258–61; skepticism and, 261; social issues and, 256–59; South Africa and, 246, 250–52, 255, 258; specialists and, 240–41, 254, 261; standard operating procedure (SOP) and, 247–49; strategic clinical use of, 236–61; technology and, 238, 249; testing and, 247, 250–51, 256, 261; training and, 240; transmission and, 252, 255–56, 343nn20–21; Uganda and, 240–43, 246, 251, 255–56, 258; UNAIDS and, 257, 343nn19–20; willful, 236, 238, 261

inclusiveness/inclusion, 315; of clinical trials, 113; of family members in treatment, 280, 296–98; healthcare policy and, 102; of researchers from poorer countries, 159, 290, 310

India, 41, 61–62, 169

infection: coinfection, 15, 63, 107, *110*, 125, 147, 153–54, 294; diagnostics on, 3, 12–13, *83*, 150, 164, 214, 244, 317; disciplining and, 211, *212*, 213–14, 218–24, 228–31; ethics and, 270, 274–76, 279, 285; exposure and, 3, 7, *110*, 111, 344n5; guidelines and, 1, 3–4, 7, 10–15, 18–22, 32, 326n8, 326n10; hygiene and, 22, *84*, 93, 254, 331n14; ignorance and, 244, 247, 250–52, 255–57, 343n19; moral issues and, 291, 294, 300, 304, 314, 344n5; opportunistic infection (OI), 10, 13–15, 48, 63, 69, 107, 125, 153, 161, 291, 298, 307; peak of new, 21; PMTCT and, 125, 205, 210–12, 215–16, 219–21, 261, 292, 339nn2–3, 340n16, 345n13; rates of, 1, 230; rule proliferation and, 92–93, 107–9, *110*; standards and, 36–38, 41–42, 47–52, 55, 61, 63, 67, 73, 327nn9–10, 328n17, 328n19; transmission and, 10–14, 37, 125, 135, 152, 205, 211, 219–20, 252, 255–56, 276, 279, 326n7, 328n19, 344n5; trustworthy data and, 164; universals and, 22–23, 94, 123, 125, 133, 135, 144, 147, 150–54, 162, 336n27

informed consent: disciplining and, *212*, 229; ethics and, 270, 344n5; ignorance and, 239–45, 248, 259, *260*; patients' rights and, *82*, *86*, 102, 122, 180, 188,

212, 229, 239–45, 248, 259, *260*, 270, 338n15, 344n5; rule proliferation and, *82*, *86*, 102, 122; trustworthy data and, 180, 188, 338n15

Institute of Medicine (National Academy of Medicine), 7, 9, *82–83*, 88–89

institutionalization effects, 143, 146, *148*

institutional review boards (IRBs): Bobbi Campbell Clinic and, 53, 55; disciplining and, 217; ethics and, 23, 262, 266–68, *278*, 282–85, 343n1; ignorance and, 240–45, 261, 341n2, 341n5; moral issues and, 289, 301–3, 308, 313–14, 345n14; Robert Rafsky Clinic and, 49–50; rule proliferation and, 99–100, 105, 114, *116–17*, 120, 332n32; standards and, 49–50, 53, 55; trustworthy data and, 174, *182*, 188–89, 201, 203

insurance: America's Health Insurance Plans, 330n5; deductibles, 96; disciplining and, 213, 216, 229; employer-sponsored, 96; ethics and, 264, 275; faculty practice plans and, 96–97; guidelines and, 14, 22; HIPAA and, 216–17, 275, 344n9; ignorance and, 243; increasing profits and, 95–96; premiums, 95–96; Robert Rafsky Clinic and, 49; rule proliferation and, *80–85*, 95–96, 101–2, 121; standards and, 49–52, 72; trustworthy data and, 190; Universal Coverage Scheme and, 56, 328n14

International AIDS Conference (IAC): Bangkok, 10, 60, 127, 305, 310, 332n4; conference themes, 334n11; Durban, 127; melding structure of, 127; moral issues and, 290–92, 304–6, 312; "One World, One Hope" theme, 127; Paris, 127; Toronto, 220, 305; universals and, 334n5; Vancouver, 127, 291–92; Washington, DC, 332n4

International AIDS Society (IAS), 332n26, 333n3, 334n11, 346n20

International Antiviral Society–USA (IAS–USA): disciplining and, 209–10, 340n9; rule proliferation and, *108*, 332n26; universals and, 141–42

International Council for Harmonisation of Technical Requirements for Pharmaceuticals for Human Use (ICH), *116*, 119, 332n31

International Health Regulations (IHR), 37

International Maternal Pediatric Adolescent AIDS Clinical Trials (IMPAACT), 327n10

Irwin Memorial Blood Bank, 3

isolation, 203, 335n21

JAMA (*Journal of the American Medical Association*), 88, *108*, 134, 340n9

Japan, *116*, 118–19, 313, 327n6

Joint Clinical Research Center, 307

Joint Commission on Accreditation of Healthcare Organizations (JCAHO): as compliance bureaucracy, 98; disciplining and, 208; international affiliate (JCI), 331n21; legal issues and, 16; rule proliferation and, *81*, *85–86*, 92, 94, 98–99, 331n19, 331n21, 332n22

Kaletra, 305

Kampala, 65–66, 247, 258, 329n26

Kampala Declaration, 38

Kapita, Bila, 127, 333n3

Kaposi sarcoma (KS), 326nn10–11, 328n12

Kefauver-Harris Amendment, 99

Kenya, 288

kidneys, 250, 336n1

Kinshasa, 21, 333n3

Kleinman, Arthur, 245

Klug, Heinz, 18–19

Knorr Cetina, Karin, 171

Koop, C. Everett, 44

Krause, Monika, 274–75

Kyaddondo, David, 275

lactic acidosis, 157, 225–28, 250, 252, *260*, 336n32

Laos, 60

Latinos, 47, 275

Latour, Bruno, 171, 181

law and legal issues: access to justice, 26–27; administrative constitutionalism, 99; anti-discrimination law, 6, 325n2; antritrust law, *80*, *84*, 95, 346n18; Baby Doe Law, 207, 339n6; binding rules, 1–2, 77, 104, *109*, *115*, 119; *Canterbury v. Spence*, 102; clinics and, 23–29; disciplining, 205–35, 340n12, 341n22; doctors and, 13; EEO law, 267–68; endowments, 2, 287, 306, 344n1; ethics, 264–72, 275–76, 283, 286; experience of legalization, 104–6; external control, 79, 88–91; fiscal responsibility, 91–94; gaps in, 25–29, 285–86, 289–90; gay rights, 3; globalization, 1, 16–20, 30, 287; *Griswold v. Connecticut*, 102; guidelines, 1–33 (*see also* guidelines); hard versus soft law, 17, 19, 77, *85*, 91, 112, *116–17*, 120, 173, 205–35, 302–3; 315; health and healthcare law, 76–87, 102–4, 122, 332n25; Helsinki Rules, *115–16*, 118–20, 266, 300, 306, 314, 332n33, 333n38; ignorance, 236–40, 246; locus of discretion, 233–34; malpractice, 20, 89–90, *108*, 131, 207, 209, 288; medicine and, 1–2, 9, 13, 16–33, 36, 77–78, *87*, 103, *116*, 119, 131, 202, 206–7, 210–22, 230–38, 287–315, 330n3, 339n5; moral, 287–315, 344n1; neutrality, 344n1; novices, 230–33; Nuremberg trials, 93; law on books versus in action, 25–27, 173, 264, 285–86; patients' rights, 6, 8, 78, *86*, 101, 177, 207, 297; practice variations, 28; promise of law, 313–15; public pressure, 101–2; *Quinlan, In re*, 102; reform, 18–19, 26, *85*, 266, 297, 345n10; research administration, 106–20; *Roe v. Wade*, 102; rule of law, 13, 26, 206, 289; rule proliferation, 76–79, *83–87*, 91, 94–95, 99–108, *109*, 112–22, 330n3; scientific claims, 288–89, 292–97, 305–6, 309; social, 2–5, 12, 14, 18, 21–22, 27, 32, 47, *86–87*, 101–2, 147, 213, 223, 234, 269, 289, 293, 303–9, 317–20, 332n25; soft law, 19–20, 77, *80*, 112, *117*, 120, 172–73, 202, 234, 293, 302–3, 315, 330n1; standards, 35–36, 41, 45, 47, 50–51; statutes, 1–6, 9, 18, 78, *86*, 99, 114, *116*, 119–22, 189, 198–99, 221–22, 266, 271, 281, 287, 289, 315, 330n11; surveillance, 18, 20, 327n4; testing, 3–13; trustworthy data, 166, 173, 183, 197–204, 337n8; uncharted medical territory, 222–24; universals, 129–31, 134, 147, 158, 163; US Constitution, 98

layered backstages, 245–49, *260*

legitimacy: ethics and, 269; ignorance and, 248, *260*; social movements and, 306–9; social order and, 16; trustworthy data and, 168, 175, 204, 337n10; universals and, *140*, 141, 145–46, *149*, 158–61, 336n30

Lempert, Richard, 27, 344n1

lipodystrophy, 251, *260*

literacy, 56, 240

Louw, Ronald, 215

Luhman, Niklas, 336n4

Lutaaya, Philly Bongoley, 329n26

Lütz, Susanne, 41

Lynch, Michael, 171

Makerere University Medical School, 65

malaria: guidelines and, 15; ignorance and, 342n9; moral issues and, 288, 344n2; standards and, 37, 71; trustworthy data and, 199; universals and, 154

Malawi, 5, 275, 319

malpractice: disciplining and, 207, 209; guidelines and, 20; legal issues and, 20, 89–90, *108*, 131, 207, 209, 288; moral issues and, 288; rule proliferation and, 89–90, *108*; universals and, 131

Mandela, Nelson, 305

Manguzi Hospital, 206

Marburg virus, 36

March, James G., 237–38

Mbeki, Thabo, 13, 44, 60, 157, 168, 205, 220, 327n7

McCarran-Ferguson Act, 95

McMasters University, 89

Medicaid: Bobbi Campbell Clinic and, 52, 54; compliance bureaucracies and, 98–99; fiscal responsibility and, 91–94; guidelines and, 9; moral issues and, 303; Robert Rafsky Clinic and, 49; rule proliferation and, *81–86*, 91–98, 102–3, 331n20; universals and, 132

medical-industrial complex, *82, 85*, 95–96

medical records: efficiency and, 104; electronic, 97; Gugu Dlamini Clinic and, 64; rule proliferation and, 97, 104, 106; trustworthy data and, 180, 191–97; universals and, 138–39, 153–56

Medicare: Bobbi Campbell Clinic and, 52, 54; compliance bureaucracies and, 98–99; fiscal responsibility and, 91–92; guidelines and, 9; Robert Rafsky Clinic and, 49; rule proliferation and, *81–86*, 88, 91–98, 103, 331n20; universals and, 132

medicine: antibiotics, 37, 63, 337n8; clinics and, 23–29; disciplining and, 205–35; discretion and, 233–34; ethics and, 270, 343n3; European Medicines Agency, 327n6; evidence-based, *83*, 89 (*see also* evidence-based medicine (EBM)); globalization of, 1, 16–20, 36, 287; guidelines and, 1–2, 7, 9, 13, 16–33; ignorance and, 238, 254, 257–59, 342n13, 343n20; legal issues and, 1–2, 9, 13, 16–33, 36, 77–78, *87*, 103, *116*, 119, 131, 202, 206–7, 210–22, 230–38, 287–315, 330n3, 339n5; locus of discretion and, 233–34; moral issues and, 287–90, 297–99, 303–5, 346n19; practice variations and, 28; rule proliferation and, 77–79, *80–83, 87*, 88–90, 103, *116*, 119; side effects and, 4–8, 15 (*see also* side effects); standards and, 35–37, 42, 69, 73; switching regimens and, 224–26; trustworthy data and, 165, 168–69, 177, 193, 202, 337n7; universals and, 123, 128–31, 141–46, 151, 153, 333n3, 334n9; Western, 28, 165, 168–69, 270, 337n7. *See also specific medicines*

Medicines Act, 346n19

Medicines Control Council (MCC), 335n20

meningitis, 126, 153, 337n8

MERS (Middle Eastern respiratory syndrome), 37

Merton, Robert, 165

middle-income countries, 7, 36–37, 41, 305, 343n20

Ministry of Public Health (MOPH), 328n16

Minow, Martha, 27

"modifier 25" issues, 54, 155

Montagnier, Luc, 166–67, 170

moral claims, 292–94, 305–6

moral issues: activists, 293, 297, 303–8, 315, 345n10; AIDS, 288–98, 301–5, 310, 314–15; ART, 288, 292–95, 300–304, 307; ARV, 291, 297, 300, 305–6; biology, 309; Bobbi Campbell Clinic, 295–96; CD4, 294, 298; CDC, 291, 294, 298; Cha-on Suesum Clinic, 295–96, 309–12, 346n26; clinics, 387–95; compliance work, 311; consent, 313; counseling, 298; Declaration of Helsinki, *115–16*, 118–19, 300, 332n33, 333n38; DHHS, 297; discretion, 295, 313; discrimination, 287; disease, 288–94, 298–99, 304, 309; doctors, 288, 291–94; drugs, 288–312, 315, 345n16, 346n21; empowerment, 308; epidemics, 30–34, 290, 292; ethics, 288, 299–301, 313–14, 345n14; evidence-based medicine (EBM), 297, 303; FDA, 291, 293, 303, 345n16, 346n17; globalization, 287, 293; Good Clinical Practice (GCP), 289; governance, 315; Government Pharmaceutical Organization (GPO), 295, 310, 346n26; Gugu Dlamini Clinic, 296–97, 309–12; healthcare, 287–89, 292, 294, 297–98, 302, 309, 314, 345n10; Hippocratic Oath, 249; hospitals, 294, 297, 307, 312; human rights, 287, 297, 302, 307; IAS, 346n20; infection, 291, 294, 300, 304, 314, 344n5; IRBs, 289, 301–3, 308, 313–14, 345n14; legal issues, 287–315, 344n1; malaria, 288, 344n2; malpractice, 288; Medicaid, 303; medicine, 287–90, 297–99, 303–5, 346n19; norms, 289; nurses, 290, 311, 346n24; opportunistic infection (OI),

moral issues (*continued*)
291, 298, 307; patients' rights, 6, 8, 78, *86*, 101, 177, 207, 297; pediatricians, 296, 310; PEPFAR, 290–92, 296, 306, 344n4, 346n26; pharmaceutical companies, 290–95, 299, 302–15, 346nn18–21; Philly Lutaaya Clinic, 296, 309–12; physicians, 290, 294–95, 301, 303, 307–8, 311–15, 345n6, 345n10, 346n17; PMTCT, 292, 345n13; poorer countries, 288–89, 294, 298–313, 314–15, 344n2, 345n11, 346n23; pregnancy, 293, 300; promise of law, 313–15; protocols, 289, 299, 306–9, 344n6; regulations, 287, 289, 293, 298–99, 302, 307, 311–15; research conduct, 299–301; richer countries, 289, 292–93, 298–314, 344n2, 346n23; Robert Rafsky Clinic, 294–96, 301, 308, 346n24; rules, 287–315; scientific claims, 288–89, 292–97, 305–6, 309; side effects, 291, 294, 299, 303, 310, 344n5, 345n12; skepticism, 311; social issues, 289, 293, 301–11, 317–21; South Africa, 292, 297–98, 304–5, 310–13, 346n19; specialists, 311, 313; standard operating procedure (SOP), 287, 289, 298–99; TAC, 292, 304, 346n19; testing, 292–93, 298, 308; Thailand, 304–5, 307, 310–11, 396; training, 290, 296–98, 309; transmission, 292, 300, 304; treatment equity, 294–98; TRIPS, 311; tuberculosis, 294, 344n2; Uganda, 288, 296, 298, 301–4, 307, 310–14; UNAIDS, 292, 306, 344n5; universals, 303–6; VCT, 298; WHO, 288, 292, 294, 297–98, 308, 344n2, 345n9; WTO, 289, 292, 305–6, 311
moral order, globalized, 287, 293
moral worth, 2, 33, 287, 290, 299, 309, 313
mucosal swabs, 213
Mulago Hospital, 65
Multicenter AIDS Cohort Study (MACS), 57
Museveni, Yoweri, 44, 269

National Guidelines Clearinghouse (NGC), 89, 330nn5–6

National Health Service, *83*, 88
National HIV/AIDS Clinicians' Consultation Center, 214
National Institute of Allergies and Infectious Diseases (NIAID), 327n10
National Institutes of Health (NIH): community advisory boards and, 23; as compliance bureaucracy, 98; DAIDS, 68, 327n10, 331n13; disciplining and, 209; ethics and, 265; fiscal responsibility and, 93; guidelines and, 23; Robert Rafsky Clinic and, 47–50; rule proliferation and, *80*, *84*, 93, 98, *116*, 118–19, 331n15, 331n18; standards and, 47–50, 57–61, 68, 70, 327n10; trustworthy data and, 172, 180, 185, 195, 203
Nazis, 114, 118, 313
NEJM (*New England Journal of Medicine*), 205
nevirapine, 124–25, 135, 152, 211, 220, 252, 339n1, 345n11
New York Civil Liberties Union, 9
New York Times, 12, 166, 344n2
90-90-90 program, 10–11, 293, 306, 325n6, 345n8
95-95-95 program, 10, 293, 306, 326n6, 345n8
norms: communal, 5; disciplining and, 230; ethics and, 272, *278*, 282; globalization and, 18; guidelines and, 5, 12, 18–19, 27, 29; institutional policies and, 12; moral issues and, 289; respect for, 197–202; rule proliferation and, 90, 104, 112, *117*; skepticism and, 197–202; standards and, 42, 46; trustworthy data and, 165, 167, *182*, 186–87, 195, 197, 200–203; universals and, 147
Norvir, 305, 346n21
Nuremberg Code, 114, *115*, 118, 266
Nuremberg trials, 93
nurses: advance practice, 38; discharge, 54; disciplining and, 211, *212*, 216–17, 221, 230–33; ethics and, 263, 273–75, 277, 282–83; ignorance and, 240–44, 254; moral issues and, 290, 311, 346n24; overworked, 35; rule proliferation and, 90, 97, 106, 331n17;

standards and, 38–41, 46, 48–50, 54, 69, 72; trustworthy data and, 171, 179–80, 184–92, 195–200, 203, 338n16, 338n21, 339n23, 339n28; universals and, 124, 130, 133, 136, 153

nursing homes, 331n21

Office of Human Research Protections (OHRP): as compliance bureaucracy, 98–100; ethics and, 267–68; rule proliferation and, *86*, 94, 98–100, *116*, 120

Office of Scientific Integrity (OSI), 166

"One World, One Hope" (conference theme), 127

opportunistic infection (OI): guidelines and, 10, 13–15; moral issues and, 291, 298, 307; rule proliferation and, 107; side effects and, 63, 107; standards and, 48, 63, 69; universals and, 125, 153, 161

O'Reilly, James T., 76

organizational boundaries, 106, 253, 254–58, *260*

orphans, 63, 118, 122, 223, 301

ownership effects, 145–46, *149*, 158

pandemics: COVID-19, 36–37; HIV, 12, 20, 34; UNAIDS and, 325n2

paperwork, 53, 97, 105, 237, 240

pap smears, 59, 228, 339n23

Paris conference (IAC), 127

patients' rights: Baby Doe Law and, 207; cultural context for, 297; informed consent, *82*, *86*, 102, 122, 180, 188, *212*, 229, 239–45, 248, 259, *260*, 270, 338n15, 344n5; public outcry for, 78, 101, 177; recruitment and, 32, 38, 117, 175–76, 183, 190, 240–44, 263, 269, 272, 282, 341n1; testing protocols and, 6, 8

PCP (pneumocystis carinii pneumonia), 15, 125, 153, 326nn10–11

pediatricians: Baby Doe Law, 207, 339n6; codifying, 341n18; disciplining and, *212*, 219, 222–24, 228, *232*, 339n3, 341n18; ethics and, 276; moral issues and, 296, 310; rule proliferation and, 121, 332n30; standards and, 63, 68,

327n10; uncharted medical territory and, 222–24; universals and, 126, 136–37, 147–51, 159–60, 336n30

Pepin, Jacques, 21

pestilence, 1

Petryna, Adriana, 245

Pfaff, Colin, 206

Pfizer, 333n4, 337n8

pharmaceutical companies: Abbott Laboratories, 3, 305, 346n21; Aspen, 40; disciplining and, 210; ethics and, 264, 281; GlaxoSmithKline, 346n21; ignorance and, 248, 250; moral issues and, 290–95, 299, 302–15, 346nn18–21; Pfizer, 333n4, 337n8; philanthropy and, 52, 163, 210, 293, 295, 337n9; profit and, 292, 336n1; rule proliferation and, 96, 102; standards and, 40–41, 45, 49, 52, 56, 59; trustworthy data and, 164, 167, 173, 180, 336n1, 337n9, 339n24; universals and, 127, 333n4

pharmacies, 24, 62, 153

philanthropy: pharmaceutical industry and, 52, 163, 210, 293, 295, 337n9; program rules and, 14, 39; richer countries and, 14, 39, 52, 163, 210, 274, 293–96, 337n9

Philly Lutaaya Clinic: ABC program and, 246; ART and, 137; ARV and, 67, 69, 139; description of, 66–67; disciplining and, 214, 218, 222, 227–28, 340n14; ethics and, 266–70, 274, 279, 282–85; food at, 67; formation of, 68; funding, 68; health visitors and, 67–68; ignorance and, 240–43, 246–51, 256–58; moral issues and, 296, 309–12; NIH and, 68, 70; pediatric program of, 68–69; pregnancy and, 67–68; research and, 65–72, 121, 138, 141, 147, 156, 159, 161, 176, 180, 185–87, 191, 196, 199, 214, 240–43, 268–70, 274, 279, 282–85, 296, 309–12, 338n14; security at, 66; staff concerns at, 69–70; standards and, 65–70, 329n26, 330n32; trustworthy data and, 176, 180, 185–91, 196, 199, 201, 338n14; universals and, 123, 127, 136–42, 146–63, 334n5, 335n23 physicians: disciplining and, 211, 226–33, 340n17; ethics and, 264, 279, 283–84, 344n6; guidelines and, 12, 22, 24–25, 31, 326n8; Hippocratic Oath and, 249; ignorance and, 243, 253, 258; moral issues and, 290, 294–95, 301, 303, 307–8, 311–15, 345n6, 345n10, 346n17; primary care, 38, 47, 53, 72, 154, 171, 264, 279, 311; research administration and, 106–20; rule proliferation and, 75, 77, 79, *84–85*, 88–90, 97, 100, 103–7, *115*; standards and, 38, 41, 45–47, 51–54, 69, 72; trustworthy data and, 179–81, 187, 191, 198, 200, 338n16, 338n21; universals and, 123, 126–27, 130–34, 139, 141, 152–55, 159–60, 163, 335n16

Piot, Peter, 257

placebos, 88, 118–19, 244

Plato, 79

pluralism, 2, 24, 27, 118

pneumonia, 15, 125–26, 132, 153, 326nn10–11

police, 19–20, 145

polygynous relationships, 247

poorer countries: clinic access and, 35; Declaration of Helsinki and, *115–16*, 118–19, 300, 332n33, 333n38; disciplining and, 219, 222, 341n20; ethics and, 270, 280, 285; globalization and, 36–37; guidelines and, 1, 14–15, 20, 22, 26, 28, 31; healthcare administration and, 1; ignorance and, 243, 247–48, 252–57, 342n14; moral issues and, 288–89, 294, 298–315, 344n2, 345n11, 346n23; philanthropy and, 14, 39, 52, 163, 210, 274, 293–96, 337n9; practice variations in, 26; rule proliferation and, 90–92, 118, 120, 333n15; salvage regimens and, 15; standards and, 35–41, 51–53, 56–57, 60, 62, 71, 73, 329n25, 330n28; TRIPS and, 14; trustworthy data and, 173, 185, 188–91, 197, 202, 338n18; universals and, 124–29, 136, 139, 155, 163, 336n30

Popovic, Mikulas, 166, 170

Population and Community Development Association, 328n17

Porter, Theodore, 177

poverty, 167, 254

Power, Michael, 177

pregnancy: breastmilk after, 219, 255–56; disciplining and, 206, 211, *212*, 214, 219–21, 228; ethics and, 270, 273, 343n2; guidelines and, 7, 14–15; ignorance and, 240, 252, 255, 343n20; moral issues and, 293, 300; mother-to-child effects, 67, 69, 118, 125, 152, 159, 205, 210–12, 215–16, 219–21, 252, 255, 261, 269, 292, 304, 328n19, 333n35, 339nn2–3, 340n14, 340n16, 343n20, 345n13; Philly Lutaaya Clinic and, 67–68; rule proliferation and, 107, *110*, 118, 332n30; standards and, 50, 64, 67–68; thalidomide and, 250; transmission and, 7, 14, 67–68, 118, 135, 152, 159, 211, 219–22, 252, 255, 269, 300, 343n20; universals and, 124–26, 135, 144, 152, 159

President's Commission on HIV/AIDS, 44

President's Emergency Plan for AIDS Relief (PEPFAR): disciplining and, 229; fiscal responsibility and, 92; funding, 335n17; Gugu Dlamini Clinic and, 63–64; guidelines and, 45, 50, 63–64; ignorance and, 246, 248, 342nn9–10; moral issues and, 290–92, 296, 306, 344n4, 346n26; rule proliferation and, *82, 84*, 92; universals and, 157, 159, 335n17

preventing mother-to-child transmission (PMTCT): disciplining and, 205, 210–12, 215–16, 219–21, 339nn2–3, 340n16; dual anti-retroviral prophylaxis and, 205; Gugu Dlamini Clinic and, 220–22; HAART and, 125; ignorance and, 261; moral issues and, 292, 345n13; universals and, 125

principal investigator (PI), 171, 180, 199, 201, 262–63, 271

prison, 118, 127, 243, 273, 304, 335n19, 343n2, 344n5

privacy: ethics and, 275; guidelines and, 7; HIPAA, 216–17, 275, 344n9; rule proliferation and, *81–82, 86*, 102; standards and, 52, 57, 62; trustworthy data and, 339n23 protocols: CPR, 24; differing, 4; disciplining and, 207–8, 226, 229, 341n18; ethics and, 270–75; geographic acceptance of, 5; Good Clinical Practice (GCP), 113, *116*, 119–20, 172, 179, *182*, 188, 217, 289, 333n28, 338n17, 339n24; guidelines and, 1, 4–6, 14, 15, 22, 24, 30, 32; hard law, 17, 19, 77, *85*, 91, 112, *116–17*, 120, 302–3, 315; ignorance and, 240, 247, 252; moral issues and, 289, 299, 306–9, 344n6; PICT, 6–7, 11; poorer countries and, 309–13; rule proliferation and, *80*, 107, 114, 117, 120; soft law, 19–20, 77, *80*, 112, *117*, 120, 172, 173, 202, 234, 293, 302–3, 315, 330n1; standards and, 35–39, 49, 57, 64, 70–72; training and, 6, 24, 32, 71, 133, 146, 184, 187–90, 226, 309; trustworthy data and, 164, 168, 172, 177, 179–90, 196–203, 338n15; universals and, 129–33, 146, 152, 155–56; VCT, 4–12, 15, 22, 213–14, 298, 325nn4–5

provider-initiated counseling and testing (PICT), 6–7, 11

Public Health Service Act (Public Law 10), 93

quality assurance/quality control (QA/QC): trustworthy data and, 175, 180, 187–93, 196; universals and, *148*, 156

Rafsky, Robert, 327n8, 338n13

randomized clinical trials (RCTs), 79, *80*, *83*, 88

Reagan, Ronald, 44, 166, 327n7

recognition gaps, 289–90

reform, 18–19, 26, *85*, 266, 297, 345n10

regulations: compliance bureaucracies and, 98–101; decentralization and, 89, 120, 326n12; disciplining and, 207–8, 211, 213–16, 221–22, 226, 230, 234, 339n6; ethics and, 264–69, 276, *278*, 280–85, 343n1; fiscal responsibility and, 91–94; guidelines, 1–3, 10, 13–18, 22–33, 326n9, 326n12; ignorance and, 236–41, 248, 259–61, 341n4; moral issues and, 287, 289, 293, 298–99,

302, 307, 311–15; Nuremberg Code, 114, *115*, 118, 266; relational, 27; rule proliferation and, 76–87, 90–95, 98–107, 112–16, 119–22, 33cn7, 331n14, 333n39; skepticism and, 32; standards and, 35–37, 40–45, 50, 54, 56, 65, 70, 73–74, 326n2; trustworthy data and, 165–67, 170–73, 177–86, 191–98, 201–3, 337n11; universals and, 123, 129, 144, 159–60, 335n22

renal disease, 91

repeat players versus one-shotters, 27, 95, 105, 308–9

research: accountability in, 16, *84*, 144, 149, 155–57, 161, 165, 173–79, 183, 204, 216, 238, 338n12; administration and, 106–20; Bobbi Campbell Clinic and, 52–53, 55, 71–72, 141, 146, 151, 155, 159, 176, 197, 241, 274, 279, 338n14; care overlap and, 72–73; Cha-on Suesum Clinic and, 56–60, 71–72, 121, 136, 141, 146, 156, 159–61, 173, 176, 188, 191–97, 217, 243, 270, 295–96, 309–12, 346n26; conduct, 299–301; disciplining and, 205–35; downstream effects and, 166–70; early controversies in, 166–70; ethics and, 262–86; evidentiary packages and, 179–202; gray boxes and, 338n19; Gugu Dlamini Clinic and, 61, 64–65, 71–72, 141, 156–61, 176, 247, 274, 309–12, 329n21; guidelines and, 1–33; ignorance and, 236–61; monitoring regimes and, 173–79; moral issues and, 287–315; Philly Lutaaya Clinic and, 66–72, 121, 138, 141, 147, 156, 159, 161, 176, 180, 185–87, 191, 196, 199, 214, 240–43, 268–70, 274, 279, 282–85, 296, 309–12, 338n14; poorer countries and, 309–13; public payment for, 91–94; records and, 192–97; recruiting subjects for, 32, 38, 117, 175–76, 183, 190, 240–44, 263, 269, 272, 282, 341n1; rules and, 75 (*see also* rules); scientific reputations and, 166–70; skepticism and, 165–69, 174–202; standards and, 34–74; trustworthy data and, 164–204; uniform work plans and, *182*, 183–87; universals and, 123–63 richer countries: disciplining and, *212*, 220, 222, 231; education and, 22, 27, 56; ethics and, 270, 280, 343n20; globalization and, 36–37; guidelines and, 1–2, 5–6, 15, 22, 26–28, 32; ignorance and, 252, 255; moral issues and, 289, 292–93, 298–314, 344n2, 346n23; philanthropy and, 14, 39, 52, 163, 210, 274, 293–96, 337n9; repeat players and, 27, 95, 105, 308–9; rule proliferation and, 90, 118, 120, 332n30, 333n35; standards and, 35–41, 49–51, 56–57, 60–61, 73, 330n32; trustworthy data and, 338n18; universals and, 123, 128–29, 138–39, 144, 151–52, 173, 186, 191, 196–97, 336n30

Rittel, Horst, 264

ritual surplus, 239–45, 259, *260*

Robert Rafsky Clinic: ART and, 47; ARV and, 132–33; clinical trial units (CTUs) and, 176; description of, 47; disciplining and, 216; "double billing" at, 51; duty allocation at, 48; ethics and, 262–68, 271–75, 277, 280, 283; funding, 47–49; ignorance and, 241, 243, 250; insurance and, 49; IRBs and, 49–50; Medicaid and, 49; Medicare and, 49; moral issues and, 294–96, 301, 308, 346n24; NIH and, 47–50; PEPFAR and, 50; research methodology at, 46–52; rule proliferation and, 75–76, 100, 106, 121; standards and, 46–53, 55, 71–72, 327n8; statistics on, 46–47; study visits at, 48–49; trustworthy data and, 168, 175–76, 185–95, 198, 200, 203, 338nn13–14; universals and, 121, 132–34, 139–42, 146–63

Roe v. Wade, 102

Rosenthal, Elisabeth, 96

routine counseling and testing (RCT): disciplining and, 213–14, 340n14; guidelines and, 6–12, 325nn3–4

rule of law, 13, 26, 206, 289

rule proliferation: activists and, *82*, *86*, 101–2, 122, 333n4; AIDS and, *82–86*, 92–93, 106–7, *108*, 111, 332n26; AIDS Education and Training Centers (AETC) and, *109*, 111–13; AMA on, *85*, 89; biology and, 123; Bobbi Campbell Clinic and, *109–10*, 112–13, 121; CDC and, 92, *108–9*, 111; compliance bureaucracies and, 98–101, 105–6; consent and, *82*, *86*, 101–2, 105, 114, 122; counseling and, 107, *110*, 113; DHHS and, *108–10*, 111–12, *116*, 120; discretion and, *80*, 97, 114; disease and, 91–93, 101, 107, 122, 331n21; doctors and, 90, 97, 104, 111, 114; drugs and, *80–86*, 88, 92, 96–99, 111, 114, 118, 332n24; education and, 100, 112, 122, 331n19, 332n26; efficiency and, *83–84*, 88, 104; empowerment and, 113; epidemics and, 90, 122, 333n3; ethics and, 78, *87*, 93–94, 100, 105, 107, 113–20, 333n40; evidence-based medicine (EBM) and, 79, *80–83*, 88–91; experience of legalization, 104–6; external control and, 79, 88–91; FDA and, *80–81*, *85–86*, 98–99, 119, 331n14, 332nn23–24; fiscal responsibility and, 91–94; Good Clinical Practice (GCP) and, 113, *116*, 119–20, 333n38; governance and, 75–77, 103, 113, 121; Gugu Dlamini Clinic and, *110*, 112–13, 121; healthcare and, 76–78, *80–87*, 89–106, 112–13, 121–22, 330nn5–9, 331nn16–17, 332n25; health law and, 78, *80–82*, *87*, 102–4, 122; hospitals and, 75, 77, *84–85*, 93–96, 105–11, 122, 331n21, 332n32; human rights and, 113–14, *115*; IAS and, *108*, 332n26; increasing profits and, 95–98; infection and, 92–93, 107–9, *110*; informed consent and, *82*, *86*, 102, 122; insurance and, *80–85*, 95–96, 101–2, 121; IRBs and, 99–100, 105, 114, *116–17*, 120, 332n32; legal issues and, 76–87, 91, 94–95, 99–108, *109*, 112–22, 330n3; malpractice and, 89–90, *108*; Medicaid and, *81–86*, 91–98, 102–3, 331n20; medical records and, 97, 104, 106; Medicare and, *81–86*, 88, 91–98, 103, 331n20; medicine and, 77–79, *80–83*, *87*, 88–90, 103, *116*, 119; NIH and, *80*, *84*, 93, 98, *116*, 118–19, 331n15,

331n18; norms and, 90, 104, 112, *117*; Nuremberg Code, 114, *115*, 118, 266; nurses and, 90, 97, 106, 124, 331n17; OHRP and, *86*, 94, 98–100, *116*, 120; opportunistic infection (OI) and, 107, 125; organizational boundaries and, 106; pediatricians and, 121, 332n30; PEPFAR and, *82, 84*, 92; pharmaceutical companies and, 96, 102; physicians and, 75, 77, 79, *84–85*, 88–90, 97, 100, 103–7, *115*; poorer countries and, 90–92, 118, 120, 333n15; pregnancy and, 107, *110*, 118, 332n30; privacy and, *81–82, 86*, 102; protocols and, *80*, 107, 114, 117, 120; public pressure and, 101–2; randomized clinical trials (RCTs) and, 79, *80, 83*, 88; rapid rise of, 75–76; regulations and, 76–87, 90–95, 98–107, 112–15, *116*, 119–22, 330n7, 331n14, 333n39; research administration and, 106–20; richer countries and, 90, 118, 120, 332n30, 333n35; Robert Rafsky Clinic and, 75–76, 100, 106, 121; Ryan White HIV/AIDS Program and, *82, 84*, 92, 94, 96, 102, *109*, 111–13; side effects and, *84*; social issues and, *80–81, 86–87*, 90, 101–2, 332n25; South Africa and, *109*, 110–13; specialists and, 103–7; technology and, *80*, 100; testing and, 100, 107, *110*, 113, 122; Thailand and, *109*, 110–11, *116*, 119; training and, 75, 77, *87*, 93, 97, 100, 104, *109*, 110–13, 119, 122, 330n7, 332n31; transmission and, 118; tuberculosis and, *110*; Uganda and, *109*, 110–11; WHO and, *108–10*, 111–12, *115*

rules: binding versus nonbinding, 1–2, 77, 104, *109*, *115*, 119; codes and, 1, 6, 23, 53–54, 114–18, 121, 217, 258, 262, 266, 282, 284; Common Rule, 94, *116*, 120, 267, 343n2; disciplining and, 205–35; "double billing" and, 51, 54; ethics and, 262–86; *farang*, 217; globalized medicine, 16–20; guidelines and, 1–33; hard law, 17, 19, 77, *85*, 91, 112, *116–17*, 120, 205–35, 302–3, 315; Helsinki Rules, *115–16*, 118–20, 266, 300, 306,

314, 332n33, 333n38; history of, 13–16; ignorance and, 236, 239, 245, 247–49, *260*; lagging, 213–16; moral issues and, 287–315; as naturalized/denaturalized, 24, 91, 146, 187; official rigidity and, 224–26; pluralism and, 2, 24, 27, 118; practice variations and, 28; research conduct, 299–301; skepticism and, 28; social movements and, 303–9; soft versus hard law, 19–20, 77, *80*, 112, *117*, 120, 172–73, 202, 234, 293, 302–3, 315, 330n1; standard operating procedure (SOP) and, 1, 13–16, 32, 70, *117*, 129, 154, 172, 183–89, 207, 247, 249, 266, 271, 289, 298–99; trustworthy data and, 164–204 (*see also* trustworthy data); uniform work plans and, *182*, 183–87; universals and, 144, *149*, 154, 158, 163; VCT, 5, 8, 15, 22

Ryan White HIV/AIDS Program: Bobbi Campbell Clinic and, 52–53; fiscal responsibility and, 92; funding and, 52–53, *82, 84*, 92, 94, 96, 102, *109*, 111, 113, 133, *148–49*, 155, 295, 328n12, 345n16; rule proliferation and, *82, 84*, 92, 94, 96, 102, *109*, 111–13; universals and, 133, *148–49*, 155

Sackett, David, 89
Sanders, Joseph, 27, 344n1
Santos, Boaventura de Sousa, 19
SARS (severe acute respiratory syndrome), 37
Sauder, Michael, 174
science/technology studies, 36, 170–72
security, 66, 326n2, 329n27
Sen, Amartya, 308
Senegal, 288
sequestered knowledge: credible routines and, 245–49; ignorance and, 236–49, *260*; participant construction and, 239–45
serious adverse event (SAE), 186, 198–99, 338n15
sex tourism, 22
sexual transmission, 5, 7, 21, 255, 276, 279, 344n5
sex workers, 1, 42, 45, 56, 328n16

Shilts, Randy, 3
side effects: adverse event (AE) and,
114; ART and, 48; disciplining and,
213, 225–26, 228; Hippocratic Oath
and, 249; ignorance and, 238, 240,
249–54, 258–61; intolerable, 15; life-
threatening, 125; meriting attention,
131; moral issues and, 291, 294, 299,
303, 310, 344n5, 345n12; opportunistic
infection (OI) and, 63, 107; optimum
therapy and, 134; rule proliferation
and, *84*; severe, 291; standards and,
47–48; trustworthy data and, 168, 178,
192, 336n1; universals and, 125, 131,
134–35, 150–51, 158, 161, 336n32
Simon, Herbert A., 237–38
skepticism: credibility and, 165–69,
174–202; ethics and, 270; evidentiary
packages and, 179–202; ignorance
and, 261; institutionalized, 31, 165,
178–202; Merton on, 165; monitoring
regimes and, 173–79; moral issues
and, 311; norms and, 197–202; public,
165; records and, 192–97; regulations
and, 32; rules and, 28; standards and,
329n27; systematic errors and, 185;
training and, 187–92; trustworthy data
and, 165–69, 174–202; uniform work
plans and, *182*, 183–87
social issues: disciplining, 213, 223, 234,
341n18; ethics, 264–66, 269, 277–81,
278, 285; guidelines, 2–5, 11–18, 21–22,
27–32; ignorance, 256–59; legal, 2–3, 5,
12, 14, 18, 21–22, 27, 32, 47, *86–87*, 101–2,
147, 213, 223, 234, 269, 289, 293, 303–9,
317, 319, 320, 332n25; legitimacy, 16;
moral issues, 289, 293, 301–11, 317–21;
role of, 1; rule proliferation, *80–81*,
86–87, 90, 101–2, 332n25; standards, 34,
46–48, 53, 63, 68–69; stigma, 4–5, 12,
32, 122, 131, 215, 217, 250–51, 255, 328n12,
329n20; trustworthy data, 169–73, 180,
189, 338n19; universals, 122–23, 127, 141,
145, 147, 151, 161–62
social movements: guidelines and, 18;
moral issues and, 293, 301, 303–9; rule
proliferation and, *80–81*, *86–87*, 101–2,
332n25; transnational, 18

sociolegal studies, and law and society
scholarship, 26–28, 35, 173, 264
South Africa: Aspen and, 40; denialism
and, 328n19; disciplining and, 205–6,
211, *212*, 213–29, 339n1, 339n3, 340n12;
doctor qualifications and, 130; drugs
and, 14, 40, 42, 45, 52, 71, 111, 136,
158, 169, 205–6, 211, 219–23, 279, 292,
298, 304–5; Durban, 60–64, 127, 247,
329n20, 334n5; education and, 62;
ethics and, 279; Gugu Dlamini Clinic,
60–65 (*see also* Gugu Dlamini Clinic);
guidelines and, 1–2, 5–6, 13–14, 30;
HIV and, 1–2, 5–6, 13–14, 30, 34, 44–
45, 52, 60–61, 71–72, 111, 113, 130, 152,
157–58, 168, 205–6, *212*, 215, 218–22,
226–29, 251–52, 255, 276, 279, 292, 298,
328n19, 329n23, 340n12; ignorance and,
246, 250–52, 255, 258; KwaMashu, 62;
KwaZulu-Natal (KZN), 61, 205–6, 220,
339n3; Mandela and, 305; Mbeki and,
13, 44, 60, 157, 168, 205, 220, 327n7;
Medicines Act, 346n19; Medicines
Control Council (MCC), 335n20;
moral issues and, 292, 297–98, 304–5,
310–13, 346n19; political history of, 60–
61; poorer economy of, 14; population
demographics of, 61; research
methodology in, 45; rule proliferation
and, *109*, 110–13; standards and, 34, 40–
45, 52, 55, 60–64, 70–72, 327n7, 328n19,
329n23; trustworthy data and, 168–69,
338n21, 339n23; Umlazi, 62; universals
and, 130, 136–41, 146–49, 152, 154,
334n5, 335n16, 335n20
specialists: disciplining and, *232*, 233; ethics
and, *278*, 282–83; guidelines and, 38;
health law, 103; ignorance and, 240–41,
254, 261; increase of, 38; moral issues
and, 311, 313; rule proliferation and, 103–
7; staff support and, 105; standards and,
38; trustworthy data and, 171, 181, 191,
201; universals and, 130, 137, 145
Squires, James D., 164
standard operating procedure (SOP):
disciplining and, 207, 211; ethics and,
266, 271; guidelines and, 13–16, 32;
history of, 13–16; ignorance and,

247–49; mismatches and, 35; moral issues and, 287, 289, 298–99; rules and, 1, 13–16, 32, 70, *117*, 129, 154, 172, 183–89, 207, 247, 249, 266, 271, 289, 298–99; security and, 66, 329n27; trustworthy data and, 172, *182*, 183–89, 203; universal precautions and, 22–23, 94, 144, 152, 336n27

standards: abstinence and, 44, 330n32; activists and, 41, 44, 46, 327n8, 329n20; AIDS and, 34, 41–49, 52, 55, 57, 60, 63, 68, 72, 327nn7–10, 328n12, 328n17, 328n19, 329n20, 329n26; AIDS Clinical Trials Group (ACTG) and, 327n10; ART and, 41, 47–48, 55, 62–64, 71, 328n19; ARV and, 56, 67; Bobbi Campbell Clinic and, 52–55, 71–72, 328n12; CD4 and, 55, 63; CDC and, 68, 327n9; Cha-on Suesum Clinic and, 56–60, 71–72, 328n17; clinics and, 34–74; confidentiality and, 46, 71, 328n18; consent and, 67; counseling and, 47, 62–63; denialism and, 44, 60, 327n7; discrimination and, 328n17; disease and, 44–50, 55–56, 63, 67–73, 327n4, 327n10, 328n17; doctors and, 35, 38–39, 48–50, 54, 59, 66, 69; drugs and, 34, 37, 40–45, 48–52, 55–57, 64–68, 71, 327n8, 329n23; education and, 55–56, 62; efficiency and, 53, 60; empowerment and, 65, 328n12; epidemics and, 41–47, 55–56, 60–61, 328n12; ethics and, 38, 50, 61; FDA and, 40, 329n23; globalization and, 35–41; governance and, 36, 41; Government Pharmaceutical Organization (GPO) and, 56, 71, 328n15; Gugu Dlamini Clinic and, 60–65, 71–72, 329nn20–21, 330n32; healthcare and, 34–41, 52, 56, 73; heterosexuals and, 35, 42, 47, 61; hospitals and, 34, 38, 42, 48, 51–53, 56, 61–72; human rights and, 37; infection and, 36–38, 41–42, 47–52, 55, 61, 63, 67, 73, 327nn9–10, 328n17, 328n19; insurance and, 49–52, 72; IRBs and, 49–50, 53, 55; legal issues and, 35–36, 41, 45, 47, 50–51; malaria and, 37, 71; medicine and, 35–37, 42, 69, 73;

mismatches and, 35; NIH and, 47–50, 57–61, 68, 70, 327n10; norms and, 42, 46; nurses and, 38–41, 46, 48–50, 54, 69, 72; opportunistic infection (OI) and, 48, 63, 69; pediatricians and, 63, 68, 327n10; pharmaceutical companies and, 40–41, 45, 49, 52, 56, 59; Philly Lutaaya Clinic and, 65–70, 329n26, 330n32; physicians and, 38, 41, 45–47, 51–54, 69, 72; poorer countries and, 35–41, 51–53, 56–57, 60, 62, 71, 73, 329n25, 330n28; pregnancy and, 50, 64, 67–68; privacy and, 52, 57, 62; protocols and, 35–39, 49, 57, 64, 70–72; regulations and, 35–37, 40–45, 50, 54, 56, 65, 70, 73–74, 326n2; research methodology for, 65–70; richer countries and, 35–41, 49–51, 56–57, 60–61, 73, 330n32; Robert Rafsky Clinic and, 46–53, 55, 71–72, 327n8; skepticism and, 329n27; social issues and, 34, 46–48, 53, 63, 68–69; South Africa and, 34, 40–45, 52, 55, 60–64, 70–72, 327n7, 328n19, 329n23; specialists and, 38; TAC and, 329n20; technology and, 36, 42; testing, 34, 63, 337n7; Thailand and, 42–45, 56–59, 328n15; training and, 38–39, 44–48, 60–65, 69, 71; transmission and, 37, 67–69; TRIPS and, 41, 56; tuberculosis and, 36–37, 63, 71, 329n23; two-drug, 205, 211, 220, 339n1; Uganda and, 34, 42–45, 55, 60, 64–71, 329nn25–26; UNAIDS and, 328n16; WHO and, 38, 327nn3–4

Starr, Paul, 77, 208

State Department, 44

Statesman, The (Plato), 79

sticky notes, 195, 339n18

stigma: AIDS and, 4–5, 12, 215, 328n12, 329n20; confidentiality and, 215; discrimination and, 3–7, 12, 250, 259, 267, 287, 325n2, 328n17; gay men and, 4–5, 12, 215, 328n12, 329n20; healthcare and, 131; health visitors and, 250–51; sexual practices and, 255; social issues and, 4–5, 12, 32, 122, 131, 215, 217, 250–51, 255, 328n12, 329n20

Stinchcombe, Arthur, 143

strategic decompiling, 237, 249–54, *260*, 343n18

subsidies, 56, 102, 337n9

Suesum, Cha-on, 328n17

support groups, 63, 224, 329n20

surveillance, 18, 20, 327n4

Swidler, Ann, 7

technology: ignorance and, 238, 249; rule proliferation and, *80*, 100; standards and, 36, 42; trustworthy data and, 164, 171; universals and, 128

tenofovir, 251

testing: activists and, 4; antibody, 3–4, 213, 256, 291, 304; barriers to, 3–13; breakpoints and, 11; client-initiated, 6, 11, 215; confidentiality in, 4 (*see also* confidentiality); consent and, 5 (*see also* consent); diagnostic, 3, 12–13, *83*, 150, 164, 214, 244, 317; differences in, 4; disciplining and, 210–23, *232*, 340n10, 340n12, 340n14, 341n19; ethics and, 268, 273, 275–76; guidelines and, 2–14, 22, 30; human rights and, 4, 6, 9; ignorance and, 247, 250–51, 256, 261; legal issues and, 3–13; low, 11, 22; moral issues and, 292–93, 298, 308; PICT, 6–7, 11; rapid, 9; rule proliferation and, 100, 107, *110*, 113, 122; screening, 5, 7, 9, *83*, 175, 188, 214, 240; silent, 5, 276; standards and, 34, 63, 337n7; trustworthy data and, 164–65, 168, 179, 183, 189–90, 195, 204; universals and, 126–27, 130, 135–36; VCT, 4–12, 15, 22, 213–14, 298, 325nn4–5

Thailand: ART and, 328n15; Cha-on Suesum Clinc, 56–60 (*see also* Cha-on Suesum Clinic); disciplining and, 217, 219, 225; doctor qualifications and, 130; drugs and, 14, 42, 45, 57, 111, 135–36, 219, 296, 304–7; education in, 56, 328n17; ethics and, 270, 282, 340n15, 345n10; Fifteenth International AIDS Conference and, 60; GPO-VIR and, 56, 71, 135, 151, 295, 310, 328n15, 335n18, 346n26; HIV and, 2, 14, 30, 34, 42,

45, 56–57, 59, 111, 130, 219, 304–5, 310, 317–18, 328n17; moral issues and, 304–5, 307, 310–11, 396; poorer economy of, 14, 42, 56–57, 219, 270, 304–7; research methodology in, 45; rule proliferation and, *109*, 110–11, *116*, 119; sex workers and, 1, 45; standards and, 42–45, 56–59, 328n15; sticky notes and, 339n18; trustworthy data and, 180, 193, 195; Universal Coverage Scheme and, 56, 328n14; universals and, 130, 135–36, *140–41*, *148*, 151; Viravaidya and, 305

thalidomide, 250

The AIDS Support Organization (TASO), 292, 304, 329n26

Thompson, James D., 184, 253

3 by 5 plan, 10, 128, 292, 306, 325n6, 334n12

toxicity, 15, 118, 135, 158, 335n18, 340n17

toxoplasmosis, 125

Trade Related Aspects of Intellectual Property Rights (TRIPS): guidelines and, 14, 22, 326n9; moral issues and, 311; standards and, 41, 56

training: certification and, 29, 41, 112, 181, 188–89, 192, 203, 267; disciplining and, 207, 210–13, 217–18, 221, 225–26, 231, *232*, 235, 340n13; ethics and, 262, 266–68, 272–73, 276, 282; expert work and, 226–30; guidelines and, 6, 17–18, 20, 24, 29, 31–32; ignorance and, 240; moral issues and, 290, 296–98, 309; poorer countries and, 309–13; protocols and, 6, 24, 32, 71, 133, 146, 184, 187–90, 226, 309; resources and, 31, 71, 111–12, 123, 134, 136, *140*, 141, 152, 188, 190, 210, 262, 297–98, 339n23; rule proliferation and, 75, 77, *87*, 93, 97, 100, 104, *109*, 110–13, 119, 122, 330n7, 332n31; skill and, 226–30; standards and, 38–39, 44–48, 60–65, 69, 71; task shifting and, 226–30; trustworthy data and, 170, 181–84, 187–92, 195, 203–4, 338nn21–22, 339nn23–24; universals and, 123, 126, 128, 130–36, 139–42, 145–52, 163, 335n23

transfusions, 3, 138–39, 207, 328n17

transmission of HIV: blood, 21, 336n27; disciplining and, 205, 211, 215, 219–22, 226, 233, 340n14; ethics and, 269, 276, 279; hygiene and, 22, *84*, 93, 254, 331n14; ignorance and, 252, 255–56, 343nn20–21; IHR and, 37; infection and, 10–14, 37, 125, 135, 152, 211, 219–20, 252, 255–56, 276, 279, 328n19, 344n5; likelihood of, 10, 135, 255, 325n6, 326n7; moral issues and, 292, 300, 304; mother-to-child, 67, 69, 118, 125, 152, 159, 219–22, 252, 255, 269, 292, 304, 328n19, 333n35, 340n14, 343n20 (*see also* preventing mother-to-child transmission (PMTCT)); pregnancy and, 7, 14, 67–68, 69, 118, 125, 135, 152, 159, 211, 219–22, 252, 255, 269, 292, 300, 304, 328n19, 333n35, 340n14, 343n20; rate of, 10–13, 205, 220, 326n7; rule proliferation and, 118; sexual, 5, 7, 21, 255, 276, 279, 344n5; standards and, 37, 67–69; universal precautions and, 22–23, 94, 144, 152, 336n27; universals and, 125, 135, 150, 152, 159, 336n27, 336n30

Treatment Action Campaign (TAC): disciplining and, 206, 220; moral issues and, 292, 304, 346n19; standards and, 329n20; universals and, 335n16

trustworthy data: accountability and, 165, 173–79, 181, 183, 204, 338n12; activists and, 168; adverse event (AE) and, 188, 199–201; AIDS and, 164, 166, 167–70, 176, 337nn6–7; AIDS Clinical Trials Group (ACTG) and, 176, 185, 193, 327n10, 331n13, 338n14; Bobbi Campbell Clinic and, 176, 197, 201, 338n14; Cha-on Suesum Clinic and, 173, 176, 188, 191–97; clinical trials and, 170–73; compliance work and, 177–78, 204; confidentiality and, 338n17; consent and, 180, 188, 194–95, 338n15; credibility and, 164–205; denialism and, 167–70; DHHS and, 166; discretion and, 177, 199–202, 338n16; disease and, 164–68; doctors and, 160, 164, 180,

195, 198, 338n21, 339n23; downstream effects and, 166–70; drugs and, 164, 167–72, 177–79, *182*, 183, 190, 193–94, 198, 336n1, 337nn8–9; early research controversies and, 166–70; education and, *182*, 188, 336n4, 337n9; efficiency and, 168, 173; empowerment and, 337n6; epidemics and, 165, 168; ethics and, 168, 172–73, 189–90, 337n8; evidentiary packages and, 179–202; FDA and, 164, 168, 172, 177, 179–80, *182*, 193–94, 339n27; Good Clinical Practice (GCP) and, 172, 179, *182*, 188, 338n17, 339n24; governance and, 177, 202; Gugu Dlamini Clinic and, 169, 176; healthcare and, 174, 202; HIV and, 165–74, 194, 202; hospitals and, 169, 184, 191, 196, 198, 337n8, 338n18; infection and, 164; informed consent and, 180, 188, 338n15; insurance and, 190; IRBs and, 174, *182*, 188–89, 201–3; legal issues and, 166, 173, 183, 197–204, 337n8; legitimacy and, 168, 175, 204, 337n10; malaria and, 199; medical records and, 180, 191–94; medicine and, 165, 168–69, 177, 193, 202, 337n7; monitoring regimes and, 173–79; NIH and, 172, 180, 185, 195, 203; norms and, 165, 167, *182*, 186–87, 195–203; nurses and, 171, 179–80, 184–92, 195–200, 203, 338n16, 338n21, 339n23, 339n28; pharmaceutical companies and, 164, 167, 173, 180, 336n1, 337n9, 339n24; Philly Lutaaya Clinic and, 176, 180, 185–91, 196, 199, 201, 338n14; physicians and, 179–81, 187, 191, 198, 200, 338n16, 338n21; poorer countries and, 173, 185, 188–91, 197, 202, 338n18; privacy and, 339n23; protocols and, 164, 168, 172, 177, 179–90, 196–203, 338n15; QA/QC and, 175, 180, 187–93, 196; records and, 192–97; regulations and, 165–67, 170–73, 177–86, 191–98, 201–3, 337n11; richer countries and, 338n18; Robert Rafsky Clinic and, 168, 175–76, 185–95, 198, 200, 203, 338nn13–14; rules and, *182*, 183–87; scientific reputations and, 166–70;

404 ‹ INDEX

trustworthy data (*continued*)
side effects and, 168, 178, 192, 336n1; skepticism and, 165–69, 174–202; social issues and, 169–73, 180, 189, 338n19; South Africa and, 168–69, 338n21, 339n23; specialists and, 171, 181, 191, 201; standard operating procedure (SOP) and, 172, *182*, 183–89, 203; systematic errors and, 185; technology and, 164, 171; testing and, 164–65, 168, 179, 183, 189–90, 195, 204; Thailand and, 180, 193, 195; training and, 170, 181–84, 187–92, 195, 203–4, 338nn21–22, 339nn23–24; tuberculosis and, 339n23; Uganda and, 180, 185–86, 196–99, 338n21; uniform work plans and, *182*, 183–87

Tshabalala-Msimang, Manto, 220

tuberculosis: disciplining and, 227–28; guidelines and, 15; moral issues and, 294, 344n2; rule proliferation and, *110*; standards and, 36–37, 63, 71, 329n23; trustworthy data and, 339n23; universals and, 124–25, 147, 153–54, 335n21

Uganda: boda-bodas of, 65, 67; denialism and, 44; disciplining and, 214–15, 218–19, 222–27, 340n14, 340n16, 341n19; doctor qualifications and, 130; drugs and, 14, 42, 45, 64–65, 68, 71, 111, 124–25, 147, 219, 223, 227, 243, 279, 288, 296–304, 307, 312; ethics and, 268–70, 275, 279; guidelines and, 1–2, 14, 30, 325n4; heterosexuals and, 1; HIV and, 1–2, 14, 30, 34, 44–45, 60, 67–68, 71, 111, 124, 130, 141, 152, 214–15, 219, 222, 227, 243, 246, 251, 255–56, 269, 275, 279, 298–304, 312, 317–19, 329n26, 340n16, 341n19; ignorance and, 240–43, 246, 251, 255–56, 258; Joint Clinical Research Center in, 307; Kampala, 38, 65–66, 247, 258, 329n26; Makerere University Medical School, 65; moral issues and, 288, 296, 298, 301–4, 307, 310–14; Mulago Hospital, 65; Museveni and, 44, 269; Philly Lutaaya Clinic, 65 (*see also* Philly

Lutaaya Clinic); poorer economy of, 1, 14, 42, 71, 124, 139, 149, 185, 219, 222, 255–56, 298–304, 307, 314, 329n25; research methodology in, 45–46; rule proliferation and, *109*, 110–11, 122; standards and, 34, 42–45, 55, 60, 64–71, 329nn25–26; trustworthy data and, 180, 185–86, 196–99, 338n21; universals and, 123–25, 130, 137–41, 147–49, 152, 156, 159, 335n23

UK Medicines for Human Use (Clinical Trials) Regulations, 119

UN Declaration of Human Rights, 114, 118

UN General Assembly Special Session on HIV/AIDS (UNGASS), 8, 325n3

uniform work plans, *182*, 183–87

United Nations Programme on HIV/AIDS (UNAIDS): ART and, 10; disciplining and, 209, 211, 229, 340n7; guidelines and, 6–12, 325nn2–3, 326n13; ignorance and, 257, 343nn19–20; moral issues and, 292, 306, 344n5; RCT and, 7; standards and, 328n16; universals and, 142, 334n12, VCT and, 6; WHO and, 7–10

Universal Coverage Scheme, 56, 328n14

universal precautions, 22–23, 94, 144, 152, 336n27

universals: accountability and, 129, 131, 144, 146, *149*, 150, 155–61; activists and, 127–28; AIDS and, 127–29, 132–33, 137, 143–47, 150–54, 157–63, 333n3, 335n19, 336n30; AIDS Education and Training Centers (AETC) and, 141; ART and, 124–25, 137, 142, 153–54; ARV and, 125, 139, 152; biology and, 123, 161–62, 167; Bobbi Campbell Clinic and, 133–36, 139–42, 146–63, 336n28; CD4 and, 124–26, 136–37, 151, 335n19; CDC and, 141–42, 336n27; Cha-on Suesum Clinic and, 135–36, 139–42, 146–63; clinical variations in, 132–63; confidentiality and, 151; coordination effects and, 144, 146, 152, 155; DHHS and, 134, 141–42; discretion and, *149*; disease and, 123, 126, 128–33, 141–52, 161, 163, 333n3, 336n27; disease-novelty effects and, 143–44, 146, 150; doctors and,

123–25, 130, 135–36, *149*, 152–53, 157, 335n19, 336n32; drugs and, 124–31, 134–37, 141, 147, 150–51, 153, 157–58, 163, 334n6, 336n29; education and, 137, 139, 162, 334n13; efficiency and, 131, 143–44; empowerment and, 145, 162; epidemics and, 151, 163; ethics and, 335n23; evidence-based medicine (EBM) and, 131–32, 141, 143–44, 146, 155, 158; Government Pharmaceutical Organization (GPO) and, 135, 151, 335n18; Gugu Dlamini Clinic and, 136–42, 146–63; healthcare and, 123, 131, 133, 137, 142–43, 152, 162–63, 334n14, 335n25; hospitals and, 124, 131, 133, 137, 143, *148*, 149–55, 335n21, 336n28; IAS and, 141–42, 333n3, 334n11; infection and, 123, 125, 133, 135, 144, 147, 150–54, 162, 336n27; institutionalization effects and, 143, 146, *148*; legal issues and, 129–31, 134, 147, 158, 163; legitimacy and, *140*, 141, 145–46, *149*, 158–61, 336n30; local, 163, 202, 335n24; malaria and, 154; malpractice and, 131; Medicaid and, 132; medical records and, 138–39, 153–56; Medicare and, 132; medicine and, 123, 128–31, 141–46, 151, 153, 333n3, 334n9; moral issues and, 303–6; norms and, 147; nurses and, 124, 130, 133, 136, 153; opportunistic infection (OI) and, 125, 153, 161; ownership effects and, 145–46, *149*, 158; pediatricians and, 126, 136–37, 147–51, 159–60, 336n30; PEPFAR and, 157, 159, 335n17; pharmaceutical companies and, 127, 333n4; Philly Lutaaya Clinic and, 123, 127, 136–42, 146–63, 334n5, 335n23; physicians and, 123, 126–27, 130–34, 139, 141, 152–55, 159–60, 163, 335n16; PMTCT and, 125; poorer countries and, 124–29, 136, 139, 155, 163, 336n30; pregnancy and, 124–26, 135, 144, 152, 159; protocols and, 129–33, 146, 152, 155–56; QA/QC and, *148*, 156; regulations and, 123, 129, 144, 159–60, 335n22; richer countries and, 123, 128–29, 138–39, 144, 151–52, 173, 186, 191, 196–97, 336n30; Robert

Rafsky Clinic and, 132–33, 139–42, 146–63; rules and, 144, *149*, 154, 158, 163; Ryan White HIV/AIDS Program and, 133, *148–49*, 155; side effects and, 125, 131, 134–35, 150–51, 158, 161, 336n32; social issues and, 123, 127, 141, 145, 147, 151, 161–62; South Africa and, 130, 136–41, 146–49, 152, 154, 334n5, 335n16, 335n20; specialists and, 130, 137, 145; standard operating procedure (SOP) and, 146, 154–55; TAC and, 335n16; technology and, 128; testing and, 126–27, 130, 135–36; Thailand and, 130, 135–36, *140–41, 148*, 151; training and, 123, 126, 128, 130–36, 139–42, 145–52, 163, 335n23; transmission and, 125, 135, 150, 152, 159, 336n27, 336n30; treatment equity and, 127–32; tuberculosis and, 124–25, 147, 153–54, 335n21; Uganda and, 123–25, 130, 137–41, 147–49, 152, 156, 159, 335n23; UNAIDS and, 142, 334n12; WHO and, 135–37, 141–42, 334n12, 334n14

urine, 213

US Agency for International Development (USAID), 44

US Constitution, 98

US News & World Report, 103

Vancouver conference (IAC), 127, 291–92

Vienna Declaration, 334n6

Vietnam, 60, 136, 188

Viravaidya, Mechai, 305

voluntary counseling and testing (VCT): disciplining and, 213–14; guidelines and, 4–12, 15, 22, 325nn4–5; moral issues and, 298

Watkins, Susan, 7

Webber, Melvin, 264

Wennberg, John, 88

West Nile virus, 36

Whyte, Michael A., 275

Whyte, Susan, 275

Willowbrook, 101

Woolgar, Steve, 171, 181

World Bank, 26–27

World Food Program, 258

World Health Organization (WHO): disciplining and, 205, 209–10, 222, 229, 340n9; Geneva and, 19; guidelines and, 6–11, 19, 326n11; Kampala Declaration, 38; moral issues and, 288, 292, 294, 297–98, 308, 344n2, 345n9; rule proliferation and, *108–10*, 111–12, *115*; staging system, 326n11; standards and, 38, 327nn3–4; UNAIDS and, 7–10; universals and, 135–37, 141–42, 334n12, 334n14

World Medical Association (WMA), *115*, 119, 332n33, 333n38

World Trade Organization (WTO): guidelines and, 326n9; moral issues and, 289, 292, 305–6, 311; TRIPS and, 14, 22, 41, 56, 311, 326n9

World War I, 22

World War II, 21–22, 93

X-rays, 153, 342n14

ZDV (zidovudine), 118

Zika, 36

Zussman, Robert, 249–50

The Chicago Series in Law and Society

Edited by John M. Conley, Charles Epp, and Lynn Mather

SERIES TITLES, CONTINUED FROM FRONT MATTER:

Union by Law: Filipino American Labor Activists,
Rights Radicalism, and Racial Capitalism
by Michael W. McCann with George I. Lovell

The Sit-Ins: Protest and Legal Change in the Civil Rights Era
by Christopher W. Schmidt

Working Law: Courts, Corporations, and Symbolic Civil Rights
by Lauren B. Edelman

The Myth of the Litigious Society: Why We Don't Sue
by David M. Engel

Policing Immigrants: Local Law Enforcement on the Front Lines
by Doris Marie Provine, Monica W. Varsanyi, Paul G. Lewis, and Scott H. Decker

The Seductions of Quantification: Measuring Human Rights,
Gender Violence, and Sex Trafficking
by Sally Engle Merry

Invitation to Law and Society: An Introduction to the Study of Real Law, Second Edition
by Kitty Calavita

Pulled Over: How Police Stops Define Race and Citizenship
by Charles R. Epp, Steven Maynard-Moody, and Donald Haider-Markel

The Three and a Half Minute Transaction: Boilerplate and the Limits of Contract Design
by Mitu Gulati and Robert E. Scott

This Is Not Civil Rights: Discovering Rights Talk in 1939 America
by George I. Lovell

Failing Law Schools
by Brian Z. Tamanaha

Everyday Law on the Street: City Governance in an Age of Diversity
by Mariana Valverde

Lawyers in Practice: Ethical Decision Making in Context
edited by Leslie C. Levin and Lynn Mather

Collateral Knowledge: Legal Reasoning in the Global Financial Markets
by Annelise Riles

Specializing the Courts
by Lawrence Baum

Asian Legal Revivals: Lawyers in the Shadow of Empire
by Yves Dezalay and Bryant G. Garth

The Language of Statutes: Laws and Their Interpretation
by Lawrence M. Solan

Belonging in an Adopted World: Race, Identity, and Transnational Adoption
by Barbara Yngvesson

Making Rights Real: Activists, Bureaucrats, and the Creation of the Legalistic State
by Charles R. Epp

Lawyers of the Right: Professionalizing the Conservative Coalition
by Ann Southworth

Arguing with Tradition: The Language of Law in Hopi Tribal Court
by Justin B. Richland

Speaking of Crime: The Language of Criminal Justice
by Lawrence M. Solan and Peter M. Tiersma

Human Rights and Gender Violence: Translating International Law into Local Justice
by Sally Engle Merry

Just Words, Second Edition: Law, Language, and Power
by John M. Conley and William M. O'Barr

Distorting the Law: Politics, Media, and the Litigation Crisis
by William Haltom and Michael McCann

Justice in the Balkans: Prosecuting War Crimes in the Hague Tribunal
by John Hagan

*Rights of Inclusion: Law and Identity in the Life Stories of Americans
with Disabilities*
by David M. Engel and Frank W. Munger

*The Internationalization of Palace Wars: Lawyers, Economists, and the
Contest to Transform Latin American States*
by Yves Dezalay and Bryant G. Garth

*Free to Die for Their Country: The Story of the Japanese American
Draft Resisters in World War II*
by Eric L. Muller

Overseers of the Poor: Surveillance, Resistance, and the Limits of Privacy
by John Gilliom

*Pronouncing and Persevering: Gender and the Discourses of Disputing
in an African Islamic Court*
by Susan F. Hirsch

The Common Place of Law: Stories from Everyday Life
by Patricia Ewick and Susan S. Silbey

*The Struggle for Water: Politics, Rationality, and Identity
in the American Southwest*
by Wendy Nelson Espeland

*Dealing in Virtue: International Commercial Arbitration and the Construction
of a Transnational Legal Order*
by Yves Dezalay and Bryant G. Garth

Rights at Work: Pay Equity Reform and the Politics of Legal Mobilization
by Michael W. McCann

The Language of Judges
by Lawrence M. Solan

Reproducing Rape: Domination through Talk in the Courtroom
by Gregory M. Matoesian

*Getting Justice and Getting Even: Legal Consciousness among
Working-Class Americans*
by Sally Engle Merry

Rules versus Relationships: The Ethnography of Legal Discourse
by John M. Conley and William M. O'Barr